Social Policy

Social Policy: Reform, Research, and Practice

Edited by

Patricia L. Ewalt
Edith M. Freeman
Stuart A. Kirk
Dennis L. Poole

NASW PRESS
National Association of Social Workers
Washington, DC

Jay J. Cayner, ACSW, LISW, *President*
Josephine Nieves, MSW, PhD, *Executive Director*

First impression, March 1997
Second impression, October 1997
Third impression, June 1998

Linda Beebe, *Executive Editor*
Nancy Winchester, *Editorial Services Director*
K. Hyde Loomis, *Senior Editor*
Christina A. Davis, *Staff Editor*
Sarah Lowman, *Staff Editor*
Stephen D. Pazdan, *Staff Editor*
Marcia D. Roman, *Staff Editor*
Bill Cathey, *Typesetter*
Ronald W. Wolf and Cynthia Hargett,
    Wolf Publications, Inc., *Proofreaders*
Bernice Eisen, *Indexer*

Library of Congress Catalog Card Number
97-65987

Printed in the United States of America

Contents

PART III: CHILDREN AND FAMILIES

PART IV: HEALTH

Introduction

Social policy has received enormous national attention in recent years. Open the newspaper, turn on the television, or listen to informal discussions at social gatherings and you will be immersed in debates about social policy: the future of Social Security, Medicare, Medicaid, and programs such as the former Aid to Families with Dependent Children (AFDC). Welfare reform, health care reform, managed care, and the social safety net, once topics at academic seminars, are now front page news and common labels for complex social policy problems. Moreover, there has been vigorous debate about how much responsibility should be shifted from the federal to the state government and to the private non-profit and for-profit sectors. In this changing social policy environment, *Social Policy: Reform, Research, and Practice* focuses on issues that have a dramatic impact on consumers of social services, on society as a whole, and on social work practice. This book presents analyses of trends in health care, mental health care, child and family services, education, housing, and public welfare and what they portend for the future. This policy reader presents research on the earliest phases of current welfare reform and shows how knowledge gained from such research prepares social workers to propose social policy.

This book reflects the trends of the day. Important among these trends, for example, is an emphasis on rebuilding communities, both socially and economically, by relying on mixtures of public and private funding and governance by local residents. As with many other changes, we do not yet know what the outcomes will be. We do recognize that to address community initiatives requires collaboration between organizations and residents to a magnitude previously unknown. The research findings reported here address the mechanisms that facilitate interorganizational management and collaborative practice.

This book is organized around six areas of interest in social policy: (1) shifting governmental responsibilities, (2) welfare and work, (3) children and families, (4) health, (5) mental health, and (6) education and schools.

SHIFTING GOVERNMENTAL RESPONSIBILITIES

Major shifts in federal policy and funding decisions have occurred under the aegis of greater local control without careful consideration of what such changes mean operationally. For example, what will be the effect of these changes on federal–state and state–local relationships? How will community residents and informal leaders be involved in decision making, if at all? Will the shift in responsibilities lead to increased culturally relevant services for consumers? Will such changes in social policy lead to capacity-building for community residents?

WELFARE AND WORK

Next to changes in health care policy, welfare reforms in benefit programs and in work requirements have received the most national and local attention. The main target of welfare and work policy seems to be women and children in poverty, although it is clear other population groups receive benefits as well. Are there sufficient training and work resources to absorb the numbers affected by new work policies? What parts of private industry and the public sector can provide additional work and training opportunities for former recipients of Aid to Families with Dependent Children (AFDC), and what policies are needed to develop these opportunities? How will new mandatory lifetime restrictions for AFDC benefits be regulated? Under what extenuating circumstances, if any, can such restrictions be waived?

CHILDREN AND FAMILIES

Society has been heady with talk about valuing children and the family but myopic about what is actually happening to them. How have past social policies affected children and families, particularly those who are poor? What can social workers expect from the new policy initiatives that are being implemented? What can social workers learn from careful study and research that can help to anticipate what lies ahead?

HEALTH

Although President Clinton's health care reform initiative failed in Congress, the health care system has been transformed nevertheless at an incredibly rapid pace, affecting consumers, health care professionals, and health care organizations alike. Mergers, acquisitions, and cost containment, topics formerly associated with the corporate sector, are refashioning health care in the United States. Fee-for-service and private practice are rapidly becoming quaint memories in the face of managed care, health maintenance organizations, health care conglomerates, and restrictive reimbursement policies. These transformations are not just taking place in the private sector but are such reshaping programs as Medicare and Medicaid. Social work practitioners in the health care field are in the midst of these changes.

MENTAL HEALTH

People with mental illness, particularly those with severe disorders, have historically fallen between the health care and welfare systems because they frequently need both treatment and economic assistance. In the current policy revolution, driven by cost containment, people with mental illness are likely to be vulnerable to abandonment by social services agencies. Social work is the largest profession in the mental health care field and must stay informed about ways to improve care to this population.

EDUCATION AND SCHOOLS

Changes in education policy are affecting a broad spectrum of issues related to regular and special education programs, services integration, family support and involvement, and professional preparation and regulation of school social workers. New mandates for full inclusion require shifts in how services are conceptualized and delivered. The new policies also blur the boundaries between regular and special education. How are teachers and other school staff being prepared for and supported in regard to such changes? How will funding and policy decisions for services integration affect the role of school social workers? How will these arrangements affect interdisciplinary collaboration? Should services integration policies require community involvement or simply assume that such involvement will occur?

This book shows that social workers are actively engaged in the current debate on issues of significance to the future of social policy and the social work profession. Is it important to specify a research agenda for the profession? What should be on that agenda? What forms of advocacy are most effective in the current environment? Is family support necessary for welfare reform? How should social workers attempt to shape social policy? Is mental illness biological in origin, and how is public policy affected by the answer to that question?

Social Policy: Reform, Research, and Practice contains 47 chapters selected from the 1996 issues of *Social Work, Health & Social Work, Social Work in Education,* and *Social Work Research.* Several chapters came from two special issues, "Social Work in an Era of Diminishing Federal Responsibility" (*Social Work,* September and November), and "Welfare Reform" (*Social Work Research,* December).

This book demonstrates how social context influences the evolution of social policy. Social policy is a work in progress, and this book reflects the driving force of policy in the making.

Patricia L. Ewalt
Edith M. Freeman
Stuart A. Kirk
Dennis L. Poole

Part I

SHIFTING GOVERNMENTAL RESPONSIBILITIES

1

Social Work in an Era of Diminishing Federal Responsibility: Setting the Practice, Policy, and Research Agenda

Patricia L. Ewalt

ocial progress, it is said, is not and cannot be a principal aim of govern ment (Weisberg, 1996). To those who have lived in no era except the New Deal and its successors and who have valued progressive aims, if not always their implementation, this is a stunning reversal of purpose. What we understood previously as an occasional failure in implementation has by some been reinterpreted as a failure of intent. Credibility is increasingly awarded to the thought that, when government curtails exploitation of one group by another or redistributes opportunity among groups, it is an intrusive control of market forces. It is not simply that our means were inadequate, it is said, but also that our aims were misguided (Sleeper, 1996).

The recent widespread criticism of government has willing listeners despite the fact that people generally believe that no entity except government can or will ensure protections essential for people's health and well-being. As posed in a question by political historian David M. Kennedy (1995) shortly after the failure of President Clinton's proposals for health care reform, "Why have the American people been so consistently skeptical of centralized government power, and so resourceful in finding ways to frustrate its exercise, even when that power is manifestly the only instrument commensurate with issues whose gravity is not in dispute?" (p. 92).

In addition, the criticism of government as an instrument of social progress ignores the fact that government operations inevitably increase opportunities and protections for some at the expense of others. Actions of the Federal Reserve, for example, are more likely either to control inflation, a concern of investors, or to promote employment, a concern of poor or unemployed people.

Social work has developed its identity as a partner to government. In the past, most social workers have been employed by government or by nonprofit agencies that depend on government. More than that, social work, as evidenced by its investment in legislative advocacy, has allied with a definition of government as an instrument of social progress. Some in social work are encouraging greater development of and reliance on affiliations with nongovernment, voluntary organizations (Center for Public Sector Leadership and Service, n.d.), but these institutions are not yet sufficiently developed to ensure a threshold of public well-being.

Decreased regard for government and decreased confidence in the ability or desirability of government action for social progress create a different environment in which social work must operate in the future. As described by Edwards, Cooke, and Reid in this issue of *Social Work* (pp. 468–479), the current political, economic, and social changes are so thoroughly rooted in historical and global developments that they may be expected to continue despite the results of electoral politics. Transformation of the environment requires equivalent transformation by its occupants. This issue and the next issue of *Social Work* are designed to analyze the environmental transformations and the changes desirable and necessary for effective future practice. The articles span social policy, research, management, community development, and the various population groups of concern to social work.

Nearly 20 years ago, *Social Work* published a special issue on conceptual frameworks. According to its introduction, the issue was generated by questions arising in the profession "about a prevailing sense of concern and uncertainty among practitioners as to what social work's purposes are and what they should be . . . [and] what social workers are and should be doing" (Minahan & Briar, 1977, p. 339). The special issues of *Social Work* for September and November 1996 again ask who we are, who we should be, and what we should be doing. This time these questions are specifically grounded in analyses of the current economic, political, and social contexts. The articles in these two issues aim to increase our understanding of the present and anticipated social context to promote a transformation of social work practice sufficient for accomplishing our purposes amid the transformations that surround the profession.

REFERENCES

Center for Public Sector Leadership and Service. (n.d.). *Institute for Civil Society Development proposal*. Cleveland: Case Western Reserve University, Mandel School of Applied Social Sciences.

Kennedy, D. M. (1995, July). How FDR derailed the New Deal [Review of the book *The Supreme Court reborn: The constitutional revolution in the age of Roosevelt*]. *Atlantic Monthly*, p. 92.

Minahan, A., & Briar, S. (1977). Introduction to special issue. *Social Work, 22*, 339.

Sleeper, J. (1996, May 6). Why trust went out the window: An inquiry into the loss of public faith and what we can do to get it back [Review of the book *In defense of government: The fall and rise of public trust*]. *New York Times Review of Books*, p. 6.

Weisberg, J. (1996). *In defense of government: The fall and rise of public trust*. New York: Scribner.

This chapter was originally published in the September 1996 issue of Social Work, *vol. 41, pp. 439–440.*

2 Articulating a "New Nationalism" in American Social Policy

Bruce S. Jansson and Susan Smith

At a time when signs point toward a diminution of federal roles, it may seem futile to advocate reinvigorating federal power. Yet many social conditions suggest the need for expanded federal roles. Traditional, festering problems like the plight of inner-city residents, homeless people, and medically uninsured citizens have been joined by the problems that have accompanied the globalizing of the American economy. Economic inequality has grown dramatically in the past three decades. The restructuring of corporations, loss of manufacturing jobs, and transfer of jobs abroad have placed millions of Americans in economic uncertainty, including members of the middle class. It is not clear whether state or local governments are positioned to address these problems without federal guidance, even when given federal resources.

After tracing the growth in the power of the federal government from 1950 to 1979, this article discusses three successive assaults on it by conservatives from 1970 to the present. It articulates a rationale for augmented federal roles while acknowledging that state and local governments should often share power with federal authorities. Eight criteria are identified that can be used in tandem to gauge where specific programs should be placed on a federal-to-state continuum, and four recommendations are provided to policy practitioners to help them achieve policy goals. ("Policy practitioners" are social workers who engage in policy advocacy, whether they are direct service, administrative, community organization, or policy-specialized staff.)

BUILDING OF A FEDERALLY DIRECTED WELFARE STATE: 1950 TO 1979

The framers of the Constitution assumed that the federal government would be limited to relatively few functions, such as raising a militia and issuing a currency. They pointedly did not discuss social policy in the Constitution, implying that it (like most powers not enumerated in the document) rested with state and local governments. Aside from relatively minor functions, as well as the funding of war pensions, the American federal government remained remarkably small during the 19th century. Even progressive reformers at the turn of this century, such as Jane Addams, envisioned modest roles for the federal government, focusing on the enactment of many regulations in local and state governments instead (Jansson, 1996).

When compared with previous years, the federal government grew remarkably during the New Deal, expanding its domestic spending from a paltry 2 percent of the gross national product (GNP) in 1930 to nearly 8 percent of the GNP in 1940 (Chubb, 1985). Even this expansion of the federal government seems limited when viewed with hindsight. Most of the funds went to work relief programs for Americans who were unemployed during the Great Depression, with most people, including Franklin Roosevelt, assuming that these "emergency" programs would disappear when the economy recovered. The social insurances of the Social Security Act were self-funding from payroll contributions, requiring few expenditures from federal coffers. Conservatives took advantage of wartime conditions, as well as their control of the Congress in the postwar years, to demolish most of the New Deal programs aside from the social insurances and several welfare programs (Jansson, 1996). Federal domestic spending had been reduced to 7.5 percent of the GNP by 1954 (Rivlin, 1992).

The federal government obtained extraordinary social policy roles in the 1950s, 1960s, and 1970s, however, that placed it in a paramount position in the American federal system. With other economies of the world savaged by World War II, Americans entered three decades of unparalleled economic growth in the wake of the war; the GNP rose in constant prices by 255 percent between 1940 and 1973 (Rivlin, 1992). This economic growth provided the resources to fund a growing domestic budget, even with massive military expenditures during the cold war (Hodgson, 1976). Federal domestic spending rose to 17 percent of the GNP by 1979 (Chubb, 1985).

Rather than giving its funds to states and local governments with no strings attached, the federal government usually linked them to myriad regulations, such as requiring them to be used for so-called categorical programs like Head Start. The federal government funded 160 categorical programs in 1960, and by 1979 it funded more than 500 of them (Chubb, 1985; Rivlin, 1992). The sheer bulk of federal regulations is illustrated by the hundreds of volumes of the *Federal Register* published between 1950 and 1975. The federal government also issued many freestanding federal regulations, such as a minimum wage, requirements about working conditions, federal child care standards, and environmental regulations.

Federal authorities sometimes bypassed state and local governments by offering resources directly to individuals or to local institutions, such as its funding of community mental health centers in the 1960s and 1970s. With the enactment of Medicare in 1965, the federalizing of the Food Stamp program in 1970, and the federalizing of Aid to the Disabled through the Supplemental Security Income (SSI) program in 1972, the federal government vastly increased its direct implementation of social policy, granting local and state governments few policy roles in these huge programs.

Curiously, the number of nonmilitary federal officials remained roughly constant from 1960 to 1985 (about 2.5 million employees), unlike the staffs of state and local governments, which doubled in these years to nearly 8 million employees as federal spending and regulations increased (Chubb, 1985). (Projected cuts in federal employment will reduce staff below 1960 levels.) This anomaly should not suggest, however, that federal authorities lacked considerable power over programs that received some federal funding. Lacking administrative resources to monitor from Washington, federal agencies relied on subnational bureaucracies at state and local levels of government to implement a significant share of federal grant programs. As Chubb (1985) analyzed, even though these state and local agencies were ostensibly under the control of governors, mayors, and county officials, they often became extensions of the federal agencies. Federal officials regularly briefed and trained their staff, obtained data from them about their programs, used them as mediators between themselves and local or state officials, and relied on them to diminish misuse of their funds by local agencies. (State and local elected officials often lacked even basic information about these programs.)

Federal programs, regulations, and court rulings, in turn, encouraged the growth of advocacy structures to protect federal programs and to expand them (Peterson, 1991). The consumers and employees of federal programs provided natural constituencies that actively sought to protect and enlarge them. Once programs were in place, other advocates sought benefits from them, such as advocates who got a share of Head Start's slots earmarked for disabled children. The welfare state stimulated the formation of advocacy groups by providing expanding resources that they could tap.

These various dimensions of federal power interacted with one another to further augment federal power. As federal domestic spending increased, federal guidelines increased, as did the size of the subnational bureaucracy. The expansion of federal programs and regulations spawned additional advocacy groups who lobbied for new programs. Federal power steadily increased from 1950 to the late 1970s in this dynamic interaction.

WAS THE FEDERAL GOVERNMENT "OPPRESSIVE"?

The federal government eclipsed the power of state and local governments in the three decades after 1950. Aggregate federal domestic spending had roughly equaled the total spending of local and state governments in 1950, but it was nearly two times their combined size by 1990 (Rivlin, 1992). Why did the power of the federal government grow so markedly? Insistence on federal regulations and categorical programs had its genesis in skepticism about the ability of nonfederal governments and institutions to use federal funds correctly if left to their own devices (Conlan, 1984; Rivlin, 1992). Many federal legislators and administrators feared that the southern states would discriminate against African Americans. They also feared that state legislatures, often dominated by rural interests and meeting only every other year, would be insensitive to urban areas and would lack the ability to develop needed policies. They doubted that primitive state bureaucracies could implement or monitor policies. They doubted that local institutions, such as big-city schools, could develop responsive services for impoverished children or people of color—a cynicism that led the framers of the War on Poverty in the 1960s to bypass local institutions by creating many programs that were directly funded from Washington. Federal legislators enacted categorical programs as well to get political credit for them in their constituencies. Federal power was fostered by the sheer amount of federal tax revenues when compared with tax revenues of state and local governments.

The growth of federal power should not be exaggerated, however. Many federal funds were administered through state and local agencies, allowing some local officials to assume a role in their implementation (Chubb, 1985). The federal government delegated key policy choices to states and local governments in many programs, such as letting states determine eligibility and services in Aid to Families with Dependent Children (AFDC) and Medicaid programs. When noting that federal domestic spending rose many times between 1950 and 1980, many commentators exaggerated its actual growth by failing to note that it began from such a low base in 1950 that even modest growth engendered huge percentage increases. Moreover, most of the growth in domestic federal spending came from expenditures on social insurances and four entitlements (Food Stamps, AFDC, Medicaid, and SSI) rather than from domestic discretionary spending for social programs funded from general revenues. Even in the mid-1990s, such discretionary spending constitutes only 16 percent of the federal budget and must cover social services, aid to cities, aid to education, improvements in infrastructure, and scores of additional areas (Congressional Quarterly Service, 1993). With substantially lower tax rates and with a large portion of its funds diverted to military programs, Americans spent significantly lower amounts than Europeans for their domestic programs from World War II onward.

It is also inaccurate to portray the rise of the American welfare state merely as a liberal power play. Liberal reformers were instrumental in securing the enactment of many reforms over conservatives' opposition, but federal spending rose steadily even during the tenures of Republican presidents and often with bipartisan support. Although conservatives often opposed the enactment of specific reforms, such as Medicare, they supported their expansion and annual funding once they had been enacted. Searching for explanations for the rise of the American welfare state, some political scientists emphasized the political rewards that domestic programs gave to incumbents of both parties by allowing them credit for specific programs and projects in their districts (Conlan, 1984).

THREE SUCCESSIVE ATTACKS ON FEDERAL POWER

Even before the rise of federal spending in the three decades after World War II, conservatives had demanded that the work relief programs of the New Deal be placed under the control of the states. Arguing that the growth of federal power ran counter to the intentions of the founding fathers, they regularly called Harry Hopkins, administrator of the Federal Emergency Relief Administration, a "welfare czar" and President Franklin Roosevelt a "dictator" (Polenberg, 1966). Republicans in the 1960s sought to place the War on Poverty under control of the states, contending that federal bureaucrats sought to use its programs to promote social change. The most systematic attacks on federal power were led, however, by Presidents Richard Nixon and Ronald Reagan, as well as by current House Speaker Newt Gingrich.

Richard Nixon proposed an ambitious plan in 1971 to supplant 129 categorical programs with six block grants with virtually no federal regulations about their use, coupled with an earlier proposal for general revenue sharing to give unrestricted funds directly to state and local governments (Nathan, 1975). Rather than framing these consolidations merely as improvements in government to allow more flexible programs at the local level, Nixon characterized them as returning the nation to the limited (federal) government intended by the framers of the Constitution. Wanting to develop a conservative coalition to dominate the Congress late in his first term, he contended that the dramatic rise in federal power had resulted from a conspiracy of liberals, advocacy groups, civil servants, and legislators (Conlan, 1984).

Nixon encountered great opposition to his block grant plans. Advocacy groups feared that states and localities would be impervious to the needs of vulnerable populations. Many federal legislators of both parties did not want to rescind programs from which they had derived political credit. Advocates for specific programs feared state governments would terminate them in favor of alternative uses of block grant funds. Nixon was able to get only two small block grants and a small revenue-sharing program enacted. Noting that Congress placed new strings even on these small block grants in succeeding years, many political scientists in the 1970s doubted that federal legislators would ever enact sizable numbers of block grants (Conlan, 1984).

If Nixon broached the idea of devolution, Ronald Reagan partially achieved its realization with nine block grants in 1981 that consolidated 77 categorical programs and terminated 62 others (Conlan, 1984). Reagan succeeded by using clever political strategy. Reckoning that few politicians would be willing to vote against a larger bill that emphasized budget cutting when government spending was widely associated with the double-digit inflation of the late 1970s, he "hid" the block grants in the budget-cutting Omnibus Budget Reconciliation Bill (Stanfield, 1981a, 1981b, 1981c). Moreover, Reagan had cleverly obtained the pivotal support of the National Governors' Association for the measure by striking a deal with them whereby they agreed to let him decrease the funding of the block grants by 25 percent (when compared to the funds of the categorical programs that were folded into them) in return for enhancing their power by giving them largely unrestricted block grant funds (Stanfield, 1981c). When Reagan tried to downsize the federal government much more substantially in 1982, however, he was decisively defeated, because many governors and legislators finally realized that his proposals disguised his intention to grant the states additional responsibilities while cutting their funding (Stanfield, 1982). Moreover, to Reagan's consternation, Congress "recategorized" some older block grants by earmarking some funds for special programs.

When viewed with hindsight, Reagan did not radically downsize the federal government. Most categorical programs remained intact, and Congress had reattached strings to his block grants (Arvidson, 1990). Although spending for many domestic programs used by poor people suffered devastating cuts, aggregate domestic spending had remained roughly constant—around 16 percent of GNP—mainly due to increased spending for social insurances, Medicaid, Food Stamps, and SSI (Rivlin, 1992).

Believing that Reagan's policies had been foiled by liberals, a new generation of conservative politicians laid the groundwork in the 1980s for a renewed assault on the power of the federal government. With a dramatic takeover of both houses of Congress accomplished in 1994, they focused on three strategies: (1) a seven-year plan to balance the federal budget to force even greater cuts in domestic programs funded by general revenues; (2) "disentitling" of Food Stamps, Medicaid, and AFDC; and (3) large cuts in Medicare. Determined to implement the downsizing of the federal government as described in the Republicans' manifesto, *Contract with America* (Republican National Committee, 1994), Gingrich labeled this assault on government spending "Reagan II" because it drew on policy ideas that Reagan had initiated as well as the political tactic of hiding devolution in a budget reconciliation measure that focused on budget cutting (Jansson, 1996). (Only Clinton's veto stood in the way of Gingrich's plan in summer 1996, which passed both houses of Congress in late 1995.) Gingrich made his future intentions clear as well: to win the presidency and to retain control of Congress to allow an even greater downsizing of the federal government (Balz & Brownstein, 1996; Dreyfuss & Stone, 1996).

Whereas conservatives were the driving force behind devolution, many liberals and Democrats developed their own versions. Walter Heller, chair of the Council of Economic Advisors in the Kennedy and Johnson administrations, favored federal revenue sharing, but Alice Rivlin (Clinton's former director of the Office of Management and Budget) proposed devolving most programs (except for medical ones, as well as SSI, AFDC, and Food Stamps) entirely to the states, hoping to fund them from revenues from a common national sales (or value-added) tax that the states would divide among themselves (Rivlin, 1992). President Clinton and most Senate Democrats have agreed to devolution of AFDC under certain conditions (Congressional Quarterly Service, 1995).

TOWARD A NEW NATIONALISM

Predictions of the demise of federal domestic roles are premature. The states' implementation of block grants has been mixed, with instances of improved programs but with cases of clear neglect of poor, controversial, and powerless groups (Morial, 1983; Nathan & Doolittle, 1987; Peterson, Rabe, & Wong, 1986; Rich, 1991). Although the states have greatly improved their policy and implementation capabilities, they remain locked in competition between themselves to keep their tax rates low to retain or attract corporations (Reich, 1991; Rose-Ackerman, 1992). This desire to minimize their taxes bodes ill for programs that are completely or partially funded by them. Many state legislators fear that generous social programs will attract benefit-seeking people from states with less generous ones in the so-called magnet effect (Peterson & Rom, 1990). Many state legislatures remain insensitive to the needs of cities and powerless groups because they are dominated by rural and suburban legislators as well as by conservatives (Balz & Brownstein, 1996). After expending a huge share of their resources on prisons, roads, education, and Medicaid, states often lack resources for other programs (Levy, 1995).

Warning signs about states' implementation of block grants and social programs abound. Many states have cut welfare benefits even when their poverty rates are both relatively high and climbing, suggesting that their fear of becoming welfare magnets overrides their concern for those who are disadvantaged (Peterson, 1995). Some states have ceded their social policy responsibilities to counties, which are often ill-equipped to handle them (Moon & Schneiderman, 1995). As a result of discretion in setting benefit levels for AFDC, states chose to cut benefits by roughly 42 percent between 1970 and 1993, from $605 to $349 in 1993 dollars (Peterson, 1995). Twenty-eight states have obtained federal waivers to restrict AFDC increases for additional births to recipient families (Council on Governors' Policy Advisors, 1996). The child welfare programs of many states have been placed under court supervision in the 1990s because they have failed to provide adequate services to abused and neglected children.

Because of its superior resources as well as its national vantage point, the federal government is best positioned to establish strategies to address many problems associated with the globalizing of the nation's economy. The federal government is no panacea, as the recent conservatives' domination of Congress suggests. Unlike states, which are limited by limited revenues and competition to retain or attract corporations, federal legislators and presidents possess much larger resources and a national perspective. Nor does Rivlin's (1992) plan to get states to join together to enact a common tax appear feasible when many state-level politicians seek tax cuts (Shannon & Kee, 1989).

The nation has many social problems. Many citizens will continue to need income and food supplementation and other survival programs during an era of growing economic uncertainty. To redress the nation's mounting economic inequality, new expenditures are needed for opportunity-enhancing and redistributive programs, not to mention changes in the tax code to lessen disparities between affluent and poor citizens (Barlett & Steele, 1994). Families and their children will need expanded economic assistance as well as an array of social services (Kamerman & Kahn, 1996). The nation needs expanded public health programs to cope with sexually transmitted diseases and growing rates of diseases like tuberculosis, new and expanded programs to help aging Americans, and programs to help citizens in impoverished areas in rural and urban settings (Frieden, 1995; Johnson, 1989).

A new nationalism is also needed in the fiscal years of the 20th century because of the globalizing of the economy. European nations and Japan have no inhibitions about establishing national policies to help their citizens compete in the global economy, such as national funding of job training programs, publicly funded child care, economic planning, and large subsidies for education. Americans need to consider radical changes in their educational system from preschool onward so that all citizens receive sophisticated education throughout their life spans (Krugman, 1990). Other changes are needed, such as transferring the financing of American health benefits from corporations to government, because the current system places American corporations at a disadvantage with nations with government-funded health insurance (Aaron, 1991).

CONTINUUM OF RELATIONS AMONG LEVELS OF GOVERNMENT

Conservatives have often framed relationships of federal and nonfederal governments in either-or terms. Recent policy history suggests that many permutations are possible, given that actual relations between the federal government and states can be depicted on a continuum (Stenberg & Walker, 1977). At one end, the federal government completely funds and implements specific policies, such as Food Stamps, Social Security, and SSI. At the other end, state or local governments completely fund and implement specific policies, such as local recreation programs and most of the nation's secondary schools. Between these ends, power is shared in various ways, as different kinds of block grants suggest. Power tilts toward federal authorities if they earmark funds for specific programs, write many regulations, and monitor programs, whereas it tilts toward the states if few federal directions accompany federal funds. Or the federal government can retain ultimate policy power but grant "waivers" to states to implement specific programs in ways that deviate from federal policy (Iglehart, 1995). These waivers in AFDC, Medicaid, and other programs tilt toward federal authority if they are closely monitored and revocable but toward states if they are granted with little surveillance and for long periods (Towns, 1995).

Eight criteria can be used to place specific programs on this continuum: (1) whether the federal tax code can be used as an incentive to induce behaviors necessary for solving a problem (Witte, 1985), (2) whether programs address the basic survival needs of citizens (Ladd & Doolittle, 1982), (3) the likelihood that states will discriminate against specific populations (Peterson, 1995), (4) the extent to which specific programs require large resources (Aaron, 1991), (5) the extent to which economic competition among states inhibits socially responsive policies (Rose-Ackerman, 1992), (6) the extent to which specific problems are linked to global competitiveness (Reich, 1991), (7) the extent to which local inputs and partnerships between public and nonpublic entities are needed (Peterson et al., 1986; Stanfield, 1982), and (8) the extent to which social programs are service intensive (Table 2-1). In addition to these eight criteria, attention must be given as well to the actual performance of state and local governments: If they endanger the well-being of citizens by not funding or poorly administering programs, the federal government should take corrective action, such as developing regulations, monitoring their programs, or contributing greater resources.

Sole Federal Funding and Implementation

National authorities should fund and implement programs to supply resources to avert "starvation and dire suffering," a phrase frequently used by President Franklin Roosevelt to defend work relief programs during the Great Depression. Safety net resources (SSI, Food Stamps, and social insurances) should not be left to local preferences, not only because they require vast resources, but also because state governments are likely to discriminate against poor people. If waivers are granted, they should be granted only for short periods, with intense federal monitoring and safeguards for recipients. Implemented by the federal government, these programs' funding should be protected by entitlement status so they receive necessary resources no matter what the current state of the budget is.

TABLE 2-1

Orienting Framework Criteria for Placing Social Policies on the Federal-to-State Continuum

Criteria	Sole Federal	Devolved with Federal Tilt	Devolved with State/Local Tilt	Sole State or Local
Extent to which federal tax code is used	X			
Extent to which program addresses survival needs	X	X		
Likelihood that states will discriminate	X	X		
Extent to which problem requires large resources	X	X	X	
Extent to which economic competition between states inhibits socially responsive policies	X	X	X	
Extent to which problem is linked to global competitiveness	X	X	X	
Extent to which local inputs and partnerships are needed		X	X	X
Service-intensive programs		X	X	X

The size of the Earned Income Tax Credit (EITC), which provides tax credits to working poor people, should be significantly enlarged to help working people buffeted by economic uncertainty and declining wages. The federal government should also use the federal tax code as an incentive for corporations to hire or train people who are affected by corporate restructuring. These incentives should be coupled with enforcement of the civil rights of people excluded from technological jobs, such as women, people of color, and physically or mentally challenged people.

Devolved Programs Tilting toward Federal Power

Some programs require the coupling of extensive federal funding and regulations with some local discretion. For example, medical policy addresses problems that cut across state boundaries, require large resources, and affect the nation's competitiveness in world markets. The federal government has to fund Medicare and Medicaid because of their sheer cost and because the states currently lack resources even to fund adequately their Medicaid costs and medical coverage of uninsured people. Partly because medical policies influence the nation's ability to compete in the world economy, federal authorities should outlaw practices that restrict the mobility of labor, such as the disinclination of many insurers to cover employees with pre-existing conditions. Economic realities will probably force the United States to enact national health insurance at some point because, as we have noted, American corporations are placed at an economic disadvantage when they must fund health benefits of employees, unlike their European and Japanese counterparts. As long as corporate funding exists, however, federal authorities should establish uniform requirements so that states that mandate corporate coverage are not subjected to corporate migration to states that lack these mandates. States need some discretion, however, in deciding precisely how they will control medical costs while also meeting the medical needs of uninsured and poor citizens. For example, whereas one state chooses to make considerable use of health maintenance organizations (HMOs) for its Medicaid enrollees, another state might make greater use of publicly funded clinics and hospitals (Fraley, 1995; Goldman & Perry, 1995). (Nationalized systems in Australia and Canada allow variations in the implementation plans of different provinces or states.)

Education at the preschool, secondary, junior college, and college levels, as well as technical schools, provides the central economic strategy for European nations and Japan to cope with the globalizing economy (Reich, 1991). Although some local and state governments have developed innovative programs, few American high school graduates possess advanced technical skills. Federal authorities ought to fund the portions of the educational system enterprise that are particularly relevant to competition in the global marketplace and should devise national standards for its science, computer, and technical portions.

Devolved Programs Tilting toward State and Local Authorities

Many service-intensive programs, like large portions of the educational system, have been primarily implemented by state and local governments with some federal assistance. Local variations exist: For example, substance abuse is particularly prevalent in some areas, and homelessness is more prevalent in others (Stanfield, 1982). It is difficult to fashion national guidelines governing some aspects of these social services programs, such as how many children should be placed in foster care or returned to their natural homes. Such guidelines have led some local officials to reunify families ill-advisedly to retain federal subsidies (Wald, 1988). When granting local discretion, however, federal authorities must make larger subsidies to these programs, because people with mental problems, homeless people, and substance abusers do not attract widespread sympathy in local and state jurisdictions. (Even such groups as abused and neglected children find their programs greatly underfunded by states and counties, resulting in caseloads for child welfare workers that far exceed the standards of the Child Welfare League of America.) Federal authorities also need to encourage partnerships between local governments and not-for-profit agencies, corporations, and community groups in these service programs. Even in devolved programs that are tilted toward the states and localities, the federal government should establish some national standards. In the case of child welfare, for example, federal authorities should not allow exorbitant caseloads to exist when the safety of children is at stake.

In an era of global competition, many programs that traditionally fall under local or state control need to be partially funded by federal authorities. For example, correctional facilities are disproportionately occupied by African Americans. If Americans want these inmates to become productive workers, they ought to establish national policies that keep more of them out of prison in the first place, such as ending sentencing disparities between crack cocaine and cocaine users and developing preventive programs that target at-risk youths. Americans should also mandate and fund technical training for them during their incarceration or on their release. If child care is to prepare children for school, it needs to meet national guidelines that require educational components, even if local and state governments administer it. Traditionally funded only by local governments, libraries and recreation centers should receive federal funds to participate in educational programs in partnership with local schools.

Sole State or Local Funding and Implementation

We are not suggesting that important roles for states and local governments need to end. These governments should continue to administer large components of secondary education, preschool services, and correctional programs with little federal funding or guidance. Although they still possess tax revenues that in their aggregate are less than federal domestic expenditures, many states have improved their financial position during the past decade by increasing their state income taxes and making somewhat less use of regressive sales taxes. Using these enhanced revenues, states can and should fund myriad social programs that address gaps or omissions in federal and state programs, link local institutions in partnerships, and develop innovative programs (Rivlin, 1992).

Hybrid Programs

AFDC is one example of a program that could combine different points in the federal-to-state continuum. AFDC currently contains both a survival (or income-providing) component as well as a job-training and placement component. Why not divide the program into an income-providing program for single heads of families who are unemployed (funded exclusively by the federal government), while placing their job training in a broader block grant program that includes other citizens and that contains transportation and child care subsidies? Moreover, the economic needs of many employed single heads of households and their families could be met by expanding the EITC into a negative income tax. In a similar fashion, public housing can be conceptualized as combining federal tax policies, block-granted social services programs, and partnerships between local housing authorities and not-for-profit organizations funded by federal resources. Allowing a diversity of options on the federal-to-state continuum, however, does not contradict a leadership role by federal authorities, who provide pivotal resources, mandates, and regulations while ceding any choices to nonfederal governments.

STRATEGIES FOR POLICY PRACTITIONERS AND EDUCATORS

The patchwork of programs forming the American welfare state has principally evolved in three eras—inception (1933 to 1950), growth (1950 to 1979), and partial devolution and contraction (1979 to 1996). A new era is upon us—reorganization.

Policy practitioners need to be active participants in this undertaking both by lobbying for appropriate changes and by preserving the integrity of programs that remain effective. Instead of allowing conservatives to focus the debate on the downsizing of the federal government, policy practitioners need to refocus the debate toward reorganization within the rubric of a new nationalism.

Our framework for a new nationalism offers a theoretical taxonomy for preserving a high level of federal involvement in the provision of social welfare. At the same time, we recognize the validity of arguments in support of block grants to the states as well as the need for local partnerships within programs that receive substantial federal funds. Certain programmatic functions need the benefit of local input. Still, decisions around the proper level of government for social programs need to be driven by the substance of the program, not the promise of monetary savings or ideological attacks on the validity of federal roles.

As we have learned from history, the prevention of dire suffering is the principal tenet on which any welfare state is built. The national goal of remaining globally competitive adds a new rationale for a sizable federal role, because it requires an investment in the nation's human capital as well as in programs that focus on citizens whose economic well-being has been eroded by technological change. Older problems continue to require federal assistance, such as family disintegration, violence, and disease. A range of programs that run the gamut from being under full federal control to being under local control are needed to address these various social problems. To achieve these policy goals, policy practitioners and educators, including people in direct service, administration, community work, and policy-specialized positions, should adhere to four principles: (1) seek and retain central rules and funding, (2) target excessive devolution for change, (3) be principled opportunists, and (4) integrate policy practice into social work curricula.

Seek and Retain Central Rules and Funding

Although the extent of federal power can vary widely between programs, the welfare state should be constructed within a national framework. To retain and expand this national framework, policy practitioners need to emphasize federally directed lobbying through national advocacy groups and through linkages between these national groups and local ones.

Target Excessive Devolution for Change

Unwarranted or excessive devolution need not be permanent; it is common for block grants to be recategorized or for new restrictions to be placed on them (Arvidson, 1990; Farnham, 1981; Stenberg & Walker, 1977). Policy practitioners should try to rescind excessive devolution or harmful cuts in federal funding for devolved programs. What has been devolved may be re-evolved.

Be Principled Opportunists

To the extent that beneficent federal rules and funding are not enacted, policy practitioners should seek the best policy outcome for disadvantaged groups within their states or localities (Nathan & Doolittle, 1987). If liberal policy is possible in their states, they should take advantage of devolved power to move policy to the left. They should form action groups within their jurisdictions as well as stronger coalitions to work toward better state policies. Advocates' angst over conservatives' gains in Washington should fuel change efforts in states and localities.

Integrate Policy Practice into Social Work Curricula

Social work educators should train all social workers to advocate on behalf of disadvantaged people (Figueira-McDonough, 1993; Jansson, 1994). Policy and practice training must focus on advocacy, which includes not only analytic skills but also political and value clarification skills. Students also need various policy-related interactional capabilities such as skills in making presentations, organizing and working in coalitions, and developing leadership (Jansson, 1994). Awareness of the historical metamorphosis of the nation and the field must be coupled with a new conception of social policy as an interventive and applied discipline that lies at the heart of social work practice in all settings.

REFERENCES

Aaron, H. J. (1991). *Serious and unstable condition: Financing America's health care*. Washington, DC: Brookings Institution.

Arvidson, C. (1990). As the Reagan era fades, it's discretion vs. earmarking in the struggle over funds. *Governing, 8*, 21–27.

Balz, D., & Brownstein, R. (1996). *Storming the gates: Protest politics and the Republican revival*. Boston: Little, Brown.

Barlett, D. L., & Steele, J. B. (1994). *America: Who really pays the taxes?* New York: Simon & Schuster.

Chubb, J. E. (1985). Federalism and the bias for centralization. In J. E. Chubb & P. E. Peterson (Eds.), *The new direction in American politics* (pp. 273–306). Washington, DC: Brookings Institution.

Congressional Quarterly Service. (1993). *Congressional Quarterly almanac*. Washington, DC: Author.

Congressional Quarterly Service. (1995, September 16). *Congressional Quarterly weekly report*. Washington, DC: Author.

Conlan, T. J. (1984). The politics of federal block grants: From Nixon to Reagan. *Political Science Quarterly, 99*, 247–270.

Council on Governors' Policy Advisors. (1996). *The states forge ahead despite the federal impasse*. Washington, DC: Author.

Dreyfuss, R., & Stone, B. (1996, January). Medikill. *Mother Jones*, pp. 22–27, 77–81.

Farnham, P. G. (1981). The targeting of federal aid: Continued ambivalence. *Public Policy, 29*, 75–93.

Figueira-McDonough, J. (1993). Policy practice: The neglected side of social work intervention. *Social Work, 38*, 179–188.

Fraley, C. (1995). Governors looking for the key to open way for Medicaid. *Congressional Quarterly Weekly, 53*, 3813–3814.

Frieden, T. (1995). Tuberculosis in New York City: Turning the tide. *New England Journal of Medicine, 332*, 229–233.

Goldman, J., & Perry, T. (1995, November 2). Streamlined approach key to San Diego health system. *Los Angeles Times*, pp. A1, A12.

Hodgson, G. (1976). *America in our time*. Garden City, NY: Doubleday.

Iglehart, J. (1995). Health care report: Medicaid and managed care. *New England Journal of Medicine, 332*, 1727–1731.

Jansson, B. S. (1994). *Social policy: From theory to policy practice*. Pacific Oaks, CA: Brooks/Cole.

Jansson, B. S. (1996). *The reluctant welfare state: Social welfare policies: Past, present, and future.* Pacific Oaks, CA: Brooks/Cole.

Johnson, J. (1989, December 12). Health chief vows minority drive: Black health is likened to Third World nation. *New York Times*, p. A12.

Kamerman, S., & Kahn, A. (1996). *Starting right: How America neglects its youngest children and what we can do about it.* New York: Oxford University Press.

Krugman, P. (1990). *The age of diminished expectations: U.S. economic policy in the 1990s.* Boston: MIT Press.

Ladd, H., & Doolittle, F. C. (1982). Which level of government should assist the poor? *National Tax Journal, 35,* 65–84.

Levy, C. (1995, December 17). Pataki's cuts rely heavily on Medicaid. *New York Times*, p. A20.

Moon, A., & Schneiderman, L. (1995). *Assessing the growth of California's General Assistance Program.* Berkeley: California Policy Seminar of the University of California.

Morial, E. N. (1983). Grants and the "new" federalism. *Journal of Public Health Policy, 4,* 259–267.

Nathan, R. P. (1975). *The plot that failed: Nixon and the administrative presidency.* New York: John Wiley & Sons.

Nathan, R. P., & Doolittle, F. C. (1987). *Reagan and the states.* Princeton, NJ: Princeton University Press.

Peterson, P. E. (1991). The rise and fall of special interest groups. *Political Science Quarterly, 4,* 539–556.

Peterson, P. E. (1995). State response to welfare reform: A race to the bottom? In I. V. Sawhill (Ed.), *Welfare reform: An analysis of the issues* (pp. 7–10). Washington, DC: Urban Institute.

Peterson, P. E., Rabe, G. B., & Wong, K. K. (1986). *When federalism works.* Washington, DC: Brookings Institution.

Peterson, P. E., & Rom, M. C. (1990). *Welfare magnets: A new case for a national standard.* Washington, DC: Brookings Institution.

Polenberg, R. (1966). *Reorganizing Roosevelt's government: Controversy over executive reorganization, 1936–1939.* Cambridge, MA: Harvard University Press.

Reich, R. B. (1991). *Work of nations.* New York: Alfred A. Knopf.

Republican National Committee. (1994). *Contract with America.* New York: Times Books.

Rich, M. J. (1991). Targeting federal grants: The community development experience. *Publius, 21,* 29–49.

Rivlin, A. M. (1992). *Reviving the American dream: The economy, the states, and the federal government.* Washington, DC: Brookings Institution.

Rose-Ackerman, S. (1992). *Rethinking the progressive agenda.* New York: Free Press.

Shannon, J., & Kee, J. E. (1989). The rise of competitive federalism. *Public Budgeting and Finance, 9,* 5–20.

Stanfield, R. L. (1981a). Block grants look fine to states; it's the money that's the problem. *National Journal, 13,* 828–832.

Stanfield, R. L. (1981b). For the states, its time to put up or shut up on federal block grants. *National Journal, 13,* 1800–1805.

Stanfield, R. L. (1981c). Reagan's policies bring cities, states together in a marriage of convenience. *National Journal, 13,* 2224–2228.

Stanfield, R. L. (1982). Picking up block grants—Where there's a will, there's not always a way. *National Journal, 14,* 616–620.

Stenberg, C. W., & Walker, D. B. (1977). The block grant: Lessons from two early experiments. *Publius, 7,* 31–60.

Towns, E. (1995). Necessary flexibility or ad hoc decision making? *Public Welfare, 53,* 6.

Wald, M. (1988). Family preservation: Are we moving too fast? *Public Welfare, 46,* 33–38.

Witte, J. F. (1985). *Politics and development of the federal income tax.* Madison: University of Wisconsin Press.

This chapter was originally published in the September 1996 issue of Social Work, *vol. 41, pp. 441–451.*

3 Social Work Management in an Era of Diminishing Federal Responsibility

Richard L. Edwards, Philip W. Cooke, and P. Nelson Reid

One needs only to look at recent presidential and congressional election results to see a growing public unhappiness with government. In 1992 Texas billionaire Ross Perot ran for president as a third-party protest candidate and received nearly 20 percent of the vote, the largest number of votes cast for a third-party candidate in a U.S. presidential election (*NBC News*, 1993). During the 1994 midterm elections, the Republican party gained control of both houses of Congress as well as many state legislatures, ending nearly four decades of control by the Democratic party. With their new majorities, Republicans quickly worked to implement provisions of the *Contract with America* (Gingrich, Armey, and the House Republicans, 1994), which emphasized shifting many federal government responsibilities to state and local governments.

There is also a growing disaffection with what is broadly termed "welfare" and the associated public and nonprofit social work and human services organizations. Although welfare, as reflected by Aid to Families with Dependent Children (AFDC), is a small proportion of the total public expenditure, it nonetheless symbolizes the perceived failure of government to deal effectively with social realities. "Welfare bashing" is a frequent topic of radio and television talk shows. Although such popular discourse may be valuable in a democracy, it places social work professionals and managers in a defensive posture. These realities make the social work manager's job more difficult.

In the near future the changing political realities and their social and cultural context will bring additional challenges to the social work profession and to those who manage social work and human services organizations. Leaders from both political parties are responding to a common set of economic and social forces and assumptions—even though they disagree on specifics—that are driving them to seek solutions to the federal budget deficit, rampant increases in expenditures for various entitlement programs, and decades of growth in federal regulations that affect almost every aspect of Americans' lives.

It is almost certain that what is termed the "devolution revolution" (Nathan, 1995) will continue regardless of the November 1996 election outcome. Budget controls, selective tax reductions, caps on entitlement spending, and means-tested benefits tied to socially "responsible" behavior are currently being implemented. In addition, block grants with reduced funding levels and regulations and the increased use of purchase-of-service (POS) agreements and other means to draw a wide range of nonprofit and for-profit organizations into service provision will further complicate and disaggregate an already dizzying arena within which social work managers must function.

This article discusses the management challenges facing social work, including changes in the U.S. economic and social structure, changes in public policy that have greatly increased the diversity and competitiveness of social services providers, and the development of a growing public discontent with government organizations. This article reviews two management approaches—total quality management and reengineering—and considers the implications for social work management.

HISTORIC POLICIES AFFECTING SOCIAL WORK MANAGEMENT

Although it may be tempting to see these new realities as a current political and partisan phenomenon, there is a larger, historical reality underlying the developments changing social welfare.

Progressive Movement and the New Deal

The progressive movement emerged in the United States during the late 19th century (Reid, 1995). Progressives promoted a rational, public, social sciences-based government response to social problems that emphasized economic regulation, meritocracy, social insurance, and other protections, as well as the "professionalization" of services. Progressives were optimistic and humane, and they promoted an environmental view of human behavior that was in contrast to the 19th-century view of individual character and will as explanations of the shortcomings of society. The progressive view helped create the context for the development of social work as a profession and established the American social policy agenda for the 20th century (Crunden, 1982; Hofstader, 1955).

In response to the Great Depression of the 1930s, President Franklin Roosevelt's New Deal federalized many progressive-initiated state-level social programs. As a result, a new scope of program construct was created through federal legislation with significant implications for program funding and responsibility. Thus was created America's version of the welfare state. However, because of a multilevel government structure, the American version was more diverse and pragmatic than its European counterparts, and without the class politics of the European welfare states, the country was unable to sustain political support for the growth of the social welfare system after the Great Depression waned. Consequently, the two decades following the passage of the Social Security Act in 1935 were characterized by a relatively slow expansion of social welfare, with the social insurances the focus of growth and political support (Reid, 1995).

During this time, social services were generally nonmarket, professional services to individuals and families who met an income requirement or had other defined special needs. Services related to rehabilitation, child welfare, protection, or care and advice and were provided by religious, secular nonprofit, or government providers. Recipients were typically called "clients" or "patients" (not "consumers"), and the problems of nonmarket or functional monopoly provision were rarely considered (Reid, 1971).

Primary management tasks involved organizing the delivery of services, accounting for the dollars spent, and relating to the funding and authority sources. Accountability was largely upward and internal, from worker to supervisor to director to board or legislative authority. External interests were represented on policy or advisory boards. Workers were not accountable to clients, who typically had little choice in consumption and little voice in program design or operations. Funding at the federal and state levels was categorical (that is, specific to a particular service in a particular problem context). The job of a manager in this context was comparatively simple in that the important actors were visible and near, continuity was ensured from year to year, and the system was closed to the intrusion of competitors or evaluators searching for evidence of cost-effectiveness.

Great Society and New Federalism

In the 1960s American social welfare changed. The nation found a surrogate for labor-based class conflict in the issues of race and poverty. The War on Poverty, with its emphasis on community-level initiatives, activism of the poor population, programs targeted to need, and an opportunity construct of poverty reduction, was a dramatic departure from the welfare state model of social security and nationalized services (Dobelstein, 1996; Patterson, 1985). The Economic Opportunity Act of 1964 was about community-level social reform that would break down barriers to opportunity and create a political presence for poor people. The result was new social programming and a recast social policy.

By the early 1970s, the United States was approaching European levels of social welfare expenditures as a percentage of its gross domestic product (GDP), a remarkable achievement for a country without a national health care program (U.S. Bureau of the Census, 1994). Total governmental expenditures, tax rates, and the number of interest groups vying for a share increased at startling rates. The context for social work or human services organizations and managers became complex, with the federal government at the center of the system for policy making, allocation of resources, and control.

Adding to the complexity, the rapid increases in expenditures and sources of funding and support did not occur within a consistent concept of social welfare development. Indeed, by the 1960s, it was already apparent that the Beveridge welfare state construct of "institutional" social welfare (Wilensky & Lebeaux, 1965), with its emphasis on universalism and citizen-based, non–means-tested benefits, would not be the basis for American social welfare.

In 1967 Congress included in amendments to the Social Security Act a provision that allowed states to contract for delivery of services or the carrying out of certain administrative tasks. By 1974 the Nixon administration had consolidated four previous titles providing for categorical services and federal funding of the Social Security Act into Title XX (Plotnick & Skidmore, 1975), which provided for a block of funds to be used in ways determined by state governments and requiring a state funding match. In addition, states were required to devote only half of the funds to providing services for poor people. These provisions greatly increased state latitude and expenditures and expanded services to include day care for children and adults, transportation, home health and homemaker services, job training and education, mental health counseling, and information and referral services.

In 1981, Congress enacted the Omnibus Budget Reconciliation Act (OBRA), which was consistent with the new federalism policies of the Reagan administration. OBRA eliminated 57 social programs that were funded by categorical grants, compressing them into seven block grants: social services; community services; alcohol, drug abuse, and mental health services; maternal and child health services; community development services; primary health services; and preventive health services (Dickinson, 1995).

Notably, none of the newer service areas that emerged in the 1970s and early 1980s was specific to the poor population, and almost all had parallels in the private market, which was producing services for paying consumers or for third-party reimbursement. Some analysts and policymakers questioned whether services for individual consumption (for example, health, legal, financial, and self-development) could be more efficiently and effectively produced in competitive markets for poor and nonpoor clients alike.

Once the overlap of services between the poor and nonpoor populations was apparent and the social control-public interest aspect of social services was rendered less important than individual consumption and change, the "commercialization of the social market" (Gilbert & Gilbert, 1989, p. 32) happened. This commercialization presumed the desirability of competition and market allocation and depended on a diversity of providers, requiring the destruction of the monopolistic social services model based on public service provision and rendering the state as broker–contractor or provider of vouchers or third-party reimbursements.

Experience in the health services sector suggests that no necessary connection exists between personal income and service consumption in a private provider market (Stoesz, 1987). As long as public or private insurance exists, people can be supported in consumption and given access to existing markets. In this situation there is no need for the government to produce services.

The search for an alternative to traditional public social service provision has taken a number of forms. The initial response to bureaucracy and unresponsive services was to render such services more accountable through political devices. The "maximum feasible participation" rule in the Economic Opportunity Act of 1964 envisioned agencies accountable to boards composed of poor people and providing services through "indigenous" workers in neighborhood organizations that represented the poor population (Patterson, 1985). Citizen participation provisions were later incorporated into the Model Cities Program; became the basis for "community control" of the New York City schools; and were incorporated in some form through advisory committees, review panels, and public hearing requirements into most areas of federal governmental rule-making and policy implementation (Dobelstein, 1996). These requirements increased the necessity for social work managers to have skill in communicating with and resolving conflicts between various constituencies or stakeholders.

Whereas the passion for participation of the poor population and citizens in general lasted only a few years, the policies requiring such processes far outlived the hope that such reforms would transform social services in meaningful ways. Meanwhile, there was a growing perception that public provision of social or human services was less efficient, less effective, and less responsive to individual consumers than market-based provision, which was growing rapidly (Levine, 1972). For example, in the child welfare arena, foster care, group homes, and residential or institutional care have been provided for many years both by nonprofit and for-profit nongovernment organizations. Indeed, by the 1980s, about 30 percent of such services were provided by government POS agreements with for-profit organizations (Abramson & Salamon, 1986). The involvement of for-profit organizations in other social and human services arenas has been increasing as well. Employment training, transportation, day care, and health and mental health services have been provided on a for-profit basis, giving rise to an expansion of private practice in social work and a new wave of human services corporations in home health care, nursing homes, and hospitals (Stoesz, 1986). Major for-profit organizations have also emerged in the day care and corrections fields.

Of course, POS contracting or third-party reimbursement through insurance is not the same as competitive market provision. For example, in health care, public and private insurance provision has set prices and removed any savings incentives to consumers, leading to efforts to replace the lost market elements through such mechanisms as diagnosis-related groups and managed care (Edinburg & Cottler, 1995). Purists have argued for vouchers or refundable medical savings accounts and have applied this economic logic to public schools, Medicare, and Social Security retirement benefits (Bendick, 1989; Ferrara, 1982). However, although the logic has become accepted wisdom in some areas, the policy prescriptions have not.

SOCIAL WORK MANAGEMENT IN THE NEXT CENTURY

Although many individuals and groups in the United States have not fared well, the 20th century has been kind to the nation as a whole. No wars have been fought on U.S. soil, the country has emerged as the world's major military and economic power, and overall the standard of living has risen dramatically. For most of the century, the country has been the envy of the world. Yet, as the beginning of the 21st century nears, Americans—and the rest of the world—are feeling a certain unease.

Before the turn of the century, in 1896 the country was in the midst of the most rapid population increase in its history, an increase driven by vast amounts of undeveloped land in the West and an open immigration policy. Cities grew by leaps and bounds, and the majority of the people in the largest cities were not born in the United States. Factories were the center of the economy, and sweat shops, low wages, child labor, crowded tenements, urban crime, and labor strife were the dominant social images of the time. Many Americans felt a sense of crisis over the dramatic transformations that they believed threatened democracy and promised permanent social conflict.

In the midst of the 1996 presidential election campaign, many Americans are expressing similar concerns about immigration, the economic structure, and a range of social problems, all of which many perceive as threats to democracy and the American way of life. Profound changes are again affecting the country: economic transition and globalization, a dominant middle-class culture and conservative movement, and the decline of welfare state ideology and the political structure supporting it.

Economic Transition and Globalization

The U.S. economy, which was built on large-scale standardization and manufacturing, has moved dramatically to service and communications, a shift in emphasis from skill and labor to speed, knowledge, abstraction, analysis, and planning. Whereas the economy is increasingly based on the manipulation of words and numbers, the U.S. population as a whole is not well suited by education or social experience for this new world. In addition, the economy has been affected by the increase of women in the workforce, the emergence of an urban underclass, and the growth of a culture that is obsessed with work and consumption.

Also, Americans are concerned that the nation has lost ground to the growing economies of Asia and the European Community and that the next century will see Americans' living standards decline even as their work time and productivity increase. The consequences of economic pressures for family life, community, and growing societal inequalities are already apparent.

Growth of the Middle Class and the Conservative Movement

The increasing economic success of the middle class, coupled with increasing social welfare expenditures with no apparent decline in social problems and a sense that social programs may have negative effects on individual and societal development, have led to a conservative movement in every Western nation. Drawing support both from cultural conservatives, who fear that social changes are destructive to valuable traditions, and from a market-minded business sector, the conservative movement has established the public policy agenda of high-GDP nations during the past 20 years.

Decline of the Welfare State

Most of the increases in social welfare expenditures in the late 1960s and early 1970s were in social security, AFDC, Medicaid, Medicare, and the Food Stamp program. In retrospect, one can see that what caught the imagination of social reformers at that time was not a reinvigorated welfare state, but rather an open society, free of the divisiveness of race and class, that provided opportunity and high standards of living for everyone. What seemed to energize reformers was the "promise of an American life" (Croly, 1909).

In 1967 Congress enacted the Work Incentive (WIN) program amendments to Title IV of the Social Security Act, creating the first work incentive program for adults receiving AFDC (Plotnick & Skidmore, 1975). The creation of the WIN program shifted the focus of AFDC from a child welfare program concerned with stabilizing a parental role and compensating for an absent parent to a program of work, opportunity, and behavioral reform for adults. Much of the current rhetoric about welfare reform can be seen as an extension of the policy shift begun in 1967.

The decline in traditional manufacturing and the size and influence of organized labor have left the welfare state without the economic structure that created its base of political support (Ehrenreich, 1985). With less political support and rejection by social and business conservatives, the ideology of the welfare state has eroded dramatically in the United States and Europe. Social work, which was central to U.S. social policy for poor and dependent people during the first third of the century, was largely relegated to service provider in a broader social welfare system in the middle third of the century. During the final decades of the century, the social work profession has often been on the outside of policy processes.

Replacing the social welfare state model is the "new consensus" or "new paradigm," which eliminates the main conservative criticisms of the welfare state (high taxes, economic stagnation, centralization and bureaucracy, suppression of labor participation) and promises a smaller, reinvented government and the end of unnecessary regulation, more reliance on local and private initiatives, greater use of market allocation for public purposes, and the end of "dependence." In this model, the government defines social objectives but no longer protects citizens from the ravages of capitalism. Rather, the government embraces the concept and operations of the free-market economy and uses it for desirable social ends. In this new paradigm the welfare state becomes the "enabling" state (Gilbert & Gilbert, 1989).

Implications for Social Work Management

Over the past few decades these changes have transformed the character of social services. That transformation, including a progressive diminishment of federal responsibility and control, has required a reconceptualization of the role and character of the social services enterprise and its management.

Some fear that such a transformation will encourage a "race to the bottom," a drastically lowered public investment in services and what Nathan (1995) characterized as a "turning away from the poor and minorities" (p. 15). Those concerned about this possibility fear that the shift in responsibility for social and human services and caps on grants will create incentives for states to cut benefits and services (Weaver & Dickens, 1995). Others have argued that such block grant funding and the accompanying increased latitude will produce innovation and experimentation in the states that will allow a comparative and empirical basis for selecting among policy options (Wiseman, 1993). However, much will depend on the political landscape in the states and regions and their capacity to respond to reductions in federal funding.

This situation will likely accelerate management changes that are already apparent in response to the shift of social policy. Downsizing or "right-sizing" is occurring in many social services organizations, a process driven by both budget constraints and the necessity for organizations to compete on service-product cost. The result is smaller and flatter organizations in which fewer people supervise more workers with fewer middle management positions (Ginsberg & Keys, 1995).

Such a process is possible because developments in information technology have radically increased speed and access to information used in decision making and rendered obsolete many positions that were once devoted to processing, storing, retrieving, and disseminating information. Enhanced computer capabilities, electronic mail, pagers, facsimile machines, and cellular telephones all affect today's work (Butterfield, 1995; Schoech, 1995).

Substantial changes have also occurred in the composition of the workforce in gender, race, and ethnicity. These changes require culturally competent managers who understand the issues presented by diversity and possess the skills to help their organizations and their workers effectively resolve those issues (Bailey, 1995).

Contemporary social work managers must function in an atmosphere of increasing ambiguity and paradox. Managers are confronted almost daily with the need to satisfy different and sometimes competing values and stakeholder interests, all in a context of diminishing resources and organizational security within the service system (Austin, 1995; Edwards, 1987; Edwards & Austin, 1991). Social work managers must learn "to negotiate, in a context of competing values, to achieve a broad consensus about organizational vision, mission, and strategy. There needs to be a process for identifying and then selecting change challenges that will be addressed" (Edwards & Eadie, 1994, p. 122). Addressing loss of security has become a primary management focus, leading to an increase in time spent dealing with external conflicting demands at the expense of internal matters (Menefee & Thompson, 1994).

In addition, social work managers must be prepared to perform different and sometimes conflicting or competing roles. These include roles that have to do with relating to the organization's environment, such as those involved in entrepreneurship and strategic management, and roles concerned with internal operations, such as creating a positive human relations climate and a smooth-functioning, well-coordinated workplace (Edwards & Austin, 1991).

Furthermore, social work managers must be market oriented. They must be able to accurately assess the place of their organization with respect to supply and demand in their field or service sector, and they must adopt a "bottom-line" mentality that has characterized the for-profit sector. Both public and nonprofit social work organizations are competing with for-profit organizations. Public organizations will become less likely to be involved in direct service delivery, and POS agreements between public agencies and nonprofit and for-profit providers will continue and expand. As is evident from the health care services sector, the operational distinction between nonprofit and for-profit organizations is no longer clear: The future of social work provision seems the same.

NEW MANAGEMENT APPROACHES

In such a context, managers of social and human services organizations are often urged by policymakers, board members, or the public to adopt the latest management fad sweeping the for-profit business sector. One key task for social work managers is to determine which management strategy can be applied to their social work organization. Gummer and McCallion (1995) observed, "the management field is . . . fraught with uncertainties and insecurities, and . . . schemes for transforming organizational forms and practices come and go on a regular basis. In the past quarter-century alone, the list of management 'break-throughs' includes program-planning-budget systems, management-by-objectives, matrix management, quality circles, zero-based budgeting, the one-minute manager, and reinventing government" (p. vii).

To be useful in social work, a management construct must provide a framework that allows an organization to identify changes and monitor results and must reorient workers to a new mission concept and relationship to its users, funders, and overall environment. Currently, two models of organizational change are being used in social work organizations—total quality management (TQM) and reengineering. Both represent substantive approaches to change management, seem generally compatible with social work values, and provide a framework that can facilitate the reorientation of social workers to the new realities.

Total Quality Management

Gunther and Hawkins (1996) suggested that TQM is more than a new management approach or philosophy; it represents a paradigmatic shift to a wholly new approach to organizational management. Whether this is true remains to be seen, but it is clear that TQM represents a significant change in approach for social work organizations. Like many other management approaches or techniques, TQM was first developed in the private business sector. It has been widely described in both popular and professional literature; has been the subject of numerous management training programs; and has been implemented in a wide range of public, nonprofit, and for-profit organizations in the health, education, and social services sectors (Ginsberg & Keys, 1995; Gummer & McCallion, 1995; Gunther & Hawkins, 1996; Keys, 1995; Moore & Kelly, 1996).

In defining TQM, Sashkin and Kiser (1993) suggested "that the organization's culture is defined by and supports the constant attainment of customer satisfaction through an integrated system of tools, techniques, and training. This involves the continuous improvement of organizational processes, resulting in high-quality products and services" (p. 39). For an organization using the approach, TQM is a continuous, integrated, and self-directed way of establishing, maintaining, and improving quality and service delivery.

Swiss (1992) discussed several basic tenets of TQM:

- The customer, or consumer, is the ultimate determiner of quality.
- Quality assurance is built into the service production process from the beginning rather than at the point of or after delivery.
- There is an absence of variability in services produced and delivered (that is, there is an error-free environment).
- People in the organization work collectively and not individually to improve quality.
- Mechanisms and procedures are in place for continuous improvement of system inputs, processes, and outputs and monitoring in each area.

- Participation in quality improvement by both professionals and staff is substantial in time and depth.
- There is a total organizational commitment, and continuous quality improvements are incorporated into the culture of the organization.

TQM is designed to help organizations survive and prosper in increasingly competitive and uncertain environments. Many private-sector businesses have found that becoming customer oriented and establishing a continuous pursuit of quality have enabled them to maintain a competitive edge. TQM has also been implemented in government organizations to assist them in overcoming a general loss of credibility. In general, TQM can aid social work organizations by integrating quality monitoring with their production processes and allowing their client-consumers to define quality. The combination of a model with emphasis on broad-based participation and a client–consumer focus consistent with the social work commitment as expressed in the *NASW Code of Ethics* (NASW, 1994) is attractive to many in the profession.

Gummer and McCallion (1995) noted that "TQM is more overtly consistent than other management approaches with the activities and interests of social services agencies and the expressed values of the social work profession" (p. xi). TQM is based on a humanistic philosophy and is participatory, nonhierarchic, and nonmechanistic. It does not rely on task analysis, time and motion studies, or other alienating processes, and it is consistent with the philosophical foundations of social work practice. Social work applications of TQM include the development of multidisciplinary health teams to improve practice (Vinokur-Kaplan, 1995), revitalizing a public child welfare organization (Austin & Cohen, 1995), improving client satisfaction with a county social services agency (O'Neil, Hasset, & Austin, 1995), developing a strategic plan for a Red Cross organization (Mulroy & Halpin, 1995), and establishing a continuous process improvement procedure for case management (Hayden & McCallion, 1995).

To respond to the long-standing criticism that social work services have insufficient focus on client–consumer interests (Moore & Kelly, 1996; Reid & Gundlach, 1983), TQM can provide ways to identify client interests and operationalize their self-determination (Keys, 1995). However, one problem associated with TQM in social work organizations is the inherent difficulty in sorting out the actors who may be regarded as client–consumers.

Social work organizations, both historically and presently, have a strong external element—that is, they actually and symbolically provide satisfaction to others in addition to their direct service to client–consumers. This accounts, at least in part, for the fact that social work organizations and services typically have been organized as accountable to interests other than clients and is expressed in the need for a social mandate as a basis for legitimacy (Reid & Gundlach, 1983).

However, the new paradigm of diminished federal responsibility deemphasizes the external, social, and community aspect of services in favor of a more individual consumption model (President's Commission on Privatization, 1988). This requires not only a reworking and restructuring of social work organizations, but a revised conceptualization of the professional aspects of so-cial work as well. A profession is, after all, not a business accountable only to customers, investors, and law; rather, it is a social covenant committed to the larger society. That covenant is expressed in all professions through standards enforced through professional organizations and recognized by society through licensing and certification procedures.

Social work managers face a major challenge in identifying their organiza-tions' client–customers and sorting out their expectations about their products and services. Given the variety of stakeholders of most social work organiza-tions, this is not an easy task. Narrowly defining as customers only those who use social work services (that is, those traditionally referred to as "clients" or "patients") is not likely to serve social work well in the present environment. Yet who are social work's customers? Are they the policymakers who created the organizations and programs, the funders, the public bodies in POS agree-ments, the insurance companies that give third-party reimbursement, the cli-ents and patients, the board members, or the general taxpaying public or com-munity? However difficult to achieve, clarity of focus on customers as direct consumers of services is critical in successful application of TQM in social work organizations. Once customers and their expectations have been identified, so-cial work managers must develop mechanisms for defining and measuring prod-uct quality, which is not an easy task (Brannen & Streeter, 1995; McGowan, 1995).

Reengineering

Reengineering, described as "the next management revolution" (Corbin, 1993, p. 26), complements TQM. Hale and Hyde (1994) defined *reengineering* as "revi-talizing an organization's core work processes to accomplish significant and rapid improvements in operating and support costs, service levels and cycle of work completion time, product and quality innovation, and employee respon-sibilities for service and organizational goals" (p. 127). Mechling (1994) defined *reengineering* as "the fundamental redesign of the work process involved in pro-ducing a product or service, rapid and large-scale performance improvements in the process being redesigned, and, often, the aggressive use of information technologies" (p. 189). In reengineering, efforts are made to bring about changes in an organization's business processes (that is, activities that produce a specific service for a specific customer), and these changes affect "job definitions, orga-nizational structures, management and control systems, information technol-ogy systems and applications, worker skill requirements, and organizational beliefs and behaviors" (Linden, 1994, p. 150). In a true reengineering effort there are no sacred cows.

As an approach to renewing organizations and systems, reengineering builds on the technologies and processes of strategic planning, quality management, participative management, project management, and classical organizational development (Hale & Hyde, 1994). Although there is as yet no clear prescrip-tion of a "right" way to reengineer an organization, Caudle (1994) identified guidelines for a successful reengineering effort, including the collaborative

development of an organizational mission that incorporates service quality specifics and identifies customers, the development of a governance structure capable of designing and implementing the change management effort, the selection of a strategy on the basis of a clear definition of desired performance outcomes,
and a focus on the organizational processes most likely to influence service quality and effectiveness. Hammer and Champy (1993) suggested that reengineered
organizations are characterized by flattened management, with employees participating on teams that have a high degree of cohesion and morale: "Managers
stop acting like supervisors and behave more like coaches" (p. 65).

To effectively implement a reengineering process, managers must have a high
level of confidence and competence, because the process involves a fundamental challenge to every procedure and assumption currently in place (Linden,
1994). What is required is a focus on possibilities, rather than constraints, through
innovation and adaptation of new ideas, technology, and processes.

Marriage of TQM and Reengineering

Both TQM and reengineering rely on "process management, customer feedback,
performance measurement, teamwork, and data-driven decision making. . . .
The differences are ones of scope and pace" (Hale & Hyde, 1994, p. 129). Given
that social work organizations are functioning in an environment of rapid and
profound change, the creative application of these management approaches or
strategies may help social work managers better position their organizations
for survival.

Proponents see TQM as promoting a grassroots, bottom-up, incremental, inclusive, and continuous change process that involves all levels of the organization. Such an approach is fundamentally consistent with social work values.
Proponents see reengineering as a more selective, upper-level-management-
driven, less-inclusive approach that operates on the premise that organizations
can change rapidly through a redesign of work or production processes.
Reengineering lends itself to more rapid organizational change than TQM and
thus is well suited to a rapidly changing environment (Hale & Hyde, 1994).

We believe that many elements of both TQM and reengineering can prove
valuable to social work managers struggling to adapt to their changing environment. However, the key to making appropriate use of these and other management approaches or models is the commitment to beginning with a clean
slate and "out-of-box" thinking (Linden, 1994). Social work managers must be
realistic about the changes confronting them and the organizations they lead
and be willing and able to challenge a range of fundamental assumptions.

CONCLUSION AND IMPLICATIONS FOR SOCIAL WORK

Far-reaching changes are taking place in the role of the federal government in
the provision of social services. The devolution revolution is under way, characterized by diminished roles for the federal government in providing and funding services. Block grants, with reduced federal funding and increased autonomy
and flexibility for state and local governments, will likely accelerate the trend
toward POS contracting by public organizations. Furthermore, the for-profit

sector is increasingly involved in social services delivery through such contracts, bringing about competition between public and nonprofit organizations and their for-profit counterparts. General public dissatisfaction with the role of government is leading to an increased focus on effectiveness and efficiency and a new fixation on results and outcomes.

When considering how social work management is being affected by the changes in federal responsibility, it is worth noting that a passion for rules and job descriptions, a devaluation of personal characteristics as immaterial to productive work, and a disregard for personal relationships among workers have tended to characterize American organizations over the course of this century. From Taylor's "scientific management" to "management by objectives" to more recent fads, popular management theory and practice have reflected these emphases (Hampden-Turner & Trompenaars, 1994). Such companies as the Big Three American automobile makers, McDonalds, and IBM are examples. Although the larger, cultural sources of these management emphases are beyond the scope of this article, those who fail to recognize that the United States has a distinctive management style that has been consistent over the past century will fail to understand a major source of the nation's economic success as well as the present limitations in the ability to adapt to the demands of a rapidly changing organizational environment.

The ability of social work to endure in the years ahead will depend on the profession's success in developing a sound body of knowledge and a capacity to apply that knowledge, bounded by the professional value system, in ways that address human and social problems effectively and efficiently. The changing environment for social work organizations and managers has implications for practice and education.

In practice, social work managers must be proactive; they must be able to create and articulate organizational vision and be skilled in strategic management, a blend of strategic planning and change management (Edwards & Eadie, 1994). In addition, social work managers must be able to manage in an organizational context that involves an increased emphasis on information technology. More than ever, social work managers need to be skilled fundraisers and coalition builders. They need to be adept at conducting market analyses and leading their organizations to focus on performance measures and output quality. Furthermore, social work managers need to be able to bring about significant changes in organizational culture in response to a rapidly changing environment.

In education, the qualities and skills needed by social work managers must be incorporated into curricula that will prepare managers for contemporary practice realities. Too often, schools of social work have lagged far behind in their approach to management education. Schools of social work must restructure their management curriculum to make it relevant to management practice in a changing and competitive environment. Schools must focus on preparing their students to manage in public, nonprofit, and for-profit organizations and provide courses and field education learning experiences that build students' problem-solving skills and abilities. Schools must offer course work in strategic management; fundraising; coalition building and interdisciplinary teamwork;

and management knowledge and skill areas including information technology, financial management, workplace diversity, and legal issues. Students must be prepared to manage organizations in which such trends as managed care, third-party reimbursement, POS agreements, performance measurement, and determination of output quality are integral. Furthermore, students must be taught how to identify their client–customers and how to package and market their organizations' services.

All of this presents a dilemma for social work educators struggling to creatively introduce more content within the curriculum constraints imposed by CSWE's accreditation standards (CSWE, 1994). However, if the profession does not adapt its curricula, there are likely to be far fewer social workers in management positions. Instead, many more managers of social work organizations will be products of schools or departments of business, public administration, and nonprofit management. This will be a serious loss for the social work profession and for those served by social work organizations.

REFERENCES

Abramson, A., & Salamon, L. (1986). *The non-profit sector and the new federal budget*. Washington, DC: Urban Institute.

Austin, D. M. (1995). Management overview. In R. L. Edwards (Ed.-in-Chief), *Encyclopedia of social work* (19th ed., Vol. 2, pp. 1642–1658). Washington, DC: NASW Press.

Austin, M. J., & Cohen, B. (1995). Using TQM principles in revitalizing public child welfare organizations. In B. Gummer & P. McCallion (Eds.), *Total quality management in the social services* (pp. 257–274). Albany, NY: Rockefeller College of Public Affairs and Policy.

Bailey, D. (1995). Management: Diverse workplaces. In R. L. Edwards (Ed.-in-Chief), *Encyclopedia of social work* (19th ed., Vol. 2, pp. 1659–1663). Washington, DC: NASW Press.

Bendick, M. (1989). Privatizing the delivery of social services. In S. Kamerman & A. Kahn (Eds.), *Privatization and the welfare state* (pp. 41–56). Princeton, NJ: Princeton University Press.

Brannen, S. J., & Streeter, C. L. (1995). Doing it with data: Total quality management and the evaluation of human services. In B. Gummer & P. McCallion (Eds.), *Total quality management in the social services* (pp. 59–88). Albany, NY: Rockefeller College of Public Affairs and Policy.

Butterfield, W. H. (1995). Computer utilization. In R. L. Edwards (Ed.-in-Chief), *Encyclopedia of social work* (19th ed., Vol. 1, pp. 594–613). Washington, DC: NASW Press.

Caudle, S. L. (1994). Reengineering strategies and issues. *Public Productivity & Management Review, 18*, 149–162.

Corbin, L. (1993). Reengineering: The next management revolution. *Government Executive, 25*(9), 26–32.

Council on Social Work Education, Commission on Accreditation. (1994). *Handbook of accreditation standards and procedures*. Alexandria, VA: Author.

Croly, H. (1909). *The promise of American life*. New York: Macmillan.

Crunden, R. (1982). *Ministers of reform: The progressives' achievements in American civilization, 1889–1920*. New York: Basic Books.

Dickinson, N. S. (1995). Federal social legislation from 1961 to 1994. In R. L. Edwards (Ed.-in-Chief), *Encyclopedia of social work* (19th ed., Vol. 2, pp. 1005–1013). Washington, DC: NASW Press.

Dobelstein, A. W. (1996). *Social welfare policy and analysis*. Chicago: Nelson-Hall.

Economic Opportunity Act of 1964, P.L. 88-452, 78 Stat. 1524.

Edinburg, G. M., & Cottler, J. M. (1995). Managed care. In R. L. Edwards (Ed.-in-Chief), *Encyclopedia of social work* (19th ed., Vol. 2, pp. 1635–1642). Washington, DC: NASW Press.

Edwards, R. L. (1987). The competing values approach as an integrating framework for the management curriculum. *Administration in Social Work, 11*(1), 1–13.

Edwards, R. L., & Austin, D. M. (1991). Managing effectively in an environment of competing values. In R. L. Edwards & J. A. Yankey (Eds.), *Skills for effective human services management* (pp. 5–22). Washington, DC: NASW Press.

Edwards, R. L., & Eadie, D. C. (1994). Meeting the change challenge: Managing growth in the nonprofit and public human services sectors. *Administration in Social Work, 18*(2), 107–123.

Ehrenreich, J. H. (1985). *The altruistic imagination: A history of social work and social policy in the U.S.* Ithaca, NY: Cornell University Press.

Ferrara, P. J. (1982). *Social security reform: The family security plan.* Washington, DC: Heritage Foundation.

Gilbert, N., & Gilbert, B. (1989). *The enabling state: Modern welfare capitalism in America.* New York: Oxford University Press.

Gingrich, N., Armey, D., & the House Republicans. (1994). *Contract with America.* Washington, DC: U.S. House of Representatives, Committees, and House Organizations, www.house.gov/org.pubs.htmc.

Ginsberg, L., & Keys, P. R. (Eds.). (1995). *New management in human services* (2nd ed.). Washington, DC: NASW Press.

Gummer, B., & McCallion, P. (Eds.). (1995). *Total quality management in the social services.* Albany, NY: Rockefeller College of Public Affairs and Policy.

Gunther, J., & Hawkins, F. (1996). *Total quality management in human service organizations.* New York: Springer.

Hale, S., & Hyde, A. C. (Eds.). (1994). Reengineering in the public sector. *Public Productivity & Management Review, 18,* 127–131.

Hammer, M., & Champy, J. (1993). *Reengineering the corporation.* New York: HarperCollins.

Hampden-Turner, C., & Trompenaars, F. (1994). *The seven cultures of capitalism.* London: Piatkus.

Hayden, W., Jr., & McCallion, P. (1995). Total quality management: Continuous process and improvement in case management. In B. Gummer & P. McCallion (Eds.), *Total quality management in the social services* (pp. 307–323). Albany, NY: Rockefeller College of Public Affairs and Policy.

Hofstader, R. (1955). *The age of reform: Populism, progressivism, and the New Deal.* New York: Alfred A. Knopf.

Keys, P. R. (1995). Quality management. In R. L. Edwards (Ed.-in-Chief), *Encyclopedia of social work* (19th ed., Vol. 3, pp. 2019–2025). Washington, DC: NASW Press.

Levine, R. (1972). *Public planning: Failure and redirection.* New York: Basic Books.

Linden, R. M. (1994). *Seamless government: A practical guide to re-engineering in the public sector.* San Francisco: Jossey-Bass.

McGowan, R. T. (1995). Total quality management: Lessons from business and government. *Public Productivity & Management Review, 18,* 321–332.

Mechling, J. (1994). Reengineering government: Is there a "there" there? *Public Productivity & Management Review, 17,* 189–197.

Menefee, D. T., & Thompson, J. J. (1994). Identifying and comparing competencies for social work management: A practice-driven approach. *Administration in Social Work, 18*(3), 1–26.

Moore, S. T., & Kelly, M. J. (1996). Quality now: Moving human service organizations toward a consumer orientation to service quality. *Social Work, 41,* 33–40.

Mulroy, E. A., & Halpin, M. (1995). Implementing total quality management: A case study in strategic planning. In B. Gummer & P. McCallion (Eds.), *Total quality management in the social services* (pp. 285–306). Albany, NY: Rockefeller College of Public Affairs and Policy.

Nathan, R. P. (1995). *Hard road ahead: Block grants and the "devolution revolution."* Albany, NY: Nelson A. Rockefeller Institute of Government.

National Association of Social Workers. (1994). *NASW code of ethics.* Washington, DC: Author.

NBC News. (1993, December 14). New York: NBC.

Omnibus Budget Reconciliation Act of 1981, P.L. 97-35, 95 Stat. 357.

O'Neil, R. R., & Hasset, S., & Austin, M. J. (1995). Clients as customers: A case study of a county social services agency listening to its primary constituency. In B. Gummer & P. McCallion (Eds.), *Total quality management in the social services* (pp. 275–284). Albany, NY: Rockefeller College of Public Affairs and Policy.

Patterson, J. (1985). *America's struggle against poverty, 1900-1984*. Cambridge, MA: Harvard University Press.

Plotnick, R., & Skidmore, F. (1975). *Progress against poverty: A review of the 1964–1974 decade*. New York: Academic Press.

President's Commission on Privatization. (1988). *Privatization: Toward more effective government*. Washington, DC: U.S. Government Printing Office.

Reid, P. N. (1971). Reforming the social services monopoly. *Social Work, 17*(6), 44–54.

Reid, P. N. (1995). Social welfare history. In R. L. Edwards (Ed.-in-Chief), *Encyclopedia of social work* (19th ed., Vol. 3, pp. 2206–2225). Washington, DC: NASW Press.

Reid, P. N., & Gundlach, J. (1983). The measurement of consumer satisfaction with social work services. *Journal of Social Service Research, 7*, 37–54.

Sashkin, M., & Kiser, K. J. (1993). *Putting total quality management to work: How to use it and how to sustain it over the long run*. San Francisco: Berrett-Koohlen.

Schoech, D. (1995). Information systems. In R. L. Edwards (Ed.-in-Chief), *Encyclopedia of social work* (19th ed., Vol. 2, pp. 1470–1479). Washington, DC: NASW Press.

Stoesz, D. (1986). Corporate welfare: The third stage of welfare in the United States. *Social Work, 31*, 245–250.

Stoesz, D. (1987). Corporate health care and social work. *Health & Social Work, 12*, 151–163.

Swiss, J. E. (1992). Adapting total quality management (TQM) to government. *Public Administration Review, 52*, 356–362.

U.S. Bureau of the Census. (1994). *Statistical abstract of the United States*. Washington, DC: U.S. Government Printing Office.

Vinokur-Kaplan, D. (1995). Social workers' adoption of quality management in a multidisciplinary host setting. In B. Gummer & P. McCallion (Eds.), *Total quality management in the social services* (pp. 231–256). Albany, NY: Rockefeller College of Public Affairs and Policy.

Weaver, R. K., & Dickens, W. T. (1995). *Looking before we leap: Social science and welfare reform*. Washington, DC: Brookings Institution.

Wilensky, H. L., & Lebeaux, C. N. (1965). *Industrial society and social welfare*. New York: Free Press.

Wiseman, M. (1993). Welfare reform in the states. *Focus, 15*(1), 15–21.

This chapter was originally published in the September 1996 issue of Social Work, *vol. 41, pp. 468–479.*

Community Building: Building Community Practice

Marie O. Weil

Social work in the United States faces extraordinary challenges in the current era of diminishing federal responsibility. Political leaders view block grants as a means of transferring decision-making power about social programs and human services to the state and local levels. But with the opportunity for increased local decision making comes the challenge to "do more with less" as human services are targeted for drastic cuts in the federal budget. The pressure for increased local autonomy has been coupled with a backlash against poor people and social services for them. The framework of federally articulated entitlements to basic supports and services evolving since the 1930s will be reduced and may be so altered that policy concepts of equality of access and equity in treatment are at risk.

At the same time, grassroots and local movements for community-based social change grounded in empowerment approaches are escalating. Social workers will be called on to respond to both the continued dismantling of the federal safety net and local concerns for economic and social development that sustains and supports families and communities.

The challenge for the social work profession is to respond to these changing conditions in ways that are proactive, advocate for vulnerable populations, and emphasize and expand skills in community-focused practice that connect empowerment strategies with social and economic development. These new strategies must create and reshape human services systems so that they strengthen the connections among the public, nonprofit, and for-profit sectors; plan effectively for local service coordination and integration; and focus on quality of care for those who cannot care for themselves. The central means for making these proactive shifts is through community practice strategies: providing liaison with communities, organizing geographic and functional communities, investing in social and economic development strategies, planning political and social action, and building coalitions.

Community practice strategies have been a critical but often underused method of practice from the inception of the profession in the settlement house and Charity Organization Society movements. But these methods have received too little attention in practice and in social work education during the past two decades. Strong emphasis on interventions at grassroots and interorganizational levels is necessary if the profession is to remain relevant to the needs of low-income and other vulnerable populations in the changing political, social, and economic context. Social workers must see that state and local decisions maximize the use of scarcer resources to meet critical needs for vulnerable populations and communities. Community practice can be a major means toward this goal.

Community building refers to activities, practices, and policies that support and foster positive connections among individuals, groups, organizations, neighborhoods, and geographic and functional communities. The Committee for Economic Development (1995) defined community building as "an ongoing comprehensive effort that strengthens the norms, supports, and problem-solving resources of the community" (p. 3). Given the current level of political divisiveness; the growing chasm between poor and lower-middle-class people and very wealthy people; the tenacity of racism; and the disappearance of jobs for low-skilled, low-literacy workers, there is a great need to find ways to reconnect people and communities into a more civil and just society.

This article delineates proactive social work responses to strengthen families and communities through community practice at grassroots and interorganizational levels. The article presents ideas for strengthening and expanding community practice, connects community practice and social development, describes the relationship between community practice and policy directions, and specifies needed research.

SOCIAL FORCES AND THE NEED FOR POSITIVE SOCIAL CHANGE

Ironically, the increasing alienation of U.S. citizens and the decline of democratic participation is occurring during a period of increasing efforts to establish democracies throughout the world. In global democratization, it is critical not only that ideas and the drive to create free markets be exported and adapted but also that infrastructures for community development and nongovernmental organizations to support democracy and participation be established or renewed.

All parts of the nation are seeing effects of the globalization of the economy, largely through the shifting of jobs overseas to lower-cost labor markets. There is increasing disparity in income between workers who are technologically prepared and service industry workers who have few benefits, often work part-time, and receive low wages. There is great need here and abroad for needs-based local economies in addition to global trade. All countries face great challenges in finding ways to pursue sustainable economic development that does not destroy the environment or place populations at risk.

The nation needs strategies and interventions at all levels to build viable communities that meet the basic needs of their members. These strategies and interventions must result in "civil societies" that develop and continually reshape effective infrastructures and mediating institutions. A *civil society* is "the communal infrastructure that underlies strong public, private and voluntary organization" (Bailey, Johnson, Smith, Wood, & Yankey, 1996, p. 1).

The nonprofit sector can provide creativity and responsiveness for addressing both local and global problems if adequately supported by private and government funding. The public sector needs to provide governance and the basic safety net for individuals, families, and communities. The for-profit sector needs to be accountable for resources and to employees; it must act with social responsibility to support communities. Each of the three sectors needs to contribute to the common good as U.S. society and the global society move into the next century.

Historical Issues

The postindustrial world is rapidly moving into the Information Age. History can be summed up in three major technological revolutions: (1) from hunting and gathering to agriculture, (2) from agriculture to manufacturing and agribusiness (the Industrial Revolution), and (3) from manufacturing and agribusiness to information generation and processing (Davis, 1996; Gore, 1996). With the rapid rise of the information industries, the speed at which information becomes obsolescent is escalating and the need for a commitment to lifelong learning is an increasingly important reality both socially and economically.

Social Work in the Information Age

Social workers need skills to stay ahead of rapid information development and social change. Continuing education strategies will become more important, and schools of social work will need to integrate new methods of learning. They must prepare for this revolution by teaching practice methods that help clients cope with accelerating social change and that help people understand local, national, and global changes so they can find sustainable niches in the growing global economy.

Social workers need skills to help break down the social alienation of poor and middle-class groups. The profession needs to invest in community practice strategies that can help diminish the negative impact of what Vice President Al Gore (1996) has described as the "digital divide" between those who have access to computers and information (and therefore jobs and resources) and those who do not. The growing power of information technology can promote positive social change and development, but the risks are also great. How can this technology be used effectively for human good and for social justice? How can it generate sustainable development and work for human and natural survival?

Theoretical Framework for Community Building

Futurists have been discussing the issues of social justice and sustainable development for some time. Metaphysician and theologian Matthew Fox (1994) discussed the negative power of the Newtonian mentality and metaphor that conceive of both mind and body as machine. In the postindustrial age, the Newtonian metaphor has lost much of its power. However, Western civilization is still locked in a Cartesian separation of mind and body, and these dated perspectives have not been replaced with human perspectives to help current and succeeding generations negotiate the rapid changes at the end of the 20th century.

Society must build philosophical frameworks to recreate a holistic human notion of the connected mind and body. Fox (1994) argued that the world is entering an "Environmental Age," which will focus on "holism" of mind and body, of individual and community, of humanity and nature. He argued that sustainable development is critical and articulated the need for renewed emphasis on participation and democracy, local decision making, and a balance or harmony with nature that harks back to the pre-modern age. Fox asserted that individuals must choose between jobs and work—"jobs" represent the vestiges of the Newtonian mechanism that reduces people to their labor, and "work" represents the possibility of wholeness. He argued that society must rebuild and recreate community and reinvent work as "real work" focused on human and sustainable development.

Social workers have a great deal to contribute to this vision. Social work relates to human potential and to wholeness in individuals, families, and communities. Our mission reflects the values of self-determination and mutual interdependence, and our goals are grounded in social justice. Although the challenge is great, with increased emphasis on community practice at grassroots and interorganizational levels social work can play a major role in the transformation of society.

Information Technology

There are strong forces to be harnessed for positive social change. Information technology can be used by grassroots groups and coalitions to network and exchange information with other organizations, to secure information about funding opportunities, to gather information and relevant research, to problem solve with other members of coalitions, and to learn from the experiences of comparable groups. The following strategies to improve practice and contribute to positive changes in the social, political, economic, and environmental systems should be emphasized to help clients, communities, and organizations adapt to social changes: educational, coaching, and empowerment methods in direct practice; capacity-building structures in and for grassroots and nonprofit organizations; emphasis on political and social participation in community life; a joining of social and economic development strategies; and expansion of research efforts to encompass the best means of capacity building and environmental sustainability.

Devolution of Social Programs to the States

All indications are that the United States will experience a devolution of dollars and programs to the state level; this change represents a major shift in policies that have been part of the basic federal social welfare fabric since the administration of Franklin D. Roosevelt. Antigovernment perspectives are being expressed from many political vantage points. There is a growing backlash against poor people, immigrants (particularly undocumented workers), and the services that provide supports for these and other vulnerable groups. Wage disparities have increased between traditional manufacturing workers and professional and technical workers. The distinctions between the salaries and perks of major chief executive officers and their seconds in command now concern even mainstream and conservative news journals (Boroughs, 1996; Byrne, 1996; Egan, 1996; Roberts, 1996). The decline in economic security resulting from corporate downsizing, job loss and displacement from the postindustrial economy, and the movement of jobs overseas produces fear and concerns with personal and societal instability for nonworking poor people, working poor people, and the middle class. These economic shifts are happening not only to low- and moderate-wage earners but also to professionals and previously well-paid industrial workers.

Block Grants and State Control. Social and political leaders are challenging the social safety net provided by government programs at the federal level. Block grants are seen as the wave of the future. Loss of the concept and scope of basic entitlement programs seems inevitable. Dollars will devolve to the states—but far fewer dollars—with the real risk of losses of federal protections, fair hearing procedures, and basic efforts to develop equity in programs and benefits and equal access across states.

More local control can bring more responsive and more flexible programs. However, local decision making does not guarantee humane decision making, as the history of racial discrimination and exclusion of African Americans from voting and from services in the southeastern United States attests. Members of Congress and some governors have propagated flawed assumptions that the states can do more with less, eliminate categorically bound services, and respond effectively to local needs (Federal News Service, 1996).

But the assumption that states can provide services adequate to escalating social problems (including AIDS, joblessness, and homelessness) with very reduced funding packages is highly problematic to say the least. The assumptions that the nonprofit sector can "pick up the slack" and that privatization and expansion of the for-profit human services sector will result in more efficient and effective services have not yet been tested.

Whatever the outcome of national and state-level political debates and decision making in the near future, several trends will continue to shift social welfare policy. Public funding for human services will decline. Growth in the for-profit human services sector will occur, at least initially, with an increased focus on managed care. The economy will continue to globalize, and the job market will continue to split into a lower-paid service economy and a higher-paid information-based economy.

Public human services will initially decline through both downsizing of staff and pressure to focus only on required services. More recent efforts to strengthen the prevention focus in health and human services (such as family-centered in-home public health services and family support and family preservation services) will be at considerable risk, because historically it has been difficult to prove to decision makers the effectiveness and cost savings of prevention. Public agency staff will increasingly focus on monitoring contracted services. Some of these shifts will increase hardships and crises for poor people and the growing segment of economically marginal workers and their families. The shifts in the responsibilities of the public, for-profit, and nonprofit sectors will also create crises in organizations in each sector. With all of these trends, the nonprofit and government sectors, in which most social workers practice, will face great challenges in dealing with local social problems and needs.

Social work practitioners, managers, students, and faculty must be prepared to recognize and seize the opportunities in these crises and to use knowledge, research, and practice skills to develop and strengthen community-based practice and service models. They will also need to build policy and research agendas grounded in community and family development and to document changes, risks, and problems arising from current change efforts. The central challenge is to think and practice both locally and globally and to develop and steer programs and projects that protect the most vulnerable populations through social and economic development strategies.

Private Charity and Local Programs. Observers of block grants strategy note with some irony that many dedicated human services and policy professionals and cutting-edge foundation initiatives have worked diligently over the past decade on the concepts of connecting service systems more closely to the community and of increasing local responsibility, involvement, and governance. However, the visionaries and pioneers in these efforts did not conceive of taking on increased responsibilities in local planning and governance with drastically fewer resources.

The entire concept of entitlement to basic human and health services as a basic right is shifting back to the assumption that charity can respond better (or at least more cheaply) to local social problems than public services can. It is evident that private giving through nonprofit federated fundraising and to local programs is one of the strengths of U.S. society. In comparison to western Europe and the developing world, the scale, vibrancy, and diversity of our nongovernmental organizations devoted to improving the quality of life are remarkable. Americans are more organized about and more generous in giving to local charities and nonprofit social programs than many other nations (Brilliant, 1990; Glaser, 1994; McGrath, 1996). Even though United Way contributions have not yet recovered from the 1992 crisis in confidence caused by misappropriation of funds, federated fundraising and support of the nonprofit sector remain a strong practice and a valued social norm (Glaser, 1994; McGrath, 1996).

The impulse to charity, both in donations of money and in volunteers' commitment of time, is a valuable part of the U.S. social fabric. However, depending on charity to meet the basic social needs of an increasing underclass, marginalized working poor families, and larger populations of children and elderly people living with disabilities and major chronic illnesses raises serious issues of equity and access as well as of resources and allocation. This very basic question is a critical concern especially when disparagement of poor people has reached new heights and when racist beliefs and practices have escalated and become more sophisticated.

Trends to cut the size and scope of government operations and movements toward privatization or "outsourcing" (contracting out) of human services program operations are rampant. The nonprofit sector is touted as able to absorb the "slack," despite documentation and testimony from numerous sector leaders that there will be too much slack to take up. National leaders of Catholic Charities USA and other voluntary sector leaders have testified to Congress that the nonprofit sector cannot make up for massive federal cuts in human services (Federal News Service, 1996).

Over the past 50 years, the role of the nonprofit sector has been more and more that of innovator, demonstrator, and tester of new program ideas and methods of service delivery. That capability will be severely tested if the sector is expected to take over the administration of basic human services programs previously handled by the public sector in addition to its current work. From the 1960s to the mid-1990s, the balance of government programs focusing on income support, child and elder abuse and neglect, foster care, adoption, and other basic social services was designed to ensure access to entitlements. With the changes in the system, many of these entitlements will vanish in a "leaner, meaner" public sector. Contracting with the nonprofit sector for specialized services will have a major impact on the entire human services sector and on the lives of clients, consumers, and constituencies. These shifts will also shape the context of social work practice and education; challenge the creativity of practitioners, faculty, and students; and test their commitment to primary social work values and professional mission.

SOCIAL WORK AND COMMUNITY PRACTICE

To respond to the current political, social, economic, technological, and environmental context and to engage in practice that is oriented toward the next millennium, social work practice needs to reclaim and stress community building and community practice and to move decisively into both social and economic development. This community practice and social development agenda includes a shift in the orientation of policy practice and shifts in the research agenda. In the future, social work must seek and establish the best means "to help people help themselves," to quote Jack Tate, a business leader and advisory board chair at a school of social work (Stancil, 1996). To achieve this mission, our professional values, knowledge base, methods of practice, and skills emphases need to be examined and expanded.

Values and Philosophy of Community Practice

Community practice in social work includes social planning, organizing, social and economic development, and social change directed toward expanding social justice (Weil, 1994). Historically, community practice in social work has striven in two major arenas to build bridges within and across communities. One major branch of community practice growing out of the settlement movement involves direct community work—organizing and social planning and economic and social development—within a geographic or functional community. The other major branch, growing out of the Charity Organization Societies, has focused on interorganizational work—interagency planning, fundraising, and resource development and coordination to provide services to a community or region. These two arenas of practice are particularly important if society is to achieve social justice and participatory democracy characterized by inclusiveness, an end to racism, and nonsexist communities and institutions.

Community-Building Methods

Currently, there is a great need to rebuild geographic communities and revitalize and develop functional communities dedicated not only to their particular causes but also to social justice and the basic human rights of all people. With the growing divisions in society, current practice has much to learn from community work pioneers. Mary Parker Follett argued strongly and early on for the need for people from different walks of life, ethnic groups, and socioeconomic groups to understand each other's positions. She coined the term "psychological interpenetration" to illustrate the need for mutual understanding in interorganizational and intergroup work (Syers, 1995). Much of early community work was grounded in group discussion and problem solving. During the 1940s and 1950s, intergroup work was an important aspect of community practice. In the 1960s the War on Poverty sparked considerable work in intergroup relations (Rothman, 1971), but the issue is not currently receiving sufficient attention in practice or in social work education. Intergroup work, mediation, conflict resolution, and group-community problem solving need to be reclaimed as part of social work practice.

Shared Values. Social work needs to reaffirm common values—democracy, social justice, equal rights. These values, articulated in policy and practice models and community problem solving, can help social workers rebuild communities at all levels. Community building originates in the development and articulation of a community's shared values and grows into skills development so that groups and organizations can successfully cope with problems of increasing variety and complexity (Rubin & Rubin, 1992). Finding common ground in values such as the well-being of children or environmental protection and maintenance requires a willingness to take risks and opportunities to explore ideas and issues (beyond sound-bite depth). Responsive community-based service networks can promote community-building activities. These activities can take place in schools through programs that help parents focus on children's and community needs, in and among religious institutions, in projects such as Habitat for Humanity, and through civic organizations and community advocacy groups. With increasing residential segregation by socioeconomic status and often race, it is important that community building take place not only within homogenous communities but across varied communities as well.

Gardner (1994) emphasized the importance of shared values in regenerating communities. He argued, "No society can remain vital or even survive without a reasonable base of shared values" (p. 5); he noted that values are generated and sustained in face-to-face interactions, and communities can either nurture or disregard ideals such as compassion and justice. Sociological traditions hold that humans acquire their sense of identity and self at least partly from their culture and their relationships with others in their community (Berger & Neuhaus, 1991; Nisbett, 1980). Community, therefore, can provide stimulus for individual identity and create a sense of belonging and security.

Increased mobility, according to Gardner (1994), has taken a toll on social anchors. Freedom cannot survive without a sense of continuity and shared values, and freedom, he cautions, is not a natural condition but a social construction, as are trial by jury and the tradition of a free press. Indeed, all the practices that ensure personal freedom are social constructions (Gardner, 1994).

Intermediary Structures. Sociologists Nisbett (1980) and Berger and Neuhaus (1991) are among the principal social theorists who have argued for the necessity in a democratic society for intermediary organizations and structures to provide supports and protections for individuals and groups against abuses of government power. Healthy communities are one kind of intermediary structure (Gardner, 1994). The nonprofit sector, where much social work takes place, also provides critical and numerous intermediary structures.

Social workers need to understand their responsibilities as intermediaries and work with the factors and values that are critical for the survival of democratic societies; this work needs to take place at the family, community, and interorganizational levels. Most social workers work in or lead organizations that are important intermediary structures for supporting families and communities.

Family–Community Links. It is important to consider how families and communities can be supported and renewed in the generation and preservation of value systems. Confronted by accelerating social change, many groups in the United States are focusing on preserving values that may always have been honored more in the breach than in practice. Coontz (1992), for example, clearly illustrates that even the picture of "rugged, individualistic" and entirely "self-sufficient" pioneer families was a myth. She carefully documents the government supports—land and other resources—granted to pioneer Euro-American families at the expense of American Indian groups.

Despite the many signs of the decline of community, Coontz (1992) notes that people wish to live in more supportive environments and to contribute to their communities. As counterarguments to cynicism, assumptions of rampant self-interest, and die-hard prejudices, she cites the many researchers who have demonstrated that

> human beings are capable of both nuanced decision making and extensive cooperation when they are not paralyzed by authoritarian hierarchies, conflicting cues, or impersonal structures that diffuse individual responsibility, or when they are involved in decision-making processes that involve *constructing* preferences rather than merely registering them. Social history also demonstrates that people are capable of changing their minds and working through deeply held prejudices to collaborate with people they formerly scorned. (Coontz, 1992, p. 285)

She points out that many programs succeed in helping children, adolescents, and families reduce "rotten outcomes," lead productive and successful lives, and contribute to their communities (Coontz, 1992; Schorr, 1988); such programs include Head Start; programs to reduce school dropout, teenage pregnancy, and family violence; Homebuilders' family preservation models; Resource Mothers; and local Prenatal and Early Infancy Projects (Coontz, 1992; Cooper, 1990; Milton S. Eisenhower Foundation, 1990; Schorr, 1988). Melaville (1991), Melaville and Blank (1993), and the Wilder Research Center (1992) have presented practical means to increase and strengthen collaboration among organizations serving families and communities. The Children's Defense Fund and other local and national organizations are often successful in providing information, lobbying, and marshaling support for children and families (as the "Stand for Children" rally on June 2, 1996, illustrated).

Direct service programs, local collaboration efforts, public education, and local and national social and political action are needed to support families and regenerate communities as viable institutions. These organizations often move from a family focus. Gardner (1994) argued from a community focus. Social workers must devise programs that connect and combine these micro and macro foci in an integrated strategy. The tradition and current literature of community practice have much to offer in guiding needed efforts.

Ingredients of Community Building

Gardner (1994, pp. 15–27) recommended the following 10 ingredients for building community:

1. wholeness incorporating diversity
2. a reasonable base of shared values
3. caring, trust, and teamwork
4. effective internal communication
5. participation
6. affirmation
7. links beyond the community
8. development of young people
9. a forward view
10. institutional arrangements for community maintenance.

Gardner suggested steps for the development of each of these ingredients of community, many of which can be incorporated into social work practice and into agency, organizational, and community interaction. A broad review of the community practice literature reveals additional ingredients for building and strengthening local leadership. Local leaders increasingly need to be savvy about resource development and means for securing funding for projects (Rubin & Rubin, 1992). They need increased and more sophisticated skills in verbal, written, and networking communication (Mondros & Wilson, 1994). Leaders and community workers need a strong grounding in and understanding of the community (Rivera & Erlich, 1995) and experience in intergroup and interorganizational relations as well as skills in organizing, planning, and implementing campaigns and projects (Alcorn & Morrison, 1994; Gamble & Weil, 1995; MacNair, Gross, & Daniels, 1995; Morrison, Alcorn, & Nelmus, 1996). Local leaders and community workers need skills to build widespread participation and ownership of group efforts as part of empowering communities to work toward their goals (Staples, 1990). It is important that they be able to facilitate group processes of analyzing problematic situations and assessing community needs and strengths and able to guide priority-setting processes such as nominal group technique (Gamble & Weil, 1995). It is critical that group members be able to move from a general plan to concrete steps to achieve goals, be able to link the group to other organizations within and outside the community, and be able to ensure that the group learns to give needed attention to both tasks and processes (Weil, 1988).

In the future, because of separations resulting from mobility and disparities in income, most communities will have to consciously work through educational and civil institutions and programs to "build and continuously repair the framework of shared values" (Gardner, 1994, p. 17). All members of society, especially historically disadvantaged or oppressed groups, need full acceptance as citizens and participants in the community. Beyond that, society needs structures and strategies to build consensus, form coalitions, and reacknowledge the necessity in democratic societies for collaboration and compromise; social workers can play a considerable role in these activities.

A central element of community building is shared tasks; when people invest in their community, their bond is strengthened. As Gardner (1994) stated, *"Community problem-solving activities build community"* (p. 19). Coalitions of social agencies are in a good position to provide common meeting grounds. Much of the tradition of community practice is grounded in building citizen participation (Gamble & Weil, 1995). Gardner recommended action steps including civic education, voter registration and get-out-the-vote drives, and forums to work through issues.

All intermediary organizations need links beyond their own community. Community development groups, community-based and social programs, neighborhood organizations, and grassroots communities "can and should define their own problems [and] exercise their own initiative in working toward solutions . . . but they must have recourse to larger networks—and must play their role in strengthening the larger systems" (Gardner, 1994, p. 25). Information technology is rapidly becoming one useful means to strengthen communication among nonprofits and grassroots groups. Social work has a major role to play in capacity building in communities. Community practitioners can contribute to efforts to enhance leadership skills among organized, participating community residents and work to recruit new participants and potential leaders. Community workers can facilitate and teach group problem solving; guide collaborative efforts; and provide research and analysis of community assets, problems, and opportunities (McNeely, 1996).

An Example of Community Building

Habitat for Humanity is one example of community building; it brings together young and older people, volunteers from various backgrounds, the future occupants of each Habitat house, and families who have already moved into Habitat houses. Habitat stresses the investment of sweat equity by potential home owners and the investment of volunteers from the business and religious communities to increase the affordable housing stock. The project builds on values that can be shared across many groups, and although it has sometimes been viewed as a small effort, it has contributed significantly to the housing stock. According to Herget (1996), "For those who had little faith in Habitat when it started building one house at a time in a small Georgia town in the early '80s, they may be surprised to know that the organization is now the nation's fifth largest builder of affordable homes. Habitat expects to build 60,000 homes nationwide this year" (p. 1D). Sponsors pay for materials, land, and fees; provide much of the labor; and serve as mortgage holders. Habitat does not charge interest, and a portion of each small monthly payment is placed in a revolving fund to finance other homes.

Habitat illustrates the promise and problems of community-building efforts. Programs like it can galvanize local groups to contribute to low-income housing stock and can bring together those who need homes with those who can work to help build them and those who can assist in financing. It is a bridge across socioeconomic and racial divides. The importance of efforts such as Habitat is not only the building of houses, but also the building of communities of interest with shared values about the need for and methods of developing affordable housing.

However, with the possible dismantling of the U.S. Department of Housing and Urban Development and many inside and outside the government pressing for such action, the challenge to find ways to provide affordable housing is serious. Although Habitat is a very successful program with a very low dropout rate, the scale of building does not equal the need for affordable housing. Habitat and other housing program volunteers need to advocate for and support a national affordable housing policy.

This period in the nation's history may require that many policy initiatives be "grown" from the local, county, or state level until sufficient political will can be again galvanized to set federal directions and standards for equity, fairness, and access. A central issue in this time of shifting political will is finding ways to connect successful locally grown ideas and programs to policy directions at the state and federal levels.

PRACTICE ORIENTATIONS

Three major practice orientations need to be increased and strengthened to rebuild community: empowerment practice, community practice, and social development practice.

Empowerment Practice

Empowerment practice at both micro and macro levels is needed to focus intervention on family and community development—to make connections from case to cause and to connect direct practice interventions to macro-focused social development change strategies. "Empowerment" has become a much-used word, and its meaning often seems to be reduced to how clients feel. It is much more. Solomon (1976) defined *empowerment* as

> a process whereby the social worker engages in a set of activities with the client . . . that aim to reduce the powerlessness that has been created by negative valuations based on membership in a stigmatized group. It involves identification of the power blocks that contribute to the problem as well as the development and implementation of specific strategies aimed at either . . . the reduction of the effects from indirect power blocks or the reduction of the operations of direct power blocks. (p. 19)

As this definition indicates, empowerment practice focuses on helping clients make actual changes that reduce the blocks to power in their lives. Human beings need to know themselves as their own agents and to be able to effect positive change in their environments. The empowerment approach "presumes that oppressed people and communities yearn for freedom, justice and fulfillment" (Simon, 1994, p. 3). Simon identifies the following five elements of practice in the empowerment tradition:

1. Collaborative partnerships with clients, client groups, and constituents;
2. A central practice emphasis on the expansion of clients' capacities, strengths, and resources;
3. A dual working focus on individuals and their social and physical environments;
4. The operating assumption that clients are active subjects and claimants;
5. The selective channeling of one's professional energies toward historically disempowered groups and individuals. (p. 24)

Empowerment practice is responsive to clients' presenting requests. It helps develop and encourage clients' involvement in peer networks, which build community. Empowerment practice always emphasizes the "centrality of clients' agency in promoting and sustaining change" (Simon, 1994, p. 181).

Lee (1994) presents a conceptual model of empowerment practice that includes the intermediary structures of family, group, subculture, and community processes to mediate between people and their environments. Social workers can connect community processes to environmental issues, can connect people to intermediary structures, and can connect people and intermediary structures to collective action strategies.

Family social and skills development needs to be accomplished by community economic development to build both family self-sufficiency and community interdependence. Connecting these two arenas means more than just helping people develop skills in interviewing for jobs; it also relates to working with communities to create enterprises, microenterprises, and cooperatives that fill longer-term niches in the local and global markets, that create and support community infrastructure, and that strengthen the nonprofit and community-based services sector to continually invest in the development of human capital. Such a development focus can enable people currently on a thin economic margin to live with greater economic security in rural or urban areas and can help to create communities that are viable and sustainable socially and economically.

At this juncture, social work needs to both reclaim its roots in community-based practice from the settlement and rural development movements and to embrace a major family, community, and social development agenda. On the interorganizational level, there is a need to revitalize local human services planning councils and to connect federated fundraising and allocation agencies to the development agenda.

To build empowerment practice, the following investment strategies are called for:

■ investments in programs focused on early childhood and family development that can promote healthy child development and develop marketable work skills and parenting skills.

- investments in programs focused on school-based or school-linked services to coordinate services for children and families.
- investments in youth-focused programs—These programs need to connect directly with community social and economic development; young people will bond more to communities when communities invest in them and when they themselves can give back.
- investments in urban models of community building, community reinvestment, and locally directed and focused economic development.
- investments in rural models that can help families and communities farm productively, develop new agricultural products that are economically and environmentally sustainable, and develop economic strategies that support ecological balance.

Investment strategies can be straightforwardly economic, as in the growing microenterprise movement and efforts to establish cooperatives, providing means for low-income groups to secure an economic foothold. Or they can be based on the types of individual development accounts (IDAs) urged by Sherraden (1991) to give low-income children a better opportunity to achieve long-term goals for education and job training through asset-based welfare. IDAs would be "optional, earnings-bearing, tax-benefited accounts in the name of each individual, initiated as early as birth, and restricted to designated purposes" (p. 220). Sherraden recommended that children receiving IDAs be trained in school to plan their own goals and to use their financial resources to support those goals. Investment strategies are also preventive strategies—for example, investing in family support programs rather than waiting for high-risk families to face necessities of foster care or investing in preventive health care early to save health care costs later. Major investment is needed in programs that enable families to get out of poverty, not just programs that will reduce the size of the welfare rolls. This kind of investment will take vigorous work to connect the nonprofit, for-profit, and government sectors in united strategies to help families gain economic security.

With regard to populations at high risk, Schorr (1988) stated that the social work profession is experienced in putting together intensive, multiservice human investment programs that can help break cycles of dependency. These human investment strategies must be coupled with economic development strategies. Strong, intensive, community-based programs (for example, the Comprehensive Head Start programs and exemplary adolescent pregnancy–parenting programs) that connect child, family, and economic development strategies should be adapted to urban and rural communities and expanded in neighborhoods throughout the nation.

In addition to program development, mission-oriented practice that is built on reflective practice and that consistently connects interventions to research is needed. The Homebuilders model for family preservation provides an exemplar of this practice direction (Fraser & Leavitt, 1990).

Community Practice

In the coming period of diminishing federal responsibility, community practice methods become even more important strategies to find local solutions and to strengthen local communities. Community practice encompasses work with individuals, task groups, organizations, and communities to produce positive social outcomes in neighborhoods, human services, and communities.

Table 4-1 illustrates eight current models of community practice (Weil & Gamble, 1995). In addition, Rothman (1995) revised his seminal three models of community organization—locality development, social planning, and social action—to encompass mixed models such as action-planning and development-planning and illustrated how value perspectives affect practice strategies. His revision and expansion provides guidance for engaging in community intervention.

The primary processes in community practice—organization, planning, development, and change—take place in all community practice efforts and reflect its scope. Organization involves the processes of empowerment and community organizing that engage citizens and communities in projects to change social and political conditions. Planning engages citizens, advocacy groups, advocate planners, and public and voluntary sector planners in the design of services that are appropriate to given communities, counties, or regions. Planning also relates to the design of more effective services, the coordination of services, and the major reform of human services systems. Development focuses on enabling and empowering citizens to work in united ways to change their lives and environments in relation to living conditions; economic conditions; and social, employment, and opportunity structures. Change defines the actions taken by groups to alter social, economic, and political institutions. Change includes social action, pluralism and participation, and leadership development and embraces all levels of change (Weil, 1994).

Both direct practitioners and specialized macropractitioners must be involved in neighborhood and community organizing and in organizing functional communities. Most direct service workers are involved in program development and community liaison work: designing services, conducting needs and strengths assessments, and working collaboratively with communities and constituencies to ensure the relevance of services. Increasingly, they are working with consumers in mutually planned and governed programs and services. The rapidly developing family support movement gives indications of these roles and trends.

Direct service workers and macropractitioners are typically involved in work with coalitions. Whereas macro specialists may be engaged in organizing coalitions, for example, to support health care or to improve services and conditions for homeless people, direct service practitioners may also be involved in those same coalitions. The increasing responsibility of direct service workers for case management or care coordination requires the careful development of collaborative services networks and systems interventions to ensure quality services. Case management responsibilities bear considerable resemblance to the roles and responsibilities involved in building coalitions.

More specialized macro roles are often involved in organizing in both functional and geographic communities. Special skills are needed to facilitate social and economic development projects and social planning. Major roles in advocacy and leadership development are typically taken on by social workers who specialize in political and social action work, coalition development and leadership, and full-time social movement work.

Table 4-1

Current Models of Community Practice for Social Work

Comparative Characteristics	Models			
	Neighborhood and Community Organizing	Organizing Functional Communities	Community Social and Economic Development	Social Planning
Desired outcome	Develop capacity of members to organize; change the impact of citywide planning and external development	Action for social justice focused on advocacy and on changing behaviors and attitudes; may also provide service	Initiate development plans from a grassroots perspective; prepare citizens to make use of social and economic investments	Citywide or regional proposals for action by elected body or human services planning councils
System targeted for change	Municipal government; external developers; community members	General public; government institutions	Banks; foundations; external developers; community citizens	Perspectives of community leaders; perspectives of human services leaders
Primary constituency	Residents of neighborhood, parish, or rural county	Like-minded people in a community, region, nation, or across the globe	Low-income, marginalized, or oppressed population groups in a city or region	Elected officials; social agencies and interagency organizations
Scope of concern	Quality of life in the geographic area	Advocacy for particular issue or population	Income, resource, and social support development; improved basic education and leadership skills	Integration of social needs into geographic planning in public arena; human services network coordination
Social work roles	Organizer Teacher Coach Facilitator	Organizer Advocate Writer/communicator Facilitator	Negotiator Promoter Teacher Planner Manager	Researcher Proposal writer Communicator Manager

SOURCE: Reprinted with permission from Weil, M., & Gamble, D. N. (1995). Community practice models. In R. L. Edwards (Ed.-in-Chief), *Encyclopedia of social work* (19th ed., Vol. 1, p. 581). Washington, DC: NASW Press.

Models			
Program Development and Community Liaison	Political and Social Action	Coalitions	Social Movements
Expansion or redirection of agency program to improve community service effectiveness; organize new service	Action for social justice focused on changing policy or policy makers	Build a multiorganizational power base large enough to influence program direction or draw down resources	Action for social justice that provides a new paradigm for a particular population group or issue
Funders of agency programs; beneficiaries of agency services	Voting public; elected officials; inactive/potential participants	Elected officials; foundations; government institutions	General public; political systems
Agency board or administrators; community representatives	Citizens in a particular political jurisdiction	Organizations that have a stake in the particular issue	Leaders and organizations able to create new visions and images
Service development for a specific population	Building political power; institutional change	Specified issue related to social need or concern	Social justice within society
Spokesperson Planner Manager Proposal writer	Advocate Organizer Researcher Candidate	Mediator Negotiator Spokesperson	Advocate Facilitator

Nonprofit Sector. A major arena for community practice is the nonprofit sector, which needs to develop strong new programs. The nonprofit sector provides most of the person-power for organizing neighborhoods and geographic and functional communities. The nonprofit sector also is engaged in most grassroots and community-based program innovation. Community practice strategies in program planning stress consumer and constituency involvement in planning, governance, and evaluation of services and interventions. The nonprofit sector will bear much of the burden for developing new strategies to deal with social problems after federal downsizing and implementation of block grants.

Public Sector. As the federal government turns social program decision making over to state and local governments, many public sector social workers will find their jobs reorganized to focus on monitoring external contracts, and public sector social work planners and managers will likely be increasingly involved in community work and interorganizational work to strengthen collaboration among public agencies, to strengthen partnerships between the public and nonprofit sectors, and to build effective collaboration at local and state levels. Collaboration and service coordination at local and state levels will take on even greater importance as agencies seek to do more with less and to use a community's resources most strategically. If the expectation that block grants will bring greater flexibility to service planning at state and local levels comes to fruition, there will need to be even more emphasis on joint service planning, pooling of funding and other resources, and development of effective collaboration.

A number of initiatives throughout the country support stronger collaboration. The Healthy Start model developed in Hawaii has spread to other states as Healthy Families America. The Hawaii Healthy Start model builds from early intervention, prevention, child mental health, and community practice models. The program incorporates a community approach and places much emphasis on extended family interventions and development of mutual support among families. Healthy Start has many factors in common with other family support programs but is more comprehensive and more grounded in community-building strategies. The nationally funded family preservation and family support initiative, another example of collaborative planning, is active in most states.

Building coordinated services, interagency collaboration, shared governance, and community accountability requires intensive work on the local level. Collaborative groups spanning service sectors should play major roles in advocacy for clients and communities through more local decision-making processes. Practitioners will need to learn to use information effectively and educate the public and elected officials about the realities of issues clients and constituencies face.

Social Development Practice

In the past social and community development practice combined action research with community development and community work throughout the developing world (Addams, 1910, 1930; Deegan, 1988; Lappin, 1985; Ross, 1955; Ross & Lappin, 1967). The social development perspective is of major importance for community practice. It is universalistic and comprehensive and focuses on "the community or society, and on wider social processes and structures" (Midgley, 1995, p. 23). It focuses not only on those in need but on whole populations and is geared toward processes of change and growth. As Midgley noted, "Social development offers a comprehensive macro-perspective that focuses on communities and societies, emphasizes planned interventions, promotes a dynamic change-oriented approach which is inclusive and universalistic, and above all seeks to harmonize social interventions with economic development efforts" (p. 8). This effort to make positive connections between economic development and human development and opportunity is needed as much in the United States as it is in any developing nation. Estes (1993) noted that economic development needs to be sustainable—that is, not damaging to the natural environment and supportive of human life and communities. Hoff and McNutt (1994) provided theoretical analyses and action strategies related to environmental and sustainable development.

Given the expected changes in social services policy, it will be increasingly important for social workers to be engaged in social and economic development projects and to incorporate sustainable development concepts into practice. Communities will need economic development programs with staff who are knowledgeable about community needs and able to work with populations who face increasing economic risk (National Congress for Community Economic Development, 1991). Social workers have always been involved in social development and bring considerable skill to that area. Social workers have also been involved in economic development but in smaller numbers. The current political, economic, and technological shifts challenge the profession to engage very actively in economic development for the benefit of low-income communities and at-risk populations. Family support programs and family resource centers offer one way to connect families and economic development. Other program areas need to find connections to help low-skilled youths and adults find avenues into the mainstream economy and ways to create microenterprises or cooperatives. Social workers must connect more effectively with housing coalitions, the microenterprise movement, and other similar efforts to invest in communities and develop resources.

The profession needs to support and staff community-based agencies and community development programs that are engaged in building local infrastructure for poor and dispossessed people and help groups plan and implement projects that promote social development and environmental protection. In rural Tyrrell County in eastern North Carolina, for example, an ongoing project combines social and economic development with environmental protection for a community-based sustainable development program. Nature Conservancy staff assisted local groups in achieving their goal of moving from a standard "tourism effort" to an eco-tourism project. Three years into the project's operations, it has become a training and employment program for local youths, has increased community pride and collaborative work, and has reclaimed a valuable network of coastal waterways (personal communication with M. Seager, coordinator, Resourceful Communities Program, Conservation Trust of North Carolina, April 1996).

POLICY PRACTICE ISSUES

Given the evolving political–economic–technological shifts, it is important for policy practice to receive increased attention, particularly policy practice at local and state levels. Although federal dollars will be lost in the implementation of block grants, the possibilities for flexibility and creativity in local service design and delivery can increase. There are more creative and appropriate ways to respond to specific community needs than extant categorical program funding sources have allowed. Advocates for children and families have long supported the notion that "dollars should follow families" rather than categorical funding streams. Maryland, Ohio, and Virginia have redesigned systems to increase interagency (primarily public agency) teamwork in service planning for families, deployment of a single case manager per family, and pooled funding for families across the agencies.

Several foundations such as Annie E. Casey, Kellogg, and Edna McConnell Clark have funded initiatives to reform human services for families and children and to develop community "ownership" of services and family interventions through community-based governance structures. Rockefeller and MacArthur, as well as Kellogg and Ford (among others), have invested in community and economic development strategies. These streams of foundation investment in community and service system initiatives offer exciting positive directions for changes in policy.

One of the critical challenges in the current climate is finding the most effective means to educate policymakers and the public about successful strategies and to determine the best means to adapt and transfer successful strategies to other communities. It is more important than ever to take policy practice and advocacy to the state and local levels so that providers, consumers, and volunteer leaders can actively influence and shape local services, build stronger community collaboration, focus on family outcomes, and develop community governance and ownership of programs and initiatives.

RESEARCH DIRECTIONS

To support these policy and practice agendas, new directions and emphases are needed in research. Direct practice models need to adapt and adopt the mission-oriented practice–research approach recommended and documented by Fraser and Leavitt (1990). A variety of other emerging research strategies are also needed to strengthen practice and document community change.

A range of methods are emerging that provide more sophisticated approaches to building capacities in local groups, organizations, and communities to conduct and interpret their own research. Highlander Center and its staff in Appalachia have long engaged in helping community groups develop fact-finding and research approaches to deal with a range of issues from community education to documentation of the dangers of hazardous waste dumps (Gaventa, 1980). For years researchers and community practitioners have worked with local agencies and groups to help develop community assessments and research strategies that can illuminate community problems and issues.

Assessment Methods

A fund of literature is evolving that emphasizes the productive partnerships that can be developed between academic researchers and community groups or interorganizational collaboratives for evaluating reforms and fostering self-determination. Johnson (1994) called these partnerships the scholar–advocate approach. In policy practice, Usher (1995) and Usher, Gibbs, and Wildfire (1995) developed and implemented self-evaluation strategies in interagency and community-based collaboratives for system reform in initiatives sponsored by the Annie E. Casey Foundation and the Kellogg "Families for Kids" initiative in North Carolina.

Fetterman, Kaftarian, and Wandersman (1996) collected examples of empowerment evaluation strategies from a number of fields. Earlier, Fetterman (1994) defined *empowerment evaluation* as "the use of evaluation concepts and techniques to foster self determination. The focus is on helping people help themselves. Evaluators teach people to conduct their own evaluations and thus become more self-sufficient. The process desensitizes and demystifies evaluation and ideally helps organizations internalize evaluation principles and practices, making evaluation an integral part of program planning" (pp. 2–3). Evaluation approaches are designed to assist community groups, interagency collaboratives, or governance bodies in articulating their research-assessment-evaluation needs, designing straightforward methods to meet these needs, and working with groups to conduct research and interpret results for the group's efforts in community change and service system improvement and reform.

Within social development approaches, assessment methods such as Participatory Rural Appraisal (World Neighbors, 1995) and Rapid Rural Assessment are being used to help residents in developing countries understand and assess community, economic, and environmental problems. Noponen (1996) developed and implemented an overall community assessment tool for the Self-Employed Women's Cooperative in India that is used in planning and program development; the instrument can be used by women who are not literate. If knowledge is power, then these evaluation, assessment, and research strategies truly bring "power to the people."

Research Partnerships

A variety of partnerships illustrate ways to conduct community-based research directed toward positive social change. The Our Children Today and Tomorrow community assessment project (Region A Child and Youth Planning Council, 1993) brought together volunteers from agencies and civic groups in the seven westernmost counties in North Carolina. Sponsored by the Southwest North Carolina Economic Development Council, this project moved from an assessment process that involved hundreds of residents in the seven counties and the Eastern Band of the Cherokee in interviews, surveys, and focus groups of adults, children, and youths to development of successive community intervention initiatives. Initially the report to the people of western North Carolina was widely distributed in the region; the information has been successfully used in applications for and implementations of a Smart Start early childhood initiative and a regional family preservation–family support project that is developing community-responsive services on the reservation and throughout the seven counties.

In the development of services for battered women, Mauney, Williams, and Weil (1993) used a participatory research model and involved a partnership of practitioners, researchers, and the North Carolina Domestic Violence Coalition to document women's needs and programs' developmental needs to help battered women move beyond crisis to self-sufficiency. Bailey and Koney (1995, 1996) have worked in service coordination collaboratives and developed capacity-building evaluations for early childhood intervention programs in Cleveland. In many areas of the United States, information management systems to strengthen interagency record keeping, joint service planning, and service system evaluation are being developed through practitioner–academic partnerships (Kirk, 1996; McCroskey & Meezan, 1996; Usher et al., 1995; Whittaker, Kinney, Tracy, & Booth, 1990).

It is becoming evident that assessment and evaluation skills are no longer the purview of the academic community (Kahn, 1982). Much more work is needed to develop user-friendly assessment and evaluation tools for communities. As academic researchers and community and agency groups learn to build stronger partnerships for assessment and evaluation, far more fruitful research may emerge from capacity building, self-evaluation, and empowerment evaluation strategies.

SOCIAL WORK EDUCATION

Social work education needs to respond vigorously to the challenges and changes in policy and practice that will result from the diminishment of federal responsibility in human services. Schools can respond in a variety of ways to assist public sector and nonprofit sector programs in adapting to the changes with the least damage to client populations and working with the practice community on investment and development strategies. Faculty and students should also be involved in advocacy for the needs of oppressed populations, for positive social policy for the human services, and for stronger connections between social and economic development efforts.

Curriculum

Schools and departments of social work should critically examine their curricula to ensure that they teach content that enables students to be effective in service provision, planning, management, and advocacy. The strongest response will focus curriculum much more directly and intensively on community practice values, knowledge, methods, and skills and on policy practice and action-oriented research. The profession must dedicate itself to producing leaders and developing collaborative leadership in the nonprofit and public sectors. The social work curriculum also needs to focus explicitly on empowerment practice with individuals, families, and groups. Each of these areas of knowledge, methods, and skills is focused on strength, resilience, and helping people solve their own problems.

Community practice needs to be explicitly incorporated into generic macro practice courses. All students need to understand the community liaison-program development model and the principles of involvement of clients and community in program planning, implementation, governance, and evaluation. Although all students may not engage in direct community organizing, many will be engaged in collaborative work with neighborhood organizations, and most social workers will be engaged in work with functional communities. Each of these functional communities has missions and goals closely aligned with the purposes of social work, and students need to learn how to work effectively with, work to empower, and advocate for these groups.

All students in macro-focused concentrations or specializations need a thorough understanding of the processes of social planning, organizing, and working with geographic and functional communities. In their efforts to build responsive services and reform systems to focus on client needs and outcomes, social workers will require the skills to work with community collaboratives that focus on families or specific populations or on service system development.

All students need a background in diversity and multicultural practice to engage in community work (Rivera & Erlich, 1995). With ethnic separations on the rise, it is increasingly important for social work schools and departments to teach students methods of conflict resolution, mediation, and intergroup relations. These issues should be major parts of the practice sequence courses.

Specialized courses in community practice and social planning provide a needed complement to management and administration skills. Courses in citizen participation and social or sustainable development provide major substance and process skills for community practitioners, and courses or material in resource development, budgeting, research methods, and information management systems provide needed technical skills.

Continuing Education

The need for continuing education will rapidly escalate with policy shifts and the increasing demands of the Information Age. Workers must prepare for the realities of changing practice methods, issues, and technologies; new skills are especially needed to enable direct practice staff to make the transition into community practice and leadership positions.

Schools should expand their continuing education offerings to include specific courses on community practice and social planning, community and economic development, nonprofit organizational development and management, information management, needs assessment and program evaluation, resource development, and program planning. Such courses should be open to program graduates, agency staff, and grassroots leaders. Basic courses in these topics would also be useful to experienced direct practitioners making a transition to program development and grassroots leadership work.

CONCLUSION

For the profession to respond to the challenges related to diminishing federal responsibility in human services and social policy, it is necessary to reinvest in community practice strategies to help build communities, strengthen local- and state-level social planning, and make connections between social and economic development. Stronger connections across these groups and program areas can help people build coalitions and take action for a more responsive human services system and for community-based social and economic development initiatives. As decision making for social welfare devolves to the local level, representatives of oppressed groups and communities and social workers must be included in the planning, governance, and evaluation of programs and in cross-system collaboratives.

Although reduced funding will create real crises, it also provides the opportunity for social workers to contribute to the transformation of democracy in communities. The expanding state and local focus of policy development and intervention design provides both opportunity and challenge for students, practitioners, educators, and researchers to engage intensively at local and state levels in program improvement, interagency collaboration, and positive system reform to improve outcomes for clients and to build more functional and responsive communities. The current crises also present opportunities for social workers and social work education programs to form partnerships not only with their traditional collaborators but also with the broader range of development and change-focused agencies. Community practice methods in organizing, planning, development, and change offer an opportunity both to return to our roots and to develop practice methods more appropriate for the coming information-service economy.

If the profession responds to the current policy and economic changes by refocusing on social, economic, and sustainable development in community contexts, much stronger models of intervention and support can be developed that are universally applicable. The quality of our future in a period of diminishing federal responsibility depends on re-engaging in community life, in community building, and in community practice. Social work has a major role to play in revitalizing communities and reorganizing the intermediary structures necessary for civil society. Whether trained primarily in direct service or macro methods, social workers must be involved in building mutually supportive groups, programs, and institutions that can support and empower families, vulnerable groups, and communities economically at risk.

The opportunity in the current crisis is to examine our roots, to reconnect case to cause and private troubles to public issues, to consider the needs of the future, to adapt social work interventions and education to community-based models, and to focus social work on its historical mission of working with people to improve the quality of their lives and to build community and social justice.

REFERENCES

Addams, J. (1910). *Twenty years at Hull-House*. New York: Macmillan.
Addams, J. (1930). *The second twenty years at Hull-House*. New York: Macmillan.
Alcorn, S., & Morrison, J. (1994). Community planning that is "caught" and "taught": Experiential learning from town meetings. *Journal of Community Practice, 1*(4), 27–43.
Bailey, D., Johnson, A., Smith, R., Wood, Z. B., & Yankey, J. A. (1996). *The Institute for Civil Society Development proposal.* Cleveland: Case Western Reserve University, Mandel School of Applied Social Sciences, Center for Public Sector Leadership and Service.

Bailey, D., & Koney, K. (1995). Community-based consortia: One model for creation and development. *Journal of Community Practice, 2,* 21–42.

Bailey, D., & Koney, K. (1996, February). *From community collaboratives to public policy: Lessons from two stories in process.* Paper presented at the Association for Community Organization and Social Administration Symposium, Council on Social Work Education, Washington, DC.

Berger, P. L., & Neuhaus, J. (1991). *The structure of freedom: Correlations, causes, and cautions.* Grand Rapids, MI: W. B. Eerdmans.

Boroughs, D. L. (1996, January 22). Winter of discontent. *U.S. News and World Report,* pp. 47–54.

Brilliant, E. L. (1990). *The United Way: Dilemmas of organized charity.* New York: Columbia University Press.

Byrne, J. A. (1996, April 22). How high can CEO pay go? *Business Week,* p. 100.

Committee for Economic Development, Research and Policy Committee. (1995). *Rebuilding inner-city communities: A new approach to the nation's urban crisis.* New York: Author.

Coontz, S. (1992). *The way we never were: American families and the nostalgia trap.* New York: Basic Books/HarperCollins.

Cooper, K. (1990, April 30–May 6). 52 years of giving kids a Head Start. *Washington Post* [National Weekly Edition], pp. 1–3.

Davis, R. (1996, April 18). *Future of the information age.* Paper presented at the North Carolina State University Annual Emerging Issues Forum, Raleigh.

Deegan, M. J. (1988). *Jane Addams and the men of the Chicago School, 1892–1918.* New Brunswick, NJ: Transaction Books.

Egan, J. (1996, April 8). Those !!$%&?! CEO salaries. *U.S. News and World Report,* p. 63.

Estes, R. J. (1993). Toward sustainable development: From theory to praxis. *Social Development Issues, 15*(3), 1–29.

Federal News Service. (1996, February 20). *Hearing of the Human Resources Subcommittee of the House Ways and Means Committee: Subject—Governors' welfare proposal.* Washington, DC: Federal Information Systems Corporation, Author.

Fetterman, D. M. (1994). Empowerment evaluation. *Evaluation Practice, 15,* 1–15.

Fetterman, D. M. (1996). Empowerment evaluation: An introduction to theory and practice. In D. M. Fetterman, S. J. Kaftarian, & A. Wandersman (Eds.), *Empowerment evaluation, knowledge, and tools for self-assessment and accountability* (pp. 3–46). Thousand Oaks, CA: Sage Publications.

Fetterman, D. M., Kaftarian, S. J., & Wandersman, A. (1996). *Empowerment, evaluation, knowledge, and tools for self-assessment and accountability.* Thousand Oaks, CA: Sage Publications.

Fox, M. (1994). *The reinvention of work: A new vision of livelihood for our time.* San Francisco: Harper & Row.

Fraser, M., & Leavitt, S. (1990). Creating social change: "Mission" oriented research and entrepreneurship. In J. K. Whittaker, J. Kinney, E. M. Tracy, & C. Booth (Eds.), *Reaching high risk families: Intensive family preservation in human services* (pp. 165–178). New York: Aldine de Gruyter.

Gamble, D. N., & Weil, M. O. (1995). Citizen participation. In R. L. Edwards (Ed.-in-Chief), *Encyclopedia of social work* (19th ed., Vol. 1, pp. 483–494). Washington DC: NASW Press.

Gardner, J. W. (1994). *Building community for leadership studies program.* Washington, DC: Independent Sector.

Gaventa, J. (1980). *Power and powerlessness: Quiescence and rebellion in an Appalachian valley.* Champaign: University of Illinois Press.

Glaser, J. S. (1994). *The United Way scandal: An insider's account of what went wrong and why.* New York: John Wiley & Sons.

Gore, A. (1996, April, 18). *The information age.* Speech presented at North Carolina State University Annual Emerging Issues Forum, Raleigh.

Herget, J. B. (1996, April 21). Turning hope into homes. *Raleigh News & Observer,* p. 1D.

Hoff, M. D., & McNutt, J. G. (Eds.). (1994). *The global environmental crisis: Implications for social welfare and social work.* Brookfield, VT: Avebury.

Johnson, A. K. (1994). Linking professionalism and community organization: A scholar/advocate approach. *Journal of Community Practice, 1*(2), 65–86.

Kahn, S. (1982). *Organizing: A guide for grassroots leaders.* New York: McGraw-Hill.

Kirk, R. (1996). Evaluation of intensive family preservation services. In *North Carolina Family Preservation Annual Report, June 1996.* Raleigh: North Carolina Department of Human Resources.

Lappin, B. (1985). Community development: Beginnings in social work enabling. In S. Taylor & R. Roberts (Eds.), *Theory and practice of community social work* (pp. 59–94). New York: Columbia University Press.

Lee, J.A.B. (1994). *The empowerment approach to social work practice.* New York: Columbia University Press.

MacNair, R. H., Gross, J., & Daniels, M. C. (1995). State promotion of advocacy organizations: A comparative analysis of four case studies in Georgia. *Journal of Community Practice, 2*(2), 77–97.

Mauney, R., Williams, E., & Weil, M. (1993). *Beyond crisis: Developing comprehensive services for battered women in North Carolina.* Winston-Salem, NC: Z. Smith Reynolds Foundation.

McCroskey, J., & Meezan, W. (1996). *Family preservation and family functioning.* Washington, DC: Child Welfare League of America.

McGrath, T. (1996, April). Talking with Elaine Chao: Rewriting the rules at the United Way. *USAIR Magazine,* pp. 12–16.

McNeely, J. B. (1996). Where have all the flowers gone? In R. Stone (Ed.), *Core issues in comprehensive community building initiatives* (p. 86–88). Chicago: Chapin Hall Center for Children.

Melaville, A. I. (1991). *What it takes: Structuring interagency partnerships to connect children and families with comprehensive services.* Washington, DC: Education and Human Services Consortium.

Melaville, A. I., & Blank, M. J. (1993). *Together we can: A guide for crafting a profamily system of education and human services* (Report prepared for U.S. Department of Education, Office of Educational Research and Improvement, and U.S. Department of Health and Human Services, Office of the Assistant Secretary for Planning and Evaluation). Washington, DC: U.S. Government Printing Office.

Midgley, J. (1995). *Social development: The development perspective in social welfare.* Thousand Oaks, CA: Sage Publications.

Milton S. Eisenhower Foundation. (1990). *Youth investment and community reconstruction: Street lessons on drugs and crime for the nineties.* Abilene, KS: Author.

Mondros, J. B., & Wilson, S. M. (1994). *Organizing for power and empowerment.* New York: Columbia University Press.

Morrison, J. D., Alcorn, S., & Nelmus, M. (1996, February). *Empowering community-based programs for youth development: Is social work interested?* Paper presented at the Association for Community Organization and Social Administration Symposium, Council on Social Work Education, Washington, DC.

National Congress for Community Economic Development. (1991). *Human investment—Community profits* [Report and recommendations of the Social Services and Economic Development Task Force]. Washington, DC: Author.

Nisbett, R. E. (1980). *Human inference: Strategies and shortcomings of social judgment.* Englewood Cliffs, NJ: Prentice Hall.

Noponen, H. (1996, May 18). *Participatory monitoring and evaluation: A prototype internal learning system for grassroots micro-finance programs.* Paper presented at the Women, Community and Sustainable Development Forum, University of North Carolina at Chapel Hill.

Region A Child and Youth Planning Council. (1993). *Our children today and tomorrow: A call-to-action for the children of western North Carolina.* Bryson City: Southwestern North Carolina Planning and Economic Development Commission.

Rivera, F. G., & Erlich, J. L. (Eds.). (1995). *Community organizing in a diverse society* (2nd ed.). Boston: Allyn & Bacon.

Roberts, S. V. (1996, January 22). Workers take it on the chin. *U.S. News and World Report,* pp. 44–46.

Ross, M. G. (1955). *Community organization: Theory and principles.* New York: Harper & Row.

Ross, M. G., & Lappin, B. W. (1967). *Community organization: Theory, principles, and practice* (2nd ed.). New York: Harper & Row.

Rothman, J. (Ed.). (1971). *Promoting social justice in the multigroup society.* New York: Association Press and the Council on Social Work Education.

Rothman, J. (1995). Approaches to community intervention. In J. Rothman, J. L. Erlich, & J. E. Tropman (Eds.), with F. M. Cox, *Strategies of community intervention* (5th ed., pp. 26–63). Itasca, IL: F. E. Peacock.

Rubin, H. J., & Rubin, I. S. (1992). *Community organizing & development* (2nd ed.). New York: Macmillan.

Schorr, L. (1988). *Within our reach: Breaking the cycle of disadvantage.* New York: Doubleday.

Sherraden, M. (1991). *Assets and the poor.* Armonk, NY: M. E. Sharpe.

Simon, B. L. (1994). *The empowerment tradition in American social work: A history.* New York: Columbia University Press.

Solomon, B. H. (1976). *Black empowerment: Social work in oppressed communities.* New York: Columbia University Press.

Stancil, J. (1996, April 23). School of social work makes its mark. *Raleigh News & Observer,* p. 1A.

Staples, L. (1990). Powerful ideas about empowerment. *Administration in Social Work, 14*(2), 29–42.

Syers, M. (1995). Mary Parker Follett (1868–1933). In R. L. Edwards (Ed.-in-Chief), *Encyclopedia of social work* (19th ed., Vol. 3, p. 2585). Washington, DC: NASW Press.

Usher, C. L. (1995). Improving evaluability through self-evaluation. *Evaluation Practice, 16,* 59–68.

Usher, C. L., Gibbs, D. A., & Wildfire, J. B. (1995). A framework for planning, implementing and evaluating child welfare reforms. *Child Welfare, 74,* 859–876.

Weil, M. (1988). Task group skills in community practice. In M. Leiderman (Ed.), *Roots and new frontiers* (pp. 131–148). New York: Haworth Press.

Weil, M. (1994). Preface. In A. Faulkner, M. Roberts-DeGennaro, & M. Weil (Eds.), *Diversity and development in community practice* (pp. xi–xix). New York: Haworth Press.

Weil, M., & Gamble, D. N. (1995). Community practice models. In R. L. Edwards (Ed.-in-Chief), *Encyclopedia of social work* (19th ed., Vol. 1, pp. 577–594). Washington, DC: NASW Press.

Whittaker, J. K., Kinney, J., Tracy, E., & Booth, C. (1990). *Reaching high-risk families.* New York: Aldine de Gruyter.

Wilder Research Center, Amherst H. Wilder Foundation. (1992). *Collaboration: What makes it work—A review of research literature on factors influencing successful collaboration.* St. Paul, MN: Author.

World Neighbors. (1995). Learning with the community through Participatory Rural Appraisal. *World Neighbors in Action: A Newsletter for Project Personnel, 24*(1E). (Available from World Neighbors, 4127 NW 122nd Street, Oklahoma City, OK 73120-8869)

This chapter was originally published in the September 1996 issue of Social Work, *vol. 41, pp. 481–499.*

5 Multicultural Community Organizing: A Strategy for Change

Lorraine Gutierrez, Ann Rosegrant Alvarez,
Howard Nemon, and Edith A. Lewis

The literature on social work practice in the 21st century depicts a grim picture. Demographic projections suggest growth in three populations disproportionately affected by poverty: single-parent families, older people, and people of color (Murdock & Michael, 1996). Projections suggest that income inequality will grow as the movement to reduce government spending leads to decreased federal responsibility and a decentralized, residual welfare state (DiNitto, 1996; Hasenfeld, 1996; Murdock & Michael, 1996). Therefore, the need for human services will increase while resources are eliminated; social work practice will become privatized and focused on methods of serving increasing numbers of people from diverse backgrounds in a context of limited resources (Hasenfeld, 1996).

This future vision of a reactive social work profession adapting to a situation of increasing injustice is chilling. Gaining perspective on these trends can provide a vision for proactive practice, policy, education, and research that can fulfill the profession's mission and purpose. What alternatives exist for those committed to increasing social justice and access to needed social supports? An alternative perspective can be developed from studying how social workers can affect these larger trends. By improving the lives of single-parent families, older people, and people of color, social workers can reduce inequality and the need for increased services. This reduction requires developing effective methods for working with diverse communities to influence policy and practice.

The scholarship on the future of social work practice has not adequately focused on the implications of these trends for community practice (Raffoul & McNeece, 1996). The increasing shift from federal to local administration of social welfare services suggests greater power for local communities in resource allocation and a significant role for community practitioners in the evolving welfare state. However, the growing ethnic, cultural, and racial diversity of society presents a challenge for community workers. Skills for working in a multicultural environment are important if communities are to be well represented in the planning process.

This article identifies how multicultural organizing can help improve the lives of individuals, families, and communities. A literature review on multicultural community practice identifies its dimensions, scope, and methods. Ways in which multicultural organizing can be pivotal for affecting positive change are discussed.

MULTICULTURAL PERSPECTIVE ON COMMUNITY PRACTICE

Community organization methods are designed to create social environments that support social justice through influencing policies, developing programs, or governing locally. Although the target of change is the community, the forum for change can be individuals, families, groups, or organizations. Organizers emphasize the importance of individual contact in building community change efforts (Burghardt, 1982; Staples, 1984). These contacts can lead to the development of social action organizations that can influence policy affecting economic and social institutions. Community change efforts can range from short and focused activities such as public hearings to long and sustained projects such as the development of alternative services (Kettner, Daley, & Nichols, 1985; Mondros & Wilson, 1994).

The concept of social justice is central to the practice of community organizing. *Social justice* refers to equity, equality, and fairness in the distribution of societal resources (Flynn, 1995). Social justice includes a focus on the structures and outcomes of social processes and how they contribute to equality, places explicit value on achieving social equity through democratic processes, and assumes that the social work role is to develop policy and practice that contribute to these goals (Flynn, 1995; Van Soest, 1994). Although community organizers may work toward local or short-term goals, the overall goal is social justice and social equality.

Models for community practice in social work have identified methods to facilitate this type of change. These models have focused primarily on typologies of practice (Rothman, 1995), levels of conflict (Warren, 1971), or the primary methods used (Mondros & Wilson, 1994). Within these models little attention has been paid to how race, gender, ethnicity, or social class affect the organizing effort. This oversight has hindered organizers from working effectively with communities of color (Bradshaw, Soifer, & Gutierrez, 1993; Burghardt, 1982; Gutierrez & Lewis, 1994; Rivera & Erlich, 1995). By ignoring how issues of culture and oppression affect their work, community organizers can perpetuate the objectification and exploitation of people of color (Burghardt, 1982). For example, organizers who view communities of color in stereotypical ways will be ineffective in building leadership or working as partners (Bradshaw et al., 1993; Gutierrez & Lewis, 1994; Rivera & Erlich, 1995). In this way community practice perpetuates the problems it is designed to solve.

Although the community-organizing literature has been relatively silent on the multicultural dimensions of practice, people of color have always worked to improve conditions within their communities (Gutierrez & Lewis, 1994; Medoff & Sklar, 1994; Rivera & Erlich, 1995). These efforts often arose from community leaders who built on existing networks. For example, the movements for equality and civil rights in communities of color during the mid- and late 20th century built on existing relationships in churches, voluntary organizations, and workplaces (Evans, 1980; Munoz, 1989; West, 1990; Withorn, 1984). Urban communities today are organizing on issues of neighborhood violence, economic issues, and environmental issues (Brown & Ferguson, 1995; Heslan & Heffner,

1987). The use of existing family, organization, and community networks in communities of color is critical to multicultural organizing.

Multicultural organizing is a perspective on community organization that builds on these traditions; it recognizes and values the experiences and contributions of different social groups in an organization or community while working to bring groups together when necessary. However, the multicultural perspective goes beyond pluralism by recognizing and working to eliminate social injustice and oppression based on specific group membership (Gutierrez & Nagda, 1996; Jackson & Holvino, 1988). Structural inequalities are responsible for strengthening ethnic borders as groups develop a culture that is oppositional to oppressive forces. Unless these inequalities are eliminated, ethnic competence will not be able to build bridges across cultural barriers. Therefore, a multicultural perspective recognizes and values cultural diversity while working to dismantle structures of inequality (Gutierrez & Nagda, 1996).

MULTICULTURAL ORGANIZING SKILLS

Multicultural organizing is not associated with any one perspective on community work; instead, it mixes and phases in different approaches to community organization according to a community's needs, strengths, and resources (Bradshaw et al., 1993). Therefore, multicultural organizing builds on and emphasizes skills required for all community organization practice. Of particular importance are skills to develop cultural competence to learn from the community, which involves understanding one's own and the community's culture and social location, recognizing and building from community strengths, working as a partner, and dealing with conflict in and between groups. The community organizer approaches the community to understand and facilitate change (Bradshaw et al., 1993; Green, 1995; Rivera & Erlich, 1995).

Understanding Culture and Social Location

The multicultural perspective requires an understanding of the significance of social location in shaping human experience (Barbarin, 1981; Devore, 1981; Green, 1995), including valuing one's own cultural heritage and having respect for and interest in others' cultural heritages (Green, 1995). Acknowledging the importance of one's own culture helps one recognize its importance to others. When one realizes what values and worldviews one holds, the dynamics of intergroup relationships become more apparent. Without seeing one's own position, it is impossible to really grasp the position of others (Devore, 1981).

Gaining knowledge of other cultures is essential for multicultural organizing. Knowledge includes awareness of the history, traditions, and values of other groups. Because ethnicity is formed from historical and social influences, learning about these external and internal factors helps one understand problems and strengths. Respect for another's culture means that one not only acknowledges the importance of the other's culture, but also shows interest in gaining knowledge about the differences. Through ethnic competence, community organizers can cultivate a respect for diversity among different groups, which will facilitate cooperation and break down barriers, and can maximize a group's potential through coordinated efforts with other groups.

Awareness of one's own social location is also critical for multicultural organizing. Rivera and Erlich (1995) have proposed that the level of one's involvement should be linked to one's relationship with the community. If the community organizer is a member of the community, then primary contact, which
involves intimate and personal grassroots work, is appropriate. A community
organizer who is of a similar ethnic or racial background but is not of the community would be involved on a secondary level, which involves participation
as a liaison or "link person" between the community and the larger society. A
tertiary level of contact would be most appropriate for those who are not members of the group on any dimension. These individuals can provide valuable
contributions through consultation and the sharing of technical knowledge.

Recognizing and Building from Community Strengths

Recognizing and building from community strengths is an important skill. Building from strengths includes identifying areas of positive functioning, particularly those that have been unnoticed or unrewarded, and using them as a basis
for the organizing effort (Gutierrez, DeLois, & GlenMaye, 1995; Saleebey, 1991).
Community organizers must recognize that most communities and families of
color have been involved in a struggle against oppressive structures and that
the struggle has required many strengths. By analyzing elements of the struggle
and how families and communities have survived, strengths can be more easily
identified and mobilized.

The collectivist worldview and family and community support networks of
many communities of color can be the basis of multicultural practice (Delgado
& Humm-Delgado, 1982; Levitt, Guacci-Franco, & Levitt, 1993). A worldview
focused on the needs and resources of collectivities such as families, neighborhoods, or communities can lead to well-developed support structures. Multicultural organizing can build on these networks by recognizing their existence
and asking community members how they can be mobilized. For example,
mobilizing natural support systems in Latino communities—such as extended
family systems, *bodegas* (ethnic groceries), and social clubs—can be used as a
strategy for assessing needs or developing services (Delgado & Humm-Delgado,
1982). Building on these strengths can result in organizing that is organic to the
community.

Working as a Partner

While working with differences, the multicultural community organizer must
act as both facilitator and learner (Green, 1995; Gutierrez & Lewis, 1994). The
process of empowerment requires that individuals and groups develop their
own strengths and solutions. Just as those who live their own cultural reality
understand it better than anyone else, groups living in a multicultural community also are conscious of how they interact with each other. Through a
facultative approach, the community organizer can help them overcome cultural obstacles and foster a positive collaboration. An effective facilitator must
adopt a humble and open attitude. This cooperation between the organizer
and the community can raise consciousness and generate solutions (Rivera &
Erlich, 1995).

An example of this process is the work of the Dudley Street Neighborhood Initiative (DSNI) in Boston. In *Streets of Hope* (Medoff & Sklar, 1994), DSNI board member Paul Bothwell explained three factors that led to the success of their multicultural organizing efforts. First, they put the heart before the head. If community organizing is conceived as demanding only administrative, assessment, and management skills, then its chances for success are slim. A community organizer in a multicultural environment must relate as a human being and reach people with real feelings as well as ideas. Second, being is more important than doing. This subtle concept reflects the difference between existential and actional worth. People and their cultures have an inherent value that cannot be detracted from, no matter what their social situation. Belief and trust in individuals and groups will create a collective trust that is essential for bringing together a diverse community. Third, they value collectivity over individuality. Doing things together and remaining united empower the entire community and lead to its integration.

Dealing with Conflict

Recognizing and working with inter- and intragroup conflict is critical for effective multicultural work. Community organizing is particularly challenging when it involves bringing together multiple groups. The history of segregation in the United States has resulted in little meaningful interaction between people from different races, classes, ethnic groups, or sexual orientations (Rivera & Erlich, 1995). Multicultural community organizing to break down these boundaries to build alliances requires recognizing and embracing the conflict that characterizes cross-cultural work.

Conflicts arise both within organizations that have been successful in reaching diverse groups and between the organization and the larger community, which may be threatened by multiracial and multiethnic coalitions. In some respects, the emergence of conflict indicates that meaningful cross-cultural work is taking place. However, the sources and resolution of conflict will affect the outcomes. The extent to which the community organizer can anticipate and use conflict constructively determines whether his or her efforts are successful (Gutierrez & Lewis, 1994; Ristock, 1990; West, 1990).

Conflict also includes the discomfort many community organizers feel when they are the sole person from a different ethnic or class background in a group or when they participate in an event that has previously been attended solely by community members. Organizers must recognize that they may be tested by community members to determine their level of commitment and their intentions. Giving to the community on its terms through volunteer or other service efforts can be an important means of entering a community (Gutierrez & Lewis, 1994).

Conflict will be especially difficult for individuals who have not previously experienced cross-cultural activities. Conflicts reflect choices about fact, value, and strategy alternatives that people face intra- or interpersonally. Avoidance behaviors only temporarily delay conflicts, which will resurface if issues are not addressed directly. Addressing a conflict is different from confrontation, which refers to a minimization or attack on a party with whom there is conflict. This minimization, either at the personal or political level, can easily be perceived as a threat, which inevitably leads to an escalation of the conflict rather than a dialogue about its nature (Weingarten & Leas, 1989).

Addressing conflict directly requires active-listening and consensus-building skills and involves taking various views of the situation from all involved in the conflict and then reaching a consensus about how to proceed. Reaching a consensus often means being open to differing conflict styles and hearing the content of the messages being presented rather than reacting only to the feelings with which they are presented. This requires openness to different styles for handling conflicts. Conflict avoidance techniques may be valued for their ability to offset the attack, whereas confrontation approaches may be valued for their ability to focus immediate attention on the conflict (Weingarten & Leas, 1989).

Dealing with conflict is difficult but valuable. It requires the ability to know oneself and to be open to knowing others. Dealing with community backlash and conflict also requires taking risks to speak out in support of community efforts. The inability to resolve conflicts can result in the death of organizations or can minimize the ability to work in coalitions.

IMPLICATIONS FOR SOCIAL WORK EDUCATION

Multicultural community organizing has implications for all levels of social work education, including the schools that educate future practitioners, the kinds of available field placements, the process and content of classroom education, and the focus and dissemination of social work research.

Implications for Schools of Social Work

The Association for Community Organization and Social Administration (ACOSA) (Pine & Mizrahi, 1996) recently reported that only 15 of 101 MSW programs in the United States offer a concentration in community practice or social administration. If multicultural community organizing is to affect economic and demographic trends, courses that develop competent community practice should be available to all students.

Part of this effort must include raising the consciousness of social work faculty and staff about the meaning, importance, and viability of community practice. Potential community practitioners can be discouraged by faculty who advise them that there are no jobs in the field or that those that exist are comparable to missionary work, offering barely subsistence-level compensation. Faculty meetings, informational lunches, and informal conversation can all be used to educate faculty and staff about placement and job opportunities and to promote the viability of community practice as a professional focus.

Implications for Field Practice

Field practice staff as well as faculty sometimes underestimate and overlook the availability of professional training opportunities in community practice. Dynamic placements can be overlooked when community practitioners do not have an MSW, which the Council on Social Work Education requires of field supervisors. Because of the diversity of the field and its historic reliance on experience versus credentials, many grassroots community activists do not have graduate degrees or have bachelor's or master's degrees in related fields, including education, psychology, business, law, sociology, and urban planning.

Establishing and maintaining field placements in community practice requires a commitment and a creative approach to such placements. One approach has been to have individual students supervised by faculty who closely monitor the placement experience. Another possibility is to establish learning laboratories under faculty supervision that would enable a group of student interns to rotate through various settings and work with a variety of issues. No doubt there are many ways to deal with this issue; the starting point is to commit to developing relationships and models so that students can receive solid field training in community practice.

Implications for the Classroom

In addition, more individual courses should address community-level issues and practice. An approach that encourages self-awareness and self-reflection is important to develop the sensitivity required in multicultural practice. The classroom provides the ideal forum for exploration of one's own cultural background and how that affects interactions with others (Green, 1995).

Teachers can provide opportunities for students to develop and carry out multicultural community-organizing projects. Students relish the chance to learn from involvement with the community while also being useful. In these opportunities community priorities must be honored, and the benefits of student projects must be reciprocal. Furthermore, in many communities, residents have been disappointed and alienated by continuous documentation of neighborhood circumstances followed by the conspicuous lack or shortage of programs and services to meet needs and build on strengths.

In the classroom setting, those who teach sensitive multicultural practice should be effective models. A parallel process can be used in which students can experience the activities and experiences involved in multicultural organizing. For example, cooperative-learning activities that involve diverse groups of students can be used to develop the skills to work across differences. This form of teaching can be challenging, especially when it is not supported by the institution or when students are unfamiliar with the approach. Even those students who most fervently extol an empowerment model, including the use of facultative rather than authoritarian leadership, will sometimes resist an interactive, experiential format and express a preference for a straightforward cookbook or lecture. This tendency can be usefully discussed and analyzed in class with parallels drawn to the community context. When given the opportunity, students can often relate this very effectively to their own placement experiences.

Implications for Research

More research is needed on multicultural community organizing, and the findings and reports should be disseminated to a wider audience. There is a tendency for community practice in general to be undocumented, which negatively affects the visibility and credibility of both the field and its practitioners. A number of factors contribute to this problem. Practitioners, caught up in pressing work, may lack the time to reflect on their experiences, write about them, and submit them for publication. In addition, practitioners may lack the professional credentials that would lead them to do research or to write about their work. Furthermore, they may not value such efforts, feeling that they are trivial and not likely to advance their causes. Although understandable, this stance ignores the reality that information dissemination can be a powerful tool for validating the work, recruiting students and other practitioners, and improving the quality of ongoing efforts.

Participatory research, including action research, has much appeal and relevance for application to research on multicultural community organizing (Brown, 1994; Delgado-Gaitan, 1993; Flynn, Ray, & Rider, 1994; Sohng, 1992; Yeich & Levine, 1992). This methodology can help make research useful and compatible even to practitioners who have been resistant previously. Because the research and action activities and outcomes are intertwined, the researcher—whether student or practitioner—can expect participant and community empowerment, capacity building, and change to result from these efforts. As with community-based action projects, students often welcome the opportunity to contribute to the community while expanding their own learning. For their own and the community's benefit, students must be educated in participant research methodology.

Research on multicultural community practice presents challenges in such basic areas as definition of terms. Consensus about meanings cannot be assumed. For example, practitioners have differing definitions not only of the phrase "multicultural community organization" but also of each term separately (Alvarez & Gutierrez, 1996). Consensus may be neither possible nor desirable, but continued exploration of differing interpretations and their implications is necessary.

Another area for research involves standards for the evaluation of community practice, specifically multicultural community organizing. Past efforts have been judged harshly on their "lack of success," and funding decisions have reflected these judgments. The success of community-level efforts has often been judged according to standards that can require the appearance of a totally unified and model community. Because communities include transient individuals and people with a multitude of problems, it seems neither just nor pragmatic to hold the community to a standard of accomplishment of levels of physical, economic, and relational health that are difficult to accomplish for individuals, let alone the aggregate. There is, however, a tendency to do just this, perhaps in part because a "dysfunctional community" may be much more visible than a "dysfunctional individual," and its "pathologies" or problems may have greater and more dramatic spillover effects on others.

People have not abandoned therapeutic counseling as a viable approach, in spite of the fact that few individuals attain a model level of psychic health and that treatment may be very long term. Similarly, community-level interventions should not be discarded because they do not provide fast and miraculous cures. Rather, community organizers may need to establish different and more varied criteria on which to assess their effectiveness. For example, in some communities just to have created a viable multiethnic coalition can justify the effort and resources.

CONCLUSION

What does social work's knowledge of multicultural organizing suggest for influencing growing income inequalities and the shift from federal to local administration of social welfare services? The objective for organizing diverse ethnic groups in a community is to achieve reciprocal empowerment so that together the groups can work toward social justice. Given the social situation in the United States, this effort implies a complete transformation of the social structure, constructing equitable and just political, economic, and intergroup relationships. In this process, diversity must be understood and respected and its strengths put to good use in forging unity. Through unity in diversity and social change, multicultural community organizers can be instrumental in promoting greater equity.

This promise of multicultural practice will remain unfulfilled if social workers continue to only react to societal changes and maintain the current structure of profession and education. Multicultural community practice will require redesigning social work education and practice. Significant changes must occur in how social workers educate students for collaborative, empowerment-based practice. It also requires the participation of social workers in nontraditional settings as activists, advocates, and mobilizers of community potential. Although these shifts may appear risky, they have the potential to reap great benefits for communities, the profession, and society at large.

REFERENCES

Alvarez, A. R., & Gutierrez, L. (1996, March). *Building bridges: Participatory research to developing training for multicultural community organizers.* Paper presented at the Annual Program Meeting of the Council on Social Work Education, Washington, DC.

Barbarin, O. (1981). Community competence: An individual-systems approach to institutional racism. In O. Barbarin (Ed.), *Institutional racism and community competence* (pp. 6–19). Rockville, MD: U.S. Department of Health and Human Services.

Bradshaw, C., Soifer, S., & Gutierrez, L. (1993). Toward a hybrid model for effective organizing in communities of color. *Journal of Community Practice, 1,* 25–42.

Brown, P. (1994). Participatory research: A new paradigm for social work. In L. Gutierrez & P. Nurius (Eds.), *Education and research for empowerment practice* (pp. 291–302). Seattle: University of Washington, Center for Policy and Practice Research.

Brown, P., & Ferguson, F. (1995). Making a big stink: Women's work, women's relationships, and toxic waste activism. *Gender and Society, 9,* 145–172.

Burghardt, S. (1982). *The other side of organizing.* Cambridge, MA: Schenkman.

Delgado, M., & Humm-Delgado, D. (1982). Natural support systems: Source of strength in Hispanic communities. *Social Work, 27,* 83–89.

Delgado-Gaitan, C. (1993). Researching change and changing the researcher. *Harvard Educational Review, 63,* 389–411.

Devore, W. (1981). *Ethnic-sensitive social work practice.* St. Louis: C. V. Mosby.

DiNitto, D. (1996). The future of social welfare policy. In P. Raffoul & A. McNeece (Eds.), *Future issues for social work practice* (pp. 254–265). Boston: Allyn & Bacon.

Evans, S. (1980). *Personal politics.* New York: Vintage Books.

Flynn, B., Ray, D., & Rider, M. (1994). Empowering communities: Action research through healthy cities. *Health Education Quarterly, 21,* 395–405.

Flynn, J. (1995). Social justice in social agencies. In R. L. Edwards (Ed.-in-Chief), *Encyclopedia of social work* (19th ed., Vol. 3, pp. 2173–2179). Washington, DC: NASW Press.

Green, J. (1995). *Cultural agencies in the human services* (2nd ed.). Englewood Cliffs, NJ: Prentice Hall.

Gutierrez, L., DeLois, K., & GlenMaye, L. (1995). Understanding empowerment practice: Building on practitioner-based knowledge. *Families in Society, 76,* 534–542.

Gutierrez, L., & Lewis, E. (1994). Community organizing with women of color. *Journal of Community Practice, 1*(2), 23–44.

Gutierrez, L., & Nagda, B. (1996). The multicultural imperative in human services organizations. In P. Rafford & A. McNeece (Eds.), *Future issues for social work practice* (pp. 203–213). Boston: Allyn & Bacon.

Hasenfeld, Y. (1996). The administration of human services—What lies ahead. In P. Rafford & A. McNeece (Eds.), *Future issues for social work practice* (pp. 191–202). Boston: Allyn & Bacon.

Heslan, A., & Heffner, R. (1987). Learning about bilingual, multicultural organizing. *Journal of Applied Behavioral Sciences, 23,* 525–541.

Jackson, B., & Holvino, E. (1988). *Multicultural organizational development.* Ann Arbor: University of Michigan, Program on Conflict Management Alternatives.

Kettner, P., Daley, J., & Nichols, A. (1985). *Initiating change in organizations and communities.* Monterey, CA: Brooks/Cole.

Levitt, M., Guacci-Franco, N., & Levitt, J. (1993). Convoys of social support in childhood and early adolescence. *Developmental Psychology, 29,* 811–818.

Medoff, P., & Sklar, H. (1994). *Streets of hope: The fall and rise of an urban neighborhood.* Boston: South End Press.

Mondros, I., & Wilson, S. (1994). *Organizing for power and empowerment.* New York: Columbia University Press.

Munoz, C. (1989). *Youth identity and power: The Chicano movement.* London: Verso.

Murdock, S., & Michael, M. (1996). Future demographic changes: The demand for social welfare services in the 21st century. In P. Raffoul & A. McNeece (Eds.), *Future issues for social work practice* (pp. 3–18). Boston: Allyn & Bacon.

Pine, B., & Mizrahi, T. (1996). *A memo to ACOSA members.* New York: Association for Community Organization and Social Administration.

Raffoul, P., & McNeece, A. (Eds.). (1996). *Future issues for social work practice.* Boston: Allyn & Bacon.

Ristock, J. (1990). Canadian feminist social service collectives: Caring and contradictions. In L. Albrecht & R. Brewer (Eds.), *Bridges of power: Women's multicultural alliances* (pp. 171–182). Philadelphia: New Society.

Rivera, F., & Erlich, J. (1995). *Community organizing in a diverse society* (2nd ed.). Boston: Allyn & Bacon.

Rothman, J. (1995). Approaches to community intervention. In J. Rothman, J. Erlich, & J. Tropman (Eds.), *Strategies of community intervention* (pp. 26–63). Itasca, IL: F.E. Peacock.

Saleebey, D. (1991). *The strengths perspective in social work practice.* New York: Longman.

Sohng, S. (1992). Consumers as research partners. *Journal of Progressive Human Services, 3*(2), 1–14.

Staples, L. (1984). *Roots to power.* New York: Praeger.

Van Soest, D. (1994). Peace and social justice. In R. L. Edwards (Ed.-in-Chief), *Encyclopedia of social work* (19th ed., Vol. 3, pp. 1810–1817). Washington, DC: NASW Press.

Warren, R. (1971). *Truth, love, and social change and other essays on community change.* Chicago: Rand McNally.

Weingarten, H., & Leas, S. (1989). *Levels of marital context* (PCMA Working Paper). Ann Arbor, MI: University of Michigan, Center for Research and Social Organizations.

West, G. (1990). Cooperation and conflict among women in the welfare rights movement. In L. Albrecht & R. Brewer (Eds.), *Bridges of power: Women's multicultural alliances* (pp. 149–171). Philadelphia: New Society.

Withorn, A. (1984). *Serving the people: Social services and social change.* New York: Columbia University Press.

Yeich, S., & Levine, R. (1992). Participatory research's contribution to a conceptualization of empowerment. *Journal of Applied Social Psychology, 22,* 1894–1908.

This chapter was originally published in the September 1996 issue of Social Work, *vol. 41, pp. 501–508.*

6

Interorganizational Community-Based Collaboratives: A Strategic Response to Shape the Social Work Agenda

Darlyne Bailey and Kelly McNally Koney

In 1992, the Assembly Democratic Economic Prosperity Team, a group of California legislators and business leaders, issued a report proposing ways to manage the state's economic dilemmas. The report stated that "traditional ways no longer suffice in today's complex global economy. Neither the standard, stereotypical Republican laissez-faire model nor the standard, stereotypical Democratic command and control model works any more. . . . We learned that only a third voice—the way of trust, partnership, and collaboration—offers us any hope for our future" (cited in Dreher, 1996, p. 132). This quote sums up the essence of this article: With constant change characterizing today's world and heightened uncertainty about tomorrow's, the organizational unit that offers the most hope for meeting these challenges and at the same time achieving its own goals is the interorganizational collaborative. Whether it is a for-profit "PAL" (that is, pooling, allying, and linking across companies) as prescribed by Kanter (1989), a nonprofit community-based consortium (Bailey & Koney, 1995a), or a social change coalition (Mizrahi & Rosenthal, 1992), interorganizational collaboratives more often are being recognized as the system of choice.

On the basis of a longitudinal field study (Bailey & Koney, 1995a), this article supports the relevance of interorganizational community-based collaboratives in addressing the challenges facing social work. Further, it identifies eight major components of community-based collaboratives and explores the paradoxical nature of these highly interdependent components to help social workers and other professionals conceive and maintain collaborative efforts. The article begins with an analysis of the current and forecasted political environment and presents interorganizational collaboratives as a highly appropriate vehicle for proactive work in this rapidly changing context. The authors conclude with recommendations for enhancing social work education and practice to better prepare the profession to create and lead these much-needed interorganizational entities.

FROM PAST TO PRESENT: ASSESSING THE CHALLENGES OF THE POLITICAL CONTEXT

Examining the Push toward Devolution

In many ways, the current political climate is reminiscent of the early 1980s. Spending cuts are a priority, this time to balance the federal budget. Emphasis is being placed on reducing the role of the federal government, returning power to the states, and cutting taxes. Given the policy priorities of today, political dialogue is centering more frequently on decentralization and devolution to describe "new" approaches to government reform. As in earlier decades, the idea of American federalism is being redefined once again.

Recommendations for dramatic reductions in federal grants and the creation of new block grants are key features of the proposed Republican plan to achieve these goals. As part of this plan, block grants are being touted as the best way to reform the welfare system. Block grants are not new. However, the emphasis placed on large-scale block granting of entitlement services by House Speaker Newt Gingrich and the 104th Congress, in conjunction with other cost reduction and decentralization efforts, has led to the characterization of today's political environment as the "devolution revolution" (Nathan, 1995).

Three central elements of the proposed Republican plan to achieve these goals pose significant threats to community-based services. First, discretionary funding for domestic programs is expected to be reduced annually for the next seven years. Projections suggest funding cuts averaging a minimum of 6 percent beginning in 1996, increasing to as much as 30 percent by the end of the seven-year period (Nathan, 1996).

Second, as part of this devolutionary plan, the federal government would transfer authority to the states for entitlement programs, including Medicaid and Aid to Families with Dependent Children, while simultaneously reducing future growth in program expenditures by capping state spending through the block grant process. Each state would be responsible for determining its own eligibility and benefits criteria. However, federal-state matching requirements would be eliminated. Therefore, in recessionary periods or other intervals of increased need, states would be faced with three choices in administering welfare programs: (1) expend additional state funds (at 100 percent rather than the 45 percent currently spent by most states under the federal matching program), (2) restrict program eligibility, or (3) reduce benefits (G. E. Peterson, 1995).

Finally, the federal evaluation and reporting requirement for these programs would be eliminated (G. E. Peterson, 1995). Consequently, one method of cost containment may be an inevitable decrease in program evaluation requirements at the state level.

Increasing Competition among Community-Based Organizations

With the focus on expanding state control of welfare and reducing social spending, competition for finite resources is increasing as well. Community-based organizations are particularly vulnerable to these changes. This does not mean that all competition is bad. Optimally, competition for funding allows agencies who provide the "best" services to survive while those providing inferior services fail. Yet who determines what services are the best? What criteria are used in this determination? Do the best organizations serve the greatest number of people? Do they provide services at the lowest cost? Or are there other criteria by which they are judged?

The optimistic view the proposed welfare reforms as new opportunities for innovation and creativity in program implementation at the state level. In addition, devolution brings decision making closer to the communities, with potential benefits for service delivery and community autonomy. Yet program evaluation requirements are in jeopardy as part of this process. Therefore, it is imperative that the community be actively involved in program planning and decision making. Unless consumers, social workers, and other local leaders provide input into these processes, there remains a substantial risk that decentralization and competition will inevitably perpetuate a quantity-over-quality approach to service delivery or cause the states to engage in a "'race to the bottom'—a race to cut welfare benefits faster than their neighbors, thereby endangering the well-being of the most marginal members of society" (P. E. Peterson, 1995, p. 1).

Highlighting the Role of Interorganizational Collaboration

As competition increases, collaboration is gaining attention as a method whereby local health and social services organizations, community leaders, and neighborhood businesses can increase their access to resources and policymakers. The goal of these partnerships is to influence the direction of program creation and policy decisions to enhance service delivery. Through collaboration, community members become active participants in these processes.

Collaboration among social services organizations is not a new phenomenon. Organizations have formed partnerships to influence policy or enhance service delivery systems for decades (for example, Armstrong, 1982; Black, 1983; Emery & Mamerow, 1986; Kaplan, 1986; Roberts-DeGennaro, 1986; Sink & Stowers, 1989; Stoecker, 1995; Weisner, 1983). However, many of these earlier collaborative efforts were voluntary partnerships, whereas many more recent collaborations are being mandated. The development of broad-based interorganizational collaboration for project planning and implementation often is a condition of funding in today's requests for proposals from both public and private institutions. Further, to ensure that new initiatives are community based, consumer involvement and resident participation frequently are mandated as well (Health Resources and Services Administration, 1991; Schietinger, Coburn, & Levi, 1995). To the extent that funders, including the federal government, are mandating partnerships and community involvement, public policy is beginning to reflect the importance of interorganizational community-based collaboration as a strategy for service delivery and resource maximization.

Given the current political environment and forecasted policy shifts, interorganizational collaboration to integrate programs and services is critically important. Acknowledging the theoretical bases for collaboration, these efforts enhance potential for resource exchange, greater efficiency of product and service delivery, and realignment of power with a move toward power parity among the members and a heightened competitive advantage for the collaborative in the community (Alter, 1990; Benson, 1975; Knoke, 1990; Warren, 1967). Community agencies can increase their chances of survival in an increasingly competitive social services arena through collaboration aimed at cutting program costs, sharing expenses for new technologies, and improving services.

Now more than ever, the salience of community and consumer input in planning and decision making for enhanced service delivery and ultimately policy recommendations is paramount. Without community participation, duplication of services may be reduced, but services targeted to specific issues may fail to respond to the individuality and uniqueness of communities. Interorganizational community-based collaboration is one means whereby communities can be active members and leaders of these efforts.

FORMULATING A PRELIMINARY UNDERSTANDING OF INTERORGANIZATIONAL COLLABORATIVES

Defining Interorganizational Collaboration

The implications of the current political situation point to the need for social work education and practice to begin focusing on collaboration and the development of interorganizational community-based collaboratives. "Collaboration is a process through which parties who see different aspects of a problem can constructively explore their differences and search for solutions that go beyond their own limited visions of what is possible" (Gray, 1989, p. 5). "It is characterized by mutual benefit, interdependence, reciprocity, concerted action, and joint production. Ideally, collaboration entails a common vision; a jointly developed structure; and the sharing of work, resources, and rewards. . . . An *interorganizational collaboration* is a group of independent organizations who are committed to working together for specific purposes and tangible outcomes while maintaining their own autonomy" (Abramson & Rosenthal, 1995, p. 1479). Whether called consortia, coalitions, alliances, networks, or federations, interorganizational collaborative efforts are all interactive structures that emphasize the creation of a partnership among parties in which joint participation ideally leads to the achievement of a common goal (Bailey & Koney, 1995a; Mizrahi & Rosenthal, 1992).

In a political and social climate where individual input often is overshadowed by larger, more organized groups, the community-based collaborative structure allows individuals and local organizations to work together, thereby increasing their collective power and resources to effect change. Ensuring the active participation of consumers, residents, or neighborhoods in these collaboratives makes them community based. Yet to be successful as community-based initiatives, these collaboratives must transcend the policy mandate for collaboration and resident input to become truly community-guided programs, with residents and local organizations directly affecting public policy and service delivery.

Social work professionals are in a key position to take the lead in forming these collaborative, community-guided initiatives. As advocates for social justice as well as individual and community empowerment, social work professionals bring essential skills and values to the task of developing interorganizational community-based collaboratives. Further, social workers possess both knowledge of and relationships in local neighborhoods to enable them to serve as links among community agencies, their consumers, and local residents.

Identifying the Eight Core Components
of Interorganizational Collaboration

In developing interorganizational community-based collaboratives, social workers must consider eight core components: leadership, membership, environmental linkages, strategy, purpose, tasks, structure, and systems (Bailey & Koney, 1995a). The definitions of the eight components underscore the interconnection among them. A change in one component creates corresponding challenges in other components. Therefore, it is imperative that social workers understand the components individually but focus appropriate attention on acknowledging the interdependence among all eight.

A community-based collaborative's *leadership* are the individuals and organizations who formally and informally guide and direct the collaborative. The *membership* are the individuals and organizations who work with the leaders within the collaborative unit. The leadership and membership components represent the primary stakeholders of the collaborative. *Environmental linkages* are the relationships between the collaborative's leaders and members and external organizations and individuals. These linkages connect the collaborative with the rest of its stakeholders and as a result expand the collaborative's full range of stakeholders. *Strategy* refers to the means and models for maintaining a share of the market and for achieving the collaborative's purpose. Ideally embodying the shared values of the leadership and members, the collaborative's *purpose* is described in its mission and overall goals. *Tasks* are the specific activities that operationalize the collaborative's strategy and, when collectively completed, accomplish its purpose. *Structure* refers to the way people and tasks are divided within the collaborative to achieve its purpose. Finally, the *systems* are the operating ties that hold the collaborative structure together. Systems include the established mechanisms for resource allocation, decision making, communication, planning, administration, human resource management, and evaluation.

EXPLORING THE PARADOXICAL NATURE
OF INTERORGANIZATIONAL COLLABORATIVES

Defining Paradox

According to *Webster's Ninth New Collegiate Dictionary* (1988), a *paradox* is "a statement that is seemingly contradictory or opposed to common sense and yet perhaps is true" or "something (as a person, condition, or act) with seemingly contradictory qualities or phases" (p. 853). Expanding on these definitions, a paradox is a dilemma that reflects competing realities. A dilemma, unlike a problem, presents different approaches to an issue. Whereas a problem tends to have good and bad or right and wrong solutions, a dilemma usually represents multiple truths with degrees of rightness and wrongness.

Sometimes paradoxes are implied beneath layers of subtlety, sometimes they are recognized easily but not understood, and other times they are quite obvious to acknowledge and address. Yet paradoxes cannot be resolved as if they were problems; rather, at best, paradoxes must be managed.

Discovering the Paradoxical Realities of the Eight Core Components

"We used to think that we knew how to run organizations. Now we know better . . . the organization of the future may not be recognizable as such" (Handy, 1994, pp. 34-35). As Handy, an expert in the area of organizational leadership, goes on to explain, the organization of the future is an embodiment of paradox. In fact, all systems of thought and deed create and even perpetuate their own paradoxes.

Correspondingly, interorganizational systems create and maintain their own paradoxes. Therefore, the eight components of collaboratives can be understood as eight paradoxical realities—realities that ideally are recognized and honored by all stakeholders and that at a minimum must be managed by leadership to facilitate the sustainability of the collaborative. The preliminary definitions offered earlier provide one framework for exploring these paradoxes, and they begin to facilitate an enhanced description of the relationship among the components and the evolution of interorganizational community-based collaborative systems.

Leadership. In an effective community-based collaborative, leadership is both assertive (guiding and directing) and responsive. Unlike autocratic leadership, good leadership is good followership. This type of leadership is sometimes called "servant leadership" (Greenleaf, 1973). Thus, a wise and effective leader stays open and attentive at the same time, following the lead of the other stakeholders.

Leaders of interorganizational community-based entities also must be pathfinders. They must see the many possibilities available to them and help others focus on the challenges of working in what for many is a new and often more complex system. Leaders must perpetuate and continue to articulate the larger vision while constantly being aware of its smaller elements and how all the elements relate to the whole.

Instead of succumbing to dualism and taking a win-lose perspective, a collaborative's leadership must regard the whole as complementary and not just as conflicting opposites. Leaders must recognize that conflict is an inherent and potentially positive aspect of collaboration. The leadership must acknowledge all issues and areas of conflict as part of the collaborative's existence and know that whether the outcome of the conflict turns into something good or bad depends on how they themselves respond to it. For favorable outcomes, leaders need to model conflict management by seeking the common ground, encouraging all stakeholders to rise above their individual and organization-specific interests, and using the power of the collaborative to empower all.

Leadership of interorganizational systems must simultaneously hold on to the knowledge and skills of leading and yet be ready to let go of it all, trusting that the essence of the collaborative and the best way of leading it wait to be "dis-covered." The power of effective leadership comes through cooperation with others and yet independence of service. Attending to the paradoxical nature of a collaborative's leadership by working with a sense of selflessness actually evokes a greater power of self.

Membership. The membership of collaboratives must work with the leaders and also must be leaders. To effectively develop and implement an interorganizational collaborative system, individual members need to have legitimate authority and credibility in their own organizations or reference groups. Similarly, all organizational members must recognize and continually acknowledge the valuable resources each brings to the system.

The membership of an organizational unit actually comprises multiple memberships. Individual and organizational members must recognize their sometimes competing "hats" and know when to wear which one. Members must realize that creating a harmonious system requires that each and all first form a vision of what that harmony would look like for the collaborative. Even when the visions are different, holding to the goal and principle of harmony sets in motion a ripple effect that operates because of the nature of the collaborative. Everyone influences everyone else. Powerful visions serve as powerful influences.

Environmental Linkages. A single organization's linkages to its surrounding environment are usually seen as external to the organization and therefore as less important to its overall effectiveness than most of its other components. In an interorganizational unit, the environmental linkages are critical to its existence. In fact, the resources available to the collaborative from its environmental linkages often exceed those available from its members.

Because of the true interdependence between the collaborative and the community, it is increasingly essential that environmental linkages are solid and intentional while simultaneously remaining fluid and emergent. In addition to the leadership and membership, the key stakeholders outside of the collaborative need to be identified at the outset, with attention given to whom a strong connection is necessary with and why. These connections must be reinforced with information continuously going out of and into the collaborative and in from and back to those in the community. Despite the purposive nature of these linkages, a healthy collaborative monitors them to minimize obstacles to the flow of information and is always ready to create new linkages as the needs of and demands on the collaborative evolve and change over time.

Strategy, Purpose, and Tasks. The strategy of a collaborative articulates the means and models through which the collaborative intends to increase its market share and, paradoxically, to increase its ability to share the market. Often organizations delude themselves into believing that their services or products can fulfill all the needs of a targeted population. In health care, social services, and even education, many organizations project the fantasy that to be the sole provider of products and services is good and is their goal. Interorganizational units know better. Their fundamental strategy is to collaborate, literally to co-labor (from the Latin *com-* plus *laborare*), or work together, to increase the impact of the services and products.

Often stakeholders of a collaborative (leaders, members, and the community) forget its essence. Even members and leaders alike sometimes get so involved with implementing the tasks of the unit that the symbols or reminders of its reason for being appear to be forgotten. Neither the purpose nor the strategy of the collaborative can be achieved without first accurately identifying the tasks appropriate to fulfilling these objectives and without effectively carrying out these specific activities.

The outcomes of the individual tasks are the basis for achievement of the larger goals. Yet when the collaborative's stakeholders maintain too narrow a focus without recognizing the relationship between these tasks and the overall purpose and strategy, numerous losses may result for the collaborative: The collaborative's loss of direction often is accompanied by a loss of creativity and innovation, a decline in member motivation, and a weakening of the collaborative's environmental linkages. The net result is usually a decrease in the collaborative's quality of performance. Thus, tasks must focus both on details and on the big picture.

In articulating an organization's purpose, leaders and members often describe the overall goals with emphasis on an end result. However, in effective interorganizational units manifestations of the purpose are everywhere, embodied in all of the components. Who the participants are, what they do, and how they all come together to do it are actually different ways of articulating the mission and goals of the collaborative. It is safe to assume that the collaborative's stakeholders remain invested because the benefits of their participation outweigh the costs. Therefore, the purpose of this unit must simultaneously serve as the ground on which the unit is built and provide the overriding shared values that serve as the glue that holds the collaborative together. Therefore, the purpose is the foundation for the development of the collaborative's components as well as the synthesis of these components. Periodically revisiting the components with the unit's purpose in mind provides the leadership, membership, and other interested stakeholders with criteria for assessing the collaborative's ability to achieve its mission.

Structure and Systems. An effective interorganizational structure and its corresponding systems have areas of tightness and looseness as well as openness and closedness. Handy (1994) referred to this form as reflecting a new balance of power that

> seeks to be both big in some respects and small in others, to be centralized in some respects and decentralized in others . . . to be local in its appeal and in many of its decisions, but national or even global in its scope . . . to maximize independence, provided there is a necessary interdependence, to encourage difference, but within limits; it needs to maintain a strong [leadership] center, but one devoted to the service of its parts; it can, and should, be led from that center but has to be managed by the parts. (p. 110)

The interorganizational collaborative reflects unity as well as diversity in an entity whose viability depends on the ability to keep the potential complexity of its structure and systems simple as it interacts with itself, evolving over time. Pragmatically this suggests that some collaboratives may function best when organized closer to a professional bureaucracy, whereas others may be akin to a divisional form or even an "adhocracy" (Mintzberg, 1979). In interorganizational units, unlike the old adage "form follows function," structure and systems work in partnership with leadership, membership, linkages, purpose, strategy, and task.

Focusing on Interconnection

No one component is more important to the effectiveness of the collaborative than any other; a change in any one component affects all others. The paradoxical nature of these components contributes to the potency of the interorganizational collaborative. Community-based organizational forms must embody clear and firm values and operate with maximum flexibility. Such entities demonstrate a high tolerance of ambiguity relative to their single-organization counterparts. Interorganizational collaboratives are best positioned to serve as catalysts for change by first articulating the needs of the community, procuring and distributing the new products of the federal-to-state devolution, and then translating the many findings of the collaborative's work into proposed policy recommendations. And when operationalized, these policies must begin to satisfy community needs.

FROM PRESENT TO FUTURE: ENHANCING SOCIAL WORK EDUCATION AND PRACTICE

Challenging Existing Paradigms

For social work professionals concerned with addressing the needs of underserved individuals and communities, the formation and maintenance of interorganizational community-based collaboratives may sound like an old idea. Certainly as organizational forms, they are not new, nor is the research conducted on them (Alter & Hage, 1993; Galaskiewicz, 1985; Katz & Kahn, 1966; Thompson, 1967; Whetten, 1981) or their inherent components. However, articulating organization–community collaboration strategies and effectively achieving mutual input in planning and decision making are not necessarily the same thing. To succeed, these collaboratives must transcend the policy mandate for local participation. They must challenge existing paradigms to establish what for many organizations and community leaders is a fundamentally new approach to planning and service delivery. Only when residents and local organizations actively engage in the political debate and participate in the decisions that directly affect them will these initiatives be truly community based and community beneficial.

Refining Social Work Education and Research

To facilitate this practice, the agenda for social work education and research must include furthering our knowledge about these collaboratives. Knowing under what conditions, how, and with whom to organize, for example, would heighten the probability of establishing effective interorganizational systems. Such activities also can serve to increase the connection between the profession, schools, and the community. For example, schools' foundation courses need to work through the entire continuum of human systems from individuals, families, and groups to organizations, interorganizational collaboratives, and communities. Including this material will ensure that all students, in macro and direct practice alike, will be exposed to the full spectrum of systems.

Moreover, a course in the methods sequence of the social work curriculum focusing on the theory and practice of collaboration would support students' preparation for responding to current challenges. Including material on the theoretical underpinnings of collaboration and the developmental phases of community-based collaboratives (Bailey & Koney, 1995b) would provide students with a theory-in-practice understanding of this organizational form.

Also, teaching on participatory action research (Park, Brydon-Miller, Hall, & Jackson, 1993) and theory-based evaluation (Weiss, 1995) in research sequences exposes social workers to effective alternative methodologies. Such participatory approaches to research, wherein researchers and community members partner in the study of the community, provide researchers with the opportunity to enhance the community-based initiatives they work with and to assist communities in organizing to make their voices heard in the public policy debate.

However, particularly because current policy changes may be eliminating mandatory evaluations, it is not sufficient for social work researchers alone to use this methodology. As Johnson (1994) proposed, using a scholar–advocate approach to social work practice would provide all social work professionals with the skills and knowledge regarding participatory action research to engage in community-based collaborative activities directed toward social change. Even if beyond the scope of their current position, social workers can undertake these efforts as volunteer members of or consultants to community initiatives. Further, all social work professionals must be diligent in supporting the validity of the issues and recommendations for program and policy determination resulting from such research efforts.

These suggestions for enhancement of social work education and practice were supported at a recent Midwestern Deans and Directors Forum held in Cleveland in October 1995. During this conference, the issue of the social work profession's future directions in research, public policy, curriculum, and community service were discussed. The ideas emanating from this dialogue underscored the need for participatory research methodologies and principles. The need to better integrate the educational sequences was argued so that learnings obtained from the community could trigger ideas for teaching and research and so that findings from these two arenas could be fed back to the community, thus demonstrating a truly holistic approach to social work practice. This approach would most effectively bring the community more fully into social work classrooms.

Revisiting the Devolution Revolution

The dictionary defines *devolution* as the "transference (as of rights, powers, or responsibility) to another; esp: the surrender of powers to local authorities by a central government" (*Webster's Ninth New Collegiate Dictionary*, 1988, p. 348). Further, one definition of *revolution* is "a: a sudden, radical, or complete change, b: a fundamental change in political organization, . . . c: activity or movement designed to effect fundamental changes in the socioeconomic situation" (p. 1010). Given these definitions, it is apparent that our nation is indeed in the midst of a devolution revolution.

Forecasting the implications of the proposed policy changes for the nation, Nathan (1995) observed,

> There is ammunition to support critics who fear social program cuts and problems for the poor as a result of this [public policy] shift, sometimes called a "shift and shaft" policy. On the other hand, there are likely to be large opportunities for state governments to reform and integrate delivery systems for domestic programs, in the process strengthening the ties people have to their state and local communities. (p. 24)

However, the extent to which this movement truly results in the redistribution of power and authority to the communities will determine the degree to which these changes actually improve the socioeconomic situation of all members of U.S. society.

From history it is evident that initiatives focusing on community-based collaboratives for planning and service delivery have given communities a head start as federal legislative policy once again begins to emphasize the decentralization of the government. As this happens, the arena for politics moves closer to the community. However, Handy (1994) cautioned, "We cannot wait for central government to give away its power; we have to do what we can without it. In the world ahead we shall increasingly have to make our own connections" (p. 272). These connections must include ones that until recently have been considered strange bedfellows. Connections now must be forged between the for-profit, local and state government, and nonprofit sectors of the community.

The jury is still out as to how proposed changes will affect service delivery. However, regardless of how the impacts of these changes are experienced by local communities, interorganizational community-based collaboration remains the best response for meeting the challenges. Social work professionals and interorganizational community-based collaboratives must work together to include the voices of the community. Such a union heightens the probability that the needs and ideas of communities will be heard in the debates throughout the different sectors of local and state communities and in the federal debate regarding public policy and service delivery. Such a union heightens the probability that communities will be better prepared to accept the challenges that lie ahead. Only with a partnership between the social work profession and interorganizational collaboratives will the community be at the forefront and will the current devolution revolution movement portend change for the better in our communities.

REFERENCES

Abramson, J. S., & Rosenthal, B. (1995). Interdisciplinary and interorganizational collaboration. In R. L. Edwards (Ed.-in-Chief), *Encyclopedia of social work* (19th ed., Vol. 2, pp. 1479–1489). Washington, DC: NASW Press.

Alter, C. (1990). An exploratory study of conflict and coordination in interorganizational service delivery systems. *Academy of Management Review, 33,* 478–502.

Alter, C., & Hage, J. (1993). *Organizations working together.* Newbury Park, CA: Sage Publications.

Armstrong, R. P. (1982). Using agency coalitions to integrate services for children. *Social Work in Education, 4*(3), 59-68.

Bailey, D., & Koney, K. M. (1995a). Community-based consortia: One model for creation and development. *Journal of Community Practice, 2*(1), 21-42.

Bailey, D., & Koney, K. M. (1995b). An integrative framework for the evaluation of community-based consortia. *Evaluation and Program Planning, 18,* 245–252.

Benson, J. K. (1975). The interorganizational network as a political economy. *Administrative Science Quarterly, 20*(1), 229–249.

Black, T. R. (1983). Coalition building—Some suggestions. *Child Welfare, 62,* 263–268.

Dreher, D. (1996). *The tao of personal leadership.* New York: HarperCollins.

Emery, K. J., & Mamerow, D. C. (1986). Making services integration work at the local level: The partnership in Dayton, Ohio. *New England Journal of Human Services, 6*(2), 12–15.

Galaskiewicz, J. (1985). Interorganizational relations. *American Sociological Review, 11,* 281–304.

Gray, B. (1989). *Collaborating: Finding common ground for multiparty problems.* San Francisco: Jossey-Bass.

Greenleaf, R. K. (1973). *The servant as leader* (rev. ed.). Cambridge, MA: Center for Applied Studies.

Handy, C. (1994). *The age of paradox.* Harvard, MA: Harvard Business School Press.

Health Resources and Services Administration. (1991, May). *Guidance for the Healthy Start Program.* Rockville, MD: U.S. Department of Health and Human Services.

Johnson, A. K. (1994). Linking professionalism and community organization: A scholar/advocate approach. *Journal of Community Practice, 1*(2), 65–86.

Kanter, R. M. (1989). *When giants learn to dance.* New York: Simon & Schuster.

Kaplan, M. (1986). Cooperation and coalition development among neighborhood organizations: A case study. *Journal of Voluntary Action Research, 15*(4), 23–34.

Katz, D., & Kahn, R. L. (1966). *The social psychology of organizations.* New York: John Wiley & Sons.

Knoke, D. (1990). *Organizing for collective action: The political economics of associations.* New York: Aldine de Gruyter.

Mintzberg, H. (1979). *The structuring of organizations: A synthesis of the research.* Englewood Cliffs, NJ: Prentice Hall.

Mizrahi, T., & Rosenthal, B. (1992). Managing dynamic tensions in social change coalitions. In T. Mizrahi & J. D. Morrison (Eds.), *Community organizing and social administration: Advances, trends, and emerging principles* (pp. 11–40). New York: Haworth Press.

Nathan, R. P. (1995, October). *Hard road ahead: Block grants and the "devolution revolution."* Paper presented at a seminar for journalists, Brookings Institution, Washington, DC.

Nathan, R. P. (1996). The "devolution revolution": An overview. In *Rockefeller Institute Bulletin, Symposium on Federalism* (pp. 5–13). Albany: State University of New York, Nelson A. Rockefeller Institute of Government.

Park, P., Brydon-Miller, M., Hall, B., & Jackson, T. (Eds.). (1993). *Voices of change: Participatory research in the United States and Canada.* Westport, CT: Bergin & Garvey.

Peterson, G. E. (1995, April). *A block grant approach to welfare reform* (Welfare Reform Brief No. 1). Washington, DC: Urban Institute.

Peterson, P. E. (1995, May). *State response to welfare reform: A race to the bottom?* (Welfare Reform Brief No. 8). Washington, DC: Urban Institute.

Roberts-DeGennaro, M. (1986). Factors contributing to coalition maintenance. *Journal of Sociology and Social Welfare, 13,* 248–264.

Schietinger, H., Coburn, J., & Levi, J. (1995). Community planning for HIV prevention: Findings from the first year. *AIDS & Public Policy Journal, 10*(3), 140–147.

Sink, D. W., & Stowers, G. (1989). Coalitions and their effect on the urban policy agenda. *Administration in Social Work, 13*(2), 83–98.

Stoecker, R. (1995). Community organizing and community-based redevelopment in Cedar-Riverside and East Toledo: A comparative study. *Journal of Community Practice: Organizing, Planning, Development & Change, 2*(3), 1–23.

Thompson, J. D. (1967). *Organizations in action.* New York: McGraw-Hill.

Warren, R. (1967). The interorganizational field as a focus for investigations. *Administrative Science Quarterly, 12,* 396–419.

Webster's Ninth New Collegiate Dictionary. (1988). Springfield, MA: Merriam-Webster.

Weisner, S. (1983). Fighting back: A critical analysis of coalition building in the human services. *Social Service Review, 57,* 291–306.

Weiss, C. H. (1995). Nothing as practical as good theory: Exploring theory-based evaluation for comprehensive community initiatives for children and families. In J. P. Connell, A. C. Kubisch, L. B. Shorr, & C. H. Weiss (Eds.), *New approaches to evaluating community initiatives: Concepts, methods, and context* (pp. 65–92). Washington, DC: Aspen Institute.

Whetten, D. A. (1981). Interorganizational relations: A review of the field. *Journal of Higher Education, 52*(1), 1–28.

This chapter was originally published in the November 1996 issue of Social Work, *vol. 41, pp. 602–611.*

Part II

WELFARE AND WORK

7

Taking New Directions to Improve Public Policy

Susan Hoechstetter

Early last year the Republican House Council held a reception for newly elected Republican members of the U.S. House of Representatives. Sheldon Goldstein, then NASW executive director, and I attended the evening event at a hotel not far from NASW's national office on Capitol Hill. After brief conversations with several new members, including a particularly warm one with the one new Republican member endorsed by PACE (NASW's Political Action for Candidate Election), Representative Bob Ney (R-OH), we met a conservative member from the East who was eager to talk welfare policy with social workers. We spoke for about 20 minutes with little agreement. The representative returned consistently to one theme—to get people off welfare, they must be pushed off. Everyone, including recipients, would be better off if those on welfare were forced to work and support themselves. Taxpayers would be better off, he said, because they would have to pay fewer taxes as a result of cuts in welfare, and they would not be cheated out of their hard-earned money by people taking advantage of the system. One by one we presented our arguments, and one by one he rejected them. Finally, I said that there just were not enough well-paying jobs available to allow everyone to make enough money to support themselves and their families. He shrugged his shoulders and said, "That's too bad."

The memory of that troubling conversation has remained with me as symbolic of the problems encountered with the Republican leadership and their supporters in the 104th Congress. This Congress is collectively committed to restricting access to social programs but not to tackling the causes of dependency on the programs. The newly elected member of Congress seemed to not care about the ultimate drawbacks of his thinking. Either his constituents also do not care, or there is another reason. I think the reason is that his constituents do not have adequate information about and understanding of the welfare issue. If they did, they would have challenged him during the campaign on the question of the availability of jobs and forced him to develop a better response or to change his position.

How important is the need to promote social policy that addresses underlying causes of social problems? How informed is the public about social policy issues and the leaders who make policy? What can the social work profession do to meet the critical challenges to obtaining its social policy objectives in the current political climate?

One answer to the last question is to work to elect candidates to office in 1996 who will support policies promoted by the social work profession. PACE, the political action arm of NASW, has undertaken that task with social workers throughout the country. But we need to do more. The problems of an inadequately informed public and congressional avoidance of the root causes of social problems will not go away easily. They also existed during the 103rd Congress, whose leadership received political support from social work.

THE ECONOMY AND SOCIAL WELFARE

NASW and other advocates are lobbying intensely to maintain a social safety net while Congress attacks funding and federal standards for social programs. It is a critical role, but it has limits. Instead of taking the holistic social work approach of working with the person in his or her environment—that is, advocating for policies that deal with the integrated effects of the economy, inadequate housing, discrimination, commercialism, conflicting values, and a host of other factors—social workers are forced to use our resources to fight to save specific social programs from being destroyed. Many congressional welfare proposals either insufficiently address or ignore the critical factors that contribute to putting people on welfare; the proposals instead focus mainly on restricting Aid to Families with Dependent Children and other benefits. Antipoverty efforts are doomed to fail if they do not address the issues and weaknesses of the economy as a whole.

Unemployment is relatively low, and the gross domestic product (GDP), the measure of U.S. market activity, is high, so many political leaders, via the media, are saying that the U.S. economy is in good shape. By doing so they contribute to public misunderstanding about the availability of economic opportunities for poor people. The problem is that workers' wages are stagnating or declining. Both Republican presidential hopeful Pat Buchanan and Clinton administration Labor Secretary Robert Reich have been pointing this out to a public that knew it by the size of their own paychecks. As the economy has shifted from a manufacturing base to a service and information base, many workers have found themselves not out of work but displaced into different work that pays less than the old factory jobs. Corporate downsizing has added to the problem. So far in the 1990s, about one in every 20 workers has lost their jobs, an increase even from the 1980s, when the number was roughly one in every 25 workers (Nardone, cited in Uchitelle & Kleinfield, 1996). Only about 35 percent of displaced workers are finding jobs at pay equal to or higher than the jobs they lost, according to U.S. Department of Labor statistics. The median U.S. wage, adjusted for inflation, was actually 3 percent higher in 1979 than it is today (Uchitelle & Kleinfield, 1996). These statistics are alarming for workers.

The economy is doing well for some people. Corporate profits are up from $526.9 billion in the fall of 1993 to $609.6 billion in the summer of 1995. Workers' wages are not gaining, but corporate shareholders and executives are receiving handsome increases. The result is a widening of the economic gap between wealthy and nonwealthy people.

To change this trend, we must develop and advance new policies that systematically reverse the transfer of resources to wealthy people and that create more opportunity for nonwealthy people. Discussions of income distribution tend to degenerate into old arguments based on views of capitalism versus socialism, leaving little room for useful interchange of ideas. Creative ways to link the economy to social welfare issues in the eyes of the public and its leaders are needed. For example, in October 1995 the *Atlantic Monthly* published an article entitled "If the Economy Is Up, Why Is America Down?" In promoting the use of a "genuine progress indicator" as the national indicator of progress, Cobb, Halstead, and Rowe (1995) added over 20 factors to the traditional GDP, including income distribution, family breakdown, crime, and pollution. The writers fantasize about television news anchor Peter Jennings delivering the evening news: "The nation's output increased," he says, "but parents worked longer hours and so had less time with their kids. Consumer spending was 'up sharply,' but much of the difference went for increased medical costs and repairing the rubble left by hurricanes and floods" (p. 72). I would add having Jennings say that although production was up, more workers were working at lower wages and unable to support their families. It might give pause to promoting economic gains that cause so much pain in other ways.

INFORMATION AS POLITICAL EMPOWERMENT

It takes information to make good choices about which policies and candidates to support and to be empowered to take action once choices have been made. Recent surveys have shown the public's appalling lack of political knowledge. A recent *Washington Post* article entitled "Who's in Control? Many Don't Know or Care" put into words my concerns about the public's lack of political knowledge (Morin, 1996). The article reported the results of a 1995 survey that found that 40 percent of the population did not know who is the vice president of the United States. Two-thirds did not know who served in the U.S. House of Representatives from their district. Knowledge about issues was also extremely poor (unless respondents perceived the issue to affect them directly). Only 28 percent of those surveyed knew that the number of employees in the federal government had decreased in the past three years.

Last year some members of Congress proclaimed that they were pushing for cuts in certain social programs because their constituents wanted a balanced budget. Surveys at the time reported that, yes, the public did want a balanced budget, but when asked about the cuts proposed in specific programs to balance the budget, they were much more hesitant. Many people did not examine how some of the budget proposals would affect programs they wanted maintained but instead simply supported the broader goal. Some members of Congress were therefore able to use public sentiment in an inauthentic way to rationalize cuts that their constituents really did not want.

Uninformed constituents' poor understanding of the real impacts of certain policy proposals leads them to elect members of Congress who do not represent their interests. According to political scientist Michael Delli Carpini, among low-knowledge voters there was "virtually no relationship" between the political issues that they said mattered most to them and the positions of the candidates they voted for on those issues (Delli Carpini, cited in Morin, 1996). Morin also reported that the more knowledgeable the citizen, the more likely he or she is to participate in the political system through voicing opinions on issues or through elections.

It is not surprising that it is difficult for people to keep up with complex policy issues and political processes and to act effectively to influence federal policymakers. It is not easy even for lobbyists or congressional offices to keep track of all of the intricacies of the legislative process to which the numerous proposals are subjected. How much more difficult it is for citizens not involved through their work with the process to spend the time needed to be fully informed. With more information the public can make better choices about which policy directions best match their personal interests and which politicians best represent those interests. And with more information, people can see how their own interests are often tied to the well-being of others.

Better knowledge of political issues can be a catalyst for more effective public commentary on the issues. We should get to the point where any political leader who speaks of the need to push people off welfare is barraged with media and constituent questions as to how he or she would bring about changes in the economy to enable most welfare participants to find jobs that pay enough for self-sufficiency.

NEW DIRECTIONS FOR SOCIAL WORK

A Holistic Social Policy Approach

It is not enough to fight just to save social programs in isolation from the broader picture. Social work advocates have to develop a more holistic policy advocacy approach that connects social programs to other important influences on individuals' ability to improve their lives, including the economy. The approach, like that of NASW's national health care campaign, should be proactive rather than only responsive to others' initiatives. I am not suggesting that social workers become economists or specialists in other fields, but rather that the profession learn more about the economic system and how it operates to advocate in a more holistic manner for economic opportunity for everyone. We need to make it a priority to collect the relevant information, teach the need for the holistic approach in social work policy classes, develop proactive policy proposals for fairness in the American economy, and work to promote those proposals. Protecting effective social programs should be only one piece of legislative policy strategy.

Advocacy for economic fairness is as much in the social work tradition of fairness and equal opportunity as is advocacy for maintaining affirmative action and ending discriminatory policies in the workplace. Many social workers already take this approach, but it is time to focus on it more as a profession—in research, policy development, advocacy, and social work education. NASW President Jay Cayner's public policy initiative is an important step toward that refocus. By bringing together economists, sociologists, lawyers, and political experts to discuss the current landscape and the outlook with social workers in policy forums, he is starting the process to help the profession look in a more holistic manner at the social policy challenges ahead.

Promoting Public Education

Social work's commitment to helping people change their lives for the better should also lead to facilitating public education in our practice. For people to advocate for and benefit from effective social policies, they must know what the policies are and what impact they will have. I like the definition for community organizing that social worker Edward Lindeman (quoted in Betten & Austin, 1990) gave in the early part of the century: "a conscious effort on the part of a community to control its affairs democratically" (p. 18). That control requires knowledge of the rules governing the community, how proposals would change the rules, who changes them, and how the process works to change them.

The concept is suitable to social work in various settings and types of practice. Hospital social workers, family services workers, private practitioners, school social workers, and others can help clients ultimately gain better control of their affairs by promoting their education about political issues and processes. Schools of social work also need to stress the importance of facilitating public education. If students graduating with social work degrees enthusiastically committed themselves to this concept, social workers might make an important difference in activating the public to become more informed and, because informed people participate more, to participate more in the democratic process.

More social workers might take on this challenge if the profession were to increase its focus on the principles and professional practice of community organizing. However, although a few schools of social work are building their community organization programs, professional activity related to community organizing on a national level is so little. No practice standards are being developed, and no conference tracks are being proposed for community organizing at the NASW national office. School social workers, substance abuse social workers, private practitioners, and others have formed or asked to form NASW membership sections devoted to their areas, but the same request has not come from community organizers. The profession needs to find a way to nurture this part of social work, especially now.

In working to facilitate public education, social workers need to take into consideration the potential positive and negative impacts of the new information technology. The technology offers greater and more timely opportunities to learn more about public policy. The Library of Congress system, Thomas, makes federal legislation available to the public. Anyone hooked up to the Internet can also gain access to home pages of members of Congress and the White House. And it is now possible for many constituents to communicate with their congressional representatives via e-mail. However, the new technology can increase the gap between advantaged and disadvantaged people if access to the communications systems is limited to those with more financial resources. For that reason, facilitating access to this technology is also important.

CONCLUSION

A Catholic University graduate social work student recently told me about a class discussion of a bill proposed by Sen. Edward Kennedy (D-MA) and Sen. Nancy Kassebaum (R-KS) that could provide millions of people with health insurance. Her social policy class examined one aspect of the bill—whether the bill would help uninsured people afford insurance, because most people eligible for insurance now under the Consolidated Omnibus Budget Reconciliation Act of 1985 do not buy it. A representative of the American Academy of Actuaries predicted at a recent briefing on the legislation that as few as 150,000 people are expected to purchase health insurance coverage in the first year after passage of the legislation because of lack of affordability. However, because both Republicans and Democrats want to demonstrate that they accomplished health care reform in this congressional session, they and the media are talking about the bill as if it would significantly change access to health insurance. They neglect to mention that it does nothing to address the affordability of health insurance. The student remarked how easy it is to distort the issue just by omitting some information.

Although the student was pursuing clinical social work studies, she became motivated by her social policy class to think more about the effects of policy on people's lives. She then took it one step further and wondered out loud how as a social worker she could help people become more informed about political issues and politicians. We should help her find an answer.

REFERENCES

Betten, N., & Austin, M. J. (1990). *The roots of community organization: 1917–1939*. Philadelphia: Temple University Press.

Cobb, C., Halstead, T., & Rowe, J. (1995, October). If the economy is up, why is America down? *Atlantic Monthly*, pp. 59–78.

Consolidated Omnibus Budget Reconciliation Act of 1985, P.L. 99-272, 100 Stat. 82.

Morin, R. (1996, January 28). Who's in control? Many don't know or care. *Washington Post*, pp. A1, A6–A7.

Uchitelle, L., & Kleinfield, N. R. (1996, March 3). On the battlefields of business, millions of casualties. *New York Times*, pp. A1, A26–A29.

This chapter was originally published in the July 1996 issue of Social Work, vol. 41, pp. 343–346.

Welfare Reform

Martha Ozawa and Stuart A. Kirk

Welfare reform is the latest stage in America's long struggle to deal with single women with children. A benign protector of single women and their children until the Great Depression of the 1930s, the U.S. government has become antagonistic toward them, blaming them for being poor, for the moral decay of society, and even for the country's difficulty in becoming economically competitive in the global market. In spite of evidence to the contrary, many politicians and citizens believe that our nation is threatened by women who join the welfare rolls instead of the labor force.

The Personal Responsibility and Work Opportunity Reconciliation Act of 1996 (P.L. 104-193), which President Bill Clinton signed into law on August 22, 1996, is, in large part, a societal response to the imagined threat posed by these women. The act represents the nation's retreat from its commitment to provide a safety net for this most economically vulnerable population. Under this law, the authority to develop and administer welfare programs will be transferred to the states. Eligibility for and the provision of welfare programs will become much more restrictive as the federal government's responsibility shrinks to merely providing block grants and enforcing the law.

Specifically, the act includes the following provisions:

- Welfare mothers will be required to work after two years of assistance.
- Cash payments will be provided for no more than five years during recipients' lives.
- Unwed mothers under 18 are ineligible for assistance unless they live in the home of an adult relative or in another adult-supervised arrangement.
- States will be allowed to deny cash payments to children born into families already receiving assistance.
- Eligibility for Temporary Assistance to Needy Families (TANF), which will replace Aid to Families with Dependent Children (AFDC), will not guarantee eligibility for Medicaid, although the act requires states to provide Medicaid to families who meet the income standards for AFDC.
- Criteria for children's receipt of Supplemental Security Income (SSI) will be more stringent, and maladaptive behavior will be eliminated as a medical criterion.
- Current legal immigrants will be barred from receiving SSI and food stamps until they become U.S. citizens, and those currently receiving these benefits will be screened after enactment; illegal immigrants are already prohibited from receiving these benefits.

■ Future legal immigrants will also be barred from receiving Medicaid and
other means-tested benefits for five years, and states will have the option
of extending this ban until the immigrants become citizens.

■ State control over food stamps is increased by allowing states to determine
food stamp benefits, to levy food stamp penalties on recipients who violate
TANF rules, and to deny food stamps to those who, during the preceding
36 months, have received food stamps for three months and not worked or
participated in a work or training program.

Sweeping changes such as these appear to be justified by erroneous beliefs
about why single mothers apply for and remain on welfare. For example, according to the prevailing myth, some women deliberately have more children
to remain on welfare and receive higher benefits. They opt to receive income not
from work but from reliance on government programs. In fact, women become
heads of their families because men no longer believe that it is in their interests
to establish and support families, and some women think it is feasible for them
to be economically self-sufficient enough to raise children alone. Often they are
not able to achieve this self-sufficiency because their educational levels are too
low for them to find jobs with wages that allow them to support their children.
They are forced, at least temporarily, to resort to welfare. The economic disadvantage of these women is expected to increase as the gap between the earnings
of high-skilled and low-skilled workers continues to widen.

As Gordon (1996) eloquently discussed, the origins of the current animosity
toward welfare mothers lie in the Social Security Act of 1935. On the basis of
wishful thinking that the two-parent family structure would remain intact and
the economic dependence of widowed mothers could be dealt with by Survivors Insurance, lawmakers at that time excluded income support for single
mothers from the mainstream social insurance program. Instead, they established the public assistance program, which incorporated both income and character testing. Policymakers in the 1930s and those who followed failed to address the legitimate claims that single mothers—deserted, divorced, or never
married—should have on public financial resources for raising their children.

In fact, the United States spends relatively little to support poor people. AFDC
accounts for only 0.37 percent of this country's gross domestic product (GDP). Moreover, all 80 income-tested programs, including Medicaid, account for only 4.91 percent of the GDP, which is equivalent to the expenditures for Old-Age, Survivors,
and Disability Insurance, commonly known as social security (Ozawa, 1995).

In spite of all the hoopla surrounding the preservation of "family values," the
family as it was traditionally constituted is no longer the only or even the major
family structure in the United States or in any other industrialized society. Similarly, the economic system and the wage structure are also changing rapidly.
Under these circumstances of social change, it is inevitable that some mothers
and their children will be economically dependent. Blaming them for their economic predicament and for other social problems is not only simplistic, it is a
cruel hoax. Such a blaming perspective will divert the nation's attention from
the real problems these women and their children face. It behooves Congress

and state legislatures to think carefully about the inevitable economic dependence of some women and their children and to develop workable proposals to address their needs.

Social work researchers have an important role to play in the process of restructuring welfare. As this special issue of *Social Work Research* on welfare reform demonstrates, there is much work that needs to be done to debunk welfare myths, document the legitimate needs of women and children, evaluate the outcomes of current programs, and monitor the effects of the welfare-to-work reforms that are now commencing across the nation. The articles in this issue are a worthy sample of the kind of careful research that must continue. One article describes, for example, the actual characteristics of welfare recipients, which bear little resemblance to the pervasive stereotype of those on welfare. Another shows that poor children are the poorest group in this country, that their standard of living is considerably below the poverty line, and that it is considerably lower than that of poor elderly people. A third article delineates how effective the use of a package of universal social welfare programs would be in reducing poverty and dependence on welfare.

Underlying these articles is the premise that women with children go on welfare because of very difficult economic circumstances that neither they can, nor we should, abide. It is essential for social welfare researchers to help sort out the complex causes of welfare dependence and find just and effective solutions to the problem.

REFERENCES

Gordon, L. (1996). How "welfare" became a dirty word. In R. Albelda & N. Folbre (Eds.), *The war on the poor: Defense manual* (pp. 108–112). New York: New Press.

Ozawa, M. N. (1995). Public spending on income-tested social welfare programs for investment and consumption purposes. *Journal of Sociology and Social Welfare, 22,* 133–146.

Personal Responsibility and Work Opportunity Reconciliation Act of 1966, P.L. 104-193.

This chapter was originally published in the December 1996 issue of Social Work Research, *vol. 20, pp. 194–195.*

Welfare Reform: The Bad, the Ugly, and the Maybe Not Too Awful

Dennis L. Poole

Every reform, however necessary will . . . be carried to an excess, that itself will need reforming.

—Samuel Taylor Coleridge

N o one can deny the need for welfare reform. The current U.S. welfare system discourages work and independence, replaces pride with stigma, and exiles poor people from community life. However, the reform embodied in the Personal Responsibility and Work Opportunity Reconciliation Act of 1996 goes too far. Rather than invest another $10 billion in America's welfare program, which the Clinton administration pledged in 1994, the new law cuts nearly $55 billion in federal dollars over the next six years. Nearly all of the savings will come from reductions in the Food Stamp program, Supplemental Security Income (SSI), and assistance to legal immigrants.

Scheduled to go into effect next year, P.L. 104-193 introduces several major changes that almost certainly will harm people in need of public assistance. At the same time, the new law ushers in a few changes that could make parts of the system work for the better.

FEDERAL BLOCK GRANT

One major change in the welfare system will be the shift from categorical funding to a federal block grant. Aid to Families with Dependent Children (AFDC), emergency assistance, and the Job Opportunities and Basic Skills Training program will be replaced with the Temporary Assistance for Needy Families (TANF) block grant. TANF will give states broad authority to create and manage their own welfare programs. In congressional testimony governors argued that states know better than Washington how to put people to work and get them off welfare. Several impressive reforms that originated in the states backed up their argument.

However, TANF will probably slow down rather than speed up welfare reform. Before the new law, states could design their own welfare programs only if Washington approved a waiver to federal requirements. This approach began to pay off in the Clinton administration when the federal government got more flexible with waivers, and states were treated as partners in welfare reform. Stalemates between the two levels of government gave way to compromise, which resulted in some meaningful reforms. This sort of compromise will be difficult now. As written, the new law nearly eliminates the federal government as a partner in welfare reform. Hence, the U.S. welfare system may soon become a hodgepodge of funding levels and eligibility requirements—50 states all doing different things—with national chaos outpacing reform.

States also post a poor track record with federal block grants, falling far short of the mark in community-based mental health care and struggling now with the federal block grant for child welfare (nearly half of the states are under court supervision for not taking proper care of children who had been abused or neglected) ("Some Look at the Welfare Plan," 1996). This track record will likely get worse with the welfare block grant. The federal government now pays 55 percent of all AFDC benefits, with no cap on the number of recipients. Under the new law, states will receive a fixed sum from the federal government regardless of the number of recipients. Over the next six years, this cost-saving measure will cut by one-third the total amount of federal funding that would have been used to support state welfare programs under current law (NASW, 1996).

Another impediment to reform is the provision that permits states to cut their own welfare spending up to 25 percent without suffering any federal penalty. In the past, if states reduced such spending, they lost as much or more in federal support. The new law gives states an open invitation to take money out of their welfare programs. Not all states will bend to this temptation, but some will. It is much easier for states to cut welfare benefits than to raise taxes for welfare reform.

WORK AND POVERTY

Replacing guaranteed cash payments with strings-attached assistance may prove the most significant change ushered in by the new law. Welfare recipients must begin working within two years of receiving aid or have their benefits reduced; lifetime federal cash assistance must not exceed five years, and able-bodied adults must work or their food stamps will be terminated. States can grant exceptions to working for mothers with young children and can extend lifetime assistance to up to 20 percent of their caseloads.

Questions remain about the potential effects of these requirements on poverty in America. One widely cited study by the Urban Institute (Zedlewski, 1996) predicted that the new law will push 2.6 million people into poverty, nearly half of whom will be children. However, this assumes that work requirements will not alter the behavior of people on welfare. Simply asking mothers to look for work can reduce caseloads by a modest percentage. The study also assumes that states and localities will not use their own money to continue aid after federal assistance expires. Most probably won't, but some will.

Still, there is little evidence that this radical departure from the past has much chance of success. The U.S. economy does not produce enough jobs for recipients to get off welfare and escape poverty; the bottom has been falling out of low-wage jobs for the past two decades. Moreover, when recipients find jobs, most of them still need assistance, because the jobs they fill are usually low-wage, part-time, or both (Lehman & Danziger, 1994). These and other structural flaws in the economy—not the unwillingness to work—push the majority of poor people onto public assistance.

Moving people off welfare demands large investments in training, education, and job creation. Conservative governors in California, Wisconsin, and other states spearheading promising reforms in their own welfare systems have already learned this lesson. But federal funding falls about $12 billion short of what will be needed over the next six years to meet the work requirements of the new law (NASW, 1996).

In the meantime, if this radical departure from the past fails, poor people will undoubtedly suffer the most. More than half of the reductions in welfare spending will be taken from families whose annual income is less than $6,490, or less than half the federal poverty line. The nation will suffer as well. America already has one of the highest rates of child poverty in the industrialized world. These rates will likely worsen under the new welfare law. Given the direct relationship between poverty and ill health (Fitzgerald, Lester, & Zuckerman, 1995), the nation also will have more children with stunted growth and physical and mental disabilities and more children dying in childhood. Savings in public assistance will drive up public costs in other areas such as health care.

LEGAL IMMIGRANTS

Another significant change is the termination of many benefits for legal immigrants. Most current and future legal immigrants will be ineligible for SSI, food stamps, and Medicaid until they become U.S. citizens or have paid social security taxes for 10 years. Mothers with dependent children could be eligible for cash assistance, but this is an option left to the states. Undocumented immigrants will not be directly affected, because they were ineligible for most major entitlement programs under previous law.

Of course, this part of the law has nothing to do with welfare reform. It was conceived by the Republican leadership in Congress as a federal budget-saving measure and as a way to curb immigration to the United States. The first of the two objectives will almost certainly be accomplished. The new law will save the federal government about $22 billion over the next six years by denying food stamps, SSI, and Medicaid to most legal immigrants. The second objective will be more elusive, however. Immigrants will still come to the United States, legally or illegally. U.S. conditions that appear harsh look better than many conditions elsewhere. The struggle now is over which level of government will pay the bill. Obviously, cutting $22 billion out of the federal welfare budget will force border states and their communities to cover a disproportionate share of this national expense.

President Clinton should use the line-item veto to strike this item from the new law. Otherwise, nearly half a million elderly and disabled legal immigrants will lose their SSI benefits. By 2002 an estimated 260,000 elderly legal immigrants, 65,000 people with disabilities, 175,000 other adults, and 140,000 children who would be eligible for Medicaid under current law will be denied this benefit under the new law (NASW, 1996).

The health implications alone are staggering The American Hospital Association predicted that hospitals will be forced to absorb an additional $10 billion in uncompensated care over seven years (Weissenstein, 1996). Similarly, public health departments will be forced to make difficult choices when the federal government no longer provides compensation for prenatal care and other treatment to legal immigrants.

Then, of course, there is the issue of social justice. The new law violates a principle that has guided America's treatment of legal immigrants for many years. The president of the National Council of La Raza, a Hispanic service organization, explains the issue this way: "It's always been a principle [in the U.S.] that you treat aliens the same way you treat everyone else. You expect them to serve in the armed forces, pay taxes, and live up to other responsibilities. You don't say, 'You're a citizen, you don't have to pay taxes'" ("Some Look at the Welfare Plan," 1996, p. 26). Legal immigrants should not be treated as scapegoats for the federal budget deficit in America.

TEENAGE PREGNANCY

Unmarried teenage mothers will receive federal public assistance benefits under the new law only if they attend school and live with an adult. It is not surprising that welfare reform law draws special attention to the issue of teenage pregnancy. A comprehensive report by the U.S. General Accounting Office (GAO) (1995) indicated that families headed by teenage mothers represent almost half of all families receiving welfare. These families are more likely to receive public assistance for longer periods than other families at great cost to public institutions. In 1992, for example, the federal government spent $34 billion in AFDC, Medicaid, and food stamp benefits to support families started by teenagers—a 17 percent increase from 1991 and a 36 percent rise from 1990. This in part reflects spiraling trends in births to unwed teenagers over the past three decades; between 1960 and 1992 the birth rate for unmarried women ages 15 to 19 increased threefold in the United States.

There is considerable debate—and uncertainty—about how best to solve this problem. One factor identified in the GAO report is that low-income teenage mothers stand a better chance of avoiding long-term dependency if they obtain a high school diploma. Active monitoring and follow-up of school attendance, along with financial incentives and sanctions, seem to increase high school or general equivalency diploma completion rates—hence the new rule that teenage mothers must attend school and live under adult supervision to receive welfare benefits. Child care is a critical factor as well—hence the appropriation of an additional $14 billion to help pay for this support.

However, other factors reported by the GAO that help teenage mothers overcome obstacles to high school completion are not addressed in the new law. Transportation assistance, school- and home-based services, and alternative educational programs receive no additional federal funding. Preventive services are noticeably missing as well. Regarding adult supervision, states will be responsible for locating and assisting an adult-supervised setting for teenagers, but no additional funding will be available for establishing "second-chance homes."

REALITIES

In our efforts to prevent these welfare reform changes from being carried to an excess, social workers must face five realities. First, there is little hope that the near future will bring an end to the federal welfare block grant. The devolution of social policy, which for the past 15 years has been shifting power and responsibility to states and localities, will probably not end in this decade. Economic forces are too strong. In addition, the majority of the voting public believes that the federal government has become too big and is too incompetent to operate certain large-scale programs. The political pendulum has swung toward decentralization; bringing it back to center in welfare reform will be difficult.

Second, as the federal government backs off from cash guarantees to poor people, much of the burden will fall to states and communities. Therefore, we must help local voters confront the question of what to do about people who are willing to work but cannot find a job. We also must help build new arrangements between government entities and nonprofit agencies, churches, and business organizations, which have long been absent in welfare system reform (Jennings & Zank, 1993). For vision, we can turn to the public health social workers in South Carolina who have built partnerships to put health social work in the middle of social change in their state and its communities.

The third reality is that the U.S. welfare system desperately needs reform. Most recipients are, indeed, exiled from community life. State welfare agencies, not communities, own their needs and problems. Worse yet, the system provides few opportunities for people on public assistance to reciprocate through work. This problem cuts deep across the grain of America, where work and reciprocity reflect prized values in the culture. The challenge then becomes one of society meeting its obligation to provide jobs to people who can and should work—and adequate income to sustain their families when they do.

The fourth reality is that no society can ignore the fact that caring for citizens is a shared responsibility. Efforts by any level of government to abdicate its share of the responsibility in welfare reform will ultimately fail. Contrary to popular perception, most increases in federal domestic spending this century have come from the states. States ask Washington for more money when they are unable to meet the needs of their own citizens; states ask Washington to get out of their way when they want to save money. Therefore, we can expect states to go to Washington again soon for more money. We must be prepared to strike excess reform from the law and to bring the federal government in as a meaningful partner in welfare reform.

Finally, there is little doubt that Americans as a people have turned inward. Some even argue that our culture indulges in narcissism. Maybe the new law will heal us somewhat. A certain losing of self is essential to serving people in need. Perhaps sending more responsibility to our communities will force Americans to look once again beyond ourselves, to neighbors and strangers near home who need help. Helping requires sacrifice, but sacrifice makes us more fully human, brings peace in ourselves, and strengthens communities. This may be America's best hope for the welfare reform of 1996.

REFERENCES

Fitzgerald, H. E., Lester, B. M., & Zuckerman, B. (Eds.). (1995). *Children in poverty: Research health, and policy issues.* New York: Garland Press.

Jennings, E. T., & Zank, N. S. (Eds.). (1993). *Welfare system reform: Coordinating federal, state, and local public assistance programs.* Westport, CT: Greenwood Press.

Lehman, J., & Danziger, S. (1994, October). *Ending welfare as we know it: Problems and prospects.* Paper presented at the fall meeting of the National Association of Deans and Directors of Schools of Social Work, Myrtle Beach, SC.

National Association of Social Workers. (1996, August 27). *Personal Responsibility and Work Opportunity Reconciliation Act of 1996 (H.R. 3734), Public Law 104-193: Summary of provisions* [Government Relations Update]. Washington, DC: Author, Office of Government Relations.

Personal Responsibility and Work Opportunity Reconciliation Act of 1966, P.L. 104-193.

Some look at the welfare plan with hope, but others are fearful. (1996, August 4). *New York Times,* p. 26.

U.S. General Accounting Office. (1995, September 29). *Welfare to work: Approaches that help teenage mothers complete high school* (GAO/HEHS/PEMD-95-20). Washington, DC: U.S. Government Printing Office.

Weissenstein, E. (1996, July 29). Hospitals opposing welfare bill provision. *Modern Healthcare,* p. 16.

Zedlewski, F. (1996, July 26). *The potential effects of congressional reform legislation on family incomes.* Washington, DC: Urban Institute.

This chapter was originally published in the November 1996 issue of Health & Social Work, *vol. 21, pp. 243–246.*

10 Poverty, Work, and Community: A Research Agenda for an Era of Diminishing Federal Responsibility

Claudia J. Coulton

The process of shifting responsibility for entitlement programs such as Aid to Families with Dependent Children (AFDC) to state and local governments is well under way. Even though these programs have not yet been turned into block grants, the majority of states now have waivers that allow significant latitude in the way they administer entitlements. At least 31 states, for example, have a waiver for some type of time limit on benefits or stringent work requirements (Center for Law and Public Policy, 1996). The theme underlying much of the reform is to make AFDC a temporary benefit and move large numbers of recipients who have been out of the labor force for extended periods of time into employment.

The income transfers provided through the AFDC program have been a cornerstone of antipoverty policy in the United States through much of the 20th century. Although their effectiveness in actually lifting families' incomes above the poverty threshold has diminished in recent decades (Danziger & Weinberg, 1994), AFDC and related entitlements have provided an important safety net for families and children. For social workers and others working with poor people, AFDC has represented the economic floor below which few families could fall and from which they could rise economically.

The limitations and constraints now being placed on AFDC and related benefits will fundamentally alter the lives of low-income families, the conditions in low-income communities, and the demands placed on local governments and nonprofit organizations. The agencies administering public assistance and related programs will be challenged to redefine their missions and redesign their services. Social workers will need new skills and knowledge to help large numbers of individuals move into the labor market and to enable communities to foster and sustain employment opportunities.

To respond to the challenges of the new era, social workers need a greater understanding of how to enhance employment opportunities for welfare recipients and low-wage workers. More intricate knowledge of the workings of low-income communities and low-skill labor markets is required, particularly knowledge about how these factors support or undermine individuals' chances of finding a job that provides a living wage. It is within these contexts that effective programs and practices will need to be crafted.

This article discusses the relationship among poverty, welfare, and work and the factors that allow communities to foster employment opportunities, enhance accumulation of wealth, and provide a safety net for families. In addition, this article outlines the research needed to raise the understanding of how communities and labor markets affect work and poverty and the process through which communities can change to meet the challenges of devolution. The agenda set forth is not exhaustive but focuses on the contexts in which low-income people, whether working or on welfare, try to raise and support their families. The agenda assumes that social workers have an important role to play in helping create community and opportunity structures that allow all families to thrive.

POVERTY AND WORK

Welfare Recipients and Poor Working People

To respond to the increasing emphasis on work and self-sufficiency, it is important to recognize that work, welfare, and poverty are intricately interwoven, dynamic, and fluid. Poverty is not solely a problem of joblessness. Although welfare recipients are the poorest population group, a sizable portion of the poor population is employed. Approximately 40 percent of poor individuals age 16 and older have jobs (U.S. Bureau of the Census, 1993), but their incomes do not rise above the poverty line because of low-wage jobs or part-time status.

Working families and welfare families are often thought of as two distinct groups, but there is actually considerable overlap between work and welfare. A slight majority of welfare recipients receive wages and welfare either simultaneously or sequentially and ultimately leave welfare for work (Harris, 1993). However, many recipients who work also return to welfare periodically. Over one-quarter of women who leave welfare return within a year, primarily because they lost a job (Harris, 1996).

These rates of official work among welfare recipients belie the fact that many additional welfare recipients work in the cash economy to supplement their welfare benefits (Edin, 1995). Their unreported jobs are typically without benefits, temporary, and part-time. Nevertheless, living on the meager amount of welfare cash benefits is not possible for most families, and they almost universally supplement their incomes (Edin, 1995).

Mandatory, broad-coverage welfare-to-work programs seem capable of moving modest proportions of welfare recipients into employment who would not have done so on their own (Gueron & Pauly, 1991). However, even the most successful programs leave more than half the participants jobless at the end of three years and do little to raise incomes above the poverty line (Friedlander & Burtless, 1995). Indeed, impressive results of mandatory broad-coverage programs have been achieved only when there has been a high demand for low-skill labor in the local economy (Bane & Ellwood, 1994).

Despite the high level of work effort in the welfare population and the fact that most people who apply for welfare leave before two years have elapsed, the majority of an AFDC caseload at any given time are long-term recipients (Bane & Ellwood, 1994). Thus, state or federal action that imposes time limits will force many individuals to seek jobs who would have remained on welfare for longer periods.

Low-Skill Labor Markets

Conditions in low-skill labor markets have a powerful effect on the employment and earnings of welfare recipients and working poor people. Although the aggregate demand for labor has grown steadily in the United States, low-skill workers have experienced a growing disadvantage in their wages. The effect has been most devastating for male high school dropouts, whose average wages fell by 13 percent during the past decade (Blank, 1994). Although deindustrialization is partially responsible for this trend, even within industries the size of the wage gap between high school graduates and college graduates nearly doubled in the 1980s (Murphy & Welch, 1993), reflecting the overall increase in demand for high-skill workers and severe slackening of demand for workers without postsecondary education in services, manufacturing, and other sectors (Blackburn, Bloom, & Freeman, 1990). Men of color with low education levels have been the most severely affected by this process. Their rate of unemployment more than doubled in the 1980s, reaching almost 50 percent by the end of the decade (Kasarda, 1989).

The wages of low-skill women have not fallen during this time. However, their earnings started out much lower and remain below those of low-skill men because of their segregation into lower-paying occupations and part-time work. Women's labor force participation has been growing steadily and reached almost 60 percent in 1990 (Blank, 1994; Caputo, 1995). For two-earner families, women's earnings have helped maintain family income despite falling wages for men. For single-earner families, especially those headed by women, incomes are disproportionately low (Danziger & Weinberg, 1994).

An additional important feature of low-skill labor markets is their changing geography. Nearly three-quarters of poor people live in urban areas (U.S. Bureau of the Census, 1993), where deindustrialization and the shift of low-skill jobs to outlying areas have increased the distance between poor people and employment opportunities (Galster & Mincey, 1993; Kasarda, 1993). Central-city residents have less access to employment than suburban residents as measured by the ratio of jobs to people within neighborhoods and by average travel times (Holzer, 1991). Youths, who tend to work closer to home, and African American men and women have been particularly disadvantaged by this suburbanization of jobs (Ellwood, 1986; Ihlanfeldt & Sjoquist, 1989, 1990).

The implementation of time limits and work requirements in the AFDC program will push even more low-skill workers into local labor markets in the short run. A fundamental question is how quickly these former welfare recipients can be absorbed into local labor markets without displacing current employees. Regions differ considerably in this regard, and making such projections requires numerous assumptions. Nevertheless, reports on two regions suggest that the gap in available jobs is severe. A study of the metropolitan Chicago labor market estimated that there would be approximately six job seekers for every entry-level job if all adult welfare recipients sought work (Carlson & Theodore, 1995). The Cleveland-Akron labor market was projected as needing to double its number of entry-level jobs to absorb just recipients in the region who were on AFDC for more than five years (Bania & Leete, 1995). Furthermore, this sudden influx of low-skill workers was expected to further depress the wages of both new and existing workers competing for these types of jobs (Mishel & Schmitt, 1995).

Poor people cycle in and out of low-wage jobs and public assistance programs. As time limits and work requirements go into effect, more families will have to rely primarily on work for their incomes. However, given the current conditions in low-skill labor markets, many will be confined to a tenuous and marginal employment status. Traditional welfare-to-work programs will be insufficient to help large numbers of recipients compete for steady jobs at nonpoverty wages. Many reforms are needed in the communities in which poor people reside and in the connections of these communities to regional labor markets.

COMMUNITY AS SOURCE OF OPPORTUNITY

A growing body of research has identified the community and neighborhood as a factor in the reproduction of social and economic disadvantage (Furstenberg, 1996). Understanding what needs to be done to create and support opportunity within communities, however, requires a focused and multidisciplinary program of community research. To date little of the research on welfare dynamics and welfare-to-work programs has been embedded in a social context.

The studied determinants of welfare and labor force participation have been the human capital characteristics of the single mother on the one hand and the services, benefits, and sanctions of the welfare system on the other. Most extant studies have focused on the individual as an autonomous decision maker, but the findings of relatively weak effects for incentives and programs suggest that the influences on employment are much more complicated. One important omission is that these studies have looked at the single woman without regard to community influences (Harris, 1993, 1996; Oliker, 1995a, 1995b).

To anticipate and accommodate the changes in entitlements, it is important to have much more information about the features of the local situation that affect the opportunities for poor men and women, both welfare recipients and poor workers. It is within the constraints and supports provided by these local contexts that the fate of poor families will be determined.

Social welfare and social work research must focus on the community and how the structures and processes affect whether low-income families can find work and achieve a living wage. Before strategies for change can be formulated, it is necessary to refine the understanding of the various ways in which communities affect work. The following sections discuss community influences on employment and income and how changes in communities can occur. This article focuses on urban communities because that is where the majority of poor people live. The author recognizes that there is considerable variation in economic and social conditions among communities, particularly in the factors that produce the preconditions for work, enable preparation and support for work, provide access to work, and provide ongoing support for working families.

Community Preconditions for Work

Socialization to Behaviors and Attitudes Conducive to Work. Through socialization processes communities affect the chances that residents will work. Wilson (1987) argued that as working role models have disappeared from some low-income communities, there has been a disruption in the socialization of children and youths into the world of work. More recently Wilson (1991) argued that jobless communities do not transmit the ideas of scheduling, regularity, and organization of daily routines necessary to be successful in the world of work.

Socialization within communities may be an important mechanism for fostering the ability to hold a job. Studies have shown that the presence of middle-class families and professional and managerial workers in neighborhoods raises the achievement levels of poor children and youths (Brooks-Gunn, Duncan, Klebanov, & Sealand, 1993; Crane, 1991; Duncan, 1993). Exposure of youths to relatively large numbers of successful and working people is believed to be necessary for the transmission of norms and behaviors required for entry into the mainstream economy.

Research is needed that reveals how these socialization processes can be encouraged in communities where joblessness is high and there are few middle-class and successful role models. Can the influence of a few available role models be spread more widely through community efforts such as involving these individuals in schools, youth programs, and family centers, so that other residents can be exposed to their know-how? How can communities retain working individuals, who have a tendency to move to more affluent communities as they achieve more success? How effective are programs that involve mentors from outside the community in socializing at-risk youths in inner-city communities to employment? How important is it that these socialization processes occur through coresidence in the same communities as opposed to creating linkages across communities?

Expectations and Definitions of Success Consistent with Work. Communities create preconditions for work to the extent that they transmit expectations and definitions of success that include preparing for and entering a career. However, there is concern that in many low-income communities the realities have interfered with such aspirations. Evidence comes from the fact that successful families in poor communities promote achievement in their offspring by actually isolating them from local relationships and influences (Jarrett, 1995). Instead, these families go to considerable effort to link their children to influences and opportunities in distant and more affluent communities.

As Burton, Obeidallah, and Allison (in press) found, many low-income communities present expectations and definitions of success that result in a lack of fit between mainstream institutions and businesses and community residents. For example, an accelerated life course in many poor neighborhoods and families leads adolescents to take on adult roles and responsibilities for family and self. These expectations for adult behavior create a misfit between adolescents and the institutions that traditionally prepare them for work, such as schools and training programs. Furthermore, these sets of adult obligations may interfere with building the basic skills that foster successful careers.

In addition, the lack of good jobs and the dangers inherent in the underground economy may have given rise to alternative definitions of success that do not necessarily include career. For example, just surviving, caring for family members, and being creative in hobbies are alternative criteria that Burton et al. (in press) found prevalent in poor communities. Although they undoubtedly make a positive contribution to self-esteem, these successes cannot substitute for paid work as a route to economic self-sufficiency.

What are the consequences for the community of the social isolation of the most successful families? Are there ways that these families could enrich and help transform the predominant expectations and definitions around them? Can other residents benefit by adopting the successful families' strategies of exposing their offspring to activities in more advantaged communities? How can institutions and services build on the positive base of existing aspirations while reducing their incompatibility with employment? How responsive will these expectations and definitions of success be to real changes in the opportunity structure? To what extent will they serve as barriers to accurate perceptions of labor market realities if they do not change?

Informal Control of Conditions That Threaten Resident Safety and Business Development. Crime and disorder interfere with residents' abilities to work and discourage business development. They raise the costs of doing business for residents and firms alike. For single mothers, dangerous neighborhoods are a reason they will not leave their children at home while they work (Oliker, 1995a).

Communities with strong internal structures are better able to control crime and disorder and make their residents feel safe (Sampson & Groves, 1989). Community organization is a function not simply of the economic status of residents but also of stable populations, an advantageous ratio of adults to children, and resident participation in organizational and civic affairs (Coulton, Korbin, Su, & Chow, 1995; Korbin & Coulton, in press).

Unfortunately, efforts to reduce crime in highly disorganized neighborhoods through external interventions such as police patrols or citizen-organized patrols have been relatively unsuccessful (Skogan, 1990). Instead, it is necessary to restore the more fundamental structures on which internal control is based.

How can informal social control be rebuilt in communities in which it has been lost? Mobilization of residents and institutions is a beginning, but research is needed on the most effective actions they can take: redesign of physical space, zoning changes, community partnerships with law enforcement. Moreover, it is important to discover how these actions can be undertaken in communities where the nature of the disorder differs. For example, do organizing strategies need to differ if disorder is caused mainly by residents or outsiders or by individuals or organized groups?

The highly organized community appears to limit disorder both by exerting normative influences on residents and by monitoring who comes into the community. Research evidence is needed about how this vital precondition for fostering business development and resident employment can be achieved in high-crime and disorganized communities.

Preparation and Support for Work

Institutions That Build Human Capital. The quality and effectiveness of schools, training programs, and postsecondary educational institutions available to community residents have a powerful effect on employment. The rapidly rising skill requirements in the labor market mean that now, more than ever, workers need considerable preparation to compete for jobs that pay a living wage. Demands for literacy and numeracy are high, and many jobs require specific technical skills. Raising the level of basic and technical skills among low-income workers is a vital strategy for moving them out of poverty (Caputo, 1995).

All too often, however, the academic performance of students whose schools are located in poor communities is too low to qualify them for well-paying jobs (Murnane, 1994). Access to compensatory and postsecondary education and job training is uneven and not always effective.

Educational reform at the community level is gaining increased attention as an approach to improving school outcomes. However, little is known about how communities themselves can create institutional change. Nevertheless, even in poor neighborhoods, parents have been able to promote the success of their individual children by becoming deeply involved in school activities and serving as advocates within the school for their children (Jarrett, 1995). Thus, the methods and consequences of increasing parent and community involvement in schools and related institutions deserve considerable study.

Schools and training programs are often embedded in larger systems. How can communities effectively strengthen these systems to make them more responsive to community needs and supportive of residents' efforts to work? Research is needed on how resources can be increased and directed more effectively as a result of community involvement.

A major concern about employment training and services is that the system is fragmented and insufficiently linked to jobs or to community residents. One model for producing more effective services is community-based, interorganizational collaboration (Bailey & Koney-McNally, in press). Although collaboration is widely advocated, research is needed on how it actually raises the quality of services and programs to improve outcomes for residents. With respect to building human capital, it needs to be demonstrated how collaboration can lead to community residents who are better prepared with the skills, attitudes, and behaviors needed for work.

Social Networks and Supports That Enable Work. Social networks and supports in the community influence employment possibilities. Working, especially for single parents, complicates the performance of household and family care responsibilities (Oliker, 1995b). The most common service needed to enable a person to work is affordable and acceptable child care (Berrick, 1991; U.S. General Accounting Office [GAO], 1994). Many welfare mothers choose to defer work until they can reduce the emotional and economic costs of child care (Edin, 1995).

Time limits and work requirements for AFDC will produce increased demand for child care, and it is unlikely that subsidized day care slots will be available for all who need them (GAO, 1994). Research is needed on how communities can increase the supply of child care resources. More thorough investigation is needed on the prevalence and quality of informal child care arrangements and how these can be strengthened and expanded. There is evidence that much of the informal child care in low-income communities is supplied by AFDC recipients (Edin, 1995). How will this system be sustained when time limits and work requirements go into effect?

Social support networks are often considered important aspects of the community that support working. Although such networks have been found helpful in coping with personal crises and everyday stresses, they have not been shown to be particularly facilitative of employment (Wellman & Wortley, 1990). One study found that families in poor neighborhoods with high unemployment reported more social support from friends than residents of more affluent neighborhoods did, suggesting that social support alone does not foster the ability to work (Boisjoly, Duncan, & Hofferth, 1995). Indeed, network relationships, especially if they are with other unemployed individuals, may actually be disruptive of work commitments (Oliker, 1995b).

Even though social networks do not promote employment per se, they do seem to foster a sense of mutual obligation and trust (Wellman & Wortley, 1990) that is thought to form the basis for social capital (Putnam, 1993). We need to learn more about the role that social capital can play in enabling poor and low-skill individuals to work and earn adequate wages. Furthermore, it needs to be determined how social networks can be enriched for individuals entering the labor market so that the relationships are conducive to work rather than undermining employment efforts.

Access to Work

Flow of Information to Job Seekers and Employers. The world of work is dynamic, and there is considerable instability for low-wage workers and people who cycle on and off welfare. Making employment transitions requires information about job openings and opportunities and about how these jobs can be obtained. Informal networks are by far the most important sources of information about jobs, and employers rely on these networks to find employees, especially those in the lower-skill categories (Holzer, 1987; Sullivan, 1989). There is evidence that employers, especially those in the suburbs, rely on statistical and geographic stereotyping (Kirschenman & Neckerman, 1991). For example, African American men from inner-city neighborhoods are not recruited by these employers because they are assumed to have bad attitudes or work habits. So an additional challenge for communities is to investigate how to channel information to employers that will diminish these stereotypes.

More research is needed on how informal networks transmit information and how to improve the accuracy and usefulness of this information. Effective methods of linking people who have been out of the labor force to job information networks should be the focus of research as well. Studies also should address how networks can be widened to reach beyond the confines of the central city into the suburban areas of job growth.

In addition to providing information to job seekers, it is important to understand how employers get information about potential entry-level employees.

Can community agencies acting as intermediaries help reduce stereotyping by pre-screening applicants? Can employers be helped to use fairer methods of identifying employees with the attitudinal qualities they want? These possibilities need to be evaluated.

It is also important to investigate the distrust of employers that seems prevalent among some inner-city residents of color (Kirschenman & Neckerman, 1991). To what degree does information flow contribute to this distrust, and what role does it play in the job-seeking process? An employee who thinks the worst of a potential employer's motivations responds to events in a negative way that may stand in the way of advancement. Are there ways that the community can reduce distrust and the experiences that foster it on both sides?

Regional Infrastructure for Connecting People to Jobs. Poor people rely on public transportation to a greater degree than other workers. Yet public transportation is not well suited to reaching jobs in suburban locations (Hughes, 1991, 1995). One study found that only 6 percent of a region's entry-level jobs could be reached within 45 minutes on the bus from the low-income areas of the central city (Bania & Leete, 1995).

There are few studies of community efforts to improve transportation to jobs in the region (Ihlanfeldt, 1994), and many significant research questions remain unanswered. Are there examples of communities working with local transportation authorities to expand routes to the suburbs? If so, has employment increased as a result? What promising models of employer-supplied transportation can be confirmed by research? Can community-sponsored car-pooling programs reduce barriers to regional employment? Studies of model programs and small-scale experiments are needed to determine the costs and feasibility of various arrangements and their results in terms of employment in low-income communities.

Job Creation and Business Investment. The possibility of working, especially for new or marginal labor force participants, is affected by the demand for workers. The decline in the numbers of jobs in central-city neighborhoods (Kasarda, 1989) has led to various strategies to attract new businesses or to expand the size of existing businesses (Hughes, 1995). Included among these strategies are tax incentives and business supports for empowerment zones and enterprise communities, the work of community development corporations in business and retail development, and various industrial retention and business support programs. Although many studies have examined how these programs promote business investment (Ladd, 1994), relatively little is known about how they improve employment opportunities for poor people (Vidal, 1995).

Studies are needed to determine which strategies have the greatest benefits for neighborhood residents, both directly through providing employment and indirectly through changing neighborhood conditions. It is also important to examine the role that the social structures in neighborhoods play in determining whether these business promotion and investment strategies are successful (Lynn, 1994).

What kinds of organizations and networks have been effectively involved in these strategies, and does their involvement make a difference in the degree to which local residents become employed? How important is resident involvement in the governance process to the ultimate success of the investment strategy?

In studying these strategies it is particularly important that researchers be alert to unintended consequences and to barriers to an incentive or benefit being used. For example, studies of a targeted jobs tax credit that gave incentives to companies to hire disadvantaged workers found that the program was extremely underused because of the stigma associated with subsidized workers (Burtless, 1985). Research needs to be designed so that negative as well as positive effects can be understood.

Ongoing Support for Working Families

Mechanisms That Provide a Safety Net for Families. Devolution implies transferring responsibility downward; increasingly, the safety net for families will be centered in communities. Even communities with the features that promote economic opportunity will need to provide security for residents' basic needs. Protecting the vulnerable population is a function of community that contributes to the residents' sense of security that allows them to seek employment and educational opportunities.

Most communities have some degree of infrastructure for hunger and shelter programs, free medical clinics, emergency aid programs, and the like, and these will play an important role as entitlement programs are restricted. Studies of what has happened to general assistance recipients after programs were restricted or eliminated have found that many former recipients survive by relying on family, friends, and community programs (Coulton, Crowell, & Verma, 1993; Danziger & Danziger, 1995). Nevertheless, the burden on communities is going to grow. Research is needed on whether and how communities increase their capacity to provide a safety net for families. Furthermore, it will be important to document the degree to which basic human needs go unmet and families and children are harmed. This type of extensive documentation can support advocacy for remedies.

Subsidized Employment. Public and community services jobs need to be available as employment of last resort to individuals who are unable to find work. Unfortunately, the controversy that has surrounded past public employment programs such as the Comprehensive Employment and Training Act of 1973 (P.L. 93-203) means that communities have little recent experience in this area (Maynard, 1995). Although there have been some promising experiments with human services employment (Bell & Orr, 1994; Coulton, Frierson, & Griffey, 1996), mounting public service employment on a large scale will require a significant increase in load capacity. Research will be needed to determine how communities can expand such employment and to identify features of public service employment that lead to skills enhancement and transition into market employment.

Mechanisms That Allow for the Accumulation of Assets. The accumulation of assets has been found to lead to attitudes and choices that promote employment. Confidence about the future and the tendency to make specific plans about work result from having assets. Assets promote the creation of social capital through connectedness with the community and its institutions and the creation of human capital through investment in education (Yadama & Sherraden, 1996).

Wealth or assets are distributed more unequally than income (Oliver, 1995). Poor people seldom have the property, savings, or investments that foster the behaviors associated with career advancement, in part because of the dearth of asset-generating mechanisms in many low-income communities (Sherraden, 1991).

Research is needed on the success of existing efforts to create or expand access to capital in low-income neighborhoods. How have community development banks, credit unions, or housing investment programs helped poor families accumulate assets? Has the accumulation of assets helped families achieve more satisfying and remunerative employment?

Communities also play a role in maintaining and enhancing the value of assets held by residents (Finn, Zorita, & Coulton, 1994). A house, for example, is the major asset of most families. The appreciation of this asset is dependent on a stable or improving neighborhood. Research is needed on how residents of low-income communities protect and enhance the value of their investments.

CONCLUSION

Welfare time limits and strong work requirements will leave large numbers of families in extremely precarious economic circumstances unless many of the barriers to employment for men and women currently in the low-skill labor force and moving on and off welfare are reduced. This problem cannot be approached piecemeal or with an individual focus; it requires a comprehensive approach to rebuilding the opportunities and supports for work in low-income communities.

The process of community change needs to get foremost attention by social work researchers and practitioners as they respond to devolution. Currently, too little attention is being paid to the community context in welfare reform discussions and research. Some advocates of devolution believe that communities hold the promise of better welfare solutions, but they have not looked realistically at the challenges facing low-income communities. The discussions and analyses have not been clear about the efforts, resources, and mechanisms that must be in place to respond effectively to these challenges. Communities' capacities to support opportunity will need to be raised, but knowledge about effective ways to do that needs to be built as well.

Social workers must take the lead in changing the focus of welfare-related research from individual capacity to community capacity. This refocusing can be accomplished by including measures of the local community employment capabilities in all studies related to welfare reform. Welfare demonstration projects should be targeted not only at changing individual behavior but also at enhancing communities' abilities to provide access to and support for work. The research must convincingly demonstrate that individual success is, in part, contingent on community assets.

Social workers must advocate at the state and federal level to broaden the scope of welfare-related research. Randomized experiments have been the dominant paradigm in recent decades, but this methodology often precludes the study of community change. With the individual as the unit of randomization, the many aspects of communities that are important for work cannot be taken into account. Policymakers and decision makers need to be convinced that other research methods are needed to deepen the understanding of these important contextual factors.

There are many important new roles for social workers in community-building initiatives. These initiatives incorporate traditional methods of community organizing and development but include community-based services to families and children as well. They take a comprehensive approach to the whole community and work on restoring the multiple forces that provide opportunity.

The premises outlined in this article have several limitations. First, urban communities have been the reference point for most of the discussion. The barriers to work in rural communities are probably different in type and scope. Second, there are many policy issues that also call for investigation, because policy support for community building is essential if it is to be successful on a large scale and if work is to be a viable alternative to welfare. Although these policy research questions are beyond the scope of this article, it is important for researchers concerned with welfare policy to appreciate its interconnection with urban, neighborhood, and community policy.

Finally, the research agenda formulated in this article will be in vain if it is not formulated in action terms. Although some basic community processes need to be better understood first, the primary intent must be community change. Much of this change has to occur by building the capacity of communities to support opportunity. All research, therefore, must be framed to answer the questions that communities have about how best to achieve their goals. Ultimately, the findings must support and guide communities in their efforts to respond to devolution by supporting and increasing opportunity.

REFERENCES

Bailey, D., & Koney, K. M. (in press). Interorganizational community-based collaboratives: A strategic response to shape the social work agenda. *Social Work.*

Bane, M. J., & Ellwood, D. T. (1994). *Welfare realities: From rhetoric to reform.* Cambridge, MA: Harvard University Press.

Bania, N., & Leete, L. (1995). *The impact of welfare reform on local labor markets.* Cleveland: Case Western Reserve University, Mandel School of Applied Social Sciences, Center on Urban Poverty and Social Change.

Bell, S., & Orr, L. (1994). Is subsidized employment cost effective for welfare recipients? Experimental evidence from seven state demonstrations. *Journal of Human Resources, 29,* 42–61.

Berrick, J. D. (1991). Welfare and child care: The intricacies of competing social values. *Social Work, 36,* 345–351.

Blackburn, M. L., Bloom, D. E., & Freeman, R. B. (1990). The declining economic position of less-skilled American men. In G. Burtless (Ed.), *A future of lousy jobs: The changing structure of U.S. wages* (pp. 31–76). Washington, DC: Brookings Institution.

Blank, R. M. (1994). The employment strategy: Public policies to increase work and earnings. In S. H. Danziger, G. D. Sandefur, & D. H. Weinberg (Eds.), *Confronting poverty: Prescriptions for change* (pp. 168–204). New York: Russell Sage Foundation.

Boisjoly, J., Duncan, G. J., & Hofferth, S. (1995). Access to social capital. *Journal of Family Issues, 16,* 609–631.

Brooks-Gunn, J., Duncan, G. J., Klebanov, P. K., & Sealand, N. (1993). Do neighborhoods influence child and adolescent development? *American Journal of Sociology, 99,* 353–395.

Burtless, G. (1985). Are targeted wage subsidies harmful? Evidence from a wage voucher experiment. *Industrial and Labor Relations Review, 39*(1), 105–114.

Burton, L. M., Obeidallah, D. A., & Allison, K. (in press). Ethnographic insights on social context and adolescent development among inner-city African-American teens. In R. Jessor, A. Colby, & R. Shweder (Eds.), *Essays on ethnography and human development.* Chicago: University of Chicago Press.

Caputo, R. K. (1995). Gender and race: Employment opportunity and the American economy, 1969–1991. *Families in Society, 76,* 239–247.

Carlson, V. L., & Theodore, N. C. (1995). *Are there enough jobs? Welfare reform and labor market reality.* Unpublished manuscript, University of Illinois at Chicago, Center for Urban Economic Development.

Center for Law and Public Policy. (1996). *Updated waiver information* (Working draft). Washington, DC: Author.

Comprehensive Employment and Training Act of 1973, P.L. 93-203, 87 Stat. 839.

Coulton, C. J., Crowell, L., & Verma, N. (1993). How time-limited eligibility affects general assistance clients. *Public Welfare, 51*(3), 29–38.

Coulton, C. J., Frierson, T., & Griffey, C. (1996). *Cuyahoga County's WPA program: Participants' satisfaction, employment, and use of public assistance: Summary report.* Cleveland: Case Western Reserve University, Mandel School of Applied Social Sciences, Center on Urban Poverty and Social Change.

Coulton, C. J., Korbin, J. E., Su, M., & Chow, J. (1995). Community-level factors and child maltreatment rates. *Child Development, 66,* 1262–1276.

Crane, J. (1991). The epidemic theory of ghettos and neighborhood effects on dropping out and teenage childbearing. *American Journal of Sociology, 96,* 1226–1259.

Danziger, S. H., & Weinberg, D. H. (1994). The historical record: Trends in family income, inequality, and poverty. In S. H. Danziger, G. D. Sandefur, & D. H. Weinberg (Eds.), *Confronting poverty: Prescriptions for change* (pp. 18–50). New York: Russell Sage Foundation.

Danziger, S. K., & Danziger, S. (1995). Will welfare recipients find work when welfare ends? *Welfare Reform Briefs, 12,* 1–4.

Duncan, G. J. (1993). *Families and neighbors as sources of disadvantage in the schooling decisions of white and black adolescents.* Ann Arbor: University of Michigan, Institute for Social Research.

Edin, K. J. (1995). The myths of dependence and self-sufficiency: Women, welfare, and low-wage work. *Focus, 17*(2), 1–9.

Ellwood, D. T. (1986). The spacial mismatch hypothesis: Are teenage jobs missing in the ghetto? In R. Freeman & H. Holzer (Eds.), *The black youth unemployment problem* (pp. 147–185). Chicago: University of Chicago Press.

Finn, C., Zorita, P., & Coulton, C. (1994). Assets and financial management among poor households in extreme poverty neighborhoods. *Journal of Sociology and Social Welfare, 21,* 75–94.

Friedlander, D., & Burtless, G. (1995). *Five years after: The long-term effects of welfare-to-work programs.* New York: Russell Sage Foundation.

Furstenberg, F. (1996, January). *The influence of neighborhoods on children's development: A theoretical perspective and a research agenda.* Paper presented at a meeting on Youth Development and Neighborhood Influences: Challenges and Opportunities, sponsored by the National Research Council and Institute of Medicine, Washington, DC.

Galster, G. C., & Mincey, R. B. (1993). Understanding the changing fortunes of metropolitan neighborhoods: 1980 to 1990. *Housing Policy Debate, 4,* 303–348.

Gueron, J. M., & Pauly, E. (1991). *From welfare to work.* New York: Russell Sage Foundation.

Harris, K. M. (1993). Work and welfare among single mothers in poverty. *American Journal of Sociology, 99,* 317–352.

Harris, K. M. (1996). Life after welfare: Women, work and repeat dependency. *American Sociological Review, 61,* 407–426.

Holzer, H. J. (1987). Informal job search and black youth unemployment. *American Economic Review, 77,* 446–452.

Holzer, H. J. (1991). The spacial mismatch hypothesis: What has the evidence shown? *Urban Studies, 28,* 105–122.

Hughes, M. A. (1991). Employment decentralization and accessibility: A strategy for stimulating regional mobility. *Journal of the American Planning Association, 57,* 288–298.

Hughes, M. A. (1995). A mobility strategy for improving opportunity. *Housing Policy Debate, 6,* 271–297.

Ihlanfeldt, K. (1994). The spatial mismatch between jobs and residential locations within urban areas. *Cityscape: A Journal of Policy Development and Research, 1,* 219–244.

Ihlanfeldt, K., & Sjoquist, D. (1989). The impact of decentralization on the economic welfare of central city blacks. *Journal of Urban Economics, 16,* 110–130.

Ihlanfeldt, K., & Sjoquist, D. (1990). Job accessibility and differences in youth employment rates. *American Economic Review, 80,* 267–276.

Jarrett, R. L. (1995). Growing up poor: The family experiences of socially mobile youth in low-income African American neighborhoods. *Journal of Adolescent Research, 10*(1), 111–135.

Kasarda, J. D. (1989). Urban industrial transition and the underclass. *Annals of the American Academy of Political and Social Science, 510,* 26–47.

Kasarda, J. D. (1993). Inner-city concentrated poverty and neighborhood distress: 1970 to 1990. *Housing Policy Debate, 4,* 253–302.

Kirschenman, J., & Neckerman, K. M. (1991). "We'd love to hire them, but . . .": The meaning of race for employers. In C. Jencks & P. E. Peterson (Eds.), *The urban underclass* (pp. 203–233). Washington, DC: Brookings Institution.

Korbin, J., & Coulton, C. (in press). Neighbors, neighborhood, and child maltreatment. *Journal of Social Issues.*

Ladd, H. F. (1994). Spatially targeted economic development strategies: Do they work? *Cityscape: A Journal of Policy Development and Research, 1,* 193–218.

Lynn, L. E. (1994). Social structures as economic growth tools. *Cityscape: A Journal of Policy Development and Research, 1,* 245–265.

Maynard, R. A. (1995). Subsidized employment and non-labor market alternatives for welfare recipients. In D. S. Nightingale & R. H. Haveman (Eds.), *The work alternative: Welfare reform and the realities of the job market* (pp. 109–136). Washington, DC: Urban Institute Press.

Mishel, L., & Schmitt, J. (1995). *Cutting wages by cutting welfare* (Briefing paper). Washington, DC: Economic Policy Institute.

Murnane, R. J. (1994). Education and the well-being of the next generation. In S. Danziger, G. D. Sandefur, & D. H. Weinberg (Eds.), *Confronting poverty: Prescriptions for change* (pp. 289–307). New York: Russell Sage Foundation.

Murphy, K. M., & Welch, F. (1993). Industrial change and the rising importance of skill. In S. Danziger & P. Gottschalk (Eds.), *Uneven tides: Rising inequality in America* (pp. 101–132). New York: Russell Sage Foundation.

Oliker, S. J. (1995a). The proximate contexts of workfare and work: A framework for studying poor women's economic choices. *Sociological Quarterly, 36,* 251–272.

Oliker, S. J. (1995b). Work commitment and constraint among mothers on workfare. *Journal of Contemporary Ethnography, 24,* 165–194.

Oliver, M. L. (1995). *Black wealth/white wealth: A new perspective on racial inequality.* New York: Routledge.

Putnam, R. D. (1993). The prosperous community: Social capital and public life. *American Prospect, 13,* 35–42.

Sampson, R. J., & Groves, W. B. (1989). Community structure and crime: Testing social-disorganization theory. *American Journal of Sociology, 94,* 775–802.

Sherraden, M. (1991). *Assets and the poor: A new American welfare policy.* Armonk, NY: M. E. Sharpe.

Skogan, W. G. (1990). *Disorder and decline: Crime and the spiral of decay in American neighborhoods.* Berkeley: University of California Press.

Sullivan, M. L. (1989). *Getting paid: Youth crime and work in the inner city.* Ithaca, NY: Cornell University Press.

U.S. Bureau of the Census. (1993). *Poverty in the United States: 1992.* Washington, DC: U.S. Government Printing Office.

U.S. General Accounting Office. (1994). *Child care: Child care subsidies increase likelihood that low-income mothers will work* (No. B-256750). Washington, DC: Author, Health, Education, and Human Services Division.

Vidal, A. C. (1995). Reintegrating disadvantaged communities into the fabric of urban life: The role of community development. *Housing Policy Debate, 6,* 169–230.

Wellman, B., & Wortley, S. (1990). Different strokes from different folks: Community ties and social support. *American Journal of Sociology, 96,* 558–588.

Wilson, W. J. (1987). *The truly disadvantaged: The inner city, the underclass, and public policy.* Chicago: University of Chicago Press.

Wilson, W. J. (1991). Public policy research and the truly disadvantaged. In C. Jencks & P. E. Peterson (Eds.), *The urban underclass* (pp. 460–481). Washington, DC: Brookings Institution.

Yadama, G. N., & Sherraden, M. (1996). Effects of assets on attitudes and behaviors: Advance test of a social policy proposal. *Social Work Research, 20,* 3–11.

This chapter was originally published in the September 1996 issue of Social Work, *vol. 41, pp. 509–519.*

11 State Welfare Reform for Employable General Assistance Recipients: The Facts behind the Assumptions

Anthony P. Halter

More and more states are choosing to eliminate, reduce, or time limit their general assistance (GA) programs for their designated employ able populations. Many governors and legislators believe that to motivate this population to find work, they must either eliminate or place time limits on general assistance. Additional assumptions are that a significant portion of this population is employable and that jobs exist if unemployed people only make the effort to search them out.

In 1982 Pennsylvania was one of the first states to lower general assistance costs by limiting the benefit period for its employable population to 90 days in any 12-month period. In 1991 and 1992, 22 states reduced or eliminated their GA programs (Gold, Lav, Lazere, & Greenstein, 1992). These legislative changes included discontinuing cash assistance for employable people, limiting the benefit period, or reducing the level of benefits. These reforms were the impetus for numerous studies on the effects of the legislation on former GA recipients by government and academic institutions in Pennsylvania, Michigan, and Ohio. This article discusses the results of these studies in terms of the diversity of the GA population, availability of employment, barriers to employment, and effects of GA reductions on human services agencies.

DIVERSITY OF THE GA POPULATION

The public impression of GA recipients as men in their twenties who have trouble keeping a job ignores about 75 percent of the population (Kossoudji, Danzinger, & Lovell, 1993). This fact is verified by other studies (Coulton, Verma, Rowland, & Crowell, 1992; Stagner & Richman, 1986) that found that GA recipients came from a wide variety of backgrounds. In these studies, 30 percent had previously worked in a full-time job before applying for general assistance, and 16 percent had received either unemployment compensation, Aid to Families with Dependent Children, or disability benefits.

AVAILABILITY OF EMPLOYMENT

The belief that a significant number of individuals who lose general assistance benefits will find employment is not borne out by the facts. Studies conducted in Pennsylvania (Commonwealth of Pennsylvania, 1984), Michigan (Hansen,

1992), and Ohio (Coulton, Crowell, & Verma, 1992) indicated that over 80 percent of the GA population did not find work.

Motivation

In Michigan welfare dependency stemmed not from lack of motivation but from inability to find employment that would provide a decent living (Kossoudji et al., 1993). Another study (Coulton, Verma, et al., 1992) indicated that most GA recipients wanted to work. The studies demonstrated that lack of motivation and desire to work were not the problem (Howe & Waller, 1993). Rather, other factors influenced whether GA recipients were able to find jobs.

Unemployment Rates

Increases in the GA rolls correlated positively with increases in unemployment rates (Richmond, Nazar, & Douglass, 1983). Some of those on general assistance had previously collected unemployment insurance. For some, GA became the unemployment insurance of last resort. One study of the GA population in Chicago (Stagner & Richman, 1986) indicated that 16 percent had collected unemployment insurance before applying for general assistance. The average time between conclusion of the last full-time job and the initial GA interview was 19 months. Most former recipients were less employable 15 months after termination of assistance than they were immediately after termination of employment (McDonald et al., 1993).

Insufficient Earnings

The earnings reported by those who found work were not enough to allow them to become self-sufficient. In Ohio average wages were between $5.00 (Coulton, Crowell, et al., 1992) and $5.50 per hour (Howe & Waller, 1993), and in Michigan the average hourly wage was $4.40 (McDonald et al., 1993). One early study (Commonwealth of Pennsylvania, 1987) showed that minimum-wage jobs were not sufficient to support individuals and that jobs with limited benefits and opportunities for wage or position advancement would not provide long-term supports. This fact was reinforced by another study (Halter, 1989) that showed that, of those removed from GA who did find work, 78.5 percent had income low enough to remain eligible for food stamps or Medicaid.

Most former GA recipients held minimum-wage jobs in the service and retail sectors (Coulton, Crowell, et al., 1992). However, Ohio Bureau of Employment Security projections estimated that only 31 percent of job growth would be in the low-skill range (Coulton, Crowell, et al., 1992). In addition, in Ohio, "if the GA terminees were the only new entrants to the low-skill labor force in this region, it would take 7.4 years for all the employable GA recipients to be absorbed at the projected rate of expected growth" (Coulton, Crowell, et al., 1992, p. 17).

Over half of Michigan's GA recipients resided in three manufacturing communities with high unemployment (McDonald et al., 1993). Studies conducted in Ohio and Michigan indicated that the heaviest concentration of individuals on general assistance was in urban areas (Coulton, Crowell, et al., 1992; Kossoudji et al., 1993), which had not generated the kinds of jobs for which recipients were qualified (Kossoudji et al., 1993).

BARRIERS TO EMPLOYMENT

Anderson and Risko (1989) stated that many members of the GA population had limited work skills. McDonald and colleagues (1993) pointed out that they were likely to have multiple barriers to employment, including health problems, lack of transportation, and lack of education, as well as responsibility for care of disabled family members, active enrollment in substance abuse treatment programs, and serious mental illness. One study (Halter, 1992) of a small group of individuals discontinued from general assistance who did not find work and became homeless showed that the longer the individuals remained homeless, the less employable they became because of the debilitating effects of living on the street.

Health Problems

Many GA recipients suffered from health problems that made it extremely difficult for them to find work but did not entitle them to disability benefits. A substantial minority (21 percent) had some chronic physical or mental health problem (Kossoudji et al., 1993). The Commonwealth of Pennsylvania (1984) reported that 25.8 percent of the respondents were in poorer health after losing GA benefits. In Michigan nearly two of three GA recipients reported health problems, with 40 percent having seen a doctor within the past month, 42 percent having visited an emergency room, and 62 percent having taken medication (Hansen, 1992).

In Ohio, one-third of GA recipients had been in an emergency room during the preceding six months, one-sixth had been admitted to a hospital, and two-thirds over age 45 had been taking prescribed medication for chronic health problems (Howe & Waller, 1993). Another Ohio study (Coulton, Crowell, et al., 1992) pointed out that nearly 30 percent of GA recipients had one or more chronic conditions requiring medical supervision and prescription medications, and one of four required ongoing care for chronic illness.

In Ohio the level of chronic illness and medical need in the GA population was much higher than the level of confirmed disability, and the percentage of recipients reporting that they had to forgo medical treatment rose 13 percent after the April 1992 terminations (Coulton, Crowell, et al., 1992). Also, 58 percent were most concerned about the lack of medical care from general assistance, with one in five experiencing a significant health problem (Summit County Department of Human Services, 1992).

A Chicago study of GA recipients indicated that health problems decreased employability; absence of a disability or health problem was one factor associated with returning to work (Stagner & Richman, 1986). In a qualitative study of Pennsylvania's GA reductions (Halter, 1992), respondents reported more types of health problems, and the longer they remained without financial support, the less employable they became because of the hardships they experienced. For the most part, these hardships were specifically related to health problems.

Lack of Transportation

The limited transportation services available to employable poor people hampers their employment efforts. Inadequate public transportation and lack of a driver's license or an automobile hindered many respondents' opportunities to find and keep jobs. In Michigan many employment opportunities were in suburban areas, where public transportation was nonexistent. In Pennsylvania, the mass transit services were very limited in many counties (Richmond et al., 1983). In Michigan employment rates for people on general assistance were highest for those who had a driver's license or a car, twice the rate of those who had neither (Hansen, 1992).

In Ohio inadequate transportation was one of the main barriers to a recipient's maintaining employment, with 23 percent of the respondents lacking transportation to the job (Summit County Department of Human Services, 1992). Howe and Waller (1993) found that in Cincinnati transportation was an impediment for about 30 percent of the GA population studied.

Lack of Education

The majority of studies indicated that about 45 percent to 50 percent of the GA population lacked a high school diploma. In Michigan Kossoudji and colleagues (1993) found that half were not high school graduates. In Michigan those living in urban areas were less likely to have diplomas than those living elsewhere (McDonald et al., 1993).

In Ohio fewer than half of GA recipients had a high school diploma or general equivalency diploma (GED) (Howe & Waller, 1993); the Summit County Department of Human Services (1992) indicated that only 46 percent of the GA recipients had completed the requirements for a high school diploma or GED. In Pennsylvania 48 percent had not completed high school (Commonwealth of Pennsylvania, 1987). In Chicago possessing a high school diploma or GED was a factor that positively influenced returning to work (Stagner & Richman, 1986), and in Michigan a high school diploma was mandatory for even the lowest skilled jobs (Kossoudji et al., 1993).

Illiteracy was another barrier to employment. In Ohio 68 percent of those completing a job application were unable to read the instructions, 57 percent could not write out all the answers, and 77 percent did not understand how to answer the questions (Summit County Department of Human Services, 1992).

Homelessness

In Michigan, local communities and private emergency services were not able to meet the increased need for services, and the elimination of general assistance appears to have created shelter problems for 29,000 former recipients in Wayne County and 4,000 in Geneseo County (McDonald et al., 1993). The number of GA recipients eliminated in Michigan increased the levels of homelessness: 20,000 former GA recipients were evicted following termination of the GA program (Hansen, 1992). The percentage of homeless former GA recipients increased from 2 percent to 25 percent within six months after the GA program ended (Hansen, 1992).

One study (Halter, 1992) of the impact of time-limiting general assistance in Pennsylvania reported that some recipients who were discontinued possessed significant barriers to employment and consequently became homeless. The longer these individuals were without some means of financial support, the less employable they became as a result of the adversities experienced because of their homelessness. With few finding jobs, many had become additional burdens on already impoverished families and friends (Coulton, Crowell, et al., 1992; Halter, 1992).

EFFECTS OF GENERAL ASSISTANCE CUTS ON HUMAN SERVICES AGENCIES

Although reducing or eliminating general assistance may initially produce a savings for state budgets, the ultimate result may be more spending for increased human services. The number of those served by other nonprofit and private human services agencies increased by 19 percent, and many agencies reported serving more former GA recipients, newly unemployed workers, and working poor people.

Ninety percent of emergency services providers in Michigan expected the needs of their communities to increase during the next six months (Hansen, 1992). Notable expansions in services occurred in medical and mental health services, and agencies' waiting lists increased.

In Pennsylvania, utility shutoffs and evictions went from 9.4 percent for GA recipients before discontinuance to 18.4 percent after (Commonwealth of Pennsylvania, 1984). When the respondents lost assistance, the percentage of GA recipients receiving loans from family, friends, charity, and social organizations increased from 24.2 to 36.6 percent (Commonwealth of Pennsylvania, 1984). In addition, whereas 9.7 percent lived with relatives or friends while they received cash assistance, 45.0 percent did so after benefits ceased. The percentage of former GA recipients who received financial help from friends, relatives, and social or charitable organizations increased from 11.4 percent to 17.0 percent after cash assistance stopped. Also, the proportion of recipients living with friends or relatives and making contributions toward housing costs declined from 83.2 percent to 37.1 percent (Commonwealth of Pennsylvania, 1984). Although it is too early to tell whether the legislative changes will have a negative effect on human services agencies, early indications are that most of the agencies in Michigan have experienced an increase in potential clients. Additional research is needed to assess the economic effect of these reductions on human services agencies.

RECOMMENDATIONS

The recipients of general assistance are a diverse population. Consideration of the complexity of this population should be an integral part of any policy-planning strategy. States may need to develop a broader array of services to address these diverse needs, such as assistance in the completion of job and disability applications and advocacy for housing (Kossoudji et al., 1993).

Some GA recipients have exhausted their unemployment compensation benefits before applying for assistance (Stagner & Richman, 1986). Strategies for legislators and policy advocates should include providing emergency cash benefits in geographical areas with high unemployment or implementing work programs that pay adequate salaries. New methods to decrease unemployment in these areas should be pursued, such as tax incentives for businesses that locate in such areas.

One of the primary problems in finding employment is that many jobs are in areas that are inaccessible to poor people. Improving the opportunities for mass transit would also alleviate some of the problems experienced by this population.

Because almost 50 percent of the GA recipients lacked a high school diploma, emphasis should be placed on developing programs that provide a combination of skills training in existing jobs and educational development toward high school equivalency. Employability is dramatically enhanced by a high school diploma (Stagner & Richman, 1986).

States should also improve their definitions of employability. A more effective means of assessing the mental and physical health of GA recipients should be developed. Factors such as job availability, education, and transportation accessibility also should be included in an employability assessment.

CONCLUSION

The present policies of eliminating, reducing, or time-limiting general assistance are based on assumptions that are not borne out by the literature. General assistance was developed for members of society who fall through the "safety net." However, many of them are not truly employable. The belief that this population is unmotivated ignores the majority of GA recipients who have significant problems that limit their ability to find work. Legislators should consider the realities and likely long-term effects of welfare reform legislation before proposing changes that may be economically damaging to the state as well as to the individuals who are directly affected.

REFERENCES

Anderson, S., & Risko, R. (1989). *Review of general assistance cases with persons aged 18—5* (Memorandum to Michigan House Subcommittee on Social Services Members). Lansing: Michigan House Fiscal Agency.

Commonwealth of Pennsylvania. (1984). *Joint study of Act 75: The impact of welfare reform.* Harrisburg, PA: Act 75 Interagency Evaluation Subcommittee, Department of Labor and Industry, Department of Public Welfare, Department of Revenue and Community Affairs, the Governor's Office of Policy Development, and the Governor's Office of the Budget.

Commonwealth of Pennsylvania, Department of Public Welfare. (1987). [Working paper on Act 75-1982 effects]. Harrisburg: Author.

Coulton, C., Crowell, L., & Verma, N. (1992). *General assistance program reductions in Cuyahoga County: Summary report.* Cleveland: Case Western Reserve University, Mandel School of Applied Social Sciences, Center for Urban Poverty and Social Change.

Coulton, C., Verma, N., Rowland, D., & Crowell, L. (1992). *Who are the general assistance recipients in Cuyahoga County?* Cleveland: Case Western Reserve University, Mandel School of Applied Social Sciences, Center for Urban Poverty and Social Change.

Gold, S., Lav, I., Lazere, E., & Greenstein, R. (1992). *The states and the poor: Budget decisions hurt low income people in 1992.* Washington, DC: Center on Budget and Policy Priorities.

Halter, A. (1989). Welfare reform: One state's alternative. *Journal of Sociology and Social Welfare, 16*, 151–161.

Halter, A. (1992). Homeless in Philadelphia: A qualitative study of the impact of state welfare reform on individuals. *Journal of Sociology and Social Welfare, 19*, 7–20.

Hansen, K. (1992). *The impact of elimination of the general assistance program in Michigan: Interim report.* Lansing: Michigan League for Human Services.

Howe, S., & Waller, M. (1993). *General assistance in Hamilton County: Executive summary.* Cincinnati: University of Cincinnati, Institute of Policy Research.

Kossoudji, S., Danziger, S., & Lovell, R. (1993). *Michigan's general assistance population: An interim report of the General Assistance Termination Project.* Ann Arbor: University of Michigan, School of Social Work.

McDonald B., Parks, S., Conyers, G., Mutchler, W., Killips, P., Kulcharek, T., & Hansen, K. (1993). *The impact on individuals and communities of the reductions in social services in Michigan in 1991–1992.* Lansing: Michigan League for Human Services.

Richmond, F., Nazar, K., & Douglass, K. (1983). *Pennsylvania trends in the average number of persons dependent on public assistance.* Harrisburg: Pennsylvania Department of Public Welfare.

Stagner, M., & Richman, H. (1986). Reexamining the role of general assistance. *Public Welfare, 44*(2), 26–32.

Summit County Department of Human Services. (1992). *Summit County general assistance survey.* Akron, OH: Author.

This chapter was originally published in the January 1996 issue of Social Work, *vol. 41, pp. 106–110.*

12 Confronting Welfare Stereotypes: Characteristics of General Assistance Recipients and Postassistance Employment

Julia R. Henly and Sandra K. Danziger

Long before the 1996 welfare reform debates, public assistance programs had been the target of budget reductions. Since 1970 benefits under Aid to Families with Dependent Children (AFDC) have decreased by an average of 40 percent nationwide (Lav, Lazere, Greenstein, & Gold, 1993). Likewise, general assistance (GA) programs run by county or state governments have faced severe reductions as well. GA and AFDC programs have been particularly hard hit in the 1990s. For example, in 1991 nine states instituted AFDC grant reductions at a level unparalleled since those imposed by the Reagan administration a decade earlier (Berrick, 1995). Similarly, GA benefit levels were reduced in 14 states in 1991 and eight states in 1992 (Lav et al., 1993), and time limits on GA enrollment have been imposed (for example, in Illinois and some counties in California) (Halter, 1996). In some cases (for example, in Michigan and Ohio), GA has been eliminated altogether (Halter, 1996; Kossoudji, Danziger, & Lovell, 1993).

Why are welfare programs serving poor people so often targeted for benefit reductions and, more recently, even termination? Although several factors enter into the policy process, the absence of a strong political power base in support of welfare programs (Heclo, 1994); self-interest on the side of voters (Kluegel & Smith, 1986); and generally negative public views of poor people, of welfare programs, and of welfare recipients (Shapiro, Patterson, Russell, & Young, 1987; Smith, 1987) all contribute to the precarious status of public assistance programs. This article critically examines the stereotypes of welfare recipients that support a negative portrayal of welfare and compares that stereotype with empirical data on recipients of general assistance in Michigan, who lost their benefits when the program was terminated in 1991.

Some findings reported in this article were also reported in earlier project reports of the General Assistance Termination Study. The authors acknowledge the Ford Foundation and the Michigan Department of Social Services for their support during earlier stages of the study. We also thank Jim Kunz and Todd Franke for consultation and assistance with this article and the anonymous reviewers for their valuable comments.

STEREOTYPES OF WELFARE RECIPIENTS

According to the commonly held stereotype, poor people are poor because of individual character faults. In particular, welfare recipients are presumed to be lazy, able yet unwilling to work, and lacking appropriate family values (Goodwin, 1983; Handler & Hasenfeld, 1991; Katz, 1989). The dominant American values of individualism and self-sufficiency (Lipset, 1967; Williams, 1979) contribute to the unpopularity of welfare programs and support the popular opinion that welfare recipients are responsible for their impoverished condition and undeserving of assistance (Feagin, 1975; Hasenfeld & Rafferty, 1989; Kluegel & Smith, 1986; MacDonald, 1972).

In addition to this emphasis on the cultural and individual value deficits of impoverished individuals, the political debate about welfare centers on the role that welfare programs play in contributing to and reinforcing the presumed negative moral and behavioral patterns of poor people (Mead, 1986; Murray, 1984). In particular, the availability of welfare, it has been argued, serves as a disincentive to workforce participation and the formation of traditional households (see Bane & Ellwood, 1994, for a review of the disincentive perspective). Thus, the public discourse about the "welfare problem" suggests both that individuals receiving welfare are "undeserving" and that welfare programs reinforce the negative behavioral tendencies of welfare recipients by the choices they provide.

Such concerns are certainly not new. In fact, American responses to poor people throughout U.S. history have reflected this reluctance to provide aid out of concern that state-sponsored assistance would encourage dependency and negatively affect the core American values of individualism, hard work, and family responsibility (Katz, 1989; Trattner, 1994). The "principle of less eligibility," whereby relief was never to be a more attractive alternative than regular work, resulted in 19th-century attempts to abolish outdoor relief (in particular, cash assistance to poor people) (Katz, 1989; Trattner, 1994). Similarly, the Charity Organization Societies of the progressive era preferred "character building" to the provision of financial assistance in their efforts to improve the circumstances of poor urban residents at the turn of the century (Iglehart & Becerra, 1995; Lubove, 1965). The United States has developed a welfare state over time, to be sure, but these traditional assumptions about who welfare recipients are and why they are not succeeding on their own have remained.

It is important to note, however, that the deserving–undeserving distinction evident throughout social welfare history does not view all poor people in an equally negative light (Cook, 1979; Handler & Hasenfeld, 1991; Katz, 1986, 1989; Trattner, 1994). In fact, some social welfare programs do not reflect the aforementioned emphasis on individual moral deficits or concerns over program dependency. This differentiation between the deserving and undeserving poor revolves around the question of whether an individual is poor because of his or her rejection of mainstream values (for example, laziness or single parenthood) or because of external factors or insurmountable individual incapacities (for example, physical disability).

From the deserving–undeserving perspective, disabled individuals and elderly people have traditionally been viewed as worthy of assistance, and their inability to earn wages through employment is generally accepted (Handler & Hasenfeld, 1991; Katz, 1989). In contrast, single, able-bodied nonworking poor people (for example, GA recipients) and single mothers with children (for example, most AFDC recipients) continue to dominate the public image of the welfare problem. This distinction has been discussed by Handler and Hasenfeld (1991) in terms of the inclusiveness versus the exclusiveness of programs. Whereas programs that serve so-called deserving populations have become more substantial since their inception (for example, Supplemental Security Income and social security benefit levels are both indexed to inflation and have broadened in scope over the years), programs designed to help the "undeserving" poor population have more stringent eligibility requirements, lower benefit levels, and far greater social control mechanisms.

Because GA is believed to serve able-bodied, single individuals, it is popularly regarded as a program for undeserving poor people. Yet it is plausible that some GA recipients are not able-bodied, but instead have a disability or health problem for which they are not receiving disability assistance, either because they do not meet the eligibility criteria or because they have not successfully completed the application process (see Berkowitz, 1987; Block, 1992; and Nelson, 1994 for discussions of the problems individuals have successfully attaining disability benefits). Thus, although GA is not a disability program, this article explores the extent to which recipients relying on the program in Michigan were truly able-bodied.

Conventional Gender Roles

The deserving–undeserving distinction is shaped by conventional gender role ideology. Research on the welfare state clearly demonstrates the role of gender role ideology in the development of AFDC policy (Abramowitz, 1988; Gordon, 1990; Nelson, 1990). In the welfare state, a woman's deservingness has been defined primarily by her marital status, whereas a man's deservingness has been judged by his connection to the labor force (Abramowitz, 1988; Nelson, 1990). The changing role of women in the labor market has not gone unnoticed in AFDC policy, as evidenced by the increased attention to job training and work requirements; however, a woman's orientation toward marriage and the rise in out-of-wedlock births continue to dominate discussions of the welfare problem. For example, the newly passed Personal Responsibility and Work Opportunity Reconciliation Act of 1996 (P.L. 104-193) includes penalties for certain categories of women who fail to subscribe to mainstream behaviors (for example, prohibiting the formation of independent households for unmarried teenage mothers) (NASW, 1996).

This article argues that, like AFDC, the negative conception of GA recipients can similarly be explained, in part, by such gender biases. However, in the case of GA, it is dominant ideology about appropriate male roles that is likely to contribute to the negative image of GA recipients: the belief that the program serves primarily men and that GA is a program for single, able-bodied, nonworking men who do not fulfill their conventional breadwinner roles through successful labor force attachment. Women are seldom viewed as part of the GA population because their needs are believed to be already served by AFDC programs. One might argue that to the extent that women are recognized as part of the GA population, they are viewed in a particularly bad light, as they are believed to be neither mothering nor working.

Racial Attitudes

In addition to the role of gender, race plays a central part in shaping the current welfare stereotype. Before the 1960s War on Poverty, low-income African Americans were excluded from most welfare programs (Abramowitz, 1988; Handler & Hasenfeld, 1991; Iglehart & Becerra, 1995). The role of race in the welfare debate heightened during the 1960s as legal challenges to discriminatory welfare practices were successfully fought, resulting in increased welfare participation rates among people of color (Handler & Hasenfeld, 1991). Stereotypes of welfare recipients have since become imbued with racial content, and stereotypes of African Americans in particular include welfare-related content (Devine & Baker, 1991; Edsall & Edsall, 1991).

Moreover, there is a growing body of literature on white Americans' racial attitudes that suggests a correlation between negative racial attitudes and opposition to welfare (Bobo & Smith, 1994; Gilens, 1996; Kluegel & Smith, 1986). For example, Bobo and Smith argued that "the term 'welfare' and its negative connotations stem from an implicit link to how one feels about blacks" (p. 391). Moreover, white Americans view African Americans as less deserving of assistance than their white counterparts (Iyengar, 1990), providing further evidence that there is a racial component to the unpopularity of welfare programs.

Thus, race and gender ideology, along with strongly held values of independence and self-sufficiency, are paramount to the current welfare stereotype. Arguments against AFDC and GA stem from a perceived violation of normative roles and as such are fueled by belief systems that hold welfare recipients to be undeserving by nature of their race, their family and work status, and their poverty. From such a perspective, it is not surprising that GA programs and AFDC programs have been targets of punitive reforms, whereas programs for the so-called deserving poor, who do not suffer the same welfare stereotyping, have been for the most part spared.

METHOD

Using data from a sample of individuals who relied on Michigan's GA program before it was terminated in October 1991, this article examines the extent to which these stereotypic images of welfare recipients reflect actual characteristics of GA recipients. In particular, it explores the extent to which former GA recipients in Michigan conformed to the stereotypic profile of the typical GA client—that is, young, African American, male, and unwilling but able to work. It also examines the degree of workforce participation in the year following the termination of GA and explores the role of age, race, gender, work experience, and health status in the probability of finding posttermination employment. The analyses in this article rely on data collected from three sources: (1) administrative records of the entire Michigan GA population, (2) a survey conducted with a random sample of former GA recipients, and (3) in-depth interviews with a subsample of survey participants.

Administrative Data

A Michigan Department of Social Services administrative data file of active recipient and case files as of March 1991 was used for the demographic analysis of the GA population. All cases facing termination on October 1, 1991, were analyzed ($N = 106,812$).

The March 1991 population was used to avoid inducing a bias from the use of records from the last program month, September 1991. Recipients who stayed on the GA rolls through the end of the program may have differed from those who had been on the program but left between the time that the termination was announced and the actual termination. In particular, some recipients may have been forced off the rolls by caseworkers preparing for the termination or may have left voluntarily after termination plans were publicly announced. The March population was also selected because March had typically high enrollment levels. Using this group as a base population ensured that a wide range of individuals formerly using the GA program would be eligible for study participation (Kossoudji et al., 1993). In addition, the state of Michigan automatically folded cases categorized as either GA-disabled and GA-family into two new state programs, State Disability Insurance and State Family Assistance. These cases did not lose benefits and were therefore excluded (Kossoudji et al., 1993).

Survey

Using the administrative records, a stratified random sample of GA recipients from five counties was drawn, resulting in an initial pool of 1,297 GA recipients; 54.7 percent ($n = 710$) of those originally drawn were identified, and 74.6 percent of those identified completed the survey ($n = 530$). The most recent telephone and address information from the Michigan Department of Social Services records was used to track former recipients; this information was often not sufficient. Of the 710 identified, 25.4 percent ($n = 180$) did not complete the interview because of refusal to participate ($n = 105$), movement out of the sampling area ($n = 47$), imprisonment ($n = 17$), or death ($n = 11$) (Danziger & Kossoudji, 1994).

Face-to-face interviews that lasted from 30 to 90 minutes were conducted from August to October 1992. All participation was completely voluntary, and respondents were compensated financially for their participation.

The survey included questions that covered eight general areas: (1) background information, (2) health status and health care, (3) experience with the GA program, (4) education and training, (5) employment, (6) income and resources, (7) coping and social support, and (8) psychological well-being. This article focuses on health, employment, and experience with the GA program.

In-Depth Interviews

Within each urban county sampled as part of the survey, men and women of three different age groups (under 26, 26 to 40, and over 40 years of age) were randomly selected to participate in the qualitative portion of the study, such that there were 10 eligible participants across the three counties in each gender and age category. This resulted in a total of 60 eligible participants.

Of the 60 respondents selected to participate, 46 completed the interviews. Of the 14 incomplete interviews, 10 eligible respondents were not identified, two refused to participate, one was too ill to be interviewed, one was in an inpatient rehabilitation program. The data from two interviews were lost because of technical problems.

Face-to-face semistructured interviews were conducted from May to August 1993. The in-depth interviews lasted from 40 minutes to two hours and were audiotaped and later transcribed. All participation was completely voluntary, and interviewees were compensated financially.

RESULTS

To determine the accuracy of the common stereotype of GA recipients, we first examined the administrative data to provide a demographic description of the population. Subsequently, we reviewed survey data on health and disability to discern whether the respondents were able-bodied. Finally, to address the work ethic aspect of the stereotype, work history and reported reasons for GA use were examined with the survey data, and narrative accounts of the value placed on work and independence were examined with the qualitative interview data.

Demographic Profile of Michigan GA Recipients

We have argued that the stereotype of GA recipients included explicit reference to their demographic characteristics. In particular, we suggested that GA clientele were viewed as primarily young African American men. However, the Michigan GA population was quite diverse with respect to race, gender, and age (Table 12-1). The GA population was 39.8 percent female. The racial and ethnic makeup of the population was as follows: 42.6 percent of former recipients were non-Hispanic white people, and 53.7 percent were African American. This overrepresentation of African Americans is probably attributable to the higher rates of poverty among African Americans and the concentration of African Americans in urban areas, where the majority of GA recipients resided. Consistent with the general ethnic makeup of Michigan, only 3.7 percent of the population was some other racial or ethnic group, most frequently Latino or Latina (1.8 percent) and American Indian (0.4 percent). Moreover, instead of being a primarily young clientele, 39.0 percent of the GA population was over 40, and only 20.4 percent were 25 years old or younger. Female GA recipients were concentrated in the over-40 age group, whereas men were more likely to be in the middle age group (26 to 40).

Comparing the demographic make-up of the survey sample with administrative data on the total population, we found that African Americans were slightly oversampled (58.9 percent compared with 53 percent of the total GA population), and recipients over 40 were oversampled (48.1 percent compared with 39 percent). Recipients under 26 were undersampled (13.9 percent compared with 20.0 percent). Male and female study participants correctly reflect

Table 12-1

Population at Risk of Termination: Race, Gender, and Age Group as a Percentage of Total GA Population: March 1991

Age Group	All[a]	White Women	African American Women	White Men	African American Men
16–25 years	20.4	4.6	4.4	5.5	4.9
26–40	40.5	5.2	6.6	10.2	17.3
41–65	39.0	9.2	9.7	8.0	10.6
All ages		19.0	20.8	23.6	32.9

SOURCE: Reprinted with permission from Kossoudji, S., Danziger, S. K., & Lovell, R. (1993). *Michigan's general assistance population: An interim report of the GA Termination Project.* Ann Arbor: University of Michigan.

NOTE: This table is based on GA recipients in the state's administrative caseload who were not identified as either disabled or a parent of dependent children by the state as of March 1991.

[a]The percentages and total population size in the first column include recipients of all races. Of the total cutoff population, 0.4 percent were American Indian, 1.8 percent were Latino, and 1.4 percent were of other unknown races. Altogether there were 100 recipients age 66 or over. Of these, 53 were white and 27 were African American.

the gender breakdown of the population, which was 59.2 percent men and 40.8 percent women (Kossoudji et al., 1993).

The greater success at locating older respondents and the difficulties identifying younger respondents may have led to an overrepresentation of age-related health and disability problems and an underrepresentation of current employment. Offsetting to some extent these potential biases toward a comparatively less functional sample, the unidentified respondents were likely to be more transient and without stable housing, given past research demonstrating higher rates of health problems and higher unemployment rates among transient populations (Blau, 1992). Thus, although the stereotype suggests that the typical recipient of GA was a young African American man, the data showed that this profile was consistent with only 5 percent of the total caseload.

Health Status and Disability

Important to the stereotype of GA recipients is the belief that program recipients are able-bodied. We examined several survey measures of health and disability. The extent of chronic illness was measured by asking respondents to report all health problems experienced in the past year that required the attention of a physician. These open-ended responses were subsequently categorized as "chronic" or "not chronic" according to the International Classification of Diseases criteria (U.S. Department of Health and Human Services, 1991; see also Verma & Coulton, 1992). We were particularly interested in whether the chronic conditions mentioned had lasted longer than one year so that we could infer that the respondents were ill while they were receiving GA benefits. In keeping with national disability surveys (for example, Wolfe, 1994), we also explored the degree to which respondents reported that health problems interfered with their ability to work. The final approximation of health and disability status was obtained by examining data on past applications for disability programs.

Over one-half (58.7 percent) of the 530 respondents reported experiencing a chronic illness that lasted more than a year. Typical health problems included hypertension, asthma, and back injuries. Over one-half (53.7 percent) of the participants also stated that sickness and heath problems limited their activities and their ability to work. Specifically, 30.9 percent reported that sickness interfered somewhat with their ability to work, and 22.8 percent indicated that illness completely disrupted their ability to work. This level of distress is higher than in comparable national samples of poor individuals (Wolfe, 1994). Examining respondents' efforts to obtain disability benefits provided further evidence that many of them were not able-bodied. One-fifth of the sample (21.5 percent) reported having unsuccessfully applied for disability benefits before GA's termination, suggesting that GA had been acting as a disability program for this group.

Thus, it is clear that the GA program was assisting many individuals who did not view themselves as able-bodied. These findings on health and disability provide compelling evidence against the stereotypic assumption that GA recipients were uniformly able to work.

Work Ethic

A final stereotypic assumption is that GA recipients eschewed American values of work and independence (that is, that GA recipients lacked a work ethic). Using data from the survey, we examined both direct and indirect aspects of the work ethic question by exploring recipients' work search behaviors as well as their actual work experiences.

More than three-fourths of the 530 respondents (76.9 percent) had been working at some point before GA was terminated. Of the small minority of respondents who reported having never held a steady job, either before or after GA ended ($n = 66$), health problems (42.4 percent) and problems attributed to the economy (for example, a lack of available jobs) (33.3 percent) were most frequently identified as reasons for this lack of work. Another 10 percent who had never worked reported lacking the proper skills to find a job, and an additional 12.1 percent reported child care and family responsibilities as interfering with their ability to enter the labor force. Only 10.6 percent of respondents without work history could be classified as potentially lacking a desire to work. These seven respondents reported that they had "never tried" to find work, that they "couldn't hold onto a job," or that they felt no "need" to work. It is unclear whether these responses indicated an unwillingness to work on the part of the respondents or reflected some other nonmotivational reason. (The percentages add up to more than 100 because some respondents listed more than one reason for not working.)

The work ethic question can also be addressed by examining the reasons for initial entry onto GA rolls. Respondents reported that they applied for GA not because of motivational deficiencies but rather for economic or health-related reasons. One-fifth of the 530 respondents (21.5 percent) cited health reasons, and 49.6 percent reported interruptions in employment—most typically being laid off or not being able to find work once unemployed. Another subgroup (11.5 percent) reported other income-related reasons for applying for GA (for example, needed money, food, or housing) without indicating what it was that led to their economically insecure situation. The remainder of respondents (17.0 percent) pointed to a status change (for example, moved from another welfare program, most often AFDC; divorce or separation; becoming an adult; or returning to school).

These findings do not support the argument that GA recipients eschewed the American value of work, but rather indicate that GA was primarily an option for individuals facing employment problems and poor health conditions. In fact, the in-depth interviews carried out with a subsample of survey respondents suggest that this reliance on welfare during times of economic hardship was viewed as a necessary but undesired condition. This ambivalence toward GA was expressed by the majority of interviewees who spoke of the importance they placed on their own independence and self-sufficiency, while simultaneously viewing government assistance as necessary because of limited labor market opportunities, health problems, or a lack of resources within their families.

For example, Marissa, a Hispanic female in the oldest age group, reported searching for work while on GA but being able to find only volunteer work. Marissa spent her GA check mostly for rent and feared that losing GA would make the medications she needed for her diabetes unaffordable. Her family was a source of support, both before and after GA ended, but they were also struggling economically, and her overreliance left her fearful. Marissa stated, "God, I was so scared, you know [when GA was about to end]. What's going to happen to me? . . . And uh, and not being able to find a job and, and uh, I think I was, I was, they still gave us the, you know, they cut the [check] which was my main concern, which was that they cut off the money for the apartment, but they gave us food stamps. And that, but the money part, you know was really hard, too. I was borrowing from my family and uh, not knowing what more, or if they were going to have it, [if] it was going to be there for me."

In addition to complications from health problems and unsuccessful job searches, Marissa's desire to be independent and self-sufficient was similar to many other recipients. For Marissa it was emotionally quite difficult to turn to welfare or family members for assistance. When asked whether she considered living with her family during times of serious economic insecurity, Marissa replied, "No. No. I like to be on my own. I, I'd rather be dead. That's the honest to God truth. I'll go out and live in the streets before I go and live on my family. . . . 'Cause I don't like to be a burden to anybody, and I know I was a burden at the time."

This theme of self-sufficiency was reflected in the majority of interviews, although experiences with the labor market suggested that living by such a principle was difficult. For respondents who had worked most of their lives, making it on their own was an especially crucial element of who they were and wanted to be. For example, Dorothy, who had worked most of her life in home health care and other related jobs, stated, "I don't like to [ask for help]. I never did. I always like to've been, you know, doing my own." Similarly, Walter, a white male in the oldest age group, stated, "I like to help myself. I don't like asking nobody for nothing, you know. I try to do it myself."

The theme of independence was common throughout the interviews but was especially prevalent for respondents over 25 years of age. The younger respondents had spent fewer cumulative years away from their families and less time in the workforce before entering GA, and, as a result, their independence was less crucial to their self-definition. However, although interviews with these younger participants reflected a less-developed work identity, they still suggested a strong attachment to a work ethic. For example, Allen, an African American man in the youngest age group, lived with his mother's friend and paid her approximately 90 percent of his GA check for rent. He reported receiving a great deal of financial and instrumental help from his father and did not suggest that this help was difficult for him to accept. At the same time, however, Allen continued to search for work, participated in mandatory job training programs, and did odd jobs when he could find them. Thus, the themes of self-reliance and independence were less salient for Allen compared to many of the older respondents, but his attachment to the work ethic seemed equally strong.

These quantitative and qualitative findings on the work ethic suggest that respondents maintained a strong orientation toward work and a discomfort with dependency but encountered many barriers to getting jobs and achieving self-sufficiency. Adding these findings on the work ethic to the previous discussion of demographic characteristics and health and disability, it is evident that the GA population is far more heterogeneous and their lives far more complex than the picture drawn by common stereotypic assumptions.

Post-GA Employment Success

To address the popular argument that limiting the availability of welfare will correspond with heightened levels of self-sufficiency, we examined the survey data on the degree of work activity in the year following the GA termination. Two logistic regression models tested the extent to which respondents' demographic characteristics were related to the likelihood of working. Thus, the dependent measure of interest is post-GA employment. Employment was measured by a dichotomous variable that reflected whether a respondent reported having worked at any time after the GA program ended in a formal sector job (described to respondents as work in jobs where taxes are taken out of their paychecks). Rather than measuring success at obtaining long-term employment, this variable measured the occurrence of any regular employment, regardless of its length, between the time GA was terminated and the point at which the survey was conducted.

Findings reveal that posttermination employment was the exception rather than the norm. Fewer than one-third of the 530 respondents (31.4 percent) had found employment in the year following GA termination. Much of this employment was unstable, as evidenced by the fact that when the survey was conducted, only one-fifth of the sample (20.9 percent) was currently employed.

Relationship of Individual Characteristics to Employment

Although the stereotype suggests that the GA clientele is a relatively young group, the youngest group, was, in fact, the smallest group. The large proportion of older participants significantly lowers the potential employability of the sample. Older people generally have a greater number of health problems, especially poor people, who generally receive less comprehensive medical care (Dunkle & Kart, 1990). In fact, a significant percentage of respondents reported suffering health problems, and these are overrepresented in the older age groups in our sample. Thus, age and health status are likely to be important predictors of post-GA employment success.

Gender may also influence post-GA employment; almost two-fifths of Michigan GA recipients were women. Women may face a different employment climate than men, either because they bring different skills to the workplace or because of the potential for differential hiring practices of employers toward women and men.

In addition, given past literature on the barriers African Americans face in the labor market, there is precedent to assume that African American respondents would have a more difficult time gaining access to jobs than white respondents after the termination of GA. Racial segregation and discrimination both continue to be significant barriers to finding employment for African Americans (Kirschenman & Neckerman, 1991; Massey, 1994; Turner, Fix, & Struyk, 1991; Wilson, 1987). In addition, some literature suggests that African American men are particularly disadvantaged in the labor market because of employer preferences for almost any other group (Kirschenman & Neckerman, 1991; Waldinger, 1995).

To measure the unique effect of individual characteristics (race by age, gender, work experience, and health-disability status) on postprogram work behavior, we created a set of dummy variables that allowed a comparison of white men to African American men, African American women, white women, other-race men, and other-race women to test the possibility that race effects are conditioned on gender. To capture work experience, the number of years of past work experience prior to receiving GA was collapsed into three categories (less than one year, one to five years, and over five years). Because extensive information on the duration of past work experience is available only for a subset of survey respondents, the use of this variable restricts the sample size to 134 of the 530 survey respondents.

The measure of health-disability status was formed by creating a dichotomous variable indicating whether a respondent was unhealthy or disabled (either had applied for a disability program before GA ended or reported health problems that interfered with their ability to work) or able-bodied (neither had a health problem nor had applied for disability insurance prior to GA).

Table 12-2 reports the findings from two logistic regression models that test the effects of these characteristics on employment success. The first model examines the effects of race (for men and women separately), age, and health status on the likelihood that respondents had worked since the GA program ended. The second model restricts the sample to those respondents for whom we were able to calculate the number of years of work experience ($n = 134$). This second model is identical to the first with the addition of the work experience variable.

TABLE 12-2

Logistic Regression Results of Models 1 and 2: The Effect of Race, Gender, Age, Health–Disability, and Work Experience on Post-GA Employment

Variable	Model 1 (N = 511)				Model 2 (N = 134)			
	β	p	Odds Ratio	CI	β	p	Odds Ratio	CI
Age								
(Under 26 years)								
26–40	−0.696	.022	0.499	.27, .90	ns	ns	ns	ns
Over 40	−1.915	.0001	0.147	.02, .28	−2.187	0.009	0.112	.02, .58
Health								
(Poor health)								
Able-bodied	1.146	.0001	3.144	2.03, 4.86	1.130	0.016	3.096	1.24, 7.73
Race and Gender								
(White men)								
Black women	−0.801	.018	0.449	.23, .87		ns		
Black men	−0.902	.002	0.406	.23, .73	−1.310	0.017	0.270	.09, .79
White women		ns				ns		
Other women		ns				ns		
Other men		ns				ns		

NOTE: Work experience was not significance in either model; ns = not significant
[a]Reference categories for interpretation of odds ratios are in parentheses.

Health–Disability. As the results of models 1 and 2 illustrate, after controlling for the effects of the other variables, being able-bodied greatly increased the likelihood of having post-GA employment. The odds of having found work are about three times greater for able-bodied individuals compared to unhealthy or disabled individuals, and as model 2 indicates, this effect does not diminish when work experience is taken into account (odds-ratio = 3.14 in model 1, 3.10 in model 2; $p < .01$).

Age. The findings also demonstrate that age is a significant factor in post-GA employment. As model 1 shows, the probability of having found employment is lower for respondents in the middle (odds ratio = 0.499, $p < .02$) and older (0.147, $p < .01$) age groups compared with respondents in the youngest age group, controlling for the effects of race, gender, and health-disability status. Considering the additional role of work experience, model 2 continues to reflect a significant effect of age, such that respondents over 40 were less likely to be working after GA ended than those under 26 (0.112, $p < .01$), although the odds of having found work are no longer different for middle-aged compared to young respondents.

Race and Gender. The findings for race and gender reveal that compared to white men, African Americans, regardless of gender, have a lower probability of posttermination employment. As model 1 indicates, the odds of having found work are significantly lower for African American men (0.406, $p < .01$) and African American women (0.449, $p < .02$) compared with white men (Table 12-2). Model 2 demonstrates that this race difference is dependent to some extent on work experience, such that controlling for work experience, the odds of working continue to be lower for African American men compared to white men (0.27, $p < .02$); however, there is no longer a significant difference in the likelihood of working between African American women and white men. As models 1 and 2 indicate, other-race men and women do not differ from white men in their likelihood of having found work.

Work Experience. Interestingly, model 2 demonstrates that once the effects of age, gender, race, and health status are taken into account, there is no additional effect of work experience. That is, respondents who reported having worked between one and five years prior to receiving GA were no more likely to work than those who reported less than one year of work experience; likewise, those respondents who had an extensive work history (that is, six years or more) were no more likely to have found employment than those with less than one year of prior employment.

DISCUSSION

Taken together, the results reported in models 1 and 2 suggest that simply removing the welfare option will not result in a significant extent of workforce participation. Quite to the contrary, our data suggest that factors other than the availability of welfare must account for unemployment, as jobless rates remained high after GA was terminated. The current models could test only for the effect of a set of individual characteristics on employment success. We found that race, gender, age, and health status contributed to different probabilities of entering the workforce.

Somewhat surprisingly, work experience did not increase the likelihood of working. There are at least two possibilities for this finding. First, it may be that our measure of work experience was too crude and that a more critical measure involving not only the cumulative years of past employment but also the quality of that experience would have proved meaningful. However, recent work on employer hiring patterns suggests that work experience may not be the primary criterion on which employers in low-skilled sectors of the labor market rely. In particular, informal hiring networks (more than work experience) and social capital (even more than human capital) seem to be of utmost importance to these employers (Kirschenman & Neckerman, 1991; Waldinger, 1995).

Yet beyond the individual characteristics measured in this study, factors external to the respondent (for example, job availability, family demands) would increase our understanding of perhaps the most significant finding that we have presented: that a substantial portion of respondents, regardless of demographic subgroup, were not employed at any time after the first year of GA termination. Future research efforts might take into account these environmental considerations to better understand barriers to employment among former welfare recipients.

Past research on AFDC has also had mixed success in accounting for postprogram employment using individual-level models. Human capital and demographic models do differentiate AFDC recipients who leave welfare for work from those who remain dependent; however, they have trouble predicting whether those who leave welfare for work will subsequently return to the welfare rolls (Bane & Ellwood, 1994; Pavetti, 1993). Clearly, variables external to recipient characteristics are important to consider in future research on the employment of welfare recipients.

CONCLUSION

We have argued that there is a pervasive but unfounded stereotype of welfare recipients, GA recipients in particular, that supports a public "get tough" attitude regarding welfare benefits. In particular, this stereotype suggests that GA recipients are a homogenous group of young, able-bodied African American men who depend on welfare and, in doing so, demonstrate their unwillingness to live by American values of hard work and self-sufficiency. The remedy to this problem has been the reduction or, as in the case of Michigan, the termination of state government welfare benefits, with the intention of providing an incentive to behave in accordance with these values.

The data presented in this article contradict these stereotypic assumptions about the GA population. A diverse population—male and female, African American and white, young and old—used the GA program and did so for a variety of reasons. Health problems had led many recipients to apply for disability benefits; however, when requests were not granted, GA became an alternative. Little evidence in this study points to a lack of attachment to values of work and self-sufficiency. Rather than a "preference for welfare over work," the behavior of former GA recipients in our survey reflected a desire to live by conventional American values but also demonstrated the difficulties in living by such a philosophy. Thus, when GA ended, employment was hard to obtain for significant numbers of recipients.

Our data do not allow us to examine whether the overall proportion of respondents who reported having found work since GA ended is significantly different from the proportion who would have left GA and found work in any given "typical" program year (the work disincentive argument). If the GA program had not been terminated, some proportion of the sample would have still left the program and entered the workforce, but because pretermination levels of leaving GA for work are not available, this welfare disincentive argument cannot be adequately tested. Yet despite this data limitation, our findings on the overall degree of work behavior after the program ended clearly indicate that the vast majority of respondents had not become self-sufficient. To the contrary, the majority of recipients were without work in the paid labor force, and those that did work faced unstable employment prospects.

Terminating welfare appears to be an ineffective policy option for this diverse population. Even the minority of recipients who were working one year after the program ended had found jobs in low-wage, often unstable employment sectors. These jobs are likely to be short-term, potentially leaving this group again without employment and without the option of turning to public assistance. Moreover, an improved economic climate still would not address the needs of former GA recipients with health problems who are unsuccessful in obtaining disability assistance yet are unable to work. Policy planning and development can be based on realistic and accurate assessments of recipient needs rather than on popular conceptions and misconceptions about the motivations of people applying for assistance. Current welfare reforms that attempt to reduce or eliminate benefits without an empirical basis for doing so, however, reflect a general disregard for such a rational approach to addressing social problems.

REFERENCES

Abramowitz, M. (1988). *Regulating the lives of women.* Boston: South End Press.

Bane, M. J., & Ellwood, D. T. (1994). *Welfare realities: From rhetoric to reform.* Cambridge, MA: Harvard University Press.

Berkowitz, E. D. (1987). *Disabled policy: America's programs for the handicapped* (A Twentieth Century Fund study). New York: Cambridge University Press.

Berrick, J. D. (1995). *Faces of poverty: Portraits of women and children on welfare.* New York: Oxford University Press.

Blau, J. (1992). *The visible poor: Homelessness in the United State.* New York: Oxford University Press.

Block, F. S. (1992). *Disability determination: The administrative process and the role of medical personnel.* Westport, CT: Greenwood Press.

Bobo, L., & Smith, R. (1994). Antipoverty policy, affirmative action, and racial attitudes. In S. H. Danziger, G. D. Sandefur, & D. H. Weinberg (Eds.), *Confronting poverty: Prescriptions for change* (pp. 365–395). Cambridge MA: Harvard University Press.

Cook, F. L. (1979). *Who should be helped? Public support for social services.* Beverly Hills, CA: Sage Publications.

Danziger, S. K., & Kossoudji, S. A. (1994). *What happened to former GA recipients? The second interim report of the General Assistance Termination Project.* Ann Arbor: University of Michigan.

Devine, P. G., & Baker, S. (1991). Measurement of racial stereotype subtyping. *Personality and Social Psychology Bulletin, 17,* 44–50.

Dunkle, R. E., & Kart, C. (1990). Health services. In A. Monk (Ed.), *Handbook of gerontological services* (2nd ed., pp. 201–227). New York: Columbia University Press.

Edsall, T. B., & Edsall, M. D. (1991, May). When the official subject is presidential politics, taxes, welfare, crime, rights, or values . . . the real subject is race. *Atlantic,* pp. 53–86.

Feagin, J. R. (1975). *Subordinating the poor: Welfare and American beliefs.* Englewood Cliffs, NJ: Prentice Hall.

Gilens, M. (1996, August 29–September 1). *"Race coding" and white opposition to welfare.* Paper presented at the Annual Meetings of the American Political Science Association, San Francisco.

Goodwin, L. (1983). *Causes and cures of welfare: New evidence on the social psychology of the poor.* Lexington, MA: Lexington Books.

Gordon, L. (Ed.). (1990). *Women, the state, and welfare.* Madison: University of Wisconsin Press.

Halter, A. P. (1996). State welfare reform for employable general assistance recipients: The facts behind the assumptions. *Social Work, 41,* 106–110.

Handler, J. (1995). *The poverty of welfare reform.* New Haven, CT: Yale University Press.

Handler, J. F., & Hasenfeld, Y. (1991). *The moral construction of poverty: American welfare reform.* Newbury Park, CA: Sage Publications.

Hasenfeld, Y., & Rafferty, J. (1989). The determinants of public attitudes toward the welfare state. *Social Forces, 67,* 1027–1048.

Heclo, H. (1994). Poverty politics. In S. Danziger, G. D. Sandefur, & D. Weinberg (Eds.), *Confronting poverty: Prescriptions for change* (pp. 396–437). Cambridge, MA: Harvard University Press.

Iglehart, A. P., & Becerra, R. M. (1995). *Social services and the ethnic community.* Boston: Allyn & Bacon.

Iyengar, S. (1990). Framing responsibility for political issues: The case of poverty. *Political Behavior, 12,* 19–40.

Katz, M. (1986). *In the shadow of the poorhouse.* New York: Basic Books.

Katz, M. (1989). *The undeserving poor: From the war on poverty to the war on welfare.* New York: Pantheon.

Kirschenman, J., & Neckerman, K. M. (1991). "We'd love to hire them, but . . . ": The meaning of race for employers. In C. Jencks & P. E. Peterson (Eds.), *The urban underclass* (pp. 203–234). Washington, DC: Brookings Institution.

Kluegel, J. R., & Smith, E. R. (1986). *Beliefs about inequality: American views of what is and what ought to be.* New York: Aldine de Gruyter.

Kossoudji, S., Danziger, S. K., & Lovell, R. (1993). *Michigan's general assistance population: An interim report on the General Assistance Termination Project.* Ann Arbor: University of Michigan.

Lav, I. J., Lazere, E., Greenstein, R., & Gold, S. (1993). *The states and the poor: How budget decisions affected low income people in 1992.* Washington, DC: Center on Budget and Policy Priorities.

Lipset, S. M. (1967). *The first new nation.* Garden City, NY: Doubleday.

Lubove, R. (1965). *The professional altruist: The emergence of social work as a career: 1880-1930.* Cambridge, MA: Harvard University Press.

MacDonald, A. P. (1972). More on the Protestant ethic. *Journal of Consulting and Clinical Psychology, 39,* 116–122.

Massey, D. S. (1994). America's apartheid and the urban underclass. *Social Service Review, 68,* 471–487.

Mead, L. M. (1986). *Beyond entitlement.* New York: Free Press.

Murray, C. (1984). *Losing ground: American social policy 1950–1980.* New York: Basic Books.

National Association of Social Workers, Office of Government Relations. (1996). *Personal Responsibility and Work Opportunity Reconciliation Act of 1996 (H.R. 3734), Public Law 104-193: Summary of provisions.* Washington, DC: Author.

Nelson, B. J. (1990). The origins of the two channel welfare state: Workmen's compensation and mothers' aid. In L. Gordon (Ed.), *Women, the state, and welfare* (pp. 123–151). Madison: University of Wisconsin Press.

Nelson, W. J., Jr. (1994). Disability trends in the United States: A national and regional perspective. *Social Security Bulletin, 57,* 27–41.

Pavetti, L. A. (1993). *The dynamics of welfare and work: Exploring the process by which women work their way off welfare* (Malcolm Weiner Center for Social Policy Working Papers: Dissertation Series). Cambridge, MA: Harvard University Press.

Personal Responsibility and Work Opportunity Reconciliation Act of 1966, P.L. 104-193.

Shapiro, R. Y., Patterson, K. D., Russell, J., & Young, J. T. (1987). The polls: Public assistance. *Public Opinion Quarterly, 51,* 120–130.

Smith, R. W. (1987). That which we call welfare by any other name would smell sweeter: An analysis of the impact of question wording on response patterns. *Public Opinion Quarterly, 51,* 75–83.

Trattner, W. I. (1994). *From poor law to welfare state: A history of social welfare in America* (5th ed.). New York: Free Press.

Turner, M. A., Fix, M., & Struyk, R. J. (1991). *Opportunities denied, opportunities diminished: Discrimination in hiring.* Washington, DC: Urban Institute.

U.S. Department of Health and Human Services. (1991). *ICD-9-CM official guidelines for coding and reporting* (9th ed.). Washington, DC: Author.

Verma, N., & Coulton, C. (1992). *Levels of chronic illness and medical care need in the general assistance population: An analysis of medical assistance claims in Cuyahoga County.* Cleveland: Case Western Reserve University.

Waldinger, R. (1995). *Black/immigrant competition re-assessed: New evidence from Los Angeles.* Unpublished manuscript, University of California, Los Angeles, Department of Sociology.

Williams, R. M., Jr. (1979). Change and stability in values and value systems: A sociological perspective. In M. Rokeach (Ed.), *Understanding human values* (pp. 15–46). New York: Free Press.

Wilson, W. J. (1987). *The truly disadvantaged: The inner city, the underclass, and public policy.* Chicago: University of Chicago Press.

Wolfe, B. L. (1994). Reform of health care for nonelderly poor. In S. Danziger, G. D. Sandefur, & D. Weinberg (Eds.), *Confronting poverty: Prescriptions for change* (pp. 253–288). Cambridge, MA: Harvard University Press.

This chapter was originally published in the December 1996 issue of Social Work Research, *vol. 20, pp. 217–227.*

13 Predictors of Employment and Earnings among JOBS Participants

Peter A. Neenan and Dennis K. Orthner

During the past several decades, the United States has embarked on a series of policy and program initiatives to help many poor people find work. Efforts have ranged from programs targeted to specific populations such as youths, teenage parents, or underskilled men to broad-based programs targeted to large percentages of mothers receiving assistance from Aid to Families with Dependent Children (AFDC). The programs themselves have also varied significantly. Some have focused on low-cost job search and placement strategies (for example, the Work Incentive Program), whereas others have incorporated more extensive human capital investment strategies that require participation in education, training, and job search activities (for example, the Saturation Work Initiative Model).

This latter approach formed the basis for the Family Support Act of 1988 (P.L. 100-485) and its Job Opportunities and Basic Skills Training (JOBS) program, which attempted to reconcile then-divergent philosophical political approaches toward welfare support through the notion of reciprocal obligation. On the one hand, this congressionally developed consensus recognized that welfare recipients are obligated to become self-sufficient to the maximum extent possible. On the other hand, it recognized that the state is responsible for providing appropriate educational and training programs and, through the provision of necessary support services, for enabling participants to pursue economic self-sufficiency for themselves and their families.

The architects of the Family Support Act assumed that poverty had multiple causes and that barriers to employability needed to be overcome for single mothers to move successfully from public assistance to earnings as a primary basis for self-sufficiency. Research during the 1970s and 1980s pointed to the difficulty of making this transition for single mothers, particularly those who had education and training deficits (Gueron & Pauly, 1991; Orthner & Kirk, 1995). Thus, the Family Support Act, and especially JOBS, adopted a more comprehensive programmatic emphasis. JOBS focused on providing and enhancing human capital through increased basic education, skills training, and postsecondary schooling and also helped overcome the barriers to both human capital development and employment by providing more extensive child care, transportation, and other assistance.

This article examines a longitudinal study of JOBS participants to determine the factors associated with employment and earnings after participants left the program. Data were collected on the background characteristics participants brought to the program, their attitudes toward welfare and work, their motivation for change, and their personal and social strengths. Participants' enhancements in education and training were assessed during the program, and their employment and earnings were measured after the program.

PREDICTORS OF EMPLOYMENT AND EARNINGS

Research on the noneconomic factors that predict job placement, employment continuity, and earnings among single mothers receiving AFDC has been relatively weak (Moffitt, 1992). Although interest has been long standing, much of the data have come from large-scale databases using administrative data. Thus, many analyses have not included psychosocial factors but have instead relied on the demographic and economic indicators available in the databases (Moffitt, 1992) or in longitudinal studies of income and earnings patterns (Bane & Ellwood, 1983). The status of current research is very much like that described by Sawhill (1988) in her review of research on poverty in the United States: "From a scientific perspective, we still understand very little about the basic causes of poverty—whether it is a matter of genetic or cultural inheritance, a lack of human capital, a choice variable related to work and family decisions, a result of macroeconomic failures or of social stratification based on race, sex, or family background" (p. 1113).

Basic demographic characteristics of the family have been consistently associated with employment rates among single-parent women. Mothers with preschool children, for example, have been less likely to find and keep employment (Floge, 1989; Rexroat, 1995), and their employment spells tend to be shorter, often because of the lack of reliable child care (Bane & Ellwood, 1994; Kimmel, 1995). Employment effects are also somewhat influenced by race. The employment rate among never-married white mothers in poverty tends to be greater than that among never-married African American mothers (Bane & Ellwood, 1994).

In addition, previous work experience tends to be associated with employment rates among single mothers. Women who have held more part-time jobs in the past are more likely to seek and achieve new jobs compared to those who have had more limited or no employment experience (Harris, 1996).

Another set of variables that tend to predict employment are human capital characteristics, including level of literacy, education, labor force experience, and training competency. The JOBS program and other human capital development strategies have promoted these kinds of experiences (Hagen & Davis, 1995). Single mothers with enhanced human capital tend to enter the labor force more quickly, stay in the labor force longer, and receive higher levels of earnings (Friedlander & Burtless, 1995). Level of education, in particular, is a significant determinant of employment and earnings among women, whatever their family structure (Moffitt, 1992). Previous work experience also contributes significantly to labor force participation, and those who have completed skills training have a significant advantage over those who have not (Orthner et al., 1995).

There are two major dilemmas, however, in the literature on single-parent human capital investments. First, much of the research on human capital factors and employment comes from data on married women or women who are not in poverty (Zimmerman, 1992). These results, although relevant to the issue, are problematic in terms of their interpretation for single mothers receiving AFDC, many of whom have significant barriers that limit the realization of their human capital. Second is the recent significant pressure to move women receiving AFDC from public assistance into employment. Although welfare employment programs targeted to women receiving AFDC have been developed over the past three decades, most have targeted volunteers or the most employment ready of the women receiving public assistance (Gueron & Pauly, 1991). The evidence from controlled studies, however, indicates that the effects of human capital investments on the employment rates of single mothers on AFDC have been relatively small, with the most significant effects on those who were most job ready (Bane & Ellwood, 1994; Friedlander & Burtless, 1995).

Attitudes toward work and welfare and psychological well-being are even less understood as factors in promoting movement toward employment among single mothers in poverty. Issues related to motivation have rarely been included in research, except in qualitative studies (Hagen & Davis, 1995). In one investigation, work-related values were not found to have a significant impact on employment rates (Isralowitz & Singer, 1986), whereas other studies found modest effects of work motivation and values on employment (for example, Goodwin, 1983). Studies have consistently found that single mothers in poverty have higher levels of psychological distress and depression than women not in poverty or those who are poor but married (for example, McLanahan & Booth, 1995). Self-esteem and mastery are also lower among these women, but the effects of unemployment are less clear, with some research finding no differences in psychological well-being due to employment (for example, Shamir, 1986) and others reporting improved well-being among employed women (for example, Voydanoff, 1995).

Unfortunately, the results of many of these studies are inconsistent and inconclusive (Bane & Ellwood, 1994). Few studies have examined both economic and psychosocial factors in the same research. Even fewer have been longitudinal, measuring the effects of personal, family, and human capital characteristics over time, especially into postprogram activity.

From a theoretical perspective, the present investigation is guided by the hypotheses of rational choice theory, a theory that suggests that individuals face economic choices and evaluate them according to their preferences, selecting the option that offers the greatest utility or satisfaction (Moffitt, 1992). The human capital assumptions underlying the Family Support Act are built on rational choice (Bane & Ellwood, 1994) and propose that individuals will weigh the costs and rewards of their personal and family strengths when deciding to enter the labor market. Based on these assumptions, we hypothesized that employment and earnings after JOBS participation would be influenced first by the background characteristics and experiences single mothers bring into the program, then by the work and personal attitudes and values that influence their progress and employment-related goals, and finally by the improvements in human capital they develop while in the program.

METHOD

Study Design

A multiyear, longitudinal tracking study was conducted in 15 North Carolina counties during the initial years of JOBS implementation in the state. The study was designed to assess changes in women's personal and family well-being while in JOBS and to observe how these indicators, including levels of economic self-sufficiency, changed after JOBS participation. Primary sources of data consisted of confidential, self-administered surveys completed by participants in the early weeks of their JOBS participation; a uniform intake assessment tool used by case managers in their initial contacts with new participants; initial case manager assessments of participants' social competence; state-level component tracking systems for participants; and monthly earnings data reported to the state's unemployment insurance system. Instruments designed to be completed by both case managers and JOBS participants were field pretested at JOBS sites in counties that were not included in the evaluation. The participant surveys were comprehensible at a fourth-grade reading level, and evaluation staff were available to answer participants' questions by collect telephone call.

Sample

The sample consisted of 664 women receiving AFDC in 15 North Carolina counties who began and ended their JOBS participation between October 1991 and June 1993 and did not later re-enter the program. The length of time spent in JOBS ranged from three to 630 days, with an average duration in the program of 196 days. New entrants to JOBS were invited to voluntarily enroll in the study; about two-thirds of all new JOBS participants in the study counties agreed to take part. Analysis of demographic characteristics and welfare recipiency patterns revealed no statistically significant differences between study participants and other female participants who enrolled in these counties' JOBS programs but did not elect to enlist in the study.

Earnings reported to the state's unemployment insurance system were tracked for each former JOBS participant during a 12-month period from July 1, 1993, to June 30, 1994. A total of 413 (62.2 percent) of the participants had earnings reported during this period that ranged from $6.39 to $27,127. The mean earnings level was $5,131, and the median was $3,868.

Data Analysis

A hierarchical multiple regression approach was used to assess the unique effect of groupings of variables on changes in earnings during the 12-month period. These variables were entered into the regression analysis in order of their temporal precedence before JOBS participation in accord with the hypotheses of the study; hence, demographic characteristics of participants were considered first, followed by indicators of human capital stock acquired before JOBS participation. Attitudinal dispositions of participants and indicators of personal and social strengths possessed at the beginning of JOBS participation were considered next in the model, followed by assessment of the unique contribution of

JOBS human capital enhancement activity undertaken by participants in relation to their subsequent earnings experience.

Given that JOBS emphasized a human capital development strategy, it was deemed conceptually important to assess separately the effects of enhancements participants acquired during program participation over the level of human capital stock they had acquired before JOBS. This technique allowed factors to be held constant so that a purer measure of relationship between and among variables could be obtained. The technique also used a forward-entry block approach, so that the relative effect of each category of participant characteristics and human capital enhancement on earnings could be observed. Because of the wide variation in length of time in which individuals participated in JOBS, this analysis controls for length of participation.

The strengths of the study design come from the ability to examine the effects on employment and earnings on the basis of characteristics that single mothers receiving AFDC brought with them to the JOBS program in comparison to the human capital achievements they made during participation. The use of hierarchical multiple regression with a longitudinal sample strengthens the ability to compare the value that was added from both economic and demographic factors with attitudinal and psychosocial strength factors. Previous research has been limited in not being able to incorporate this range of variables in a longitudinal data set. The design also permits continued study of this sample of single mothers over time to determine longer-range effects beyond those of the outcome evaluation period in this study.

Several limitations to this study should be noted. First, a longer-term earnings period may result in somewhat different earnings patterns. Recent results from multiyear follow-up studies indicate that human capital investment programs result in different earnings patterns depending on the population served and the program model used (Friedlander & Burtless, 1995). There is also a potential selection problem in JOBS programs such as in North Carolina. Many participants were able to select themselves both in and out of the program as they chose. Also, outcomes such as those described here may be different in other states with different benefit levels.

Predictor Variables

Demographic Characteristics. Demographic characteristics included age of participant in years, number of children living in the household, and age in years as of next birthday of the youngest child living in the household. Race of the participant was treated as a dummy variable, with nonwhite as the reference category.

Labor Force Experiences and Attitudes toward Work and Welfare. Variables in this cluster included intrinsic job satisfaction for present or most recent employment for those who had held a job, perceived adequacy of welfare as an income support, and self-assessed probability of future welfare receipt. Intrinsic job satisfaction was measured by a three-item Likert-type scale adapted from the work of Seashore, Lawler, Mirvis, and Cammann (1982): Respondents indicated their level of satisfaction with their most recent job's provision of chances to (1) learn new things, (2) do something worthwhile, and (3) do something that made them feel good about themselves. Responses ranged from 1 = very dissatisfied to 4 = very satisfied. When summed, these items formed a unifactor scale (α = .84). Possible scores ranged from 3 to 12, with higher scores indicating higher levels of intrinsic job satisfaction.

Perception of welfare as an adequate income support was measured by a single item asking, How well does welfare meet the needs of you and your family? Five responses were possible, ranging from 1 = it meets none of my and my family's needs to 5 = it meets all of my and my family's needs. Participants were also asked to assess the probability that they would be receiving welfare one year in the future. Responses ranged from 1 = no chance to 6 = certain. Both measures were adapted for the JOBS evaluation based on their utility in prior studies of welfare populations' attitudes and beliefs (Neenan, Orthner, & Ferguson, 1994).

Human Capital Stock. Human capital variables included participant's level of formal educational attainment as reported by the participant to her case manager during the employability assessment phase at the beginning of JOBS participation and case worker ratings of a participant's level of social competence. Assessment of social competence was undertaken by seven semantic differential adjective pairs. Case managers rated each new JOBS participant on a 10-point scale anchored by the following adjective pairs: lacks confidence–confident, attractive–unattractive, does most things well–does few things well, undependable–dependable, self-reliant–dependent, possesses social skills–lacks social skills, and lacks job skills–possesses job skills. When recoded to ensure unidirectionality, these items form a unidimensional scale (α = .92). Possible scores ranged from 0 to 70, with higher scores indicating a higher rating of social competence by the case manager.

Personal and Social Strengths. Personal and social strength variables included participant's level of self-determination or mastery, level of depression (Barnes & Prosen, 1984), and coping competence (Orthner & Blankenship, 1990). Mastery was assessed by a seven-item scale (α = .72) adapted from Pearlin, Menaghan, Lieberman, and Mullen (1981) in which respondents were asked to indicate whether the following seven statements were descriptive of themselves: (1) There is no way I can solve some of the problems I have, (2) I feel I am being pushed around in life, (3) I have little control over the things that happen to me, (4) I can do anything I really set my mind to, (5) I feel helpless in dealing with the problems of life, (6) what happens to me in the future depends on me, and (7) there is little I can do to change the important things in my life. Possible responses for each item ranged from 1 = not at all like me to 3 = a lot like me. Following recoding of items to ensure unidirectionality, the resultant scale has values ranging from 7 to 21, with higher scores indicating higher levels of mastery.

Depression was measured by a 20-item scale developed by the Center for Epidemiological Studies (Radloff, 1977). Possible scores on the recoded scale (α = .79) range from 0 to 60, with higher scores indicating higher levels of depression. Coping competence was assessed by a three-item scale (α = .68) that asked participants to assess the degree to which they felt confident of positive outcomes under conditions when (1) things had to get done, (2) tough problems were faced, and (3) the participant was going through a rough period. Possible scores on this measure range from 3 to 21, with higher scores indicating higher levels of self-assessed coping competence.

Human Capital Enhancement. Successful completion of the component activity designed to enhance employability included education below postsecondary, certifiable skills training, and postsecondary education certified by degree. These items were tracked using the state's Employment Programs Information System, which records JOBS activity and statuses for participants.

Dependent and Control Variables

Earnings covered by the state's unemployment insurance system for the 12-month period was the dependent variable. Length of time enrolled in JOBS before July 1, 1993, was the control variable.

Model

Table 13-1 presents measures of central tendency and dispersion for each variable. Before specification of the hierarchical regression model used in this analysis, examination of bivariate relationships among all the variables to be incorporated in the model was performed to detect possible multicollinearity. These interrelationships were generally modest (Table 13-2). Following specification of the hierarchical regression analysis, an analysis of residuals was performed in a further effort to detect the possible existence of nonlinearity and multicollinearity that would have the effect of spuriously suppressing relationships. The results of this analysis showed a near-normal plot of residuals, with a mean of .00 and a standard deviation of .95. Finally, to assess the possibly confounding interrelationship between the duration of participants' enrollment in JOBS and their personal and social strengths and demographic characteristics, a first-stage regression model was specified with number of days enrolled in JOBS as the dependent variable and the predictor variables as independent variables. The resulting model was not statistically significant [$R^2 = .02$, $F(11, 652) = 1.32$], suggesting the absence of interdependence.

FINDINGS

Approximately 24 percent of the overall variation in postprogram earnings is accounted for by the five categories of predictor variables included in this analysis. Table 13-3 summarizes the relative contribution of each category of variables to earnings variation.

Step 1: Length of Time in JOBS

To control for the effects of duration of participation in JOBS, the number of days between entry and exit from JOBS was entered as the initial step in the hierarchical regression model. The total variation explained in postprogram earnings attributable to length of JOBS participation accounted for approximately 3 percent of the variation in earnings for the sample ($R^2 = .03$). Length of time in JOBS remained significantly associated with earnings at all stages of the model.

TABLE 13-1
Variables' Univariate Descriptive Measures (N = 664)

Variable	M	Median	SD	Range
Predictor variable				
Demographic characteristics				
Age, years	29.8	28	7.6	18–59
Number of children	1.8	2	.94	1–6
Age of youngest child, years	5.9	4	4.7	1–19
Race (69.4% nonwhite)				
Labor force experience and work and welfare attitudes				
Employed at entry (8.4%)				
Employed full-time in the past (64.3%)				
Intrinsic job satisfaction	8.8	9	2.3	3–12
Adequacy of welfare	2.7	3	.81	1–5
Probability of future welfare receipt	2.2	2	1.3	1–6
Human capital stock				
Formal education level	11.1	12	1.7	2–16
Social competence	41.9	42	13.7	7–70
Personal and social strengths				
Mastery	16.6	17	2.8	8–21
Depression	19.4	18.5	10.8	0–51
Coping competence	12.8	13	2.9	5–21
Human capital enhancements				
Education below postsecondary (17.5% completed)				
Skills training (10.1% completed)				
Postsecondary education (9.4% completed)				
Control variable				
Days in JOBS	196.2	167	137.7	3–630
Dependent variable				
Earnings, dollars	3,160.45	903.92	4,500.85	0–27,127.39

NOTE: JOBS = Job Opportunities and Basic Skills Training program.

Step 2: Demographic Characteristics

Demographic characteristics accounted for an additional 4 percent of explained variation in earnings ($R^2 = .07$). At the second stage of model specification, when only length of participation in JOBS and demographic characteristics of participants were considered, neither the participant's age nor number of children in the family were significantly associated with subsequent earnings experience. Both race ($\beta = .11$) and age of youngest child ($\beta = -.11$) were significantly associated with postprogram earnings experience at this stage ($p < .05$), although these relationships attenuated as the model was further specified.

Step 3: Attitudes toward Work and Welfare

Participants' attitudes toward work and welfare accounted for an additional 5 percent of variation in postprogram earnings ($R^2 = .12$). Individuals predicting

TABLE 13-2
Interitem Correlations among Variables

	1	2	3	4	5	6	7	8	9	10	11	12	13	14	15	16	17	18	19
1	—																		
2	.16	—																	
3	.75	-.11	—																
4	.11	.17	.13	—															
5	.13	.05	.05	.04	—														
6	.18	-.04	.20	-.04	—	—													
7	.08	.16	.19	.25	—	-.04	—												
8	-.11	-.09	-.11	-.17	-.03	.01	.11	—											
9	.03	.07	.00	-.08	-.02	.05	.03	.01	—										
10	.18	-.04	.05	.20	.08	.16	-.12	-.08	.01	—									
11	.09	.05	.05	-.03	.03	.05	-.16	.01	-.08	.37	—								
12	.13	-.11	.14	.08	.05	.30	.04	.07	.01	.23	.33	—							
13	.00	.09	-.05	.02	-.08	-.18	-.05	-.04	.07	-.11	-.15	-.35	—						
14	.02	.05	-.03	-.11	.14	.11	.21	-.10	-.04	.07	-.06	.11	-.16	—					
15	-.04	.03	-.04	.04	-.05	-.20	.04	.03	-.10	-.35	-.13	-.10	.06	-.09	—				
16	-.05	.02	-.03	.13	-.07	-.08	.00	.07	.03	.13	.08	.01	-.12	-.11	.02	—			
17	-.03	.03	-.05	-.06	.03	.04	-.03	-.02	.07	.29	.29	.16	-.13	-.09	-.16	-.06	—		
18	.16	.02	.04	.10	-.13	.07	-.09	-.01	-.02	.13	.08	.00	-.05	-.04	.18	.09	.23	—	
19	.07	.00	.01	.04	.10	.15	.06	.05	-.10	.29	.24	.21	-.12	.07	-.11	.04	.12	.07	—

NOTE: 1 = age, 2 = no. of children, 3 = age of youngest child, 4 = race, 5 = employed at entry, 6 = employed full-time in the past, 7 = intrinsic job satisfaction, 8 = adequacy of welfare, 9 = probability of future welfare receipt, 10 = formal education level, 11 = social competence, 12 = mastery, 13 = depression, 14 = coping competence, 15 = education below postsecondary, 16 = skills training, 17 = postsecondary education, 18 = time in JOBS, 19 = earnings after JOBS.

TABLE 13-3

Hierarchical Multiple Regression Predicting Postprogram Earnings for JOBS Participants (Beta Values, Controlling for Length of Time in JOBS)

Variance	Step 1	Step 2	Step 3	Step 4	Step 5	Step 6
Time in JOBS						
Days	.18**	.18**	.23**	.14**	.15**	.13**
Demographic characteristics						
Age		.07	.07	.06	.05	.04
Race		.11*	.08	.03	.04	.05
Number of children		−.06	−.06	−.03	−.03	−.04
Age of youngest child		−.11*	−.09	−.09	−.06	−.05
Attitudes toward work and welfare						
Welfare adequate			−.22**	−.28**	−.27**	−.25**
Receive welfare in future			−.12**	−.12**	−.08*	−.09*
Intrinsic job satisfaction			.06	.08*	.07	.08*
Human capital: Stock						
Formal education				.16**	.13**	.13**
Social competency				.21**	.19**	.18**
Personal and social strengths						
Mastery					.18**	.19**
Depression					−.15**	−.16**
Coping competence					.03	.02
Human capital enhancements						
Education below postsecondary						.03
Skills training						.07
Postsecondary education						.08*
R^2	.03	.07	.12	.19	.22	.24
R^2 change		.04	.05	.07	.03	.02

NOTE: JOBS = Job Opportunities and Basic Skills Training program.
$*p < .05.$ $**p < .01.$

that they would be still be receiving welfare one year in the future ($\beta = -.12$) and those who were more likely to view welfare as an adequate income support for themselves and their families ($\beta = -.22$) experienced significantly lower postprogram earnings from employment ($p < .01$).

Step 4: Human Capital Stock

Human capital stock acquired by participants before JOBS accounted for an additional 7 percent of explained variation in postprogram earnings ($R^2 = .19$). Both formal education before JOBS ($\beta = .16$) and caseworker-rated level of participant social competence ($\beta = .21$) were significantly associated with higher earnings ($p < .01$).

Step 5: Personal and Social Strengths

Personal and social strengths of participants accounted for an additional 3 percent of explained variance ($R^2 = .22$). Both sense of mastery ($\beta = .18$) and level of depression ($\beta = -.15$) were significantly associated with postprogram earnings ($p < .01$).

Step 6: Human Capital Enhancements

The final block of variables to be entered into the model was human capital enhancements acquired by participants while in JOBS. These consisted of three formal educational programs, successful completion of which is evidenced by a certificate, degree, or diploma. Successful completion of at least one of three component activities contributed an additional 2 percent of explanation in variation on postprogram earnings ($R^2 = .24$). Only the successful completion of postsecondary education was significantly associated with postprogram earnings ($\beta = .08$, $p < .05$). Neither successful completion of educational activity below the postsecondary level ($\beta = .03$) nor skills training ($\beta = .07$) was significantly associated with postprogram earnings.

Model

When the fully saturated model is considered, it appears that no single category of participant characteristics by itself is substantially predictive of earnings outcomes from employment following JOBS program participation. Factors associated with more favorable earnings after JOBS participation appear to be associated not only with human capital stock before JOBS, which may be enhanced during program participation, but also with the personal strengths and attitudes and beliefs that participants have concerning control over their own destiny and the rejection of welfare as an adequate support system.

However, it is important to remember that approximately three-quarters of the overall variation in participants' postprogram earnings remains unexplained by this model. The addition of macrolevel characteristics (for example, labor market dynamics, income transfer support levels, and preferences for working) may account for additional sources of variance.

DISCUSSION

Two of three of the single-parent women on AFDC who exited JOBS had earnings during the defined outcome evaluation period. The most significant factors contributing to employment and earnings were the women's characteristics and attitudes before entering the JOBS program. Of the total variance explained in the model ($R^2 = .24$), 79 percent of that variance is explained by the factors that the women brought with them to the program. Prior labor force experience and work-related attitudes accounted for 29 percent of the explained variance, and human capital characteristics accounted for another 21 percent of the variance.

The personal and social strengths of the women contributed very little to their employment and earning outcomes ($R^2 = .03$). As the overall correlation matrix indicates, personal and social strengths are associated with labor force experience and human capital characteristics. However, when the variance explained by these strengths is accounted for after the other factors are considered, they contribute very little additional variance beyond that which is already explained.

In contrast, the human capital enhancement contributed to employment and earnings but added only 8 percent to the total explained variation. One reason why this contribution is not higher is that many of the women left the JOBS program before they had achieved significant gains in their education, training, or job readiness. Thus, for many of the women, the earnings experience was much more likely to be influenced by the characteristics they brought into the program than by the enhancements they achieved as a result of JOBS activities.

IMPLICATIONS FOR POLICY AND PRACTICE

Short-term employment outcomes from programs such as JOBS are unlikely to lift most families out of poverty, even when individuals have higher levels of motivation and human capital. The majority of the single mothers in this study left JOBS for wages that were too low to substantially improve their economic conditions beyond that of public assistance. The JOBS program itself, although laudable in its attempt to improve education and training, had too few participants who achieved significant enough gains in their education and training competence to substantially improve their economic self-sufficiency.

One question that these results raise is whether voluntary welfare employment programs can be effective in promoting economic self-sufficiency without strong sanctions or participation requirements. Participants in this program, as well as those in many other states (U.S. General Accounting Office, 1995), were able to leave without making substantial gains in their human capital. Their success in getting jobs therefore depended more on the motivation and experience that they brought into the program than the improvements they garnered as a result of the program. Thus, the motivation and competencies that encouraged their participation may also have increased their employment and earnings rather than the program itself.

Another implication is that human capital development that focuses solely on basic education attainments below postsecondary levels may not be cost-effective in terms of employment outcomes. Completing a basic education curriculum or general equivalency diploma had no significant effect on the employment and earnings of these single mothers. To some degree, this may represent the current conditions in the economy in which some level of basic education is assumed in entry-level jobs and having a degree or certificate may not improve one's competitive advantage in the labor market. Some jobs today can be accomplished with very low levels of literacy. Therefore, a welfare program probably requires a set of education and job competencies that go beyond this basic level to be able to offer a higher employment and earnings capacity.

Finally, this study suggests the importance of incorporating psychosocial factors into research designs that probe the relationships between welfare employment program enrollment and subsequent employment and earnings experiences for former participants. Even though personal mastery, depression, and coping competence did not add significant additional contributions to statistical variance after other factors were accounted for, these conditions are related to other characteristics and attitudes that single mothers bring into their education, training, and employment preparation. Related research has pointed to their possible role as mediating factors in facilitating JOBS program participation and successful completion (Orthner & Neenan, 1996). The attitudes of the women toward work and welfare also appear to be important contributors to progress toward economic self-sufficiency; this suggests the utility of incorporating these insights into welfare employment research and practice.

REFERENCES

Bane, M. J., & Ellwood, D. (1983). *The dynamics of dependence: The routes to self-sufficiency* (Report to the U.S. Department of Health and Human Services). Cambridge, MA: Urban Systems Research and Engineering.

Bane, M. J., & Ellwood, D. (1994). *Welfare realities: From rhetoric to reform.* Cambridge, MA: Harvard University Press.

Barnes, G. E., & Prosen, H. (1984). Depression in Canadian general practice attenders. *Canadian Journal of Psychiatry, 29,* 2-10.

Family Support Act of 1988, P.L. 100-485, 102 Stat. 2343.

Floge, L. (1989). Changing household structure, child-care availability, and employment among mothers of preschool children. *Journal of Marriage and the Family, 51,* 51-63.

Friedlander, D., & Burtless, G. (1995). *Five years after: The long-term effects of welfare-to-work programs.* New York: Russell Sage Foundation.

Goodwin, L. (1983). *Causes and cures for welfare.* Lexington, MA: Lexington Books.

Gueron, J. M., & Pauly, E. (1991). *From welfare to work.* New York: Russell Sage Foundation.

Hagen, J. L., & Davis, L. V. (1995). Another perspective on welfare reform: Conversations with mothers on welfare. In *Rockefeller Institute bulletin* (pp. 23-32). Albany: State University of New York, Nelson A. Rockefeller Institute of Government.

Harris, K. M. (1996). *Teenage mothers and welfare experience: Transitions into and out of welfare dependency.* Philadelphia: Temple University Press.

Isralowitz, R., & Singer, M. (1986). Unemployment and its impact on adolescent work values. *Adolescence, 21,* 145-158.

Kimmel, J. (1995). *Child care costs as a barrier to employment for single and married mothers.* Unpublished manuscript, W. E. Upjohn Institute for Employment Research, Kalamazoo, MI.

McLanahan, S., & Booth, K. (1995). Mother-only families: Problems, prospects, and politics. In G. L. Bowen & J. F. Pittman (Eds.), *The work and family interface: Toward a contextual effects perspective* (pp. 191-211). Minneapolis: National Council on Family Relations.

Moffitt, R. (1992). Incentive effects of the U.S. welfare system: A review. *Journal of Economic Literature, 30,* 1-61.

Neenan, P. A., Orthner, D. K., & Ferguson, M. R. (1994). *North Carolina JOBS evaluation, longitudinal participant study: The participant at entry to JOBS.* Chapel Hill: University of North Carolina at Chapel Hill, School of Social Work, Human Services Research and Design Laboratory.

Orthner, D. K., & Blankenship, D. (1990). *Soldier and spouse survey scale characteristics* (AFRP Analysis Plan, Appendix D). Research Triangle Park, NC: Research Triangle Institute.

Orthner, D. K., & Kirk, R. (1995). Evaluations of welfare employment programs. In R. L. Edwards (Ed.-in-Chief), *Encyclopedia of social work* (19th ed., Vol. 1, pp. 2499-2507). Washington, DC: NASW Press.

Orthner, D. K., & Neenan, P. A. (1996). Children's impacts on stress and employability of mothers in poverty. *Journal of Family Issues, 17,* 667–687.

Orthner, D. K., Neenan, P. A., Deang, L. P., Flair, K. A., Ferguson, M. R., Stafford, R. E., & Ingle, J. M. (1995). *Impact evaluation of the North Carolina JOBS evaluation.* Raleigh: North Carolina Department of Human Resources.

Pearlin, L. I., Menaghan, E. G., Lieberman, M. A., & Mullen, J. T. (1981). The stress process. *Journal of Health and Social Behavior, 22,* 337-356.

Radloff, L. S. (1977). The CES-D Scale: A self-report depression scale for research in the general population. *Applied Psychological Measurement, 1,* 385-401.

Rexroat, C. (1995). Race and marital status differences in the labor force behavior of female family heads: The effect of household structure. In G. L. Bowen & J. F. Pittman (Eds.), *The work and family interface: Toward a contextual effects perspective* (pp. 212-221). Minneapolis: National Council on Family Relations.

Sawhill, I. V. (1988). Poverty in the United States: Why is it so persistent? *Journal of Economic Literature, 26,* 1073-1119.

Seashore, S. E., Lawler, E. E., Mirvis, P., & Cammann, C. (Eds.). (1982). *Observing and measuring organizational change: A guide to field practice.* New York: John Wiley & Sons.

Shamir, B. (1986). Self-esteem and the psychological impact of unemployment. *Social Psychology Quarterly, 49,* 61-72.

U.S. General Accounting Office. (1995). *Welfare to work: Most AFDC training programs not emphasizing job placement.* Washington, DC: Author.

Voydanoff, P. (1995). Economic distress and family relations: A review of the eighties. In G. L. Bowen & J. F. Pittman (Eds.), *The work and family interface: Toward a contextual effects perspective* (pp. 331-344). Minneapolis: National Council on Family Relations.

Zimmerman, S. L. (1992). *Family policies and family well-being: The role of political culture.* Newbury Park, CA: Sage Publications.

This chapter was originally published in the December 1996 issue of Social Work Research, *vol. 20, pp. 228–237.*

14 Work and Automobile Ownership among Welfare Recipients

Paul M. Ong

Welfare reform is enmeshed in a policy conundrum (Ellwood, 1988). Although Americans generally believe that government should provide a helping hand to people who need temporary assistance, they are frustrated by a welfare system that has perpetuated long-term dependency and has grown larger over the years. Aid to Families with Dependent Children (AFDC), established in 1935 to provide income support to children of widows, has expanded dramatically since the 1960s. In the early 1990s, AFDC covered 5 million adults and 9 million children at a cost of about $23 billion a year (U.S. House of Representatives, 1993). AFDC-FG (Family Group) is the major component. Nearly all AFDC-FG recipients reside in female-headed households. In California in 1993, AFDC-FG was 87 percent of state's welfare caseload.

Despite a political consensus that the welfare system should be restructured to increase employment among AFDC recipients, a heated partisan debate exists over how to promote greater economic self-sufficiency. Opposing sides differ sharply on issues such as time limitations on benefits, type and amount of support and training services, and extent and nature of jobs available to welfare recipients. Policies and programs should not be based on unrealistic assumptions rooted in ideological polemics; instead, they should be anchored in the employment realities facing recipients.

One barrier to employment is geographic isolation. A disproportionate number of welfare recipients live in the inner city, isolated from the expanding employment opportunities in suburban areas (Kasarda, 1980). These residents are "spatially mismatched" with the suburbanized jobs and "skills mismatched" with the jobs remaining in the central business districts. Inner-city welfare recipients must compete for relatively few jobs, most of which pay low wages. For example, the South Central community of Los Angeles is home to 7 percent (about 660,000 people) of the region's population, many of whom are poor and people of color. However, the community is the site of only 3 percent of the region's jobs, a disproportionate number of which pay low wages (Ong, 1993). The difficulty in finding employment in the inner city is further aggravated by a tendency by businesses to avoid low-income, minority neighborhoods in their recruitment and hiring of workers (Kirschenman & Neckerman, 1991).

Of course, not all welfare recipients reside in inner-city neighborhoods. Osterman (1991) found that in low-income neighborhoods with a high employment rate, which he interpreted as a proxy for the availability of jobs, relatively fewer female-headed households were receiving welfare. However, the relationship between local employment opportunities and welfare use is complicated. Welfare recipients may be more likely to find jobs in areas rich in employment opportunities; high employment rates may also be associated with a community norm that stigmatizes welfare use, thus reducing participation in AFDC. In an analysis of Chicago's Gautreaux program, which helps low-income black families move from public housing into private-market housing largely in the suburbs, Rosenbaum and Popkin (1991) found that residential location matters. Among the female heads of household involved in the program, those who had moved to suburban areas were more likely to be employed than those who remained in the city. Those who left the inner city stated that it was easier to find employment in the suburbs because there were more jobs there.

Residential mobility as a policy option, however, has limitations (Leadership Conference Education Fund, 1995). Many in the Gautreaux program experienced difficulties adjusting to their new, predominantly white environment and felt isolated from their old social and familial networks. The U.S. Department of Housing and Urban Development has been committed to supporting residential mobility, but Congress has been less supportive. Moreover, joblessness among welfare recipients is not simply the product of uneven spatial distribution of jobs between suburban and inner-city areas. Many suburban areas are primarily residential communities, yet these neighborhoods do not suffer high joblessness because their residents have the means to commute to distant employment.

Urbanization in the United States has produced a metropolitan structure in which long commutes to work are the norm. In 1990 the national average for a one-way commute was 11 miles and 20 minutes (Pisarski, 1992). The average commuting time in the major metropolitan areas of Chicago, Los Angeles, New York, San Francisco, and Washington, DC, was slightly lower than the national average (22.4 minutes versus 28.5 minutes, respectively) (Rossetti & Eversole, 1993). Traveling alone by car is the most widely used means to get to work, accounting for 73 percent of all work commutes in 1990. Even among working poor people, three-fifths drove to work alone in 1990. Public transportation can be an effective alternative, but inner-city residents are likely to rely on poor public transportation, which seriously restricts employment opportunities (Taylor & Ong, 1995).

Access to good transportation enables people to conduct geographically broader job searches, to accept employment offers farther away from home, to improve work attendance, and to keep the commute burden to a reasonable level. Thus, car ownership is an important factor in improving the employment status of welfare recipients. The lack of this resource may help explain the lack of employment stability among recipients. Although a few studies have identified the transportation problems encountered by welfare recipients, no empirical study has focused on the impact of automobile ownership on welfare and work.

This article analyzes a recent survey of AFDC recipients in California in terms of automobile ownership and presents findings for several employment outcomes. Implications for programs and policy are discussed.

METHOD

Data for this study came from a survey sponsored by the California Department of Social Services and conducted by the Survey Research Center at the University of California, Berkeley (Schink & Snow, 1994; Survey Research Center, 1994). The survey, conducted from October 1993 to September 1994, is based on a stratified sample of AFDC-FG recipients from four counties (Alameda County and Los Angeles County are highly urbanized, San Bernardino County is becoming urbanized, and San Joaquin County is agriculturally based) in December 1992, with an oversampling of AFDC-Unemployed Parent cases.

The survey questionnaire contained more than 500 items, including questions on employment, assets (including automobile ownership), and travel to work. The questionnaire was administered over the telephone in English and Spanish. A total of 2,214 interviews were completed. The person interviewed was usually the adult female head of household.

This article examines a subsample of the interviews based on the following criteria: (1) The family was receiving AFDC-FG; (2) the family was headed by a woman age 18 or older who was white, Latina, or African American; and (3) the woman did not have a health problem that prevented her from working. A total of 1,112 women met these criteria (however, some of the following analyses used only a subsample either by design or because of missing data). Twenty-seven percent responded positively to the question, "Do you own a reliable car?"

A dichotomous variable indicated whether a respondent had worked during the month before or the week of the interview (many welfare recipients move frequently between welfare and work; Bane & Ellwood, 1994; Harris, 1993). Additional information was provided by data on the number of hours worked during the past month. Earnings data were total pretax income for that month, and only responses of reported earnings of less than $1,600 were used because higher reported earnings may be caused by recording errors (the maximum allowable earnings for recipients varied by household size and equaled up to 185 percent of the minimum household budget estimated by the state; $1,600 is about the level for a household of five). Hourly wage was estimated from reported monthly hours and earnings, and outliers (less than $1.50 per hour or more than $20 per hour) were deleted. For women with no estimated wage level, hourly wage information for the week of the interview was used when available.

Initial analyses were based on statistical tests of means for respondents with and without an automobile and statistical tests of bivariate distributions. Multivariate analyses were used because the employment outcomes are influenced by factors other than automobile ownership. On the basis of the literature on labor and the effects of public assistance (see Moffitt, 1992), this study used the following independent variables: years of schooling, age, presence of an infant (ages one to two), years on AFDC, race, presence of a health problem that limits type or amount of work, county of residence, and programmatic status. Years on AFDC was calculated for the most recent receiving period. It was expected that the presence of an infant or a health problem would hinder employment searches and the ability to accept some job offers. On the other hand, a greater amount of human capital (years of schooling and age) could lead to more job offers at higher wages, thus increasing the likelihood of employment. (Given the lack of continuous employment for welfare recipients, this study does not use the calculated potential years of labor market experience, which is commonly used in empirical studies of labor market outcomes.)

County of residence captured variations in the local economic base and level of unemployment. Programmatic status indicated whether a respondent was covered by California's 1992 welfare reform legislation or by older provisions (although most AFDC recipients were covered by the legislation, several thousand remained under the old regulations as a control group to evaluate the effects generated by the changes). Respondents covered by the new regulations were classified as belonging to the experimental group. The women in this category would be more likely to work because they had more economic incentives to do so (for example, the tax on earned income was lowered, and the maximum allowable earnings while on welfare was increased).

The weighted results are reported for all analyses, although the unweighted results are consistent. Logit regressions were used to model the dichotomous employment variable:

$$Pr_i\ (WORKED) = e^{\beta X_i}/(1 + e^{\beta X_i})$$

for WORKED $\supset$ (1, 0),

where $e(\ldots)$ is the exponential function, i is the ith observation, X is the vector of independent variables, and β is the vector of estimated coefficients. Linear regressions were used to model hours worked in the past month, monthly earnings, and hourly wages, and the analysis was limited to the observations with nonzero values for the dependent variables. The same set of independent variables was used for both the logit and linear regression models. For earnings and wages, the models were estimated using both the linear and log form of the dependent variable. Although the latter is the standard approach in labor economics, the former is easier to interpret. The estimated coefficients reported in this article are based on the dependent variables reported in dollars, and the findings are consistent with those from the model using the log of the dependent variables.

RESULTS AND DISCUSSION

Automobile Ownership and Employment Outcomes

Welfare recipients who owned an automobile enjoyed a statistically significant advantage in terms of having worked in the past month, mean hours worked in the past month, and mean monthly earnings (Table 14-1). The difference in mean hourly wage between women with and without an automobile was not statistically significant. One interpretation for these results is that

TABLE 14-1

Employment Characteristics of Welfare Recipients Who Owned and Did Not Own an Automobile

Characteristic	Owned Automobile	Did Not Own Automobile	p
Worked during past month (%)	37	23	< .001
Mean hours worked in past month	91.4	64.4	< .001
Mean monthly earnings ($)	370	237	< .001
Mean hourly wage ($)	6.41	5.74	.106

an automobile can provide access and mobility but cannot impart skills needed for higher wages.

An advantage remains even after controlling for the independent variables (Table 14-2). The coefficients were largely consistent with the predicted effects. The presence of an infant was a barrier to holding a job but did not affect the other employment outcomes. Health problems depressed both employment probability and hours worked. The human capital variables—years of schooling and age—increased employment probability and hourly wage. The unreported regression using the log of hourly wages as the dependent variable indicated that each additional year of schooling increased hourly wages by about 3 percent, which is about half the rate for women not receiving welfare (Gronau, 1988; O'Neill, 1985). Each additional year of age increased hourly wages by a little more than 1 percent, which is understandable given the lack of continuous employment and access to on-the-job training for most welfare recipients.

Although the coefficients for the counties indicated that local economic conditions influenced employment outcomes, the estimates were statistically insignificant. These variables may be too crude to capture the labor market conditions most relevant to welfare recipients. Finally, membership in the experimental group was statistically insignificant, perhaps due in part to the relatively brief time that the provisions of welfare reform had been in place before the survey.

Automobile ownership was highly significant in terms of having worked during the past month, hours worked, and monthly earnings. The estimated coefficients for the logit model can be converted into marginal changes in probability by using the following equation:

$$\Delta Pr / \Delta x = C(p(1-p)),$$

where C is the estimated coefficient for variable x and p is the observed employment probability for the total sample. Using this equation, the estimated impact of automobile ownership, after controlling for the other independent factors, is 12 percentage points, which is close to the observed unadjusted difference of 14 percentage points. The coefficients from the linear regressions can be interpreted directly, and they indicate that automobile ownership increased hours worked in the past month by 23 and monthly earnings by $152, which are sizeable and statistically significant differences.

TABLE 14-2

Results of Multivariate Models on Employment Outcomes

Independent Variable	Worked during Past Month	Hours Worked during Past Month	Monthly Earnings	Hourly Wage
Constant	−2.754***	15.3	119	1.27
Experimental group	−0.225	3.8	−18	−.38
Black	0.270	12.2	115*	.05
Latino	0.242	7.4	98	−.86
Owned automobile	0.607***	23.4***	152***	−.02
Years of schooling (¥ 10)	0.096***	14.4	8	2.18***
Non–English speaker	0.170	23.7*	−4	−.50
Years on AFDC (¥ 10)	−0.300	−9.6	−26	.81
Age (¥ 10)	0.246***	8.6**	16	.84***
Health problem	−0.439**	−44.4***	−176***	−.45
Infant present	−0.482***	9.8	29	−.19
Alameda County	−0.112	−24.3*	−62	.08
San Bernardino County	−0.342	0.9	109*	.57
San Joaquin County	0.332	3.9	36	.51
N	1,110	234	254	218
Adjusted r^2	NA	.147	.073	.163

NOTE: AFDC = Aid to Families with Dependent Children. NA = not applicable.
*$p < .10$. **$p < .05$. ***$p < .01$.

The small number of respondents who worked (and who reported monthly earnings and calculated hourly wages) precluded testing the robustness of the positive effects of automobile ownership on three of the four outcome measures; however, the total sample was sufficiently large to examine the effect on employment probability for several subgroups. A more restricted logit model was used that included only the more statistically significant independent variables (automobile ownership, years of schooling, years on AFDC, and presence of infant and county of residence when appropriate). This model was estimated separately for each racial group, county of residence, years of schooling (zero to eight years, nine to 11 years, high school graduate, and some college), presence of an infant, and years on AFDC (zero to two years, three to five years, and six or more years). Of the 16 logit regressions, every coefficient for automobile ownership had a positive sign; 11 were statistically significant at the .10 level, and eight were statistically significant at the .05 level. This indicated a remarkable consistency, and the lack of statistical significance for some models can be attributed to small numbers of observations for particular subsamples.

Automobile ownership had no effect on hourly wage; in fact, the sign is negative, and the associated probability is .965. Moreover, the estimated coefficient for this variable remained insignificant for both a more parsimonious model (using only automobile ownership, years of schooling, years on AFDC, age, and residence in the two urban counties) and a model using the log form of hourly wages. These findings imply that car ownership is not correlated with some unmeasured individual quality that would affect productivity and therefore hourly wages. Consequently, automobile ownership was not likely to increase the hourly incentives for recipients to work. On the other hand, the findings are consistent with the assertion that automobile ownership helps broaden job searches and improves work attendance, which would increase employment probability and hours worked.

Owning an automobile also reduces travel time to work (Table 14-3). Whereas 37 percent of the welfare recipients without automobiles took 45 minutes or more to travel one way to work, only 15 percent who owned automobiles traveled this long. A total daily commute of at least an hour and a half is substantial given that many welfare recipients work only part-time.

Dynamics of Automobile Ownership

Automobile ownership is not causally independent of a welfare recipient's employment status. Unfortunately, it was not possible to estimate a structural model because the data set did not contain information on the required excluded variables and because there were methodological problems estimating simultaneous equations with only dichotomous dependent variables. Ideally, data would be available on geographic and racial variations in the cost of insurance and inheritance of assets from others or from a divorce. Nonetheless, the data do indicate that welfare recipients with the greatest employment and earning potential are best situated to becoming automobile owners.

Both employment probability and owning an automobile increase with years of schooling (Table 14-4). Despite this apparent correlation, a further breakdown of the sample by automobile ownership reveals important differences. The employment rates for the welfare recipients who owned an automobile were consistently lower than for those who did not own an automobile across educational levels, indicating that ownership is not entirely endogenous or merely an epiphenomenon of more fundamental factors that increase the employment rate.

Although automobile ownership and employment are causally linked, it is not likely that they occur simultaneously. It is more likely that one precedes the other, setting up a dynamic and cumulative causal interaction. One possible path is from exogenously produced employment to automobile ownership. The survey data used by this study are not rich enough to test this assertion, even indirectly; however, there is supporting evidence from reverse-commute programs, which are designed to help inner-city residents overcome spatial barriers through subsidized, group-based transportation (Rosenbloom, 1992). Reports from two programs indicated that after securing employment, some participants

TABLE 14-3

Welfare Recipients' One-Way Travel Time to Work

Minutes	Automobile Owner (%)	Automobile Passenger (%)	Other Means (%)
Less than 15	38	52	14
15–25	33	41	27
30–44	14	7	21
More than 45	15	1	37

Note: $\chi^2(6) = 24.92$, $p < .001$.

TABLE 14-4

Employment Outcomes, by Years of Schooling and Years on AFDC

Years	% Who Owned Automobile	% Who Worked in Past Month	% Who Worked	
			Without Automobile	With Automobile
Of schooling				
0–8	14	20	18	31
9–11	22	22	19	32
High school graduate	27	28	25	36
Some college	51	34	26	42
On AFDC				
0–2	27		24	28
3–5	26		23	40
6 or more	30		17	43

NOTE: AFDC = Aid to Families with Dependent Children.

were able to purchase an automobile when it became financially feasible. This action can be interpreted as a sound decision based on a rational calculation in which the derived benefits outweigh the additional costs. This choice is understandable because the reverse-commute programs rely on time-consuming, group-based modes. Moreover, owning an automobile provides better access to a multitude of activities that improve the overall quality of life.

The data presented in Table 14-4 suggest another process in which initial capital endowment leads to greater disparities in employment with length of time on AFDC. The automobile ownership rate is consistent across groups defined by years on AFDC, but the percentage who worked in the past month is not. Among the women with the fewest years on welfare, the employment rate of those without an automobile who worked is nearly identical to the rate for those with one. However, the relative differences increase dramatically with length of time on welfare. There is a slight decline among the women without an automobile, but there is sizeable increase among those with an automobile. Furthermore, these figures may underestimate the differences in employment rates between groups, because owning an automobile appears to be associated with exiting welfare, particularly during the first year or two on welfare (the exit rates are based on 156 usable observations of women who were off AFDC at the time of the interview). Among those who were on welfare for no more than two years and then exited, 42 percent owned an automobile at the time of the interview, compared to 27 percent of those who remained on welfare. Unfortunately, it is not known if the women owned their own cars before exiting.

There are limits to imputing longitudinal dynamics to cross-sectional data, but there is a sound theoretical or conceptual reason for the above-mentioned hypothesis. The higher the direct out-of-pocket costs and the perceived costs of travel time, the less likely a person is to undertake a job search, to secure employment, and to remain on the job. People without an automobile face considerably higher transportation-related barriers; therefore, those facing this high cost could become increasingly discouraged over time.

Although there are systematic and causal relationships between employment and automobile ownership, there are also important exogenous and less-predictable factors beyond the control of individuals. Unexpected disruptions in employment caused by firm or economywide fluctuations and personal crises would undermine the financial ability to maintain ownership. Moreover, automobile owners may suffer from accidents, thefts, and major breakdowns. One could presume that welfare recipients who owned an automobile are more likely to be uninsured than the general population, making a single accident a catastrophic event. Left without reliable transportation, welfare recipients' jobs and later their automobile ownership could be in jeopardy. These shocks in employment and ownership can produce cumulative outcomes that create greater welfare dependency.

CONCLUSION

Certainly, the above analyses can be improved with additional data. The cross-sectional nature of the data is less than ideal for analyzing the underlying dynamic relationship between automobile ownership and employment. What is not known is whether there is a pattern of frequent movement between owning and not owning an automobile, the relationship between fluctuations in ownership and employment, and the role of exogenous shocks. Also, more information is needed about the process of saving that leads to the purchase of an automobile. The analysis of spatial barriers is incomplete because there is no information on the economic base of the local community, the availability and quality of public transportation, and geographic variations in insurance premiums and other relevant costs.

Despite the limitations of the data and analyses, one finding stands out: Owning an automobile is instrumental to employment. This remains true even if ownership is not causally exogenous to employment. This conclusion should not be surprising given that the labor market reflects the sprawling, automobile-oriented structure of modern metropolitan areas. With limited income from welfare benefits, most AFDC recipients are forced to find housing in low-income, inner-city neighborhoods, whose residents suffer from a spatial and skills mismatch. Although the inability to address the simultaneity problem prevents determining whether providing an automobile would have an independent and dramatic impact on employment, the evidence is sufficiently strong to argue for welfare policies and programs that facilitate automobile ownership. The following proposals should not be viewed as new entitlements; instead, the policies and programs, some of which are relatively inexpensive as compared to existing efforts, promote the ultimate goal of economic self-sufficiency.

Existing eligibility requirements for new AFDC recipients prevent an individual from owning an automobile worth more than $1,500. This policy forces a person with a higher-valued automobile to sell or exchange it for a less-valued one before qualifying for benefits. The rationale for this regulation is to force individuals to rely first on their assets; however, an automobile worth $1,500 is not likely to be reliable. A sound policy should recognize that a reliable car of reasonable value is not a luxury but rather an instrument to future employment.

California's welfare reform raised the allowable value for an automobile from $1,500 to $4,500, but this applies only to those already receiving AFDC.

Policymakers should also consider programs that make it easier for welfare recipients to operate and maintain a reliable car, including providing training for do-it-yourself maintenance, referrals to reliable and honest automobile repair services, and access to reasonable insurance. Some assistance should be given to people encountering temporary needs caused by unforeseen disruptions to employment or major automobile repairs, including providing temporary transportation assistance. Improving the continuity of employment and automobile ownership can prevent short-term crises from transforming into prolonged joblessness.

Finally, it is worth reconsidering transportation-based programs to overcome the spatial mismatch with the objective of promoting automobile ownership: "The importance of convenient, fast, and reliable home-to-work transportation should not be overlooked" (Scholfer & Wachs, 1972, p. 56). Such programs should complement other programs, such as skills training and job development. Although public agencies should not give individuals their own cars, these agencies can provide group-based transportation to facilitate job searches and to provide a means of commuting to work during the first several months of employment. The ultimate goal, however, is independence through both employment and automobile ownership.

REFERENCES

Bane, M. J., & Ellwood, D. T. (1994). *Welfare realities: From rhetoric and reform.* Cambridge, MA: Harvard University Press.

Ellwood, D. T. (1988). *Poor support: Poverty in the American family.* New York: Basic Books.

Gronau, R. (1988). Sex-related wage differentials and women's interrupted labor careers—The chicken or the egg? *Journal of Labor Economics, 6,* 277–301.

Harris, K. M. (1993). Work and welfare among single mothers in poverty. *American Journal of Sociology, 99,* 317–352.

Kasarda, J. (1980). The implications of contemporary redistribution trends for national urban policy. *Social Science Quarterly, 61,* 373–400.

Kirschenman, J., & Neckerman, K. M. (1991). "We'd love to hire them, but . . .": The meaning of race for employers. In C. Jencks & P. E. Peterson (Eds.), *The urban underclass* (pp. 203–232). Washington, DC: Brookings Institution.

Leadership Conference Education Fund. (1995, April). *Urban property and civil rights.* Workshop sponsored by the Leadership Conference Education Fund, Greenbriar, WV.

Moffitt, R. (1992). Incentive effects of the U.S. welfare system: A review. *Journal of Economic Literature, 30,* 1–61.

O'Neill, J. (1985). The trend in the male-female wage gap in the United States. *Journal of Labor Economics, 3,* S91–S111.

Ong, P. M. (1993). *The economic base of south central Los Angeles.* Los Angeles: City of Los Angeles, Human Relations Department.

Osterman, P. (1991). Welfare participation in a full employment economy: The impact of neighborhood. *Social Problems, 38,* 475–491.

Pisarski, A. (1992). *Travel behavior issues in the 1990s.* Washington, DC: U.S. Department of Transportation, Office of Highway Information Management.

Rosenbaum, J. E., & Popkin, S. J. (1991). Employment and earnings of low-income blacks who move to middle-class suburbs. In C. Jencks & P. E. Peterson (Eds.), *The urban underclass* (pp. 342–356). Washington, DC: Brookings Institution.

Rosenbloom, S. (1992). *Reverse commute transportation: Emerging provider roles*. Washington, DC: University Research and Training Program.

Rossetti, M., & Eversole, B. (1993). *Journey to work: Trends in the United States and its major metropolitan areas, 1960–1990*. Springfield, VA: National Technical Information Service.

Schink, W., & Snow, B. (1994). *Demonstration project overview*. Berkeley: University of California and California Department of Social Services.

Scholfer, J., & Wachs, M. (1972). *Job accessibility for the unemployed: An analysis of public transportation in Chicago*. Chicago: Mayor's Committee for Economic and Cultural Development of Chicago.

Survey Research Center. (1994). *California Work Pays demonstration project survey: English/Spanish interviews, 1993–1994 preliminary version codebook*. Berkeley: University of California, Author.

Taylor, D. T., & Ong, P. M. (1995). Spatial mismatch or automobile mismatch? An examination of race, residence, and commuting in the U.S. metropolitan areas. *Urban Studies, 32,* 1453–1473.

U.S. House of Representatives, Committee on Ways and Means. (1993, July 7). *Overview of entitlement programs*. Washington, DC: U.S. Government Printing Office.

This chapter was originally published in the December 1996 issue of Social Work Research, *vol. 20, pp. 255–262.*

Part III

CHILDREN AND FAMILIES

15 The New Politics of Child and Family Policies

Sheila B. Kamerman

Although the details are not yet known, three monumental legislative changes of the 104th Congress will have major implications for social policies and programs affecting children and their families, especially those with very low or modest incomes. Regardless of whether these changes constitute a historic watershed or represent short-term developments that will be reversed or significantly modified within a few years, they constitute a dramatic shift in the premises underlying public child and family policies and the terms of public debate.

The first of these changes is the likely enactment of the most significant cuts in federal spending for low-income children and families that the country has ever experienced. The goal of eliminating the federal budget deficit over the next seven years has taken precedence over almost all social protection goals. Whether the cuts occur as reductions in projected growth or decreases in direct funding, they probably will be tied to the proposed elimination of the entitlement status of several programs: Aid to Families with Dependent Children (AFDC), Medicaid, and possibly the Food Stamp program. These caps, which would not take account of inflation or demographic changes (or would do so only in part), will in effect reduce actual dollars available. Depending on what figures are used, funding for the major social programs benefiting low-income children and their families is expected to be 25 percent to 30 percent less in 2002 than it would have been if existing programs were left unchanged (Ellwood & Gold, 1995). Because the cuts are "backloaded" (that is, they increase over time), the effects will be especially severe in the first years of the next century.

The second major change is what has been termed "the devolution revolution" (Nathan, 1995), whereby primary responsibility for social protection of low-income children and their families is transferred from the federal government to state and local governments. Through the device of block grants, federal social programs would be turned into funding streams for the states to use largely as they see fit within general program categories (financial assistance and health care) and with only limited constraints. In turn, the states get an opportunity to be creative and innovative in their use of these funds and in the programming options open to them.

The third change is a significant philosophical shift in some quarters in the premises underlying social protection policies. In a process that has been under way for several decades, the problem of poverty has been largely redefined by some groups in Congress and elsewhere in society from an unfortunate condition resulting from external social and economic factors to a problem that results mostly from the immoral and irresponsible behavior of individuals. And the solution has been transformed, for those who hold such views, from a search for effective social policies to an emphasis on individual change. Indeed, to some extent, the current concern with illegitimacy can be explained as a concern about women having children whom they cannot support financially.

The elimination of the entitlement status of the major social benefits and the return to a pre-New Deal discretionary status may be interpreted as almost a full return to late-19th-century social welfare policies. The emphasis on work reminds some observers of the moral "work tests" (tests to see if someone really wanted to work) of the 19th century but is a sensible response to social change for others (deSchweinitz, 1943). The nature of particular work programs reflects these differences. Legislators with a "remoralization" agenda would, for example, combine behavioral rules such as a family size cap with work rules.

Even if the expected social policy changes are not as draconian as expected, it is probable that people who use social benefits and services will have fewer guarantees than they have had for more than 30 years, that states will have far more discretion and flexibility in setting child and family policies than has been the case, that there will be few requirements for accountability to the federal government, and that states will have fewer resources than they have had for the past 20 years. Moreover, states are likely to find themselves in a new policy environment with little federal support and no additional federal funds to carry out planning, capacity building, community outreach, and monitoring and tracking of outcomes. Voluntary sector leaders and entrepreneurs and child advocates will encounter greater difficulties in carrying out their programs. And most important, social protection for the most vulnerable citizens will be severely constrained.

Once these policy changes are in place, many states will already have established or will be in the process of installing alternative programs. Some may try to glide into the new pattern by keeping their existing programs, albeit at lower benefit levels, by curtailing eligibility, or by reducing the duration of benefits. In effect, they may choose to sustain what they now have but provide less to fewer people, perhaps for briefer periods. Others, however, may decide to eliminate what is now in place and, starting with a tabula rasa, to invent a new social protection system for children and families. Many states probably will adopt positions somewhere in between.

This article discusses some preliminary ideas on a program-by-program basis, recognizing at the outset that only the basic outline of proposed policy changes is in place. The details are not yet fixed, and changes in each of the major policy domains have consequences for the others. The objective is to identify alternative paths worth exploring in what will be the new domains of welfare, health care, child care, child nutrition, and child welfare. The primary goal is to provide social work professionals—policy scholars, practitioners, advocates, and educators—with knowledge that can help them shape their responses to these changes. The ultimate goal is to minimize harm to children and maximize child and family well-being. Social workers will want to participate in the large task ahead—helping and influencing states as they exercise their options. There is a similarly demanding task of helping voluntary sector leaders and community advocates adapt to a new policy environment.

AID TO FAMILIES WITH DEPENDENT CHILDREN

AFDC, Title IV-A of the Social Security Act, is the program usually referred to as "welfare"; it is the means-tested cash benefit program providing grants to aid financially needy children and their parents or caretakers, overwhelmingly their mothers. In 1993, more than 14 million individuals were receiving AFDC, including 9.5 million children and 5 million families. AFDC is an entitlement program in that those who qualify have a legally enforceable right to benefits. In addition, unlimited federal matching funds are authorized in response to state expenditures to cover benefit and administrative costs as well as the costs of child care for young children (three years and older) of recipients who are required to work or study.

AFDC is financed through a combination of federal, state, and sometimes local payments. It is not indexed, so the real value of AFDC benefits declined by 43 percent between 1970 and 1993 (U.S. House of Representatives, 1994). (And even when coupled with food stamps, which are indexed, the package has been cut by almost 30 percent.) Although AFDC coupled with food stamps has been ineffective in reducing the child poverty rates since 1983, these two benefits have had a significant effect on reducing the poverty gap—the gap between family income and the poverty threshold. Since 1979 AFDC and food stamps together have reduced the poverty gap by 41 percent to 45 percent each year for recipient families.

Congressional Proposals

The primary objectives of the proposed new assistance program, Temporary Assistance to Needy Families (TANF), as stated in several congressional initiatives (H.R. 4, S. 1795) are to help needy families with minor children, to provide job preparation and employment opportunities for these families, and to reduce the rate of out-of-wedlock pregnancies and births. Federal funding is proposed at about $16 billion annually (Burke, 1995, 1996). States are given some partial financial protection against population growth but none against recession or increased unemployment, and the funding cuts incorporated into the conference bill are substantially deeper than those contained in the Senate bill.

The core provisions of TANF include the following:

- repealing AFDC, the Job Opportunities and Basic Skills Training (JOBS) program, emergency assistance, and the 1988 provision in Medicaid legislation that limits AFDC benefit reduction and replacing them with fixed block grants to states for TANF
- eliminating the entitlement status of cash assistance
- conditioning receipt of TANF benefits after two years on work and requiring specified rates of participation in work activities by TANF families by that time

- limiting lifetime receipt of TANF to a maximum of five years
- permitting states to pay families moving into the state from a state paying lower benefits at the same level as the lower-benefit state for up to one year
- placing severe restrictions on legal immigrants' ability to qualify for benefits
- repealing the $50 disregard from child support payments
- permitting the transfer of up to 30 percent of assistance funds to the child care block grant (Burke, 1996; Kamerman & Kahn, 1996).

The major differences between the House and Senate bills are that the House bill excludes unwed mothers under 18 and their children and any additional child born to a woman receiving TANF, whereas the Senate bill is permissive with regard to these provisions; the conference bill is closer to the Senate version. The Senate bill requires states to maintain their expenditures for TANF at a level equal to 80 percent of their prior contribution to AFDC, but the House bill does not; the conference bill sets the requirement at 75 percent and as low as 67 percent under certain circumstances. The conference bill (H.R. 3507, S. 1795) reduces the proportion of families that states can exempt from the five-year time limit because of hardship from the Senate-proposed 20 percent to 15 percent.

In return for the states' loss of unlimited matching funds and the constraints listed earlier, the states gain significantly in flexibility. They can set eligibility criteria, benefit levels, benefit duration (up to the maximum specified in the law), income and asset limits, and rules about earnings as they wish. And they can restructure the administrative organization of their assistance programs, keeping them autonomous and freestanding, linking them with employment and training programs, or linking them with social services and child care. If they deem it desirable or, in contrast, if they find the process difficult, they can enact miniature versions of the federal legislation and channel block grants to their local governments, leaving it to them to cope with poverty and assistance problems at the community level.

Possible State Actions

Given the federal cuts that will accompany the block grants, only states willing to add to their current AFDC expenditures or states with a rapidly improving job picture will avoid facing a lower program budget. No such states have been identified. State policymakers would have the choice of cutting caseloads, cutting levels of aid, or limiting benefit duration even further, and some may decide to accept penalties because they do not achieve the required work participation rates.

As an alternative, states may follow Americans' historical preference for in-kind benefits over cash by substituting higher health care and child care benefits (and increasing food stamp use, if outside the block grants). Indeed, some states are actively proposing this. The availability of food stamps as an entitlement will be critical if assistance recipients are to have any protection.

Given the decline in AFDC caseloads in many states over the past year, some states assume that they can phase in any changes slowly. Some other states are simply imposing significant cuts in all social programs on the assumption that adaptation and readjustments can be made once changes are in place. Still others have instituted significant new programs. Indeed, some states—including Iowa, Michigan, Minnesota, Vermont, and Wisconsin—have already begun the change process through their AFDC waiver experiments; these states have been given waivers from existing regulations by the U.S. Department of Health and Human Services so that they can redesign their programs (Greenberg, 1996). These states have launched programs that are worth closer examination and monitoring.

A major focus of most new initiatives and waiver experiments is an emphasis on work (Greenberg, 1996). Some set time limits for receipt of welfare or for beginning to work, some increase earnings disregards and thus create stronger work incentives, some eliminate exemptions from work requirements that previously existed (for example, by defining women with infants as employable). Some states are considering extending eligibility for benefits beyond welfare recipients in an effort to avoid the creation of new inequities and resentments among low-income working people.

None of the proposed programs is cheap, however. At the other end of the range of state responses, a report of the proposed Mississippi program indicates how limited some state responses are likely to be. For example, the AFDC benefit in Mississippi is $120 a month for a family of three (less than one-fourth of the median benefit in 1993), with a $24 a month addition for another child (Sack, 1995). The state would eliminate that supplement for a child born to a mother already receiving AFDC.

Peterson (1995, 1996) argued that there is a strong likelihood of a "race to the bottom" across the states. He found that from 1976 to 1989, AFDC benefits were cut $19 and Medicaid benefits decreased $10 per family for every year that a state's benefits exceeded that of the contiguous state's average by $100. Illustrating this point, Governor George Pataki of New York announced that the state's AFDC benefits would be cut by 26 percent to match the benefit level of its neighboring state, New Jersey (Dao, 1995; Levy, 1995). Nonetheless, benefit values still vary enormously across states, and states like Wisconsin and Minnesota are projecting potentially generous health care plans.

MEDICAID AND HEALTH CARE

Medicaid has become an increasingly central program for children and their families. In 1992, 25 percent of all children, including almost three-quarters of low-income children under age six and 60 percent of low-income children aged six to 18, were covered by Medicaid. Medicaid now is the largest children's program, and $78 billion, more than half of these funds, are federal (U.S. House of Representatives, 1994).

Children and their families constitute more than 70 percent of the total of Medicaid beneficiaries but account for only 30 percent of total expenditures ($132 billion in 1993) (Mann, 1995; University of Wisconsin, 1996). Children alone constitute almost half of Medicaid recipients (49 percent) but account for only 16 percent of expenditures. Over one-third of all births are paid for by Medicaid, as are the medical costs of one-third of infants and toddlers.

More than half of the children on Medicaid live in families with working parents. According to the U.S. Census Bureau (1995), the proportion of children covered under employer-provided private health insurance declined from 63.2 to 57.6 percent between 1989 and 1993, and 90 percent of uninsured children had working parents or caretakers. Compared with children covered by private health insurance, uninsured children are less likely to receive early preventive health care services, including routine childhood immunizations, and are more likely to be treated in a hospital emergency room when a health problem becomes a crisis.

As employers have downsized medical coverage or dropped dependent coverage, Medicaid has picked up the slack. Between 1989 and 1993, Medicaid increased its coverage of children under 18 years old by 54 percent; the number of children covered rose from 8.9 million to 13.8 million, largely because of federal mandates for the coverage of low-income children (Mann, 1995; University of Wisconsin, 1996).

Medicaid spending has increased dramatically. The federal share quadrupled during the 1980s and now constitutes 40 percent of all federal grants to state and local governments. The projected growth of Medicaid expenditures is estimated at 11 percent a year over the next seven years (University of Wisconsin, 1996)—the "crisis" spurring the cuts. Medicaid has become a major financial burden for states and localities, accounting for 20 percent of average state expenditures.

There was periodic talk of federalization long before the *Contract with America* (Republican National Committee, 1994) chose the alternative of block-granting, perhaps without entitlement. If Medicaid funding is capped and frozen and if employer-provided health insurance for children continues to decline at the rate of about 1 percent a year, the achievements brought about by the congressionally mandated Medicaid enhancements of the Reagan and Bush years will be reversed (Mann, 1995). Much will depend on the final shape of the Medicaid legislation, because eight times the funds of AFDC are involved, and Medicaid has met many social services costs in addition to strict medical care.

Congressional Proposals

To save about $170 billion (proposed in the budget reconciliation bill vetoed by President Clinton) between 1995 and 2002, the congressional proposals (H.R. 4) would give each state a reduced sum of money annually to provide health care for its low-income citizens and would allow each state to decide what benefits to offer and who would qualify (Burke, 1995, 1996). The current mandates—to cover all low-income children by phasing in coverage beginning with those born in 1983, to cover all children under age six in families with incomes up to 133 percent of the poverty threshold, and to extend Medicaid coverage for one year to families leaving AFDC for jobs—would be eliminated in the House bill; the Senate bill would preserve the coverage currently available to children under 12 and pregnant women. Although the projected cuts are in fact reductions in the rate of growth between 1995 and 2002 (5 percent growth instead of the projected 11 percent), the net effect is that by 2002 the average federal payment would be about 30 percent lower than it would have been if the program had continued in its present form.

Moreover, although the conference bill includes federal standards for nursing homes and health care coverage for pregnant women, children aged 12 and under, and low-income people with disabilities, it does not provide health care for adolescents and does not specify a minimum package of medical services that states must offer.

Possible State Actions

Focusing only on the aspects of Medicaid involving children and their families, the following discussion offers a brief summary of some possibilities. The theory underlying the Medicaid block grant is that, in addition to limiting the increase in federal expenditures for Medicaid and therefore limiting the federal contribution if health care costs rise more rapidly than anticipated, the block grant provides greater flexibility. With more flexibility in designing and administering Medicaid, according to the theory, the states would institute so many efficiencies and innovations that they would not miss the federal dollars.

There are several alternative paths for states to choose if they reorganize their Medicaid systems or supplement their Medicaid funding with additional public or private funds. These include a managed care system for Medicaid, a maternal and child health care system, and a supplementary child health insurance or health care program using public or private funds or both (National Governors' Association [NGA], 1995).

Much media attention has featured the adoption of a managed care system to provide Medicaid coverage at a known cost, provoking anxieties about coverage and quality. New York's problems in implementing such a plan—in particular, the inability to move large numbers of people into health maintenance organizations (HMOs) and the substandard care provided at some HMOs—are evidence of the potential downside. In contrast, Hawaii and Oregon, among others, offer examples of a more positive experience in reforming their health care delivery systems.

An alternative approach would be to establish a statewide maternal and child health prevention and primary care system. A state could package its maternal and child health care block grant, community neighborhood and migrant health centers funds, and the portion of its Medicaid budget over which it might have a measure of control to create a statewide network of centers for primary care. These centers would offer prenatal care; regular infant, toddler, and preschooler checkups and immunizations; outreach; and health visits. Specialist services for Medicaid families could then be covered under major medical health insurance policies funded in various ways.

Still another option is to build on the delinking of Medicaid from AFDC begun in 1989. In recent years, with federal matching support, some states have established expanded Medicaid programs to cover child health care, and others, including Minnesota, Pennsylvania, and Washington, have established new public child health insurance programs. Still others (for example, Colorado and Florida) have established new private child health insurance or mixed public and private programs. One important result of these efforts has been significantly improved child health outcomes. By delinking general assistance and

Medicaid, states could choose to do what several states have proposed—namely to cover all low- or modest-income children and their families regardless of enrollment in AFDC or TANF. Providing access to low-income working families with no employment-related health insurance would provide an essential form of social protection while creating a work incentive and would eliminate the work disincentive created under AFDC and Medicaid for low-skilled women.

Planning cannot go very far until it is clear how state Medicaid block grants will be determined, how they will be divided among user categories, and just what (if any) mandates will come with the block grants to create "semi-entitlements." Will there be a straight block grant to the states or the more protective per capita cap as proposed by both the president and the NGA that would allow funding to grow?

Even if Medicaid remains an entitlement program, it is likely to experience significant funding cuts, and states will probably be given more flexibility in designing variations. It is particularly important that state officials be reminded that children are a very inexpensive group to cover with health insurance or health care and that the payoff is significant. Most programs that have already been established include low-cost preventive health services such as well-child visits and immunizations in their benefits packages. These services not only are important in and of themselves, but also may save additional dollars in acute care services later.

Finally, regardless of future policy changes, the new innovative state child health programs will build on the foundation of the existing Medicaid program and its funding. If these funds are constrained and existing Medicaid coverage curtailed, the numbers who apply for the new state programs are likely to increase, and the costs of the program will rise accordingly.

CHILD CARE

In 1993 almost 60 percent of women with young children under age six and 55 percent with children under age three were in the labor force. Consequently, the demand for child care services has increased dramatically over the past 15 years (Blank, 1996; Children's Defense Fund, 1995; National Association for the Education of Young Children, 1995; Spar, 1995; U.S. House of Representatives, 1994). Since enactment of the Family Support Act of 1988 (P.L. 100-485), women with children aged three and older have been expected to be available for work provided they have access to child care. Under current law, three child care programs are authorized as part of AFDC: AFDC child care, transitional child care, and at-risk child care (U.S. House of Representatives, 1994).

A recent U.S. Census Bureau study (Casper, Hawkins, & O'Connell, 1994) found that low-income families who paid for their preschool-aged children's child care spent 26 percent of their income on such care in 1991, more than in 1990, when comparable families spent 22 percent (Clark & Berkowitz, 1995), but almost four times the portion of income spent by nonpoor families. Almost half the families (46 percent) receiving AFDC, food stamps, general assistance, or benefits from the Special Supplemental Food Program for Women, Infants, and Children (WIC) paid for child care, compared with 57 percent of those not receiving benefits, and they spent an average of $50 a week on child care, compared with $78 spent by those not receiving benefits (U.S. Bureau of the Census, 1995).

Congressional Proposals

Proposed federal child care expenditures in fiscal year 1995 included $900 million for the Child Care and Development Block Grant (CCDBG), $542 million for AFDC child care, $154 million for transitional child care, and $300 million for at-risk child care, a total of almost $2 billion—a substantial increase from child care expenditures in 1990, before almost all these programs were put in place (Clark & Berkowitz, 1995). The Dependent Care Tax Credit for middle- and upper-income working families would almost double this ($3.8 billion), and Head Start would add another $3.4 billion, an almost 50 percent increase since 1990 in constant 1995 dollars. Title XX of the Social Security Act would provide about another $600 million for child care. At this writing, the Child and Dependent Tax Credit appeared untouched, Head Start spending would be cut modestly, and Title XX was expected to be cut by 20 percent (about $3 billion over five years) (Spar, 1995).

The conference bill, like the Senate version of TANF, would define women with children who are one year old and older as employable, but the House bill would permit states to require a single mother to find employment from the time her baby is only 13 weeks old (Spar, 1995). Neither bill provides any guarantee of child care availability or any provision for protecting child care quality. Moreover, although more low-income mothers would be required to work, federal child care funding for low-income families would be cut.

The CCDBG would subsidize child care for low-income working families, including those in which the parents are in training or education programs. The conference bill creates a single child care program (to be run by the lead state agency operating the CCDBG) with two funding streams totaling $17 billion over seven years (Spar, 1995). One of the funding streams is a capped entitlement funded at $10 billion over seven years, and the other is a discretionary program funded at $7 billion over seven years. Overall, funding levels would be about $2 billion less than in the Senate bill (Child Care Action Campaign, 1995a, 1995b). (A subsequent proposal offered by the NGA [1995] would add $4 billion more for child care.)

Under the current law, child care is guaranteed for AFDC recipients who are working or participating in an approved training or education program and for one year for those leaving AFDC for a job. The conference bill does not guarantee assistance recipients child care and expects parents with young children to work a 35-hour week instead of the 20 hours a week required in the Senate bill. However, the conference bill would not permit a reduction or termination of benefits to a single custodial parent of a child under age six if child care were unavailable. Whether quality standards of child care would be imposed and what those standards would be are not clear.

The increased expectations about work are likely to lead to greater demand for child care. An analysis of the impact on New York City of proposed higher work requirements for AFDC beneficiaries found that public expenditures for child care would need to increase fivefold if just one-third of all AFDC mothers (including those with children under age three) were required to take jobs; expenditures would be far higher if the proportion expected to work were the proposed 80 percent or 85 percent (Kobin, Waldfogel, & Kamerman, 1996).

Nationally, in 1994, about 56 percent of AFDC adults were classified as exempt from work requirements (because they had a child under age three, were incapacitated, or cared for an incapacitated family member). Yet even among the 44 percent considered employable, only 13 percent were working (Kobin et al., 1996). Stretching the proposed funds to pay for more child care is likely to lead to still greater use of custodial rather than developmentally oriented child care, with likely negative consequences. The risk of abuse is also likely to rise. It may be some time before the negative effects are visible; however, given the requirement in some states for women with babies to work (in Michigan, just a few weeks after birth), the effects may show up sooner.

Possible State Actions

For states expecting women with very young children to have a job by the time their youngest child is two—and even younger—availability of child care will be critical. Access to care will be especially important for low-income working people. How can states address the issue of availability?

States can either supplement the federal funds for child care or fail to meet the requirements for getting welfare mothers with very young children into the workforce (and pay the penalty but reduce expenditures for assistance-related child care). They can exclude mothers with children under age one or even age two (if they began to receive assistance only after their babies were born) from the work requirements and so reduce demand for expensive infant and toddler care. States could even choose to lower assistance benefits but invest more in child care.

Beyond this, states can reduce the child care cost level they are prepared to cover or raise parent copayments. States could give up "child development" standards and instead cover, as some have suggested, the maximum amount of unregulated, low-standard babysitter child care in support of a major work program thrust or public workfare policy. The rationale would be that children must pay this price to give their mothers a "push" into self-sufficiency or that current programs, with some major exceptions, are already of poor quality (Brown, 1996; Greenberg, 1996).

Finally, states could follow the continental European example and reorganize their child care system, placing it under public education auspices and expanding prekindergarten programs delivered at or through primary school for two-, three-, and four-year-olds with wraparound services for children whose mothers work longer or later hours. This program, of course, would require an infusion of state funds but from a different stream, namely education, and would be an investment in a universal strategy.

FOOD STAMPS AND CHILD NUTRITION

The Food Stamp program is intertwined with welfare and the proposed TANF program because recipients are primarily welfare beneficiaries. About 42 percent of food stamp recipients have no income other than AFDC, 91 percent have incomes below the poverty threshold, and 61 percent are children (U.S. House of Representatives, 1994). Families with children receive 82 percent of all food stamp benefits. Food stamps reduce the poverty rate of children and their families by about 15 percent, almost as much as the 18 percent reduction effected by AFDC and Supplemental Security Income (SSI) (U.S. House of Representatives, 1994). The Food Stamp program has been an entitlement program, with federal funding provided according to needs.

Congressional Proposals

Although the conference bill does not mandate block-granting the Food Stamp program, it does make dramatic changes in its structure, imposes draconian cuts on funding, and provides an opportunity for states to choose a block grant option if at least 80 percent of the funds go to food aid and if they have a statewide electronic benefit system. The Senate and House bills also greatly expand states' administrative flexibility and their ability to operate a simplified program for assistance recipients and to coordinate administrative procedures with TANF. Work rules are made more stringent, the basic guarantee is lowered, and more constraints are placed on legal immigrants (Richardson, 1995).

In the conference bill, child nutrition funds would be included in a block grant with funding constraints and targeted far more toward very low-income children. Funding would be reduced by $2 billion more than was contained in the Senate bill (from $8.3 billion over seven years to a proposed $6 billion). Funding would be cut for meal subsidies in family day care homes, and the inflation index would be suspended for subsidies going to higher-income families (Congressional Research Service, 1995; Richardson, 1995).

Effects on State Programs

Given significantly lower federal subsidies, will family day care homes drop out of the program and go underground to avoid the licensing and tax-paying requirements on which federal food subsidies are now contingent? States electing to block grant the Food Stamp program would have their funding frozen at the level of 1994 expenditures, and no adjustments would be made if there were a recession, if a state's population increased, or if food prices rose (Richardson, 1995).

If the states opted for a block grant, they could choose to reduce benefit levels or restrict eligibility. States that chose the block grant would see the funds go directly to the state (a short-sighted if superficially attractive option), whereas the states maintaining the entitlement would find more money going directly to very low-income recipients.

For child welfare advocates, the Food Stamp program may be the only safety net left, and it is likely to become increasingly important in the new social policy environment. Indeed, if the entitlement is preserved, some states that choose to lower TANF benefits will be able to use food stamps to absorb 30 percent of the cuts and not deprive TANF recipients as much.

SUPPLEMENTAL SECURITY INCOME

Since the 1990 Supreme Court decision in *Sullivan v. Zebley*, which mandated child-specific functional assessments and reversed a policy under which children were being denied assistance under adult criteria, there has been an explosion of child disability cases under SSI (now totaling over 1 million) (Parrott, 1995). The child component of SSI has become largely an income support program for low-income families of children with mental retardation and other mental disorders, with diseases of the nervous system, and with congenital abnormalities. Except in the rare instances of adequate parental insurance, SSI also pays all hospital costs of premature and low-birthweight babies defined as disabled because of multiple problems. Eligibility continues for a year without a means test (Parrott, 1995).

In a move to cut costs and deal with other SSI problems (for example, benefits to adult alcoholics and substance abusers), the conference bill would restrict eligibility for SSI by narrowing the types of disabilities that would enable a child to qualify, thus reducing expenditures (Parrott, 1995). Moreover, the bill would reduce SSI benefit levels for children by about 25 percent over the next seven years.

At present SSI is an important alternative for families with children who qualify. Under the new proposals, some of these children would be ineligible. There could also be major spillover effects on special education and early intervention programs. State options are unclear as yet.

CHILD WELFARE

Congressional Proposals

Although the Senate bill retained the provisions of the Adoption Assistance and Child Welfare Act of 1980 (P.L. 96-272, Title IV-E of the Social Security Act) as an entitlement, the conference bill does so only in part. Foster care maintenance payments (payments that cover the living expenses of foster children) remain an entitlement, but preventive services and administrative expenses (including funds for research and training, data processing, and the recruitment and training of staff) are included in a proposed block grant (H.R. 3507, S. 1795).

Effects on State Programs

If women are forced off assistance without jobs and subsidized child care, they could be accused of neglect and caught up in the child protection system. States in which the need for child protection resources increases substantially would either have to raise state spending or scale back services for abused and neglected children. Alternatively, states could gear up for an "institutionalization" alternative (mother–child group homes), a costly choice. Or homeless shelters could be confronted with an increase in demand by single mothers and their children.

CROSS-CUTTING ISSUES

Clearly, state and local planners will need to devote attention to cross-cutting issues, no matter which programs they select. Social work planners and policy analysts need to participate in the process of identifying options and influencing decisions.

The first issue is the allocation of scarcer and diminishing resources. Should states rearrange and recombine funding streams and, if so, on what principles? Many service reformers have long urged the advantages of decategorization (pooling categorical funds to integrate services). On what basis should allocations be committed? To what extent should funding cuts be balanced by lowering per capita expenditures and grants and by changing the basis (or duration) of eligibility to decrease caseloads?

Second, should jurisdictions begin with the restructuring of specific programs (for example, welfare, food stamps, employment, child care, child health, child nutrition, or child welfare) and their interrelationships and then deploy the available resources? Wisconsin and Minnesota, for example, have chosen to subsume or link their cash assistance program with their employment services (Kamerman & Kahn, 1996). Some states are also considering policies that go beyond welfare recipients and include low-income working people in jobs, health care, and child care programs. Others may choose to relink cash assistance with social services (casework services), although the absence of a federal match and the proposed cut in Title XX (the Social Services Block Grant) funds will certainly make it harder to do. Obviously, basic policy orientation and philosophies will be involved in considering or rejecting any proposal. States may want to break out of traditional programming patterns, however.

Third, intrastate devolution also belongs on the immediate agenda. The Congress and the governors are preoccupied with undoing some of the developments in federal–state relations of the past 60 years. But periodically in U.S. history, and certainly in every decade since the 1960s, an effort has been made to devolve resources, power, or initiatives to local communities or neighborhoods, variously defined as community action, model cities, community development block grants, and empowerment zones. States may wish to seize the opportunity of the current devolution to reconsider their relationships to "lower" tiers and how such relationships should affect their general strategies.

Fourth, information systems will require early redesign to sustain either planned resource reallocation or major restructuring of programs and their administrative apparatus, as well as future analysis of the effects.

Fifth, reorganized program governance and administration may also be possible. Advocates of reshaped priorities (more prevention) and services integration have long bemoaned the obstacles created by federal legislation and mandates. Thus far, efforts at integrating child and family social services have been implemented without attention to the welfare waiver initiatives. Could this change? Is this a time of opportunity?

Sixth, although this article has concentrated on federal-state entitlement programs and on potential state-locality actions to build on new flexibility or to cope with effects of cuts, the biggest impact on all social welfare programs will probably be from the overall decreases in federal appropriations. A full list of cuts will become apparent after appropriation bills are passed and budget reconciliation is completed. Will the supplementation of the incomes of low-income working people ("make work pay") by means of the Earned Income Tax Credit be cut as much as has been proposed?

Finally, preparing for interactive and spillover effects will be an essential component of each state's or locality's planning. It will be impossible to consider what to do about any one program without considering interactions. As put by Professor Donald F. Kettl, University of Wisconsin (cited in Pear, 1995),

> Welfare reform will not work unless it is supported by job training programs. Job training will not work unless trainees can obtain child care for their children and transportation to both training and work. And welfare recipients will have little incentive to move from welfare to work unless their children receive health care. The governors and state legislatures will not only have to figure out how to manage these programs. They will have to learn to dance the intricate minuet connecting them. (p. 3)

Any initiative with regard to assistance benefits, eligibility, or duration will have consequences for child care; any curtailment of access to child care will create barriers to work; any changes in the Food Stamp program will have consequences for welfare; and any failure to delink Medicaid from welfare will also result in reciprocal effects. These systems are interrelated and must be monitored from that perspective. No matter what the specifics are, states are likely to be confronted with painful choices between basic cash assistance, health care, child care, child protection, and child nutrition.

Whatever new policies are enacted, there will surely be cuts in funding. Any significant reduction in public funding for social protection will significantly increase the numbers of poor and vulnerable people and in turn will increase the flow of needy consumers to the voluntary agencies. Which people with what problems will come to them? How can these agencies survive when public funding is cut? What will happen to people seeking help when neither public nor private agencies have the resources to respond?

IMPLICATIONS FOR SOCIAL WORK

No matter what their opinions are about the proposed changes in federal social policy, public officials and voluntary-sector leaders will want to maximize the potentials of the new flexibilities, whether through devolution and block grants, waivers, or amendments to the entitlement programs and concomitant increases in state discretion. They must also begin to confront and cope with newly created funding shortfalls, obstacles, and problems for their services and clients. Social workers should play an active and visible role in the process. Planning, implementation, and advocacy must begin at once if jurisdictions and social agencies are to avoid difficulties or loss of opportunities.

If social workers are to play a role, they must first be informed. NASW and other professional organizations in which social workers participate need to monitor legislative developments at national and state levels and make this information available to their colleagues on a regular and timely basis. Special services on the Internet, such as HandsNet, can play an important role as well. Social workers need to be aware of the leading policy research, analysis, and advocacy organizations.

As states become increasingly important players, practitioners and advocates must add specific state-level information to their national picture. Because the child poverty rate is especially high in urban areas (particularly in the very large cities of New York, Los Angeles, Miami, and Chicago), and because the Congress appears insensitive to the needs of cities, monitoring developments and the consequences for children in cities is especially important. Given the slowdown in the legislative process at the close of 1995 and in early 1996, it remains unclear precisely what to expect from Congress. This insecurity and potential volatility make regular and ongoing monitoring of developments even more critical as the year unfolds.

Second, child advocates must speak with a common voice "to work together to protect children's well-being, not just one set of services," according to Eve Brooks, president of the National Association of Children's Advocates (personal communication, July 27, 1995). Otherwise, "advocates may end up successfully protecting funds for child care, for example, but at the expense of funds for child health care" or welfare. Social work child advocates need to keep this principle in mind as they move to lobby on issues of particular concern, and they need to keep the big picture in view all the time. For social work child advocates confronting the proposed changes, protecting the entitlement status of the major programs should be the primary focus—in particular, Medicaid and the Food Stamp program, then AFDC, then child welfare. These constitute the child and family policy infrastructure in this country, the critical foundation on which all other policies depend.

Third, in advocating against block grants or against funding cuts, social workers must be ready to support their criticisms with data and to propose viable alternatives. This requires analyses of the effects of the proposed initiatives and data on how they would hurt children as well as detailed plans of alternative proposals including their costs and benefits. The analysis by the Office of Management and Budget, the U.S. Department of Health and Human Services, and other agencies (1995) of the effect of the proposed welfare changes on child poverty and the finding that the conference bill would add more than 1 million children to the numbers now in poverty had a major influence on slowing down the congressional process and the Republican initiatives. When similar changes are proposed in the states, social workers and other child advocates need to confront the public with comparable data on the increase in child poverty, in child morbidity, in malnutrition, in incidents of child abuse, or in school failure. Up-to-date information, analytic capacity, and quantitative skills will become especially important.

Fourth, social work researchers should become involved in state and local as well as national monitoring efforts, paying particular attention to quantifying effects on children and families, tracking children across systems, and comparing child outcomes across jurisdictions.

Fifth, social workers, along with others concerned with the well-being of children and families, must begin to plan for new systems and programs that can be developed within the current political and social context. It will be easiest to move toward new systems in areas where all parents, not just low-income parents, are facing the same problems, such as health care and health insurance. In short, social workers should target not only welfare recipients but also low-income working people and families with children and others who need public aid. Additional opportunities could emerge with regard to child care, family preservation and support, and the tax system. In time the nation should again be able to turn to the tax system for more creative support, for example, in the form of a refundable child tax credit.

Finally, social work practitioners need to remember that they are the eyes and ears of the profession. If the worst occurs and some or all of the entitlement programs are eliminated and funding is cut, social work practitioners will be among the first professionals to see the effects on children and their families. Although numbers tell an important story, it is the personal stories of individuals in their daily lives that often make the difference. No profession has the access to these stories that social workers have. Social workers must then, as always, be a voice for children.

REFERENCES

Adoption Assistance and Child Welfare Act of 1980, P.L. 96-272, 94 Stat. 500.

Blank, H. (1996). *The welfare reform debate: Implications for child care.* Washington, DC: Children's Defense Fund.

Brown, H. (1996, May 7). Wisconsin welfare boomerang. *New York Times* [Op-Ed], p. A23.

Burke, V. (1995, October 4). *Cash welfare for families with children: Comparison of House and Senate versions of H.R. 4* (Report for Congress). Washington, DC: Congressional Research Service.

Burke, V. (1996, June 6). *Family cash welfare: H.R. 4, H.R. 3507/S. 1795, and draft Clinton bill* (Report for Congress). Washington, DC: Congressional Research Service.

Casper, L. M., Hawkins, M., & O'Connell, M. (1994). *Who's minding the kids? Child care arrangements, Fall 1991* (U.S. Bureau of the Census, Current Population Reports, P70-36). Washington, DC: U.S. Government Printing Office.

Child Care Action Campaign. (1995a, October 6). *Legislative alert on child care* [Memorandum]. New York: Author.

Child Care Action Campaign. (1995b, November 21). *Legislative alert on child care* [Memorandum]. New York: Author.

Children's Defense Fund. (1995). Comparisons of key Senate child care provisions, House provisions, and current law, October 1995. *CDF Reports, 17*(1).

Clark, R. L., & Berkowitz, R. E. (1995). *Federal expenditures on children, 1960–1995.* Washington, DC: Urban Institute.

Congressional Research Service. (1995). *Child nutrition* [Issue brief]. Washington, DC: Author.

Dao, J. (1995, December 3). Pataki to propose sharply reducing welfare benefits. *New York Times* [Weekend edition], sec. 1, p. 1.

deSchweinitz, K. (1943). *England's road to social security.* Philadelphia: University of Pennsylvania Press.

Ellwood, D. A., & Gold, S. (1995). *Children and the balanced budget amendment.* Albany, NY: Center for the Study of the States.

Family Support Act of 1988, P.L. 100-485, 102 stat. 2343.

Greenberg, M. (1996). *Welfare reform in an urban environment.* Washington, DC: Center on Law and Social Policy.

Kamerman, S. B., & Kahn, A. J. (1996). *Whither American social policy?* New York: Columbia University.

Kobin, N., Waldfogel, J., & Kamerman, S. B. (1996). *Special analysis of impact of proposed welfare reform initiatives on child care needs, demands, costs, and use in New York City.* Unpublished manuscript, Columbia University, School of Social Work, New York.

Levy, C. (1995, December 16). Pataki budget has sharp cuts in aid to poor. *New York Times*, p. A1.

Mann, L. (1995). *A Medicaid block grant is likely to lead to an inequitable distribution of federal funds.* Washington, DC: Center on Budget and Policy Priorities.

Nathan, R. P. (1995). *Hard road ahead: Block grants and the "devolution revolution."* Unpublished manuscript, Nelson Rockefeller Institute of Government, Albany, NY.

National Association for the Education of Young Children. (1995). *Comparisons of child care provisions in the current law, and the bills passed by the House and Senate.* Washington, DC: Author.

National Governors' Association. (1995). *Innovative state health initiatives for children.* Washington, DC: Author.

Office of Management and Budget, U.S. Department of Health and Human Services, and other agencies. (1995). *Potential poverty and distributional effects of welfare reform bills and balanced budget plans.* Washington, DC: Author.

Parrott, S. (1995). *The House Ways and Means welfare proposal.* Washington, DC: Center on Budget and Policy Priorities.

Pear, R. (1995, October 29). Shifting where the buck stops. *New York Times* [Weekend edition], sec. 4, p. 3.

Personal Responsibility and Work Opportunity Act of 1995, H.R. 3507/S. 1795, 104th Cong., 2nd Sess. (formerly H.R. 4).

Peterson, P. (1995).*The price of federalism.* Washington, DC: Brookings Institution.

Peterson, P. (1996). Budget deficits and the race to the bottom. In S. B. Kamerman & A. J. Kahn (Eds.), *Wither American social policy?* (pp. 43–63). New York: Columbia University.

Republican National Committee. (1994). *Contract with America.* New York: Times Books.

Richardson, J. (1995, August 10). *Food stamp reform* (Report for Congress). Washington, DC: Congressional Research Service.

Sack, K. (1995, October 23). In Mississippi, will the poor grow poorer with state welfare plan? *New York Times,* p. A1.

Spar, K. (1995, September 20). *Child care: A comparison of House and Senate welfare reform legislation* (Report for Congress).Washington, DC: Congressional Research Service.

Sullivan v. Zebley, 110 S. Ct. 885 (1990).

University of Wisconsin, Institute for Research on Poverty. (1996, Spring). *Focus, 17* (Special issue on Medicaid).

U.S. Bureau of the Census. (1995, October 6). *Child care costs greater burden for the poor* [Press release]. Suitland, MD: Author.

U.S. House of Representatives, Committee on Ways and Means. (1994). *1994 green book: Overview of entitlement programs.* Washington, DC: U.S. Government Printing Office.

This chapter was originally published in the September 1996 issue of Social Work, *vol. 41, pp. 453–465.*

16 The Impact of Federal Policy Changes on Children: Research Needs for the Future

Lynn Videka-Sherman and Pamela Viggiani

Through a convergence of factors—a president who vowed in his 1992 campaign to "end welfare as we know it," a majority Republican Congress who pledged to reform welfare in its policy manifesto *Contract with America* (Gingrich, Armey, & the House Republicans, 1994), and an impending November 1996 election creating pressure for candidates from both parties to make good on those earlier promises—the federal government will soon enact the most sweeping revision of social welfare policy since the New Deal. President Clinton has signed the Personal Responsibility and Work Opportunity Act of 1996, ending Aid to Families with Dependent Children (AFDC) and instituting far-reaching changes in aid to needy people and immigrants in this country.

This new law is one thread in a far-reaching change in the federal policy fabric, that of "devolution" of policy making to states. *Devolution* means that the federal government will give more discretion to the states and will maintain less oversight of social policy as implemented by states. Devolution could lead to great variations in social policy the likes of which we have not seen in this century. Although health care, Medicaid, and child welfare policy, especially foster care, have yet to see major federal legislative changes, numerous bills have been considered at the federal and state levels.

Although many of these changes are not described in terms of children's policy, they will affect children disproportionately. These policy revisions are aimed at the poor population, and children are the majority of the poor population in the United States. Analysts have estimated that two of every three people affected by welfare reform will be children (Center on Budget and Policy Priorities, 1996).

DEVOLUTION REVOLUTION AND WELFARE REFORM

If the "devolution revolution" (Nathan, 1996) proceeds as outlined, welfare and other major federal programs will be delegated to the states. Nathan, McGrath, and O'Heaney (1996), in a concise and cogent history of federalism in the 20th century, credited Presidents Lyndon Johnson and Richard Nixon with instituting federalist policies in the first "block grant" programs such as Johnson's Law Assistance Block Grant in 1967 and Nixon's State and Local Fiscal Assistance Act of 1972 (which expired in 1986), the Community Development Block Grant, and Title XX of the Social Security Act. According to Nathan et al., the philosophy behind the Johnson–Nixon brand of federalism was that greater flexibility for states and localities would allow them to reform government-sponsored social services in ways that would improve coordination and efficiency and allow the local community to determine needs and set priorities in selected areas of social policy. President Nixon felt strongly that certain public-sector responsibilities should remain centralized, including health, welfare, and the environment. Under Nixon's new federalism, funding was increased to states and localities while categorical programs and restrictions were relaxed or eliminated in the new block grant programs.

The late-1990s brand of federalism differs from its precursors in several ways. First, the welfare and health programs considered sacred by earlier federalists are now the objects of devolution, breaking down a national standard for support of poor people, including health care. Second, today's devolution of power in matters of social policy is combined with drastic reductions in federal revenues to support the states' new discretion. States will be freer to devise and implement welfare and health programs for poor people, but they will have up to 20 percent less federal support to do so, pushing the burden to state and local taxes or resulting in dramatically reduced programs for poor families.

It is not coincidental that these changes are taking place at a time when economic forces and the power base in this country are shifting. Conservative states in the South and West are booming economically, whereas the eastern and western coastal states are struggling to restructure their economies to promote technological and service industries. Several midwestern states have experimented creatively with state programs for poor adults and with federal AFDC and Medicaid waivers to try new approaches to deal with poverty. Studies show that these programs reduce state expenditures by a mere fraction of the goals of their champions, or about 10 percent (Danziger, Johnson, & Newman, 1995; deParle, 1995). They also show that greater numbers of families go to work as a result of these programs but that these families do not move out of poverty because they typically hold low-paying, insecure jobs. These families' economic status is worse off welfare than on (Danziger et al., 1995; deParle, 1995). It is clear that the most creative welfare-to-work programs will have small effects and will not end poverty. Welfare reform in the 1990s is a hybrid of the zeal for tax reductions among the middle and upper classes and a resurgence of doubts about whether poor people deserve help.

Wade Horn (1996), secretary of the U.S. Department of Health and Human Services during the Bush presidency, traced the history of the goals of public welfare. The pre-New Deal welfare for widows and their children and the original Aid to Dependent Children program were aimed at enabling widowed mothers to stay out of the workforce. As rates of divorce increased the population of single mothers and as cultural mores concerning mothers in the workforce changed, second-generation federal welfare programs under the Family Support Act of 1988 were aimed at putting welfare mothers to work. Both Horn (1996) and Kondrata (1996) agreed that the 104th Congress's version of welfare reform is aimed at reducing single parenthood, teenage parenting, and subsidies for nonworking poor people.

CHILDREN'S POLICY INITIATIVES

Other than child labor protection and public education funding, federal policymakers have developed few special policies for children. The current devolution debates have vacillated on whether to include foster care and other child welfare programs in block grant provisions. The House of Representatives has usually included child welfare in its block grant provisions; the Senate has always removed this provision. Child welfare and foster care are not block granted in the Personal Responsibility and Work Opportunity Act of 1996.

At the state level, several states (such as Maryland) have already moved to contain foster care and children's services costs through service consolidation and block grants to localities. States are searching for managed care financing models to apply to child welfare services.

Health Care Reform

Although President Clinton's national health care reform failed in 1995, health care is changing rapidly. The move to managed care, including in Medicaid programs, through federal waivers is one strategy to contain still-soaring health care costs. Attempts to reduce eligibility for Supplemental Security Income will directly affect disabled children in the United States.

Child Abuse and Neglect

Federal support for community-based services for children at risk of child abuse and neglect has diminished in recent years. Although foster care expenditures have increased dramatically, the National Center for Child Abuse and Neglect has vastly reduced its discretionary funding program. The number of abused and neglected children in foster care has grown, but preventive, community-based services have been cut.

Family Preservation

The Personal Responsibility and Work Opportunity Act of 1996 protects funding for family preservation (Title IV-B) and foster care (Title IV-E). Family preservation is a program that has expanded in the past four years, yet most states are still dramatically underfunded for family preservation services. Research findings on the effectiveness of these services have been mixed (Schuerman, Rzepnicki, & Littell, 1994).

Family Values and Federal Policy

In addition to family self-sufficiency and "personal responsibility" for one's own economic fate, the conservative emphasis on traditional family values has fostered bills that would protect and strengthen the United States's already strong protections of family privacy. The Family Privacy Protection Act (H.R. 1271) would require prior written parental consent for a youth to participate in any federally funded research that included "questions on sexual behavior or attitudes, psychological problems, religious beliefs, and illegal, antisocial, or self-incriminating behavior." Several states require or are considering requiring parental notification before a minor can seek an abortion.

RESEARCH PRIORITIES

Research on the effects of policies on children that goes beyond counts of affected children is essential. Research will be even more difficult to conduct than it currently is because of the loosening of reporting provisions and the weakened or eliminated federal oversight provisions in the devolution craze.

Documenting Poverty Outcomes and Intervening Variables for Children

Detailed follow-up of the effects of devolution on children is essential. Longitudinal studies of families' experiences as devolution is implemented must be conducted. Information on families' experiences under current welfare practices must be collected now to best compare the effects of policy changes. This research program should document not only family income and employment status changes, but also effects on family interaction, children's school attendance and performance, and child care arrangements and quality.

It is even more important to conduct research that will inform a conceptual understanding of the effects of changes in the federal safety net and consequences for children. Many studies identify poverty status as a "marker" or correlate of undesirable outcomes such as lower educational attainment, higher rates of school failure, and juvenile delinquency. One priority of research in the future is study of variation in the effects of poverty on children with an aim to explaining this variation. Poverty research will need to be informed by theoretical understanding of family process and other buffers of the effects of poverty on children.

The next generation of research on the effects of poverty on children must be informed by knowledge of family relationships. Research on the resiliency of children in toxic environments (Garbarino, 1995; Garmezy, 1983) has shown that some children excel despite growing up with economic and emotional deprivation and abuse. What enables these children to escape the ravages of their experiences? How can these factors inform future policies? We must answer these questions if research is to inform policy choices that enhance child well-being.

Detailing State Variation in Devolution

With devolution there may be more policy variation among states than ever before. Researchers must seize the opportunity to study this variation in all its phases—design and implementation as well as outcome. Multistate comparison studies will be essential and will be most informative if they focus on comparisons of definable differences in policy provisions across sites. For example, states that maintain current levels of benefits to families and children must be compared to states that enact the most drastic reductions allowed under the Personal Responsibility and Work Opportunity Act of 1996.

Descriptive studies of the variations in state policies will be important, as will knowledge of how states are proceeding with devolution. State variations in programs, services, administration, financing, and state and local tax support will be essential to describe and measure.

Policy implementation and outcomes should be studied. Nathan (1982) described "field network evaluation," a methodology that extends case study methodology to the multisite implementation of new policies. Field network evaluation uses on-site field associates to collect qualitative and quantitative data from multiple states or locations to compare locations' implementation of a new policy. Researchers interview key informants, including policymakers, agency managers, and clients. The field associates from each site apply a "site perspective" to the policy implementation. The central research team consolidates the findings of the field associates and provides a multistate or national perspective. This approach is appealing because it combines local perspectives and national comparison. It requires substantial funding to support study staff in each site as well as national staff who travel extensively to achieve the integrated analysis of and balance between local and national perspectives. This methodology has been used to study the Family Support Act of 1988 (Hagen & Lurie, 1993).

A rich area for social work study is to examine the perspectives on policy initiatives of administrators and service delivery staff at national, state, and local agencies. The professional training and agency auspices of local child services staff may vary widely. For example, family preservation services caseworkers may have a bachelor's degree in a field other than social work, a high school diploma, or a graduate degree in social work. These caseworkers may be employed in public social services agencies or not-for-profit agencies that contract with public agencies to deliver family preservation services. How does each practitioner understand the policy initiative? How does a policy change affect the intervention approach used by the practitioner? Do the practitioner's actions change with a policy shift? Do the services offered under family preservation differ from the services offered before family preservation? These important questions link policy and practice, and social workers have much to contribute to an understanding of these factors.

Studying Effect Reduction in Wide-Scale Policy Implementation

Numerous studies have indicated that wide-scale policy implementation almost invariably leads to reduced program effects when the same program is compared to the small demonstration that spurred the development of the particular policy. This has been found to be true for family preservation programs (Schuerman et al., 1994), community-based child abuse and neglect intervention programs (Berkeley Planning Associates, 1976), and substance abuse prevention among youths (Tobler, 1994). The gap between small-scale demonstration implementation and national policy implementation is fertile ground for study. We need to know much more about how policy initiatives are implemented and how they vary at the local level, particularly when they involve services delivered by practitioners to clients.

Monitoring Correlates of New Policy Initiatives

It is important to study the unintended and intended effects of the new policies on children. Of particular concern is whether the time limits and reduced benefits included in the Personal Responsibility and Work Opportunity Act of 1996 result in increases in the number of children being shunted to foster care. This law may lead to the ballooning of child welfare rolls if, as other resources and benefits shrink, families are driven to use the child welfare system as a last resort for obtaining services.

Analyzing Outcomes and Cost–Benefits

It is imperative that the social work profession continue to build knowledge about service outcomes. We need to know which approaches to family preservation are most effective. We need to move beyond looking at large-scale outcomes, which have been disappointing for so many child intervention programs (Berkeley Planning Associates, 1976; Schuerman et al., 1994), and begin to study program variation. What characterizes the most successful intervention sites? What amounts of variation are present in the degree of program success?

Future research should focus on explaining program variation and variables—client, practitioner, and administrative—linked with success. Lipsey (1994) explained a methodology for secondary analysis using meta-analysis techniques. He examined differential outcomes in programs that serve juvenile delinquents and showed that the most effective programs had commonalities in program structure and elements, client characteristics, and practitioner characteristics. Tobler (1994) demonstrated similar findings for substance abuse interventions for teenagers. Schorr and Schorr (1989) used a qualitative approach in their discussion and case illustrations of effective community-based family and child social services programs. To be able to use these approaches to study program and outcome variation, several features must be available, including the following:

- There must be an accepted criterion for program success. This criterion must be applicable across a wide range of programs.
- Data must be available or obtainable for a reasonably large number of programs to make studies of outcome variation possible.
- There must be a knowedge base and a conceptual framework that identify explanatory variables of interest. Theory must inform research.

To meet these demands, the profession must be involved in conducting the original studies on which a synthesis can be based. Archiving data in national archives such as the Child Abuse and Neglect Data Bank at Cornell University (Cappelleri, Eckenrode, & Powers, 1993) can help investigators gain access to original studies.

Multisite study consortiums are another promising tool for the study of the effects of new federal policy changes on children. Social work researchers from across the United States should collaborate to seek federal and foundation funding for such studies. This approach can enhance sample sizes and representativeness.

Social work must increasingly focus on cost–benefit analyses of social programs. Big costs and small effects—this is the reputation of all too many social programs, particularly those that target women and children. We need to add a social work perspective to cost–benefit analysis that would ensure that social benefits and costs are included in econometric models. If the promising research on the prevention of social problems is ever to influence future policies, we must communicate the success of early intervention in deterring the larger social costs of later intervention. This argument has had some success in Head Start, child health, and substance abuse prevention programs.

Schuerman (1995) identified improper targeting of social services as a primary reason that program effects appear small in many cases. Targeting involves delivering limited resources (services) to people who manifest the problem targeted by the policy (or who are at great risk for developing the problem) *and* who are likely to benefit (attain desired outcomes) from the program. Presuming that a policy initiative is clear enough to identify a target population and program outcomes, we need to know much more about which clients are best suited to the program—that is, which will receive the services and make the desired changes. Research on client variation in outcomes along with the development of cogent theoretical models and valid, sensitive measures will make this knowledge building possible.

GETTING THE MESSAGE TO THE PEOPLE

The rise of the conservative social agenda over the past 10 years is due to local diligence in promoting conservative issues through local school boards (Richards, 1995) and through successful media campaigns. The rise of conservative think tanks such as the American Enterprise Institute and the Manhattan Institute, along with their success in reaching the public through the print and electronic media, has swayed public opinion toward conservatism. There are lessons to be learned from social conservatives' approach. If social work research is to influence public policy and support a sense of social justice in this society, social work researchers must develop new dissemination strategies. Like it or not, this society is saturated with information and with sophisticated marketing approaches. These marketing approaches have shaped public opinion on such matters as health care services, higher education, and legal services.

Research concerning policies that affect children must be disseminated in modern ways. The profession's reliance on publications in scholarly journals will not shape public policy in the future. In addition to scholarly journal publication, social workers must disseminate the findings of their research through newspapers and radio reports that reach diverse audiences, including those not traditionally in "liberal" ideological camps. Talk shows and other nontraditional forms of dissemination must be tapped. Crisp, to-the-point program reports should be used to influence the opinions of public officials. These program reports need to be presented in a style very different from the traditional detailed, technical, and lengthy narrative.

The bottom line is that information that emerges from quality data must be collected and analyzed in rigorous, state-of-the-art ways, but researchers must take the next step with this data. It must be packaged in multiple forms targeted to specific audiences—policymakers, local communities, the general public. Dissemination pieces need to be brief and clear, and they must catch the eye. Those who cringe when thinking about "advertising" the results of social work research must remember that public policy is shaped by public opinion, and public opinion is shaped by perceptions of this society.

CONCLUSION

We are embarking on a sea of change in U.S. social policy. Local control and diminished resources are givens in the new social policy formula, representing an unprecedented opportunity for social work researchers. Strong ties forged with public social services entities will position social workers in many states to be partners with state governments in evaluating the effects of welfare reform on children. Perhaps our biggest research challenge is to disseminate research results so that the American public will support policies that promote the well-being of children; Horn (1996) reminded us that child well-being is clearly not a goal of the present policies on welfare reform. Social workers can make a unique contribution to future public policy by informing legislators and executive staff how policies are translated into practice and what effects they have on clients. There is tremendous opportunity for social workers to join together across states and localities to develop consortia studies that will command public attention and sway public opinion. All that is left is to do it!

REFERENCES

Berkeley Planning Associates. (1976). *The effectiveness of child maltreatment interventions in five states.* Boston: Author.

Cappelleri, J. R., Eckenrode, J., & Powers, J. C. (1993). The epidemiology of child abuse: Findings from the second national incidence and prevention study of child abuse and neglect. *American Journal of Public Health, 83,* 1622–1624.

Center on Budget and Policy Priorities. (1996). *The conference on the welfare bill* (rev. ed.). Washington, DC: Author.

Danziger, S., Johnson, J. H., & Newman, K. S. (1995). Overcoming poverty: What research demonstrates. In *Proceedings of a Congressional Breakfast Seminar.* Washington, DC: Consortium of Social Science Associates.

deParle, J. (1995, December 3). Less is more: Faith and facts in welfare reform. *New York Times,* pp. 4–1, 4–16.

Family Support Act of 1988, P.L. 100-485, 102 Stat. 2343.

Garbarino, J. (1995). *Raising children in a socially toxic environment.* San Francisco: Jossey-Bass.

Garmezy, N. (1983). Stressors of childhood. In N. Garmezy & M. Rutter (Eds.), *Stress, coping and development in children* (pp. 43–84). New York: McGraw-Hill.

Gingrich, N., Armey, D., & the House Republicans. (1994). *Contract with America.* Washington, DC: U.S. House of Representatives, Committees, and House Organizations, www.house.gov/org.pubs.htmc.

Hagen, J. L., & Lurie, I. (1993). *Child care service and jobs: Local implementation.* Albany, NY: Nelson A. Rockefeller Institutes of Governing, State University of New York at Albany.

Horn, W. F. (1996, Summer). Assessing the effects of the "Devolution Revolution" on children and families. *National Center for Children in Poverty: News and Issues,* p. 1.

Kondrata, A. (1996). Reflections on national welfare policy and state reform options. In S. B. Kamerman & A. J. Kahn (Eds.), *Planning a state welfare strategy under waivers or block grants.* New York: Columbia University School of Social Work, Cross National Studies Research Programs.

Lipsey, M. (1994). *Meta-analysis for explanation.* Newbury Park, CA: Sage Publications.

Nathan, R. P. (1982). The methodology for field network evaluation studies. In W. Williams (Ed.), *Studying implementation: Methodological and administrative issues.* Chatham, NJ: Chatham House.

Nathan, R. P. (1996, March 13). *"Devolution Revolution": Private charities can't pick up the slack— No way!* Paper presented at the Annual Meeting of the Cincinnati United Way and Community Chest, Cincinnati.

Nathan, R. P., McGrath, M. J., & O'Heaney, W. C. (1996, June 12). *The "nonprofitization move-ment": An examination of the effects of devolution on nonprofit organizations.* Paper presented at the New Partnership Project, Center on Philanthropy, Indiana University, Indianapolis.

Personal Responsibility and Work Opportunity Act of 1996, H.R. 3507, S. 1795.

Richards, C. (1995, September 29). *Developing alliances: Standing up to the radical right.* Paper presented at the Bi-Annual Meeting of the National Association of Deans and Directors of Schools of Social Work, San Antonio, TX.

Schorr, L., & Schorr, D. (1989). *Within our reach: Breaking the cycle of disadvantage.* New York: Anchor Books.

Schuerman, J. R. (1995). *The problem of targeting.* Unpublished manuscript.

Schuerman, J. R., Rzepnicki, T. C., & Littell, J. (1994). *Putting families first: An experiment in family preservation.* Hawthorne, NY: Aldine de Gruyter.

Tobler, N. S. (1994). *Meta-analysis of school-based substance abuse prevention for youth* (Final report to the National Institute for Drug Abuse, Report No. R01-DA05505). Rockville, MD: National Institute on Drug Abuse.

This chapter was originally published in the November 1996 issue of Social Work, *vol. 41, pp. 594–600.*

17 Effects of Assets on Attitudes and Behaviors: Advance Test of a Social Policy Proposal

Gautam N. Yadama and Michael Sherraden

In his 1994 welfare reform proposal, President Clinton included a number of measures to increase asset limits and create special savings accounts called "individual development accounts" (IDAs). These proposals, presented as legislation, were sponsored by Senators Daniel Moynihan (D-NY) and Edward Kennedy (D-MA), Representatives Sam Gibbons (D-FL) and Dick Gephardt (D-MO), and others. Other proposals for IDA demonstrations had already been introduced by Representatives Tony Hall (D-OH), Bill Emerson (R-MO), and Cardiss Collins (D-IL) and by Senator Bill Bradley (D-NJ). Almost every welfare reform proposal, Republican and Democrat, would raise asset limits to encourage saving. This bipartisan emphasis on asset building is a new and untested approach to antipoverty policy.

Assets are typically viewed as a storehouse for future consumption, but they may have important psychological and social effects as well. A fundamental theme in American culture suggests that wealth and property holding may have positive effects on personal well-being, social status, and citizen participation. This theme has deep historical roots and a long-lasting influence on public policy. It is an idea that was expounded by Thomas Jefferson; recorded in the observations of Alexis de Tocqueville; and later invoked as a rationale for such policies as the Homestead Act, government-backed home mortgage lending programs, employee stock ownership plans, and proposals for ownership of public housing. Related proposals in public policy regarding the idea of capital accounts, primarily for youths, have been suggested by Tobin (1968), Haveman (1988), and Sawhill (1989). These proposals are for a single lump-sum distribution, to be given to recipients late in adolescence, that might be thought of as a multipurpose voucher for health, welfare, and education choices. However, the intention of these proposals is to provide a fund for welfare consumption choices. Effects of asset holding, other than for consumption choices, have not been discussed by these authors.

Analysis for this article was made possible by a faculty research grant of the George Warren Brown School of Social Work, Washington University, St. Louis. An earlier version of this article was presented at the Seventh International Conference of the Society for the Advancement of Socio-Economics, Washington, DC, April 7–9, 1995. The authors thank David Gillespie, Deborah Page-Adams, Shanta Pandey, Robert Plotnick, and two anonymous reviewers for their helpful comments.

Specification of the psychological and social effects of asset holding is not well developed. Typically, effects of asset holding have been presented as broad normative statements (for example, by Thomas Jefferson) or as sweeping narrative observations (for example, by Alexis de Tocqueville). To be sure, a number of eminent scholars, including Adam Smith, Karl Marx, Max Weber, Thorstein Veblen, and William James, have commented in various ways on the effects of property holding, but clear propositions have seldom been formulated. The discussion has been more in the realm of social philosophy than the social sciences. The study described in this article provides an empirical test of the effects of assets on attitudes and behaviors.

STUDIES OF ATTITUDES, BEHAVIOR, AND ECONOMIC STATUS

In related research, several studies have been undertaken to assess relationships among attitudes, behaviors, and subsequent changes in labor force participation and income. Duncan and Hill (1975) examined the extent to which attitudes such as efficacy, trust, aspiration and ambition, risk avoidance, connectedness, time horizon, and economizing behavior affect economic status. Their study examined the effect of attitudes, behaviors, and economic status over a five-year period between 1968 and 1972. These researchers concluded that the effects of attitudes and behaviors on economic status are negligible and that "despite the fact that some attitudes and behavior patterns had statistically significant effects on income change, they did not have powerful effects" (Duncan & Hill, 1975, p. 99). Andrisani (1977, 1981) studied the relationship between internal and external attitudes and labor market experience. On the basis of modest effects, he concluded that internal and external attitudes are systematically related to labor market experiences such as growth in average hourly earnings and occupational attainment. Duncan and Morgan (1981), on the other hand, concluded that attitudes are not important in explaining economic success.

In looking at this research overall, two features are evident. First, most of the studies focused on effects of attitudes and behavior on subsequent economic status rather than vice versa (although occasionally researchers have examined effects of income on social and psychological factors; see Duncan & Hill, 1975). Second, most of the measures of economic status are based on some measure of income or an income-to-needs ratio. There is little systematic research on assets and their possible relationships with attitudinal and behavioral variables.

STUDIES RELATING ASSETS WITH SOCIAL AND PSYCHOLOGICAL VARIABLES

There is a long history of cross-national research on correlates of property holding in anthropology and sociology (Rudman, 1992, provides an excellent review). Most of the work is ethnographic, although limited systematic studies have appeared in the past half-century. The unit of analysis in these studies is not at the individual or household level, and the work generally does not speak to attitudinal and behavioral variables. Much of this body of work has a marked ideological bias, either categorizing the harmful results or extolling the virtues of private property.

In modern sociology there is a large literature associating assets with social power (Domhoff, 1971; Kolko, 1962; Mills, 1956), but the focus is typically on the social power of the upper class, where assets are concentrated. There is little attempt to examine effects of asset holding among other population groups or to specify propositions that might be tested in heterogeneous populations. However, there are some noteworthy exceptions, in which the authors stated clear hypotheses and used empirical data. Kohn, Naoi, Schoenbach, Schooler, and Slomczynski (1990) systematically tested psychological effects of asset holding, including self-directedness and intellectual flexibility, in Japan, Poland, and the United States, and Vosler and Page-Adams (1993) tested the relationship between property holding and depression among auto workers in the United States. In both of these studies, significant effects of asset holding were found after controlling for income and education.

As an additional step toward formulating this idea in terms that are accessible to systematic analysis, Sherraden (1990, 1991) developed propositions regarding attitudinal and behavioral effects of asset holding. The suggested effects include greater household stability, increased long-term thinking and planning, increased effort in maintaining and enhancing assets, increased human capital development, increased risk taking, greater personal efficacy and self-esteem, increased social status, increased community involvement, and increased political participation. These propositions are stated at a general level, but they invite systematic tests. Haveman (1992) suggested that Sherraden may have had "the signs on the relevant coefficients correct" (p. 1521) but that confirmatory evidence was lacking.

For obvious reasons, it is very desirable to test asset-based policy proposals in advance, using any available empirical data. However, because assets and their effects have not been a focus of previous theory and research, most data sets do not offer opportunities for such tests. Fortunately, between 1968 and 1972, and only in these years, the Panel Study of Income Dynamics (PSID) included a wide range of attitudes and behaviors. When combined with PSID asset measures of savings and house value, the opportunity exists—as far as we know the only opportunity—for a longitudinal test. In addition, we can simultaneously test for two major alternative explanations. The first alternative explanation is that attitudes and behaviors cause assets rather than vice versa. The second alternative explanation is that income, not assets, affects attitudes and behaviors. These different explanations are not mutually exclusive. It is likely that both income and assets affect attitudes and behaviors in similar directions, but to some extent independently, and the relationship between assets and attitudes and behaviors probably works both ways (Sherraden, 1991).

In this article, we take a step toward testing the general theoretical statement that assets have effects on certain attitudes and behaviors (usually thought of as positive). Taking into account the theoretical statement and the two alternative explanations, we tested for the effect of assets on attitudes and behaviors, the effect of attitudes and behaviors on assets, the effect of income on attitudes and behaviors, and the effect of attitudes and behaviors on income.

DATA AND PROCEDURES

A large proportion of the research on attitudes, behavior, and economic status is based on the PSID, an ongoing longitudinal survey of 5,000 families that began in

1968 and was conducted by the Survey Research Center at the University of Michigan (Hill, 1992). The study began with 4,802 households—1,872 low-income households were drawn from the Survey of Economic Opportunity and another 2,930 households were drawn from the national sampling frame of the Survey Research Center (Hill, 1992). Heads of household from PSID were selected to study the relationship between assets and attitudes and behaviors. We arrived at the final sample of 2,871 cases after filtering the data for accuracy and for those who were heads of household in both 1968 and 1972. The mean age of study participants was 43 years. Overall, 75 percent of the household heads were men and 25 percent were women. Regarding race, 66 percent were white; 32 percent were black; and the remaining 2 percent were Puerto Rican, Mexican, or other.

It is possible to use the PSID to explore effects of assets on attitudes and behaviors and vice versa. Specifically, we could examine the effects of assets on prudence, efficacy, horizons, connectedness, and effort. However, the analysis is constrained by certain limitations in the data set. As with Duncan and Hill (1975), we restricted our analysis to a five-year period from 1968 to 1972 because data on attitudes and behaviors have not been collected after 1972. (More reliable data on assets were gathered in 1984; however, because PSID data on attitudes and behaviors precedes the more reliable data on assets, it is not possible to examine the effect of assets on attitudes and behaviors after 1972.)

The PSID data set also enabled us to examine simultaneously the two major alternative explanations. Accordingly, we examined the effect of income while testing for the effect of assets on attitudes and behaviors, and we also tested for the second alternative explanation, that attitudes and behaviors affect assets rather than vice versa. All the effects were simultaneously estimated as a path model of directly observed variables using LISREL 8. A causal model with directly observed variables, such as the one tested here, is classified in LISREL as submodel 2 (Jöreskog & Sörbom, 1989), a class of models in which the dependent and explanatory variables are directly observed.

Variables such as house value and income are directly observed and are used as such in the path model. All of the attitude and behavior variables and the savings variable are indices derived from other observed variables. Every index used in this analysis was derived by the PSID staff from a combination of weighting and aggregation of responses to specific sets of observed variables. The primary reason for using the PSID indices is that they have been used in previous analyses (Andrisani, 1977; Duncan & Hill, 1975; Duncan & Morgan, 1981), enabling us to compare our results with the relevant research. Each index in the present study is used as an observed variable. Computation of a measurement model is not relevant because we used each of the indices as an observed variable; therefore, we use a path model instead of a structural equation model with latent variables.

Unlike traditional path models, it is possible to simultaneously estimate all effects in a path analysis model for directly observed variables using LISREL. In the traditional path-analytic model, one obtains reduced-form equations first and then solves for the structural parameters (Jöreskog & Sörbom, 1989), whereas in LISREL, a path model is considered as a system of equations, and all structural coefficients are estimated directly and the reduced form obtained as a byproduct (Jöreskog & Sörbom, 1993). In causal models of directly observed variables, there are no latent variables, only directly measured variables: ys and xs. Because there are no latent constructs, a measurement model and the associated factor loadings (represented in $\lambda\text{-}x$ and $\lambda\text{-}y$ matrices) and correlations of measurement error (represented in $\theta\text{-}\delta$ and $\theta\text{-}\varepsilon$ matrices) are not relevant and therefore not estimated. Matrices representing factor loadings are fixed to identity, and matrices of measurement error are fixed to zero (Bollen, 1989). Moreover, in this submodel, the covariance matrix of independent constructs is assumed to be an unconstrained free covariance matrix of x variables (Jöreskog & Sörbom, 1989).

We estimated the effect of assets in 1968 on all the attitudes and behaviors in 1972 while controlling for the effects of the respective attitudes and behaviors in 1968. Similarly, we estimated the effects of attitudes and behaviors in 1968 on assets in 1972 while controlling for time 1 effects of assets and income. Both sets of effects were tested simultaneously in the same model. In addition, we simultaneously estimated the effects of income in 1968 on attitudes and behaviors in 1972, and vice versa, in the same model.

Control Variables

Age, race, gender, education of the head of household, and a variable indicating the presence of young children in the family were used as control variables. Age was the reported age of the head of household, and education was the number of years of school completed by the head of household. Race (1 = white, 0 = person of color) and gender (1 = male, 0 = female) were ordinal variables that had been dummy coded. The question "How old is the youngest child under 18 in the family unit?" was used as a control for the presence of young children in the family. Values for this variable ranged between 1, indicating the presence of a child less than two years old, and 9, indicating the presence of no children under age 18. These control variables were of no theoretical or policy interest in the present discussion. Nonetheless, controls were used here to remove doubt about the independence of asset effects.

Variables of Theoretical and Policy Interest

The variables in this study were house value, savings, income, prudence, efficacy, horizons, connectedness, and effort. House value, savings, and income in 1968 were independent variables affecting attitudes and behaviors in 1972 after controlling for the effects of attitudes and behaviors in 1968. Attitudes and behaviors in 1968 were independent variables affecting assets and income in 1972 after controlling for the effects of assets and income in 1968. All of these effects were estimated while simultaneously controlling for the effects of the demographic variables identified earlier.

Attitude and behavior variables were prudence, efficacy, horizons, connectedness, and effort. Together, the five attitude and behavior variables were the closest approximations that PSID data provided to the hypothesized asset effects suggested by Sherraden (1990, 1991). Overall, these variables represented desirable personal and social attributes consistent with the aims of social policy. Horizons, connectedness, and effort were particularly relevant to the content of the current welfare reform debate. See Table 17-1 for descriptive statistics of all variables used in the analysis.

There were two attitude and behavior indices that were available in the PSID but not used in this analysis. The first, an aspiration–ambition index, was not used because it has resulted in counterintuitive effects in the past and because the measure may be flawed. Duncan and Hill (1975) found a negative effect of income on the aspiration–ambition index, which they suggested was the result of certain components of the index, such as planning for or doing something about a better job, which are components generally associated with unsatisfactory income. The second index, an economizing behavior index, was not used because we could not find any proposition in the literature that suggested a relationship between asset holding and economizing behavior. Duncan and Hill (1975) discussed other possible behavioral measures at length. All indexes were developed and previously used by the Survey Research Center of the University of Michigan. Prior use of the indexes added to their usefulness in the current analysis.

House Value. The house value measure was used as an indicator of asset holdings. For respondents who did not own a home, this variable indicated a value of zero, and for those who owned a home, the actual value of the home was reflected in this variable. Whether a person lived in a rental property at the time of the study and the amount of rent they paid were assessed separately from home ownership elsewhere in the survey. Appropriate accuracy codes were used to filter out inaccurate estimates of house value, and 1968 house values were adjusted to 1972 dollars.

Savings. Household savings was the other asset variable. The savings measure was the reserve funds index, which was a measure of savings undertaken by a family. A score of 5 indicated that the family had current savings of two or more months' income, and a score of 1 indicated that the family did not have any savings. The savings reserve index was computed by the PSID staff using three other specific variables. In the first question respondents were asked if

TABLE 17-1

Descriptive Statistics of Asset, Income, Attitude, and Behavior Variables Used in the Analysis

Variable	1968		1972	
	M	*SD*	*M*	*SD*
House value	9,110.49	12,590.57	11,699.55	14,165.68
Savings	2.73	1.72	2.66	1.74
Income	8,656.49	6,925.67	10,140.22	7,776.04
Prudence	4.69	1.27	3.68	1.16
Efficacy	3.38	1.68	3.01	1.54
Horizons	4.27	1.30	4.28	1.02
Connectedness	5.89	1.70	6.02	1.64
Effort	1.85	1.30	2.13	1.49

NOTE: See text for explanation of numerical values.

they had savings in the form of checking or savings accounts or government bonds. The second question assessed the extent of savings as a proportion of income. A third variable used in the computation of the reserve funds index reflected the extent of savings in the past five years. For details on the particular variables and the computational method for the reserve funds index, see Survey Research Center (1972b, p. 261). The savings measure used in the savings reserve index was truncated. It did not differentiate those who had savings of only two months' income from those who had savings greater than two months' income. Although asset-based policy demonstrations were not limited to encouraging savings of only two months' income, we were limited by the available data on savings included in the PSID. The original reserve fund index variable was reversed to make signs consistent throughout.

Income. The income measure refers to total family money income. This includes labor market earnings, public and private income transfers, rent, and interest income for all members of the family. Income in 1968 was adjusted to 1972 dollars.

Prudence. The prudence index was a modified form of the risk avoidance index developed by the PSID staff. This index was constructed by summing the standardized responses to questions about auto insurance, medical insurance, and personal smoking habits. One other question that was used to compute the index dealt with personal savings. To avoid any measurement confounding between the risk avoidance index and one of the asset variables (savings and reserve index), we recomputed prudence by partialing out the contribution of the savings variable. Prudence was represented by a revised form of variables V397 (1968) and V2945 (1972) in our analysis. For details on the variable numbers and the specific questions used to compute this index, see Survey Research Center (1972a, p. 364) and Duncan and Hill (1975, p. 74). Risk avoidance was considered positive in this context because it "is not the potentially beneficial entrepreneurial risk but rather is undue or unnecessary risk, indicated by excessive cigarette smoking, failure to fasten seat belts, having inadequate medical insurance or savings or operating uninsured vehicles" (Duncan & Hill, 1975, p. 74). In our analysis, unlike the original risk avoidance index, the index for prudence did not incorporate the adequacy of savings as one of the proxy measures. In other words, the measure of prudence was the same as the risk avoidance index minus the reserve funds measure. We undertook this alteration in the risk avoidance index to avoid confounding variables, because one of our asset variables is the savings reserve index.

Efficacy. Efficacy was measured with the efficacy-planning index developed by PSID staff from responses to specific questions about feelings, expectations, and confidence about the future. The index was computed using five questions measuring a personal sense of effectiveness in carrying out plans and also a general future orientation of the respondent. Respondents were asked if they thought life would work out, if they generally got to carry out the plans they envisioned, and if they were future oriented or lived from day to day. In our path analysis we used the efficacy planning index for 1968 (V419) and 1972 (V2939) to assess the effect of assets while controlling for time 1 effects. For greater detail on the questions and the variables, see Survey Research Center

(1972a, p. 367) and Duncan and Hill (1975, pp. 83–89). The index reflects a respondent's satisfaction with self and confidence about the future (Survey Research Center, 1972a).

Horizons. Horizons were measured with the horizon proxies index of PSID, which included responses to questions about obtaining a new job, having more children, and having educational goals for one's children. The index was computed using responses to questions about plans to move to obtain a new job, plans to have more children, and educational goals for one's children. All asset effects on the horizons index were examined after controlling for the effects of prior horizons. The horizons index for 1968 is V391 and for 1972 is V2946. For greater detail see Survey Research Center (1972a, p. 364), and for prior application of the horizons index, see Ehrlich (1975, pp. 189–207).

Connectedness. The connectedness index was an index of connectedness to sources of information and help. The index assessed whether a respondent was in contact with relatives and neighbors or was active in certain organizations. The index determined the extent to which a head of household was in touch with sources of information and help. "Contact with relatives and neighbors belonging to organizations, and use of the media are hypothesized to enhance opportunities for information and its potential use" (Survey Research Center, 1972a, p. 363). This index was computed using nine specific variables that assessed attendance at organizations, use of the media, acquaintance with neighbors and relatives, and participation in any labor union (Duncan & Hill, 1975, p. 113; Survey Research Center, 1972a, p. 363). The connectedness index was represented by variables V393 (1968) and V2947 (1972). Both the horizon proxies index and the connectedness index have been termed "advantageous behaviors" in prior research (Duncan & Hill, 1975).

Effort. Effort was measured using the real earning acts index, which was composed of behaviors that resulted in nonmoney income or investment in human capital (Survey Research Center, 1972a, p. 364); effort has been termed a "coping behavior" by Duncan and Hill (1975). The index was constructed from responses to questions on the extent of home repair, car repair, home gardening, and other productive money-saving or human capital accumulation activities undertaken in one's spare time. The index was calculated from responses to four specific questions (see Duncan & Hill, 1975, pp. 94–96). The effort index was represented by variables V395 (1968) and V2943 (1972). In the current analysis, we did not distinguish between advantageous behaviors and coping behaviors (for a discussion of the content and construction of indexes used in this analysis, see Survey Research Center, 1972a, pp. 363–372, and 1972b, pp. 787–792).

RESULTS

The overall fit of the baseline structural equation model was adequate. The model had a goodness-of-fit index (GFI) of .96, adjusted goodness-of-fit index (AGFI) of .81, comparative fit index (CFI) of .94, and a relative fit index (RFI) of .74. Although the GFI indicates a very good fit, the chi-square measure of fit indicated a less than adequate fit [$\chi^2(48, N = 2,871) = 1,115.40, p = .00$]. Discrepancy among measures of fit can be easily explained. It is known that some measures of model fit—chi-square is foremost among them—are prone to sample size effects. As sample size becomes large, so does the chi-square statistic, leading one to falsely reject a model even if the model has an adequate fit (Yadama & Pandey, 1995). Because our analysis is based on a large sample size (N = 2,871), it is reasonable to expect large chi-square values. Therefore, we relied on other measures of fit that are not as affected by sample size.

Our results indicate that several of the errors in equations (ζs) predicting the dependent variables are correlated. Errors in equations predicting income and house value were allowed to correlate, and so were errors in equations predicting savings and horizons. The final model, with the loss of only two degrees of freedom, is a markedly improved model with excellent indicators of fit. The fit of our model improved on freeing these error terms [$\chi^2(46, N$ = 2,871) = 383.22, p = .00, GFI = .99, AGFI = .93, CFI = .98, RFI = .91]. The root mean square residual for the final model is low (.021), and the root mean square error of approximation is .051 (p value for test of close fit = .40), both indicating a good overall fit.

Table 17-2 reports the results of our analysis testing for the effects of income and assets on attitudes and behaviors and vice versa. Effects of each asset variable on the five attitude and behavior measures were assessed only after controlling for age, race, gender, education, age of youngest child, and the effect of the time 1 score of a given dependent variable. Coefficients for control variables are not reported here because they are not of analytical interest. (However, the effects of assets actually increased in the presence of control variables, whereas effects of income diminished.) As stated earlier, income is included in the analysis as an alternative explanation for attitudes and behaviors.

In this analysis we found a number of significant but modest effects (Table 17-2). Five of the 10 standardized coefficients relating the two asset variables and five attitude and behavior variables were significant, all in the expected direction. As predicted, savings had a significant positive effect on prudence (b = .20, $p \le$ .01), efficacy (b = .10, $p \le$ .01), horizons (b = .19, $p \le$ .01), and connectedness (b = .05, $p \le$ .05). The other proxy asset variable, house value, had one significant effect on horizons (b = .07, $p \le$ .01). Effort was the only variable not related to either of the asset variables.

As alternative explanations, we turned first to the possibility that it is income rather than assets that affects attitudes and behaviors. Looking at standardized path coefficients (Table 17-2), two of the five effects of income on attitudes and behaviors were significant and positive: prudence (b = .05, $p \le$ .05) and horizons (b = .05, $p \le$ .05). Efficacy, connectedness, and effort were not significantly related to income. Although there were some income effects, as anticipated, the income effects were overall not as prominent and strong as the savings effects (Table 17-2).

We considered next the possibility that attitudes and behaviors cause assets rather than vice versa. We estimated the effects of attitudes and behaviors on savings, house value, and income (Table 17-2). Four of the 10 effects relating to assets were significant: prudence had a significant positive effect on house value (b = .05, $p \le$ .01) but not on savings, efficacy had a significant positive effect on savings (b = .05, $p \le$ .01), connectedness had a significant positive effect on savings (b = .04,

TABLE 17-2

Standardized Path Coefficients for Changes in Attitudes, Behaviors, Assets, and Income at Time 1 (1968) on Attitudes, Behavior, Assets, and Income at Time 2 (1972)

Variable	Prudence (1972)		Efficacy (1972)		Horizons (1972)		Connectedness (1972)		Effort (1972)		House Value (1972)		Savings (1972)		Income (1972)	
	b	t	b	t	b	t	b	t	b	t	b	t	b	t	b	t
Prudence (1968)	.37**	21.88	—	—	—	—	—	—	—	—	.05**	4.17	-.02	1.39	.04**	3.04
Efficacy (1968)	—	—	.35**	20.07	—	—	—	—	—	—	-.01	-.63	.05**	3.72	.03**	2.72
Horizons (1968)	—	—	—	—	.08**	4.43	—	—	—	—	.01	1.08	.02	1.00	.07**	5.26
Connectedness (1968)	—	—	—	—	—	—	.41**	23.70	—	—	-.02	-1.61	.04**	2.62	.01	.55
Effort (1968)	—	—	—	—	—	—	—	—	.33**	18.22	.03*	2.13	-.06**	-4.19	.00	-.17
House value (1968)	.04	1.75	.04	1.75	.07**	3.35	.03	1.35	.02	.71	.62**	40.48	.04*	2.07	.11**	7.60
Savings (1968)	.20**	10.17	.10**	4.72	.19**	9.13	.05*	2.32	-.01	-.49	.06**	4.09	.46**	24.75	-.02	-1.67
Income (1968)	.05*	2.09	.03	1.14	.05*	2.50	.00	.08	-.03	-1.28	.14**	9.24	.06**	2.97	.61**	40.32
R2	.25**		.23**		.26**		.22**		.14**		.62**		.43**		.64**	

NOTE: All of the reported effects are after controlling for race, gender, age, education, and age of youngest child in the family unit. Estimates are computed using LISREL 8. $N = 2,871$.

SOURCE: Data are from Panel Study of Income Dynamics, heads of household in 1968 and 1972 (Survey Research Center, 1972a, 1972b).

*$p \le .05$. **$p \le .01$.

$p \leq .01$), and effort had a significant effect on house value ($b = .03, p \leq .05$). One relationship was significant in the opposite direction: effort had a significant negative effect on savings ($b = -.06, p \leq .01$). Overall, the effects of attitudes and behaviors on assets were in the predicted pattern, but quite modest.

DISCUSSION

Although this test of asset effects is far from perfect, it does have two highly desirable features: it is longitudinal, and it simultaneously considers two alternative explanations. All of this occurs in a single statistical test. In this regard, the design of the analysis is as concise and elegant as one could hope. Seldom in social sciences research is there an opportunity for a simultaneous test of key competing theories. We are very fortunate indeed that a data set existed that made the test possible.

Results support some of the hypothesized effects. One of the asset variables—savings—has significant effects in the predicted direction on three of the attitude and behavioral variables. House value has a significant positive effect on prudence. Also, the savings and house value effects on attitudes and behaviors occur beyond the effects of income. In addition, because of the construction of the statistical tests across longitudinal data, savings at one point affects attitudes and behaviors at a second point. A similar conclusion can be drawn for the effect of house value on prudence.

In this study, savings stands out as being particularly important in possibly influencing attitudes and behaviors. These effects are consistent with Sherraden's (1991) broadly stated propositions that assets have a positive effect on expectations and confidence about the future; influence people to make specific plans with regard to work and family; induce more prudent and protective personal behaviors; and lead to more social connectedness with relatives, neighbors, and organizations. Clearly, much more work remains to be done in theoretically specifying and confirming these asset effects, but overall results suggest that the thinking is on the right track.

One of the dependent variables, effort, is unrelated to assets. The general proposition is that when people have assets, they put forth more effort in maintaining those and other assets. Although the home ownership and other literature largely supports this view, the current study does not. As an alternative proposition, perhaps when people have assets they tend to purchase services (home repair, car repair) and do not try as hard for human capital improvements (training for a new job, going back to school). This question is certainly fundamental to any consideration of asset-based social policy, and more studies are needed.

Looking at the first alternative explanation, the effects of income on attitudes and behaviors are not as strong as the effects of savings. This finding deserves considerable attention. Social policy in Western welfare states is dominated by the provision of income, either as "social insurance" or means-tested transfer. If savings provide equal or stronger effects on attitudes or behaviors—and at the same time, economic development of households—then perhaps more social policy should promote asset accumulation in this form.

In a test of the second alternative explanation—that attitudes and behaviors cause assets—we found that attitudes and behaviors do have some significant effects on asset accumulation. Thus, without overstating the strength of the findings, it appears that assets lead to more positive attitudes and behaviors, and the same attitudes and behaviors lead to more assets. This is perhaps an empirical glimpse of a "virtuous circle" in household development—assets lead to more positive attitudes and behaviors, which in turn lead to more assets, and so on.

Turning to research issues, these results, although not overwhelming, suggest that assets deserve as much attention as income in studies that relate economic status with psychological and social variables. Moreover, the traditional emphasis on studying economic status as an outcome of attitudes and behaviors should be expanded to include the reverse proposition: in this case, that assets positively affect certain attitudes and behaviors.

Considering the restricted five-year period used in this analysis, it is also possible that the observed effects could be different—either larger or nonexistent—over a longer period. Ideally, future longitudinal tests should incorporate a longer time frame (although absence of attitudinal and behavioral measures in the PSID since 1972 is a problem in this regard). Future studies should also include more robust measures of attitudes and behaviors. It would also be helpful if future research examined these questions through a variety of methods.

Regarding asset-based policy demonstrations, as of this writing Iowa has passed legislation for an individual development account demonstration over five years. Several small IDA projects are under way at local agencies around the country. Evaluation designs for most IDA experiments are to include social and psychological effects. President Clinton's proposal for an IDA demonstration also would require testing social and psychological effects. Given the results of this study, we conclude that the policy demonstrations are warranted.

REFERENCES

Andrisani, P. J. (1977). Internal-external attitudes, personal initiative, and the labor market experience of black and white men. *Journal of Human Resources, 12*, 308–328.

Andrisani, P. J. (1981). Internal-external attitudes, sense of efficacy, and labor market experience: A reply to Duncan and Morgan. *Journal of Human Resources, 16*, 658–666.

Bollen, K. A. (1989). *Structural equations with latent variables.* New York: John Wiley & Sons.

Domhoff, G. W. (1971). *The higher circles: The governing class in America.* New York: Vintage.

Duncan, G. J., & Hill, D. (1975). Attitudes, behavior, and economic outcomes: A structural equations approach. In G. J. Duncan & J. N. Morgan (Eds.), *Five thousand American families: Patterns of economic progress* (Vol. 3, pp. 61–113). Ann Arbor: University of Michigan, Institute for Social Research, Survey Research Center.

Duncan, G. J., & Morgan, J. N. (1981). Sense of efficacy and subsequent change in earnings—A replication. *Journal of Human Resources, 16*, 649–657.

Ehrlich, E. (1975). Involuntary disruptions of "life-cycle" plans. In G. J. Duncan & J. N. Morgan (Eds.), *Five thousand American families: Patterns of economic progress* (Vol. 3, pp. 189–219). Ann Arbor: University of Michigan, Institute for Social Research, Survey Research Center.

Haveman, R. H. (1988). *Starting even: An equal opportunity program to combat the nation's new poverty.* New York: Simon & Schuster.

Haveman, R. H. (1992). Review of M. Sherraden, *Assets and the Poor. Journal of Economic Literature, 30*, 1520–1521.

Hill, M. S. (1992). *The panel study of income dynamics: A user's guide.* Newbury Park, CA: Sage Publications.

Jöreskog, K., & Sörbom, D. (1989). *LISREL 7: User's reference guide.* Mooresville, IN: Scientific Software.

Jöreskog, K., & Sörbom, D. (1993). *LISREL 8: Structural equation modeling with the SIMPLIS command language*. Chicago: Scientific Software International.

Kohn, M., Naoi, A., Schoenbach, C., Schooler, C., & Slomczynski, K. (1990). Position in the class structure and psychological functioning in the United States, Japan, and Poland. *American Journal of Sociology, 95,* 964–1008.

Kolko, G. (1962). *Wealth and power in America*. New York: Praeger.

Mills, C. W. (1956). *The power elite*. New York: Oxford University Press.

Rudman, F. W. (1992). Cross-cultural correlates of the ownership of private property. *Social Science Research, 21*(1), 57–83.

Sawhill, I. V. (1989). The underclass: An overview. *Public Interest, 96,* 3–15.

Sherraden, M. (1990). Stakeholding: Notes toward a theory of welfare based on assets. *Social Service Review, 64,* 580–601.

Sherraden, M. (1991). *Assets and the poor: A new American welfare policy*. New York: M. E. Sharpe.

Survey Research Center. (1972a). *A Panel Study of Income Dynamics: Study design, procedures, available data, 1968–1972 interviewing years* (Vol. 1). Ann Arbor: University of Michigan, Institute for Social Research.

Survey Research Center. (1972b). *A Panel Study of Income Dynamics: Tape codes and indexes, 1968–1972 interviewing years* (Vol. 2). Ann Arbor: University of Michigan, Institute for Social Research.

Tobin, J. (1968). Raising the incomes of the poor. In K. Gordon (Ed.), *Agenda for the nation* (pp. 77–116). Washington, DC: Brookings Institution.

Vosler, N., & Page-Adams, D. (1993, February). *A study of economic resources and depression*. Paper presented at 39th Annual Program Meeting of the Council on Social Work Education, New York.

Yadama, G. N., & Pandey, S. (1995). Effect of sample size on goodness-of-fit indices in structural equation models. *Journal of Social Service Research, 20*(3-4), 49–70.

This chapter was originally published in the March 1996 issue of Social Work Research, *vol. 20, pp. 3–11.*

18 The Relative Importance of Economic and Cultural Factors in Determining Length of AFDC Receipt

James P. Kunz and Catherine E. Born

The long-standing debate on welfare reform is far from over, but one contentious element has been decided. As a result of the enactment of the Personal Responsibility and Work Opportunity Reconciliation Act of 1996 (P.L. 104-193), limits will be imposed on the length of time (a maximum of five years in most cases) adult recipients in the Temporary Assistance to Needy Families (TANF) program—which will replace Aid to Families with Dependent Children (AFDC)—will be able to receive federally subsidized financial assistance. The debate continues, however, about the extent to which supportive services such as employment and training programs and child care are needed for welfare recipients to achieve self-sufficiency. Because of the newly mandated time limits, the question is no longer of interest solely to academicians and researchers. Instead, fiscal and implementation challenges posed by welfare reform make the question of practical importance to states.

Underlying the debate over the extent to which support services are needed is a fundamental difference in beliefs about the causes of welfare receipt and dependency. One side believes in a cultural model of welfare use and dependency and views welfare as a trap that encourages individuals to stay at home and receive benefits rather than work (Murray, 1984). Proponents of the cultural model believe that over time, welfare use itself, whether by oneself or by one's family members, friends, or neighbors, causes the stigma associated with welfare to disappear and recipients to adopt self-defeating work attitudes and poor work ethics (Mead, 1986, 1992). As a result, providing supportive services to help recipients move from welfare to work is not as important as ending or limiting a welfare system that President Ronald Reagan, quoting President Franklin Roosevelt, referred to as "a narcotic, a subtle destroyer of the human spirit" ("Transcript of President Reagan's Speech," 1986, p. A10).

Another side believes in an economic model of welfare use that emphasizes both recipients' human capital and labor market conditions that affect one's ability to become self-sufficient. Human capital factors include education, training, and the experience gained while employed, which are seen as investments that ultimately make recipients more employable and productive. "Labor market conditions" refers to the supply-and-demand factors in labor markets that make it difficult for AFDC recipients to obtain gainful employment (Danziger & Gottschalk, 1995; Wilson, 1987). Proponents of the economic model argue that there has been a decline in the number of jobs available to low-skilled workers and an increased demand for high-skilled workers. They also emphasize other barriers to employment, such as a lack of affordable child care and high transportation costs. Under the economic model, any welfare reform program that does not provide employment and training and other supportive services is thought unlikely to promote self-sufficiency.

EXISTING RESEARCH

Research that compares the relative importance of cultural and economic factors in determining the length of welfare spells among current AFDC recipients would be useful in this debate. A finding that time spent on AFDC, net of other factors, made it more difficult to leave AFDC would suggest that the imposition of time limits would be more important than providing supportive services. A finding that cultural factors made it more difficult to leave AFDC would lead one to the same conclusion. Alternatively, a finding that economic factors made it more difficult to leave AFDC would provide evidence that supportive services are needed.

Welfare researchers have only recently begun to look specifically at this question. Unfortunately, most research is hampered by data limitations in the large, nationally representative datasets that have been used to estimate the determinants of AFDC spell length. Early studies (for example, Hutchins, 1981) looked at simple models of transitions on and off the AFDC program. Bane and Ellwood (1983) are generally credited with the first comprehensive study of AFDC spells. Using data from the Panel Study of Income Dynamics (PSID), Bane and Ellwood followed a sample of female-headed households over a 12-year period, which enabled them to characterize the duration of spells and identify characteristics associated with longer spells. Ellwood (1986) examined an additional three years of data and differentiated between single and multiple spells. The findings were that most AFDC spells were short, lasting less than two years, but that a substantial number of spells were long-term and that short-term and long-term recipients differed in several respects. For example, many women use welfare only for transitional support. These women are typically the best educated, have previous work experience, and entered the welfare rolls after a divorce and at a time when they did not have very young children. But an important minority, at least one-quarter, collect AFDC for 10 or more years. These women usually did not complete high school, were never married, and had little work experience. The long-term recipients use a highly disproportionate share (almost two-thirds) of the funds spent on AFDC (Ellwood, 1986). O'Neill, Bassi, and Wolf (1987), using data from the PSID and National Longitudinal Survey of Young Women, obtained comparable results.

All of these studies used annual AFDC income, with varying thresholds, to determine whether the entire year is included in the spell. This approach overestimates use because receipt in only one month is construed as a one-year spell. To avoid this problem, Blank (1989) used monthly data from the Seattle/Denver Income Maintenance Experiment to calculate AFDC spells. She found that the mean length of spells was 3.1 years and that 62 percent of completed spells (40 percent overall) end within a year after they began. Using event history analysis, Blank also examined the question of duration dependence, that is, whether length of an AFDC spell affected the hazard rate (the probability of a spell ending at a particular time). She found some evidence of negative duration dependence, meaning that the longer one stayed on AFDC, the less likely one was to leave AFDC at any time. This finding is consistent with the notion of welfare dependency suggested by the cultural models. As with the studies mentioned earlier, Blank found that older and more educated women have higher exit probabilities, whereas households of color and households with more children have lower exit probabilities.

The existing research relies mostly on datasets that have rich information about welfare spells but less information about recipients. Thus, none of the research so far has been able to examine cultural factors. In addition, the lack of detailed information in event history analysis contributes to the likelihood of spurious negative duration dependence, that is, the possibility that what is being attributed to negative duration dependence may actually be due to unobserved differences in AFDC recipients. The concept of job readiness illustrates how unobserved heterogeneity could cause spurious negative duration dependence. If job readiness affects AFDC spell length, then those who are job ready leave sooner than those who are not, causing the hazard rate to fall over time. However, if job readiness is unobserved, the falling hazard rate will be mistakenly attributed to the effects of time itself rather than to differences in readiness.

Blank (1989) addressed this issue by estimating a model that assumed that the AFDC population consisted of two groups that differed in unknown ways. She found that one group had a very low probability of leaving at all times, whereas the other group had a high probability of leaving that began to fall after 12 months. Blank concluded that there was weak evidence of time dependence but that her results should not be interpreted as indicating that few women stayed on welfare a long time. Rather, she concurred with Ellwood (1986) that the AFDC population was exceptionally diverse, with some women leaving welfare quickly and others with few nonwelfare opportunities staying on for a considerable time.

Controlling for unobserved heterogeneity by making assumptions about the ways in which AFDC recipients might differ from one another is a valuable technique often used by researchers; however, researchers would agree that a better way to estimate duration dependence would be to measure the factors considered important to determine spell length. Thus, if job readiness indeed affects spell length, we should measure it rather than make assumptions about it.

Our research takes a step in this direction. Using a rich dataset on first-time welfare recipients in Maryland obtained in a study conducted via a long-standing partnership between the state's public welfare agency and its state school of social work, we examined duration dependence, looking at important variables not available in most databases. This study should lead to better estimates of duration dependence and provide empirical data to inform the ongoing debate about the relative importance of cultural and economic factors in welfare dependency.

METHOD

The data used in this study come from two sources: (1) an extensive interview administered to a random sample of 437 women drawn from those applying for AFDC for the first time in Maryland over a six-month period in 1987 and (2) the administrative case records for these women from the time they began receiving AFDC until April 1991. The interview contained detailed questions about demographics, family welfare history, work history, educational experience, and physical health. The administrative case records contained the dates the women went on and off welfare, from which we calculated the length of each recipient's initial welfare spell in months.

We limited the analysis to each recipient's initial welfare spell, because to use any subsequent welfare spells we would need to model AFDC entry, and our data do not allow us to do so. Limiting the analysis to the first spell means that we are underestimating AFDC use for recipients who leave and return to the program. For the majority of recipients in the study, this is not a concern; however, 19.5 percent of the recipients did have more than one spell over the time we observed them. To avoid the problem presented by *churning*—the concept that some AFDC recipients leave the program for administrative reasons—we ignored any interruptions in a spell lasting less than two months.

Besides having more detailed information about a variety of client characteristics, this dataset differs from most others in that it is limited to women receiving AFDC for the first time. For statistical reasons, this is a major advantage because it allows us to avoid the problem of left-censoring that is often present in this type of study. In general, *censoring* occurs when researchers know a client's history only between two given dates. *Left-censoring* refers to information that is missing before the initial date of data collection; *right-censoring* refers to information that is missing after the last date of data collection. Because we have data from the initial date of each client's first spell, there are no left-censored data.

Limiting our analysis to first-time recipients is also advantageous for policy reasons because it is likely that many states will phase in at least some of the new federal reforms by focusing them on AFDC/TANF recipients as they first come on the welfare rolls; however, limiting the analysis to first-time recipients means that the findings may not be representative of the AFDC caseload at any given time and will be less useful for states considering implementing welfare reform measures for their entire caseload.

As with most other studies, our data are right censored because we do not know what happened to these clients after April 1991. Fortunately, the techniques available to compensate for right-censored data are much more tractable than those for left-censored data.

An important concept in event history analysis is the *hazard rate*, that is, the conditional probability of ending a welfare spell at time t given that one is in fact in the midst of a welfare spell at time t. The hazard rate is a function of both explanatory variables and the time spent in a spell. The latter notion—duration dependence—is determined by examining what happens to the hazard rate as t increases. If the hazard rate increases, then spells are characterized as having positive duration dependence; if the hazard rate is constant or falls, then spells are characterized as having no or negative duration dependence, respectively. Another important concept is the use of parametric assumptions about the hazard rate, that is, the a priori assumptions researchers make about the form of the hazard function. We used two parametric forms, the Weibull distribution and the log-logistic distribution, commonly used in event history analysis (Lancaster, 1990).

The Weibull distribution assumes that the hazard function is as follows:

$$\text{hazard}(t) = e^{Bx} * p(e^{Bx} * t)^{p-1} \tag{1}$$

where e = natural log, B = vector of associated coefficients, x = vector of characteristics other than time that determine spell length, p = parameter that determines that distribution of the hazard, and t = time. One way to see how the hazard changes over time is to take the log of equation 1 and see how the hazard rate responds as t increases:

$$\log \text{hazard} = Bx + \log p + (p-1)Bx + (p-1)\log t \tag{2}$$

Note that the only term with t in it is the last term. This means that the log hazard, and hence the hazard rate, either falls, stays constant, or rises depending on the value of p. Specifically,

- If $p > 1$, then the hazard rate goes up with time.
- If $p = 1$, then the hazard rate does not change with time.
- If $p < 1$, then the hazard rate goes down with time.

Thus, under the Weibull form, the parameter p is the critical value to determine whether there is negative duration dependence. However, one limitation of the Weibull assumption is that it allows only for a monotonic hazard rate. Because of this restriction, another commonly assumed distribution is the log-logistic distribution, which allows for the hazard to change direction over time. The log-logistic distribution assumes that the hazard function is as follows:

$$\text{hazard}(t) = e^{Bx} * p(e^{Bx} * t)^{p-1} / (1 + (e^{Bx} * t)^p) \tag{3}$$

Under the log-logistic assumption, the hazard rate is free to change over time. Specifically,

- If $p \leq 1$, then the hazard decreases monotonically over time.
- If $p > 1$, then the hazard rate increases until the point in time when $t = (p-1)^{1/p}/e^{Bx}$.

Under both assumptions, the critical parameter is p. The larger p is, the less likely one is to characterize the population as having negative duration dependence.

Just as changes in p affect how the hazard function traces out over time, the coefficients of the vector, x, show how changes in other characteristics affect the hazard function at any given point in time. For example, if the coefficient of job readiness is positive and significant, then those with higher job readiness scores are more likely to leave AFDC at a given point in time relative to other AFDC recipients.

FINDINGS

Figure 18-1 shows the frequency distribution of welfare spells for the 437 AFDC recipients in the sample. A rising number of recipients leave AFDC during the initial months, with exits tapering off after about a year and decreasing over time. The sharp increase in spell length longer than 42 months is due to right censoring; these recipients were still in the midst of their initial welfare spell when data collection ended in April 1991. As with earlier studies, we found that about 45 percent of spells ended within one year, and 62 percent ended within two years. The remainder of the spells lasted more than two years, and, overall, 24 percent of the sample were still in the midst of their initial welfare spell when data collection ended.

Table 18-1 shows the descriptive statistics for the explanatory variables. After controlling for race, age, number of children, physical health, and the unemployment rate, we included six economic variables and six cultural variables thought to affect spell length. Number of children could be thought of as a cultural variable by those who argue that women who receive AFDC continue to have children to increase their benefit; however, this is unlikely to be the case with first-time AFDC recipients. The six economic variables were (1) education, (2) work experience, and (3) job readiness (measured by the sum of responses to a 19-item Likert scale) and whether lack of (4) available child care

FIGURE 18-1

Frequency of Welfare Spells

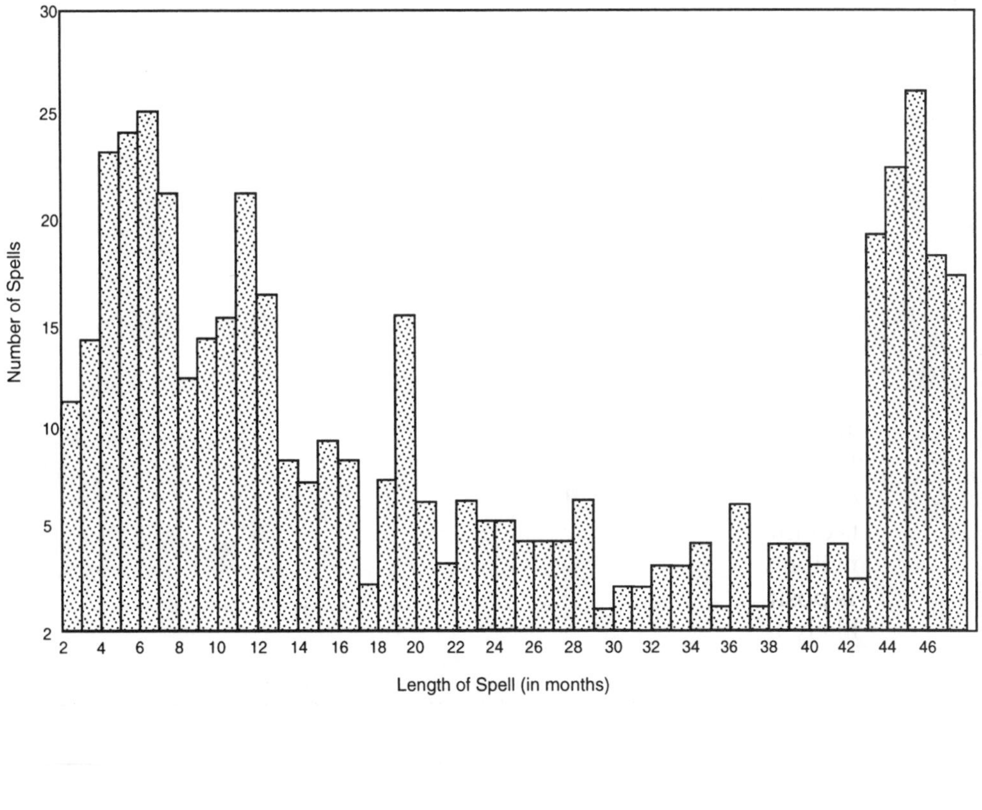

Length of Spell (in months)

TABLE 18-1

Client Characteristics (Weighted by Region)

Characteristic	%
Race	
White	41.1
Other	58.9
No. of children	
1	63.8
2	20.4
3	11.0
4 or more	3.7
Chronic medical condition	
No	72.4
Yes	27.6
High school degree	
No	41.8
Yes	58.2
Full-time job since high school	
No	30.7
Yes	69.3
Child care is barrier to work	
No	52.2
Yes	47.8
Transportation is barrier to work	
No	70.7
Yes	29.3
Loss of Medicaid is barrier to work	
No	86.8
Yes	13.2
Teenage mother	
No	44.1
Yes	55.9
Mother was teenage mother	
No	41.4
Yes	58.6
Family member receiving AFDC	
No	46.9
Yes	53.1
Friend receiving AFDC	
No	51.7
Yes	48.3
Neighbor receiving AFDC	
No	76.2
Yes	23.8
Father of first child took responsibility for child	
No	43.6
Yes	56.4

	M	SD
Age at time of interview	24.1	6.9
Unemployment rate	5.5	1.9
Job readiness score	70	9.3

and (5) transportation and (6) loss of Medicaid were perceived as barriers to employment. The six cultural factors were (1) whether the recipient was a teenage mother; (2) whether her mother was a teenage mother; (3) whether the father of the first child took responsibility for the child; and whether (4) other family members, (5) friends, or (6) neighbors received welfare. Responses for each variable were measured as of the time of the interview at the beginning of the welfare spell, except for the unemployment rate, which was the unemployment rate for the county where the recipient lived at the beginning of her spell, averaged over the $3^1/2$ years of the study period.

Table 18-2 presents the results of the event history analysis using both a Weibull distribution and a log-logistic distribution. Three striking findings emerge: (1) There is much less evidence of negative duration dependence than found in previous studies, (2) almost all of the economic factors significantly affect spell length in the expected direction, and (3) virtually none of the cultural factors is significant. Under the Weibull distribution, the value for p, the parameter for determining the effect of time itself, is 1.142, with a 5 percent confidence interval ranging from 1.001 to 1.283. Because the critical value for this parameter is 1, one can (although just barely) reject the hypothesis that there is negative duration dependence. Under the log-logistic distribution, which has a lower likelihood value and hence seems to fit the data better, the value for p is 1.681, which implies an increasing hazard during the first 14 months of welfare receipt and a falling hazard thereafter. The values under both of these distributions are higher than, for example, those found by Blank (1989) and indicate much less evidence of negative duration dependence than found previously. In fact, when we analyze the data using only the variables available from the Blank study, the values for p drop to 1.085 using the Weibull specification and 1.405 using the log-logistic specification, providing evidence of spurious negative duration dependence.

Even more striking is a comparison of the coefficient for the remaining explanatory variables. Five of the six economic factors are significant under both distributions. As has been found in previous studies (Ellwood, 1986), recipients with a high school degree or post-high school education were more likely to leave AFDC at any given point in time. In addition, those who scored higher on the job readiness scale were also more likely to leave AFDC. Those who cited the lack of affordable child care or transportation costs as barriers to employment were significantly less likely to leave AFDC. The only economic factor that was not significant was the perceived loss of Medicaid as a barrier to employment.

On the other hand, only one of the cultural factors was significant, a result that was not robust across specifications. Under the Weibull distribution, those who had a close friend on AFDC were less likely to leave AFDC at any point in time; however, this factor was not significant under the log-logistic distribution. The other five factors were insignificant under both distributions. In addition, the unemployment rate was significant under both specifications, which also suggests that length of welfare is affected more by economic factors, including those beyond the control of the recipient, than by cultural factors.

TABLE 18-2

Event History Analysis of Duration of Welfare Spells

Variable	Weibull Specification	SE	Log-Logistic Specification	SE
Constant	–3.909*	0.579	–3.749*	0.598
Age	–0.012	0.010	–0.007	0.012
Race (1 = nonwhite)	–0.332*	0.093	–0.387*	0.107
No. of children	0.125*	0.062	0.105	0.071
Chronic medical condition (1 = yes)	0.093	0.101	0.112	0.115
Unemployment rate	–0.074*	0.027	–0.073*	0.028
Education (1 = high school degree)	0.350*	0.107	0.376*	0.116
Work experience (1 = held full-time job since leaving high school)	0.330*	0.123	0.342*	0.124
Job readiness score	0.016*	0.006	0.168*	0.006
Child care is barrier to employment (1 = yes)	–0.361*	0.105	–0.351*	0.112
Transportation is barrier to employment (1 = yes)	–0.232*	0.108	–0.265*	0.120
Loss of Medicaid is barrier to employment (1 = yes)	0.181	0.141	0.302	0.167
Teenage mother (1 = yes)	–0.050	0.109	–0.080	0.127
Mother was teenage mother (1 = yes)	0.136	0.095	0.078	0.104
Family member receiving AFDC (1 = yes)	–0.029	0.100	–0.080	0.109
Friend receiving AFDC (1 = yes)	–0.197*	0.097	–0.165	0.108
Neighbor receiving AFDC (1 = yes)	–0.093	0.113	–0.051	0.119
Father of first child took responsibility for child (1 = yes)	0.068	0.097	0.152	0.108
p	1.142	0.072	1.681	0.089
Confidence interval for p	1.001, 1.283		1.508, 1.855	
Log likelihood	–599		–578	

NOTE: $N = 437$.

*$p < .05$.

CONCLUSION

Because of limitations in the datasets on which they were based, most empirical studies of duration dependence in the AFDC program have used artificial methods to account for client characteristics and other factors thought to be associated with length of welfare spells. Our study did not suffer this common constraint, because we were able to measure and incorporate six economic and six cultural factors in the analysis.

The inclusion of actual data rather than assumptions results in findings that are notably different from those of many other studies. We found little or no evidence that either time on AFDC itself or the presence of a "welfare culture" of friends, family, and neighbors on AFDC induces welfare dependency. Instead, we found that recipients' human capital characteristics and the extent to which child care and transportation pose barriers to employment are much more important contributors to the length of clients' first welfare spell. In addition, we found that the local unemployment rate also has a significant impact on the duration of initial AFDC spells.

These findings lend support to the argument that if client self-sufficiency is truly a goal, meaningful welfare reform must go beyond the imposition of time limits on benefit receipt. The findings suggest that an investment strategy in education, work preparedness, job training, and public-sector jobs, along with the provision of supportive services such as child care and transportation, would be most productive in moving families toward true economic independence.

The findings suggest three dilemmas that states committed to meaningful welfare reform will face as they attempt to plan for and implement the new national law. First, it seems clear that, except for high school or alternative education for teenagers, education will not be a permissible use of federal block grant funds. Instead, only "vocational education activities" qualify, and only a fraction (20 percent) of those enrolled in these activities may be counted toward the mandated work participation rates. Second, the law limits the time period in which a client's participation in education activities may be counted as work to 12 months. Third, the law provides $13 billion less than it projected would be needed to meet the work requirements and $1.4 billion less than what would be needed to provide child care (Center on Budget and Policy Priorities, 1996).

How should the states proceed? One important, immediate step should be to identify recipients who empirical research and practical wisdom suggest most need and could most benefit from the receipt of noncash supportive services, that is, clients who, without such intervention, are most likely to reach the time limits. Constructing a profile of those recipients is beyond the scope of this study. However, if the massive changes embodied in the new welfare reform law are truly meant to do more than just save money, our findings strongly suggest that efforts to identify and intervene with these at-risk families would be a far more effective self-sufficiency strategy over time than the mere imposition of time limits.

REFERENCES

Bane, M. J., & Ellwood, D. (1983). *The dynamics of dependence: The routes to self-sufficiency.* Cambridge, MA: Urban Systems Research and Engineering.

Blank, R. (1989). Analyzing the length of welfare spells. *Journal of Public Economics, 39,* 245–273.

Center on Budget and Policy Priorities. (1996). *The new welfare law.* Washington, DC: Author. (Available from http://www.cbpp.org/wecnf813.html)

Danziger, S., & Gottschalk, P. (1995). *America unequal.* Cambridge, MA: Russell Sage Foundation and Harvard University Press.

Ellwood, D. (1986). *Targeting "would-be" long-term recipients of AFDC.* Cambridge, MA: Harvard University, Mathematica Policy Research.

Hutchins, R. (1981). Entry and exit transitions in a government transfer program: The case of Aid to Families with Dependent Children. *Journal of Human Resources, 16,* 217–237.

Lancaster, T. (1990). *The economic analysis of transition data.* Cambridge, MA: Cambridge University Press.

Mead, L. (1986). *Beyond entitlement: The social obligations of citizenship.* New York: Free Press.

Mead, L. (1992). *The new politics of poverty: The working poor in America.* New York: Basic Books.

Murray, C. (1984). *Losing ground: American social policy, 1950–1980.* New York: Basic Books.

O'Neill, J. A., Bassi, L. J., & Wolf, D. A. (1987). The duration of welfare spells. *Review of Economics and Statistics, 69,* 241–248.

Personal Responsibility and Work Opportunity Reconciliation Act of 1996, P.L. 104-193.

Transcript of President Reagan's speech to Congress on the state of the union. (1986, February 5). *New York Times,* p. A10.

Wilson, W. J. (1987). *The truly disadvantaged.* Chicago: University of Chicago Press.

This chapter was originally published in the December 1996 issue of Social Work Research, *vol. 20, pp. 196–202.*

Family Support as an Intervention with Female Long-term AFDC Recipients

Catherine F. Alter

Although a majority of families who ever receive Aid to Families with Dependent Children (AFDC) rely on ben-efits for a relatively short period of time, about 30 percent are long-term recipients who receive public assistance for three or more years (Duncan & Hoffman, 1988; Ellwood & Bane, 1986). For politicians and policymakers, long-term recipients are the core of the "welfare problem," because at any single point in time they constitute a majority of the AFDC caseload (Murray, 1984). Even modest reductions in the number of long-term recipients produce large welfare savings, because they consume the bulk of AFDC dollars (Ellwood, 1986, 1988). Current welfare reform efforts are therefore testing new methods to help long-term recipients shorten the length of time they depend on AFDC.

Federal policy toward long-term welfare recipients changed with the passage of the Family Support Act of 1988 (FSA) (P.L. 100-485), which acknowledged that leaving welfare is often a lengthy and difficult process for long-term recipients and requires more than traditional employment strategies (Gueron & Pauly, 1991; Hagen, 1995). The vast majority of long-term recipients are single mothers who do not have the concrete resources needed for a transition to work, such as child care and reliable transportation. In addition, many do not have the job skills or the personal competencies to enable them to manage work and parenting successfully. The FSA viewed leaving welfare as a deliberate and incremental process of personal growth, education, and training and suggested that welfare-to-work programs for long-term recipients focus first on the intermediate steps to self-sufficiency and then on continuous support for the transition to independence (Gueron & Pauly, 1991). This policy of the FSA was implemented through the Job Opportunities and Basic Skills Training (JOBS) program, which provided matching funds to states for a broader range of employment services, including specially targeted educational opportunities and intensive support services such as child care, transition work incentives, and other support services. The theory behind both FSA and JOBS was that education with

Preliminary analyses of the data in this article were presented at meetings of the National Association of Family-Based Services, Boston, 1993, and Chicago, 1994. This article reports findings from an evaluation conducted by the Institute for Social and Economic Development (ISED) and funded by the Annie E. Casey Foundation, the Charles Stewart Mott Foundation, and the Wesley and Irene Mansfield Charitable Foundation. John Else, president of ISED, was project director. A copy of the evaluation is available from ISED, 1901 Broadway, Suite 303, Iowa City, IA 52240.

support services would increase recipients' human capital, thus increasing their ability to obtain higher wages and enabling them to move out of poverty and into economic stability and independence.

Evaluation research in recent years has focused on state efforts to reduce AFDC rolls by increasing recipients' earning power (Hagen, 1994). In a review of four state welfare-to-work initiatives of the 1980s, Friedlander and Burtless (1995) found that the three narrowly focused Work Incentive programs were not effective in increasing earned income five years after recipients exited their programs. In contrast, a review of nine broad coverage programs showed differential results depending on the subgroup of recipients (Gueron & Pauly, 1991). In general, the smallest program effects were achieved by the least disadvantaged group of women—that is, those who were receiving AFDC benefits for the first time and who had recent work experience; even without assistance they tended to stay on welfare for relatively brief periods of time. By contrast, the moderately disadvantaged women—that is, those who had received AFDC before, were reapplying, and had some employment history—exhibited the most consistent positive effects. The most disadvantaged women—that is, those who were long-term recipients and had the weakest employment histories—did not show consistent or large earnings gains (Gueron & Pauly, 1991).

The research on 1980s programs looked at programs that attempted rapid job placement. Comprehensive programs that provide long-term recipients with education and support represent a different approach, one that has not been rigorously evaluated. This article asks two questions: (1) Does family support enable long-term recipients to develop the personal competencies and the job skills necessary for successful job entry? and (2) Once employed, is their earning power sufficient to make self-sufficiency a realistic alternative to public assistance? The first question addresses the efficacy of family support as a method of achieving job readiness, an approach that has not been studied to date. The second question suggests that single mothers may not willingly give up their benefits unless their earned income has equivalent purchasing power in terms of food, housing, and medical care for their children.

IOWA FAMILY DEVELOPMENT AND SELF-SUFFICIENCY PROGRAM

The Family Development and Self-Sufficiency (FaDSS) Program is a component of Iowa's welfare reform initiative. It provides family support and other services to female long-term AFDC recipients. FaDSS involves participant families in an intense relationship with a specially trained family development specialist who assists them with personal growth activities—planning for the future, learning to obtain social services and education, and building assertiveness skills. FaDSS is based on the premise that family support helps parents achieve personal self-sufficiency, which in turn enables them to achieve economic self-sufficiency (Bruner, 1989). Family support, in this context, shifts the focus of involvement from the problems of the individual AFDC recipient to a family-centered perspective, and the entire family participates in program activities. The overall strategy is to build on each family's individual strengths, treat parents as partners, provide access to comprehensive services, and integrate families into their communities (Alter, Deutelbaum, Dodd, Else, & Raheim, 1990; Dunst, Trivette, & Deal, 1988; Weiss, 1992).

At the psychological level, family support buffers or absorbs some of the extraordinary stress experienced by family members, which, in turn, enables them to develop better coping skills and a future orientation (Thoits, 1986). The central assumption of FaDSS is not new—that the power of the personal relationship between a family development specialist and the long-term recipient enables the latter to organize and focus her energy to achieve personal competence and ultimately economic self-sufficiency (Perlman, 1971). The application of family support to long-term public assistance recipients is new.

The theoretical model on which the FaDSS program plan is based (Alter, Losby, & Yarbrough, 1996) draws from theories of life-cycle development (Bronfenbrenner, 1979), chronic stress (Cole, 1980; Colten & Gore, 1991; Mirowsky & Ross, 1989), social support (Caplan, 1981; Thoits, 1986; Weiss, 1992; Zigler & Black, 1989), family empowerment (Dunst et al., 1988; Gutierrez, 1990; Pinderhughes, 1983; Rappaport, Swift, & Hess, 1984), and family-based services (Hartman & Laird, 1983). According to the model, parents who participate in FaDSS experience two kinds of program effects. The first hypothesized effect is intermediate changes, including internal psychosocial changes and behavioral changes. Participants are expected to become more efficacious or able to accomplish the tasks required for meeting the needs of themselves and their families; to be more successful in accomplishing these tasks and thus feel greater competence and mastery; and, therefore, to be more self-confident in themselves and their capacity to have fulfilling family lives. As a result of assistance and coaching from the family development specialists, FaDSS participants are also expected to exhibit behavioral changes: to improve the housing situation of their families, to increase their level of education, and to obtain employment in greater numbers and earn higher wages than those in the control group. The second hypothesized effect is that in the long run, participants will achieve self-sufficiency faster than nonparticipants.

The 10 Iowa nonprofit agencies that began delivery of FaDSS services between 1989 and 1991 offer the same in-home service components—family assessment, goal setting, ongoing family support, and advocacy—as well as specialized group and center-based activities. The program's intermediate objective of building personal competencies is also sought through referral to other community agencies and networking with formal and informal helping networks, so that each participant is linked to all the services she needs. Home visits continue until the family requests that they end or until 90 days after the family is no longer receiving AFDC benefits.

This article reports findings about the effectiveness of the FaDSS Program and thus sheds some light on the efficacy of family support with female long-term recipients or those at risk of long-term dependency. It presents information on only the intermediate and longer-term effects of the program on its participants. Other findings from the evaluation are in preparation: the nature of and activities inherent in the family support approach (Alter, Yarbrough, & Losby, 1996), descriptions of the instruments used to measure FaDSS effects (Alter et al., 1996), and a study of the reliability of self-reported AFDC history (Losby & Alter, 1996).

EVALUATION OF FaDSS

Methods

The evaluation of the FaDSS Program used a randomized control group design. For three years starting from the initiation of the program in January 1989, the grantee agencies recruited long-term AFDC recipient families. In the summer of 1993, the researchers randomly selected respondents for the evaluation from the two groups, and during the fall they conducted one-hour interviews.

Procedures

The evaluation design used a three-step process. The grantee agencies recruited participants from lists of AFDC recipients supplied to them by the Iowa Department of Human Services (IDHS). The individuals on these lists were those who met the established criteria for long-term dependency or for being at risk of long-term dependency. AFDC parents who agreed to participate were informed that they might be placed in a control group. The agencies then sent the lists of those who agreed to participate back to the IDHS central office, where they were randomly assigned to the FaDSS group ($n = 384$) or control group ($n = 319$). AFDC recipients who were assigned to the control group did not receive FaDSS services, but they were eligible for all other welfare-to-work programs available in the state, including those of the Iowa PROMISE JOBS program. Members of the control group were not contacted again by anyone from the FaDSS grantee agencies.

The second step took place in 1993 when the research team obtained the lists of all FaDSS and control respondents from the four largest programs and randomly selected two research groups—the FaDSS group ($n = 300$) and the control group ($n = 300$).

The third step occurred between September 1, 1993, and December 17, 1993, when we attempted to reach all 600 respondents in the research groups for telephone interviews. Each of the four research agencies provided its most current addresses and telephone numbers for the research families before the interviewing period began, and they sent a letter explaining the nature of the evaluation to every family. As the interviewing period continued, follow-up mailings encouraged families to participate in the interview. If letters were returned marked "address unknown," we consulted telephone directories, and if this was unsuccessful, we contacted directory assistance to obtain the telephone number of relatives who might put us in touch with the respondents. Families without telephones were interviewed at agency offices. All participants who completed the interview were compensated with a $10 gift certificate from a local merchant.

We located 200 respondents in the FaDSS group and 150 in the control group who were willing to participate in the study, for a completion rate of 67 percent and 50 percent, respectively. Given the constraints we were under—the FaDSS Program had been in operation for three years before the evaluation, and the members of the control group had had no contact with any staff person during that period of time—the completion rate is as high as can be expected and is similar to other studies that have targeted similar populations (Maynard, 1993; Maynard & Fraker, 1987).

Possible Bias. We identified two sources of potential bias in the sample selection procedures used. One occurred during the first step, when one grantee began working with all the individuals in its first batch of recruits rather than waiting for the names of those who had been randomly assigned to the FaDSS group. This meant that 32 individuals who should have been in the control group were reclassified as members of the FaDSS group, and this accounts for the unequal numbers of individuals in the two groups.

We reasoned that a possible source of bias might stem from the fact that the offending grantee was located in a geographic area with a better job market and more educational opportunities, thus giving the individuals in the FaDSS Program a better chance of achieving favorable outcomes. To investigate this possibility, we compared the outcomes of FaDSS group members served by the offending grantee with those served by the other grantees. There were only minor differences, and these pointed away from bias. For example, we looked at the proportion of months during the research period that families were off AFDC and found that the offending agency's clients were off AFDC an average of 28 percent of the months, whereas the balance of the FaDSS group was off 30 percent of the time. We concluded that the recruitment and random assignment procedure did not bias the sample.

Our other concern was bias resulting from nonresponse—the inability of interviewers to locate respondents. To investigate this possibility, we compared the respondent group to the nonresponse group for both the experimental group and the control group. The only data item available for respondents and nonrespondents alike was the number of months they had been on AFDC prior to assignment to a group. Because this is one indicator of subsequent AFDC dependency (Ellwood, 1988), we used it as a measure of comparability. We found that in the FaDSS group, respondents had received AFDC benefits an average of 13.5 months, whereas nonrespondents had received benefits for an average 12.7 months; in the control group the average for respondents was 14.1 months and 13.3 months for nonrespondents. These are small differences and are perhaps the result of the nonrespondents' moving out of state for work or marriage. In any case, the difference is equal in both magnitude (less than a month) and direction for the experimental and control groups and for the respondents and nonrespondents.

Representativeness. In assessing the representativeness of the sample, we found only one difference between the respondents in the FaDSS and control groups at the time of assignment. The two groups were similar with regard to age, years of education, number of children, years on AFDC prior to assignment, and ethnicity. Comparison of marital status, however, showed that more FaDSS participants had never married and proportionately more control group members were separated, divorced, or widowed or married or living with a partner (Table 19-1). This difference in marital status may have occurred

TABLE 19-1

Characteristics of FaDSS Participants and Control Group at Time of Assignment (*N* = 348)

Characteristic	FaDSS Participants (*n* = 199)		Control Group (*n* = 149)	
	M	*SD*	*M*	*SD*
Age	28.3	6.6	28.2	6.5
Years of education				
completed	12.0	1.7	11.9	1.7
Number of children	2.0	1.1	2.1	1.1
Years on AFDC				
prior to assignment	6.2	4.9	6.6	4.6
	n	%	*n*	%
Ethnicity				
White	179	89.9	138	92.6
Other	20	10.1	11	7.4
Marital status				
Never married	72	36.1	34	22.8
Separated, divorced,				
or widowed	81	40.7	73	48.9
Married or living				
together	46	23.1	42	28.2

NOTES: FaDSS = Family Development and Self-Sufficiency Program. The original sample included 350 respondents. On inspection, it was discovered that two participants were men, one each in the FaDSS and control groups. They were excluded from the analysis, producing a sample size of 348. Statistical difference between the FaDSS group and the control group, $\chi^2 = 7.0$, $p < .05$.

because one program targeted individuals who were at risk of long-term AFDC dependency, and most of these were unwed teenage mothers. A breakdown of the groups into age categories shows that 38.7 percent of the FaDSS group were under 24 years of age, whereas only 33.6 percent of the control group fell into this category, and virtually all of these participants were single parents. Although this difference may be a source of bias, it points away from program effectiveness, because we expected teenagers to take longer to become self-sufficient than mothers in their late twenties and thirties.

Measures of Intermediate Effects

Self-Efficacy. Many families in poverty are continuously vulnerable to major crises because of relatively small problems and needs. For example, the 10-year-old car breaks down and the parent does not have the $150 needed for repairs, so she cannot get to work, the rent does not get paid the next month, and the family is evicted from their apartment. Stabilization of the family's living arrangements and the meeting of basic needs are therefore the first steps in the path to personal and economic self-sufficiency (Bruner & Berryhill, 1992). The family development specialists first assist participants in stabilizing their living situations and then in building their self-efficacy; they impart information about services and resources available in the community, coach participants on how to obtain the services they need, teach home management and assertiveness skills, and advocate for participants when necessary.

The FaDSS Program assumes that participants who have knowledge of community resources and know how to obtain and manage them will perceive themselves and their families to be less in need. To test this assumption, we developed a five-item scale in which participants were asked to rate how able they were to meet their families' needs (financial situation, transportation situation, own education, children's food needs, and children's education) before enrollment (or assignment) and at the time of the interview. We used a three-point scale (1 = poor, 2 = adequate, 3 = excellent) and then calculated the difference between the responses for the two points in time. The analysis compared these difference scores for the two groups across time.

Competence. Family development specialists frequently encounter women who are overwhelmed by the enormity of providing for the needs of their children and themselves. Living with poverty takes an enormous toll on single parents, and its effects are often low self-esteem, feelings of helplessness, depression, and social isolation. The FaDSS Program focuses on building personal competence and sense of control—often termed a "process of empowerment" (Gutierrez, 1990). Family development specialists assist participants in actively accomplishing tasks of daily living, assuming that a sense of mastery grows from the successful completion of these tasks and that the process is a spiral—small achievements become the foundation for larger achievements, which together undergird an increasing sense of control over daily life (Herr & Halpern, 1991).

To measure respondents' perceptions of their feeling of mastery, we developed a 12-item scale, each item focusing on a specific task associated with the daily care of children or self. Respondents were asked to respond yes or no to whether they thought they were able to accomplish the following 12 tasks at the two points in time: (1) find and keep permanent employment, (2) avoid destructive relationships, (3) create and stick to a budget, (4) find and use community services, (5) feel a part of the community, (6) get teachers to listen when they were talking about their children, (7) find and keep good friends, (8) keep themselves healthy, (9) have satisfying relationships with their children, (10) take their children to the dentist twice a year, (11) take their school-age children to the doctor when needed, and (12) take their preschool children to the doctor for annual checkups. This scale was analyzed and scored in the same way as the self-efficacy scale.

Self-Confidence. Family development specialists begin to learn the parents' secrets once they establish rapport with their families (for example, childhood histories of neglect, abuse, and family violence). In addition, many of the single mothers have men in their lives who themselves experienced childhood abuse, delinquency, and academic failure. These relationships are maintained even when they are unhealthy, because these women lack the resources and self-confidence needed to break away and live independently. The FaDSS Program assumes that as women experience success in meeting the basic needs of their families and begin to better organize and cope with day-to-day life, they gain confidence and learn that they are strong and capable. This change in self-image, in turn, enables them to overcome their need for a relationship at any cost and to seek out other support in healthy ways. They also become more consistent and less physical in disciplining their children and enjoy more the leisure time they spend together (Bruner & Berryhill, 1992).

We constructed a self-confidence scale drawing from the work of Caplan (1981) on self-confidence; Pearlin, Lieberman, Menaghan, and Muller (1981) on mastery; and Rosenberg (1965) on self-image. We selected 12 items that measure respondents' confidence in their ability to plan and shape their futures and those of their children. In the telephone interview, the women were read 12 statements (for example, "You have a plan for the future," "You can do anything you set your mind to," "You are confident that you will be able to reach your goals," "You are able to do things as well as most other people," "What happens to you in the future mostly depends on you," "You feel responsible for your future and your children's future"). Respondents were then asked whether they agreed or disagreed with the statement as it applied to them at the time of their enrollment (or assignment) and then were asked if their agreement or disagreement was "strong" or "slight." This scale produced responses on a four-point scale ranging from 1 = strongly disagree to 4 = strongly agree. It was repeated to apply to the day of the interview. We scored and analyzed the scale responses in the same way as the other two scales. Like the self-efficacy and competence scales, the self-confidence scale is a self-assessment—respondents' perceptions of how much they had changed between the time of their enrollment and the day they were talking with the interviewer.

Housing. Poor families may regularly face eviction or loss of their homes. Moving frequently or, conversely, remaining in an unsafe living situation is one measure of family instability and inability to gain control over needed concrete resources. Because housing is such a critical factor contributing to family stability, we created a separate scale to measure how respondents perceived their current housing situations. If the respondent said that she was not satisfied with her family's housing, she was then asked to identify specifically what was unsatisfactory and what she was doing about it. It was expected that FaDSS participants' growing competence and self-confidence would enable them to be more proactive in solving their housing problems.

Education. Education is one path to personal and economic self-sufficiency, and it is therefore a major focus of the family development specialists' work with FaDSS participants. We asked participants a short series of questions about their educational attainment during the research period and expected that a greater percentage of FaDSS participants would have enrolled in educational programs and completed more years of school than members of the control group.

Employment. Employment is the other intermediate path to self-sufficiency. FaDSS participants are expected to gain employment in greater numbers, to have better jobs (full-time with benefits), and to receive higher wages than members of the control group. We categorized the ability to find employment as an intermediate effect of the FaDSS Program, rather than as a program outcome, for the following reason: In an earlier study of AFDC recipients in Iowa, Fisher, Forkenbrock, Pogue, and Tracy (1989) found that to fully replace the purchasing value of public assistance for a family with two children in Iowa—including AFDC, food stamps, Medicaid, and housing subsidies—a woman would have to earn approximately

$10.32 per hour, a wage reached by few long-term recipients, and then not until after many years of work. It therefore seemed reasonable to measure employment as a step toward self-sufficiency and not an end in itself.

Measures of Longer-Term Effects: Economic Self-Sufficiency

The desired longer-term outcome of the FaDSS Program is economic *self-sufficiency*, defined as coming off, and staying off, the AFDC program. The telephone interview therefore contained items that asked respondents to recall the dates they were first on and off AFDC and then the starting and ending dates for all subsequent spells. From this information we calculated the total number of months recipients had received AFDC benefits before and after assignment.

In pursuing the assessment of validity, we sought a criterion for the reliability of these self-reported AFDC data and obtained from IDHS the electronic administrative file containing the month-by-month records of AFDC checks sent to the 350 respondents for the preceding six years. We compared the self-reports with the electronic data and found there was not a high level of agreement between the two, especially beyond the first spell (Losby & Alter, 1996). We concluded that, although not perfectly reliable, the administrative file was a more accurate source of information on AFDC history than were respondents' memories. All of the outcome data reported here are therefore taken from the IDHS AFDC records.

Although by February 1995 we had had the AFDC records for 74 months, we did not have six years of postassignment history for each respondent, because they enrolled in FaDSS (or were assigned) at different times between January 1989 and December 1991. We put all respondents in the same time frame, regardless of what month and year they were actually assigned, and found that there were 42 months of AFDC history for all of them. (For each month after the 42nd month, we had a reduced sample size.) We simply calculated the percentage of respondents who were off AFDC (for the last time during the research period) in each month, stopping at the 60th month when the sample size became too small.

Validity and Reliability of Interview Schedules

Before starting the interviews, we investigated the content validity of the interview schedule with members of Iowa's Family Development and Self-Sufficiency Council, program staff, and other colleagues with knowledge of and experience with family support programs. To assess face validity we pilot-tested the three intermediate effect scales with AFDC recipients who were not involved in FaDSS but who resided in the same geographic areas and had similar AFDC histories. Feedback from both of these assessments provided the basis for numerous changes in the interview schedule; these processes and the results are described in Alter, Yarbrough, and Losby (1996).

We also investigated the internal consistency of each of the scales. The self-efficacy scale had the highest level of reliability (Cronbach's alpha = .86), followed by the self-confidence scale (Cronbach's alpha = .85) and the competence scale (Cronbach's alpha = .75).

RESULTS

Intermediate Outcomes

Self-Efficacy. Members of the control group reported a higher aggregate score for self-efficacy ($M = 1.97$) than did the FaDSS group ($M = 1.89$) at the first point in time. By the interview date, however, the FaDSS participants rated themselves higher ($M = 2.29$) than the control group members did ($M = 2.20$). Both of these differences are statistically significant. This pattern held across time. The FaDSS participants reported a greater increase in their perceived ability between their assignment and the interview (.40) than did the control group (.23), and the difference between these gains was also statistically significant. In addition, there was a statistically significant interaction effect [$F(1, 348) = 16.25, p < .0001$] between program participation and time, indicating that, overall, FaDSS clients felt they had improved significantly over the course of their participation in their ability to meet concrete family needs, and this change was greater for FaDSS parents than it was for members of the control group (Table 19-2).

Competence. FaDSS participants and control group members judged their competence quite similarly at the time of their assignment but significantly differently at the time of the interview [$F(1, 348) = 7.09, p < .0081$]. When comparing the indices across time, both groups felt they were more competent at the second point, although the gain of the FaDSS participants was greater (0.20) than it was for the control group (0.14). Overall, there was an interaction between treatment and time, indicating that there was a significant difference in perceived competence between FaDSS parents and control group members across time [$F(1, 348) = 7.64, p < .0060$] (Table 19-2).

Self-Confidence. The self-confidence score was the same for the FaDSS and control groups at the time of the assignment, and there was also no difference between the two groups at the time of the interview. There was, however, a small difference between FaDSS participants and control group members in terms of how much their scores improved across time. The FaDSS participants' index score increased by 0.33, whereas the control group's score increased by only 0.12. This difference was not large enough, however, to produce an overall interaction between treatment and time (Table 19-2).

Housing. A larger proportion of the FaDSS parents (47.7 percent) said they had been dissatisfied with their housing than did the control families (38.7 percent). FaDSS participants and control parents were similar in regard to the reasons for their dissatisfaction—amount of space, maintenance of the residence, and safety—but there were differences in what they did about these problems. A significantly larger percentage of control parents with housing problems did nothing (75.9 percent) compared with FaDSS participants who did nothing (27.4 percent). Of those who took action to solve their housing problems, a greater proportion of FaDSS parents looked for another place to live, filed a complaint with their landlord, or filed for subsidized housing. The modal response of control parents was to try to fix the problem themselves (Table 19-3).

Education. Members of the control group, although starting with almost the same level of education ($M = 11.9$ years) as the FaDSS group ($M = 12.0$ years),

TABLE 19-2

Differences in Perception of FaDSS Participants and Control Group Members on Three Scales at Assignment and Time of Interview and Changes across Time (N = 348)

Scale and Variable	FaDSS Participants (n = 199)		Control Group (n = 149)		F	p
	M	SD	M	SD		
Self-efficacy scale						
Simple effect for participants and control group	FaDSS Participants		Control Group			
Then	1.89	.34	1.97	.38	7.60	.0062
Now	2.29	.36	2.20	.41	8.68	.0034
Simple effect for time	Then		Now			
FaDSS participants	1.89	.34	2.29	.36	213.6	.0001
Control group	1.97	.38	2.20	.41	53.52	.0001
Participation × time interaction F(1, 348)					16.25	.0001
Competence scale						
Simple effect for participants and control group	FaDSS Participants		Control Group			
Then	.70	.21	.72	.22	1.55	.2134
Now	.90	.13	.86	.16	7.09	.0081
Simple effect for time	Then		Now			
FaDSS participants	.70	.21	.90	.13	171.7	.0001
Control group	.76	.22	.86	.16	59.17	.0001
Participation × time interaction F(1, 348)					7.64	.0060
Self-confidence scale						
Simple effect for participants and control group	FaDSS Participants		Control Group			
Then	2.76	.70	2.87	.74	1.94	.1645
Now	3.09	.49	2.99	.41	1.31	.2539
Simple effect for time	Then		Now			
FaDSS participants	2.76	.76	3.09	.40	17.68	.0001
Control group	2.87	.74	2.99	.41	1.59	.2084
Participation × time interaction F(1, 348)					3.21	.0740

NOTE: FaDSS = Family Development and Self-Sufficiency Program.

gained only 0.6 years of additional education between their enrollment and the interview date, compared with 1.1 years for the FaDSS participants. This is a statistically significant difference [$F(1, 348) = 10.9, p < .01$]. More FaDSS participants enrolled in educational programs (61.0 percent) than did control group members (46.7 percent), and 43.5 percent of FaDSS participants enrolled in either community colleges or four-year institutions, compared with only 26.0 percent of the control group (Table 19-3).

TABLE 19-3

Changes in Housing and Education between Assignment and Interview by FaDSS Participants and Control Group Members

Area of Change	FaDSS Participants ($n = 199$)		Control Group ($n = 149$)		F	df
	n	$\%$	n	$\%$		
Housing						
Dissatisfied with family's housing	95	47.7	58	38.7		
Did nothing	26	27.4	44	75.9	71.3***	1, 348
Did something	69	72.6	14	24.1	15.9***	1, 348
Looked for another place to live	29	30.5	0	0.0		
Filed complaint with landlord	19	20.0	1	1.7		
Fixed the problem themselves	15	15.8	13	22.4		
Filed for subsidized housing	6	6.3	0	0.0		
Total	69	72.6	14	24.1		
Education						
Total enrollments	173	86.5	78	52.0	17.6***	1, 348
Total enrolled in an educational						
program	122	61.0	70	46.7	7.1**	1, 348
PROMISE JOBS	29	14.5	10	6.7	5.3*	1, 348
JTPA program	29	14.5	8	5.3	7.6**	1, 348
Community college	59	29.5	26	17.3		
College or university	28	14.0	13	8.7		
Technical or vocational school	13	6.5	6	4.0		
Completed high school or						
GED courses	15	7.5	15	10.0		
	M	SD	M	SD		
Education gain (in years)	1.1	1.3	.6	.9	10.9*	1, 348

NOTE: FaDSS = Family Development and Self-Sufficiency Program; JOBS = Job Opportunities and Basic Skills Training program; JTPA = Job Training Partnership Act; GED = general equivalency diploma.
*$p < .05$. **$p < .01$. ***$p < .0001$.

Employment. There were no statistically significant differences between the FaDSS participants and control group members in terms of employment. At assignment, one-quarter to one-third of both groups were working, whereas at the time of the interview, 53.5 percent of FaDSS participants and 51.3 percent of control parents had jobs. Slightly more of the FaDSS participants had full-time jobs, however. The only statistical difference was for wages: FaDSS participants gained considerably more in their earned wages ($3.41 per hour) than did control group members ($2.22 per hour) (Table 19-4).

Longer-Term Outcome: Self-Sufficiency

Our analysis of the IDHS AFDC grant history file showed that there were no differences between the treatment and control groups in the proportion that exited AFDC after assignment, at least for five years after assignment. In fact, a larger percentage of control group members were off AFDC at each six-month increment, and this trend did not begin to reverse until the 54th month (Figure 19-1).

TABLE 19-4

Changes in Employment between Assignment and Interview by FaDSS Participants and Control Group Members

Employment	FaDSS Participants (n = 199)		Control Group (n = 149)		χ^2
	n	%	*n*	%	
Employed at time of assignment	57	28.6	49	33.1	
Employed at time of interview	107	53.5	77	51.3	
Employment gain	50	24.9	28	18.2	
Current job					
Part-time	33	30.8	30	39.0	
Full-time	74	69.2	47	61.0	
Health care benefits	49	45.8	37	48.0	
No health care benefits	58	54.2	40	52.0	
Wages	*M*	*SD*	*M*	*SD*	
Average hourly wage at time of assignment	$2.32	$2.50	$2.92	$2.74	
Average hourly wage at time of interview	$5.73	$2.92	$5.14	3.02	
Wage gain	$3.41	$4.06	$2.22	$4.34	4.14*

*$p < .05$.

Subsequent analysis led us to develop three mutually exclusive categories for respondents depending on whether they (1) found employment and went to work (job group), (2) enrolled in school and worked part-time (job and school group), or (3) went neither to work nor to school (neither group). Repeating the analysis in Figure 19-1 using these three categories, we obtained the results shown in Table 19-5.

Sixty-one of the 192 members of the FaDSS group (32 percent) and 62 of the 147 members of the control group (42 percent) chose the job path. Of all job-path respondents who reached self-sufficiency by the 60th month (for whom we had records), a larger percentage of the FaDSS group than of the control group reached self-sufficiency (78 percent compared with 63 percent). Until the 48th month, a larger percentage of the control group had exited AFDC, but then their numbers began to decline, whereas the FaDSS group had an increase in the percentage who were exiting. The difference between the treatment and control job-path subgroups in the 60th month was significant at the $p < .10$ level.

One hundred twelve of the FaDSS participants (58 percent) and 68 of the control group members (46 percent) returned to school and worked part-time. Of those who took advantage of educational opportunities, 46 percent of the FaDSS participants and 38 percent of the control group had exited AFDC by the 60th month.

Nineteen of the FaDSS participants (10 percent) and 17 of the control group members (12 percent) neither returned to school nor went to work. Of this last

FIGURE 19-1

Percentage of FaDSS Participants and Control Group Members off AFDC Each Six Months from Assignment across 60 Months (N = 339)

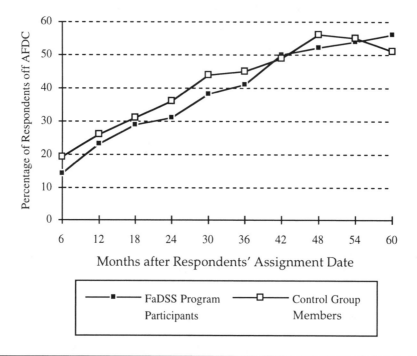

SOURCE: Iowa Department of Human Services (IDHS) AFDC records.

NOTES: FaDSS = Family Development and Self-Sufficiency Program; AFDC = Aid to Families with Dependent Children. The sample size for this figure (N = 339) is less than the number in the tables (N = 348) because the IDHS file is missing nine records. For 48, 54, and 60 months, the number of individuals declined because they had assignment dates in 1991 and therefore had not had more than four years of postassignment AFDC history. Between months 48 and 60, the total of 339 declined to 218.

group, only 40 percent of the FaDSS participants were self-sufficient, compared with 56 percent of the control group, by the 60th month.

We went back to the demographic data to see if there were personal characteristics or other factors that would explain individual trajectories off AFDC by any of these paths. Of the demographic variables that accounted for trajectory (for example, age of subject, age of subject at birth of first child, number of children at assignment, education level of subject at assignment, and so forth), we found two that differentiated the women who went neither to school nor to work from those who did. The first factor was having a child with a serious health problem or disability. The second factor was the number of children; at the time of the interview, the latter group had significantly more children ($M = 2.3$) than the other two groups ($M = 1.8$). Apparently this subgroup of the FaDSS and control groups had greater child care responsibilities than others did, and this was a barrier to moving toward self-sufficiency.

TABLE 19-5

Percentage of FaDSS Participants and Control Group Members off AFDC at the End of Each Six Months, by Employment Category (N = 339)

Off AFDC at End of	FaDSS Participants				Control Group			
	Job (n = 61)	Job and School (n = 112)	Neither (n = 19)	Total (N = 192)	Job (n = 62)	Job and School (n = 68)	Neither (n = 17)	Total (N = 147)
6 months	28	8	5	14	29	12	18	19
12 months	44	14	5	23	34	16	35	26
18 months	54	20	16	29	42	21	35	31
24 months	53	22	11	31	53	25	24	36
30 months	57	32	16	38	58	35	29	44
36 months	64	32	21	41	65	32	24	45
42 months	69	45	26	50	73	36	24	49
48 months[a]	68	49	14	52[b]	71	43	44	56[c]
54 months	67	49	38	54[d]	67	46	44	55[e]
60 months[f]	78	46	40	56[g]	63	38	56	51[h]

Source: Iowa Department of Human Services (IDHS) AFDC records.

Note: AFDC = Aid to Families with Dependent Children; FaDSS = Family Development and Self-Sufficiency Program.

[a] The sample size for Table 5 (N = 339) is less than on the previous tables (N = 348), because the IDHS file is missing nine records. For 48, 54, and 60 months, the number in each cell declined because some participants had assignment dates in 1991 and therefore had not had more than four years of postassignment AFDC history. Between months 48 and 60, the total sample of FaDSS participants declined to 218.

[b] N = 153.

[c] N = 109.

[d] N = 148.

[e] N = 105.

[f] Mean differences between participants and control group members were not statistically significant at p < .05. The small sample size makes detecting significant differences difficult. However, the within-group difference between the "job" and "school and job" groups is significant at the p < .06 level, and the difference between the treatment and control "job" groups is significant at the p < .10 level.

[g] N = 129.

[h] N = 89.

We used two regression models to determine if program factors had a significant effect on the probability of participants getting off AFDC. The first model used demographic variables only at the time of participants' enrollment in FaDSS (Table 19-6). The second model added program variables: path off AFDC, duration of enrollment, and support of the FaDSS worker. The dependent variable was participants' months off AFDC as a percentage of the total months they could have been off AFDC between enrollment and 48 months after enrollment, the last time we analyzed IDHS files of benefit checks.

DISCUSSION

This evaluation has provided some evidence to validate the assumptions of the FaDSS Program model and to answer the study questions. In regard to the first question, the study showed that FaDSS participants achieved a greater increase in competence and self-efficacy than recipients who were not assigned to the family support program. Significantly more FaDSS participants reported feeling more confident about their ability to cope with everyday life, to meet the concrete needs of their families, to improve their housing situation, and to take advantage of educational opportunities.

Participants made considerable progress toward stability and independence, a feat that does not fit the stereotype of the long-term welfare recipient. Current debate about welfare reform in the press and among politicians often characterizes welfare recipients as unmotivated and content to live indefinitely on public assistance. We found the opposite to be true: After participation in FaDSS, most respondents made substantial improvements in their lives. Fewer than 10 percent of the respondents (a total of 19 individuals out of 200) failed to find employment or go back to school during the period of the study, and half of these had more children than the others or had a child with a disability.

In regard to the second study question, the FaDSS participants' movement toward the desired outcome—being off AFDC without returning—was slower than policymakers would like. After two years in FaDSS, only 30 percent were self-sufficient, and at three years, only 40 percent were economically independent. It was not until $3^1/2$ years after enrollment that half of the FaDSS respondents were off AFDC. This is also the point when the FaDSS group started outperforming the control group.

These outcomes may disappoint some, but it is necessary to understand the findings within the context of prior research. Friedlander and Burtless (1995) found that in the one broad-based program they included in their study (California's San Diego Saturation Work Initiative Model), the experimental group had 21 percent greater earnings in the first year of the study and 29 percent in the second year, five years *after* their exit from the program. In contrast, this study at present has only $1^1/2$ years of postprogram AFDC history for all the FaDSS respondents (assuming an average of two years of program participation). It will take another three to four years of AFDC history to be able to assess conclusively whether family support is effective when self-sufficiency is the outcome measure.

This study found preliminary indicators of positive outcomes, however. The trend lines in Figure 19-1 suggest that the FaDSS group may achieve greater economic independence in the long run, and the difference between the two groups is approaching statistical significance (Table 19-5). Given more time and the capacity to follow the two groups, we will have an assessment of whether family support coupled with generous education and training provisions is successful with female long-term welfare recipients.

Perhaps the most important finding is that it takes time for this population to exit AFDC. Long-term recipients are a very disadvantaged group of women, even when compared to the rest of the AFDC population. These women grew up in poverty and are raising their children in poverty; impoverished environments often inflict considerable stress and misfortune on women and children. In seeking evidence for this assumption, we mailed our respondents a straightforward yes–no checklist of stressful events (Greenspan, Weider, Lieberman, Nover, Lourie, & Robinson, 1987). We obtained a response rate of 57.3 percent. The women reported extraordinarily high levels of emotional abuse as adults (71.3 percent), physical abuse as adults (57.9 percent), physical (41.1 percent) and sexual (39.3 percent) abuse as children, and homelessness as adults (19.6 percent). On average, the respondents said they had suffered 4.5 of the 10 stressors listed. This high level of stress and its associated scars greatly disadvantage these women in their quest to believe that they can control their lives and plan an alternative future for themselves and their children.

There are factors other than personal stress that also account for continued AFDC dependency. For one, young girls are socialized to want to be good mothers, and in our culture, especially among lower socioeconomic groups, good mothers take care of their children themselves—they do not turn them over to kin or to strangers. In qualitative focus group data we have from these women, there is evidence that many are willing to absorb the stigma and sanctions of prolonged welfare dependency to be full-time mothers, often the only role in which they feel comfortable and fulfilled. For them, gaining the confidence to take on another role, being able to ask for help, and learning to use it effectively all take time. For the FaDSS participants who returned to school (61 percent), the move toward self-sufficiency was necessarily delayed by the number of years they were in school. This is a plausible explanation for why the percentage of FaDSS participants exiting AFDC surpass the control group until 42 months after enrollment.

The other path off AFDC was via employment. A considerable number of women found employment (without going back to school), in spite of the fact that they had young children. As a subcategory of this cohort, it is not surprising that they achieved self-sufficiency faster than those who returned to school, and for them employment was thus the best short-term strategy. Five years after assignment, however, the proportion of this group who were off AFDC was starting to decline, and it remains to be seen whether the large percentage of this cohort who achieved self-sufficiency can continue doing so. Following the respondents for another five years will answer this question and thus reveal the better long-term strategy for these AFDC recipients—jobs or school.

TABLE 19-6

Two Regression Models of Self-Sufficiency on Demographic Variables at Enrollment, and Demographic and Program Variables during Participation (N = 199)

Model and Independent Variable[a]	b	SE	p
Model with demographic variables only			
1. No. of prior spells on AFDC	−.58	.00	< .0001
2. Employed	.27	.03	< .0001
No = 0			
Yes = 1			
3. Marital status	−.17	.01	.0008
Married = 1			
Divorced, separated,			
or widowed = 2			
Never married = 3			
4. No. of children	−.10	−.01	.0499
$R^2 = .54$, Adj. $R^2 = .53$,			
$F(1, 191) = 55.3, p < .0001.$			
Model with demographic and program variables			
1. No. of prior spells on AFDC	−.63	.00	< .0001
2. Employed	.11	.03	.0085
No = 0			
Yes = 1			
3. Marital status	−.14	.00	.0010
Married = 1			
Divorced, separated,			
or widowed = 2			
Never married = 3			
4. No. of children	.00	NA	NA
5. Path off AFDC	−.25	.02	< .0001
Job = 1			
School and job = 2			
Neither = 3			
6. No. of months enrolled	−.17	.00	.0002
% personal support of			
FaDSS worker	.10	.04	.0126
$R^2 = .72$, Adj. $R^2 = .71$,			
$F(1, 191) = 80.6, p < .0001.$			

NOTE: AFDC = Aid to Families with Dependent Children; NA = not applicable; FaDSS = Family Development and Self-Sufficiency Program.

[a]The dependent variable is participants' months off AFDC as a percentage of the total months they could have been off AFDC between enrollment and 48 months after enrollment (see Table 19-5), the last time we analyzed the Iowa Department of Human Services files of AFDC benefit checks.

In the end, however, it is important to remember that FaDSS participants, three-quarters of whom are single women with school-age children, cannot themselves overcome the structural problems in the job market—decreasing numbers of well-paying full-time jobs with benefits and increasing numbers of part-time, low-paying jobs without benefits. If it is the case that FaDSS participants are no more likely to be self-sufficient in the long run than members of the control group, we may be looking at the effects of a constricting job market and declining resources for child care rather than a failure of the FaDSS Program. What we do know is that FaDSS is successful in increasing participants' ability to cope with the everyday problems of being a parent, and that in itself is an important success.

A major caveat remains, however. Simply put, it is the issue of where federal and state authorities draw the AFDC eligibility line and how the program is administered. If a society is genuinely concerned about the welfare of poor children and families, exiting public assistance should mean exiting poverty. If families are pushed and prodded off public assistance by tighter rules, more stringent work requirements, and limitations on the duration of receipt of benefits, then defining these people as "self-sufficient"—because they are off AFDC—is a mean-spirited delusion. If being self-sufficient means that families must suffer the stresses and repression of poverty, then, as a concept, it is morally indefensible. Unfortunately, this evaluation did not address this issue, and it remains on the research agenda.

Can we generalize these preliminary findings to family support programs that target long-term recipients in other states? No, unless the states are similar, with comparable levels of adult education, unemployment rates, and percentages of poor families. The evaluation model we used (Alter, Losby, & Yarbrough, 1996), however, could be used by other states even though environmental conditions vary. Do these findings speak to the cost-effectiveness of family support within the context of welfare-to-work programs? No; this study did not collect data on program costs for either the FaDSS or control groups. Friedlander and Burtless (1995) found that gains in participants' earnings were several times larger than net program costs, but we did not have the resources to do a cost–benefit analysis.

Given the current debates about welfare reform, it is nevertheless increasingly important to look at the long-term differential effects of providing AFDC recipients with educational and personal development opportunities, as Iowa has done, versus the limited job-placement programs of many states. If family development and a human assets approach (Sherraden, 1991) are going to survive the current political atmosphere, it will depend to a large extent on the availability of cost–benefit analyses that show that the costs of long-term solutions are offset by their benefits. Therefore, these analyses should also be part of our research agenda.

REFERENCES

Alter, C., Deutelbaum, W., Dodd, T., Else, J., & Raheim, S. (1990, September). *Integrating three strategies of family empowerment: Family, community, and economic development.* Paper presented at the National Conference on Family Empowerment, University of Iowa, School of Social Work, Iowa City.

Alter, C., Losby, J. L., & Yarbrough, D. (1996). *Iowa's Family Development and Self-Sufficiency (FaDSS) Program: An evaluation of family support as an intervention with long-term AFDC recipients.* Manuscript submitted for publication.

Alter, C., Yarbrough, D., & Losby, J. L. (1996). *Measuring the steps toward self-sufficiency for long-term AFDC recipients.* Manuscript in preparation, Institute for Social and Economic Development, Iowa City, IA.

Bronfenbrenner, U. (1979). *The ecology of human development*. Cambridge, MA: Harvard University Press.

Bruner, C. (1989). *Iowa's family development grant program*. Des Moines, IA: Child and Family Policy Center.

Bruner, C., & Berryhill, M. (1992). *Making welfare work: A family approach*. Des Moines, IA: Child and Family Policy Center.

Caplan, G. (1981). *Support systems and mutual help: Multidisciplinary explorations*. New York: Grune & Stratton.

Cole, F. (1980). The family life cycle of the multiproblem poor family. In E. A. Carter & M. McGoldrick (Eds.), *The family life cycle* (pp. 343–381). New York: Gardner.

Colten, M. E., & Gore, S. (1991). *Adolescent stress: Causes and consequences*. New York: Aldine de Gruyter.

Duncan, G. J., & Hoffman, S. D. (1988). The use and effects of welfare: A survey of recent evidence. *Social Service Review, 24*, 238–257.

Dunst, C., Trivette, C., & Deal, A. (1988). *Supporting and strengthening families*. Cambridge MA: Brookline Books.

Ellwood, D. T. (1986). *Targeting "would-be" long-term recipients of AFDC*. Princeton, NJ: Mathematica.

Ellwood, D. T. (1988). *Poor support: Poverty in the American family*. New York: Basic Books.

Ellwood, D. T., & Bane, M. J. (1986). Slipping into and out of poverty: The dynamics of spells. *Journal of Human Resources, 21*, 1–23.

Family Support Act of 1988, P.L. 100-485, 102 Stat. 2343.

Fisher, P., Forkenbrock, D., Pogue, T., & Tracy, M. (1989). *Welfare reform in Iowa: Options and opportunities*. Iowa City: University of Iowa, Public Policy Center.

Friedlander, D., & Burtless, G. (1995). *Five years after: The long-term effects of welfare-to-work programs*. New York: Russell Sage Foundation.

Greenspan, S. E., Weider, S., Lieberman, A. F., Nover, R. A., Lourie, R. S., & Robinson, M. E. (Eds.). (1987). *Infants in multirisk families: Case studies in preventive intervention*. Madison, CT: International Universities Press.

Gueron, J. M., & Pauly, E. (1991). *From welfare to work*. New York: Russell Sage Foundation.

Gutierrez, L. M. (1990). Working with women of color: An empowerment perspective. *Social Work, 35*, 149–153.

Hagen, J. L. (1994). JOBS and case management: Developments in 10 states. *Social Work, 39*, 197–205.

Hagen, J. L. (1995). Implementing JOBS: From the rose garden to reality. *Social Work, 40*, 523–532.

Hartman, A., & Laird, J. (1983). *Family-centered social work practice*. New York: Free Press.

Herr, T., & Halpern, R. (1991). *Changing what counts: Re-thinking the journey out of welfare*. Evanston, IL: Northwestern University, Center for Urban Affairs and Policy Research.

Losby, J., & Alter, C. (1996). *Self-reported AFDC history versus state administrative files: Is there a difference?* Manuscript in preparation, Institute for Social and Economic Development, Iowa City, IA.

Maynard, R. A. (1993, September-October). Prevalence and causes of repeat pregnancies among welfare-dependent teenage mothers. *Family Planning Perspectives*, pp. 7–29.

Maynard, R. A., & Fraker, T. (1987). The adequacy of comparison group designs for evaluations of employment-related programs. *Journal of Human Resources, 22*, 33–46.

Mirowsky, J., & Ross, C. (1989). *Social causes of psychological distress*. New York: Aldine de Gruyter.

Murray, C. (1984). *Losing ground*. New York: Basic Books.

Pearlin, L., Lieberman, M., Menaghan, E., & Muller, J. (1981). The stress process. *Journal of Health and Social Behavior, 22*, 337–356.

Perlman, H. H. (1971). *Perspectives in casework*. Philadelphia: Temple University Press.

Pinderhughes, E. (1983). Empowerment for our clients and ourselves. *Social Casework, 64*, 331–338.

Rappaport, J., Swift, C., & Hess, R. (Eds.). (1984). *Studies in empowerment: Steps toward understanding and action*. New York: Haworth Press.

Rosenberg, M. (1965). *Society and the adolescent self-image.* Princeton, NJ: Princeton University Press.

Sherraden, M. (1991). *Assets and the poor: A new American welfare.* Armonk, NY: M. E. Sharpe.

Thoits, P. A. (1986). Social support as coping assistance. *Journal of Consulting and Clinical Psychology, 54,* 416–423.

Weiss, M. D. (1992, December). Reducing poverty: Alternative approaches. *Current,* pp. 31–57.

Zigler, E., & Black, K. (1989). America's family support movement: Strengths and limitations. *American Journal of Orthopsychiatry, 59,* 6–19.

This chapter was originally published in the December 1996 issue of Social Work Research, *vol. 20, pp. 203–216.*

How Safe Is the Safety Net for Poor Children?

Martha N. Ozawa and Yat-sang Lum

One of the most important developments in the American family since the end of World War II has been the widening disparity in income status among generations. Public policy intervention to ensure income security for elderly people through social security created a new generation of elderly people who could live independently on their own incomes. Rapid increases in social security benefits during the late 1960s and the early 1970s, the provision of cost-of-living increases in benefits since 1974, and the enactment of Supplemental Security Income (SSI) under the 1972 Amendments to the Social Security Act and the Employee Retirement Income Security Act of 1974 (P.L. 93-406) further improved the income status of the elderly population.

In contrast, the income status of children has declined. Because more children live in female-headed families as a result of increasing divorce rates and out-of-wedlock births, the income status of children has deteriorated (Danziger & Gottschalk, 1985; Hernandez, 1995). The declining total fertility rate means that children are concentrated among fewer and younger families, who are traditionally worse off economically than adults and elderly people. The worsening of the income status of children is compounded by the growing inequality in earnings since the early 1970s, with young workers' wages declining relative to those of older workers (Haveman & Wolfe, 1994). Fuchs and Reklis (1992) demonstrated that from 1960 to 1988, the median household income per child decreased from 67 percent to 63 percent of the median household income per adult aged 18 to 64 and from 84 percent to 68 percent of the median household income per elderly person (65 and older). In the meantime, the official poverty rate of children surpassed that of elderly people in 1974 and reached 21.9 percent in 1992, a rate 1.7 times that of elderly people (U.S. House of Representatives, 1994).

Along with the dynamically changing economic circumstances of different generations, the direction of social policy on public income transfers is changing rapidly. Under the banner of the Contract with America, the Republican-led House of Representatives passed, on March 24, 1995, the Personal Responsibility Act (H.R. 4) to tighten eligibility for Aid to Families with Dependent Children (AFDC) and SSI (Burke, 1995a, 1995b; Solomon, 1995; Storey, 1995). On September 19, 1995, the Senate passed the Work Opportunity Act (S. 1305), which is a milder version of the House welfare reform bill. In particular, the Senate bill allowed the states to choose to implement, whereas the House bill required the states to enforce, the family cap in AFDC (meaning that welfare mothers who have additional children are denied additional benefits) and to deny cash payments to teenage mothers who have children out of wedlock. The Senate bill, unlike the House bill, required the states to continue to contribute at least 80 percent of their current spending for AFDC and made only immigrants who arrived after the enactment of the bill ineligible for AFDC (Burke, 1995b; Seib & Frisby, 1995). Both the Senate and House bills ended SSI benefits for substance abusers, restricted SSI eligibility for disabled children, and ended benefits for most illegal immigrants (Burke et al., 1995).

Although Congress spent considerable legislative energy in passing H.R. 4, President Clinton vetoed the bill on January 9, 1996. A conference bill, the Personal Responsibility and Work Opportunity Reconciliation Act of 1996 (P.L. 104-193), will have been sent to the president and signed into law by the time this article is published. This bill would provide block grants to states for AFDC and limit payments to two years per episode and five years during the lifetime of a recipient, thus ending the entitlement principle. As a result, the economic standing of low-income children is expected to be adversely affected because, as of 1993, 9.3 million children were enrolled in AFDC, and 770,000 low-income disabled children were benefiting from SSI (Social Security Administration, 1994).

Although the intent of the current congressional initiatives is to reduce the budget deficit and ultimately the national debt, the public should be concerned about the effect of these initiatives on the deteriorating income status of children. This concern should heighten as the nation enters a new century and simultaneously faces growing international economic competition and the impending retirement of the baby boomers, each of whom will have to be supported by only two workers, instead of the current three (Board of Trustees, 1996). It does not seem plausible that any nation could produce an ultraproductive labor force from a population of children who have been losing ground economically relative to adults and elderly people.

The study presented in this article investigated the income status of children in poverty, particularly how effectively public income transfers provide a safety net for children compared with adults and elderly people. To address this central question, the following research questions were asked:

■ What are the levels and sources of income of poor children, and how do they differ from those of adults and elderly people who are poor?

■ To what extent do public income transfers increase the income level of poor children, and how does this increase differ from that for poor adults and poor elderly people?

■ How do such transfers change the shape of income distribution among poor children? How does the equalizing effect of transfers differ for children and for adults and elderly people?

■ How do public income transfers change the economic stratification among poor children? How does such a change differ from that for poor adults and poor elderly people?

LITERATURE REVIEW

Research on the effect of public income transfers has focused on how they reduce the poverty rate and equalize the income distribution among specified demographic groups. Little research has been conducted on how such transfers raised the income level of the poor population to the current level or changed the economic stratification among poor people. These are major focuses of the present study.

Studies have shown that, of all types of transfers, social insurance benefits, such as social security benefits, are the most effective in reducing poverty among elderly people, whereas means-tested benefits such as AFDC, SSI, food stamps, and housing benefits are the most effective in reducing poverty among nonelderly groups (Ozawa & Wang, 1994; U.S. House of Representatives, 1994). Taken as a whole, the system of public income transfers reduces the poverty rate for elderly people more effectively than for the nonelderly population, primarily because of the enormity of the social security expenditures that are targeted mainly to people over 65. Moreover, the effectiveness of public income transfers in reducing the poverty rate of elderly people has increased (Ozawa, 1995; Sawhill 1988).

Ozawa and Wang (1994) concluded that all public transfers reduce the poverty rate of apparently better-off households to a greater extent than apparently worse-off households (that is, married-couple households over female-headed households and white households over black households). Similarly, a study by the Social Security Administration (Kearnery, Grundmann, & Gallichio, 1994) found that the receipt of social security benefits and SSI resulted in a greater reduction in the poverty rate of two-parent families than of one-parent families. Ozawa and Wang reasoned that the public income transfer system creates a greater antipoverty effect for apparently better-off households because the scope of the non–means-tested portion of the system is larger, middle-class households benefit more from non–means-tested programs than low-income households do, and the pretransfer incomes of middle-class households are higher.

The equalizing effect of public income transfers has been another focus of research. Danziger and Plotnick (1977) showed that public income transfers reduce income inequality among elderly people, particularly among elderly women living alone, the group generally known as the most economically disadvantaged among this population. Radner (1987) noted that because of the steady increases in social security benefits over the years, the Gini coefficient (higher coefficients indicate greater income inequality) for elderly people declined from 1967 to 1979, although it increased slightly from 1979 to 1984, whereas the Gini coefficient for the nonelderly population increased consistently from 1979 to 1984.

Ozawa and Wang (1994) showed that together, non–means-tested and means-tested transfers reduced income inequality more effectively for aged households than for nonaged households and for apparently worse-off households than for apparently better-off households. Nevertheless, the posttransfer Gini coefficients of aged households, female-headed households, and black households were still higher than those of their counterparts. In short, research has shown that the nonaged population depends heavily on means-tested programs to reduce both the poverty rate and the degree of inequality, whereas the aged population depends heavily on non–means-tested programs, especially the social security program, to accomplish these goals.

Ozawa and Lum (1995) sought answers, based on 1991 data, to a set of questions similar to those of the present study, but they focused on the income status of poor elderly and nonelderly households. Taking households as the unit of analysis, they found that public income transfers (social insurance benefits and welfare payments) indeed provided a more effective safety net for poor elderly households than for poor nonelderly households. In particular, because of these transfers, the average income of poor elderly households, expressed in a poverty ratio, increased by 1,014 percent (from .07 to .78), and the Gini coefficient of these households declined by 85 percent (from .815 to .123); in contrast, the average income of poor nonelderly households, also expressed in a poverty ratio, increased by 118 percent (from .28 to .61), and the Gini coefficient of these households declined by 57 percent (from .624 to .265). More important, as Ozawa and Lum noted, after these transfers were distributed, the income status of elderly households was no longer correlated with any demographic variable under investigation, but that of nonelderly households was correlated with the type and size of household.

Thus, earlier studies concentrated mainly on the antipoverty and equalizing effects of public income transfers and, therefore, stopped at the point of estimating the percentage of a particular population who are poor before and after public income transfers are distributed or at the point of estimating the degree of inequality before and after such transfers are distributed. Hence, little is yet known about people, let alone children, who are poor after all public income transfers are distributed. The study by Ozawa and Lum (1995), which focused on aged and nonaged poor households, was the beginning of an inquiry into the economic lives of poor people. Using people as units of analysis and building on that study, the present study focused on children in poverty: Who are they? Where would they be if they did not receive social insurance benefits and welfare payments? What are the distributive effects of these transfers on children, and how do they differ from those for adults and elderly people?

METHODS

Conceptual Framework

To answer these questions the present study evaluated how effectively public income transfers provide a safety net for poor children, poor adults, and poor elderly people. The quantification of this concept involved two indicators: (1) the degree to which the public income transfers improved the average incomes of these groups and (2) the degree to which the transfers lessened the degree of income inequality. If public income transfers positively affected the income status of these groups on the basis of these two indicators, one could conclude that these transfers established an effective safety net. Which group of people is provided with a more effective safety net than others is an empirical question.

In this study, we investigated the income status of poor children, poor adults, and poor elderly people in their own right. Applying the methods used by Ozawa and Kono (1995) in their study on household expenditures for children in Japan, we first obtained the poverty ratio for each household by dividing household income by the poverty line. The poverty ratio so obtained was assigned to each person in the household. Then, people in all the households were cross-tabulated by age groups (children, 1 to 17 years; adults, 18 to 64 years; and elderly people, 65 and older), and the poverty ratios of people in the same age group were averaged. This procedure assumed that all people in the same household had the same income status. An advantage of using the poverty ratio instead of per capita household income (that is, household income divided by the number of people in the household) is that it incorporates the economy of scale, thus making it possible to compare the income status of a person with that of another person, regardless of the size of households both came from.

For this investigation, we targeted two types of social insurance programs (social security benefits and unemployment insurance) and all means-tested cash transfer programs (AFDC; SSI; general assistance; veterans' pensions; Indian, Cuban, or Refugee Assistance; foster child care payments; and other welfare benefits) for their distributive effects. We also included food stamps, which are generally considered near-cash benefits. We called social security and unemployment insurance benefits "social insurance benefits" and means-tested cash transfers and food stamps "welfare payments." We included social security and unemployment insurance benefits in social insurance benefits because these two benefits are a particularly important source of income for poor households; we included all means-tested cash transfers and food stamps because they are targeted to low-income households. Other types of social insurance benefits, such as workers' compensation and veterans' benefits, are treated as part of pretransfer income for the purposes of this study.

To examine the differential distributive effects of public income transfers on different generations, we categorized individuals into the three age groups—children, adults, and elderly people. To indicate how these transfers changed the income status of the three generations, we present income data for the following three sequential stages of income distribution:

1. first stage—pretransfer income (total money income minus social insurance benefits and means-tested cash transfers)
2. second stage—pretransfer income plus social insurance benefits (social security and unemployment insurance benefits)
3. third stage—the second-stage income plus welfare payments (means-tested cash transfers and food stamps).

Source of Data

Data for the study were taken from Wave 3 of the 1991 panel of the *Survey of Income and Program Participation* (SIPP), whose universe is the resident population of the United States excluding people living in institutions and military barracks (U.S. Bureau of the Census, 1992). The SIPP includes data on demographics, marital status, household relationship, race, ethnic origin, labor force activity, types and amounts of monthly income, and participation in various cash and noncash benefit programs.

For the purposes of this study, we chose people as the units of analysis and selected all people who were living in households with posttransfer income below the poverty line. To select people for this study, we first divided all people into Hispanic and non-Hispanic people and then divided non-Hispanic people into white, black, and other racial backgrounds. On the basis of these procedures, we selected Hispanic people, non-Hispanic white people, and non-Hispanic black people, excluding those of other non-Hispanic racial backgrounds. Hereafter, those selected groups of people are referred to as white, black, and Hispanic. Through these selection procedures, we chose 1,752 children, 1,932 adults, and 405 elderly people, for a total of 4,089 poor people. Data were analyzed separately for children, adults, and elderly people. We used weight procedures for all statistical analyses except for the regression analysis.

Data Analysis

The data were analyzed in three ways. First, the average poverty ratios of children, adults, and elderly people were calculated for the three sequential stages. The upward movement of poverty ratios was noted as social insurance benefits and welfare payments were added sequentially to pretransfer incomes. The upward movement in the poverty ratio indicates the extent to which the incomes of these groups of poor people move toward the poverty line as a result of receiving these two types of benefits.

Second, we obtained Gini coefficients for the poverty ratios of children, adults, and elderly people at these three sequential stages and noted changes in the Gini coefficients at the second and the third stages. A decline in the Gini coefficient indicates that the distribution of poverty ratios became less unequal as the two types of public income transfers were added sequentially to pretransfer incomes.

Third, we conducted multiple regression analyses of poverty ratios for these three stages, using as independent variables a person's age and race and the type and size of household that the person came from.

The results of the regression analyses with these independent variables are useful for understanding how social insurance benefits and welfare payments, sequentially, change the income status of children, adults, and elderly people who are poor. Also, because social insurance programs and welfare programs use different eligibility criteria and benefit formulas, it was anticipated that they would differentially affect the income status of different demographic groups of poor people within a particular generation.

FINDINGS

Level and Sources of Posttransfer Income

Households that poor children come from have the highest mean posttransfer income—$10,626, compared with $7,966 and $5,638, respectively, for households of poor adults and poor elderly people. Expressed in poverty ratios, however, the income status of children (.66) is higher than that of adults (.60) but lower than that of elderly people (.76) (Table 20-1).

Table 20-1 also shows the percent distribution of income by source, constructed from the mean household income. The sources of income of the children's households are considerably different from those for the other two age groups. For the children's households, earnings are the most important source (43.59 percent), followed by means-tested cash transfers (24.02 percent), but means-tested cash transfers plus food stamps account for 41.71 percent of the income of these households. Compared with the households of children, the households of poor elderly people rely more on social insurance benefits (social security and unemployment insurance benefits) as a source of income (70.46 percent), and the households of poor adults rely less on means-tested cash payments or food stamps and more on social security and unemployment insurance benefits. However, as is true of children's households, earnings are the most important source (44.59 percent) of income for adults' households.

Distributive Effects of Public Income Transfers

Which group of individuals benefits most from social insurance and welfare payments to reach their current income status? For elderly people, the mean pretransfer poverty ratio is .09, which is extremely low. Social insurance benefits increase their mean poverty ratio by 611 percent to .64, and welfare payments increase it by an additional 133 percent to .76 (Table 20-2). As a result, all public income transfers increase the mean poverty ratio of elderly people by 744 percent.

TABLE 20-1

Posttransfer Income Status of Poor Children, Adults, and Elderly People: 1991

Measure	Children	Adults	Elderly People
Level of annual income ($)			
Mean income	10,626	7,966	5,638
Median income	10,548	7,758	5,616
Mean poverty ratio	.66	.60	.76
Median poverty ratio	.71	.68	.81
Average household size	4.22	3.16	1.38
Share of income (%)			
Earnings	43.59	44.59	4.27
Income from assets	0.79	2.78	4.22
Social security and unemployment insurance benefits	6.63	11.29	70.46
Means-tested cash transfers	24.02	20.28	13.49
Food stamps	17.69	12.91	2.45
Other	7.27	8.15	5.11
Total	99.99	100.00	100.00

NOTE: Totals may not add to 100 percent because of rounding.

The distributive effects of public income transfers for children are less powerful than for elderly people. Before transfers, the mean poverty ratio of children is .32, which increases by 16 percent to .37 with the addition of social insurance benefits, and increases further by 91 percent to .66 with the receipt of welfare payments. As a result, for children, the mean poverty ratio increases by 107 percent as a result of receiving both types of benefits. Of the two types of transfers, welfare payments are more effective than social insurance benefits in increasing the poverty ratio of children, whereas the reverse is true for elderly people.

Public income transfers are least effective in increasing the income status of poor adults. Social insurance benefits increase their mean poverty ratio by 25 percent from .32 to .40, and welfare payments further increase this ratio by an additional 63 percent to .60. All income transfers increase their mean poverty ratio by 88 percent to .60. However, social insurance benefits increase the income status of poor adults more than that of poor children.

Median figures tell much the same story, only more so. The pretransfer poverty ratios are considerably lower and the posttransfer poverty ratios considerably higher than when mean figures are used as an indicator. In particular, the case of poor elderly people is extraordinary: Their pretransfer median poverty ratio is only .01, which surges to .81—an 8,000 percent increase—after the receipt of both social insurance benefits and welfare payments (Table 20-2). The ranking of children stays the same as when mean figures are used. The income status of children is the same as for adults before transfers, the lowest

TABLE 20-2

Effects of Public Income Transfers on Poverty Ratios of Poor Children, Adults, and Elderly People: 1991

Measure	Pretransfer Income	Plus Social Insurance Benefits[a]	Plus Welfare Payments[b]	% Change Due to All Transfers
Poverty ratio (mean)				
Poor children	.32	.37	.66	
Poor adults	.32	.40	.60	
Poor elderly people	.09	.64	.76	
Percent change (mean)				
Poor children		16	91	107
Poor adults		25	63	88
Poor elderly people		611	133	744
Poverty ratio (median)				
Poor children	.19	.32	.71	
Poor adults	.19	.39	.68	
Poor elderly people	.01	.70	.81	
Percent change (median)				
Poor children		68	205	273
Poor adults		105	153	258
Poor elderly people		6,900	1,100	8,000

[a]Includes social security and unemployment insurance benefits.
[b]Includes all means-tested cash payments and food stamps.

after the receipt of social insurance benefits, and second to that of elderly people after all transfers.

These figures indicate the powerful distributive effect of social insurance benefits—mostly social security—in helping poor elderly people achieve their current income status, which is the highest of the three age groups. Starting with only 9 percent of the poverty line, on the basis of the mean poverty ratio, elderly people achieve the highest income status after receiving social insurance benefits. When welfare payments are distributed, this group still maintains the highest income status among the three age groups.

Although poor children's income status is equal to that of poor adults before transfers, it plunges to the lowest level after social insurance benefits are distributed and then climbs above that of adults after welfare payments are distributed. This finding shows the powerful distributive effect of welfare payments on poor children. As for poor adults, after they receive social insurance benefits and welfare payments, they fall to the bottom of the economic ladder.

Effects on Gini Coefficients

Before elderly people receive social insurance benefits and welfare payments, the Gini coefficient of their poverty ratios is .791, which is extremely high. The receipt of social insurance benefits decreases the Gini coefficient by 71 percent to .226, and the receipt of welfare payments decreases it by an additional 12 percent to .134, which is extremely low (Table 20-3).

The situation of poor children is quite different from that of elderly people. Before transfers, the Gini coefficient for children (.581) is lower than that for elderly people (.791) but higher after transfers (.198 compared with .134). Of the two types of transfers, welfare payments are more effective than social insurance benefits in reducing the Gini coefficient of children, whereas the reverse is true for elderly people.

Again, public income transfers do least to reduce the income inequality of poor adults, whose pretransfer Gini coefficient is .580, almost identical to that

TABLE 20-3

Effects of Public Income Transfers on Gini Coefficients of Poverty Ratios of Poor Children, Adults, and Elderly People: 1991

Measure	Pretransfer Income	Plus Social Insurance Benefits[a]	Plus Welfare Payments[b]	% Change Due to All Transfers
Gini coefficient				
Poor children	.581	.519	.198	
Poor adults	.580	.485	.273	
Poor elderly people	.791	.226	.134	
Percent change				
Poor children		−12	−55	−66
Poor adults		−16	−37	−53
Poor elderly people		−71	−12	−83

[a]Includes social security and unemployment insurance benefits.
[b]Includes all means-tested cash payments and food stamps.

of poor children. Social insurance benefits decrease the Gini coefficient of adults by 16 percent to .485, which is lower than that of children. However, because welfare payments are less effective in reducing the Gini coefficient for adults, the posttransfer Gini coefficient (.273) of adults becomes considerably higher than that of children or elderly people.

The analysis of the income status and Gini coefficients at three stages of income distribution indicates the differential effectiveness of social insurance and welfare payments in creating the safety net for the three age groups. On the basis of the extent to which these benefits improve the income status and decrease the inequality of income, one can state that these benefits create a safety net most effectively for elderly people, less effectively for children, and least effectively for adults.

All told, the findings in Tables 20-2 and 20-3 paint a picture of poor children that is distinctly different from that of poor elderly people. In the absence of social insurance benefits and welfare payments, children would be better off than elderly people. But the distribution of social insurance benefits places elderly people considerably ahead of children, and the distribution of welfare payments maintains the economic advantage of elderly people over children. Furthermore, after all transfers are distributed, the income inequality among elderly people is the smallest of the three groups of poor people.

A cautionary note is in order with regard to the distribution of poverty ratios of elderly people. A separate analysis of data indicated that the degree of skewness of the distribution of pretransfer poverty ratios is 2.68 and that of posttransfer poverty ratios is –1.47, meaning that the distribution of pretransfer poverty ratios is skewed positively and the distribution of posttransfer poverty ratios is skewed negatively. The positive skewness in the distribution of pretransfer poverty ratios indicates that there are a few elderly people who are relatively well off, in that they have incomes closer to the poverty line, but the great majority of elderly people are extremely poor. The reverse is true with regard to the negative skewness in the distribution of posttransfer poverty ratios. Thus, in interpreting income inequality among elderly people after all transfers are distributed, one has to say that although a considerable degree of equality is attained as a result of transfers, some elderly people are still extremely poor.

Multiple Regression Analysis

Multiple regression analysis was performed at three sequential stages of income distribution to observe the changes in the economic stratification of the three groups.

Poor Children. Before transfers, race, household type, and household size are statistically significantly related to the income status of children (Table 20-4). Compared with black children, white and Hispanic children are better off ($p < .001$ and $p < .01$, respectively). In addition, children from married-couple households are significantly better off than children from female-headed households ($p < .001$), and those from large households are significantly better off than those from small households ($p < .01$).

TABLE 20-4
Multiple Regression Analysis of Poverty Ratios of Poor Children in Three Stages of Income Distribution: 1991

			Regression Coefficients and *t* Values			
	Pretransfer Income		Plus Social Insurance Benefits[a]		Plus Welfare Payments[b]	
Variable	Coefficient	t	Coefficient	t	Coefficient	t
Intercept	.0074	0.180	.0406	1.000	.5484***	17.296
Age group	.0025	1.683	.0045**	3.080	.0002	0.164
Race						
(Black)						
White	.0997***	5.146	.0775***	4.036	.0142	0.947
Hispanic	.0595**	2.881	.0487*	2.378	.0390*	2.439
Household type						
(Female headed)						
Married couple	.2841***	16.791	.2844***	16.952	.0125	0.953
Male headed	.0217	0.464	.1166*	2.511	-.0846*	-2.335
Household size	.0250**	2.818	.0267**	3.038	.0205**	2.985
N	1,752		1,752		1,752	
R^2	0.23		0.22		0.018	
F	85.412***		82.983***		5.424***	

NOTE: Reference groups are in parentheses.
[a]Includes social security and unemployment insurance benefits.
[b]Includes all means-tested cash payments and food stamps.
*$p < .05$. **$p < .01$. ***$p < .001$.

When social insurance benefits are distributed, age emerges as a significant variable ($p < .01$). Older children may be significantly better off than younger children at this stage because they tend to live in households headed by older parents, who are more likely to benefit from survivors insurance, disability insurance, and sometimes old-age insurance (Koitz, Kollman, & Neisner, 1994; National Academy of Social Insurance, 1994).

Children from male-headed households become better off than children from female-headed households at this stage as well ($p < .05$). The variables household size and race maintain their significance, although the Hispanic status becomes weaker ($p < .05$).

The distribution of welfare payments on top of social insurance benefits changes the economic stratification among poor children drastically. First, the age of children is no longer significant. Second, the significance level of race decreases further. At this stage, poor black children are just as well off as poor white children, although they are still worse off than poor Hispanic children ($p < .05$). Third, and more important, children from female-headed households become just as well off as those from married-couple households and become better off than those from male-headed households ($p < .05$). Household size maintains its significance.

Poor Adults. The regression results at the pretransfer stage for adults mirror those for children, with a few exceptions. The significance level of the difference in the poverty ratios between adults from Hispanic households and those from black households is somewhat weaker ($p < .05$) than in the case of children ($p < .01$); age is inversely related to the income status among adults ($p < .001$) but not among children (Table 20-5).

When social insurance benefits are distributed, the coefficient for age reverses its direction. At this stage, the older the adults, the better off they are ($p < .05$). In addition, Hispanic adults are no longer better off than black adults. The other variables stay the same.

When welfare payments are distributed, a drastic change occurs with regard to the variable household type. Adults who come from female-headed households become significantly better off than those from married-couple households ($p < .01$) or from male-headed households ($p < .001$). Age is no longer significant at this stage. The variable household size maintains its significance.

Poor Elderly People. The economic stratification among elderly people is distinctly different from that among children or among adults at each stage of income definitions. At the pretransfer stage, the type of household that elderly people come from has no effect on their income status, whereas this variable is significant for children and adults. As is true for adults, however, age is inversely related to the income status of elderly people: The younger they are, the better off they are ($p < .05$). White elderly people are significantly better off than black elderly people ($p < .01$). Also, household size is positively related to income status ($p < .001$) (Table 20-6).

When social insurance benefits are distributed, age loses its statistical significance. More important, the coefficient for household size reverses its direction. As was mentioned elsewhere, this change has to do with the way social security

TABLE 20-5

Multiple Regression Analysis of Poverty Ratios of Poor Adults in Three Stages of Income Distribution: 1991

| | Regression Coefficients and t Values | | | | | |
| | Pretransfer Income | | Plus Social Insurance Benefits[a] | | Plus Welfare Payments[b] | |
Variable	Coefficient	t	Coefficient	t	Coefficient	t
Intercept	.1354***	3.414	.1492***	3.631	.4359***	12.346
Age group	-.0023***	-3.698	.0015*	2.288	.0009	1.648
Race (Black)						
White	.0909***	4.589	.0693***	3.376	.0099	0.558
Hispanic	.0588*	2.499	.0414	1.696	.0376	1.795
Household type (Female headed)						
Married couple	.1560***	8.919	.1630***	8.990	-.0550**	-3.533
Male headed	.0445	1.847	.0357	1.431	-.0950***	-4.426
Household size	.0393***	6.075	.0225***	3.361	.0499***	8.653
N	1,932		1,932		1,932	
R^2	0.13		0.09		0.08	
F	47.786***		30.724***		26.311***	

NOTE: Reference groups are in parentheses.
[a]Includes social security and unemployment insurance benefits.
[b]Includes all means-tested cash payments and food stamps.
*$p < .05$. **$p < .01$. ***$p < .001$.

TABLE 20-6

Multiple Regression Analysis of Poverty Ratios of Poor Elderly People in Three Stages of Income Distribution: 1991

	Regression Coefficients and t Values					
	Pretransfer Income		Plus Social Insurance Benefits[a]		Plus Welfare Payments[b]	
Variable	Coefficient	t	Coefficient	t	Coefficient	t
Intercept	.2454*	2.206	.4058*	2.412	.8115***	6.361
Age group	−.0035*	−2.462	.0026	1.207	−.0002	−0.110
Race (Black)						
White	.0632**	2.839	.1249***	3.713	.0140	0.550
Hispanic	−.0305	−0.876	.0058	0.110	.0381	0.953
Household type (Female headed)						
Married couple	−.0362	−1.257	.0852	1.960	−.0224	−0.679
Male headed	.0094	0.368	.0341	0.886	.0436	1.495
Household size	.0505***	4.073	−.0464*	−2.479	−.0356*	−2.510
N	405		405		405	
R^2	0.08		0.08		0.04	
F	5.914***		5.616***		2.691*	

NOTE: Reference groups are in parentheses.

[a]Includes social security and unemployment insurance benefits.

[b]Includes all means-tested cash payments and food stamps.

*$p < .05$. **$p < .01$. ***$p < .001$.

benefits are distributed (Ozawa & Lum, 1995). Under social security, when the primary beneficiary (the primary insured worker) has two or more dependents, the rule of the maximum family benefit applies. Thus, social security benefits are insensitive to family size. This explains, in part, why the direction of the coefficient changes from the positive to the negative.

The greatest transformation in economic stratification occurs at the stage of receiving welfare payments, when all variables, except household size, are insignificant and the percentage of variance explained by all variables is small (4 percent). All this means that poor elderly people are a homogeneous group with respect to their posttransfer income status. This regression result echoes the finding of a large reduction in the Gini coefficient of elderly people when both social insurance benefits and welfare payments are distributed (Table 20-3).

Again, caution should be taken in interpreting the findings about elderly people, because the distributions of pretransfer poverty ratios and posttransfer poverty ratios (when both social insurance and welfare payments are distributed) are skewed considerably and thus depart from the normal distribution. Thus, the findings from the multiple regression analysis for this age group should be considered tentative.

All Poor People. To investigate whether there are statistically significant differences in the income status of poor children, adults, and elderly people, we conducted a regression analysis of all poor people, including two dummy variables for adults and elderly people. We also included the interaction terms between age group and household type and between age group and household size because the direction and the magnitude of the coefficients of household type and household size differ among the three age groups.

At the pretransfer stage, other things being equal, the poverty ratio of children is no different from that of adults or elderly people. However, when social insurance benefits are distributed, the poverty ratio of children becomes significantly lower (by .5722) than that of elderly people ($p < .001$) and lower (by .1281) than that of adults ($p < .01$). When welfare payments are distributed, the poverty ratio of children becomes slightly higher (by .0840) than that of adults ($p < .05$) but is still significantly lower (by .2432) than that of elderly people ($p < .001$) (Table 20-7).

DISCUSSION

Social Policy

The findings of this study indicate that the safety net is working most effectively for elderly people, less effectively for children, and least effectively for adults who are poor. The distribution of the posttransfer income among elderly people is considerably more equal than that among children or adults.

Social policy on public income transfers is largely responsible for the economic stratification among the three age groups of poor people. Mainly because of welfare payments, children are made slightly better off than adults. Because of social security benefits supplemented by SSI payments, elderly people are made better off than children or adults. Thus, the ranking is as follows:

TABLE 20-7
Multiple Regression Analysis of Poverty Ratios of All Poor People in Three Stages of Income Distribution: 1991

			Regression Coefficients and t Values			
	Pretransfer Income		Plus Social Insurance Benefits[a]		Plus Welfare Payments[b]	
Variable	Coefficient	t	Coefficient	t	Coefficient	t
Intercept	.0296	0.808	.0680	1.802	.5523***	17.828
Age group (Children)						
Adults	.0001	0.003	.1281**	3.136	-.0840*	-2.504
Elderly people	-.0825	-1.811	.5722***	12.167	.2432***	6.299
Race (Black)						
White	.0924***	7.291	.0771***	5.897	.0116	1.078
Hispanic	.0536***	3.679	.0445**	2.959	.0386**	3.124
Household type (Female headed)						
Married couple	.2843***	17.673	.2807***	16.904	.0132	0.967
Male headed	.0232	0.501	.1185*	2.483	-.0845*	-2.158
Household size	.0254**	2.982	.0290**	3.302	.0201**	2.795
Interaction term						
Adult + married couple	-.1380***	-6.252	-.1107***	-4.859	-.0637***	-3.406
Elderly + married couple	-.3047***	-6.155	-.2097***	-4.105	-.0524	-1.249
Adult + male headed	.0277	0.537	-.0762	-1.431	-.0099	-0.227
Elderly + male headed	-.0229	-0.358	-.1205	-1.828	.1228*	2.269
Adult + household size	.0223*	2.242	-.0083	-0.810	.0283***	3.361
Elderly + household size	.0322	1.473	-.0760***	-3.369	-.0515**	-2.782
N	4,089		4,089		4,089	
R^2	0.20		0.19		0.08	
F	80.801***		73.254***		29.025***	

NOTE: Reference groups are in parentheses.

[a] Includes social security and unemployment insurance benefits.

[b] Includes all means-tested cash payments and food stamps.

*$p < .05$. **$p < .01$. ***$p < .001$.

elderly people at the top, children in the middle, and adults at the bottom. This ranking differs from that of these three age groups in the general population. A separate analysis of data indicates that in the general population, the average poverty ratio of children (2.56) is the lowest among the three generations, with adults having the highest average poverty ratio (3.66) and elderly people having the second highest average poverty ratio (3.03).

The posttransfer economic stratification among poor children is also a product of social policy. Largely because of welfare payments, the black-white racial difference in income status disappears. The income level of children from female-headed households is brought up to the level of those from married-couple households and is higher than the level of those from male-headed households.

Similarly, welfare payments bring the income status of poor adults living in female-headed households above that of poor adults living in married-couple households or in male-headed households. On the other hand, welfare payments make the economic stratification among poor elderly people disappear almost completely.

The posttransfer income status of children, adults, and elderly people who are poor reflects the intent of U.S. social policy on income security. The federal government placed a high priority on establishing income security for elderly people and, therefore, instituted the social security program in 1935 and the SSI program in 1972. Social security was meant to replace wages lost because of retirement, and SSI was meant to ensure a national minimum income for the elderly population. The two programs operating in tandem have succeeded in creating an effective safety net for poor elderly people.

In contrast, income security for children has not been a high political priority. Thus, no income support program addresses the income needs of all poor children adequately. For example, AFDC, on which poor children heavily depend, ignores those who live in married-couple households or in male-headed households. Its payments are low and insecure compared with SSI, which benefits many poor elderly people. Except in a few states, and unlike SSI, AFDC provides no cost-of-living increases. As a result, the median state AFDC payment level declined 47 percent in real terms from 1970 to 1994 (U.S. House of Representatives, 1994). Furthermore, the parents of poor children have never been encouraged to apply for AFDC in the way elderly people have been encouraged to apply for SSI through outreach programs as mandated under the 1983 Amendments to the Social Security Act (P.L. 98-21) and the Omnibus Budget Reconciliation Act of 1989 (P.L. 101-239). What this study has revealed, therefore, is an outcome of past and current U.S. policies on income security.

Methodology

This study took a static, instead of a dynamic, view of the economic situation of poor children, adults, and elderly people, which should be recognized as a limitation of the study. As was noted earlier, a major objective of the study was to find an answer to the question, To what extent do public income transfers increase the income level of poor children? The corollary of this question was, What might the income status of poor children have been if they did not receive benefits from public income transfer programs? In search of answers to these questions, we investigated the measured effect of public income transfers. The measured effect means the difference between pre- and posttransfer income levels. Thus, this study did not consider behavioral responses to public income transfers. But one needs to be aware that some parents of children and some others may try to work more and earn more if public income transfers are not provided; conversely, some individuals may work less and earn less as a result of receiving public income transfers. Research that takes into account such behavioral responses to public income transfers adopts a dynamic view of the situation and, therefore, must use a statistical procedure that is appropriate for such a research design, an approach that is different from the one used in this study.

Another issue regarding the research methodology is that this study focused on posttransfer poor children, adults, and elderly people. We targeted these groups because they are the poor as the public knows them (those who stay poor in spite of all public income transfers) and because they are the ones to whom the current policy debate relates. However, some researchers may be interested in investigating the measured effect of public income transfers on pretransfer poor people. If this is the focus of the investigation, then the researchers must select all individuals who are poor before they receive public income transfers, some of whom may become nonpoor after transfers. Much of the research on the antipoverty effect of public income transfers focuses on such a population because the objective of this research is to investigate the percentage of pretransfer poor people who become nonpoor after transfers. Many studies in this vein were cited earlier.

In addition, however, researchers may be interested in finding an answer to a question equivalent to that raised in this study: To what extent does the income status of pretransfer poor children, adults, and elderly people improve as a result of receiving public income transfers? To shed light on this question, we produced a set of tables for pretransfer poor children, adults, and elderly people similar to those produced for the posttransfer groups (Tables 20-8 through 20-14).

Pretransfer Poor People

Generally, the findings about pretransfer poor people parallel those for posttransfer poor people in some ways but differ in many other ways. Social insurance benefits and welfare payments, together, improve the income status of elderly people most effectively, that of adults less effectively, and that of children least effectively (Tables 20-9 and 20-14). In general, social insurance benefits and welfare payments, together, equalize the distribution of incomes of pretransfer poor people to a lesser degree than the distribution of incomes of posttransfer poor people. The following discussion highlights the findings for each age group of pretransfer poor people that differ from the findings for the posttransfer groups.

Children. Of all age groups, children have the lowest income status at two stages of income distribution (after social insurance benefits are distributed and after both social insurance benefits and welfare payments are distributed) (Tables 20-9 and 20-14). Of all racial and ethnic groups of children, white children have the highest income status at all stages of income distribution (Table 20-11).

TABLE 20-8

Posttransfer Income Status of Pretransfer Poor Children, Adults, and Elderly People: 1991

Measure	Children	Adults	Elderly People
Level of annual income ($)			
Mean income	12,194	10,687	12,297
Median income	11,544	10,044	11,628
Mean poverty ratio	.77	.89	1.54
Median poverty ratio	.77	.84	1.49
Average household size	4.20	3.05	1.66
Share of income (%)			
Earnings	42.45	34.34	3.48
Income from assets	0.87	2.94	6.43
Social security and unemployment insurance benefits	12.28	28.89	73.92
Means-tested cash transfers	22.69	17.42	4.33
Food stamps	14.96	8.13	0.57
Other	6.75	8.27	11.26
Total	100.00	99.99	99.99

NOTE: Totals may not add to 100 percent because of rounding.

Children from male-headed households have a higher income status than do children from female-headed households at all stages of income distribution. Older children have a higher income status than do younger children after both social insurance benefits and welfare payments are distributed (Table 20-11). Household size does not make a difference in the income status of children at two stages of income distribution (after social insurance benefits are distributed and after both social insurance benefits and welfare payments are distributed).

Elderly People. Either on the basis of the mean poverty ratio or the median poverty ratio, elderly people attain the above-poverty income status as soon as they receive social insurance benefits and further improve it by receiving welfare payments (Table 20-9). Of all groups of elderly people from households of all types, elderly people from married-couple households have the highest income status at all stages of income distribution (Table 20-13). The income status of elderly people from male-headed households is higher than that of elderly people from female-headed households at two stages of income distribution (after social insurance benefits are distributed and after both social insurance benefits and welfare payments are distributed). The mean pretransfer income status of pretransfer poor elderly people is not as low, compared with those of children and adults, as that of posttransfer poor elderly people (Table 20-9). The income inequality among pretransfer poor elderly people that is measured after the distribution of both social insurance benefits and welfare payments is greater than among posttransfer poor elderly people at the same stage of income distribution (Table 20-10).

Adults. Of all racial and ethnic groups of adults, white adults have the highest income status at all stages of income distribution (Table 20-12). The income status of adults from female-headed households is the same as that of adults from married-couple households after the distribution of social insurance benefits and

TABLE 20-9

Effects of Public Income Transfers on Poverty Ratios of Pretransfer Poor Children, Adults, and Elderly People: 1991

Measure	Pretransfer Income	Plus Social Insurance Benefits[a]	Plus Welfare Payments[b]	% Change Due to All Transfers
Poverty ratio (mean)				
Poor children	.37	.47	.77	
Poor adults	.37	.68	.89	
Poor elderly people	.32	1.47	1.54	
Percent change (mean)				
Poor children		27	81	108
Poor adults		84	57	141
Poor elderly people		359	22	381
Poverty ratio (median)				
Poor children	.31	.45	.77	
Poor adults	.33	.64	.84	
Poor elderly people	.23	1.45	1.49	
Percent change (median)				
Poor children		45	103	148
Poor adults		94	61	155
Poor elderly people		530	17	548

[a] Includes social security and unemployment insurance benefits.
[b] Includes all means-tested cash payments and food stamps.

TABLE 20-10

Effects of Public Income Transfers on Gini Coefficients of Poverty Ratios of Pretransfer Poor Children, Adults, and Elderly People: 1991

Measure	Pretransfer Income	Plus Social Insurance Benefits[a]	Plus Welfare Payments[b]	% Change Due to All Transfers
Gini coefficient				
Poor children	.535	.493	.239	
Poor adults	.518	.483	.339	
Poor elderly people	.556	.261	.226	
Percent change				
Poor children		−8	−47	−55
Poor adults		−7	−28	−35
Poor elderly people		−53	−6	−59

[a] Includes social security and unemployment insurance benefits.
[b] Includes all means-tested cash payments and food stamps.

welfare payments. Older adults are better off than are younger adults after the distribution of social insurance benefits and welfare payments (Table 20-12).

CONCLUSION

What effect will Congress's enactment of welfare reforms have on children? Obviously, cuts in welfare programs would further lower the income status of children. In addition, the economic differences between black children and white and Hispanic children would become visible, and the income status of children

TABLE 20-11

Multiple Regression Analysis of Poverty Ratios of Pretransfer Poor Children in Three Stages of Income Distribution: 1991

	Regression Coefficients and t Values					
	Pretransfer Income		Plus Social Insurance Benefits[a]		Plus Welfare Payments[b]	
Variable	Coefficient	t	Coefficient	t	Coefficient	t
Intercept	.0411	1.062	.2264***	4.750	.6950***	16.796
Age group	.0021	1.538	.0100***	5.835	.0059***	3.965
Race						
(Black)						
White	.0982***	5.348	.1102***	4.869	.0559**	2.849
Hispanic	.0473*	2.340	.0586*	2.352	.0373	1.722
Household type						
(Female headed)						
Married couple	.2578***	16.194	.2833***	14.445	.0120	0.703
Male headed	.0992**	2.582	.1406**	2.970	.0976*	2.375
Household size	.0317***	3.836	-.0070	-0.686	-.0030	-0.340
N	2,148		2,148		2,148	
R^2	0.18		0.14		0.01	
F	77.329***		56.550***		5.201***	

NOTE: Reference groups are in parentheses.

[a]Includes social security and unemployment insurance benefits.

[b]Includes all means-tested cash payments and food stamps.

*$p < .05$. **$p < .01$. ***$p < .001$.

TABLE 20-12
Multiple Regression Analysis of Poverty Ratios of Pretransfer Poor Adults in Three Stages of Income Distribution: 1991

| | Regression Coefficients and t Values | | | | | |
| | Pretransfer Income | | Plus Social Insurance Benefits[a] | | Plus Welfare Payments[b] | |
Variable	Coefficient	t	Coefficient	t	Coefficient	t
Intercept	.1575***	4.547	.1961***	3.454	.4209***	7.678
Age group	−.0010*	−2.018	.0093***	11.133	.0094***	11.634
Race						
(Black)						
White	.0802***	4.619	.1191***	4.187	.0726**	2.642
Hispanic	.0460*	2.169	.0272	0.783	.0198	0.588
Household type						
(Female headed)						
Married couple	.1472***	10.009	.2510***	10.416	.0398	1.709
Male headed	.0169	0.801	−.0133	−0.384	−.0794*	−2.373
Household size	.0417***	7.369	−.0259**	−2.793	.0133	1.492
N	2,813		2,813		2,813	
R^2	0.10		0.13		0.07	
F	53.712***		69.966***		32.957***	

NOTE: Reference groups are in parentheses.
[a]Includes social security and unemployment insurance benefits.
[b]Includes all means-tested cash payments and food stamps.
*$p < .05$. **$p < .01$. ***$p < .001$.

TABLE 20-13
Multiple Regression Analysis of Poverty Ratios of Pretransfer Poor Elderly People in Three Stages of Income Distribution: 1991

			Regression Coefficients and t Values			
	Pretransfer Income		Plus Social Insurance Benefits[a]		Plus Welfare Payments[b]	
Variable	Coefficient	t	Coefficient	t	Coefficient	t
Intercept	.3027**	3.145	.9335***	5.158	1.1145***	6.616
Age group	-.0026*	-2.167	.0007	0.285	-.0009	-0.423
Race						
(Black)						
White	.1062***	4.529	.3431***	7.779	.2734***	6.660
Hispanic	-.0625	-1.763	-.1064	-1.594	-.0497	-0.801
Household type						
(Female headed)						
Married couple	.1007***	5.475	.6813***	19.701	.5590***	17.368
Male headed	.0394	1.627	.1174*	2.573	.1227**	2.891
Household size	.0474***	4.181	-.0626**	-2.940	.0041	0.205
N	1,911		1,911		1,911	
R^2	0.08		0.27		0.24	
F	28.731***		114.641***		98.705***	

NOTE: Reference groups are in parentheses.
[a]Includes social security and unemployment insurance benefits.
[b]Includes all means-tested cash payments and food stamps.
*$p < .05$. **$p < .01$. ***$p < .001$.

TABLE 20-14

Multiple Regression Analysis of Poverty Ratios of All Pretransfer Poor People in Three Stages of Income Distribution with Interaction Terms: 1991

			Regression Coefficients and t Values			
	Pretransfer Income		Plus Social Insurance Benefits[a]		Plus Welfare Payments[b]	
Variable	Coefficient	t	Coefficient	t	Coefficient	t
Intercept	.0593	1.729	.2419***	4.403	.6838***	13.312
Age group (Children)						
Adults	.0317	0.855	.3449***	5.806	.1465**	2.637
Elderly people	.0544	1.453	.9204***	15.361	.5275***	9.417
Race (Black)						
White	.0938***	8.493	.1639***	9.267	.1085***	6.566
Hispanic	.0353**	2.634	.0359	1.673	.0289	1.439
Household type (Female headed)						
Married couple	.2573***	16.814	.2605***	10.637	-.0073	-0.318
Male headed	.0999**	2.624	.1282*	2.104	.0858	1.506
Household size	.0326***	4.073	.0055	0.428	.0071	0.589
Interaction term						
Adult + married couple	-.1254***	-6.164	.0021	0.064	.0615*	2.021
Elderly + married couple	-.1384***	-5.799	.4548***	11.906	.5984***	16.755
Adult + male headed	-.0807	-1.867	-.1647*	-2.381	-.1944**	-3.005
Elderly + male headed	-.0611	-1.337	-.0274	-0.374	.0301	0.440
Adult + household size	.0173	1.865	-.0573***	-3.866	-.0225	-1.621
Elderly + household size	.0090	0.655	-.1045***	-4.731	-.0340	-1.647
N	6,872		6,872		6,872	
R^2	0.13		0.45		0.36	
F	75.558***		425.067***		292.339***	

NOTE: Reference groups are in parentheses.

[a] Includes social security and unemployment insurance benefits.

[b] Includes all means-tested cash payments and food stamps.

$p < .05.$ **$p < .01.$ ***$p < .001.$

from female-headed households would decrease. Similarly, the racial differences in the income status among elderly poor people would become visible.

Cuts in social security benefits—if they are ever passed by Congress—would quickly destroy the safety net for poor elderly people. Thus, Congress will inevitably face intergenerational conflict in finding ways to cut the fiscal deficit. Cuts in welfare programs would worsen the economic lives of poor children, whereas cuts in social security would destroy a vital part of the safety net for poor elderly people.

Beyond the immediate policy debate, a fundamental policy question arises: Is it in the national interest to let poor children live in economic circumstances that are clearly less adequate than those of poor adults or poor elderly people? Can this country afford to treat poor children differently, depending on their living arrangements? And with regard to all children, can this country enter the new century, in which it will face the dual predicament of global economic competition and a greater financial obligation to support the growing number of elderly people, by allowing children to be raised in considerably less favorable economic conditions than adults or elderly people experience? Obviously, something is amiss, and policymakers need to find a new approach to dealing with this dual predicament.

REFERENCES

Board of Trustees. (1996). *The 1996 annual report of the federal Old-Age and Survivors Insurance and Disability Insurance Trust Fund.* Washington, DC: U.S. Government Printing Office.

Burke, V. (1995a). *Family cash welfare: Comparison of House-passed and Senate Finance Committee versions of H.R. 4* (Report for Congress 95-691 EPW). Washington, DC: Congressional Research Service.

Burke, V. (1995b). *Welfare reform* (Report for Congress IB 93034). Washington, DC: Congressional Research Service.

Burke, V., Richardson, J., Solomon, C., Spar, K., Vialent, J., Talley, L. A., & Eig, L. (1995). *Welfare reform: The Senate-passed bill (H.R. 4)* (Report for Congress 95-991 EPW). Washington, DC: Congressional Research Service.

Danziger, S., & Gottschalk, R. (1985). Poverty of losing ground. *Challenge, 28*(2), 32–38.

Danziger, S., & Plotnick, R. (1977). Demographic change, government transfers, and income distribution. *Monthly Labor Review, 100*(4), 7–11.

Employee Retirement Income Security Act of 1974, P.L. 93-406, 88 Stat. 829.

Fuchs, V. R., & Reklis, D. M. (1992). American's children: Economic perspectives and policy options. *Science, 255,* 41–46.

Haveman, R., & Wolfe, B. (1994). *Succeeding generations.* New York: Russell Sage Foundation.

Hernandez, D. J. (1995). *America's children: Resources from family, government and the economy.* New York: Russell Sage Foundation.

Kearnery, J. R., Grundmann, H. F., & Gallichio, R. (1994). The influence of social security benefits and SSI payments on the poverty status of children. *Social Security Bulletin,'57*(2), 27–33.

Koitz, D., Kollman, G., & Neisner, J. (1994). *Status of the disability programs of the Social Security Administration, 1994* (Report for Congress 94-477 EPW). Washington, DC: Congressional Research Service.

National Academy of Social Insurance. (1994). *Rethinking disability policy: The role of income, health care, rehabilitation and related services in fostering independence.* Washington, DC: Author.

Omnibus Budget Reconciliation Act of 1989, P.L. 101-239, 103 Stat. 2106.

Ozawa, M. N. (1995). Antipoverty effects of public income transfers on children. *Children and Youth Services Review, 17*(1/2), 43–59.

Ozawa, M. N., & Kono, S. (1995). *Child well-being in Japan: The high cost of economic success* (Innocenti Occasional Papers, Special Subseries: Child Poverty in Industrialized Countries). Florence, Italy: UNICEF.

Ozawa, M. N., & Lum, Y. (1995). *Safety net and the poor: Generational differences.* Unpublished manuscript, Washington University, St. Louis.

Ozawa, M. N., & Wang, Y. (1994). Distributive effects of benefits and taxes. *Social Work Research, 18,* 149–162.

Personal Responsibility Act, H.R. 4, 104th Cong., 1st Sess. (1995).

Personal Responsibility and Work Opportunity Reconciliation Act of 1996, P.L. 104-193.

Radner, D. B. (1987). Money incomes of aged and nonaged family units, 1967–84. *Social Security Bulletin, 50,* 9–28.

Sawhill, I. V. (1988). Poverty in the United States: Why is it so persistent? *Journal of Economic Literature, 26,* 1073–1119.

Seib, G. F., & Frisby, M. K. (1995, September 19). As welfare-reform bill moves to the middle, concerns arise whether the center can hold. *Wall Street Journal,* p. A24.

Social Security Administration. (1994). *Annual statistical supplement, 1994, to the Social Security Bulletin.* Washington, DC: Author.

Social Security Amendments of 1983, P.L. 98-21, 97 Stat. 65.

Solomon, C. D. (1995). *Supplemental Security Income (SSI) children: Welfare reform in the 104th Congress* (Report for Congress 95-402 EPW). Washington, DC: Congressional Research Service.

Storey, J. R. (1995). *Welfare reform: Background and key issues* (Report for Congress 95-72 EPW). Washington, DC: Congressional Research Service.

U.S. Bureau of the Census. (1992). *Survey of Income and Program Participation (SIPP) 1991* (Panel Wave 3 core microdata file). Washington, DC: Author.

U.S. House of Representatives, Committee on Ways and Means. (1994). *1994 green book: Overview of entitlement programs.* Washington, DC: U.S. Government Printing Office.

Work Opportunity Act, S. 1305, 104th Cong., 1st Sess. (1995).

This chapter was originally published in the December 1996 issue of Social Work Research, *vol. 20, pp. 238–254.*

21

Welfare Reforms and Services for Children and Families: Setting a New Practice, Research, and Policy Agenda

Edith M. Freeman

The current political climate and economic stressors have increased pressures for results-oriented social programs (Strom & Gingerich, 1993). These pressures have led to the proposal of drastic program reforms and cost-containment policies by the 104th Congress. Social workers and other helping professionals will be required to eliminate, reorganize, or provide new services to families and children, often in less time and with fewer resources.

Political leaders blame social programs and low-income families for the continuing poverty and escalating national debt while ignoring structural barriers to self-sufficiency. Poole (1995) noted, for example, that welfare-to-work reforms may fail because "the American economy cannot produce enough jobs or enough income for welfare recipients to escape poverty without government intervention" (p. 83). Contrary to conservative rhetoric about family values and the country's desire to be supportive of families, family self-sufficiency may be less achievable today than at any other period in this century except the Great Depression (Atherton, 1992; Keigher, 1994).

This article discusses barriers to family self-sufficiency and analyzes the impact of these barriers on families. It discusses some political definitions of self-sufficiency to illustrate how these definitions encourage punitive policies and limit family self-sufficiency. This article discusses a more appropriate definition and illustrates its usefulness with an example of community research conducted to identify social support needs. The author recommends changes in social work practice and education that can enable the profession to have a stronger influence on social policy. Finally, to achieve this social justice goal and integrate policy development into clinical and community practice, the author proposes new research and policy agendas for the profession. (SWR)

BARRIERS TO SELF-SUFFICIENCY

Some barriers to family self-sufficiency have been created by a lack of clarity about what families are expected to do for themselves and what responsibilities society has in supporting families. This lack of clarity has led to questions about the appropriate balance between self-sufficiency and social supports. The economic and political climates in which these questions developed emphasize the need to re-evaluate the country's resource priorities (Poole, 1995).

264

Resource reallocations through current and proposed social program and policy reforms have created significant barriers to self-sufficiency. The barriers include the negative labeling of low-income families, limitations on service availability and comprehensiveness under managed care, perpetuation of power hoarding through block grants, and a priority on individual self-sufficiency over family or community rebuilding.

Negative Labeling of Families

Negative labeling of families has occurred because the current reforms are based on the assumption that low-income families are to blame for their lack of self-sufficiency. Proposed welfare reforms, which would affect the Aid to Families with Dependent Children (AFDC) Block Grant, the Federal–State Partnership, and the Child Protection Block Grant, would eliminate the federal guarantee of or entitlement to cash assistance for all eligible families, the requirement that states maintain current levels of funding for social programs, and the requirement that states meet a federal guarantee of foster care and adoption assistance for children (NASW, 1996). By decreasing social supports and resources in these essential areas, the reforms may decrease rather than increase self-sufficiency, leading to an escalation of the family-blaming process (Freeman, 1996a; Strom & Gingerich, 1993).

Welfare reforms also include the Personal Responsibility and Work Opportunity Act (H.R. 4, 1995), which proposes to limit AFDC benefits to a maximum of five years and requires recipients to work after a maximum of two years (NASW, 1996). Proponents of this reform assume the current welfare program has failed because a majority of recipients have exploited the program and are not interested in working and becoming self-sufficient. Many recipients want to work; however, they lack marketable job skills, training, and work opportunities (O'Donnell, 1993). Instituting welfare reform without changing the structure of the country's inequitable employment system could reinforce or increase the current pattern of labeling low-income families as the problem. Poole (1995) and Jones (1992) have observed that blaming and labeling increase when the availability and number of adequate-paying jobs are insufficient or when all groups do not have equitable access to available jobs.

Service Limitations under Managed Care Policies

Another barrier to self-sufficiency for families involves the managed care policies being implemented by most states. Managed care is a mechanism for delivering health care that is part of the proposed national health care plans and Medicaid reform (Chamberlain, 1995). Medicaid reform proposals would repeal Title XIX of the Social Security Act and eliminate consumer protections from cost-sharing requirements, creating barriers to care for families. This reform also would eliminate guaranteed eligibility for children between the ages of 13 and 18 for Medicaid coverage (NASW, 1996).

Managed care policies are designed to reduce costs and improve services in programs such as Medicaid by shifting the financial risks from states to private carriers (Saucier, 1995). Those policies are being used to privatize social programs and the health care field, including foster care, substance abuse treatment, and community support programs for clients with severe and persistent mental illness.

Although other models exist, there are two predominant types of managed care models: primary care management models and risk-based models. Under primary care management models, a primary care physician or mental health provider receives a fee to coordinate and authorize services for clients, who pay or are subsidized on a fee-for-service basis. In risk-based models, there is a set prepayment for an established package of services, so the contractor takes a financial risk for costs that exceed the prepaid amounts (Horvath & Kaye, 1995). Saucier (1995) stated that these models should be examined more closely "because they produce powerful and controversial financial incentives" (p. 1) for contractors to decrease services once the preset fees have been reached, regardless of the quantity and quality of services needed.

Thus, managed care policies may limit the comprehensiveness and availability of services being provided and, consequently, a family's ability to return to or develop self-sufficiency. Family members may be unable to resolve or fully recover from the effects of health conditions, substance abuse problems, or family violence. Moreover, the reduction of community risk factors and related structural problems may not be addressed because of these managed care service limitations (Chamberlain, 1995; Freeman, 1996a; Hawkins & Catalano, 1992).

Block Grant Funding and Power Hoarding

A third barrier to family self-sufficiency is the proposed block grant funding, which is designed to decentralize funding and return decision making to local and state control. Block grants have been proposed for programs such as child care for low-income families, community service, economic revitalization, and maternal and child health (NASW, 1996). Without strong safeguards, however, the block grant funding system may simply shift from what Freire (1983) called a monopoly by the "powerful few" (at the federal level) to a similar hoarding of power at the state and local level. Thus, the power sharing might not include the most powerless families in each community.

Power-sharing safeguards can help address structural barriers to self-sufficiency by mandating opportunities for communities to help make funding decisions. Safeguards would include community representation on policy boards to encourage meaningful family and community involvement in decisions about welfare (O'Donnell, 1993), employment (Jones, 1992), education (Chavkin & Brown, 1992), and mental health services (LeCroy, 1992). Mandating these opportunities can increase communities' self-determination and sense of well-being.

Emphasis on Individual Self-Sufficiency

A fourth barrier to family and community self-sufficiency is the emphasis by political leaders on individual self-sufficiency in isolation from the environmental context. This emphasis on individual responsibility alone ignores what Poole (1995) described as the country's shared responsibility to help rebuild families and communities. Rebuilding communities requires that a diversity of perspectives and voices be included in assessing needs and engaging in collective research and political action (Freeman & Pennekamp, 1988).

Yeich and Levine (1992) suggested that participatory research is useful for involving oppressed and vulnerable groups in the study of their collective problems and leads to empowerment as they resolve those problems. Community rebuilding can decrease stressors from bureaucratic practices in services organizations and restrictive social policies that lead to inadequate coping, family dysfunction, educational failure, school dropout, and lack of community growth and prosperity. Individually oriented reforms are needed (for example, work training and day care programs for poor people), but community rebuilding also should be a priority (Solomon, 1987).

DEFINITIONS OF SELF–SUFFICIENCY

The emphasis on individual self-sufficiency by many political leaders is based on their worldviews and value orientations, and their proposed restrictive reforms are punitive toward individuals who do not achieve their prescribed goals. These values have influenced how leaders define self-sufficiency and the reasons they stress individual responsibility in achieving this goal. Although social work embraces a different set of values related to the strengths perspective, social justice, and client self-determination, it is important for social workers to understand the worldviews and values underlying proposed social program reforms. By understanding these underlying values, social workers can help resolve barriers to self-sufficiency and influence policy development, reform, and implementation.

Norm-Based Definitions

Many Republican leaders, political conservatives, and other decision makers use a norm-based value framework in defining, assessing, and addressing problems of self-sufficiency. These policymakers define self-sufficiency as the average or "normal" individual's or family's ability to become economically self-supporting based on the values of rugged individualism and the Protestant work ethic (Poole, 1995). Other means to self-sufficiency such as creative problem solving and appropriate use of social supports are not included in this definition. People are viewed as independent beings who are capable of becoming economically self-sufficient and empowered without social supports.

This view denies that social structure contributes directly to the success of individuals who reach self-sufficiency and, conversely, that it shares any responsibility for individuals who do not achieve this goal. Not surprisingly, policymakers who share this view attribute failure to become self-sufficient to a lack of motivation or will and to value and cultural deficits (Poole, 1995). The norm framework has been applied somewhat appropriately to physical health and illness (as the medical model), but it is much less appropriate for defining mental health and social problems because of its linear cause-and-effect perspective and its failure to address people's strengths (Weick, 1985).

The framework provides decision makers with an extremely narrow and biased view for assessing families' economic and social conditions and the effectiveness of programs designed to address those conditions. For example, the norm-based definition of self-sufficiency encourages policymakers to focus on individual problems and pathology when programs such as welfare and the Work Incentive Program do not result in recipients' economic independence. The multiple factors that contribute to recipients remaining on welfare and being underemployed or unemployed even after participation in these programs (for example, program quality, conflict between social policies and program goals) are ignored by those who define self-sufficiency on the basis of norms.

Chapin (1995) described this type of biased assessment as a political construction of reality that allows policymakers to "transform people into problems" (p. 506). Two types of policies often develop out of this narrowly focused assessment process. One group of policies, including the current social program reforms, restrict access to resources for people who are assumed to have exploited their past opportunities for success. A second group of policies help preserve the resources and privilege of groups that have achieved self-sufficiency based on the norm definition of the concept. Examples of these policies include tax loopholes for businesses, farm subsidies, and education subsidies for middle-income families. Many policymakers suggest that this second group of policies are acceptable because the protections they provide are different from the supports poor families receive in social programs. These decision makers also say that the protections for more successful people help improve the overall prosperity of the country, whereas supports for poor people do not.

Internal-Standard Definitions

A second way of defining self-sufficiency is used by policymakers in a variety of arenas, including some in the political arena (even some liberal political leaders). Such policymakers define self-sufficiency as an individual, family, cultural group, or community's process of achieving its own unique level of self-actualization and development in social, psychological, and cognitive areas. Economic independence is assumed to occur in conjunction with growth in those related areas. This more humanistic definition implies that individuals and other systems have different abilities and capacities along with differential access to resources, including social supports, cultural enrichment experiences, education, employment, and training opportunities. Levels of self-sufficiency can be assessed, therefore, as the sum of the individual's or unit's development, opportunities, and experiences based on the unit's internal standard (Erickson, 1985; Rhodes, 1985). Using this definition, decisions about funding grants, providing social supports, awarding scholarships, and selecting honorees for national and international awards are made by policymakers in the education system, private foundations, self-help programs, religious groups, the human capital movement, and the national and state legislatures (Caplan & Weissberg, 1989; Carnine, Carnine, Karp, & Weissberg, 1988; Ellis, 1973; Kurtz & Powell, 1987).

Unlike norm-based definitions of self-sufficiency, internal-standard definitions acknowledge that the environment can influence people's opportunities to reach self-sufficiency. But they assume people can reach self-sufficiency and empowerment through a planned self-development process without necessarily changing barriers or other social structures (Freeman & O'Dell, 1993). Policymakers who use an internal-standard definition of self-sufficiency believe an individual's failure to become self-sufficient results from developmental or socialization inadequacies, physiological problems, or emotionally traumatic events.

Based on this definition of self-sufficiency, some decision makers' policies have helped develop programs and other opportunities for individual enrichment, assimilation, and socialization. These special initiatives include English as a second language classes, 12-step and other mutual-help groups, indigenous helper programs, entrepreneurial and other leadership development programs, professional development and remedial programs for academics and students in higher education, job readiness and work training projects, early childhood programs (Head Start and Follow-Through), and public school remedial and special education programs.

Although these programs are often effective in meeting special individual and family needs, the definition of self-sufficiency used by policymakers as a rationale for developing the programs is too narrow. Unlike norm-based definitions, internal-standard definitions do not blame or label people for failing to reach self-sufficiency, and they lead policymakers to provide certain social supports that are beneficial to families and communities. But Israel (1985) suggested that this way of defining self-sufficiency does not go beyond promoting individual change and strengthening mutual-help support systems within a community to focus on social change. Policymakers must also target social structures outside a community that limit its members' self-sufficiency and self-determination.

Person-in-Environment Definition

Norm-based and internal-standard definitions of self-sufficiency encourage policymakers to ignore the need for environmental or social change and therefore prevent an accurate assessment of what families and communities need to reach self-sufficiency. The person-in-environment (PIE) framework, used by social work and some other professions, provides a definition of self-sufficiency that clarifies how the environment should be changed to become more supportive of families. Within this framework, self-sufficiency is defined as the knowledge, skills, and personal and collective power necessary to meet needs and to function interdependently at multiple system levels, with economic self-sufficiency as one of several desirable outcomes. The framework can encourage decision makers to assess the balance between individual, family, and community needs and the environmental resources necessary for meeting those needs when existing strengths and resilience are insufficient (Germain & Gitterman, 1980).

The PIE definition and framework emphasize values such as shared responsibility, reciprocity, and mutual interdependence (Poole, 1995). These values normalize each family's need for social supports at various points in its life cycle because of the changing and dynamic goodness-of-fit between needs and resources (Germain, 1983). Critical points in families' life cycles when they may need social supports include the birth of a first child when parent education is needed (for example, the Parents as Teachers Program), catastrophic illness (for example, a comprehensive health care plan), or industrial plant closings (for example, subsidized work-retraining programs). The broad variety of needed social supports include tangible and intangible supports as well as formal and informal or mutual-help supports.

The PIE perspective provides a rationale for social policies that offer supports at the various life cycle stages and requires policies that address systemic economic and political conditions that make families less self-sufficient. Such a framework makes clear how the needs for social supports of the country's most vulnerable families are more severe because of a combination of individual and environmental factors.

PIE DEFINITION OF SELF–SUFFICIENCY APPLIED TO COMMUNITY RESEARCH

The social support needs of families with young children were the focus of a community research project in a midwestern city, where a private foundation wanted to explore ways it could serve those families more effectively. The foundation contracted with a graduate school of social work to conduct an ethnographic study of the community to clarify and analyze the residents' assessment of their needs. The foundation's emphasis on helping community residents reach their individual potential and become more self-sufficient implied they were defining this concept based on the internal standard, but this was not stated directly (Freeman & O'Dell, 1993). In this study, three issues emerged from participants' definitions of self-sufficiency. First, the participants' definitions and indicators of self-sufficiency were broader than the norm-based and internal-standard definitions frequently used by policymakers. The participants' collective definitions ranged across multiple levels, from the individual to the external environment, instead of focusing only on the individual. Their definitions focused not only on economic indicators of self-sufficiency, but also on indicators such as a greater range of personal choices and the community's role in making life better for more vulnerable families and individuals. In essence, taken collectively, the participants' definitions were more consistent with the PIE definition.

Second, although the respondents phrased some indicators from an individual perspective, indicators related to the family, community, and larger environment referred to collective or interdependent activities. For example, when one participant defined self-sufficiency related to the community, she said, "I think self-sufficiency is when we [the community] pull together for a good cause . . . like when they [the school board] was tryin' to close our high school. . . . We worked together to stop them. We didn't win, but we showed them" (Freeman & O'Dell, 1993, p. 50). This participant's response illustrates activities that increase political power and opportunities for residents to influence systems.

Third, participants either spontaneously shared examples to clarify their definitions of self-sufficiency or, when asked to elaborate on those definitions, responded with examples. Their examples included a broad range of formal and informal resources and social supports. Many of the informal resources they identified already existed in the community, whereas many of the formal resources they identified were needed. Examples of informal supports included mutual-help networks and community education about how the business and political systems worked. Job-training, health care, day care, and community-controlled social programs were identified as formal external resources or policies required to eliminate structural barriers to self-sufficiency. A combination of formal and informal supports is important for self-sufficiency and empowerment for individuals (Chang, 1993), families (Dunst, Trivette, & Deal, 1989), organizations (Gutierrez, GlenMaye, & DeLois, 1995), cultural groups (Hardy-Fanta, 1986), and communities (Solomon, 1987).

The findings from the study revealed a community that was self-sufficient in some ways but required a broader array of environmental supports for meeting its community rebuilding needs. Although many of its conditions are unique, this community had some conditions that are common to communities across the country. All community rebuilding requires new ways of defining and organizing practice that are consistent with the PIE definition and goal of self-sufficiency.

RECONCEPTUALIZING COMMUNITY PRACTICE

Rebuilding communities and providing social supports offer exciting opportunities for reconceptualizing community practice in schools, family services agencies, mental health centers, youth services organizations, and other community programs (Freeman & Pennekamp, 1988). The current sociopolitical climate and proposed reforms are emerging out of a reactive, conservative philosophy. Social work should move beyond the current crisis and anticipate future needs as resources are being eliminated or reallocated. A proactive approach involves eliminating rigid practice boundaries, forming new creative partnerships with families and other professionals that cross traditional organizational parameters, and developing community-centered service delivery systems.

Eliminating Practice Boundaries

Social work should move from conceptualizations of practice based on professional interests to those that more closely approximate clients' "lived experiences" (Freeman & O'Dell, 1993; Gulati & Guest, 1990; Segal, 1992) to "address both the personal issues of their clients as well as the policies and practices that shape the provision of services and resources" (Frey, 1988, p. 2). Although policy has always been the center of formal social supports, the current economic and political situation has heightened the impact of policy on families' lives and the need for all social workers to understand and address policy issues.

The traditional direct–indirect practice continuum has been conceptualized in terms of rigidly separate areas of practice. Keeping the areas of clinical practice, community practice, and social administration separate may have been important initially when practice activities were being delineated. However, clients' needs and life circumstances in their real environments are interrelated rather than separate. In addition, the impact of the current reforms is requiring more efficient and comprehensive approaches to helping clients cope with increased stressors when there are fewer resources available. Thus, practice needs to be more integrated by encouraging the areas of overlap and flexibility that are shown on the traditional practice continuum in Figure 21-1.

This flexibility in practice roles is required for social workers to implement five policy-related models identified by Wyers (1991). Figure 21-1 illustrates how these models parallel the areas of practice continuum with some adaptations. Wyers's models are not mutually exclusive, but they vary according to their degree of policy-related activity. "Worker as policy" refers to the direct services worker, who is the "embodiment or personification of policy" and the "artery through which policy flows in its implementation" (p. 245). The worker's "values, principles, and theoretical assumptions become the actual policies that inform the nature and quality of services provided" (p. 246). Social workers as policy conduits are "the connection through which enacted policy is translated into practice" (p. 245) as well as sounding boards who provide systematic feedback about the effects of policy on families to organizational and community policymakers. Social workers in all three traditional practice areas have access to and should share information with decision makers about the impact of policy on clients.

The social worker as internal change agent is the direct services worker who influences his or her employing agency's policies when they are not conducive to effective services or when policy gaps are identified (Wyers, 1991). The external change agent advocates policy changes in systems that are separate from their agencies of employment. External change agents can be direct service providers or administrators. Wyers noted that these change agents need more specialized policy-related skills. The social worker as policy expert conducts policy analyses, formulates social policy, and influences the policy-making process at

FIGURE 21-1

Comparison of the Traditional Direct–Indirect Practice Continuum and Wyers's Policy Practice Models

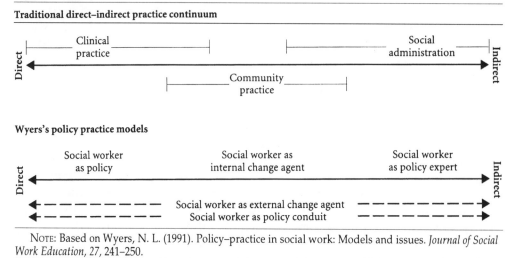

NOTE: Based on Wyers, N. L. (1991). Policy–practice in social work: Models and issues. *Journal of Social Work Education, 27,* 241–250.

community and legislative levels. The role requires policy and practice training at the macro level in schools of social work.

Regardless of whether the focus of services is clinical, community, or social administration, the social worker may need to offer services in one of the other traditional areas and fulfill one or more of Wyers's (1991) policy-related models as needed. Another option may be to work collaboratively with other social workers or helping professionals who can offer services in one of the other traditional practice areas or use another of Wyers's policy-related models. These and other options will require social workers to become more knowledgeable about how to use different policy practice models.

To illustrate how this reconceptualization of practice can be applied, an example of overlapping clinical and community practice in school–community settings is useful. The work often begins with social workers' data from clinical assessments in those settings or with information they collect during community work, such as service provision in a community program, interagency meetings, or informal community events. A person-in-environment assessment, in this blend of clinical–community practice, should include questions about factors in families' community or larger environments that support or impede the goals they desire (Freeman & O'Dell, 1993). These questions can reveal information about community or larger systems problems that are influencing the situation.

In a psychosocial assessment conducted by a school social worker, these questions revealed that a student's attendance problem was being exacerbated by the ongoing violence and drug sales near her school and the recent murder of her cousin. Another social worker in a community center noted an increase in residents' requests for transportation to center activities. By asking questions about family and community factors that were affecting the residents' participation, he learned that the transportation authority had recently eliminated several bus routes in the area. The lack of transportation was also affecting residents' efforts to get to and from work and to handle other family-related responsibilities.

In both situations, clients' self-sufficiency needs were threatened by a lack of resources. Therefore, working only at the individual level to increase their coping with violence and to find other transportation would not have been effective. The social workers needed to assume Wyers's (1991) policy conduit or external change agent roles (Figure 21-1). Assuming these roles would have involved working collaboratively with the families, other school and other community practitioners, community members, and institutions to develop collective action strategies (Freire, 1983) to change the environment—that is, an unsafe neighborhood or inadequate public transportation. These collaborative and policy-related roles are beneficial because they are more in tune with clients' environmental constraints and social justice issues (Figueira-McDonough, 1993).

Forming New Creative Partnerships

Much of the empowerment literature encourages social workers to establish new relationships with clients that do not replicate the environmental power inequities clients experience daily (Dunst et al., 1989; Gutierrez, 1990; Solomon, 1987). Even when helpers are required to involve consumers as an empowerment strategy, they may have difficulty shifting from traditional to more facilitative roles. For example, Knitzer, Steinberg, and Fleish (1990) found that parents were often discouraged from becoming involved in the decision-making and service delivery process required by federal policy for family-centered collaborative services between educational and mental health systems. These findings support the need for more equitable and involved parental roles.

Social Worker–Client Partnerships. Gutierrez (1990) recommended that, rather than social workers analyzing clients' problems and then advocating as needed to change the environment, a more power-equalizing role is needed. That role involves teaching families and then letting them teach others how to conduct and understand a power analysis of their situations. In the process families identify barriers in the immediate and larger environments that may be influencing a problem and its resolution and raise questions about who benefits and who suffers if the problem is maintained. Another step in this process is addressing the barriers through collective advocacy and community mobilization. Identifying potential sources of unacknowledged power is equally important, including forgotten skills, positive personal qualities, areas of social influence, and social supports (Gutierrez, 1990; Israel, 1985).

These strategies and partnerships can increase families' and community groups' involvement in decision making about how to influence policy and other structural changes. When the findings of the community research study discussed earlier were shared with the respondents during the member checking process to elicit their reactions, they disagreed that the family-centered early childhood program the foundation recommended was needed. Instead, they requested the foundation's financial and technical assistance in developing their political power to influence systems outside their community.

With the foundation's support, the community planned and implemented political action strategies to gain control over the parochial and public schools in their community, their first priority among their self-sufficiency needs. Their power analysis and research helped them anticipate and counter negative responses from the two education systems. They achieved their goal of gaining a community public high school as a step toward reducing the 60 percent dropout rate among their youths. They also won a multicultural curriculum and community control of the board of the community parochial school. The foundation provided social workers and other community practitioners and consultants to help the residents develop their two-year planning and structural change process. This process illustrates the new client partnerships that will be needed for community rebuilding and empowerment (Freeman, 1996b; Gutierrez, 1990; Hawkins & Catalano, 1992).

Practice–Research Partnerships. More collaboration will be needed between practitioners and researchers in community practice and other areas. Practice–research partnerships can integrate practitioners' expertise in service delivery (for example, deciding how to change the interventions being studied to meet clients' needs) with researchers' expertise in design and methodology (operationalizing the target behaviors and the interventions) (Galinsky, Turnbull, Meglin, & Wilner, 1993). Such collaboration can provide the best subjective and objective knowledge available: practice wisdom and research-based practice guidelines (Klein & Bloom, 1995). This combined knowledge can be used to influence funding and policy decisions in this period of increased competition for diminishing resources (Klein & Bloom, 1995). Also, in these new partnerships social workers train other professionals (including managed care contractors) in practice–research collaboration and policy practice roles.

Developing Community-Centered Service Systems

There is a need to shift service delivery from a community-based to a community-centered approach. *Community-based programs and systems* are defined as school-linked and integrated services models that provide a range of comprehensive services in one physically accessible school or community site (Aguirre, 1995). Although such programs often seek the community's support for their presence, they are not usually accountable to the community. *Community-centered systems* are defined as services that have "structural components that make programs accountable to community members by involving advisory boards and citizen review boards in planning, implementing, and monitoring programs . . . along with the use of peer-led services" by youths, family members, and other community residents (Freeman, 1996a, p. 4).

These programs go beyond helping meet immediate and short-term needs by focusing also on consumer-determined, long-term family and community capacity building. The shift to community-centered service systems requires workers to influence policy at state and local levels where requests for proposals and managed care contracts are developed. As policy experts in partnerships with community members and other professionals in policy–practice roles, workers should help mandate criteria for community-centered programs and prevention in funding proposals. Because some key decisions may still be made at the federal level, advocacy and lobbying at that level will be important, too (Freeman, 1996b).

CHANGES IN SOCIAL WORK EDUCATION

A number of changes are necessary in social work education to support the practice innovations discussed in this article. Murdrick, Steiner, and Pollard (1992) believed that planning for change in general is the foundation for other changes and that schools of social work should use forecasting to plan for the types of social problems and the sociopolitical climate that may exist at national, state, and local levels in the future.

Community rebuilding and capacity-building practice require that schools of social work reintroduce or develop concentrations in community practice. All social workers will need substantive knowledge about the community as a system and its impact on family and organizational functioning. This knowledge will be needed whether workers engage in direct or indirect practice primarily or become policy experts or researchers (Huber & Orlando, 1993). Social workers planning to become community practitioners will need advanced knowledge about community self-sufficiency. They will also need to understand practice theory and skills related to community practice and the collective power and skill development that communities need to influence systems change (Rogge, 1993). Specializations in school social work, school-community practice, child welfare, and children and families will require additional content and learning experiences in the community area.

The policy practice roles necessary for effective services along the direct–indirect practice continuum require new methods of integrating policy practice, practice research, and other parts of the social work curriculum. Course work and field practicum experiences should be reorganized to include content and joint micro or macro assignments that help students integrate practical learning experiences (Huber & Orlando, 1993). Policy integration should include analyzing the current political climate, decision makers' value frameworks, and policies on the basis of strengths and empowerment (Chapin, 1995).

Curriculum changes are also needed to support the proposed partnerships with clients and other professionals. To build these new coalitions and maintain facilitative empowerment-oriented roles, social workers will need information on postmodern perspectives that emphasize many ways of knowing and narrative and other strengths-based approaches to practice (Burstow, 1991). Additional courses are needed to teach new forms of collaboration consistent with these perspectives, including direct interdisciplinary and consumer participation in courses and field work (Strom & Gingerich, 1993). In addition, a curriculum is needed to teach students the tasks of collaborative relationships, including how to facilitate clients in conducting power analyses and deconstructing the value frameworks used by policymakers in their funding decisions.

FUTURE RESEARCH AND POLICY AGENDA

Research

The foundation for the research agenda is closer relationships between practitioners and researchers with improved communication and collaboration. Consensus building about the subjective and objective knowledge to be collected must be done in consultation with consumers, so that their voices are included in the agenda setting. Therefore, the agenda should not be determined before that collective process.

Some possible research agenda areas might include documenting what families and communities can and are doing for themselves, what works (best practices in formal and informal social supports), and what other supports are needed in terms of policy. The agenda would need to include culturally sensitive ethnographic research methods as needed, consumer involvement in all phases of the research process, policy impact analyses, and improved prevention evaluation technology. The effectiveness of this type of research agenda is based on a solution-focused practice research paradigm rather than a pathology-focused one (Nickerson, 1995).

Policy

A policy agenda consistent with the research agenda should involve "a more inclusive approach to policy formation and an expanded array of empowering policy options" (Chapin, 1995, p. 506). Wyers's (1991) policy models involve all direct and indirect services practitioners in policy at various level; an inclusive policy agenda would also include families and communities. Policy is more likely to reflect consumers' realities when they are on policy-making teams (Chapin, 1995). Common policy agenda areas at the national level could be identified through consensus building, such as strengths-oriented full-employment policies instead of the current punitive reforms. Local or state policy agendas that are based on self-sufficiency needs at multiple levels and that present the array of empowerment options suggested by Chapin could be identified and prioritized by each community.

CONCLUSION

Although the focus of this article is on families and community practice, the discussion has implications for all segments of society and for the profession of social work as a whole. Current political and social reforms can bring about the worst of times as well as opportunities for positive change. Blaming poor people for poverty that is maintained by systemic power and resource inequities is blaming the victims. Yet it is important to acknowledge that some social programs have not been as effective as intended in helping the majority of families achieve self-sufficiency. Reforms are inevitable, and the need for change presents an opportunity to develop more empowerment-oriented supports that do not foster dependency or stigmatize poor people.

Social work and other helping professions should widen their repertoire of policy practice roles to affect policy development at the national, state, and local levels or lose this opportunity for positive change. But a more systematic approach to change will be needed, perhaps more now than at any other time, for the profession to accomplish the necessary level of integrated, client-centered practice. A systematic approach to change requires a closer relationship between social work education and practice based on a national process of priority setting and monitoring. Such a process may make the profession more accountable and prepared for the next set of challenges from policymakers.

By using norm-based definitions of self-sufficiency, policymakers have transformed not only families but also social workers into "the problem." Therefore, working toward positive change can benefit the consumers of social work services as well as the profession itself.

REFERENCES

Aguirre, L. M. (1995). California's efforts toward school-linked, integrated, comprehensive services. *Social Work in Education, 17,* 217–225.

Atherton, C. R. (1992). A pragmatic approach to the problem of poverty. *Social Work, 37,* 197–203.

Burstow, B. (1991). Freirian codifications and social work education. *Journal of Social Work Education, 27,* 196–207.

Caplan, M. Z., & Weissberg, R. P. (1989). Promoting social competence in early adolescence. In B. H. Schneider, G. Attili, J. Nadel, & R. P. Weissberg (Eds.), *Social competence in developmental perspective* (pp. 371–385). Boston: Kluwer.

Carnine, D., Carnine, L., Karp, J., & Weissberg, P. (1988). Kindergarten for economically disadvantaged children: The direct instruction component. In C. Warger (Ed.), *A resource guide to public school early childhood programs* (pp. 73–78). Alexandria, VA: Association for Supervision and Curriculum Development.

Chamberlain, R. (1995). *Kansas mental health managed care: Enhancing client lives while controlling costs* [Executive summary]. Lawrence: University of Kansas, Office of Social Policy Analysis.

Chang, V. N. (1993). Prevent and empower: A student-to-student strategy with alcohol abuse. *Social Work in Education, 15*, 207–213.

Chapin, R. K. (1995). Social policy development: The strengths perspective. *Social Work, 40*, 506–514.

Chavkin, N. F., & Brown, K. (1992). School social workers building a multiethnic family-school-community partnership. *Social Work in Education, 14*, 160–164.

Dunst, C., Trivette, C., & Deal, A. (1989). *Enabling and empowering families: Principles and guidelines for practice.* Cambridge, MA: Brookline Books.

Ellis, A. (1973). *Humanistic psychotherapy.* New York: McGraw-Hill.

Erickson, E. H. (1985). Life cycle. In M. Bloom (Ed.), *Life span development* (pp. 35–41). New York: Macmillan.

Figueira-McDonough, J. (1993). Policy practice: The neglected side of social work intervention. *Social Work, 38*, 179–188.

Freeman, E. M. (1996a). Community practice and policy issues revisited [Editorial]. *Social Work in Education, 18*, 3–6.

Freeman, E. M. (1996b). President Clinton and the 104th Congress: The nightmare on Capitol Hill [Editorial]. *Social Work in Education, 18*, 67–70.

Freeman, E. M., & O'Dell, K. (1993). Helping communities redefine self-sufficiency from the person-in-environment perspective. *Journal of Intergroup Relations, 20*, 38–54.

Freeman, E. M., & Pennekamp, M. (1988). *Social work practice: Toward a child, family, school, community perspective.* Springfield, IL: Charles C Thomas.

Freire, P. (1983). *Pedagogy of the oppressed.* New York: Continuum.

Frey, G. (1988). *A framework for policy-related practice.* Unpublished manuscript, Portland State University, Graduate School of Social Work, Portland, OR.

Galinsky, M. J., Turnbull, J. E., Meglin, D. E., & Wilner, M. E. (1993). Confronting the reality of collaborative practice research: Issues of practice, design, measurement, and team development. *Social Work, 38*, 440–450.

Germain, C. B. (1983). *Practice in health settings.* New York: Columbia University Press.

Germain, C. B., & Gitterman, A. (1980). *Life model of social work practice.* New York: Columbia University Press.

Gulati, P., & Guest, G. (1990). The community-centered model: A garden-variety approach or a radical transformation of community practice? *Social Work, 35*, 63–68.

Gutierrez, L. (1990). Working with women of color: An empowerment perspective. *Social Work, 35*, 149–153.

Gutierrez, L. M., GlenMaye, L., & DeLois, K. (1995). The organizational context of empowerment practice: Implications for social work administration. *Social Work, 40*, 249–258.

Hardy-Fanta, C. (1986). Social action in Hispanic groups. *Social Work, 31*, 119–123.

Horvath, J., & Kaye, N. (1995). *Medicaid managed care: A guide to the states.* Portland, ME: National Academy for State Health Policy.

Hawkins, J. D., & Catalano, R. F. (1992). *Communities that care.* San Francisco: Jossey-Bass.

Huber, R., & Orlando, B. P. (1993). Macro assignment: Think big. *Journal of Social Work Education, 29*, 19–25.

Israel, B. (1985). Social networks and social work: Implications for natural helper and community-level interventions. *Health Education Quarterly, 12*, 65–80.

Jones, L. (1992). The full employment myth: Alternative solutions to unemployment. *Social Work, 37*, 359–364.

Keigher, S. M. (1994). The morning after deficit reduction: The poverty of U.S. maternal and child health policy [National Health Line]. *Health & Social Work, 19*, 143–147.

Klein, W. C., & Bloom, M. (1995). Practice wisdom. *Social Work, 40*, 799–807.

Knitzer, J., Steinberg, Z., & Fleish, B. (1990). *At the schoolhouse door.* New York: Bank Street College of Education.

Kurtz, L. F., & Powell, T. J. (1987). Three approaches to understanding self-help groups. *Social Work with Groups, 10*, 69–80.

LeCroy, C. W. (1992). Enhancing the delivery of effective mental health services to children. *Social Work, 37,* 225–231.

Murdrick, N. R., Steiner, J. R., & Pollard, W. L. (1992). Strategic planning for schools of social work. *Journal of Social Work Education, 28,* 278–290.

National Association of Social Workers, Office of Government Relations. (1996, March 4). *Social workers urged to respond to governors' proposals on welfare and Medicaid* [Government Relations Alert]. Washington, DC: Author.

Nickerson, P. R. (1995). Solution-focused group therapy [Notes from the Field]. *Social Work, 40,* 132–133.

O'Donnell, S. (1993). Involving clients in welfare policy-making. *Social Work, 38,* 629–635.

Personal Responsibility and Work Opportunity Act, H.R. 4, 104th Cong., 1st Sess. (1995).

Poole, D. (1995). Beyond the rhetoric: Shared responsibility versus the Contract with America [Editorial]. *Health & Social Work, 20,* 83–86.

Rhodes, S. (1985). A developmental approach to the life cycle of the family. In M. Bloom (Ed.), *Life span development* (pp. 30–39). New York: Macmillan.

Rogge, M. E. (1993). Social work, disenfranchised communities, and the natural environment: Field education opportunities. *Journal of Social Work Education, 29,* 111–120.

Saucier, P. (1995). *Public managed care for older persons and persons with disabilities: Major issues and selected initiatives* [Monograph]. Portland, ME: National Academy for State Health Policy.

Segal, E. A. (1992). Multineed children in the social services system [Trends & Issues]. *Social Work in Education, 14,* 190–198.

Solomon, B. (1987). *Empowerment: Social work in oppressed communities.* New York: Columbia University Press.

Strom, K., & Gingerich, W. J. (1993). Educating students for new market realities. *Journal of Social Work Education, 29,* 78–87.

Weick, A. (1985). Issues in overturning a medical model of social work practice. *Social Work, 28,* 467–471.

Wyers, N. L. (1991). Policy-practice in social work: Models and issues. *Journal of Social Work Education, 27,* 241–250.

Yeich, S., & Levine, R. (1992). Participatory research's contribution to a conceptualization of empowerment. *Journal of Applied Social Psychology, 22,* 1894–1908.

This chapter was originally published in the September 1996 issue of Social Work, *vol. 41, pp. 521–532.*

22 Mothers' Views on Child Care under the JOBS Program and Implications for Welfare Reform

Jan L. Hagen and Liane V. Davis

The recently passed Personal Responsibility and Work Opportunity Reconciliation Act of 1996 (P.L. 104-193) curtails expenditures for welfare programs (such as Aid to Families with Dependent Children [AFDC], food stamps, and Supplemental Security Income [SSI] for children) by allocating a fixed sum of federal funds to states, imposing lifetime limits on welfare benefits, and increasing the demands on states to require welfare recipients to engage in work-related activities. The debates surrounding the demands for high levels of participation in work-related activities have given little consideration to the child care services necessary for women to participate, particularly those with preschool children.

In earlier welfare legislation, child care provisions have been an important adjunct to welfare-to-work programs. Most recently, in designing the Job Opportunities and Basic Skills Training (JOBS) program under the Family Support Act of 1988 (FSA) (P.L. 100-485), Congress recognized that child care would be critical to participation in welfare employment programs by AFDC recipients and to the participants' ability to make the transition to employment (for analyses of the Family Support Act, see, for example, Chilman, 1992; Gueron & Pauly, 1991; Hagen, 1992; Stoesz & Karger, 1990). In the current context of welfare reform, it is appropriate to review earlier legislative provisions for child care services and to assess JOBS participants' experiences with those services.

As part of a three-year study on the implementation of the JOBS program (Hagen & Lurie, 1994), the authors interviewed JOBS participants in four communities to assess their experiences with the program and supportive services, including child care. Using data from our overall study on JOBS participants (Hagen & Davis, 1994), this article focuses on the women's perceptions of child care services and the effects of their participation in the JOBS program on their children. We have reported elsewhere the findings about the respondents' perceptions of the services received under the JOBS program, their evaluation of the program, and their status at the time of follow-up (Hagen & Davis, 1995).

Funding for this study was provided by the Foundation for Child Development, New York. The conclusions and opinions in this article reflect those of the authors and should not be construed as representing those of the funders. The authors wish to thank Irene Lurie, who served as coprincipal investigator for the JOBS Implementation Study, and Ling Wang, who served as the project's research associate and assisted with data analysis for this article.

Because this research used the major provisions of the legislation as its basis, this article summarizes the child care provisions and earlier research on the implementation of these provisions.

CHILD CARE PROVISIONS OF THE FAMILY SUPPORT ACT OF 1988

The Family Support Act of 1988 reflected a clear shift in work expectations for mothers with young children who receive welfare benefits. Although work incentives and requirements have been tied to receipt of AFDC since the late 1960s, earlier legislation focused on AFDC mothers with children age six and older. Under the Family Support Act, mothers with children age three or older are required to participate for up to 20 hours each week in JOBS training if child care is available. In addition, states could elect to require participation by mothers with children age one year or older. Responding specifically to the risk that minor custodial parents would become long-term welfare recipients, Congress also mandated that mothers under 20 years of age who had not completed high school or its equivalent be required to participate in educational activities, regardless of their children's ages.

Under this federal legislation, child care was guaranteed, if needed, for children of JOBS participants. In a major departure from previous legislation, Congress also authorized transitional child care for up to 12 months to families that became ineligible for AFDC because of increased earnings. Federal funding for child care, which had been severely limited under early welfare employment programs, was significantly liberalized under the FSA and was made an open-ended entitlement. State expenditures for child care services were matched by the federal government at the Medicaid rate, which ranges from 50 percent to 80 percent, depending on the state's per capita income.

Child Care under JOBS

Research findings to date suggest that women participating in the JOBS program have, indeed, found access to child care services (Hagen & Lurie, 1994). Participation rates for the JOBS program, however, were at the relatively low rates of 11 percent of nonexempt AFDC recipients, and many states were operating programs with voluntary rather than mandatory enrollment. It is possible that women volunteering for the JOBS program have fewer child care needs. Also, Hagen and Lurie (1993a) identified significant gaps in services, particularly care for infants and toddlers and care during evenings, nights, and weekends.

The most significant concern related to child care and JOBS is the adequacy of state funding. Even with the liberalized federal provisions for funding child care, a number of states have confronted funding problems that have either restricted access to the JOBS program itself or resulted in decreased availability of funding for the states' subsidized child care programs for non-AFDC low-income working families (Hagen & Lurie, 1993a).

Parental Choice in Child Care Services

Parental choice in selecting child care services also was a central premise in developing the federal legislation and the regulations, which stipulate "that consistent with individual responsibility is choice, and that parents be given a wide range of options for child care while participating in this program" (Aid to

Families with Dependent Children, 1989). Research that has considered the implementation of this provision from the perspective of administrators and front-line workers indicated that states' JOBS programs were safeguarding parental choice, with many local sites placing strong emphasis on formal or regulated care (Hagen & Lurie, 1993a; Hagen & Wang, 1994; Martinson & Riccio, 1989). Data available on service use also suggest that formal care has been emphasized (Hagen & Lurie, 1993a; U.S. House of Representatives, 1993). However, data on service use may well undercount the extent to which informal care is used by JOBS participants, particularly if state policy discourages or prohibits payment to relatives or to people providing care in the child's own home.

For parental choice to be meaningful, parents must be informed about child care services and have access to assistance in obtaining child care services if necessary. The federal legislation requires that states provide, either directly or through others, information about the types and locations of services and inform clients that assistance is available in selecting appropriate care for their children. If requested, the welfare agency must provide assistance in obtaining child care services. Although JOBS programs have responded to this provision by making some assistance available, the extent of the services and the expertise of the agencies providing the services are highly variable (Hagen & Lurie, 1994). In addition, Meyers and van Leuwen (1992), commenting on their findings from participants in California's welfare employment program, noted that

> In promoting parental choice in child care arrangements, however, it is crucial that the quality of care for children not be compromised. Many of the women in this sample had little experience finding and evaluating market care. AFDC recipients entering JOBS programs are likely to need assistance in making informed choices about their options for care and about how to evaluate the quality of various alternatives. (p. 34)

Meyers and van Leuwen found that single-parent AFDC recipients' child care preferences resembled those of other working parents and that they relied on informal and organized child care in about equal proportions. However, informal care provided by relatives and friends tended to be relied on for infants and older, school-age children. Market care was the preference for the majority of women with toddlers and preschool children.

Links with Early Childhood Education

Finally, the legislation required that state welfare agencies coordinate their efforts with existing early childhood education programs, including Head Start. This particular provision, along with the other supportive services potentially available to both adults and children, could have turned the JOBS program into a two-generational preventive one (Smith, Blank, & Bond, 1990). Children from low-income families, including welfare families, have been identified as a particularly vulnerable group. For example, Zill, Moore, Smith, Sherf, and Cario (1991) noted that "only about one-third of preschool children from welfare homes receive intellectual stimulation and emotional support from their parents comparable to that received by most children in families that are neither poor nor welfare dependent" (p. ii).

High-quality child care services are viewed as one avenue to compensate for inadequate parental stimulation. Sonenstein and Wolf (1991) found that welfare mothers were concerned that child care provide learning opportunities for their preschool children. To date, however, research suggests that few linkages have been established between JOBS programs and early childhood education programs, including Head Start (Hagen & Lurie, 1993b).

STUDY METHODS

Between November 1992 and May 1993, trained interviewers conducted face-to-face interviews with 357 JOBS participants in four local sites that were included in the larger JOBS implementation study: Minneapolis (Hennepin County); Utica, New York (Oneida County); Springfield–Eugene, Oregon (Springfield Branch); and Houston (Harris County). We selected these sites to provide some of the diversity found in JOBS programs across the country in program design, emphasis given to human capital investment or labor force attachment strategies, intensity of case management services, and extent of assistance in locating child care. In August 1993 we conducted follow-up telephone interviews to assess the women's progress while participating in the JOBS program and in locating employment. We completed telephone interviews with 283, or 79.3 percent, of the respondents.

To be included in the survey, a respondent had to be a female AFDC recipient who actively participated in educational, work training, or employment services offered under the JOBS program and who had at least one child aged three to five. We limited the survey to mothers because most adult AFDC recipients are mothers. We were interested in JOBS participants with children aged three to five because the FSA, unlike earlier legislation regarding welfare employment programs, extended participation requirements to mothers with preschool children. Mandating participation by this group of AFDC recipients created new challenges regarding the provision of child care services.

Instruments

Both surveys relied on structured instruments to collect information. In designing the instruments we followed the major provisions of the JOBS legislation and drew on other research on welfare recipients and welfare employment programs (for example, Garvin, 1974; Gilbert, Berrick, & Meyers, 1992; Goodwin, 1983; Martinson & Riccio, 1989; Maynard, 1990; Reid & Smith, 1972; Smith, Fortune, & Reid, 1975; Sonenstein & Wolf, 1991). The instruments included items specific to the JOBS program, the respondents' motivation for program participation, their satisfaction with the program, and their expectations about benefits from the program. We considered the women's experiences related to child care in depth. In addition to examining the extent to which they received assistance in finding child care, the extent of choice they had in selecting child care, and the arrangements they actually made for their children, we considered factors important to them in selecting child care and their satisfaction with the care their children received.

Analysis

We used descriptive statistics to summarize and analyze much of the data. Although this was not a random sample, we used inferential statistics (primarily chi-square and one-way analysis of variance) in the interpretation of the findings. We used these inferential statistics to make comparisons across sites or various subgroups of respondents. The significance level for all reported analyses was established at the .05 level. In comparing sites in this article, we report only those findings that were statistically significant.

Characteristics of Respondents and Site Descriptions

For over half (56.2 percent) of the women, this was their first episode on welfare under their own grant, and they had begun their current episode within the past three years. On average, the respondents had been receiving welfare for 2.5 years. The women had participated in the JOBS program for an average of 7.4 months, but the length of time differed significantly across sites (Table 22-1). Participants in Springfield–Eugene, Oregon, had the shortest length of participation, averaging 4.6 months, whereas those in Minneapolis had participated for the longest period, an average of 13.1 months. The Minneapolis site has traditionally taken a more long-term approach to welfare employment programs and emphasized education and training programs. At the time of our study, Springfield-Eugene was emphasizing helping people enter the labor market quickly. Three-fourths (75.5 percent) of the women viewed their participation in the JOBS program as voluntary, but the proportions varied significantly by site, ranging from 99.0 percent in Minneapolis to 49.1 percent in Springfield–Eugene.

It is important to note that at the time of our study, the federally mandated rate of participation for the JOBS program was only 11 percent of the nonexempt AFDC caseload. This rate was exceeded by the four states included in this study: Minnesota (16 percent), New York (12 percent), Oregon (21 percent), and Texas (12 percent) (U.S. Department of Health and Human Services, 1993). In addition, at the time of the study, state policies in many instances encouraged the enrollment of volunteers in the JOBS program (Lurie & Hagen, 1993). Other limitations to the study stem from the purposive selection of local JOBS programs, a relatively small sample restricted to active JOBS participants who were mothers of at least one child aged three to five, and reliance on client self-report. Within these limitations, the study increases our understanding of how the JOBS program and related child care services affected the lives of these mothers and their children. (For further information on study methods, respondent characteristics, and descriptions of the local JOBS programs, see Hagen & Davis, 1994.)

FINDINGS

Information and Referral Services

Most (85.5 percent) of the respondents indicated that a welfare worker or JOBS case manager had provided them with information about child care. The majority

TABLE 22-1

Selected Demographic Characteristics of JOBS Participants, by Program Site: 1992–1993

Characteristic	Minneapolis (*n* = 100)	Utica, NY (*n* = 100)	Springfield–Eugene, OR (*n* = 57)	Houston (*n* = 100)	Total (*N* = 357)
Average time in JOBS program (months)	13.1	8.6	4.6	6.1	7.4
Household					
Average number of children	2.2	2.4	2.2	2.5	5.5
Average age of children	4.7	5.9	5.6	5.9	5.5
Average size of household	2.7	2.8	2.9	3.7	3.0
Marital status (%)					
Married	2.0	14.0	12.3	11.0	9.5
Separated, divorced, or widowed	25.0	36.0	49.1	44.0	37.3
Never married	73.0	50.0	38.6	45.0	53.2
Living together as couple	16.3	16.7	28.0	4.2	14.7
Age (mean)	25.7	27.3	27.7	29.0	27.4
Age distribution (% by years)					
18 to 20	11.3	4.0	8.8	5.0	7.1
21 to 25	48.5	37.0	26.3	24.0	34.7
26 to 30	19.6	32.0	36.8	38.0	31.1
31 to 35	15.5	21.0	15.8	17.0	17.5
36 to 49	5.2	6.0	12.3	16.0	9.6
Race (%)					
White	42.3	71.7	91.1	17.0	51.1
African American	46.4	22.2	0	67.0	38.1
American Indian	8.2	3.0	7.1	2.0	4.8
Other	3.1	3.0	1.8	14.0	6.0
Hispanic origin (%)	3.0	5.0	3.5	21.2	8.7

(continued)

TABLE 22-1
Continued

Characteristic	Minneapolis (n = 100)	Utica, NY (n = 100)	Springfield–Eugene, OR (n = 57)	Houston (n = 100)	Total (N = 357)
Education (%)					
8th grade or less	0	7.0	7.0	9.0	5.6
9th through 11th grade	14.0	34.0	31.6	37.0	28.9
GED	25.0	22.0	14.0	10.0	18.2
High school graduate	24.0	20.0	17.5	30.0	23.5
Some college	29.0	17.0	28.1	12.0	20.7
Associate's degree	7.0	0	1.8	1.0	2.5
Bachelor's degree or higher	1.0	0	0	1.0	.6
Completed training for job before entering JOBS program (%)	25.0	29.0	26.3	47	32.5
Trade certificate or license (%)	18.0	20.0	14.0	33.0	22.1
Self-rating of overall health (%)					
Excellent	25.0	17.0	8.8	19.0	18.5
Very good	28.0	28.0	22.8	38.0	30.0
Good	32.0	41.0	36.8	32.0	35.3
Fair	13.0	11.0	28.1	9.0	13.7
Poor	2.0	3.0	3.5	2.0	2.5
Health problem limiting ability to work (%)	8.0	12.0	29.8	10.0	13.2

Note: JOBS = Job Opportunities and Basic Skills Training program; GED = general equivalency diploma.

of them had received information about the role of the JOBS program in helping them pay for and find child care. However, only 4.9 percent reported that they had been told that they would not have to participate in the JOBS program if they could not find child care. The noteworthy site differences are the low percentage (47.4 percent) of respondents in Springfield–Eugene who reported being told that the JOBS program would help them find child care and the relatively low percentage (50.9 percent) of respondents in Utica who reported being told about the transitional child care benefits.

Arrangement of Care for Preschool Children

We asked the women a series of questions about the child care services they were receiving for their youngest child between the ages of three and five. An average of 73.3 percent of the participants reported making their own child care arrangements when they began to participate in the JOBS program, ranging from a high of 91.2 percent in Springfield–Eugene to a low of 67.0 percent in Utica. Of those who had received assistance in making child care arrangements, 76.3 percent reported receiving help from either the lead JOBS agency or the local welfare agency.

Over two-thirds (68.3 percent) of the participants indicated that they had complete freedom of choice in making child care arrangements, and an additional 17.6 percent indicated they had a fair amount of choice in the process. Consistent with this was the report by 87.3 percent of the participants that their case workers did not try to influence their selection of child care.

Important Factors in Selecting Child Care

The participants were asked to indicate how important various factors were to them in selecting child care and to select the one factor that was most important. The importance of various factors in selecting child care was rated on a four-point scale of 1 = extremely important, 2 = important, 3 = not very important, and 4 = not at all important.

Whereas most of the factors were considered extremely important to the majority of participants, the most important were the safety of the setting and the dependability, trustworthiness, and training of the provider (Table 22-2). That the provider be someone the participant knew and trusted was extremely important for a greater percentage of the respondents in Springfield–Eugene than in Minneapolis. However, fewer of the Springfield–Eugene participants indicated that the education and training of the provider was extremely important to them than those from the other sites. The difference in the importance of the cost of child care is also noteworthy. More than twice the number of respondents in Houston identified this as an extremely important factor than did those in Minneapolis (Table 22-2).

When asked to choose the single most important factor, the women most frequently selected the safety of the setting (46.9 percent) and the provider being somebody they knew and trusted (29.2 percent). Respondents in all the sites chose these two factors in that order, except in Springfield–Eugene, where the ranking was reversed.

TABLE 22-2

Percentage of JOBS Participants Rating Child Care as Extremely Important and Expressing Satisfaction with Available Care, by Factor and Program Site

Factor	% Rating Child Care as Extremely Important						% Satisfied[a] (N = 357)
	Minneapolis (n = 100)	Utica, NY (n = 100)	Springfield– Eugene, OR (n = 57)	Houston (n = 100)	Total (N = 357)	p	
Safety of setting	92.0	94.0	98.2	93.0	93.8		99.0
Dependability of child care	86.0	80.0	86.0	84.0	83.0		97.5
Known or trusted provider	63.0	76.0	80.7	72.0	72.0	.05	98.3
Education or training of provider	74.0	70.0	52.6	78.0	70.6		95.0
Match between mothers' values and providers' values for child rearing	64.0	67.0	70.2	72.0	68.1		96.9
Extent to which provider spends time teaching child new things	70.0	51.0	59.6	73.0	63.9	.005	90.0
Convenience of hours	65.0	48.5	57.9	57.0	57.0		96.0
Convenience of location	58.6	52.0	49.1	62.0	56.2		95.0
Cost of child care	30.3	44.4	40.4	66.0	45.9	.0005	96.0
Number of children in setting	39.4	37.8	22.8	47.0	38.4		96.9

NOTE: JOBS = Job Opportunities and Basic Skills Training program.
[a]Data on participant satisfaction for individual program sites are omitted because there were no significant differences.

Type of Child Care Setting

The participants were asked to identify the primary type of child care their youngest child between the ages of three and five was receiving while they were attending the JOBS program. Overall, slightly more than two-thirds (68.1 percent) of the women relied on formal child care arrangements, including day care centers, public education preschool programs, licensed family day care, and Head Start (Table 22-3). The greatest percentage of children (44.1 percent) were in day care centers. Children in Springfield–Eugene were the least likely to be in day care centers, whereas those in Houston were the most likely. Almost one-third (32.0 percent) of the women relied on informal, home-based care.

About equal numbers of children were cared for in their own (16.6 percent) or somebody else's home (15.4 percent), most often with a relative providing the care. In these settings, the children were cared for by grandparents (32.1 percent), nonrelatives (24.8 percent), partners (19.3 percent), siblings (13.8 percent), and other relatives (10.1 percent). Home-based care was used far more often in Springfield–Eugene (51.2 percent) and Utica (40.9 percent) than in either Minneapolis (15.5 percent) or Houston (25.8 percent). In addition, far more of the home-based day care providers in Springfield–Eugene were nonrelatives (50.0 percent) than in the other sites, where nonrelatives provided less than 20 percent of this informal care: Minneapolis, 18.8 percent, Utica, 13.9 percent, and Houston, 12.0 percent.

When asked what their preferred form of child care would be if cost, distance, and availability were not concerns, the women most frequently selected licensed day care (34.6 percent). However, the major difference that would occur if all forms of child care were available, accessible, and affordable was an increase in the use of educational programming through either Head Start or other public educational preschool programs. Comparable decreases would occur in day care centers and the care of children in others' homes, in either unlicensed or licensed facilities. Of those choosing informal home-based care, the most frequently mentioned preferred caregiver was a grandparent (34.8 percent). Other relatives, including partners and siblings, were preferred by 43.5 percent.

For the women in this study, travel to the child's provider was not a significant issue. Most of the child care providers were within a reasonable distance from the participants' homes. The median time it took to travel one way between the participant's home and the child care provider was 10 minutes.

Children were with their primary child care provider on average 27 hours per week. One-fourth (25.8 percent) of respondents, however, reported that in a typical week their youngest child received child care from at least one additional provider during the time they were attending JOBS activities, bringing the average number of hours that children were in child care each week to 31, with no appreciable differences among the sites.

Reliability

The women reported relatively stable child care arrangements since they began the JOBS program; 71.1 percent reported that they had not been required to

TABLE 22-3
Percentage of JOBS Participants' Youngest Children in Various Child Care Settings

Child Care Setting	Minneapolis ($n = 100$)	Utica, NY ($n = 100$)	Springfield– Eugene, OR ($n = 57$)	Houston ($n = 100$)	Total ($N = 357$)
Day care center	45.4	40.9	30.4	53.6	44.1
Own home	6.2	21.6	26.8	16.5	16.6
Someone else's home	9.3	19.3	30.4	9.3	15.4
Public education preschool program	11.3	4.5	3.6	12.4	8.6
Licensed family day care	19.6	4.5	7.1	1.0	8.3
Head Start	8.2	9.1	1.8	7.2	7.1

NOTES: JOBS = Job Opportunities and Basic Skills Training program. Youngest children were ages three to five years.
$\chi^2(1, 15) = 60.94, p \leq .0005.$

make any changes in child care services. Of those reporting changes in child care arrangements, 55.3 reported changing only once, with an additional 30.1 percent making two changes. The most frequent reasons for changing child care providers were dissatisfaction with the child's care (17.5 percent), provider became unavailable (14.6 percent), respondent's schedule changed (10.7 percent), and travel time became too long (9.7 percent). Despite concerns mentioned elsewhere about the safety of their children when cared for by others, only 5.8 percent of those who changed reported doing so because they felt the arrangements were unsafe.

Child care was also reliable. Only 10.4 percent of the respondents reported that they had missed a JOBS activity because their provider was unavailable to provide care for the child. Of those who had missed a JOBS activity because their provider was unavailable, 45.9 percent missed only one day of activity.

When asked to indicate how satisfied they were with 10 specific aspects of their child care arrangements, the women reported a high degree of satisfaction, with no statistically significant differences among the sites (Table 22-2). When asked to make a global assessment of their child care arrangements for their preschool children, the women indicated a high degree of satisfaction. Nearly two-thirds (64.6 percent) of the women reported that they were extremely satisfied, and another 32.3 percent were satisfied.

Program Benefits to Children

Serving as positive role models for their children motivated many of the women to participate in the JOBS program. When asked to identify their major reasons for participating in the JOBS program, 77.0 percent of the women identified "setting a good example for their children" as one of two major reasons for participating in the JOBS program, the other being to receive education and training, a factor identified by 82.6 percent of the women.

The women were also asked to identify two ways in which the program had been helpful to their children. Among the 79.8 percent ($n = 285$) who identified ways in which their children benefited, the women most frequently mentioned aspects related to child care, particularly the opportunities provided for children to enhance their social and academic skills. A significant number of the respondents also identified ways in which their relationships with their children had improved, either because they now had respite from child care or had developed new skills to enable them to respond to and teach their children.

Status at Follow-Up

In August 1993 we reached 79.3 percent (n = 283) of the respondents for a follow-up telephone survey. Nearly three-fifths (55.8 percent, n = 158) of those surveyed at follow-up reported still participating in the JOBS program. Close to one-fifth (18.0 percent, n = 51) of the women were no longer in the JOBS program because they had obtained employment. An additional 6.4 percent (n = 18) of the women had completed assigned JOBS activities but had not yet found employment. The remaining 19.8 percent were no longer participating in the JOBS program for a variety of reasons, including no longer receiving AFDC benefits, health problems, or difficulties with child care or transportation.

About two-thirds (67.4 percent) of the women still participating in the JOBS program reported stable child care arrangements since the initial interview, and the remaining 32.6 percent had changed child care arrangements at least once. For most of the latter, only one change was necessary, but 28.0 percent reported two or more changes. The main reasons for changing child care were dissatisfaction with the child's care (22.1 percent), unavailability of the provider (14.3 percent), change in the schedule of JOBS activities (11.7 percent), and difficulty getting to the provider because of distance or time (7.8 percent).

In a typical week, the children spent an average of 26 hours in child care while the participants were attending JOBS activities; 53.6 percent were extremely satisfied with their child care arrangements, and an additional 35.3 percent were satisfied.

Three-fifths (61.1 percent) of the 283 follow-up respondents thought that being in the JOBS program was helpful to their children. We asked those who said that their participation was helpful to their children to specify how their children had been helped. About three-fifths (60.4 percent) of this group provided at least one specific way in which their participation had helped their children. The most frequently given reasons fell into four categories: (1) 26.8 percent indicated that their children were enhancing their social skills, generally through participating in some form of day care; (2) 21.3 percent of the respondents noted that they were now serving as positive role models for their children, especially by demonstrating the value of staying in school; (3) 15.8 percent identified ways in which their participation was benefiting their children's academic achievement (for example, their children were being exposed to a broader array of learning experiences); and (4) 12.9 percent mentioned an improvement in their relationships with their children (for example, knowing how to spend quality time with their children or being able to help them with their homework).

Only 16.1 percent (n = 37) of the 231 respondents still participating in the JOBS program thought that being in the program was harmful to their children.

This varied across the sites, however, with close to half (46.4 percent) of respondents in Springfield–Eugene indicating that their participation was harming their children, in contrast to 4.8 percent in Houston, 13.2 percent in Utica, and 16.7 percent in Minneapolis. For this small group, the primary way in which their participation hurt their children was by reducing the amount of time they had to spend with their children. Few identified specific ways in which this affected their children, citing more generalized concerns about their children feeling abandoned or not liking it when their mothers left them.

DISCUSSION

The findings presented here offer another perspective on the implementation of the JOBS program—that of the program's intended beneficiaries. The findings are limited to the four sites in which the study was conducted and to a particular subset of JOBS participants, women with at least one child aged three to five who were actively participating in a JOBS program. Although our findings have limitations, they offer an alternative to the views of policymakers, administrators, and service providers.

Many of our findings related to child care services are positive, perhaps surprisingly so, given the concerns that are frequently raised about child care services. For most women in this study, child care was dependable, reliable, relatively stable, and easily accessible. However, at least one-third of the women changed child care arrangements for their youngest children aged three to five for various reasons. Meyers (1993) identified the same reasons—dissatisfaction with care provided, changes in schedules of JOBS activities, and travel difficulties—as contributing to a mother's probability of dropping out of a welfare employment program.

Most of the women thought that parental choice was safeguarded in that the agencies did not exert pressure on them to select any particular type of care, a finding consistent with other studies (Hagen & Lurie, 1993a; Hagen & Wang, 1994; Martinson & Riccio, 1989). However, to make parental choice meaningful, mothers must have relevant information about child care options and child development.

The extent to which women received specific information in this area and the extent to which they were expected to arrange child care without this guidance were inconsistent. The findings suggest that far more assistance was provided in Houston and Minneapolis than in Utica and particularly Springfield–Eugene. One explanation for these differences was the use of child care management agencies in the Houston JOBS program and the more active involvement of the Minneapolis case managers in assisting clients with child care arrangements. The findings from Springfield–Eugene indicate that case managers and local child care resource and referral agencies gave only limited assistance to JOBS participants in arranging child care. This lack of assistance may offer a partial explanation for greater reliance on home-based care provided by nonrelatives.

The respondents in Springfield–Eugene were more likely to indicate that their participation in the JOBS program was having an adverse effect on their children. In our study, almost half the respondents in Springfield–Eugene indicated that their participation in the JOBS program was having a harmful effect on their children. This percentage compares with Skricki's (1994) finding that 31 percent of the Oregon respondents indicated that their participation in the JOBS program had a negative or very negative effect on their children. Again, these evaluations by the women in Springfield–Eugene may be related to the adequacy of the child care information and referral assistance they received initially as well as to the quality of child care they were able to obtain.

Our findings lend support to those of Meyers and van Leuwen (1992) about child care preferences. The women in this study relied more heavily on formally organized child care settings, especially day care centers, for their children in the three- to five-year-old group. Although the women expressed high levels of satisfaction with their current child care arrangements, their preference was for an increased use of educational preschool programs, including Head Start. Like Sonenstein and Wolf's findings (1991), our study suggests that welfare mothers prefer child care settings that provide learning opportunities for their preschool children.

The relatively small percentage of children aged three to five reported by the mothers to be in early childhood education programs was not unexpected. The limited linkages with early childhood education programs and Head Start have been attributed to the fact that these programs are available only during the school year and usually provide only one-half day of child care. In recent years, however, funding for Head Start has increased significantly, in part to allow for all-day, full-year care (Chilman, 1993). As these programs develop, they may increase the availability of these services to participants in welfare employment programs as well as to employed low-income families.

Although relatively little attention has been given to the quality of child care services per se under the JOBS program, many women in this study who relied heavily on formal child care services believed the JOBS program had been helpful to their children by providing their children with the opportunity to enhance their social and academic skills in child care settings. From the mothers' perspective, then, having access to the child care subsidies provided by the JOBS program resulted in an enriched environment for their children, an outcome envisioned by those who advocated positioning the JOBS program as a preventive, two-generational program (Smith et al., 1990).

CONCLUSION

Overall, the findings regarding the effect on young children of their mothers' participation in the JOBS program are encouraging: The majority of the women viewed their JOBS participation as beneficial to their children. For some, the JOBS program operated as a two-generation preventive program by enhancing the lives of welfare children, although certainly not to the extent that was envisioned by Smith et al. (1990).

We suggest that three factors—all of which are not components of the new welfare legislation—were critical in contributing to the rather positive findings about child care services under the JOBS program. First, most of the women in our study had volunteered to participate in the JOBS program; they were motivated to avail themselves of educational and training opportunities. They also believed that their preschool children were benefiting as well, primarily as a result of their involvement in formal day care services.

Second, three of the local JOBS programs were willing to undertake more long-term investments in providing education and training to many of the respondents, to individualize service packages, and to provide assistance (either directly or indirectly through others) in locating child care services. For the women in these programs, the agencies relied more on positive inducements for program participation than on negative sanctions. One local program emphasized a labor force attachment strategy in its JOBS program, provided little if any assistance with child care arrangements, placed greater emphasis on mandatory program enrollment, and did not individualize service packages. From the participants' perspective, this program was the least satisfactory.

Third, at the time of the study, states were required to serve only 11 percent of their nonexempt AFDC caseload, and achieving this level of participation was not a significant challenge for some states' JOBS programs, which already had well-developed welfare employment programs (Hagen & Lurie, 1994). In addition, these states had sufficient state funds at the time of our study to draw down the federal matching funds for both their JOBS programs and the associated child care services to meet the federal participation rate of 11 percent.

The Personal Responsibility and Work Opportunity Reconciliation Act calls for almost the opposite: an emphasis on mandatory rather than voluntary participation in welfare employment programs, an emphasis on quick entry into the labor force rather than longer-term education and training, and participation in work-related activities by 50 percent of the AFDC caseload by 2002. Drastic changes are also proposed for child care services.

The child care provisions associated with the JOBS program have four significant features: (1) an uncapped federal funding stream for child care services required by JOBS participants and those making the transition to work, (2) a "guarantee" of support for child care services if a recipient is required to participate in a welfare employment program, (3) a federal directive to provide clients with assistance in selecting and locating child care, and (4) coordination with early childhood education programs. In 1990, these provisions were supplemented by the enactment of the At-Risk Child Care Program under AFDC to support child care services for low-income, non-AFDC families who needed child care services to work and who were "at risk" of becoming eligible for welfare if child care subsidies were not provided. This was a capped entitlement program that provided federal matching funds to the states based on the Medicaid matching rate.

P.L. 104-193 eliminates provision of child care assistance as an entitlement for AFDC and other low-income families receiving cash assistance, even if they are required to participate in work-related activities. In addition, it reduces funding and caps the federal matching funding available for child care assistance (NASW, 1996), even though the percentage of recipients expected to participate in work-related activities will increase significantly. Clearly, the current law lacks both the necessary safeguards to protect vulnerable children and the necessary funds to support state efforts in meeting child care needs for poor families.

As this study suggests, the issues related to child care for women receiving welfare and expected to engage in welfare employment programs are multidimensional and complex. Social workers must keep child care issues in the forefront as welfare employment programs designed for adult recipients, most of whom are mothers with young children, begin to be instituted in the states. If the states do not ensure access to quality child care services, including the availability of child care subsidies, as part of these welfare reforms, mothers with preschool children who are welfare recipients will encounter significant, perhaps impossible, barriers to participating in work-related activities as well as in employment. And their children's life circumstances will be compromised even further.

REFERENCES

Aid to Families with Dependent Children; Job Opportunities and Basic Skills Training (JOBS) program; child care and supportive services; conforming changes to existing regulations. 54 Fed. Reg. 42146-42267 (1989) (to be codified at 45 C.F.R. §§205, 224, 233, 234, 238, 239, 240, 250, 255, and 258).

Chilman, C. S. (1992). Welfare reform or revision? The Family Support Act of 1988. *Social Service Review, 66,* 349–377.

Chilman, C. S. (1993). Parental employment and child care trends: Some critical issues and suggested policies. *Social Work, 38,* 451–460.

Family Support Act of 1988, P.L. 100-485, 42 U.S.C. §1305.

Garvin, C. C. (1974). *Incentives and disincentives to participation in the Work Incentive Program* (Final report prepared for the U.S. Department of Labor). Washington, DC: U.S. Department of Labor.

Gilbert, N., Berrick, J. D., & Meyers, M. K. (1992). *GAIN family life and child care report.* Berkeley, CA: Family Welfare Research Group.

Goodwin, L. (1983). *Causes and cures of welfare.* Lexington, MA: Lexington Books.

Gueron, J., & Pauly, E. (1991). *Reforming welfare with work.* New York: Russell Sage Foundation.

Hagen, J. L. (1992). Women, work, and welfare: Is there a role for social work? *Social Work, 37,* 9–14.

Hagen, J. L., & Davis, L. V. (1994). *Implementing JOBS: The participants' perspective.* Albany, NY: Nelson A. Rockefeller Institute of Government.

Hagen, J. L., & Davis, L. V. (1995). The participants' perspective on the JOBS program. *Social Service Review, 69,* 656–678.

Hagen, J. L., & Lurie, I. (1993a). *Child care services and JOBS: Local implementation.* Albany, NY: Nelson A. Rockefeller Institute of Government.

Hagen, J. L., & Lurie, I. (1993b). The Job Opportunities and Basic Skills Training Program and child care: Initial state developments. *Social Service Review, 66,* 198–216.

Hagen, J. L., & Lurie, I. (1994). *Implementing JOBS: Progress and promise.* Albany, NY: Nelson A. Rockefeller Institute of Government.

Hagen, J. L., & Wang, L. (1994). Implementing JOBS: The roles and functions of front-line workers. *Social Service Review, 68,* 369–385.

Lurie, I., & Hagen, J. L. (1993). *JOBS implementations: Structure and design of local programs.* Albany, NY: Nelson A. Rockefeller Institute of Government.

Martinson, K., & Riccio, J. (1989). *GAIN: Child care in a welfare employment program.* New York: Manpower Demonstration Research Corporation.

Maynard, R. (1990). The child care market for low-income parents. In R. Maynard, E. E. Kisker, & S. Kerachsky (Eds.), *Child care challenges for low-income families* (pp. 9–12). New York: Rockefeller Foundation.

Meyers, M. K. (1993). Child care in the JOBS employment and training program: What difference does quality make? *Journal of Marriage and the Family, 55,* 767–783.

Meyers, M. K., & van Leuwen, K. (1992). Child care preferences and choices: Are AFDC recipients unique? *Social Work Research & Abstracts, 28*(1), 28–34.

National Association of Social Workers, Office of Government Relations. (1996). *Personal Responsibility and Work Opportunity Reconciliation Act of 1996 (H.R. 3734), Public Law 104-193: Summary of provisions.* Washington, DC: Author.

Personal Responsibility and Work Opportunity Reconciliation Act of 1996, P.L. 104-193.

Reid, W. J., & Smith, A. D. (1972). AFDC mothers view the Work Incentive program. *Social Service Review, 46,* 347–362.

Skricki, I. (1994). *Unheard voices: Participants evaluate the JOBS program.* Washington, DC: Coalition on Human Needs.

Smith, A. D., Fortune, A. E., & Reid, W. J. (1975). WIN, work, and welfare. *Social Service Review, 49,* 396–404.

Smith, S., Blank, S., & Bond, J. T. (1990). *One program, two generations.* New York: Foundation for Child Development in partnership with the National Center for Children in Poverty.

Sonenstein, R. L., & Wolf, D. A. (1991). Satisfaction with child care: Perspectives of welfare mothers. *Journal of Social Issues, 47,* 15–31.

Stoesz, D., & Karger, H. J. (1990). Welfare reform: From illusion to reality. *Social Work, 35,* 141–147.

U.S. Department of Health and Human Services. (1993, June 10). *Job Opportunities and Basic Skills Training Program* (Information Memorandum No. JOBS-ACF-IM-93-10). Washington, DC: Author.

U.S. House of Representatives, Committee on Ways and Means. (1993). *1993 green book.* Washington, DC: U.S. Government Printing Office.

Zill, N., Moore, K. A., Smith, E. W., Sherf, T., & Cario, M. J. (1991). *The life circumstances and development of children in welfare families: A profile based on national survey data.* Washington, DC: Child Trends.

This chapter was originally published in the December 1996 issue of Social Work Research, *vol. 20, pp. 263–273.*

23   Is Shelter a Private Problem?

Elizabeth A. Mulroy and Patricia L. Ewalt

S wirling around Capitol Hill is a neoconservative smokescreen that will likely have long-term adverse ef-fects on housing and community development and on the living conditions of low-income Americans. Under the guise of deficit reduction, Congress, in the fiscal year 1996 budget, is attempting to cut housing appropriations by 25 percent. Some key provisions for change to U.S. Department of Housing and Urban Development (HUD) appropriations include

- increasing the tenant-paid share of rents in the Section 8 program
- eliminating all new certificates and antidiscrimination provisions in the Section 8 program
- cutting funds to America's homeless population by 40 percent
- eliminating funds to develop new public housing
- reducing funds to operate and modernize public housing
- repealing federal preferences that give priority for public housing to the neediest individuals and families, including homeless people and victims of domestic violence
- eliminating or weakening the Community Reinvestment Act of 1977, which requires safe and sound lending to credit-worthy borrowers in low- and middle-income neighborhoods
- prohibiting HUD from enforcing the Fair Housing Act of 1968 against property insurance redlining (National Low Income Housing Coalition, 1995).

These proposed cuts in affordable housing and community development—in combination with cuts in Aid to Families with Dependent Children; the Food Stamp program; the Special Supplemental Food Program for Women, Infants, and Children; Medicaid; and Medicare—threaten to unravel the nation's already threadbare safety net for low-income households. Advocates of these programs will likely not see all of these proposed cuts enacted in the 1995–96 legislative session. However, conservative congressional fervor for cutting these programs is expected to continue.

PHILOSOPHY

Congressional actions toward housing are part of a deliberate and incisive restructuring of the welfare state that began more than a decade ago. At the core is a philosophical redirection of public policy to eliminate the role of the federal government in housing. Underlying this perspective is the belief that deep cuts in housing are justified because, in reality, no rental housing crisis has ever existed.

This position is based on the viewpoint of conventional economic theory, which holds that home prices and rents are and should be the result of marketplace supply and demand. Overall, it is assumed that the market functions well to meet the nation's housing needs. In 1983 the President's Commission on Housing concluded that "Americans today are the best-housed people in history, with affordability problems limited to the poor" (cited in Gilderbloom & Applebaum, 1988, p. 3). Poor people are seen as responsible for their own plight; problems of affordability are attributed to individual shortcomings such as divorce or low income. A housing crisis thus is viewed as a personal problem rather than a social one meriting government intervention (Gilderbloom & Applebaum, 1988).

In the turbulence of recent politics, the neoconservative Contract with America mobilized coalitions of governors and members of Congress to seize the moment. First, they swiftly crafted legislation that would extend the conservative agenda. Second, they continue to work vigorously to implement a long-range strategy to dismantle the welfare state, including reducing eligibility, shifting responsibilities to state and local government ("new federalism"), and privatizing public functions (Wolch & Dear, 1993).

CHANGES IN HOUSING POLICY

Both Congress and HUD have proposed sweeping and complex changes in housing policy. Two key bills are the U.S. Housing Act of 1995 (H.R. 2406) and the HUD-sponsored American Community Partnerships Act.

U.S. Housing Act of 1995

The legislative intent of the proposed U.S. Housing Act of 1995 is "to repeal the U.S. Housing Act of 1937, deregulate the public housing program and the program for rental housing assistance for low-income families, and increase community control over such programs." The framers of this legislation envision a society with a strong private housing sector, limited federal role, and privatized public-housing management functions. Resources would be reallocated by revising housing programs to operate in a way that more closely resembles the private housing market. A redistribution of services would restrict eligibility solely to people who are "responsible, deserving citizens who cannot provide fully for themselves because of temporary circumstances or factors beyond their control."

American Community Partnerships Act

The high costs of rehabilitating, maintaining, and managing some of the most distressed public-housing projects have motivated HUD to propose the American Community Partnerships Act, which would transform how public housing is funded. First, the act would tie public-housing rents to a property's market value, then it would provide public-housing tenants with vouchers that encourage them to move to the private rental market (Austin, 1995). These changes will purportedly increase a tenant's housing choice, deconcentrate very poor neighborhoods, and reduce costs to HUD. Residential mobility, however, will hinge on the availability of affordable private rental housing, the enforcement of housing discrimination laws, and the willingness of landlords to rent to low-income families of color with children and to participate in a government program.

IMPACT OF POLICY CHANGES

If proponents of the broad-based neoconservative agenda are successful in deregulating housing while also eliminating $80 billion in welfare funding in seven years, the net effect will increase the number of poor people; further reduce the supply of affordable rental housing; increase homelessness; reduce basic needs services; and increase social segmentation, economic inequality, and the geographic isolation of people living in poverty (Goldsmith & Blakely, 1992).

Low-Income Families

The hardest hit will be low-income families with children who rent. The most vulnerable Americans—children in poverty—will be caught in the vise between income reductions in public assistance and shelter reductions in housing programs (Center for Community Change, 1995a, 1995b, 1995c). The vast majority of poor families now live in housing that is neither public nor subsidized and is in the private rental market. Half of all poor households with children pay more than 50 percent of their incomes for housing, leaving them unable to meet other basic needs, including food, child care, insurance, transportation, medical costs, and clothing (National Low Income Housing Coalition, 1995).

Today there are 4 million people across the country who live in public housing, and they are very poor. Their median household income is $6,420, compared with a national median household income of more than $35,000 (Gurwitt, 1995). Sixty-four percent of public-housing residents are people of color; about half are households with children, and the balance are elderly or disabled people (U.S. Department of Housing and Urban Development, 1995). Who among these people will meet the new criteria of being "responsible, deserving citizens" who are poor by virtue of circumstances beyond their control? What are their realistic chances of using tenant-based vouchers without supportive housing search services and enforcement of a federal fair housing policy?

Racial Discrimination

The persistence of racism leads us to predict that the proposed housing programs will increase inequality. Recent attacks on fair housing programs and on the Community Reinvestment Act of 1977 will increase obstacles to equal housing opportunity. An African American woman who was a Petty Officer in the U.S. Navy and a Gulf War veteran was recently denied rental housing in Washington, DC, because of her race (Inbar, 1995). What chances for fair housing might low-income African American families expect to have as they try to move out of public housing in a deregulated environment?

LESSONS FROM SUCCESSFUL HOUSING PROGRAMS

The conservative push to revamp the federal role in housing is coming at a time when demonstration projects and other innovative programs are showing how to create successful housing programs. Two areas of interest to social work are the changing role of public housing authorities (PHAs) and the use of housing subsidies to stabilize poor families.

Changing Role of PHAs

Many PHAs have broadened their scope of responsibility beyond the management of dense projects to the spatial deconcentration of poor tenants and the revitalization of poor neighborhoods surrounding public-housing developments. In Louisville, Kentucky, a PHA is bulldozing a distressed housing project and replacing it with a mixed-income development of single-family homes, townhouses, and apartments, of which one-third are reserved for low-income former tenants. Tenants who are unable to qualify for the new housing will be relocated into small-scale, scattered-site, mixed-income, multifamily units elsewhere in the city. In Denver and in Charlotte, North Carolina, similar plans include partnerships with social services agencies, public schools, and job-training programs to improve a household's overall environment—the physical and social contexts—so that poor people can lead more normal lives (Gurwitt, 1995).

Housing Subsidies

Section 8 subsidies (which allow poor families to pay 30 percent of their income for rent, with the federal government subsidizing the balance directly to landlords) are difficult for poor families to use on their own (Mulroy, 1988, 1995). However, when combined with institutionally supported housing search services, the subsidies can be used to provide safe, affordable, long-term housing for families (Sard, 1992). Examples include the following:

- Federal preferences that give homeless families a priority for Section 8 certificates have become lifelines out of homelessness and into stable, affordable, private rental housing (Rog, 1994).
- The court-ordered Gautreaux Program has placed about 5,600 racially segregated public-housing families in Chicago in the private rental market since 1976 using Section 8 certificates (Rosenbaum & Popkin, 1990).
- The Family Unification Program links Section 8 certificates with child welfare and other services to prevent out-of-home placement and to reunify families whose housing problems resulted in a child's out-of-home placement. "In its short life, this program has created unprecedented cooperation between housing authorities and child welfare authorities and has preserved and reunited families whose children would otherwise have entered out-of-home care" (Liederman, 1994, p. 2).

IMPLICATIONS FOR SOCIAL WORK

Two key factors are missing from the current housing policy debate. First is the lack of public awareness and vocal constituency for funded projects similar to those that have already shown how the housing needs of poor people can be met. Second, there is a lack of understanding that affordable, safe, nontransient, and habitable housing is fundamental to meeting all other basic needs, is a core function of government, and is in the public interest.

Social workers and others who understand and appreciate the potentially dev-astating impact of the proposed cuts in housing and community development should work assertively to influence the housing policy debate. In the May edito-rial, we will discuss further the implications of housing issues for social workers.

REFERENCES

Austin, D. (1995). *Round one of conference on VA-HUD-IA appropriations concluded.* Washington, DC: National Low Income Housing Coalition.

Center for Community Change. (1995a, November 20). *Policy alert 39.* Washington, DC: Author.

Center for Community Change. (1995b, November 22). *Policy alert 40.* Washington, DC: Author.

Center for Community Change. (1995c, December 4). *Policy alert 41.* Washington, DC: Author.

Community Reinvestment Act of 1977, P.L. 95-128, 91 Stat. 1147.

Gilderbloom, J. I., & Applebaum, R. P. (1988). *Rethinking rental housing.* Philadelphia: Temple University Press.

Goldsmith, W. W., & Blakely, E. (1992). *Separate societies: Poverty and inequality in U.S. cities.* Philadelphia: Temple University Press.

Gurwitt, R. (1995, August). The project's coming down. *Governing.*

Inbar, T. (1995, Fall). Gulf War veteran denied housing. *Fair Housing Report,* p. 1.

Liederman, D. (1994). Editorial. *Children's Voice, 3*(3), 2.

Mulroy, E. A. (1988). The search for affordable housing. In E. A. Mulroy (Ed.), *Women as single parents: Confronting institutional barriers in the courts, the workplace, and the housing market* (pp. 123–163). Dover, MA: Auburn House.

Mulroy, E. A. (1995). *The new uprooted: Single mothers in urban life.* Westport, CT: Auburn House.

National Low Income Housing Coalition. (1995). *Call to action.* Washington, DC: Author.

Rog, D. (1994). *Homeless Families Program: Interim benchmarks.* Nashville, TN: Vanderbilt Institute for Public Policy Studies.

Rosenbaum, J., & Popkin, S. (1990). *The economic and social impacts of housing integration* (Research and Policy Reports). Evanston, IL: Northwestern University, Center for Urban Affairs and Policy Research.

Sard, B. (1992, Spring/Summer). Housing the homeless through expanding access to existing housing subsidies. *New England Journal of Public Policy,* pp. 187–201.

U.S. Department of Housing and Urban Development. (1995). *Recent research results.* Washington, DC: Author, Office of Policy Development and Research.

Wolch, J., & Dear, M. (1993). *Malign neglect: Homelessness in an American city.* San Francisco: Jossey-Bass.

This chapter was originally published in the March 1996 issue of Social Work, *vol. 41, pp. 125–128.*

24 Affordable Housing: A Basic Need and a Social Issue

Elizabeth A. Mulroy and Patricia L. Ewalt

Pending cuts in the U.S. Department of Housing and Urban Development's (HUD's) fiscal year budget combined with deep funding cuts in public assistance will have a profound effect on low-income households, in turn affecting the social work profession. Low-income consumers of social work services will find that housing and employment are interrelated issues of central concern. These substantive areas will wedge their way prominently into social policy, social work methods and fields of practice, and research.

CROSS-CUTTING IMPLICATIONS

Housing

The proposed cuts in the HUD budget will reduce the supply of and access to affordable rental units. These cuts, in combination with reduced appropriations for income maintenance programs at federal and state levels for individuals and families (such as Aid to Families with Dependent Children, general assistance, and Supplemental Security Income), will make it more difficult for low-income consumers to find rental housing they can afford.

Housing has unique economic, psychological, and symbolic significance. It has a pervasive impact on quality of life beyond just the provision of shelter. Safe, affordable, nontransient housing is the key that opens the door to meeting other basic needs. Its location determines personal safety and access to commercial facilities, public and social services, transportation networks, recreational and cultural resources, quality schools, and employment opportunities (Mulroy, 1995a; Smizik & Stone, 1988).

Housing Supply. Affordable units for low-income renters have been substantially lost through the demolition of distressed public housing projects, the conversion of apartment buildings and single-room occupancy hotels to condominiums, and recently what is called "expiring use restrictions" on many private for-profit housing developments. In the 1960s, federal assistance shifted from constructing public housing to providing subsidies to private developers to construct housing for low-income people at affordable rents. Developers were allowed to opt out of these rent restrictions after 20 years. Beginning in the 1980s, in areas where market rents had increased substantially, "the owners opted out and raised rents to market levels, displacing thousands of poor tenants. When conditions had declined, owners simply undermaintained their property for additional, final profits and then allowed HUD to foreclose on deteriorated buildings" (Barton, 1996, p. 109).

Housing Affordability. Housing affordability is the ratio of a household's housing costs to its income. HUD generally considers housing to be affordable when it is 30 percent of a household's income. However, more than half of all poor renters spend at least 50 percent of their income on housing (Dreier & Applebaum, 1992).

Although public housing and housing allowances have existed for several decades to ease the rent burden on poor households, their effectiveness has been limited (Mulroy, 1995b). The majority of low-income renter households do not receive any kind of federal, state, or local rent subsidy, nor do they live in public housing (U.S. Bureau of the Census, 1990). Low-income residents in the private rental market are being squeezed by higher rents.

Cuts in public assistance benefit levels and changes in eligibility requirements will further reduce the incomes of already low-income households, leaving them less money to spend on rent. Long-term unemployed workers laid off from low-wage work will be especially vulnerable.

Affordability problems can lead to housing displacement, which occurs when a household is required to move because of circumstances beyond its control. People will be displaced from their residences because of eviction or the threat of eviction caused by rent increases that are beyond their ability to pay.

Section 8 certificates are subsidies that allow families who meet low-income eligibility requirements to pay 30 percent of their income for rent, and HUD subsidizes the balance of rent directly to the landlord. Pending legislation does not authorize any new Section 8 certificates to be issued in fiscal year 1996, so families currently doubled up and living in overcrowded conditions while on waiting lists for new Section 8 certificates may also be displaced.

Overcrowding. Long considered an indicator of housing need, overcrowding has increased in the United States after decades of decline—but dramatically so in California and Hawaii. In these two states with expensive housing, 20 percent of renters live in overcrowded conditions (Meyers, Baer, & Choi, 1996).

Homelessness, the bottom rung on the ladder of housing displacement, will likely increase for the most vulnerable consumers who experience multiple personal stressors. Special populations such as victims of domestic violence, homeless people, elderly people, and disabled people will suffer disproportionately from HUD budget cuts (Citizens Housing and Planning Association, 1996). Federal preferences that favored homeless people and victims of domestic violence as priority categories, for example, have been suspended, although local Public Housing Authorities can establish their own preference categories consistent with local housing plans.

Employment

Provisions that link low-income households to wage work are features of current legislation in public welfare, public housing, social services, and community and economic development (HUD, 1995a, 1995b, 1995c). Employment—and its attendant education, training, transportation, and child care needs—will be a key issue for low-income people who rely on public assistance or who live in public housing.

Yet two considerations, one related specifically to housing and the other to complex interorganizational arrangements, may interfere with low-income consumers' ability to become and remain employed. First, repeated housing displacement is associated with family destabilization and insecurity (Bronfenbrenner, 1986), factors that are incongruent with a routine work schedule. Stable living arrangements are a prerequisite to continuous, satisfactory workplace performance.

Second, consumers may sincerely want to participate in newly created economic development programs, but such programs will likely require sophisticated skills in understanding and negotiating a complex maze of interorganizational arrangements. Diverse public agencies with mandated responsibilities to administer public assistance, social services, economic development, and public housing programs are now programmatically tied together but may lack coordinated service integration (Alter, 1990; Alter & Hage, 1993; Glisson & James, 1992).

In addition, the increase in privatization—the purchase of public services for job training, employment placement, social services, and housing management from organizations in the nonprofit and for-profit sectors—has blurred the lines between public- and private-sector functions and roles. Accountability and clear avenues for consumer participation, grievance, and advocacy are increasingly obscured.

IMPLICATIONS FOR SOCIAL WORK

Affordable housing is a basic need and a social issue, not a private issue, for clients of social work services. As legislative changes move employment to center stage in welfare reform and in public housing requirements (Citizens Housing and Planning Association, 1996), both housing and employment are social work issues. They are also interdependent.

Social Policy

There is a socioeconomic crisis in the nation that requires new and fresh social policies to challenge the neoconservative approach to meeting human needs. First, a vision is needed that incorporates affordable, safe, nontransient housing as a basic need in society and as a goal to be achieved. If social policy "emphasizes cooperation and shared responsibility among society's institutions and its structural elements, the entire population, and the individual" (Iatridis, 1994, p. 15), then housing and employment policy should both be considered subunits of social policy. A structure should be in place through which cross-cutting implications of social policies could be analyzed, adjusted, unified, and coordinated.

Second, decentralization of decision making and government downsizing are shifting the formation of social policies to state and local levels with three effects: (1) Social workers can influence state and local decision systems directly; (2) policymakers can formulate creative solutions based on locally specific needs; and (3) progressive innovations (often initiated at the local level in response to failed federal programs) can be tested and then replicated "up" to state, regional, and national levels.

One example of local innovation is the movement to establish a social housing sector, that is, housing owned by private nonprofit corporations or limited-equity cooperatives and allocated to people according to need rather than ability to pay (Barton, 1996). Social housing uses a combination of nonprofit ownership and capital grants to provide permanently affordable home ownership and rental units for low-income people.

Generated primarily at the local level, ownership vehicles commonly used for creation of social housing include community-based nonprofit housing corporations, mutual housing associations, limited-equity cooperatives, and land trusts (Barton, 1996; Smizik & Stone, 1988). Social housing is not expected to replace the public or private sector's role in affordable housing production. However, with diminished federal responsibility for affordable housing, we will likely see an expansion of social housing as a sector.

Social Work Practice

Consumers of social work services will require practitioners to integrate three elements into their practice methods: (1) a housing element; (2) a community and economic development element; and (3) a collaborative, interorganizational element.

Housing. Children and families, elderly people, people with mental illness or disabilities, battered women, victims of child maltreatment, people with AIDS, and homeless people receiving social work services will need a housing element integrated into their service plans. This requires knowledge of the availability of affordable rental housing in a regional housing market: Who are the public, private, and nonprofit producers of affordable rental housing in the consumer's geographic area? Where are these organizations located? How can consumers get information about them, and how can they visit them? What are the eligibility criteria for any remaining federal, state, or local housing programs? Where are they being implemented?

Low-income consumers will need assistance with the housing search to have a fighting chance of competing with market renters in a deregulated housing environment. Social work services should include help in navigating the maze of public and nonprofit agencies and for-profit real estate firms in the housing business and then negotiating rents with private landlords. The more extensive the geographic search becomes, the more agencies, actors, and transactions will be required.

Community and Economic Development. Increased economic deprivation of clients, federal mandates, and revitalized agency mission statements will motivate human services agencies to continue shifting a broad range of direct services into the community. Multiple unmet needs, including housing and employment, are interrelated when the neighborhood is considered the unit of analysis.

Distressed communities with concentrations of poor people have traditionally been the target of community development, an antipoverty strategy that seeks to create new kinds of communities with strong local institutions and residents who are directly involved in planning for local needs (Sullivan, 1993). The Community Development Block Grant and the Empowerment Zone and

Enterprise Community Programs are resources for community economic development (HUD, 1995a, 1995b, 1995c). President Clinton's new National Urban Policy, articulated in "Empowerment: A Covenant with America's Communities," intends to "link families to work by bringing together tax, welfare, education, job training, transportation, and housing initiatives that help families make the transition to self-sufficiency and independence" (HUD, 1995b, p. 2). Approximately 105 locations or zones have been selected in national competition (HUD, 1995b).

Social workers should know about these community economic development initiatives for three reasons: (1) to be legitimate community representatives at the decision table in the planning and design of service structures, (2) to help clients living in these zones gain access to any available resources, and (3) to facilitate consumer participation in the planning process. Participation of resident consumers is integral to successful program outcomes in neighborhood and economic development (Bendick & Egan, 1995; Mier, 1994).

Collaborative, Interorganizational Relationships. Increased consumer needs, reduced resources for human services, trends toward community-based service delivery, and the privatization of public functions all point to a need for collaborative interorganizational relationships, irrespective of a practitioner's micro or macro perspective. New systems of care call for flexibility and for a broad knowledge of resources beyond one's own or one's agency's functional area of specialization. Adaptability and cooperative behavior are required at the organizational as well as at the interpersonal level to build and sustain collaborative interagency arrangements. Though difficult to implement in a competitive, purchase-of-service culture, collaborative service networks built on mutual trust can provide social workers with more resources and consumers with effective, integrated services (Alter & Hage, 1993; Mulroy, 1995c).

Research

The HUD budget cuts raise several issues for social work research, of which two will be discussed here—research on neighborhood poverty and research on the effects of pending legislative cuts.

First, the profession's social reform roots and the *NASW Code of Ethics* (NASW, 1994) suggest that social workers have a serious interest in understanding why urban poverty is increasingly concentrated in inner-city neighborhoods, what the neighborhood effects are on the poor people who live there (Wilson, 1987), and what strategies are effective in ameliorating problems. Scholars from many academic disciplines are examining these questions. Social workers who practice in poor communities seek guidance from social work research on the efficacy of social policies and programs and the outcomes of their work. Social workers want to know more about the characteristics of poverty neighborhoods; whether traditionally accepted indicators of housing need are still appropriate; how to measure service needs in neighborhoods and communities that are increasingly diverse and multicultural; and what housing and community development interventions strengthen families and neighborhoods, particularly from the residents' perspective. (For research in neighborhood poverty see, for example, Coulton, 1995; Coulton & Chow, 1991; Coulton, Chow, & Finn, 1990; and Sherraden, 1991.)

Finally, research is needed that examines the effects of the pending cuts in HUD and public assistance budgets on poor people. Policymakers and practitioners need to know what the effects will be of the simultaneous cuts in "place-based" housing strategies and in "people-based" income maintenance strategies. Social work researchers are well positioned to investigate these issues.

REFERENCES

Alter, C. (1990). An exploratory study of conflict and coordination in inter-organizational service delivery systems. *Academy of Management Journal, 33,* 478–501.

Alter, C., & Hage, J. (1993). *Organizations working together.* Newbury Park, CA: Sage Publications.

Barton, S. (1996). Social housing versus housing allowances: Choosing between two forms of housing subsidy at the local level. *Journal of the American Planning Association, 61,* 108–119.

Bendick, M., & Egan, M. L. (1995). Worker ownership and participation enhances economic development in low-opportunity communities. *Journal of Community Practice, 2,* 61–85.

Bronfenbrenner, U. (1986). Ecology of the family as context for human development: Research perspectives. *Developmental Psychology, 22,* 723–742.

Citizens Housing and Planning Association. (1996, January 3). *Summary of House/Senate Conference Committee Bill.* Boston: Author.

Coulton, C. (1995). Using community-level indicators of children's well-being in comprehensive community initiatives. In J. Connell, A. Kubisch, L. Schorr, & C. Weiss (Eds.), *New approaches to evaluating community initiatives: Concepts, methods, and contexts* (pp. 173–199). Washington, DC: Aspen Institute.

Coulton, C., & Chow, J. (1991). *The impact of poverty on Cleveland neighborhoods.* Cleveland: Case Western Reserve University, Mandel School of Applied Social Sciences, Center for Urban Poverty and Social Change.

Coulton, C., Chow, J., & Finn, C. (1990). *Social conditions affecting people in Cleveland's low-income neighborhoods.* Cleveland: Case Western Reserve University, Mandel School of Applied Social Sciences, Center for Urban Poverty and Social Change.

Dreier, P., & Applebaum, R. (1992). The housing crisis enters the 1990s. *New England Journal of Public Policy, 8,* 155–167.

Glisson, C., & James, L. (1992). The interorganizational coordination of services to children in state custody. *Administration in Social Work: Organizational Change and Development, 16,* 65–80.

Iatridis, D. (1994). *Social policy: Institutional context of social development and human services.* Pacific Grove, CA: Brooks/Cole.

Meyers, D., Baer, W., & Choi, S. Y. (1996). The changing problem of overcrowded housing. *Journal of the American Planning Association, 62,* 66–84.

Mier, R. (1994). *Social justice and local development policy.* Newbury Park, CA: Sage Publications.

Mulroy, E. (1995a, November 2). *Achieving the systemic neighborhood network: The community context of nonprofit interorganizational collaboration.* Paper presented at the Association for Research on Nonprofit Organizations and Voluntary Action, Cleveland.

Mulroy, E. (1995b). Housing. In R. L. Edwards (Ed.-in-Chief), *Encyclopedia of social work* (19th ed., Vol. 2, pp. 1377–1384). Washington, DC: NASW Press.

Mulroy, E. (1995c). *The new uprooted: Single mothers in urban life.* Westport, CT: Auburn House.

National Association of Social Workers. (1994). *NASW code of ethics.* Washington, DC: Author.

Sherraden, M. (1991). *Assets and the poor: A new American welfare policy.* Armonck, NY: Sharpe.

Smizik, F., & Stone, M. (1988). Single-parent families and a right to housing. In E. Mulroy (Ed.), *Women as single parents: Confronting institutional barriers in the courts, the workplace, and the housing market* (pp. 227–270). Westport, CT: Auburn House.

Sullivan, M. (1993). *More than housing: How community development corporations go about changing lives and neighborhoods.* New York: Community Development Research Center, Graduate School of Management and Urban Policy, New School for Social Research.

U.S. Bureau of the Census. (1990). *Housing characteristics of selected races and Hispanic origin households in the United States: 1987* (Series H121-87-1). Washington, DC: U.S. Government Printing Office.

U.S. Department of Housing and Urban Development. (1995a, August). *Recent research results.* Washington, DC: Author, Office of Policy Development and Research.

U.S. Department of Housing and Urban Development. (1995b, October). *Recent research results.* Washington, DC: Author, Office of Policy Development and Research.

U.S. Department of Housing and Urban Development. (1995c, December). *Recent research results.* Washington, DC: Author, Office of Policy Development and Research.

Wilson, W. J. (1987). *The truly disadvantaged: The inner city, the underclass, and public policy.* Chicago: University of Chicago Press.

This chapter was originally published in the May 1996 issue of Social Work, *vol. 41, pp. 245–249.*

25 Is the Whole Greater than the Sum of the Parts? Interaction Effects of Three Non–Income-Tested Transfers for Families with Children

Rebecca Y. Kim, Irwin Garfinkel, and
Daniel R. Meyer

For three decades the public income transfer system for families with children in the United States has been criticized for being overly targeted at extremely poor families headed by single mothers. Much of the disapproval has centered around two features of the system: its categorical nature and its reliance on income-tested benefits. Categorical eligibility requirements that limit benefits to single-parent families have been criticized as unfair to two-parent families and as discouraging marriage. Income-tested benefits have been reproached because they discourage work in that they reduce benefits by extremely high rates as earnings increase.

To remedy these shortcomings derived from overtargeting, government-sponsored studies of the U.S. welfare system in the 1960s advocated lowering the benefit reduction rate in welfare programs and extending eligibility for welfare benefits to two-parent, working poor families (see three earlier studies: President's Commission on Income Maintenance Programs, 1969; U.S. Advisory Council on Public Welfare, 1966; U.S. Congress Joint Economic Committee & Subcommittee on Fiscal Policy, 1972–74). Although the enactment of the federal Food Stamp and earned income tax credit (EITC) programs in the mid-1970s reduced overtargeting on extremely poor single-parent families, as of late 1995, the system remained highly targeted (Garfinkel, 1996). Academic studies in the 1980s generally focused on the shortcomings of income testing per se, noting that in addition to creating disincentives to work, income-tested programs did nothing to prevent poverty, stigmatized beneficiaries, and undermined social solidarity. Rather than extending welfare, these studies advocated the creation of new universal benefits that were neither income tested nor limited to single-parent families (Ellwood, 1988; Garfinkel, 1982; Garfinkel & McLanahan, 1986; Wilson, 1987).

In the late 1980s and early 1990s, universal reforms were being taken seriously in the political process. The National Commission on Children, appointed jointly by President Ronald Reagan and the U.S. Congress in 1987, agreed with previous criticisms of overtargeting and advocated a set of more universal reforms, including a $1,000 refundable income tax credit for children, some form of national health insurance, a new child support assurance system, and increases in EITC and child care benefits. (One of these reforms—child support assurance—is not truly universal in that it is restricted to families with at least one parent living apart from the child.) President Bill Clinton proposed variants of all of these reforms and made universal health care reform the centerpiece of his domestic agenda.

Although Congress enacted the EITC expansion as part of the 1993 budget bill, Clinton's proposal for universal health care was rejected in 1994, and the Republicans went on in the fall to win control of both the Senate and the House of Representatives. Universal reforms—except perhaps for a tax credit for children—are no longer on the political agenda. Instead, recent House and Senate legislation has targeted Aid to Families with Dependent Children (AFDC), the cash assistance program for children, for elimination.

Still, the effects of universal programs are of interest. At some point the U.S. political pendulum will swing back, and universal programs will again be on the political agenda. In the meantime, states have been given great flexibility in designing income transfer programs, and some may consider tradeoffs between means-tested and non–means-tested programs or consider the relative advantages of single versus multiple programs. Furthermore, in other nations, proposals abound for reducing universal programs and adopting more targeted programs, making this question relevant in the international context as well.

Although previous research has provided estimates of the benefits and costs of particular universal programs, this article is the first to address the question of whether the benefits and costs of a set or package of universal programs are equivalent to the additive effects of each program considered by itself. Advocates frequently argue that whereas the effectiveness of any single program is likely to be limited, a comprehensive approach can succeed. When several programs are combined as a package, the resulting combined effect could be equal to or greater than the sum of the single programs' effects performed alone. In other words, is the whole greater than the sum of the parts? This question has remained unanswered. This article estimates the effects of a package of three universal programs that have received considerable attention in the United States recently—a refundable tax credit for children, universal health care, and a child support assurance system. We find some evidence of positive interaction effects that strengthens the case for universality.

Although most social workers are implementers or service deliverers with little interest in promoting changes or initiating innovations in social policy (Figueira-McDonough, 1993), a part of the profession has always attended to social policy. Policy issues, such as how to allocate limited resources to populations in need, have important implications for the social work profession. Social work practice is framed by the approach adopted by policymakers. Moreover, restructuring the current welfare programs will have great impact on the vulnerable populations served by the social work profession.

LITERATURE REVIEW

The traditional approach to studying participation in income-tested programs is to posit that women examine the wages they would be able to earn in the marketplace and the income available through welfare and choose between these two options (Moffitt, 1992). A consensus of this type of research is that AFDC recipients do work somewhat less than they would if there were no AFDC program; the effects are generally small but important (see Moffitt, 1992, for a review). Prior studies of the effects of non–income-tested programs have typically used this microeconomic framework.

Several proposals for a children's allowance (equivalent from an economic point of view to a refundable tax credit for children) were made during the late 1960s (Musgrave, Heller, & Peterson, 1970; Orshansky, 1968; Schorr, 1966; Vadakin, 1968). More recently, a few scholars have again proposed a children's allowance (Ellwood, 1988; Garfinkel & McLanahan, 1986; National Commission on Children, 1991). Meyer, Phillips, and Maritato (1991) estimated that an allowance of $1,000 per child would reduce the poverty rate of poor children by 15 percent, reduce AFDC caseloads by 24 percent, and increase the mean hours worked by women receiving AFDC by 14 percent.

Although there is a large volume of research on national health insurance (NHI), we currently lack empirical estimates for the impact of NHI on children's economic status. A few studies discuss the implications of universal health care coverage for children. Holahan and Zedlewski (1991) examined the effects of Medicaid expansion; they estimated that 8 million children whose parents did not have employer-provided insurance would be enrolled at a cost of $5.3 billion (in 1989 dollars) if Medicaid were expanded to 200 percent of the poverty line. Zedlewski, Holahan, Blumberg, and Winterbottom (1993) simulated the distributional effects of alternative health care financing of NHI on different income classes, focusing on all nonelderly individuals. The authors concluded that universal coverage would redistribute the burdens of financing health care from the upper to the lower income classes.

A few studies have also provided simulations of a child support assurance system to estimate its cost and potential effects (Garfinkel, Robins, Wong, & Meyer, 1990; Lerman, 1989; Meyer, Garfinkel, Robins, & Oellerich, 1991; Meyer & Kim, 1994). These studies generally found modest effects on poverty among custodial-parent families and somewhat larger effects on AFDC recipiency.

These studies estimated the effects of only a single program on poverty, welfare participation, and work. An interesting research question is the degree to which the estimated effects would be altered if several non–income-tested programs were combined. As additional non–income-tested benefits are added, their effects could be linearly additive or magnified. The focus of this study is to examine potential interactions that result from the combined programs and to identify the direction and the size of that interaction. To separate an interaction effect from the effect of a single program, we simulated each single program separately and then simulated all three programs together.

This study builds on our prior simulation model to estimate the costs and effects of child support assurance (Meyer, Garfinkel, et al., 1991) and the children's allowance (Meyer, Phillips, et al., 1991). We go beyond our previous work by incorporating changes in the health insurance system from the current system (composed mainly of Medicaid and employer insurance for this population) to NHI and, most important, by explicitly examining the interaction effects of the three programs.

DATA AND METHOD

Data

The data used for this study were drawn from wave 6 of the 1987 panel of the Survey of Income and Program Participation (SIPP), which includes the events of September 1988. Our sample consists of families with children under 18 years. There were 4,487 families, including 3,321 husband-and-wife families, 1,034 mother-only families, and 132 father-only families.

There were several advantages of using SIPP for our study. First, SIPP was specifically designed to collect detailed information on transfer program recipiency. Questions were asked separately for each transfer program with regard to recipiency and the amount of benefits received per month. These questions allowed us to identify which families participated in the AFDC and Food Stamp programs and how much those families received in benefits in each month. This monthly information is valuable, because eligibility for most welfare programs is determined on a monthly basis. Second, SIPP provides details of health care coverage, including coverage by government programs and private health insurance. This information allowed us to place a dollar amount on the value of health care coverage for each member of our sample based on the number of people covered and the type of plan. Finally, wave 6 of SIPP contains a topical module on child support, providing such information as whether a child support agreement exists, what amount has been awarded, and what amount has been received. This information was important for simulating the child support assured benefit.

The SIPP data are the best available, but they are not perfect. We imputed information on income when it was missing. We made four types of imputations to income. First, of the 1,441 families who were eligible for child support, 386 were missing child support information. For these families, we imputed the probability of having an award, the collection rate, and child support payments based on multivariate equations estimated from SIPP, following Kim (1993). Second, we assigned AFDC recipiency to some mother-only families who were income-eligible for AFDC but did not report receiving it. We did this because AFDC recipiency is underreported in our sample by 30 percent. (Also, see Dickert, Houser, & Scholz, 1994 or Jabine, 1990 for the underreporting problem in SIPP.) Benefit amounts were determined based on the state maximum benefit level (by family size) and a tax rate on earned income (estimated by Fraker, Moffitt, & Wolf, 1985), following Kim. Third, we assigned food stamp recipiency to these imputed AFDC families because most AFDC families also receive food stamps (U.S. House of Representatives, 1993). Benefit amounts for all families were calculated based on the 1988 food stamp benefit formula. Fourth, we calculated income and payroll taxes and the EITC according to the 1988 tax law. Because data on itemization were not available, we assumed that all families took the standard deduction.

We also assigned a value to health care coverage using a market value approach. For example, we used mean state expenditures on Medicaid as a basis for assigning a value to Medicaid coverage. Mean state Medicaid expenditures per AFDC child and per AFDC adult were taken from U.S. House of Representatives (1990, p. 1302). Because members of our sample who were eligible for Medicaid but who did not receive any medical care derived an insurance value from the coverage, the state mean expenditures were adjusted to reflect a value for all eligible adults and children on AFDC. A family value of Medicaid coverage was the sum of child values and adult values. This approach resulted in an average value of $2,321 per family.

To place a value on employer-provided insurance, we used the average premium paid by employers for different types of plans from Gabel, DiCarlo, Fink, and de Lissovoy (1989). Although we would have liked to use the amount of the premium paid by the employer, this is not available in SIPP. According to Gabel et al., in 1988 employers paid an average of $1,016 annually for an individual plan and $2,510 for a family plan. If a family reported the family plan through employer coverage, we assumed that the family had a value of $2,510; if the individual plan was reported, $1,016 was assigned to the family as the value of coverage provided through the employer.

But a simple assignment of this value to all families with coverage would ignore the possibility that large families derive more value from being covered than small families. To account for this variation, we first calculated the mean value per eligible adult and the mean value per eligible child, as follows: We first assigned $2,510 and $1,016 (depending on the plan type) to each family identified with employer insurance. We then aggregated these values and counted the total number of adults and children covered through employers in our sample. This resulted in a $65 billion total premium (employer paid), 43.2 million total adults, and 40.7 million total children. We also used the ratio of per adult health expenditures to per child expenditures from Waldo, Sonnefeld, McKusick, and Arnett (1989), which is 2.1:1. If these are put together,

$$AV_e = 2.1 * CV_e$$

$$AV_e * 43.2 + CV_e * 40.7 = 65,000$$

(unit in millions),

where AV_e and CV_e are per adult value and per child value of employer insurance coverage, respectively. The solution of these equations resulted in $971 per eligible adult and $471 per eligible child as the value of employer-provided coverage. A family value was then the sum of eligible adult and child values in the family. This approach resulted in a value of $2,510 per family when an employer offered a family plan ($971 per adult and $471 per child) and $1,016 when an employer offered an individual plan.

When we valued NHI, we assumed that the value would be similar to the value of current employer-provided coverage. If the proposed NHI has benefit packages and cost-sharing arrangements similar to those in a typical employer-provided plan, the use of the current total premium paid by the employer and employee ($2,820) may not be far away from the cost required for NHI to cover a family. But an assignment of a flat amount ($2,820) to each family as the family value of NHI would ignore family size and age categories of family members. Therefore, NHI values per eligible adult and per eligible child were obtained according to the same procedure as in the valuation of employer insurance. The total adults and total children covered under NHI were counted at 63.3 million and 68 million, respectively; the family values of NHI ($2,820 each family) were aggregated at $104 billion. Plugging these figures into the previous equations resulted in NHI values of $1,078 per adult and $524 per child. These values were then assigned to each family member and summed to produce the family value of NHI. These adjusted family values did not change either the aggregate total value ($104 billion) or the family mean value, but allowed different values depending on family size and the age category of family members. This approach results in an average value of $2,821 per family under NHI.

After we made these imputations, we calculated net income, which we defined as the sum of all cash income plus the cash value of food stamps, health insurance coverage, and the EITC, minus income and payroll taxes. We compared our measure of net income to the poverty line. We used a different definition of income than is used in the official poverty figures; the largest difference is that we counted the value to health care coverage as income. Table 25-1 shows information on our resulting sample.

Method

This study uses a microsimulation model that incorporates behavioral responses. Microsimulation is a method for mapping the current tax and income transfer system and changes to it onto household-level information in a representative sample of individuals. Microsimulation models have been widely used to estimate the costs and effects of policy proposals (Citro & Hanushek, 1991).

Features of Proposed Plans. We first needed to specify program parameters under the postreform. The postreform includes an introduction of three new public benefits: a refundable tax credit for children, NHI, and an assured child support benefit. For a refundable tax credit for children, we simulated a credit of $1,000 per year per child under 18 years and treated credits as taxable income. The simulated plan also required that a family on AFDC must leave the AFDC rolls to be entitled to the refundable tax credit. We assumed that the family would choose to participate in the program that provides the higher level of economic well-being. This plan required a gross cost of $60.2 billion in 1988 dollars. We assumed that this cost would be financed in two ways: by eliminating the current tax exemptions for children and by increasing income tax rates by 1.6 percent.

For NHI, we assumed that the current system of Medicaid and employer-provided health insurance would be replaced with a single system, but people covered by Medicare would continue their current coverage under the Medicare program. The NHI plan also assumed coverage of all uninsured people in the sample, including uninsured dependents of Medicare-covered individuals.

TABLE 25-1

Sample Characteristics of Families with Children under 18 Years

Characteristic	Reported Income Definition[a]	Simulated Income Definition[b]
Poverty		
Total people in poverty (millions)	21.28	14.61
% of people in poverty	16.2	11.1
Total poverty gap ($ billions)	26.6	13.1
Income distribution (%)		
Below poverty line	16.7	11.4
Between 100% and 200% of poverty line	21.9	29.2
Between 200% and 300% of poverty line	20.2	24.8
More than three times poverty line	41.2	34.6

	Reported	Simulated	Administrative Records[c]
Aid to Families with Dependent Children (AFDC)			
Total caseloads (millions)	2.65	3.84	3.75
% of families on AFDC	7.2	10.4	10.6
Total benefits ($ billions)	11.3	16.1	16.9
Total benefits minus child support collections ($ billions)	10.7	14.8	15.5
Food stamps			
Total caseloads (millions)	3.79	4.45	4.72
% of families receiving food stamps	10.3	12.1	13.3
Total benefit payments ($ billions)	7.8	8.8	8.8

	People Covered (millions)	% of People Covered[d]	Total Value (millions)[e]	Mean Family Value[e]
Health insurance coverage type				
Medicaid	14.84	11.3	10,746	2,321
Employer-paid insurance	83.75	63.6	65,094	2,507
Medicare	0.4	0.3	1,176	2,696
Self-insured	15.81	12.0	0	0
Uninsured	19.32	14.7	0	0
National health insurance	131.73	100	104,121	2,821

	Reported	Simulated
Private child support		
Among custodial mother families (10.7 million)		
% of custodial families with awards	56.5	55.3
% of total award collected	74.7	72.6
Mean award amount ($)[f]	2,656	2,713
Mean payment ($)[f]	1,986	1,969
Among custodial father families (1.4 million)[g]		
% of custodial families with awards	NA	27.3
% of total award collected	NA	44.1
Mean awards amount ($)[f]	NA	2,272
Mean payment ($)[f]	NA	1,002

NOTE: N = 4,487; total families = 36.91 million.

[a]Reported earnings, child support, AFDC and food stamp benefits, and all other taxable and nontaxable incomes are included.

(continued)

TABLE 25-1

Continued

ᵇThe simulated income is defined as the sum of reported earnings and all other taxable and nontaxable incomes; child support payments; and calculated AFDC, food stamp, and earned income tax credit (EITC) benefits and market values of health care benefits minus calculated income and payroll taxes. This differs from the reported income in four ways: (1) AFDC benefits and food stamp benefits are imputed; (2) EITCs are calculated and included; (3) market values of health care benefits from Medicaid, Medicare, and employer-provided insurance are included; and (4) income and payroll taxes are calculated and subtracted.

ᶜFor AFDC records, see U.S. House of Representatives (1989, pp. 555 and 559). Note that $15.5 billion is calculated from total payments to single parents and unemployed parents minus total child support collections. For Food Stamp records, see U.S. House of Representatives (1991, p. 1351; 1993, pp. 1620, 1626, and 1632). Percentage records are calculated from the corresponding total caseload divided by the total number of families with children under age 18 (U.S. House of Representatives, 1991, p. 951).

ᵈThe sum of these percentages may not be 100% because some families had dual coverage. For valuation, these families are assumed to be covered through the coverage that provides the higher value.

ᵉThese values were obtained based on the market-value approach.

ᶠThese means are for custodial families with awards.

ᵍThese figures were obtained from the Wisconsin Children, Incomes, and Program Participation Survey (CHIPPS).

The benefits offered under NHI would resemble the average benefits package under current employer-provided health insurance. NHI would contain cost-sharing provisions (including coinsurance and deductibles) similar to current employer insurance. To finance the cost of NHI, a payroll tax schedule was incorporated into the simulation of NHI. We found that a new payroll tax of 7.2 percent and other associated savings would be sufficient for financing the total NHI cost of $104.1 billion for families with children. A major source of savings under NHI is the current cost of Medicaid. In addition, NHI is expected to bring additional income tax revenues because currently tax-exempted employer contributions would be considered taxable incomes.

Because we assumed that current employer-provided insurance would be replaced with national health insurance, the NHI simulation needed to determine how to treat current premium costs paid by employers. In the long run, most economists predict that employers would shift the savings directly to workers by adjusting wages by the change in health benefit costs, holding workers' total compensation constant (Zedlewski et al., 1993; see also Gruber, 1994, for wage shifting). On this premise, the hourly compensation of current employer-paid premiums was computed and added to the current gross wage. This increased wage was used as the postreform wage rate under NHI simulation.

For the assured child support benefit, we simulated a guaranteed level of $2,000 annually for the first child entitled to child support. This benefit was increased by $1,000 for the second child, $1,000 for the third, $500 for the fourth, and $500 for the fifth child. The public cost of the assured benefit was then defined as the assured level minus the amount of private child support currently received. (Note that we do not assume that an assured benefit would have an immediate effect on private child support payments.) Our simulation of the assured benefit had the following additional features: The public cost of the assured benefit was subject to the federal income tax, assured benefits were restricted only to custodial parents with awards, and a family on AFDC had to leave the AFDC rolls to be entitled to the assured benefit.

Simulation Model. Analyzing the effects of policy changes requires a model that predicts behavioral responses to the changes proposed under the reform. To predict welfare participation and labor supply decisions, we used a conventional economic utility maximizing model as described in Garfinkel et al. (1990). The static microeconomic theory of labor supply assumes that individuals choose the number of hours they will work and whether they will receive welfare benefits based on the alternative that provides the highest utility. The form of the utility function that we used to determine the response to a new public program is the augmented Stone–Geary direct utility function used by Garfinkel et al. (1990) and Meyer, Garfinkel, et al. (1991) and is given as follows: For single-mother families,

$$U(C, H, \varepsilon) = (1 - \beta)\ln(\frac{C}{m} - \delta) + \beta\ln(\alpha - \frac{H}{R} + \frac{\varepsilon}{R * (1 - \beta)}) \tag{1}$$

For married-couple families,

$$U(C, H_1, H_2, \varepsilon_1, \varepsilon_2) = (1 - \beta_1 - \beta_2)\ln(\frac{C}{m} - \delta) + \beta_1\ln(Z_1) + \beta_2\ln(Z_2), \tag{2}$$

where

$$Z_1 = \alpha_1 - \frac{H_1}{R_1} + \frac{(1 - \beta_2) * \varepsilon_2}{R_1 * (1 - \beta_1 - \beta_2)} + \frac{\beta_1 * W_2 * \varepsilon_2}{R_1 * W_1 * (1 - \beta_1 - \beta_2)} \quad \text{and}$$

$$Z_2 = \alpha_2 - \frac{H_2}{R_2} + \frac{(1 - \beta_1) * \varepsilon_2}{R_2 * (1 - \beta_1 - \beta_2)} + \frac{\beta_2 * W_1 * \varepsilon_1}{R_2 * W_2 * (1 - \beta_1 - \beta_2)}$$

In these equations, C = annual consumption of market goods; H_n = annual hours of work (1 for husband, 2 for wife; when not subscripted, this refers to single women); β_n = marginal propensity to consume leisure; δ = subsistence consumption; α_n = total time available for work; m and R = indexes that normalize C and H in accordance with the size and composition of the household; ε_n = an error term representing tastes for work; and W_n = the hourly net wage.

Maximization of the utility formulation subject to a budget constraint yields an optimal number of hours, $H = \alpha(1 - \beta)R - \beta(n - \delta m)/W + \varepsilon$, for single-mother families, and

$$H_1 = \alpha_1(1 - \beta_1)R_1 -$$
$$\beta_1(n - \delta m + W_2 * \alpha_2 * R_2)/W_1 + \varepsilon_1 \text{ and}$$

$$H_2 = \alpha_2(1 - \beta_2)R_2 -$$
$$\beta_2(n - \delta m + W_1 * \alpha_1 * R_1)/W_2 + \varepsilon_2$$

for married-couple families, where n = net unearned income (and thus $C = n + W_1 H_1 + W_2 H_2$).

Because directly estimating the parameters of this utility function was beyond the scope of our study, we drew on results from the existing labor supply literature. For our estimates of the labor supply effects, we used the results obtained by Johnson and Pencavel (1984) in their analysis of the labor supply response to the Seattle and Denver Income Maintenance Experiments (SIME–DIME). In particular, for single women we assumed $\beta = .128$; $\delta = -2,776$; $\alpha = 2,151$; $m = 1 - .401 * \ln(1 + K)$ (K being the number of children in the family under 18 years); and $R = 1 - .071P$ (P being 1 if there are preschool-age children in the family, 0 if otherwise). For married couples we assumed $\beta_1 = .2113$; $\beta_2 = .1238$; $\delta = 1,616$; $\alpha_1 = 2,587$; $\alpha_2 = 2,012$; $m = 1 + 1.069 * \ln(1 + K)$; $R_1 = 1$; and $R_2 = 1 - .051P$.

Because the optimal hours of work predicted by the equation did not match the observed hours of work for individual families, the epsilon terms (representing tastes for work) were defined as the difference between optimal hours and observed hours. The epsilon terms were then incorporated into the utility function as shown in equations 1 and 2, and this forced the observed hours to be optimal hours for more than 97 percent of the individuals in our sample.

Individuals not working presented two particular complications: First, we had no wage for them, and so we had to estimate wages (see Kim, 1993, for the estimating equations). Second, individuals not working were typically not on the margin of going to work, and so a random epsilon term was drawn from a standard normal distribution. Additional details on this procedure can be found in Garfinkel et al. (1990).

The simulation model involved several intermediate steps. First, we examined the current situation, calculating welfare program participation and current utility based on net income and the hours that the adults in the family were working at the time. We then introduced the three new public benefits—refundable tax credits for children, the assured benefit, and NHI—into the current system and predicted behavioral responses to these benefits. To make the prediction, we assumed that families considered many potential changes in work hours and welfare program participation. To do this we assumed that those not currently working considered going to work. All potential hour points were compared in terms of their utility levels, and the point of highest utility was finally selected. The selected point under the postreform defined each family's labor supply and welfare participation. Finally, the predictions for each family of income, taxes, hours worked, welfare participation and benefit amounts, and public costs of new benefits were aggregated to generate the effects of the reform.

Our model improves on the previous simulation model developed at the Institute for Research on Poverty (Garfinkel et al., 1990; Meyer, Garfinkel, et al., 1991). The original model used an exact budget line and calculated utility on each segment of the budget line. However, the use of exact budget sets becomes virtually impossible when several programs are involved. For this reason, the original model ignored food stamps, the EITC, and Medicaid. Because the present study considered both these public transfer programs and private transfers through employer-provided insurance, it did not use an exact budget line, but calculated utility at each of the potential hour points specified. This new approach enabled us to incorporate health care transfer programs as well as a broader range of income transfer programs.

The model does have some limitations. For example, the model assumes that all who desire jobs can find them. Another important limitation is that although the model now incorporates health benefits, food stamps, and the EITC, it does not yet incorporate child care benefits or expenditures for housing subsidies. One other limitation stems from our counting of health benefits as income in the poverty calculations. Although this treatment of health insurance would be problematic if the primary focus of the analysis were the absolute level of poverty, our concern is not with the absolute level of poverty or any other outcome, but rather with whether the effects of a package of non–income-tested programs are equal to the additive effects of each individual program. The final limitation comes from the microsimulation method itself, which has not developed a technique for testing statistical significance (see Citro & Hanushek, 1991).

RESULTS

To measure the interaction effect of the three non–income-tested programs, we first simulated each program separately and then the three programs together. (The same program parameters were used in each simulation.) In our results, we present the estimated effects under each single program alone, the sum of each program's effects, and the estimated effects under the three combined programs. To examine the direction and magnitude of the interaction effect of the three programs, our discussion includes a comparison of the combined effect with the sum of each program's effects.

For outcomes that involved discontinuities, such as being an AFDC or food stamp recipient or falling below a poverty line cutoff, using the sum of each program's effects as a basis for comparison raised a double-counting problem. Suppose that an AFDC family is predicted to leave welfare under the assured benefit, the refundable tax credit, and NHI. This family would be counted as an off-AFDC case in all single programs, which means that the sum of the percentage of reductions in AFDC caseloads would count this family three times. On the other hand, this family would be counted once in calculating the percentage reduction in AFDC caseloads under the combined programs. To correct this double-counting problem in sums, we identified the double-counted cases between different simulation runs and separated them in the calculation of sums. These adjusted sums were compared with the combined effects in all outcome measures. Interaction effects were then defined as the combined effects minus the adjusted sums.

Table 25-2 presents the estimated effects on poverty, AFDC, food stamps, labor supply, and income redistribution. Looking first at the effects on poverty of single programs, the number of individuals in poverty is predicted to decrease by 16.5 percent under the refundable tax credit, 19.4 percent under NHI, and 3 percent under the assured benefit. These predicted percentages add up to 38.9 percent, but this sum is adjusted to 34.6 percent when double-counted cases are taken into account. When the three programs are combined, however, we predict a larger percentage reduction in poverty—43.4 percent. This antipoverty effect under the

TABLE 25-2

Effects of Single and Combined Programs on Poverty, Welfare Participation, and Labor Supply

Measure of Effects on	Effects of Single Programs			Adjusted Sums	Effects of Combined Programs	Interaction Effects[d]
	Refundable Tax Credit ($1,000)[a]	National Health Insurance[b]	Assured Child Support Benefit ($2,000)[c]			
Poverty						
% change in poverty rate	−16.5	−19.4	−3.0	−34.6	−43.4	−8.8
% change in poverty gap	−25.8	−32.2	−3.0	−50.4	−55.5	−5.1
Aid to Families with Dependent Children (AFDC)						
% change in AFDC cases	−1.5	−1.5	−0.8	−1.9	−22.3	−20.4
% change in AFDC payments	−0.4	−0.1	−0.2	−0.2	−12.5	−12.3
Food stamps						
% change in food stamp cases	−2.9	−1.3	−0.7	−3.2	−6.0	−2.8
% change in food stamp payments	−8.6	−0.6	−1.7	−10.1	−16.7	−6.6
Labor supply						
Women originally on AFDC						
Change in mean hours	5	−5	2	2	31	29
% change	2.3	−2.2	0.9	1.0	13.4	12.4
% nonworkers who begin to work	0.4	0.7	0.1	0.8	10.5	9.7
Women not on AFDC						
Change in mean hours	−38	−25	−7	−70	−51	19
% change	−3.4	−2.2	−0.7	−6.3	−4.6	1.7
All men[e]						
Change in mean hours	−26	−24	−2	−52	−56	−4
% change	−1.3	−1.2	−0.1	−2.6	−2.8	−0.2

Redistributional Effects	Preform Mean Net Income	Differences in Mean Net Income Postreform					
Below poverty line	7,756	901	1,237	115	2,253	2,422	169
Between 100% and 200% of poverty line	16,455	552	605	139	1,296	1,461	165
Between 200% and 300% of poverty line	27,800	156	31	86	273	204	−69
More than three times poverty line	48,331	−528	−1,679	28	−2,179	−2,116	63

[a]The $1,000 refundable tax credit for children is cost neutral by eliminating tax exemptions for children and increasing the income tax rate by 1.6%.

[b]For national health insurance financing, payroll tax rate is increased by 7.2% with no exemptions for poor people.

[c]This run assumes no improvement in the child support system.

[d]This column is calculated with combined effects minus adjusted sums.

[e]A small number of men on AFDC are included in this category.

combined programs is 8.8 percentage points greater than the adjusted sum of each program's effects (last column in Table 25-2). A similar pattern is found for the effect on the poverty gap. Estimated percentage reductions in the poverty gap under single programs total 50.4 percent after the adjustment. On the other hand, the percentage reduction in the poverty gap under the combined programs is estimated at 55.5 percent, 5.1 percentage points greater than the adjusted sum.

Table 25-2 also shows the estimated effects on AFDC recipiency and benefit payments. Our estimates indicate that each program alone would have a very small effect on AFDC caseloads: a 1.5 percent decrease with the refundable tax credit, a 0.8 percent decrease with the assured benefit, and a 1.5 percent decrease with NHI. The estimated effect on AFDC benefit payments of each program alone is almost negligible—less than a 1 percent decrease. Adjusting for double counting, these estimated effects of single programs add up to a mere 2 percent decrease in AFDC caseloads and a 0.2 percent decrease in AFDC payments. Under the combined programs, however, a decrease of more than 22 percent in AFDC caseloads and a decrease of about 13 percent in AFDC payments are estimated. That is, the combined programs achieve a decrease in AFDC caseloads of more than 20 percentage points and a decrease in AFDC payments of more than 12 percentage points than the counterpart sum of each program's effects. These results indicate that the impact on AFDC under the combined programs becomes substantially strengthened due to the interaction of the three programs.

In Table 25-2, our results also indicate upward interactions for the estimated effects on food stamp recipiency and benefit payments, but smaller than for AFDC. The smaller interaction effect is probably attributable to the fact that eligibility for food stamps extends much higher in the income distribution than eligibility for AFDC.

The estimated effects on labor supply indicate that it is the interaction effect of the programs on the labor supply responses of women on AFDC that underlies the interaction effects on AFDC caseloads and payments (Table 25-2). Looking at changes in the mean hours worked by AFDC women, the refundable tax credit and the assured benefit lead to annual increases of five hours and two hours, respectively, whereas NHI leads to a decrease of five hours per year. (Note that NHI could discourage the work effort of some working AFDC recipients because of the 7.2 percent increase in payroll taxes for financing.) These predicted changes in the mean hours worked under single programs add up to an increase of two hours. Under the combined programs, an increase of 31 hours is estimated for the mean hours worked by AFDC women. In other words, the combined programs yield an increase of 29 hours (more than 12 percentage points greater) over the addition of the single programs' changes in the mean hours. The upward interaction for the work incentive under the combined programs is particularly strong for nonworking AFDC women. As seen in Table 25-2, all single programs have negligible effects on the percentage of nonworking AFDC women who begin to work. The total is less than 1 percent. On the other hand, the combined programs would entice about 11 percent of nonworking women on AFDC to begin to work. This percentage is more than 10 times as large as the sum of the single programs' effects.

Why are there such strong interaction effects on the work effort of AFDC recipients? The welfare benefits package (AFDC, food stamps, and Medicaid) in many states is far more generous than any single program reform. When each single program is implemented, its benefits plus earnings remain less attractive than the welfare benefits package. (Wage rates are typically low for these women.) Thus, despite the fact that the non–income-tested programs have lower marginal tax rates than the AFDC program, one benefit alone is not sufficient to entice most AFDC mothers to work. When the three programs are combined, however, the combined benefits package in conjunction with earnings becomes more attractive than the welfare benefits package.

For individuals not receiving AFDC, all programs are predicted to have negative effects on the mean hours worked, because any increase in unearned income would decrease the number of hours they work. (Also, increased tax rates for financing could contribute to the decrease in hours worked.) The estimated decrease in annual hours worked by women not on AFDC weakens when the three programs are combined, suggesting a counteracting interaction of the combined programs on the negative effects on labor supply responses of non-AFDC women (Table 25-2). For men, the combined programs result in a slightly greater negative effect on their hours worked than the sum of each program's effects, but the difference is very small.

Table 25-2 also presents estimates for changes in mean income for four different income classes. Under single programs, the poor and the near-poor populations increase their income levels (more with NHI and the refundable tax credit than with the assured child support benefit). NHI provides the most benefits to low-income families, because many of these families are uninsured under the current system. It should be noted that financing schedules for NHI and the refundable tax credit are incorporated; increased mean incomes mean that on average the new benefits received outweigh the increase in taxes. In the top income class, however, increased taxes are more than the benefits received under NHI and the refundable tax credit. When the three programs are combined, poor and near-poor families substantially increase their mean incomes (by $2,422 for poor families and $1,461 for near-poor families), whereas the top income class decreases its mean income by $2,116. Comparing these figures with the sums, all income classes except those between two and three times the poverty line show small upward interactions of the combined programs.

The estimated costs and savings of the simulated programs are presented in Table 25-3. The total gross cost is estimated at $60.2 billion for the refundable tax credit, $104.1 billion for NHI, and $5.7 billion for the assured child support benefit under the single program reform. The total gross cost under the combined programs is $2.6 billion greater than the addition of gross costs estimated under single programs, primarily because more AFDC families are able to move off welfare and participate in the reform program.

TABLE 25-3

Costs and Savings under Reform (in Millions of Dollars)

Measure	Under Single Programs			Adjusted Sums	Under Combined Programs	Inter-action Effects[a]
	Refundable Tax Credit ($1,000)	National Health Insurance	Assured Child Support Benefit ($2,000)			
Total gross cost	60,216	104,121	5,687	170,024	172,631[b]	2,607
Welfare savings	866	10,813	203	11,662	14,222	2,560
Total tax revenue[c]	59,350	93,308	371	153,029	154,735	1,706
Net cost	0	0	5,113	5,333	3,674	−1,659

[a]Calculated with estimates under the combined programs minus adjusted sums.
[b]Refundable tax credit: $61,543; national health insurance: $104,121; assured child support benefit: $6,967.
[c]Estimated changes in earned income tax credit as a result of labor supply responses are also included.

All reform programs generate some savings from welfare programs, including AFDC, food stamps, and Medicaid: The estimated welfare savings are $0.9 billion under the tax credit, $10.8 billion under NHI, and $0.2 billion under the assured benefit. (Medicaid savings are generated from AFDC families who leave welfare under the assured benefit and the refundable tax credit, assuming that these families lose Medicaid coverage. Because Medicaid is replaced with NHI, a large part of the estimated welfare savings under NHI comes from the Medicaid program.) The combined programs, however, show a $2.6 billion greater welfare savings than the adjusted sum of welfare savings under single programs.

Looking at the total tax revenue in Table 25-3, the estimated tax revenue under the refundable tax credit ($59.4 billion) is generated from eliminating exemptions for children and increasing income tax rates by 1.6 percent. The total tax revenue under NHI (estimated at $93 billion) primarily comes from increasing payroll taxes by 7.2 percent and eliminating current income tax exemptions for employer-paid premiums. The single program of the assured child support benefit also shows some tax revenue (about $0.4 billion) as a result of changes in labor supply in response to the new benefit. When the three programs are combined, they would again generate greater tax revenue ($1.7 billion more) than the sum of revenues under the single programs. Because of the greater welfare savings and tax revenue under the combined programs, the net cost of the three combined programs (estimated at $3.7 billion) is about $1.7 billion lower than the sum of net costs under the single programs, although the total gross cost of the combined programs is $2.6 billion greater than the sum of each program's gross costs. This gain in program cost under the combined programs is a result of the interactions of the combined programs.

CONCLUSION

This article examined three proposed programs that could have a large impact on vulnerable populations whose well-being is important to the social work profession. Of particular interest are the interaction effects of three non–income-tested programs: a $1,000 refundable tax credit for children (per child under

18 years), an assured child support benefit ($2,000 for the first eligible child), and national health insurance. Our results suggest that the effect of the programs interacting with one another would be much larger than the sum of the effects produced by each program alone. In particular, we found that these three programs, when they are implemented together, become much more effective in inducing AFDC families to work and move off welfare.

As noted earlier, this study does have weaknesses. The valuation of health care coverage is crude. Not all who want to work will find work. Microsimulation methodologists have yet to develop tests of statistical significance. Future research should address these and other shortcomings. Still, we doubt that the central policy implication of these results will be overturned by future research. Any single program reform alone is not enough to bring AFDC recipients out of poverty and off welfare dependency. Only a combined benefits package would enable many AFDC recipients to combine earnings with other public benefits and free them from relying solely on AFDC benefits.

More broadly, our results provide some support for the proposition that a multifaceted approach to reducing poverty may succeed where a single reform would fail. The benefits of a package of universal reforms are greater than the additive effects of each program alone. The whole is greater than the sum of its parts.

REFERENCES

Citro, C. C., & Hanushek, E. A. (Eds.). (1991). *Improving information for social policy decisions: The uses of microsimulation modeling.* Washington, DC: National Academy Press.

Dickert, S., Houser, S., & Scholz, J. K. (1994). Taxes and the poor: A microsimulation study of implicit and explicit taxes. *National Tax Journal, 4,* 621–638.

Ellwood, D. T. (1988). *Poor support: Poverty in the American family.* New York: Basic Books.

Figueira-McDonough, J. (1993). Policy practice: The neglected side of social work intervention. *Social Work, 38,* 179–188.

Fraker, T., Moffitt, R., & Wolf, D. (1985). Effective tax rates in the AFDC program. *Journal of Human Resources, 20,* 251–263.

Gabel, J., DiCarlo, S., Fink, S., & de Lissovoy, G. (1989). Employer-sponsored health insurance in America. *Health Affairs, 8,* 116–128.

Garfinkel, I. (Ed.). (1982). *Income-tested transfer programs: The case for and against.* New York: Academic Press.

Garfinkel, I. (1996). Economic security for children. In I. Garfinkel, J. Hochschild, & S. McLanahan (Eds.), *Social policy for children* (pp. 33–82). Washington, DC: Brookings Institution.

Garfinkel, I., & McLanahan, S. S. (1986). *Single mothers and their children: A new American dilemma.* Washington, DC: Urban Institute Press.

Garfinkel, I., Robins, P. K., Wong, P., & Meyer, D. R. (1990). The Wisconsin child support assurance system: Estimated effects on poverty, labor supply, caseloads, and costs. *Journal of Human Resources, 25*(1), 1–31.

Gruber, J. (1994). The incidence of mandated maternity benefits. *American Economic Review, 84,* 622–641.

Holahan, J., & Zedlewski, S. (1991, Spring). Expanding Medicaid to cover uninsured Americans. *Health Affairs,* pp. 45–61.

Jabine, T. B. (1990). *The survey of income and program participation quality profile.* Washington, DC: U.S. Department of Commerce.

Johnson, T. R., & Pencavel, J. H. (1984). Dynamic hours of work functions for husbands, wives, and single females. *Econometrica, 52,* 363–389.

Kim, Y. (1993). *The economic effects of the combined non-income-tested transfers for families with children: Child support assurance, children's allowance, and national health insurance.* Unpublished doctoral dissertation, University of Wisconsin-Madison.

Lerman, R. I. (1989). Child support policies. In P. H. Cottingham & D. T. Ellwood (Eds.), *Welfare policy for the 1990s* (pp. 219–246). Cambridge, MA: Harvard University Press.

Meyer, D. R., Garfinkel, I., Robins, P. K., & Oellerich, D. (1991). *The costs and effects of a national child support assurance system* (Discussion Paper No. 940-91). Madison: University of Wisconsin-Madison, Institute for Research on Poverty.

Meyer, D. R., & Kim, R. Y. (1994). *Incorporating labor supply responses into the estimated effects of an assured child support benefit* (Discussion Paper No. 1033-94). Madison: University of Wisconsin-Madison, Institute for Research on Poverty.

Meyer, D. R., Phillips, E., & Maritato, N. L. (1991). The effects of replacing income tax deductions for children with children's allowances. *Journal of Family Issues, 12,* 467–491.

Moffitt, R. (1992). Incentive effects of the U.S. welfare system: A review. *Journal of Economic Literature, 30,* 1–61.

Musgrave, R. A., Heller, P., & Peterson, G. E. (1970). Cost-effectiveness of alternative income maintenance schemes. *National Tax Journal, 23*(5), 140–156.

National Commission on Children. (1991). *Beyond rhetoric: A new American agenda for children and families.* Washington, DC: Author.

Orshansky, M. (1968). Who was poor in 1966? In E. M. Burns (Ed.), *Children's allowances and the economic welfare of children* (pp. 178–184). New York: Citizen's Committee for Children of New York.

President's Commission on Income Maintenance Programs. (1969). *Poverty amid plenty: The American paradox.* Washington, DC: U.S. Government Printing Office.

Schorr, A. L. (1966). *Poor kids.* New York: Basic Books.

U.S. Advisory Council on Public Welfare. (1966). *Having the power, we have the duty.* Washington, DC: U.S. Government Printing Office.

U.S. Congress Joint Economic Committee & Subcommittee on Fiscal Policy. (1972–74). *Studies in public welfare.* Washington, DC: U.S. Government Printing Office.

U.S. House of Representatives, Committee on Ways and Means. (1989). *1989 green book: Background material and data on programs within the jurisdiction of the Committee on Ways and Means.* Washington, DC: U.S. Government Printing Office.

U.S. House of Representatives, Committee on Ways and Means. (1990). *1990 green book: Background material and data on programs within the jurisdiction of the Committee on Ways and Means.* Washington, DC: U.S. Government Printing Office.

U.S. House of Representatives, Committee on Ways and Means. (1991). *1991 green book: Background material and data on programs within the jurisdiction of the Committee on Ways and Means.* Washington, DC: U.S. Government Printing Office.

U.S. House of Representatives, Committee on Ways and Means. (1993). *1993 green book: Background material and data on programs within the jurisdiction of the Committee on Ways and Means.* Washington, DC: U.S. Government Printing Office.

Vadakin, J. C. (1968). *Children, poverty, and family allowances.* New York: Basic Books.

Waldo, D., Sonnefeld, S., McKusick, D., & Arnett, R. (1989). Health expenditures by age group, 1977 and 1987. *Health Care Financing Review, 10*(4), 111–120.

Wilson, W. J. (1987). *The truly disadvantaged: The inner city, the underclass, and public policy.* Chicago: University of Chicago Press.

Zedlewski, S., Holahan, J., Blumberg, L., & Winterbottom, C. (1993). The distributional effects of alternative heath care financial options. In J. A. Meyer & S. S. Carroll (Eds.), *Building blocks for change: How health care affects our future* (pp. 87–144). Washington, DC: Economic and Social Research Institute.

This chapter was originally published in the December 1996 issue of Social Work Research, *vol. 20, pp. 274–285.*

Empowering Battered Women Transnationally: The Case for Postmodern Interventions

Linda Mills

International policymakers have at last committed themselves to ending gender warfare (Carrillo, 1992; Connors, 1994; United Nations, 1993). Through educational campaigns (Montano, 1992), task force and commission reports (Australian Law Reform Commission, 1993; Canadian Panel on Violence against Women, 1993), constitutional amendments (Brazilian Constitution, 1988), and other law reforms, governments around the globe are now taking conscious steps to eliminate or ameliorate the effects of intimate violence in the family.

As a leading cause of injury and death to women, violence against women by their intimate partners nonetheless remains an intractable problem. Each year, in the United States alone, at least 2 million women of all races and classes are battered by a spouse or intimate partner (Straus & Gelles, 1986). Battery by a spouse or lover is the single most common reason for women entering hospital emergency rooms, exceeding childbirth, automobile accidents, muggings, and all other medical emergencies. Studies have found that 22 percent to 35 percent of women presenting to hospital emergency departments are there because of complaints related to ongoing abuse (Randall, 1990). One of every three pregnant obstetric patients was at risk of abuse (Helton, McFarlane, & Anderson, 1987). Furthermore, in 1993, 27 percent of all violence against women was committed by intimates, that is, their lovers or ex-lovers (U.S. Department of Justice, 1994).

American women are certainly not alone in this regard. A cross-cultural study of family violence found that domestic abuse occurs in over 84 percent of the 90 societies examined (Levinson, 1988). In Canada and Guatemala, 25 percent to 40 percent of women studied had been abused by an intimate partner (Castillo, Bates, Rosales, & Alvarez; Haskell & Randall, cited in Heise, Pitanguy, & Germain, 1994). In Chile, Colombia, and Belgium, the figure ranged from 4 percent to 60 percent (Heise et al., 1994). In Europe (not counting the countries of the former Soviet Union), between 12 million and 24 million women and girls were subject to violence annually (Reilly, 1994). In Sweden, often looked to as a model country for gender equality, in 1989 a woman was reported battered by a current or former intimate partner every 20 minutes (Leander, cited in Elman & Eduards, 1991).

These alarming statistics have mobilized a number of formerly battered women and feminist advocates worldwide to address domestic violence. Together, they have shaped and influenced ideological and programmatic considerations of how and under what circumstances the law should be applied and what battered women must do to remain free of violence in their lives. The consensus within the battered women's movement on this issue has been that violence against women in the family must be treated as a crime (Zurutuza, 1993).

DOMESTIC VIOLENCE AS CRIME

The underlying value of treating domestic violence as a crime is that, at least theoretically, this response treats men and women as equals. If men who beat their neighbors are prosecuted for battery, so should men who beat their wives. Violence perpetrated almost exclusively against women is thus given the same legal status as crimes perpetrated outside the domestic sphere.

The strategy of treating woman abuse as a criminal offense has remained the primary legal intervention since the problem was first seriously addressed in the 1960s. There is, however, a danger in focusing primarily on this intervention. Battered women not only have been reluctant to file reports with the police but also too often have not sought any kind of help or delayed seeking help until long after the abuse began. Thus, it is estimated that only 14 percent of American women who experience "severe" violence ever contact the police (Gelles & Straus, 1988). Moreover, in a country like Sweden, where wife beating was made a criminal offense in 1982, only 31 percent of battered women surveyed in 1989 wanted their batterer arrested (Elman & Eduards, 1991). Taken together, this evidence suggests that international efforts to prosecute wife beaters, reform police practices, issue restraining orders, and impose mandatory arrest laws may fail to enable or encourage most battered women to seek the legal assistance they need to end the violence in their lives.

Why do so few battered women seek available legal assistance? A primary reason is that for emotional, financial, or cultural reasons they choose to remain in their existing relationships (Hackler, 1991; Kirkwood, 1993; Rimonte, 1991). Because nearly every criminal intervention, including the most innovative ones, potentially subjects the batterer to incarceration, battered women who are emotionally, financially, and culturally entangled in their abusive relationships may feel alienated from a criminal-oriented system that is inflexible in catering to their needs—needs that may or may not involve arresting, prosecuting, or incarcerating their abusers.

This article examines legal interventions instituted to respond to the problem of domestic violence and assesses the propriety of the criminal model on which they are based. Using postmodern social work theory and practice, which reject the notion that clinical certainty is either desirable or achievable (Pozatek, 1994), the article promotes the idea of a more workable alternative response to the problem—a domestic violence commission that places the power and control over her actions and reactions in the hands of the battered woman herself. The assumption is that legal and social work advocates must abandon clinical postures that claim to "know" how a battered woman feels and instead adopt a position of measured clinical uncertainty.

The conflicting loyalties experienced by most, if not all, battered women to themselves, their batterers, and their communities cry out for interventions that are more tolerant of the unpredictability generated by the trauma of intimate violence. Interpretations, advice, and remedies must respect the differences inherent in each battered woman's experience and treat the problem according to the survivor's shifting positions, but also must recognize that true empowerment for battered women may itself be transitional and uncertain. The proposal for a domestic violence commission answers that call by providing for a self-initiated and self-paced model that is fluid and flexible in its timelines and remedies.

EFFECTIVENESS OF EXISTING LEGAL INTERVENTIONS

Legal attempts to punish perpetrators of domestic violence have all come about during the past 20 years (Hart, 1994). Most of the most innovative of these strategies have been instituted in the past five years. These legal responses include police procedures designed to increase the effectiveness of civil protection orders and numerous options for prosecuting batterers, including most notably mandatory arrest.

Arrest and Prosecution

There has been a change in police attitudes; they are more likely than in the past to arrest the perpetrator when the victim is visibly injured or when there is probable cause to believe a crime has been committed. However, arrest and prosecution have not proved effective in reducing violence against women in the family. In the short term, mandatory arrest appears to reduce future battering by minor offenders but to escalate violence by more serious offenders, depending in part on factors such as whether the batterer is employed (Berk, Campbell, Klap, & Western, 1992; Sherman et al., 1992). After six months even minor offenders tend to abuse again (Sherman et al., 1992).

Civil Protection Orders

Even civil protection orders, which enjoin a batterer from further violence or threats, have only limited value as a means to curtail violence in many women's lives (Keilitz, 1994). In most states civil protection orders can be used either in conjunction with criminal proceedings or on their own in civil court (Keilitz, 1994); thus, protection orders potentially give women the means to fashion remedies according to their needs. However, a recent study of women who obtained temporary protection orders found that 60 percent experienced physical or psychological abuse in the year after the order was issued (Keilitz, 1994).

The problem with civil protection orders, prosecution, and arrest policies is that they effectively require women to terminate their abusive relationships and subject them to even more serious attacks by their batterers. Studies show that battered women who attempt to leave the abuser may be most at risk of "femicide" (Hart, 1988). Ironically, criminal strategies that seek to terminate the abuse and hence the relationship through legal interventions may prove most dangerous.

Cultural Responses

Dogmatic approaches are completely unresponsive to battered women who are incapable of leaving because of internal or cultural pressures. Some women, and particularly women of color, may be more likely to stay in abusive relationships for social or economic reasons. Not surprisingly, recent research reveals that norms of family honor and cultural barriers influence many battered women's decisions to silently endure abusive relationships (Rimonte, 1991).

In particular, women who live in cultures where community is stressed above individuality face sometimes insurmountable barriers when confronting domestic violence. This is particularly true in Middle Eastern and some Pacific Island and Asian cultures, where

> a woman abused by her husband hesitates a very long time before attempting to do anything about the violence at all. To some, her inaction (and silence) suggests collusion. In fact, it is an indication of the desperation induced by the limited vocabulary of self-definition permitted by her culture, and the terrible price she must pay to preserve her identity within her culture. (Rimonte, 1991, p. 1319)

For women caught in such a cultural web, criminal interventions as they are currently designed may be completely unresponsive to their needs.

NATIONAL AND INTERNATIONAL INNOVATIONS IN LEGAL INTERVENTIONS

Recently, several innovations that do not rely exclusively on criminal legal strategies have been implemented. These interventions seek to incorporate alternative legal and social work methods to respond to the problem of domestic violence.

U.S. Approaches

Hawaii has attempted to address family matters in a more comprehensive manner by developing a unified criminal and civil court that adjudicates woman and child abuse, divorce, and juvenile delinquency matters in one forum. This unified court has been hailed by some as a model for administering a more therapeutic justice. Yet this approach has been challenged for being unresponsive to the diverse needs of battered women. For instance, Barbara Hart, the legal director of the Pennsylvania Coalition against Domestic Violence, among others, has argued that revealing spousal abuse in one proceeding might affect a woman's credibility in another family matter (such as child custody) adjudicated by the same court (*Unified Courts*, 1994).

In November 1992 Dade County, Florida, launched a dedicated Domestic Violence Court that seems to respond to needs in more diverse ways. Though the Dade County Court focuses exclusively on issues of woman and child abuse and provides only criminal strategies, it also incorporates some social work methods ("UM Alums Help Stop the Violence," 1993). The goals of the court are to stop the violence, protect the victim and her children, make the offender accountable, and make treatment available as needed. Although this court represents some institutional progress, insofar as it uses social work methods, in other ways it does not go far enough. Civil remedies, along with administrative legal relief, could go a long way in helping battered women address criminal matters as well as family and financial concerns. The Dade County Court has been challenged on the constitutional grounds that it systematically discriminates against criminal defendants charged with battering (*A.G. v. Lederman*, 1994).

Finally, a comprehensive program in Duluth, Minnesota, uses a combined criminal and therapeutic model in an interesting way. Police are instructed to arrest batterers rather than tell them to "take a walk and cool off," and representatives from battered women's shelters and batterers' treatment programs are dispatched to talk with the parties immediately after the arrest; batterers are often ordered by courts to undergo treatment as an alternative to serving time in prison (Randall, 1991). Researchers evaluating this program have relied on such outcomes as conviction rates ("significantly increased"), number of women filing for protection orders ("tripled"), and number of batterers brought back into court for failure to comply with civil or criminal court orders ("risen tenfold") (Randall, 1991).

Approaches in Other Countries

Like Dade County's Domestic Violence Court, the Winnipeg Family Violence Court in Winnipeg, Ontario, Canada, hears only cases of child, spouse, and elder abuse (Ursel, 1994). A study of its effectiveness during its first two years concentrated only on the program's stated goals of limiting to three months the time for processing cases, reducing case attrition prior to sentencing, and imposing more appropriate sentences on abusers (Ursel, 1994). The study found that the average processing time was in accordance with the three-month goal (Ursel, 1994). However, it also found that woman abuse cases were slightly less rigorously prosecuted. This problem may arise from the fact that newly instituted police policies that frequently involve arresting and charging people accused of domestic violence too often result in weak cases and reluctant complainants (Ursel, 1994). In addition, changes in sentencing rules included a higher incarceration rate and a higher percentage of offenders sent to batterers' or alcohol treatment programs (Ursel, 1994).

The state of Sao Paulo, Brazil, offers yet another approach to draw women into the legal system that should be considered in developing a truly comprehensive solution to the problem of domestic violence. It is important to note that Brazil is the first nation in the world to target domestic violence in its national constitution; in 1988 Brazil required its state governments to "prohibit violence in the sphere of their relations." The state of Sao Paulo has translated this strong ideological stance into 41 women-staffed police stations (including female investigators and jail keepers) dedicated solely to crimes against women (Eluf, 1992). Officers investigate women's reports of assault, battery, and sex crimes, and social workers help with nonlegal needs. Since Brazil instituted these programs, complaints of woman abuse have skyrocketed (Eluf, 1992), signifying that many women think these police stations are responsive to their needs.

Two other programs are integrating legal and social work methods to provide interesting and important approaches to combating domestic violence. A program in Hamilton, New Zealand, monitors consistency in police, corrections, court, and shelter responses. In addition, it provides educational programs for abusers and support services for battered women. Thus, the New Zealand program acknowledges and responds to the complex and interacting needs of batterer and battered alike. This program shows further promise in two additional ways: It incorporates the particular needs of culturally diverse populations and encourages the native population of Maori women it serves to design a mode of intervention that meets their specific cultural needs.

In spite of the criticisms, aspects of the Hawaii Unified Court, the Dade County Domestic Violence Court, and the Winnipeg Family Violence Court provide promise for rethinking domestic violence policy that has heretofore focused exclusively on traditional criminal interventions. Taking all the evidence together, it appears that harsher or even more comprehensive criminal-oriented policies are not the panacea feminists hoped they would be. If recent homicide statistics are an indication of whether prevalent or innovative approaches to domestic violence are working, it appears that the current legal interventions protect men against violence at the hands of women but do not effectively protect battered women against the violence of men. Although fewer women have killed their male partners in the past 10 years, compared with the previous 20, men are killing their female partners at the same rate as before (Browne & Williams, 1989).

Still, programs like the women's police stations in Sao Paulo and the police and other efforts in Hamilton and Duluth have all proved useful for helping battered women confront the violence in their lives. And yet research reveals that an even more responsive approach to domestic violence, one that reconsiders legal interventionist policies from an entirely new perspective, is needed to reduce the occurrence of woman abuse (Littleton, 1993; Tifft, 1993).

A NEW PARADIGM FOR JUSTICE

Psychotherapist and political theorist Jane Flax (1992) suggested that juristic interventions for women should use relational notions of justice, that is, systems that recognize social interaction and intimate relations as their cornerstone. Many women define themselves, learn, and grow through relationships or intimate social interactions with others including mothers, fathers, husbands, lovers, children, siblings, and friends. Many women even translate work relationships into friendships to function effectively in employment contexts. Indeed, it is primarily through intimate others that women come to know themselves and learn to mediate the emotional, cultural, and even financial features of their personal well-being (Flax, 1992).

Such ways of knowing and being are not linear but subjective and interactive. They depend on the intimate presence and active, involved expression of the other (Flax, 1992). As painful (and perhaps even familiar) as it is for the legal or social work professional to acknowledge this, emotional and physical violence may not be altogether incompatible with such patterns of relating. Without prejudging how the pattern is formed and why it manifests in more extreme forms in some intimacies and not others, it is apparent that when violence erupts and the woman (or the batterer) is removed from the intimate setting, the woman is deprived of an important link to and displaced by a certain voice or lack in her self.

A Postmodern Approach

For many battered women, the violence is eminently confusing, and the abrupt removal of the batterer may be even more confusing. It is in this confusing period that battered women attempt, over and over, to leave their batterers or decide to stay and endure the abuse forever. To respond to the deep uncertainty and lack of emotional clarity a violent explosion introduces into her life, the battered woman requires above all else time and a fluid institutional response to her conundrum.

Multifaceted and multideliberative legal and social work systems that respond to the survivor's need for flexibility are necessary to help her in working through the conditions of relational ways of knowing and being and in learning specifically to distinguish in her mind and soul between violence and healthful expressions of intimacy. In this vein, interventions for battered women, both legal and otherwise, should reflect a postmodern social work approach that not only respects the possibility or likelihood of this relational structure but also provides the time and fluidity necessary for self-guided resolution. Such a system should recognize that true empowerment for battered women is achieved not through obedience to the expectations of legal or social work advocates or models but through acknowledgment of the woman's need to reconsider and re-evaluate the meaning of the trauma in a flexible time frame and a supportive environment.

Legal institutions and their relevant ideologies must be reformed to ensure that all battered women needing services are welcome and to recognize that women's relationships may be important to them, even when they involve violence.

Domestic Violence Commission

Domestic violence commissions that acknowledge the shifting uncertainty of a survivor's experience as she grapples with a multitude of conflicting loyalties are needed both nationally and internationally. Although the administrative configuration of these commissions would depend on how any given region adjudicates or prosecutes domestic violence cases and on the needs of the particular battered women it serves, a reflexive social work–oriented model should be designed to reach battered women who are, given current institutional constraints, prevented from seeking assistance from a legal system that has failed to consider the relational and associated financial, emotional, and cultural features of the abusive relationship.

Such commissions could be modeled on either dedicated domestic violence courts (Miami's approach) or unified courts (Hawaii's model). Women might bring civil, criminal, or administrative matters for adjudication, depending on what course of action they were ready to pursue. Women would file domestic violence complaints in informal but confidential and private settings, potentially with social workers at hospital emergency rooms, in (women-run) police stations, on hot lines, and in legal services offices. Their complaints would then be sent to and administered through the commission. Restraining orders and other legal remedies would be available if the women desired them. Other measures, depending on the woman's requests, would be available to ensure her safety (for example, shelter stays for either the victim or perpetrator and house surveillance, including monitoring devices).

Depending on the remedy she sought, the woman would have a choice of financial assistance (welfare, credit, alimony, or a job), assistance with other government benefits (including housing), and child care. Studies have shown that when women worldwide are not provided with concrete tools to modify their social or economic circumstances, the recurrence of maltreatment is more likely (Zurutuza, 1993). Ongoing related criminal or civil actions, once the woman was ready to file and physically and emotionally prepared to proceed, could be heard in a domestic violence court similar to that in Dade County, Florida, by judges who were trained in the complexities of adjudicating these cases.

This commission could advance domestic violence policy by empowering the battered woman herself to design a course of action she felt would eradicate violence from her life. A flexible remedy menu and time line that respected the uncertainty generated by conflicting loyalties could be just what the battered woman needs to finally face, incrementally and at her own pace, what she may have otherwise tolerated for fear that the legal system, with its essentialist and blunt criminal instruments, would do for her what she was not yet ready or willing to do for herself.

IMPLICATIONS FOR SOCIAL WORK PRACTICE

Some social work practitioners have argued that a feminist stance on violence against women in the family requires an unequivocally woman-centered approach that helps survivors become economically independent of their abusers so the women can permanently escape their abusive relationships (Davis & Hagen, 1992). One recent study revealed that the most staunch feminist battered women's advocates believe that a survivor who decided to remain married should be encouraged to change her decision (McKeel & Sporakowski, 1993). Such an approach ignores the clinical reality and rich social work tradition that treats a client in the fluid context of her relationships and recognizes that her uncertainty and emotional and cultural loyalties demand a safe and nonjudgmental space in which to explore these issues.

CONCLUSION

Social workers should take the lead in establishing legal responses to domestic violence that are premised on postmodern social work theories and practices, that provide an environment in which to explore all the battered woman's options, and that embody an institutional ethos for empowering her through self-paced and self-initiated change. Given this critical moment in gender history, when governments around the globe are searching for appropriate solutions to the problem of woman abuse, it is important that existing and innovative transnational legal strategies be more fully explored for their potential global effectiveness. Domestic violence commissions that draw on social work theory and practice and treat the battered woman with all her attending complexity should be culturally adapted. By providing a nonjudgmental approach to the problem of domestic violence and by suspending expectations of the battered woman, the commission can incrementally empower a survivor to confront the violence in her life as she explores

the emotional, financial, and cultural loyalties to which we all, to one degree
or another, feel bound.

REFERENCES

A.G. v. Lederman (Hon. Cindy S.), 643 So.2d 1091 (1994).

Australian Law Reform Commission. (1993). *Equality before the law* (Discussion Paper 54).
Sydney: Author.

Berk, R. A., Campbell, A., Klap, R., & Western, B. (1992). The deterrent effect of arrest in
incidents of domestic violence: A Bayesian analysis of four field experiments. *American
Sociological Review, 57*, 698–708.

Brazilian Constitution. (1988). Art. 226, § 8.

Browne, A., & Williams, K. (1989). Exploring the effect of resource availability and the likelihood of female-perpetrated homicides. *Law & Society Review, 23*, 75–94.

Canadian Panel on Violence against Women. (1993). *Changing the landscape: Ending violence,
achieving equality: Final report of the Canadian Panel on Violence against Women.* Ottawa: Author.

Carrillo, R. (1992). *Battered dreams: Violence against women as an obstacle to development.* New York:
United Nations Fund for Women.

Connors, J. (1994). *United Nations Fourth World Conference on Women: Background paper on violence
against women.* Unpublished manuscript, University of London, School of Oriental and
African Studies.

Davis, L. V., & Hagen, J. L. (1992). The problem of wife abuse: The interrelationship of social
policy and social work practice. *Social Work, 37*, 15–20.

Elman, A., & Eduards, M. (1991). Unprotected by the Swedish welfare state: A survey of
battered women and the assistance they received. *Women's Studies International, 40*, 413–421.

Eluf, L. (1992). A new approach to law enforcement: The special women's police stations in
Brazil. In M. Schuler (Ed.), *Freedom from violence: Women's strategies from around the world*
(pp. 199–212). Washington, DC: Overseas Education Fund International.

Flax, J. (1992). Beyond equality: Gender, justice, and difference. In J. Flax (Ed.), *Beyond equality
and difference: Citizenship, feminist politics, and female subjectivity* (pp. 192–210). London:
Routledge.

Gelles, R., & Straus, M. (1988). *Intimate violence: The causes and consequences of abuse in the
American family.* Beverly Hills, CA: Sage Publications.

Hackler, J. (1991). The reduction of violent crime through economic equality for women. *Journal
of Family Violence, 6*, 199–216.

Hart, B. (1988). Beyond the duty to warn: A therapist's "duty to protect" battered women's
children. In K. Yllö & M. Bograd (Eds.), *Feminist perspectives on wife abuse* (pp. 334–348).
Beverly Hills, CA: Sage Publications.

Hart, B. J. (1994). *State codes on domestic violence: Analysis, commentary, and recommendations.*
Upland, PA: Diane Publications.

Heise, L., Pitanguy, J., & Germain, A. (1994). *Violence against women: The hidden health burden*
(World Bank Discussion Paper 255). Washington, DC: World Bank.

Helton, A., McFarlane, J., & Anderson, E. (1987). Battered and pregnant: A prevalence study
with intervention measures. *American Journal of Public Health, 77*, 1337–1339.

Keilitz, S. (1994). Legal report: Civil protection orders: A viable justice system tool for deterring
domestic violence. *Violence and Victims, 9*, 79–84.

Kirkwood, C. (1993). *Leaving abusive partners: From the scars of survival to the wisdom for change.*
London: Sage Publications.

Levinson, D. (1988). Family violence in cross-cultural perspective. In V. Van Hasselt, R. L.
Morrison, A. S. Bellack, & M. Herson (Eds.), *Handbook of family violence* (pp. 435–456). New
York: Plenum Press.

Littleton, C. (1993). Women's experience and the problem of transition. In M. Minow (Ed.),
Family matters: Readings on family lives and the law (pp. 261–272). New York: New Press.

McKeel, A. J., & Sporakowski, M. J. (1993). How shelter counselors' views about responsibility for
wife abuse relate to services they provide to battered wives. *Journal of Family Violence, 8*, 101–107.

Montano, S. (1992). Long live the differences with equal rights: A campaign to end violence against women. In M. Schuler (Ed.), *Freedom from violence: Women's strategies from around the world* (pp. 213–226). Washington, DC: Overseas Education Fund International.

Pozatek, E. (1994). The problem of certainty: Clinical social work in the postmodern era. *Social Work, 39,* 396–403.

Randall, T. (1990). Domestic violence intervention calls for more than treating injuries. *Journal of the American Medical Association, 264,* 939–940.

Randall, T. (1991). Duluth takes firm stance against domestic violence, mandates abuser arrest, education. *Journal of the American Medical Association, 266,* 1180, 1183–1184.

Reilly, N. (Ed.), with D. Bailey, L. Fortin, S. Frost, L. M. Gracia, E. Hatton, U. Mann, L. Morris, G. Rogers, A. Romani, J. Schwarz, & S. Venkateswar. (1994). *Testimonies of the Global Tribunal of Violations of Women's Human Rights at the United Nations World Conference on Human Rights, Vienna, June 1993.* New Brunswick, NJ: Center for Women's Global Leadership.

Rimonte, N. (1991). A question of culture: Cultural approval of violence against women in the Pacific-Asian community and the cultural defense. *Stanford Law Review, 43,* 1311–1326.

Sherman, L. W., Schmidt, J. D., Rogan, D. P., Smith, D. A., Gartin, P. R., Cohn, E. G., Collins, D. J., & Bacich, A. R. (1992). The variable effects of arrest on criminal careers: The Milwaukee domestic violence experiment. *Journal of Criminal Law & Criminology, 83,* 137–168.

Straus, M., & Gelles, R. (1986). Societal change and change in family violence from 1975 to 1985 as revealed by two national surveys. *Journal of Marriage and the Family, 48,* 465–480.

Tifft, L. (1993). *Battering of women: The failure of intervention and the case for prevention.* Boulder, CO: Westview Press.

UM alums help stop the violence. (1993). *Barrister: The University of Miami School of Law Alumni Magazine, 48,* 8–10.

Unified courts: A preliminary discussion. (1994). Minutes of conference, June 1, 1994, Palmer House, Chicago.

United Nations. (1993). *Vienna Declaration and Programme of Action* (Document A/157). New York: Author.

Ursel, J. (1994). The Winnipeg Family Violence Court statistics. *Canada, 14*(12), 1–15.

U.S. Department of Justice. (1994). Domestic violence: Violence between intimates. In *Bureau of Justice Statistics, selected findings* (NCJ 149259, pp. 1–9). Washington, DC: Bureau of Justice Statistics.

Zurutuza, C. (1993). Domestic violence: Strategies used by the Latin American women's movement. In Latin American Committee for the Defense of Women's Rights (Ed.), *Women: Watched and punished* (pp. 59–77). Lima, Peru: Comite Latinoamericano para la Defensa de las Derechas de la Mujer.

This chapter was originally published in the May 1996 issue of Social Work, *vol. 41, pp. 261–268.*

27 The Ideology of Welfare Reform: Deconstructing Stigma

Frederick B. Mills

Recent welfare reform proposals (in particular, the Personal Responsibility Act of 1995) are grounded in a neoconservative critique of welfare (Gilder, 1995; Murray, 1984/1994). These legislative proposals are centered around recipients of Aid to Families with Dependent Children (AFDC) rather than focused on economic structural reform. The Personal Responsibility Act of 1995 (H.R. 4) and the Republican Party's *Contract with America* (Gingrich et al., 1994) assume that defects in AFDC mothers, not the welfare state or the structure of the U.S. economy, are to blame for the expansion of the AFDC rolls and the growing number of people living below the poverty line:

> Isn't it time for the government to encourage work rather than rewarding dependency? The Great Society has had the unintended consequence of snaring millions of Americans into the welfare trap. Government programs designed to give a helping hand to the neediest of Americans have instead bred illegitimacy, crime, illiteracy, and more poverty. Our *Contract with America* will change this destructive social behavior by requiring welfare recipients to take personal responsibility for the decisions they make. (p. 65)

This article argues that the labels associated with AFDC recipiency and rooted in these neoconservative ideas continue to serve as a political tool for the current welfare reform movement to promote a regressive welfare reform system. This article deconstructs those labels, particularly those used in the Personal Responsibility Act of 1995. In this article, *deconstruction* refers to the process of analyzing stigma into its component concepts, exposing these concepts as mere prejudice, and leaving a path open to reinterpret (that is, to construct) a new paradigm. This deconstruction has practical implications for social work because it widens the parameters of the welfare reform debate and suggests alternative interpretations of the needs of AFDC mothers.

DECONSTRUCTING STIGMA

The stigma paradigm hinges on the use of the concepts of dependence, addiction, and illegitimacy and promiscuity to describe single mothers and children whose fathers are absent. The terms' impact on the development of welfare programs is not new; however, stigma has become more difficult to expose in an era in which women are alleged to have made significant gains in economic and social equality.

Deconstructing Dependence

The concept of dependence has been used by advocates of restrictive welfare policies to refer to moral and psychological deficiencies. Dependence is a sufficient condition for being considered mentally unfit. Independence is a necessary condition for being considered mentally fit. Murray (1984/1994) even referred to those who are self-sufficient as "the good people."

The genealogy of the dependence-independence dichotomy was traced by Fraser and Gordon (1994), who found that the concept of dependence changed from a social and economic category in preindustrial society to a moral and psychological category in postindustrial society. During this shift the single-earner family was phased out; women were expected to become wage earners:

> The combined results of these developments is to increase the stigma of dependency. With all legal and political dependency now illegitimate, and with wives' economic dependency now contested, there is no longer any self-evidently good adult dependency in post-industrial society. Rather, all dependency is suspect, and independence is enjoined upon everyone. Independence, however, remains identified with wage labor. (p. 324)

Dependence did not always carry a stigma. Aid to Dependent Children (ADC), established in 1935, and an earlier version of the AFDC program discouraged the participation of women in the labor force by reducing the working recipient's grant by 100 percent of earnings. Proper motherhood and control of women's sexuality—not self-sufficiency—were the goals. Restrictions on ADC during the 1940s and 1950s included "man in the house" rules that "allowed social workers to make unannounced visits and eliminate from the rolls any woman found living with a man" (Quadagno, 1994, pp. 119–120). "Public patriarchy" (Fraser, 1987, p. 104) replaced the husband as provider for the dependent single mother, forbidding her to have sex outside of matrimony. Active, organized resistance by welfare rights groups such as the National Welfare Rights Organization in the mid-1960s led to the removal of such demeaning restrictions (Quadagno, 1994).

The ADC paradigm of the deficient woman, that is, a single mother without a man on whom to depend, is still operative. Again the social status (single parent) of the woman, not the labor market structure, is the problem. The 1967 Work Incentive Program and later the welfare-to-work focus of the Family Support Act of 1988 added to "proper motherhood" the expectation that the single mother be "self-sufficient." This expectation was driven by economic conditions as the single-earner family became less viable.

Deconstructing Addiction

The stigma of addiction is closely related to the stigma of dependence. Fraser and Gordon (1994) examined the association of AFDC with pathology. Welfare has been linked to the concept of addiction and narcotics since its inception. President Ronald Reagan, in his 1986 State of the Union Address, referred to Franklin D. Roosevelt's description of welfare as "a narcotic, a subtle destroyer of the human spirit" (cited in Rank, 1994, p. 19). After quoting Roosevelt, Reagan declared, "we must escape the spider's web of dependence" (p. 19). President

George Bush, in his 1992 State of the Union Address, paraphrased Roosevelt in the same manner. This view was articulated in the language of a House of Representatives report that accompanied the Welfare Transformation Act of 1995 (H.R. 1157). The analogy for welfare recipiency is clearly and explicitly drug addiction: "By anybody's definition, remaining on welfare for 8 years is dependency. Welfare has become a narcotic" (p. 6). It has a "narcotic effect" because it is an entitlement program. This guarantee of benefits "induces dependency" (p. 6). Notice that welfare itself and not poverty induces dependence. This is a powerful analogy; however, Rank (1994) provided empirical evidence that most mothers are off AFDC within two years.

This comparison with drug addiction has practical implications for social welfare practice in the case management of welfare-to-work programs. The *Employment and Training Reporter* ("One Trainer Says," 1994) reported that welfare as an addiction is being used as the basis of social services welfare case management training.

There is no empirical evidence that welfare is generally like an addiction, nor is there any evidence that welfare has a narcotic effect on recipients. The stigma, then, is based on weak induction, in this case, the fallacy of false generalization.

Deconstructing Illegitimacy and Promiscuity

The terms "out-of-wedlock birth" and "illegitimacy" are used specifically to stigmatize unmarried women who give birth and their children. Although two partners are involved in producing a child, unwed fathers are usually referred to as "absent," and the stigma is usually limited to the failure to pay child support. Despite a lack of empirical evidence that women on AFDC are promiscuous (Schur, 1984), conservative commentator George Gilder (1995) stated that "on the whole, white or black, these women [on welfare] are slovenly, incompetent, and sexually promiscuous" (p. 25). This alleged promiscuity becomes the basis of Gilder's critique of aggressive federal and state efforts to enforce child support: "Their [AFDC mothers'] best strategy is to seduce as many men as possible and then summon the constabulary of the welfare state to collect child support payments from the few who find jobs or win the lottery" (p. 26). Gilder maintained that "many recipients see welfare as a promiscuity entitlement" (p. 26). The assumption seems to be that if fathers were not coerced into paying child support, there would be more of an incentive for AFDC mothers to marry these fathers. Gilder stated, "With young women commanding power over income, sex, and children without marriage, why should they marry?" (p. 26). However, there is no evidence that such calculations are significant factors in decisions to separate from or divorce what Gilder calls "DNA dads" (p. 26) (see also Fraser, 1987).

The stigma of illegitimacy also applies to children. Once a mother is labeled "promiscuous" and the child "illegitimate," it becomes easier to speak of group homes for unwed mothers and orphanages for their children (see Weaver, 1994). The child, too, is the "other" (see Polakow, 1993).

The Personal Responsibility Act of 1995 would deny AFDC benefits to a child born to a mother younger than 18 or already receiving AFDC. The *Contract with America* contains similar language: "To reverse skyrocketing out-of-wedlock births that are ripping apart our nation's social fabric, we provide no welfare to teenage parents" (Gingrich et al., 1994, p. 65) (see also Havemann & Dewar, 1995; Wasem, 1995). The implication is that denying benefits under such circumstances removes an incentive to have illegitimate children.

However, there is no evidence that the availability of welfare is a significant motivation for having children. Gingrich et al. (1994) assumed that there is such evidence: "It's time to change the incentives and make responsible parenthood the norm and not the exception" (p. 75). There is also no evidence to support the assumption that cutting benefits will restore a sense of responsibility.

In addition, empirical studies have shown that higher welfare grants are not correlated with any increase in fertility ("Dethroning the Welfare Queen," 1994). According to Rank (1994), data from Wisconsin during the early 1980s indicated that the fertility rates of women receiving AFDC were significantly lower than in the national and Wisconsin populations. Rank also found that "the longer a woman remains on welfare, the less likely she is to give birth" (p. 76). The variable that most predicts childbirth while receiving welfare is not having a high school diploma. Rank's empirical data and extensive interviews offer no evidence that welfare provides a significant incentive for childbirth and suggests that other variables may account for out-of-wedlock births for AFDC mothers.

Using the U.S. Bureau of the Census (1995) definition of fertility rate, women receiving welfare have more children per thousand (2,586 for AFDC mothers as compared with 2,123 for non-AFDC mothers). However, these data merely show that in the sample studied, AFDC mothers had slightly larger families (2.6 children) than non-AFDC mothers (2.1 children). This is not evidence that AFDC provides an incentive to have larger families. In addition, the census data, although based on a national sample of about 19,000 households, provide an inflated picture of AFDC mother fertility rates because births that occurred before AFDC enrollment are included. Therefore, the fertility rate issue requires further study.

IMPLICATIONS FOR SOCIAL WORKERS

Social services workers and other frontline staff who serve in the administration and delivery of welfare programs ought to resist the reproduction of stigma associated with AFDC. This can be done by forming advocacy networks of social services workers, employment and training counselors, and support staff from public and private organizations. The network should be independent from the agencies represented; lines of authority at the job should not apply at network meetings. The mission of the network would be to advocate for the best interests of the clients and to affect local and state policy in the development of local guidelines and social services practices.

One example of such an association is the Employment and Training Advocacy Network (ETAN) of Montgomery County, Maryland. Members of ETAN (including this author) formulated recommendations for their local social services organizations, built cooperative networks to streamline the referral process for clients, and participated in committees that reported directly to social services policymakers.

On an individual level, frontline workers can treat each client as an individual with goals and not as an object or mere case. Social workers can advocate the elimination of mandatory and universal psychiatric counseling for AFDC mothers and resist the implementation of addiction models of case management. Employment and training staff can ensure that AFDC recipients have real input into their individual service strategy; the individual service strategy should be made in a partnership for success. Such a partnership recognizes that AFDC mothers need training for career-type jobs that offer medical benefits to achieve real self-sufficiency.

To empower AFDC recipients and to expose stigma labels and humanize the system, either the employment and training component or the social services component of a welfare-to-work program can create a newsletter written and edited by AFDC recipients that addresses their concerns about policy and service delivery. Such a newsletter, *Project Independence News,* was published by this author in Montgomery County in 1993 and 1994. Social services workers can also include AFDC recipients in regular staff meetings at which program recommendations are discussed.

Although some AFDC recipients do fit the anecdotal claims of fraudulent and abusive use of public funds, the stigma labels apply such anecdotes to recipients in general. These labels and their underlying ideology are so powerful that even professional social workers may be influenced by them in the administration of AFDC and welfare-to-work programs. As Freedberg (1993) pointed out, the profession that implements the ethic of care combined with theoretical knowledge may do the most good. Perhaps this deconstruction of labels may assist frontline workers in humanizing public assistance.

CONCLUSION

The labels of "dependence," "addiction," and "illegitimacy" are political tools used by Gingrich et al. (1994) as well as congressional welfare reformers who support the Personal Responsibility Act of 1995 to build public support for restrictive and punitive reform measures. Each label is rooted in the claim that AFDC itself produces more poverty and that AFDC mothers are to blame for the perpetuation of poverty.

The neoconservative critique of welfare argues that welfare is too liberal rather than that wages are too low, that subsidized child care is an unjust transfer of resources rather than that affordable day care is too scarce, and that medical assistance is a crutch rather than that access to health care in the open market is too restricted and expensive. Instead of characterizing women who choose welfare as rational agents looking out for the best interests of their children, they depict such women as promiscuous and compare them to drug addicts. Social workers and case managers can either bring alive the stigma labels or humanize the administration of AFDC and welfare-to-work programs.

REFERENCES

Dethroning the welfare queen: The rhetoric of reform. (1994). *Harvard Law Review, 107,* 2013–2030.

Family Support Act of 1988, P.L. 100-485, 102 Stat. 2343.

Fraser, N. (1987). Women, welfare and the politics of need interpretation. *Hypatia, 2,* 103–121.

Fraser, N., & Gordon, L. (1994). A genealogy of dependency: Tracing a keyword of the U.S. welfare state. *Signs: Journal of Women in Culture and Society, 19,* 309–336.

Freedberg, S. (1993). The feminine ethic of care and the professionalization of social work. *Social Work, 38,* 355–346.

Gilder, G. (1995, June). Ending welfare reform as we know it. *American Spectator,* pp. 24–27.

Gingrich, N., Armey, D., & the House Republicans. (1994). *Contract with America* (E. Gillespie & B. Schellhas, Eds.). New York: Times Books.

Havemann, H., & Dewar, H. C. (1995, June 19). Heated debate on welfare reform threatens to melt GOP solidarity. *Washington Post,* p. A4.

Murray, C. (1994). *Losing ground: American social policy, 1950–1980.* New York: Basic Books. (Original work published 1984)

One trainer says a 12-step program helps clients break welfare grip. (1994, May 11). *Employment and Training Reporter,* pp. 690–691.

Personal Responsibility Act of 1995, H.R. 4, 104th Cong., 1st Sess.

Polakow, V. (1993). *Lives on the edge: Single mothers and their children in the other America.* Chicago: University of Chicago Press.

Quadagno, J. S. (1994). *The color of welfare: How racism undermined the War on Poverty.* New York: Oxford University Press.

Rank, R. R. (1994). *Living on the edge: The realities of welfare in America.* New York: Columbia University Press.

Schur, E. M. (1984). *Labeling women deviant: Gender, stigma, and social control.* New York: Random House.

U.S. Bureau of the Census. (1995). *Mothers who receive AFDC payments—Fertility and socioeconomic characteristics* (Statistical Brief 95-2). Washington, DC: U.S. Government Printing Office.

Wasem, R. E. (1995). *Welfare reform: Adolescent pregnancy issues* (CRS Report for Congress No. 94-591 EPW). Washington, DC: U.S. Library of Congress, Congressional Research Service.

Weaver, K. (1994, Summer). Old traps: Why welfare is so hard to reform in 1994. *Brookings Review,* pp. 18–21.

Welfare Transformation Act of 1995, Report 104-81, together with dissenting views (to accompany H.R. 1157), 104th Cong., 1st Sess.

This chapter was originally published in the July 1996 issue of Social Work, *vol. 41, pp. 391–395.*

Part IV

HEALTH

28 The Governors' Dangerous Medicaid Endgame

Sharon M. Keigher

> Many public opinion surveys show that people have more trust in state government than in the federal government.
> —Larry Sabato, University of Virginia

> The governors are a special interest group, trying to maximize federal aid and increase their ability to withdraw state money from welfare and Medicaid.
> —Robert Greenstein, Center on Budget and Policy Priorities

Since October 1, when the federal fiscal year began without a budget agreement, there have been not one but two federal government shutdowns and 10 temporary, or stopgap, spending bills to either reopen it or keep it going. Nearly six months into the 1996 fiscal year, with a White House–Congressional impasse like none in recent memory, our national government still does not have a budget. And President Clinton appears to be holding firm in his resolve to veto Congress's Medicaid cuts and welfare reforms ("Medicaid Conference Reports," 1996). But don't exhale yet.

Into this impasse waded the National Governors' Association (NGA), the elected officials the people traditionally trust more than the federal government, with a Medicaid proposal even more regressive than that made by the House of Representatives last year and vetoed by the president. Hoping to resuscitate the welfare issue, the governors announced the outlines (and few details) of an allegedly new position on February 6 during a dinner with their former gubernatorial colleague at the White House. Approved by 75 percent of the governors (of whom nearly two-thirds are Republicans), their agreement was extolled as "the catalyst to break the deadlock and get everything else moving" (Pear, 1996a, p. A1).

Having embraced the Republican federal budget-cutting mania of 1994, many governors face serious budget balancing pressures in 1996. But rather than take their own medicine—cutting programs, raising state taxes, and accepting the consequences—they have proposed a complex, cheap, short-term plan to scam federal money by obtaining relief from the mandates that accompany categorical grants-in-aid. Their proposals cover welfare, Medicaid, nutrition, child care, and child protection; their Medicaid position is addressed in this column.

THE GOVERNORS' MEDICAID PROPOSALS

Medicaid is now the largest remaining open-ended entitlement program in the federal budget. Since 1965 it has grown to be a significant funder of the U.S.

health care system and an important source of coverage for people and of revenues for providers, far surpassing Aid to Families with Dependent Children (AFDC) and the block grants in state budgets. In 1993, 32.1 million people were covered by Medicaid at a cost of $112.8 billion. About 64 percent of the cost was financed by the federal government, with the balance paid directly by states. About 33 percent of all births are covered by Medicaid, as is health care for nearly 25 percent of children (*Medicaid: The health and long-term care safety net,* 1995). Medicaid finances half of all nursing home care, provides health insurance to 13 percent of the nonelderly population, and supplements Medicare for 10 percent of elderly people. Overall, 60 percent of all people living in poverty are assisted directly by Medicaid (Friedland, 1995).

The governors' proposed changes to Medicaid are artfully crafted to avoid the term "block grant" but still remove vital entitlement protections. Medicaid recipients would continue to be covered for hospital and physicians' services, nursing home care, family planning services and supplies, and laboratory services and X-rays. But states would have "complete flexibility in defining the amount, duration, and scope of services" (Pear, 1996a, p. A12). The NGA plan includes the following guidelines:

- States would have to continue to provide Medicaid for pregnant women with family incomes up to 33 percent above the official poverty level, children under age six in families with incomes up to 33 percent above the poverty line, and children ages six to 12 in families below the poverty line ($11,821 for a family of three in 1994). Coverage of children ages 12 to 18 would be optional.
- States would have to provide Medicaid for disabled people, but the states would define disability subject to approval of the Secretary of the Department of Health and Human Services.
- Recipients of AFDC and Supplemental Security Income (SSI) would be entitled to Medicaid, as they are under current law.
- People improperly denied Medicaid could appeal to a state agency and could then file suit in a state court, with a right to appeal to higher state courts and ultimately to the U.S. Supreme Court.
- States would have "complete authority" to set Medicaid payment rates for health plans, doctors, and hospitals "without interference from the Federal Government or threat of legal action" by health care providers. States would no longer need federal permission to require Medicaid recipients to enroll in health maintenance organizations or be subject to lawsuits by health care providers demanding higher reimbursement.
- Federal grants to the states for Medicaid would be adjusted for the rising cost of health care and expected changes in the number of poor people. The federal government would provide "extra money" for states with unexpected population growth (Pear, 1996a).

WHAT IS WRONG WITH THIS PICTURE?

The governors' plan is a bit like issuing invitations to a dinner party at which the host knows the food will run out before all the guests have been served. It guarantees states federal "matching" funds while dumping federal rules guaranteeing equity among beneficiaries and states. It provides the governors with a gratuitous bonanza in two ways: (1) It allows them to walk away from their long-standing fiscal responsibilities to children, families, and people with disabilities and chronic illnesses, and (2) it creates, under the guise of flexibility, new loopholes in federal law through which enterprising states could divert large amounts of federal funding for purposes other than helping needy families: "The track record of many states includes exploitation of similar seemingly innocuous provisions in federal law" (Children's Defense Fund, 1996, p. 2). The latest projections estimate these cuts would save as much as $300 billion over the next seven years relative to Medicaid spending under current law. The cash-strapped governors would become the big winners because 70 percent of the potential savings would be in state general funds (Center on Budget and Policy Priorities, 1996a).

Changing the Funding Formula

Federal categorical assistance programs are rooted in the principle that states share responsibility for financing the cost of basic help to children, families, and disabled adults. Grants-in-aid ensure this partnership by providing matching revenues of 50 percent to 83 percent of the dollars states expend on Medicaid; the poorer the state, the higher the rate of aid. Federal Financial Participation for public assistance and Federal Medicaid Assistance Participation provide states with financial incentives to be careful managers, and federal regulations delineating eligibility standards and basic obligations provide incentives for equitable administration.

The governors' proposal would dismantle this structure of matching grants by capping federal Medicaid payments and reducing the state matching requirements in the same way last year's Senate welfare and budget reconciliation bills did. Once federal payments reach the state's ceiling, or "cap," the federal government would cease providing funds, and a state would bear any additional costs it incurs in full. Because the federal caps would be set below anticipated expenditures under current law, the matching funds required for a state to secure its maximum allotment would be less than the matching funds required under current law. Consequently, states could reduce their contributions for Medicaid without affecting the amount of federal matching funds they receive.

In addition, NGA would reduce the amount of state matching funds required for at least the 25 wealthier states by raising the floor for federal matching to 60 percent of costs (the current floor is 50 percent); no states would have to pay more than 40 percent of program costs (Center on Budget and Policy Priorities, 1996a). With a 40 percent matching requirement, a state would need to provide only $2 in state funds for every $3 in federal funds it receives, whereas under the current 50 percent matching requirement, the state must put up $3 in state funds for each $3 in federal funds received. This change would allow many states to reduce their contributions by one-third without reducing the level of federal funding they secure (Center for Budget and Policy Priorities, 1996a). This change alone would permit states to reduce their funding by as much as

$214 billion over seven years without losing any federal matching funds (Center on Budget and Policy Priorities, 1996b).

Cutting Eligibility

In some ways the governors' accord would simply reify cuts many states are already making. States have been granted 37 waivers by the Clinton administration for experiments requiring or encouraging welfare recipients to work, and many states are designing Medicaid experiments to contract with private managed care plans. States have also witnessed a steady erosion of Medicaid benefits and services as a growing proportion of the population becomes uninsured and seeks medical assistance and state appropriations have not kept up with inflation. Failure to increase income ceilings each year gradually limits eligibility to people with lower and lower real incomes.

An increasing proportion of children (25 percent of those under age six) are now poor, which is why recent Congresses mandated that states expand eligibility for young children by raising the ceiling on the percent of poverty at which eligibility begins. Consequently, as the population of children under 18 grew by 3.1 million between 1988 and 1992, the proportion with private health insurance declined by 4.2 percent, and the proportion with employer-provided health insurance dropped by 4.5 percent, but the federally mandated Medicaid expansions absorbed 6 percent more of these children. The percentage without any health insurance actually declined by 0.7 percent (Newacheck, Hughes, & Cisternas, 1995). Without this coverage a much higher proportion of children would have no health insurance. The governors would drop these mandates, leaving children vulnerable again.

Creating New Loopholes

The governors also see an opportunity to use federal matching dollars to supplant cost liabilities that have been disallowed since welfare grants-in-aid to the states began in 1935. Whereas recent Congresses have sought to ban states' "creative" budgeting and accounting techniques that circumvent matching requirements to obtain additional Medicaid matching funds, the NGA proposal seeks to revive many of these. For example, the NGA plan would repeal the ban on provider donations and taxes, a technique many governors used in the late 1980s and early 1990s to generate cash for Medicaid matching. (At the request of the Bush administration, Congress barred this practice in 1991, effective January 1, 1993.) States could again take funds from providers, use them (rather than state funds) to qualify for federal matching funds, and then cycle these donations, or "taxes," back to providers while keeping the federal funds. A U.S. General Accounting Office (GAO) (1994) audit found, for example, that in one year Michigan obtained $256 million in federal funds without investing any state matching funds by soliciting "donations" from hospitals and returning an equivalent amount of funds to hospitals through "disproportionate share hospital" payments under Medicaid.

Another exploitation of federal matching funds would be to allow states to use them for a host of purposes unrelated to providing health coverage to low-income individuals such as paying the cost of operating state adult psychiatric hospitals, providing health care to inmates in state prisons, purchasing health coverage for all state workers and retirees with incomes below 275 percent of the poverty level ($41,662 for a family of four), and attracting business from other states by subsidizing health coverage for workers with incomes below 275 percent of the poverty level (Children's Defense Fund, 1996). Governors would then be able to reduce further the real state matching funds they committed to Medicaid, because any residual state spending for workers' health coverage, psychiatric hospitals, and other purposes might be counted as matching funds.

Finally, the proposal would allow a one-time-only windfall to the current governors without obliging them to plan ahead for the health needs of low-income individuals. Many of the governors of the largest states have already based their FY 1996 budgets on the arcane formula change in the welfare reform legislation that President Clinton vetoed, behaving as if they already had the billions in savings plus additional federal aid in the bank. New York State has built in savings of $1.3 billion, Michigan has included $320 million, and California has included $299 million (Families USA, 1996). These states could be sent scrambling to make up huge budget shortfalls if the NGA endgame strategy fails. NGA chair Governor Tommy Thompson (R-WI) admitted that if the reforms were not adopted during March, he did not know "what some states are going to do" (Families USA, 1996, p. 1).

Medicaid program administrators know that the most expensive care is not for children and their parents on AFDC, but rather for children, adults, and elders who are disabled as well as poor; people with AIDS and other chronic conditions; people living in nursing homes; and people with lifelong substance abuse problems and mental illnesses. Key to the whole proposal is the governors' desire to control the definition of disability and to avoid serving the most costly clients or to serve them in the least expensive ways. They want the right to "cost shift" like private insurance and managed care organizations.

A Familiar Strategy

The governors' proposal is reminiscent of Derthick's (1976) cogent analysis of gubernatorial politics, *Uncontrollable Spending for Social Service Grants*, which examined how in the late 1960s and early 1970s astute state policymakers exploited loopholes in grants-in-aid for social services under the public assistance titles of the Social Security Act to cover expenses far afield of the purposes in the law. Between 1969 and 1972, a period during which AFDC enrollments "only" doubled, states quadrupled their spending for federally matched social services. In 1969 President Nixon opened these floodgates to Republican governors in the larger states and their budget wizards. Although congressional intent had repeatedly disallowed spending of social services funds for public education and mental, correctional, and children's institutions, these were precisely the purposes to which governors quickly redirected much of the funding. The free flow ended in 1972, when Congress created Title XX of the Social Security Act (P.L. 92-512), which imposed a cap on the amount of federal matching funds states could receive annually.

In explaining how states exploited the federal largesse, Derthick (1976) concluded that "had the purpose of federal grants been clear and specific, the lack of an expenditure ceiling would not have mattered much; and had there been a limit on expenditures, the lack of purpose in the law would have mattered less than it did" (p. 106). In 1977 the federal allocation for Title XX was $2.79 billion; by 1992, after Title XX became the Social Services Block Grant, its budget was still $2.8 billion, and inflation had eroded the value of that funding by over half (U.S. House of Representatives, 1991). New block grants and capped grants-in-aid can expect a similar fate. With hindsight we see that congressional interest and support wanes over time. Lack of purpose and specificity in the law is a good way to kill the golden goose of federal aid.

REACTIONS TO THE GOVERNORS' PROPOSAL

The governors' claims of a breakthrough were immediately questioned by the *New York Times*, which observed that "what they did not achieve is a proposal that would guarantee essential security for the impoverished. A civilized, wealthy society should do no less" ("No Salvation," 1996, p. A14). But, the *New York Times* cautioned, "Under tremendous pressure to balance state budgets each year, states cannot afford to expend their own resources if they take care of the poor in ways that attract more poor families and repel taxpaying families and corporations" (p. A14). Medicaid, without an open-ended funding formula and entitlement protections, will cease to protect anyone with certainty as states rapidly engage in a race for the bottom.

A coalition of civil rights organizations assailed the plan by February 12, saying that they knew from experience to trust the federal government more than the states to care for poor people. The National Association for the Advancement of Colored People noted that "Many African-Americans remember that 'states' rights' were code words for the states' denial of basic civil rights. We are concerned that this history not return in the context of welfare reform" (cited in Pear, 1996b, p. A8).

House Democrats assailed the plan as well, as did Catholic Charities USA: "The Catholic Church, from the Pope on down through the bishops, teaches that government and society also have responsibilities: to help guarantee that people have 'suitable employment,' adequate wages and welfare benefits when jobs are unavailable," said Deputy Director Sharon Daly (cited in Pear, 1996c, p. A8).

To this Governor Thompson retorted flatly, "The Catholic Church is wrong" (cited in Pear, 1996b, p. A8).

The National Council of Senior Citizens' (1996) "Top 10 Reasons to Oppose the Governors' Medicaid Reforms" include most of the concerns cited above, but in addition, the council was concerned that enforcement of federal nursing home standards included in the Omnibus Budget Reconciliation Act of 1987 (P.L. 100-175) would be left up to the states; that the Boren Amendment requiring that states pay a fair rate to nursing homes would be repealed; and that federal oversight would be limited. Even though the federal government would be paying the lion's share of the cost, it would be unable to step in unless federal dollars were substantially misused. Other groups now assailing the plan include the U.S. Conference of Mayors and the American Academy of Pediatrics, as well as the usual coalitions advocating for children, people with disabilities and AIDS, elders, and families.

By late February, President Clinton had begun backtracking from the initially warm reception he had given his former colleagues—the governors. Still making vague favorable comments about the governors' intentions, he is questioning the Medicaid proposal's lack of guarantees of benefits to poor people, the states' freedom to curtail assistance, and the lack of legal protections for beneficiaries. Administration officials have just begun overtly criticizing it; a White House strategy for defeating the governors' pernicious plan seems to be emerging. Unfortunately, even if it works, no White House strategy can preclude the incalculable damage and pain these governors are bringing home as the next Medicaid battles shift to the statehouses.

CURRENT BUDGET DEADLOCK

Federal spending on Medicaid in 1994 was $92 billion, and by the year 2002, at present spending rates, it would grow 118 percent to $179 billion. However, the budget resolution passed by Congress last spring sought to reduce this rate of growth by more than half (to 52.8 percent). Relative to what the Congressional Budget Office anticipates under current law, this would be a 30 percent reduction in spending over seven years, and more than half (53.3 percent) of the cumulative $182 billion in reductions needed over that seven-year period would occur in the last two years (2001 and 2002) (Friedland, 1995). It was President Clinton's veto of the Medicaid bill emerging from that resolution that led directly to the present budget impasse.

The budget for 1996 is still deadlocked over the larger debate on balancing the entire federal budget in seven years and the policy differences that led to President Clinton's string of vetoes that delayed passage of six of the 13 appropriations bills for 1996 (Gray, 1996) and resulted in government shutdowns. The private negotiations between the White House and congressional leaders in December and January attempted to whittle away at these differences. The stopgap bill signed by President Clinton on January 26 expires March 15, along with the latest debt ceiling and most of the spending authority for the Departments of Veterans Affairs, Housing and Urban Development, Commerce, Justice, State, Labor, Health and Human Services, and Education. And now, perhaps, the impasse will yield to public response.

Although the public waits, generally oblivious, the stakes are increasing for elected officials who offered solutions in 1994. Freshman Representative Matt Salman (R-AZ), a rising star in conservative circles, recently noted "that some people were running away from the Contract with America like scalded cats.... We have lost our way and we need to get it back again. I think the public got a taste of what our revolution was all about during the first 100 days, but during the budget scuffle everything sort of went up in smoke" (cited in Gray, 1996, p. A10).

Indeed, it did. Surveys suggest that after a year of it, voters are turned off by much of the Republican agenda. "Dole gets no response whatsoever to returning power to the states, for the Tenth Amendment or, importantly, for achieving a balanced budget in seven years" (Greenberg, cited in Judis, 1996, p. 4). And on the same surveys, voters are alarmed by Republican efforts to slow the growth of Medicare spending, privatize Social Security, and allow corporations to divert money from workers' pension funds.

Ironically, President Clinton may be the only one still talking about deficit reduction. The Contract with America, a balanced budget, the capital gains tax cut—reportedly the big issues in 1996—have scarcely been mentioned by the candidates, "as if the Presidential campaign were stuck in some electoral Bermuda triangle where no one has heard anything about the 'revolution' of 1994" (Apple, 1996, p. B6).

Having just returned from a three-week break, Congress again appears to want to settle the budget and move on. Appropriations chairmen Senator Mark Hatfield (R-OR) and Representative Robert Livingston (R-LA) declared on February 24 that they are giving top priority to reaching an early and permanent resolution on the 1996 budget by introducing omnibus spending bills stripped of the social riders on abortion and other incendiary issues and uncoupled from the larger debate on balancing the budget in seven years. Congress may be ready to raise the debt limit, although efforts will certainly be made by the Republican governors (frequently participating in House Republican discussions) to link this to their Medicaid and welfare proposals (Gray, 1996).

CONCLUSION

In the popular anonymously authored novel floating around Washington *Primary Colors* (1996), Democratic Governor Stanton, a man "close to the people," offers his young aide, Henry Burton, his opinion about the role of governors and leaders in this new age. Henry, disillusioned by what he has seen of politics, is no longer a "true believer." But Governor Stanton, who loves "the people" as much as he loves his work, knows his value in a democracy. He pleads with Henry to stay with him for the long haul:

> Two thirds of what we do is reprehensible. This isn't the way a normal human being acts. We smile, we listen. . . . We live an eternity of false smiles—and why? . . .
>
> The opportunity to . . . make the most of it, to do it the right way—because you know as well as I do there are plenty of people in this game who never think about the folks, much less their "better angels." They just want to win. They want to be able to say, "I won the biggest thing you can win." And they're willing to sell their souls, crawl through sewers, lie to the people, divide them, play to their worst fears. (p. 364)

Elected officials who remember "the folks" and the responsibilities of government matter a great deal.

REFERENCES

Anonymous. (1996). *Primary colors*. New York: Random House.
Apple, R. W. (1996, February 25). Why the party can't stop Buchanan. *New York Times*, pp. B1, B6.
Center on Budget and Policy Priorities. (1996a, February 28). *Federal caps and state matching requirements under the governors' Medicaid proposal* [Press release]. Washington, DC: Author.

Center on Budget and Policy Priorities. (1996b, February 29). *Will states maintain the safety net? Evidence from bad times and good* [Press release]. Washington, DC: Author.

Children's Defense Fund. (1996, February 20). *The NGA welfare and Medicaid plans: A bonanza for the states* [Press release]. Washington, DC: Author.

Derthick, M. (1976). *Uncontrollable spending for social service grants.* Washington, DC: Brookings Institution.

Families USA. (1996, February 28). *Medicaid/Medicare: Delay in passage threatens state budgets* [Press release]. Washington, DC: Author.

Friedland, R. (1995, November). Medicare, Medicaid, and the budget. *Public Policy and Aging Report, 7*(1), 1–2, 14–15.

Gray, J. (1996, February 25). G.O.P. in Congress splits on tactics to regain an edge. *New York Times*, pp. A1, A10.

Judis, J. B. (1996, March 4). TRB from Washington. *New Republic, 4233*, 4.

Medicaid conference reports good news and bad news. (1996, February–March). *Action for Universal Health Care, 4*(6), 8.

Medicaid: The health and long-term care safety net, 103rd Cong., 2d Sess. (1995) (testimony of D. Rowland).

National Council of Senior Citizens. (1996, February 20). *Top 10 reasons to oppose the governors' Medicaid "reforms"* [Press release]. Washington, DC: Author.

Newacheck, P., Hughes, D., & Cisternas, M. (1995). Children and health insurance: An overview of recent trends. *Health Affairs, 14*(1), 244–254.

No salvation from the governors [Editorial]. (1996, February 7). *New York Times*, p. A14.

Omnibus Budget Reconciliation Act of 1987, P.L. 100-175, Title I, 101 Stat. 928, 930, 952.

Pear, R. (1996a, February 6). Governors' group finds agreement on Medicaid plan. *New York Times*, pp. A1, A12.

Pear, R. (1996b, February 14). Governors' plan on welfare attacked. *New York Times*, p. A8.

Pear, R. (1996c, February 21). House Democrats assail welfare plan backed by governors. *New York Times*, p. A8.

Social Security Act, P.L. 92-512, Title III, 86 Stat. 945-947 (1972).

U.S. General Accounting Office. (1994, August). *States use illusory approaches to shift program costs to federal government.* Washington, DC: U.S. Government Printing Office.

U.S. House of Representatives, Committee on Ways and Means. (1991). *Overview of entitlement programs: The green book.* Washington, DC: U.S. Government Printing Office.

RESOURCES FOR FIGHTING STATE MEDICAID CUTS

Advocacy Institute. (1995). *By hook or by crook: A guide to combat stealth lobbying.* Available from the Advocacy Institute, 1707 L St., NW, Suite 400, Washington, DC 20036. Phone: (202) 659-8475, fax: (202) 659-8484, e-mail: a1000@advinst.org. Designed to help grassroots advocates spot and turn the tables on corporate special interests and big-money lobbyists at the state and local levels. Includes useful lessons drawn from the experiences of citizen groups laboring in diverse areas. $10.

Families USA. (1996). *A Medicaid tool kit.* Available from Families USA Foundation, 1334 G St., NW, Washington, DC 20005. Phone: (202) 628-3030, fax: (202) 347-2417. Collected materials from many sources covering federal law, benefits and cost sharing, eligibility, state funding, managed care, cutting costs without hurting people, accountability, organizing, and media. The complete version costs $30; a briefer version is available.

NE Ohio Coalition for National Health Care. (1996). *Medicaid HMO brochure for Ohio.* Available from NE Ohio Coalition for National Health Care, 2800 Euclid, Suite 520, Cleveland, OH 44115-2418. Phone: (216) 241-8422, fax: (216) 241-8423. Prepared for AFDC and Healthy Family/Healthy Start recipients. Presents highly readable basic information and tips on selecting a Medicaid managed care organization (MCO) and consumer activism. Cost: $.50

for out-of-state orders. *User's guide to Medicaid managed care in Ohio.* A longer analysis of background information on managed care with comparisons of selected services of Medicaid MCOs in Ohio. Cost: $1.00 for out-of-state orders.

Perkins, J., & Rivera, L. (1995). *Medicaid managed care: 20 questions to ask your state.* Available from the National Health Law Project, 1815 H St., NW, Suite 705, Washington, DC 20006. Phone: (202) 887-5310, fax: (202) 785-6792.

This chapter was originally published in the May 1996 issue of Health & Social Work, *vol. 21, pp. 151–157.*

29 Keeping Managed Care in Balance

Dennis L. Poole

Managed care has thrown us off balance—and rightfully so. Who would have predicted 10 years ago that nearly all Americans would be covered under a managed care plan by the turn of the century? Who would have guessed that Americans, long resistant to interference in the provider–patient relationship, would abruptly sell this right for the promise of lower premiums (Burner, Waldo, & McKusick, 1992; Keigher, 1995)?

With this sudden turnabout, we as social workers must adjust quickly to the new, complex playing field of managed competition. We must know the differences among managed indemnity plans, preferred provider organizations, exclusive provider organizations, point-of-service plans, and health maintenance organization plans. We must grasp the meaning behind a new glossary of terms, such as "service bundling," "cost efficiencies," and "capitation financing."

We are also thrown off balance by the promises of managed care. Can this new system accomplish the seemingly impossible by containing costs while maintaining quality of care? Many of us remain skeptical. We were taught that one of the distinguishing characteristics of social welfare institutions was the "absence of a profit motive" (Wilensky & Lebeaux, 1965, p. 141). It does not take much digging to find the profit motive resting in the heap of many managed care plans.

CONTROLLING COSTS

To regain our balance, we first must put managed care in economic perspective. If current trends continue, health care expenditures in the United States will approach the $2 trillion mark by 2000, the equivalent of nearly 20 percent of the nation's gross national product (GNP). Left unchecked, these expenditures will soar above $16 trillion by 2030, or 32 percent of the GNP (Burner et al., 1992).

Efforts to find a more efficient system of health care than fees-for-service have been under way for a long time, most of this century in fact (Edinburg & Cottler, 1995). However, the advent of the managed care movement in the United States began with passage of the Health Maintenance Organization Act of 1973 (P.L. 93-222). The act was "directed toward establishing alternate models of health care delivery, emphasizing comprehensive health care, and utilizing a financial structure based on capitation and involving enrollment and prepayment of fees" (Caputi, 1978, p. 17).

Momentum toward managed care accelerated during the Reagan administration. The Deficit Reduction Act of 1984 (P.L. 98-369) implemented the prospective payment system, a new strategy for controlling costs in Medicare. For the first time, financial risks in Medicare moved through aggregate payments from a third-party payer (the federal government) to health care providers. Soon thereafter, health insurance companies followed suit, negotiating deals that eventually would strangle the life out of the fee-for-service system in America (Averill, 1993; Coile, 1990).

The defeat of President Clinton's Health Security Act of 1993 (S. 1757 and H.R. 3600) hastened the nation's march toward managed care. Although widely criticized on the right and left of the political spectrum, the fate of the act ultimately fell to the power of "old shibboleths about a single-payer system increasing bureaucracy, lowering quality, lessening choice, and even promoting socialism" (Mizrahi, 1995, p. 1197). This defeat shut the door on national health care reform but opened corridors of reform in state governments for managed care.

States were already reeling from a staggering threefold increase in Medicaid expenses since 1985 (Lewin-VHI, 1995). With these expenses averaging 18 percent of total state budgets and escalating rapidly, state governments moved swiftly with their own reforms to get costs under control (National Association of State Budget Directors, 1994). The federal government helped, not with new dollars, but with waivers giving states great latitude in the design and delivery of their Medicaid programs. States took full advantage of this opportunity. Swept by national trends, they opted for managed care in the hopes that this system would rescue them from spiraling Medicaid expenses. Today all but a few states have some type of managed care plan in place for Medicaid recipients (Kaiser Commission on the Future of Medicaid, 1995).

The long-term impact of the federal government's decision to balance the federal budget by 2002 should not be underestimated. Federal aid provides more revenue to states than any other single tax source, more than all revenue collected from property taxes, sales taxes, or income taxes. Under a balanced budget, state and local governments could lose almost $400 billion over a seven-year period (Center on Budget and Policy Priorities, 1995). This makes cost containment all the more urgent.

HANDWRITING ON THE WALL

States, localities, and administrators already feel the pinch of these economic forces. They see the handwriting on the wall and have begun to reposition for the impact.

To begin, states are now making distinctions between "mandatory" and "optional" services. Under Medicaid Waiver 1115, states can determine which of several optional services—and the amount—they will provide in their managed care programs (Vandivort-Warren, 1995). Naturally, states are looking for ways to trim costs in optional service categories. Social workers are not the only professionals concerned about the budget ax; optional services provided by nurses, physical and occupational therapists, physicians, speech therapists, and psychologists are on the chopping block as well.

Localities are also looking for ways to trim costs. City and county budgets face intense scrutiny, while consolidation of resources by means of the United Way and other local coordinating structures gains widespread donor support.

In addition, localities are building partnerships that they hope will manage re-sources more efficiently and deliver outcomes more effectively. Comprehensive, interagency, interdisciplinary programs are in; fragmented, departmental, discipline-specific services are out (Daka-Mulwanda, Thornburg, Filbert, & Klein, 1995; Schorr, Farrow, Hornbeck, & Watson, 1995).

Many administrators have responded to these economic pressures by restruc-turing their agencies. Shifting from hierarchically organized departmental or-ganizations to program management organizations has become a priority to them. They want their agencies to move from discipline-specific departments with different functions to flattened organizations with disciplines integrated by programs (Charns & Tewksbury, 1993). Hospital social workers understand this phenomenon well; they were first among our colleagues in health care to experience the impact. Yet in truth they are not being singled out. All hospital-based professionals have been thrown off balance by the change. Only recently have their counterparts in community-based agencies begun to feel the ripple effects of cost containment and restructuring.

WEIGHING THE EVIDENCE, IDENTIFYING OUR CONCERNS

The verdict is still out on managed care. Thus far, the evidence is mixed as to whether this system can deliver what it promises. Some studies report that man-aged care brings improvements in utilization, costs, and access (Douglass & Torress, 1994; Fox & McManus, 1992; Hurley, Freund, & Paul, 1993; Lewin-VHI, 1995; Milam, 1994; Van Gorder & Hashimoto, 1993). Yet other studies contradict these claims (Bagarozzi, 1995; Freund & Lewit, 1993; Rowland, Rosenbaum, Simon, & Chait, 1995; Wood, Halfon, Sherbourne, & Grabowsky, 1994).

Consequently, professional views on managed care balance somewhere be-tween hope and dread. Jackson's (1995) assessment best sums up the situation:

> At its worst, [managed care] is perceived as a system in which no *real* dollars are saved, and money is diverted to administrative operations and profits at the expense of needed patient services. At its best, it is perceived as a system in which appropriate structure, control, and accountability enable the most effi-cient use of health resources to achieve maximal health outcome. To date, that "best" system has not been developed, but it is clear the variety of models cur-rently in use and proposed are examples of the attempt to reach the best bal-ance. (p. 1)

In the meantime, managed care raises many concerns for social workers. For the people we serve, managed care raises a host of issues pertaining to confi-dentiality, duty to aid, self-determination, freedom of choice, access, quality of care, research protocols, informed consent, participation in treatment decisions, and client rights. Organizational adjustments linked to managed care raise other concerns as well, such as lack of professional autonomy, blurring of professional roles, and loss of job security.

MOVING FORWARD

Given that managed care is here to stay, we must find helpful ways to address such issues. Therefore, this special issue of the journal offers a fresh look at this trend-setting system of care in health and mental health. The contributors offer insights that are forward-looking, yet practical, as we attempt to regain our balance in managed care.

Clearly, the future of social work in managed care rests in great measure on our own response to change. To position our profession at the forefront, we must first maintain a constructive mind-set. Feeling victimized, or reacting as if our professional services are being singled out, will only make matters worse. All other professional groups in health and mental health share our experiences, though some more than others. We are all fighting for our professional lives.

Fallout from the fray will depend partly on economics. Professionals who demonstrate their worth in this highly competitive environment will survive at a greater rate than professionals who do not. Hence, disciplined accumulation of practice data is no longer a luxury but a necessity in today's professional market. We must redesign our performance accountability systems to measure outcomes, not merely processes or workloads. Fortunately, we have tools already available to help us in the transition.

Politics will be a major factor as well. Professionals who demonstrate political savvy will survive at a greater rate than their counterparts. It is critical, therefore, that we become promoters of change—not bystanders—in this environment. We must move out of our offices into the political space that extends beyond our professional system. Forming alliances and coalitions, staffing key committees and task forces, writing action proposals, and taking part in policy making—these and other tactical measures can win social work a place at the negotiating table of managed care.

Finally, there is the matter of ethics. Once our professional service mission is clear, we must be willing to put ourselves at odds with goals and values that run counter to that mission. Because we cannot fight every battle or advocate every cause, we must choose carefully which ones to stand firm on. This is difficult under managed care. Its powerful head winds can easily knock a nation off balance, displacing human decency for dollars and cents as the bottom line.

REFERENCES

Averill, R. F. (1993). Competition and prospective payment: A new way to control health costs. *Journal of American Health Policy, 3,* 22–28.

Bagarozzi, D. A. (1995). Evaluation, accountability, and clinical expertise in mental health managed care: Basic considerations for the practice of family social work. *Journal of Family Social Work, 1,* 101–116.

Burner, S. T., Waldo, D. R., & McKusick, D. R. (1992). National health expenditures projections through 2030. *Health Care Financing Review, 14*(1), 1–29.

Caputi, M. A. (1978). Social work in health care: Past and future. *Health & Social Work, 3*(1), 8–29.

Center on Budget and Policy Priorities. (1995). *Holding the bag: The effect on state and local governments of the emerging fiscal agenda in the 104th Congress.* Washington, DC: Author.

Charns, M. P., & Tewksbury, L. S. (1993). *Collaborative management in health care: Implementing the integrative organization.* San Francisco: Jossey-Bass.

Coile, R. C. (1990). Managed care: Ten leading trends for the 1990's. *Hospital Strategy Report, 2,* 1–9.

Daka-Mulwanda, V., Thornburg, K. R., Filbert, L., & Klein, T. (1995). Collaboration of services for children and families: A synthesis of recent research and recommendations. *Family Relations, 44,* 219–223.

Deficit Reduction Act of 1984, P.L. 98-369, 98 Stat. 494.

Douglass, R. L., & Torress, R. E. (1994). Evaluation of a managed care program for the non-Medicaid urban poor. *Journal of Health Care for the Poor and Underserved, 5,* 83–98.

Edinburg, G. M., & Cottler, J. M. (1995). Managed care. In R. L. Edwards (Ed.-in-Chief), *Encyclopedia of social work* (19th ed., Vol. 2, pp. 1635–1642). Washington, DC: NASW Press.

Fox, H., & McManus, M. (1992). *Medicaid managed care arrangements and their impact on children and adolescents: A briefing report.* Washington, DC: Child and Adolescent Health Policy Center.

Freund, D., & Lewit, E. (1993). Managed care for children and pregnant women: Promises and pitfalls. *Future of Children, 3,* 92–122.

Health Maintenance Organization Act of 1973, P.L. 93-222, 87 Stat. 914.

Health Security Act of 1993, S. 1757 and H.R. 3600, 103rd Cong., 1st Sess. (1993).

Hurley, R., Freund, D., & Paul, J. (1993). *Managed care in Medicaid: Lessons for policy and program design.* Ann Arbor, MI: Health Administration Press.

Jackson, V. (1995, August). *A brief look at managed mental health care.* Washington, DC: National Association of Social Workers, Office of Policy and Practice.

Kaiser Commission on the Future of Medicaid. (1995, April). *Medicaid and managed care: Policy brief.* Washington, DC: Author.

Keigher, S. (1995). Managed care's silent seduction of America and the new politics of choice [National Health Line]. *Health & Social Work, 20,* 146–151.

Lewin-VHI. (1995, February). *States as payers: Managed care for Medicaid populations.* Washington, DC: National Institute for Health Care Management.

Milam, S. P. (1994). *A comparative study of indigent clinics in a private, managed care delivery system and a public, neighborhood clinic-based delivery system.* Unpublished doctoral dissertation, University of Texas, Austin.

Mizrahi, T. (1995). Health care: Reform initiatives. In R. L. Edwards (Ed.-in-Chief), *Encyclopedia of social work* (19th ed., Vol. 2, pp. 1185–1198). Washington, DC: NASW Press.

National Association of State Budget Directors. (1994, February). *1993 expenditure report.* Washington, DC: Author.

Rowland, D., Rosenbaum, S., Simon, L., & Chait, E. (1995). *Medicaid and managed care: Lessons from the literature.* Washington, DC: Kaiser Commission on the Future of Medicaid.

Schorr, L., Farrow, F., Hornbeck, D., & Watson, S. (1995). *The case for shifting to results-based accountability: With a start-up list of outcome measures.* Washington, DC: Center for the Study of Social Policy.

Van Gorder, E., & Hashimoto, B. (1993). Hawaii reaches out to the multineeds child: The state's cluster system cuts through red tape. *Public Welfare, 51,* 6–13.

Vandivort-Warren, R. (1995, June). *Merging managed care and Medicaid: Private regulation of public health care* (NASW Social Work Practice Update). Washington, DC: National Association of Social Workers, Office of Policy and Practice.

Wilensky, H. L., & Lebeaux, C. N. (1965). *Industrial society and social welfare.* New York: Free Press.

Wood, D., Halfon, N., Sherbourne, C., & Grabowsky, M. (1994). Access to infant immunizations for poor, inner-city families: What is the impact of managed care? *Journal of Health Care for the Poor and Underserved, 5,* 112–123.

This chapter was originally published in the August 1996 issue of Health & Social Work, *vol. 21, pp. 163–166.*

30 Speaking of Personal Responsibility and Individual Accountability . . .

Sharon M. Keigher

It being an election year, late summer 1996 has seen a feeding frenzy of "accomplishments" fly from the 104th "Contract with America" Congress. While most of us were watching the Olympics, the Congress—deeply fearful of being labeled "do nothing"—proved that it could reform health care and "welfareasweknowit" after all ("Welfareasweknowit," 1996, p. 3).

The legislation free-falling from Capitol Hill to the White House in August echoed the themes invoked gratuitously during August's Republican National Convention—God, family, honor, duty, country—usually followed by the party mantra: personal responsibility and individual accountability. When Republican presidential candidate Bob Dole declared in his acceptance speech, "Individual accountability must replace collective excuses," he insulted social workers everywhere, implying that community-based programs, social security, and health coverage for all Americans somehow exacerbate weakness in the American character. Two pieces of legislation, the Personal Responsibility and Work Opportunity Reconciliation Act of 1996 (P.L. 104-193) and the Health Insurance Reform Act (P.L. 104-191, 1996), which emerged from conference committees in early August and which President Bill Clinton signed in late August, will operationalize these overworked clichés as thoroughly as anything else this Congress did.

That partisan refrain, personal responsibility and individual accountability, is now heard playing like a broken record on our collective consciousness—from 50 statehouses, from every local government, and in every school. It is already shaping the work of planners and budgeters; eligibility examiners; child welfare, hospital, and nursing home social workers; mental health therapists; and selfless volunteers throughout the land. Like it or not, we all are implementing these complex, probusiness, and regressive welfare statutes.

REAL INTENDED HARM: THE PERSONAL RESPONSIBILITY AND WORK OPPORTUNITY RECONCILIATION ACT OF 1996

Implications for Welfare

"Am I missing something? Throw people off welfare in the name of strengthening families and alleviating poverty?" asked *New Republic* contributor Alex Kotlowitz (1996) of the congressional welfare bill. He continued, "The 'logic' goes something like this: Ending a mother's welfare payments will force her to find a job. Bingo. We've got a working mom, and she's no longer poor. Why didn't we think of this a long time ago?" (p. 19).

Why not, indeed. The experts insisted that reforming welfare would require spending more, not less, money. Nonetheless, P.L. 104-193 will reduce federal spending by $54 billion over the next six years, with the budget savings coming chiefly from cutting food stamps, throwing more than 1 million children into poverty, increasing hunger, and preventing legal immigrants from gaining access to most federal benefits (National Health Law Program, National Center for Youth Law, & National Senior Citizens Law Center, 1996).

As passed, the legislation ends the oldest program in the safety net, Aid to Families with Dependent Children (AFDC). Although the federally assisted AFDC program dates back to 1935 and the original Social Security Act, Skocpol (1996) noted that these "mothers' pensions" date back even farther to the 1910s, when 40 states passed laws allowing local governments to make payments to impoverished widows so they could care for their children in their own homes rather than surrendering them to orphanages or foster care.

In addition to eliminating entitlement to AFDC as of October 1, 1996, P.L. 104-193 repeals the Job Opportunity and Basic Skills Training program and Emergency Assistance to Families with Children. These programs are being replaced by capped state block grants called Temporary Assistance to Needy Families (TANF), which do not go into effect until July 1, 1997. TANF's benefits are limited to a maximum of five years, with recipients required to work after two. TANF no longer guarantees assistance to everyone who meets the state's eligibility criteria. The block grant, being a finite cash amount to each state, may or may not last through the year, so states have wide discretion in restricting eligibility and coverage. The law also eliminates the "individualized functional assessment" requirement for Supplemental Security Income (SSI) eligibility and changes other criteria that in the next six years could deny SSI benefits to over 300,000 children with severe disabilities, especially those with mental and emotional or multiple impairments (National Health Law Program et al., 1996).

The law imposes major restrictions on receipt of public benefits by legal immigrants already in the United States, including elimination of eligibility for SSI and food stamps. People currently receiving SSI, an estimated 350,000 poor older people and 150,000 disabled people, will lose benefits under this provision as soon as their cases are reviewed, and nearly 1 million will lose food stamps.

The law also makes across-the-board reductions in the value of food stamps over the next six years, a change that affects all recipients. Finally, it changes the effective date of SSI applications to the month after the month in which the application is filed, automatically delaying receipt of benefits (National Health Law Program et al., 1996).

Implications for Medicaid and Health Care

NASW, along with a strong coalition of advocates in both Washington and the state capitols, worked very hard to defeat the welfare bill and to improve its Medicaid-related provisions. Senator John Chafee (R-RI) fought successfully to ensure that the Medicaid guarantee was retained for families who meet AFDC eligibility now and in the future, while Republican governors vigorously opposed him.

At the same time, unsure if they could count on a presidential veto, advocates fought hard to defeat the governors' Medicaid Block Grant proposal. Fortunately, the latter effort was successful. Without this effort, the damage would have been much worse. Congress was unable to craft a Medicaid Block Grant acceptable to the White House and is unlikely to reopen discussions again this fall.

Despite having preserved Medicaid, P.L. 104-193's complex provisions still have the effect of terminating Medicaid eligibility for hundreds of thousands of people—primarily legal immigrants. Medicaid eligibility and coverage are affected in several ways. Medicaid eligibility continues for presently AFDC-eligible families, even if they are no longer receiving cash assistance under a state's new welfare program. Since its inception, a primary purpose of Medicaid has been to provide health care coverage for specific categories of recipients of cash welfare benefits: families with children on AFDC, elderly people, and blind and disabled people receiving SSI. The link between medical assistance and AFDC has meant that even Medicaid eligibility for non-AFDC recipient children depends on AFDC rules. Thus, a bill abolishing AFDC potentially threatens guaranteed Medicaid eligibility for millions of families (National Health Law Program et al., 1996).

For Medicaid purposes, P.L. 104-193 directs state Medicaid agencies to behave as if the AFDC program had not been abolished. If a family meets the income and resource standards in effect under the state's AFDC program as of July 16, 1996, the family must still be considered eligible for Medicaid. Many states aggressively trimmed their welfare rolls during 1995-96 to minimize the number who could maintain eligibility (Families USA, 1996b).

States can adopt a joint application process for Medicaid and welfare under their new welfare programs. However, they must continue their current application process for people who are eligible under current law and wish to apply for Medicaid only. This means that local social services offices will have to perform two separate eligibility calculations—AFDC, using the state's new welfare rules, and Medicaid, using the "old" AFDC rules—potentially compromising a number of Medicaid principles. For example, Medicaid will still require "timely processing" of applications (within 45 days) and due process in the handling of complaints, even though a state's new welfare rules may not. States would be allowed to terminate Medicaid coverage for individuals (but not their children) who are in the state's new work program but are terminated because they are not working. Complying with these principles will be administratively cumbersome, so clients' rights groups will need to monitor states' processes very closely (National Health Law Program et al., 1996).

The bottom line is that abolition of federal AFDC eligibility standards poses a threat to Medicaid eligibility for parents, other caretakers, and teenagers who cannot qualify for Medicaid under current law unless they receive AFDC. These groups include some 4 million adults, 1.5 million teenagers, and nearly 65,000 grandparents who care for minor children. States are not likely to provide them with adequate medical care without the federal matching funds now lost (National Health Law Program et al., 1996).

Medicaid coverage of legal immigrants has been eliminated. Most immigrants coming into the United States after enactment will be barred from Medicaid for all but emergency medical services for five years, after which the income and resources of their legal sponsor and his or her spouse would be counted for purposes of determining eligibility. In effect, most immigrants will be ineligible for any federal means-tested programs (including Medicaid) until they become citizens.

States can choose whether or not to cover legal immigrants already in the country but cannot deny eligibility to veterans; to permanent residents with a 10-year work history who have not received public benefits; or, for five years after entry, to either refugees or asylees. These provisions will be particularly hard on the estimated 65,000 elderly legal immigrants currently residing in nursing homes. Clinicians will be burdened by red tape and moral dilemmas (National Health Law Program et al., 1996).

Medicaid coverage for disabled children has been reduced. The bill narrows the current definition of disability for establishing the eligibility of children for SSI. It is estimated that 315,000 children will lose their SSI benefits as a result of this change, including 47,000 who will also lose Medicaid coverage (because they are adolescents born before September 30, 1983, or their family's incomes are above the poverty threshold). Most will continue to be eligible for Medicaid because their incomes already fall below the poverty line (National Health Law Program et al., 1996). In addition to these details, further implications will be identified as analysts, practitioners, and advocates gain experience with the program and real concentrated hardships are imposed on the poorest and least healthy in America.

SYMBOLIC GOOD NEWS: THE HEALTH INSURANCE REFORM ACT

Meanwhile, another revolutionary piece of legislation, the Health Insurance Reform Act (P.L. 104-191, 1996), directly affects most Americans (Families USA, 1996a). Late in July, the House and Senate finally reached a compromise on legislation sponsored by retiring Senator Nancy Kassebaum (R-KS) and Senator Edward Kennedy (D-MA) to curb what were alleged to be some of the worst abuses by health insurers. The Health Insurance Reform Act got only lukewarm support from NASW, who, seeing how badly both the Clinton administration and the Congress wanted bragging rights to it, lobbied heavily instead for amendments to lift its limits on catastrophic coverage and include mental health benefits.

Although the House and Senate passed bills in April 1996, disputes over the amendments, including those on mental health, and the Republican insistence on including medical savings accounts (MSAs) delayed the process of crafting a compromise between the two versions. The final version of P.L. 104-191 was adopted by the House on August 1 (with only two dissenting votes) and unanimously approved by the Senate the next day. President Clinton signed the bill into law on August 21 (Families USA, 1996a).

The Health Insurance Reform Act will help a disputed number of Americans who are caught in "job lock," afraid to change jobs or start their own businesses because they have pre-existing conditions that would prevent them from obtaining new health insurance coverage. Under the law, insurers may not deny coverage or impose pre-existing condition exclusions for more than 12 months for any condition diagnosed or treated in the preceding six months. This 12-month exclusion is a lifetime limit: No new pre-existing condition exclusions may be imposed on anyone who maintains continuous coverage.

The law ensures the availability of individual policies for employees who leave jobs voluntarily or involuntarily and for their dependents, applying only to those who had maintained continuous private coverage for the preceding 18 months and who were ineligible for further coverage under the Consolidated Omnibus Budget Reconciliation Act of 1985 (P.L. 99-272). It prohibits insurers from denying coverage or charging higher premiums to individuals in group plans who are in poor health. It also prohibits insurers from refusing to sell plans to small employers (with two to 50 employees). It makes long-term care expenses deductible for federal income tax purposes. Qualified long-term care expenses—both nursing home costs and home health care—would be treated like other medical costs (Families USA, 1996a).

Finally, P.L. 104-191 increases the deductibility of premiums for the self-employed. Over a 10-year period, the law gradually raises the percentage of health insurance premiums self-employed people can deduct from their federal income taxes to 80 percent from the present 30 percent.

Now the Bad News

This compromise law also includes some less desirable provisions. It allows for the creation of 750,000 tax-exempt MSAs, beginning in 1997, limited to self-employed and uninsured people and workers in businesses with fewer than 50 employees. It imposes some limits on the size of the tax break and taxes (with penalties) most nonmedical withdrawals from MSAs. After four years, congressional action would be required for further expansion of MSAs, but the Democrats fear that this privatized model has the potential to erode the very bases of social insurance and Medicare itself (Families USA, 1996a).

The law criminalizes transfers of assets to qualify for Medicaid, imposing fines of up to $10,000 and jail sentences of up to one year for those who "knowingly and willingly" transfer assets to qualify for Medicaid. This provision will have a chilling effect on people needing Medicaid to pay for nursing home services and will discourage many from applying for assistance. And nursing homes are likely to use it to discourage residents from applying for Medicaid. Also, for the first time, premiums for long-term care insurance will be deductible from federal income taxes up to certain specified limits (Families USA, 1996a). This costly and unnecessary tax break for higher-income individuals gives a significant stimulus to the private long-term care insurance industry.

Finally, P.L. 104-191 lets insurers sell policies duplicating benefits. It permits insurers selling long-term care policies to sell multiple policies to unsuspecting elderly people without disclosing that the plans duplicate benefits they already have (Families USA, 1996a).

What the Act Does Not Do

Although the Health Insurance Reform Act will help people with pre-existing conditions who have been denied coverage or who fear losing coverage, it does little to ensure that they can afford these policies. And it does not help those currently covered by individual policies; the limits on pre-existing condition exclusions apply only to those who have been enrolled in group plans.

Nor is there protection for mental health coverage. In its passage of the original bill, the Senate approved an amendment sponsored by Senators Pete Domenici (R-NM) and Paul Wellstone (D-MN) requiring that benefits for mental health and substance abuse be comparable to medical benefits. Fierce lobbying by the business community, who claimed it would increase costs drastically, killed the mental health provision in conference negotiations (Families USA, 1996a).

Most important, this legislation does nothing to help the uninsured millions of Americans who are not covered by their employers or by any public program and are still unable to afford private coverage. Their numbers are still growing at an alarming rate, and P.L. 104-191 will not change that reality one iota.

HOW WILL SOCIAL WORK ORGANIZATIONS IN HEALTH CARE RESPOND?

Last spring, anticipating the congressional outcomes described earlier, NASW hosted an unusual and unofficial summit meeting in Washington. With the political future still ominously uncertain, the April 14 meeting was attended by representatives of 20 health-related social work organizations. (Market principles prevailed: Only organizations that could afford to send a representative, or already had one in Washington, participated.) These health care organizations (Table 30-1) reflect the multifaceted nature of the profession and its variegated capacities to influence health care policy.

NASW's National Government Relations staff reported that they meet almost weekly with the American Public Health Association (APHA) and the American Hospital Association (AHA) to ensure close connections, because NASW's goals are not always the same as theirs (personal minutes taken April 14, 1996). Lobbying actions have had to be largely defensive this year, but normally the less visible issues, particularly regulation changes and administrative decisions, are where input from other social work organizations is especially valuable. Discussion at the summit meeting focused on these organizations' joint potential for communication, strategic actions, and professional standards setting. How might these organizations exchange information on a regular basis? Although most agreed that NASW should facilitate this, the venues were less clear. Exchange of newsletters is one way, as is use of the Internet, fax, and other print media. Information and technology cost money, as does face-to-face networking, but most participants felt that the latter has more meaningful impact.

How might organizations collaborate in responding to legislative and regulatory threats and opportunities in a timely way? This question evoked discussion of the importance of state-level activity and regional discussion and planning. Regional (substate and intrastate) communication networks have shown some substantial successes. For example, public health social workers in the South have asserted real, visible influence on states in the face of recent threats to public services, and the Internet was used to locate psychotraumatologists in response to the Oklahoma City bombing.

TABLE 30-1

National Social Work Organizations in Health Care

Organization	Address	Telephone No.	No. of Social Workers
Alcohol, Tobacco, and Other Drugs Section	NASW 750 First Street, NE, Suite 700 Washington, DC 20002-4241	(202) 408-8600	1,400+
APHA Social Work Section	American Public Health Association 1015 15th Street, NW Washington, DC 20005	(202) 789-4500	300
Association of State and Territorial Public Health Social Workers	c/o Washington State Department of Health 1511 Third Avenue, Suite 323 Seattle, WA 98101-1632	(206) 464-7132	100
National Resource Center on AIDS	Boston College Graduate School of Social Work Chestnut Hill, MA 02167	(617) 552-4038	serves all
National Association of Perinatal Social Workers	123 Cheat Canyon Park Drive Morgantown, WV 26505	(304) 598-4899	400+
Council of Nephrology Social Workers	National Kidney Foundation 30 East 33rd Street New York, NY 10016	(800) 622-9010	900 45 chapters
Federal Social Workers Consortium	P.O. Box 6622 Columbia, MD 21045-6622	(202) 762-3116	300+
National Federation of Societies for Clinical Social Work	P.O. Box 3740 Arlington, VA 22203	(703) 522-3866	11,000 34 state societies
Society for Social Work Administrators in Health Care	American Hospital Association One North Franklin Chicago, IL 60606	(312) 422-3771	2,100

Organization	Phone	Members
American Association of Spinal Cord Injury American Paraplegic Society Association of Spinal Cord Injury Nurse and social workers American Spinal Injury Association 75-20 Astoria Boulevard Jackson Heights, NY 11370-1177	(712) 803-3782	330 Psychologists
Association of Oncology Social Work Association of Pediatric Oncology Social Work 1901 East Jefferson Street Baltimore, MD 21205	(410) 614-3990	1,000+
Hospice Social Workers National Hospice Organization 1901 North Moore Street, Suite 901 Arlington, VA 22209	(703) 243-5900	400
American Network of Home Health Care Social Workers 1187 Wilmette Avenue Wilmette, IL 60091	(847) 853-9204	1,000
National Social Work AIDS Network c/o Harlem United Community AIDS Center 207 West 133rd Street New York, NY 10030	(212) 491-9000, ext. 101	125+

How can professional standards be maintained and made relevant to all these changing services? There was overriding concern in the summit and informal meetings about developments in managed care organizations. Little is known about the differential practice climates in corporations as opposed to nonprofit health maintenance organizations. Other concerns were expressed about new reimbursement requirements, functional assessment requirements, and the increasingly task-focused and outcomes-oriented expectations of the seamless health care organization. All this is becoming part of social work's technology. There was agreement that social work skills and identities in health care settings are changing rapidly, as are social work organizations themselves.

Some organizations are older than NASW—APHA and AHA were founded in 1872 and 1898, respectively, whereas several growing organizations began in the 1980s. (The Social Work Section of the APHA was started in 1970.) Hospice social workers organized in 1991, and the American Network of Home Care Social Workers (ANHCSW) was incorporated in 1995. After eight years in development, ANHCSW held its first ever national conference in Chicago in May, drawing an attendance of over 350. The National Social Work AIDS Network was founded in 1987.

A very large health care constituency was recently blended into the new NASW Section on Alcohol, Tobacco, and Other Drugs. Several organizations publish their own specialty journals, such as *Journal of Psychosocial Oncology*, *SCI (Spinal Cord Injury)*, *Psychosocial Process*, *Hospice Journal*, and *American Journal of Public Health*, and most publish regular newsletters.

The national political typhoon dissipates as a new and energetic executive director takes the reins at NASW's national office. With the combination of repressive welfare reductions and mythical health insurance requirements now facing social workers in literally every practice setting, today's health care organizations deserve the investment of every student and professional practitioner. Our own "individual accountability" cannot be complete without the collective informational resources these various organizations all bring to an issue. And our personal sense of responsibility, our consciences, cannot be satisfied without commitments to others' well-being before our own.

NASW serves as a vital umbrella, even though it sometimes disappoints advocates of specialized and targeted agendas in specialty health care practice. The detailed implications of the welfare and health insurance reforms are perfect examples of why NASW needs specialty input. Perinatal, nephrology, and oncology social workers all have seen how the burden on a young family of unpaid medical bills compounds the socioemotional difficulties they already face. All feel the pain when denial of prophylactics and education have resulted in unnecessary abortion or aggravated debilitating conditions like hypertension and AIDS. Social workers in public health and long-term care know why only some form of public, universal (rather than private) insurance will ever protect us all. To promote unpopular collective solutions, social workers need one voice across the whole nation. Poverty and welfare are everyone's issues, collective issues. Poverty does not produce anyone's paycheck; welfare provides for fewer and fewer.

Find the organization that represents you best, join it, and help ensure that your state has a functioning chapter. With membership you will receive relevant information about reforms in your state that affect your practice and your conscience. Your country (honor, duty, family, God) needs your contributions, now more than ever.

REFERENCES

Consolidated Omnibus Budget Reconciliation Act of 1985, P.L. 99-272, 100 Stat. 82.

Families USA. (1996a, August). Medical savings accounts limited to demonstration program: Kassebaum-Kennedy health insurance bill clears Congress. *a.s.a.p. Update.* (Available from Handsnet [Online service], Families USA Foundation, 1334 G Street, NW, Third Floor, Washington, DC 20005)

Families USA. (1996b, August). Safety net shredded as food, health, income support are cut. President says he will sign punitive welfare bill. *a.s.a.p. Update.* (Available from Handsnet [Online service], Families USA Foundation, 1334 G Street, NW, Third Floor, Washington, DC 20005)

Health Insurance Reform Act, P.L. 104-191 (1996).

Kotlowitz, A. (1996, August 12). Hit and myth. *New Republic,* p. 19.

National Health Law Program, National Center for Youth Law, & National Senior Citizens Law Center. (1996, August 12). *An analysis of welfare reform and its effects on Medicaid recipients.* (Available from Handsnet [Online service], Families USA Foundation, 1334 G Street, NW, Third Floor, Washington, DC 20005)

Personal Responsibility and Work Opportunity Reconciliation Act of 1996, P.L. 104-193.

Skocpol, T. (1996, August 12). Bury it. *New Republic,* 20–21.

Welfareasweknowit [Editorial]. (1996, August 12). *Nation,* p. 3.

This chapter was originally published in the November 1996 issue of Health & Social Work, *vol. 21, pp. 304–311.*

31 The Emerging Health Care World: Implications for Social Work Practice and Education

Barbara Berkman

The cost of health care in the United States is approaching $1 trillion a year, 15 percent of the gross national product (Shortell, Gillies, & Devers, 1995). Public and private entities are calling for reforms that will limit these rising costs. The acute care hospital, once the central institution of health care delivery, is particularly challenged by today's calls for controls. In response, the decentralization of expensive diagnostic services to out-of-hospital sites has accelerated, and the use of ambulatory care for procedures that were once done only on an inpatient basis has increased. These measures have resulted in cost savings by limiting the numbers of patients hospitalized and by reducing inpatient lengths of stay. Between 1984 and 1992 hospital admissions declined 11 percent and inpatient days 20 percent (Shortell et al., 1995). Currently, it is estimated that 98 percent of all medical encounters occur in nonhospital settings and that outpatient surgeries represent approximately 70 percent of all surgical procedures (Shortell et al., 1995). Empty inpatient beds have already contributed to the downsizing of hospital staff and the closing of facilities. Between 1980 and 1993, 949 hospitals closed (American Hospital Association [AHA], 1994). These dramatic changes in patient care delivery have been stimulated significantly by advances in technology and new approaches to the financing of health care, including managed care programs insuring specific populations.

GROWTH OF MANAGED CARE

"Managed care" refers to a number of organizational structures, various financing arrangements, and regulatory devices (Mechanic, Schlesinger, & McAlpine, 1995). The key idea underlying managed care is the limiting of unnecessary health service utilization by altering treatment processes in various ways: through budget restrictions and utilization controls, through financial incentives for providers to limit services, through case management review of treatment plans against pre-established criteria, and through the use of primary care physicians as gatekeepers for access to care (Mechanic et al., 1995; Society for Social Work Administrators in Health Care, 1994).

The use of managed care organizations for the administration of private medical benefits is a fast-growing trend. It is estimated that by the year 2000, 90 percent of all medical benefits administration will be handled by managed care organizations (White, Simmons, & Bixby, 1993). Physicians are challenged by the structural constraints and inherent limitations of managed care. Choices traditionally made exclusively within the patient–physician relationship are now made through the institutional arrangements of managed care (Rodwin, 1995). As a result, many providers are trying to treat patients at that point in the continuum of care at which the greatest value is added. For the most part, this point is outside of inpatient hospital services (Shortell et al., 1995).

Capitation

One particularly significant change in managed care financial arrangements is capitation. Under this form of payment, a provider system is paid a fixed amount to care for patients over a given period. In the fee-for-service payment system, greater volume is associated with more revenue. In the new world of capitation, revenue is earned up front when the care contract is negotiated on the basis of a predetermined amount of money per member per month for a defined population of enrollees (Shortell et al., 1995). Capitation is designed to provide an incentive to providers to keep patients healthy, thereby controlling the costs of patient care by staying within a budget. Although it is assumed that under capitation this flat fee will exceed the cost of some patients' care and be insufficient to cover the cost of others, it is expected that this cost differentiation will balance out and that the provider will be adequately reimbursed.

Although capitation arrangements currently account for only 7 percent of the revenues of hospitals and medical groups, capitation growth is projected to reach 17 percent over the next two years (Shortell et al., 1995). Even today, in some hospitals, 20 percent of revenue is attributed to capitation arrangements, and there are medical groups for which capitation represents over 50 percent of revenue (Shortell et al., 1995). It is anticipated that capitation will result in the creation of networks of integrated health care delivery in which a full spectrum of services from primary to specialized care will be offered at a fixed price (Moriarity, 1993; Pear, 1993). Many hospitals have already diversified into vertical integrated networks of care by expanding or adding group practices, ambulatory care centers, home health agencies, subacute care units, and hospices. For example, between 1980 and 1992 there was a 73 percent increase in the volume of outpatient visits (AHA, 1993). Between 1972 and 1990, the percentage of hospitals offering home health services increased from 6 percent to 36 percent, and the percentage of hospitals providing subacute inpatient care increased from 9 percent to 21 percent (Robinson, 1994).

Primary Care Physicians as Gatekeepers

Within these new health care delivery systems, primary care physicians are important gatekeepers who monitor and coordinate their patients' health care. They are expected by insurers to control the access of patients to both specialized medical care and necessary community-based social and health care resources (Cassell, 1995). Unfortunately, the medical and nonmedical service systems have operated as separated and fragmented entities, raising increased concerns about accessibility, efficiency, and comprehensiveness of health care services (Itano, Williams, Deaton, & Oishi, 1991).

OLD AND NEW HEALTH CARE PARADIGMS

Traditionally, the U.S. health care system has been based on a paradigm of un-predictable acute simple disease. This model has become increasingly inappro-priate as increasing numbers of patients are presenting with multiple, chronic health problems. These patients, particularly those who are elderly, will be in-creasingly at risk of losing their ability to function independently and of living with frailty. The leading causes of morbidity and mortality are almost all related to chronic, complex processes. For example, pneumonia, once perceived pri-marily as an acute illness, is now frequently perceived as an episode in a chronic disease process such as obstructive lung disease or HIV infection (Pawlson, 1994).

In the new health care paradigm of chronic, complex illness, episodes of need for care tend to be relatively more predictable (Pawlson, 1994), and there is the recognition that chronic illnesses are determined by multiple factors, such as an individual's social, psychological, and physical environment; genetic makeup; and health care accessibility factors (Evans, 1994; Syme, 1994). The view that illness is a chronic process raises the question of whether an acute episode could have been prevented, placing much more importance on patients as consumers and partici-pants in determining their health care service needs. The focus of care is logically on primary care with an emphasis on disease prevention and health promotion (Pawlson, 1994). Screening for patients at risk for physical, social, or psychologi-cal regression becomes much more essential in this new model, and the timing of intervention by health care professionals becomes paramount.

SOCIAL WORK'S ROLE IN HEALTH CARE

Within the acute care model, illness is depicted as a single isolated event, with the patient hospitalized, treated, and discharged. It is therefore understandable that the role of the social worker in this framework was predominantly as a part of hospital inpatient services focusing on the discharge of patients and on out-comes related to reducing both lengths of stay and premature rehospitalization through provision of necessary posthospital care services and resources. Con-versely, the chronic complex illness model assumes multiple contributing fac-tors, with the basis of illness being biopsychosocial and the relationship among the health care systems being continuous. For this model to succeed, the hospi-tal must become part of a primary care network of community-oriented social services delivery systems focused on broad aspects of health care and chronic disease management (Shortell et al., 1995). This requires the restructuring of the caregiving process. The biggest challenge to this restructuring (or "clinical re-engineering," as it is often called) lies in managing multiple, complex, chronic illnesses that require a continuum of care and treatments from multiple profes-sionals in various settings. In this model, the social worker's role should be throughout the continuum of care.

At present the health care system is not adequately prepared to handle the de-mands and complexity of the psychosocial health care needs of the increasing num-bers of chronically ill ambulatory patients. Whereas primary care physicians have traditionally participated in the episodic phases of chronic illness, their physiologi-cal orientation within the acute care medical model is too restrictive in terms of the overall health concerns of their patients, making it difficult for them to play a major role in managing the patients' continuing complex needs. Concomitantly, they are often unfamiliar with the range of available nonmedical home and community-based services (Zawadski & Eng, 1988). Making in-depth psycho-social–environmental assessments; working with compliance issues; engaging the family and other support systems; and referring patients to needed services such as home health care, physical therapy, occupational therapy, financial services, day care, nursing homes, and meal and transportation services can best be addressed through the involvement and collaboration of social workers. Screening hospitalized inpatients' need for social work services has helped social workers be more effective in hospitals by making case finding more proactive (Berkman, Rehr, & Rosenberg, 1980). Similarly, in outpatient settings, screening and assessment by social workers can help increase the awareness of psychosocial and environmental issues that affect a patient's condition and lead to effective early interventions.

The biopsychosocial approach of social work in health care provides a carefully balanced perspective that takes into account the entire person in his or her environment and helps social workers assess the needs of an individual from a multidimensional point of view. Biopsychosocial assessments are going to play an increasingly important role in health planning and clinical practice. With the goals of maintaining patients' viability to live in independent settings and enhancing quality of life, greater attention is being given to standardized screening tools that use predictive factors to yield standardized scores, which lead to an assessment of at-risk patients' social health care needs.

Clinical Specialists

Dramatic changes in health care delivery have already affected the practice of social work, particularly in hospitals. Recently, the Society for Social Work Administrators in Health Care and NASW conducted a national research project to study the current impact of social work on these fast-moving changes (Berger et al., 1996). This research found that, indeed, social work clinical activity in ambulatory care is increasing but is not commensurate with the hospitals' movement toward service delivery in ambulatory care.

Departments of social work are moving away from traditional linear management, which includes directors, associate directors, assistant directors, and various other levels of managers and supervisors, to self-managed team approaches in which there are fewer managerial staff. The national study by Berger et al. (1996) noted that although there are anecdotal reports of decentralization of social work services, their data do not suggest this to be a major trend in the structure of social work services. Although this study sheds light on the effects of changes in health care on social work, we do not know the full impact of managed care development as it will influence restructuring and resizing activities.

Although the total number of health care professionals, including social workers, participating in hospital-based services will decrease because of reduced inpatient beds, a significant role for social workers in health care services still exists—that of clinical specialists, sophisticated and adaptable practitioners who can work flexibly under minimal supervision. Primary care physicians, as well as medical specialists, need the skills of social workers to handle the psychosocial and environmental aspects of illness. It is becoming more common to hear that mental states play an important role in recovery from physical illness (Chiacchia, 1993; Mumford, Schlesinger, & Glass, 1982; Williams, 1990). Concomitantly, psychological states and stimuli may have a direct influence on somatic function (Katon & Schulberg, 1992; Schnall et al., 1990). Neither medical specialists nor primary care physicians will have adequate knowledge of or training in the recognition or treatment of mental disorders such as mild depression or anxiety, which can have a negative effect on the patient's recovery from illness and his or her ability to follow necessary chronic care regimens (Magruder-Habib, Zung, & Feussner, 1990).

The social worker can be the member of the health care team, either inpatient or outpatient, who has the knowledge and skills to identify patients in need of the psychosocial help necessary to change negative behaviors and thus stop progression toward disability. Specifically, social workers are needed

- to help determine if the patient and family can manage the recommended treatment or discharge plan
- to counsel and support patients and significant others who are emotionally distraught (for example, as a result of a diagnosis or bereavement)
- to assist patients and families with decision making around ethical issues
- to educate patients and significant others regarding psychosocial issues in adjusting and responding to illness and to necessary role changes
- to assist in resolving behavioral problems that impede the ability of the patient and family to make decisions
- to assist in identifying and obtaining entitlement benefits
- to assist in identifying and obtaining nonmedical community resources
- to assist the health care team in resolving patient and family behavioral problems that impede the team's ability to care for the hospitalized patient
- to provide risk management by intervening with patients and families who are dissatisfied with their care
- to offer consultation to providers around behavioral and emotional issues.

Case Managers

In the role of case manager or care coordinator, social workers provide interventions that are short term and intensive with the goal of creating the support systems necessary to enhance and maintain social functioning (Williams, Warrick, Christianson, & Netting, 1993). Social workers have historically focused on transactions between individuals and the environment from a biopsychosocial perspective in an attempt to improve the quality of life for the individual in terms of psychosocial functioning (Hartman, 1991; Zayas & Dyche, 1992). The social work case manager addresses both the individual client's biopsychosocial status and the state of the social system in which he or she operates. It is in this position, which focuses on screening and assessing the needs of the client and the client's family, that the case manager also arranges, coordinates, monitors, evaluates, and advocates for a package of multiple services to meet the specific client's complex needs (NASW, 1992). To this end, early intervention, such as screening of patients by social workers, may determine the existence of depression, delay the physical deterioration of the patient, and help prevent hospitalization (Berkman et al., 1996; Lockery, Dunkle, Kart, & Coulton, 1994).

Furthermore, social workers can help physicians identify patients' needs more appropriately and define their problems more specifically (Azzarto, 1993; Dobrof, Umpierre, Rocha, & Silverton, 1990; Eggert, Zimmer, Hall, & Friedman, 1991; Fielden, 1992; Mayer et al., 1990; Morrow-Howell, 1992; NASW, 1992; Oktay, Steinwachs, Mamon, Bone, & Fahey, 1992; Seltzer, Litchfield, Kapust, & Mayer, 1992). For example, studies have found that somatization can be reduced with case management involvement. By addressing the social and emotional needs of patients, social work case managers are able to alleviate the demand for time and attention that such patients place on their physicians (Azzarto, 1993; Colone, 1993). In addition, the social work case manager, under managed care, must be able to manage the benefits available to the patient by understanding what services are available, what their costs are, what the benefit limitations are, and which benefits are cost-effective.

Efficiency in interdisciplinary collaboration for effective patient care both within the institution and in the community at large is a necessary practice skill for all health care professionals. Collaboration with community agencies and with programs for patients with particular diseases, including nursing and home care services, local community programs, hospices, and support groups, is even more essential for optimum social work case management practice. Neither the doctor nor the nurse has the knowledge necessary to assess social services needs or to secure and coordinate community-based services. Central to collaborative practice is the establishment of effective means of communication among all disciplines. Communication skills, particularly in conveying information electronically, are necessary.

Another important role of the case manager is to provide information about public or private resources available to clients and about ways to gain access to these resources. Social workers are trained to be aware of and use community resources to make the environment on all levels more supportive and enabling for the individual. The social worker, as case manager, is able to identify gaps in services that the client is receiving (Loomis, 1988) and has been shown to be successful in linking patients, particularly elderly ones, to the services they need (Colone, 1993; Howell, 1992; Oktay et al., 1992; White et al., 1993). Clinical case management is particularly important in gerontological social work because of the multiple problems that elderly people face and their need for supports and resources (Morrow-Howell, 1992).

Is the social worker, as a case manager or care coordinator, cost-effective? Although more research is needed to ascertain exact savings, social workers can reduce costs by means of preventive measures (Azzarto, 1993; Gropper, 1988; Loomis, 1988). Early intervention, decreased rates of hospital readmissions, and decreased emergency department visits are enormously cost-effective (Colone, 1993; Dobrof et al., 1990; Eggert et al., 1991; Migchelbrink, Anderson, Schultz, & St. Charles, 1993; Oktay et al., 1992; Wofford, Schwartz, & Byrum, 1993). Adding a social worker to a primary care practice can result in significant financial benefits for the physician. Medicare considers each patient visit as potentially billable, so a physician can free up valuable billable hours when the social worker has relieved the doctor of the need to spend time providing attention and arranging home care services, family meetings, and the like (Azzarto, 1993; Colone, 1993; personal communication with S. Shearer, program manager, Senior Care Network, Huntington Memorial Hospital, Pasadena, CA, May 10, 1996). The use of social workers to attend to the psychosocial needs of patients also benefits insurance providers because costs are decreased significantly when mental health problems are detected early. For example, early detection of mental health problems can result in the decreased likelihood that patients will misuse medical appointments for psychosocial problems (Azzarto, 1993; Clarke, Neuwirth, & Bernstein, 1986; Colone, 1993; Dobrof et al., 1990; Gropper, 1988; Loomis, 1988). Studies are needed that specifically operationalize social work interventions and tie their services to specific outcomes, including indicators of cost-effectiveness.

Benefits

The presence of a social worker in a primary care outpatient setting provides several therapeutic benefits to patients and physicians. When a social worker is able to share information about a patient's social problem, the physician is able to provide more comprehensive care. Having someone with sufficient mental health practice competency in a medical practice allows the physician to see more patients with emotional problems (Williams & Clare, 1979), thus widening the range of patients in the practice. The physician has the support of the social worker's skills when patients' presenting physical symptoms are secondary to social and emotional issues. Hence, the physician can deal with the medical aspects of care without neglecting the social and psychological needs of his or her patients (Robertson, 1992). In addition to outpatient primary care offices, there are many excellent avenues for offering outpatient case management, such as geriatric assessment clinics, mental health services, health satellite clinics, alcohol and substance abuse programs, home health care services, outreach programs, and wellness programs. There are also specialty centers for people with neurologic disorders, organ transplant patients, and oncology patients, to name a few (Rango & Kunes, 1995).

Another important aspect of social work health care services involves family members. The importance of balancing the client's capacities with informal help and formal structures so as to maximize client functioning cannot be overstated (Morrow-Howell, 1992). The social worker who is conversant in medical terminology can relate to providers and is able to explain medical jargon to patients and their families (American Hospital Association Council, 1987; Applebaum & Christianson, 1988). Assessing the relationship between the patient and caregiver is important because of the potential for caregiver burnout. A knowledgeable social worker can assess for this possibility and offer respite services. Knowing about the existence of respite services may also enable the patient to use informal support systems more fully and enable family members to be more willing and more effective in assisting their sick family member and improving his or her quality of life (Seltzer et al., 1992; Sizemore, Bennett, & Anderson, 1989).

Legal and Ethical Issues

The practice of social workers either as clinical specialists or case managers involves decisions that have legal and ethical considerations, primarily around the prolongation of life and dilemmas relative to providing information about specific types of illnesses or social concerns. In addition, the allocation of limited resources can be a source of ethical conflicts. There are no clear answers to many questions raised by new medical technologies, new illnesses, or new resource restrictions. These clinical decisions must be addressed by all health care practitioners. In addition, social workers as case managers are beginning to discuss advance directives with patients while they are in the primary care setting, before an emergency life-or-death medical crisis (Berkman et al., in press).

ROLE OF SOCIAL WORK EDUCATION

Social work practitioners must be independent players who assume a significant role on the health care team. Their training should be dynamic, addressing the changing health care environment with an anticipation of tomorrow's advances (Berkman et al., in press). Social workers will be needed who are trained to work together as members of a team in which they are able to address the needs of patients for preventive, curative, and rehabilitative services. Interdisciplinary education for advanced students should be a core component of all health professional education programs, both practicum based and school based.

The knowledge and skills required for practice as a clinical specialist in health care are well documented (Berkman et al., 1990). School-based and hospital-based models for developing a program to teach this knowledge and skills are also available (Berkman & Carlton, 1985; Caroff & Mailick, 1980). In light of the rapidly evolving changes in health care practices, it is all the more critical to review the knowledge base needed for specialist social workers and to make it a priority to learn the knowledge that is essential for both today's and tomorrow's health care world.

Theoretical Framework

The theoretical framework necessary for practice in health care should not emphasize psychopathology but instead should focus on the adaptive capacities of patients and significant others with the goals of preventing maladaptive behavior and enhancing recovery. The emphasis of practice in health care is on enhancement of coping. Pre-existing emotional problems are a focus of intervention only to the extent that they compromise coping, not as primary illnesses to be treated in and of themselves. The framework for practice in health care must include an understanding of the interaction among psychological, social, cognitive, and biological factors.

A unique critical skill necessary for social workers in health care practice is the ability to integrate physiological data. This skill is as important to social work assessment and practice as the ability to integrate psychodynamic data. The issue for education is to create an understanding of how the psychological and biological interact physiologically and behaviorally. Social work specialists must have the tools to advance their understanding and use of biomedical knowledge. For social workers to offer optimal help to patients and families, they must have knowledge of the specificity of the illness or disease and its effect. They should be able to use the numerous sources of current medical data and have an understanding of the questions that must be asked about each patient. This is particularly relevant given that advances in health care technology significantly affect patients physiologically, psychologically, and socially. At the same time it is equally important to understand the patient and family perceptions of the disease (its causes and its cures), to be able to identify common and uncommon psychosocial needs of patients and families, and to understand how they will cope with the illness. Students must enter the health care setting with an understanding of how to get the information they need. There will be little time for mentoring, and supervision will be minimal. MSW programs must provide students with a framework to enable them to understand what information is needed and how to get it.

Practice Skills

In health care practice, the social worker must be competent in using the most helpful modes of individual, family, and group therapies at the various stages of illness. During the past several decades, practice courses in master's-level education programs typically have been structured to encompass general principles that are applicable to a variety of settings. Although these generic principles are certainly basic to the learning needs of the health care trainee, preparation for actual field experience is often less than adequate. Therefore, a number of practice issues must be addressed.

The health care specialist must be able to design treatment interventions based on an assessment of the problems facing an individual or family within the specific context of the disease or disability, giving consideration to internal and external resources. In the health care setting, the emphasis is on enhancing the patient's and family's ability to cope with health problems. This may involve strengthening social support, mobilizing external resources (for example, by means of advocacy, provision of concrete services, or involvement of family and community resources), or strengthening internal resources (for example, through clarification, education of the individual and family about the illness and its implications, priority setting, and regulation of the tempo of the coping activity). Although MSW educational programs generally teach these interventions, the specific context of health care delivery systems and the context of disease and disability must also be integrated.

An important aspect of clinical work in health care is the element of uncertainty confronting increasing numbers of families as technological developments in medicine transform life-threatening diseases into chronic illnesses. An area that deserves more attention by MSW programs is the use of systemic work to better understand and intervene more effectively with families stricken by chronic illness (Leahey & Wright, 1985). Courses in chronic illness interventions should be a major focus of health care curricula. Working within a family systems perspective can be especially useful in opening lines of communication, helping family members support each other in the tension of the uncertainty, and dealing with lack of synchrony when it occurs.

There is growing acknowledgment of and use of groups in helping patients and families. Group work is significant for intervention in health care settings. Most groups in health care are used to provide information and support to their members in an effort to increase coping skills and thereby foster some behavioral change (Berkman et al., in press).

Context of Health Care

There is a significant role for social workers in primary care in the coordination of nonmedical services, particularly in the community. These efforts at providing linkages with needed services save time for doctors, nurses, and patients by enabling faster access to needed care and thus can improve consumer relations (White et al., 1993). This clinical specialist role, or "case management" as it is called, has been given little attention in current social work curricula.

An emerging structure of health care is that of patient-focused care: a patient-centered and clinically driven approach to care from preadmission through posthospitalization (Clancy, 1994; Parsons & Murdaugh, 1994). There are key elements present in patient-focused care models, including decentralization of services with self-contained patient units, clinical pathway (practice protocol) development, multiskilled workers and cross training, and organizational restructuring. Social workers, as part of interdisciplinary work teams, will have minimal supervision once licensure requirements are met. Interdisciplinary teamwork requires communication skills, both electronic and written, and an understanding of the roles and functions of core and consultative team members.

Managed care uses new tools such as clinical pathways to ensure that patient care complies with predetermined standards. Clinical pathways delineate profession–specific responsibilities in assessment and care and describe the nature of team interactions, time frames for intervention, and processes and resources by case type. Beginning with the patient's entry into the health care system, the clinical pathway also establishes review procedures that measure patient outcomes. Social workers will be expected, and will want, to participate in the development of these clinical pathways so as to define more clearly their role in patient care delivery (Colone, 1993). Although clinical pathways generally have been developed for inpatient services, there is some initial movement into primary care. The ability to conceptualize social work interventions and expected outcomes is a critical practice skill.

THE FUTURE

What does this transition in the American health care system mean for social work practice and education? What are the fundamental issues that social workers should be considering? Instead of thinking primarily in terms of acute inpatient care delivery and discharge planning, which has been the main focus of social work delivery since the advent of Medicare, social workers must now think of redistributing their services within the continuum of care. Instead of treating acute care illness episodes, social workers must offer services that are oriented toward the goals of disease prevention and health promotion. Instead of caring for individual patients, social workers should be accountable for the health status of vulnerable at-risk populations such as elderly people, people infected with HIV, abused children and adults, victims of domestic violence, and pediatric oncology patients. Instead of thinking primarily of inpatient specialty services, social workers must now think of ambulatory care services, emphasizing primary care and ongoing health care management of chronic illnesses. Finally, for those who will still be needed to work with inpatient issues, social workers must shift their focus from discharge planning to thinking in terms of what patient care issues require their services. Social workers must determine when they are the primary health care professional with the skills to deal with specific issues, such as resolving behavioral problems, that impede the ability of the patient and family members to manage recommended treatment or discharge plans. Thus, instead of thinking in terms of inpatient beds and covering beds, social workers must think about covering care at the appropriate level, and instead of managing a department, they must manage a market (for example, dysfunctional families who hinder patient care and recovery) and promote their services throughout the hospital and within the community (Shortell et al., 1995).

Although social work education has placed greater emphasis in past years on the psychological and interpersonal elements of social functioning, there is a growing substantive argument for the inclusion of both biomedical- and psychological-based knowledge as the necessary thrust of social work education. The recent trend in health care toward increased diagnostic and treatment specialization has led to the formation of social work specialty groups such as oncology social workers, renal disease social workers, HIV/AIDS workers, heart and lung transplant workers, and neonatal workers. This trend reflects the awareness that specialized, diagnostically specific knowledge and skills of both a psychodynamic and physiological nature are required for truly valued social work practice in health care.

It is evident to those who practice in health care that the content areas conceptualized as necessary in advanced health curricula must encompass a blend of cultural, social, psychological, environmental, spiritual, and biological dimensions of social functioning. The bottom line is that a strong social work specialist in health care is one who is not easily overwhelmed by organizational complexities; who is knowledgeable about and comfortable around sophisticated state-of-the-art medical care; who is able to be flexible, creative, and a leader in service delivery both in the hospital and in the community; and who can work collaboratively as a key member of the health care team. As the face of health care changes dramatically toward outpatient care for complex medical situations, social work must also expand its focus of concern and articulate a new vision for itself.

REFERENCES

American Hospital Association. (1993). *Hospital statistics* (1993–1994 ed.). Chicago: Author.
American Hospital Association. (1994). *Hospital closures: 1980 through 1993. A statistical profile.* Chicago: Health Care Information Resources Group.
American Hospital Association Council. (1987, Fall). Case management: An aid to quality and continuity of care. *AHA Council Report*, pp. 1–11.

Applebaum, R., & Christianson, J. (1988). Using case management to monitor community-based long-term care. *Quality Review Bulletin, 14*(7), 227–231.

Azzarto, J. (1993). The socioemotional needs of elderly family practice patients: Can social workers help? *Health & Social Work, 18,* 40–48.

Berger, C. S., Cayner J., Jensen, G., Mizrahi, T., Scesny, A., & Trachtenberg, J. (1996). The changing scene of social work in hospitals: A report of a national study by the Society for Social Work Administrators in Health Care and NASW. *Health & Social Work, 21,* 163–173.

Berkman, B., Bonander, E., Kemler, B., Isaacson-Rubinger, M. J., Rutchick, I., & Silverman, P. (in press). Social work in the academic medical center: Advanced training—A necessity. *Social Work in Health Care.*

Berkman, B., Bonander, E., Rutchick, R., Silverman, P., Kemler, B., Marcus, L., & Isaacson-Rubinger, M. J. (1990). Social work in health care: Directions in practice. *Social Science and Medicine, 31*(1), 19–26.

Berkman, B., & Carlton, T. (1985). *The development of health social work curricula: Patterns and process in three programs of social work education.* Boston: Massachusetts General Hospital, Institute of Health Professions.

Berkman, B., Rehr, H., & Rosenberg, G. (1980). A social work department develops and tests a screening mechanism to identify high social risk situations. *Social Work in Health Care, 5*(4), 373–386.

Berkman, B., Shearer, S., Simmons, J., White, M., Robinson, M., Sampson, S., Holmes, W., Allison, D., & Thomson, J. (1996). Ambulatory elderly patients of primary care physicians: Functional, psychosocial and environmental predictors of need for social work care management. *Social Work in Health Care, 22*(3), 1–20.

Caroff, P., & Mailick, M., with Fields, G. (Eds.). (1980). *Social work in health services: An academic practice partnership.* New York: Prodist.

Cassell, E. J. (1995). Teaching the fundamentals of primary care: A point of view. *Milbank Quarterly, 73,* 373–405.

Chiacchia, K. B. (1993). Link is found between nerves and immune cells. *Harvard Medical Area Focus, 20,* 1, 4.

Clancy, C. (1994). Patient-focused care: Part 1. Danger or opportunity? *Social Work Administration, 20*(4), 2–6.

Clarke, S. S., Neuwirth, L., & Bernstein, R. H. (1986). An expanded social work role in a university hospital-based group practice: Service provider, physician educator, and organizational consultant. *Social Work in Health Care, 11*(4), 1–16.

Colone, M. A. (1993). Case management and managed care: Balancing quality and cost control. *Social Work Administration, 19*(3), 6–13.

Dobrof, J., Umpierre, M., Rocha, L., & Silverton, M. (1990). Group work in a primary care medical setting. *Health & Social Work, 15,* 32–37.

Eggert, G. M., Zimmer, J. G., Hall, W. J., & Friedman, B. (1991). Case management: A randomized controlled study comparing a neighborhood team and a centralized individual model. *Health Services Research, 26,* 497–505.

Evans, R. C. (1994). Health care as a threat to health: Defense, opulence and the social environment. *Health and Wealth, 123*(4), 21–42.

Fielden, M. (1992). Depression in older adults: Psychological and psychosocial approaches. *British Journal of Social Work, 22,* 291–307.

Gropper, M. (1988). A study of the preferences of family practitioners and other primary care physicians in treating patients' psychosocial problems. *Social Work in Health Care, 13*(2), 75–91.

Hartman, A. (1991). Social worker in situation. *Social Work, 36,* 195–196.

Howell, N. (1992). Clinical case management: The hallmark of gerontological social work. *Geriatric Social Work Education, 18*(3–4), 119–131.

Itano, J., Williams, J., Deaton, M., & Oishi, N. (1991). Impact of a student interdisciplinary oncology team project. *Journal of Cancer Education, 6,* 219–226.

Katon, W., & Schulberg, H. (1992). Epidemiology of depression in primary care. *General Hospital Psychiatry, 14,* 237–245.

Leahey, M., & Wright, L. (1985). Intervening with families with chronic illness. *Family Systems Medicine, 3*(1), 60–69.

Lockery, S. A., Dunkle, R. E., Kart, C. S., & Coulton, C. J. (1994). Factors contributing to the early rehospitalization of elderly people. *Health & Social Work, 19,* 182–191.

Loomis, J. F. (1988). Case management in health care. *Health & Social Work, 13,* 219–225.

Magruder-Habib, K., Zung, W.W.K., & Feussner, J. R. (1990). Improving physicians' recognition and treatment of depression in general medical care. *Medical Care, 28,* 239–250.

Mayer, J. B., Kapust, L. R., Mulcahey, A. L., Helfand, L., Heinlein, A. N., Seltzer, M., Mailick, L., Leon, C., & Levin, R. (1990). Empowering families of the chronically ill: A partnership experience in a hospital setting. *Social Work in Health Care, 14*(4), 73–91.

Mechanic, D., Schlesinger, M., & McAlpine, D. D. (1995). Management of mental health and substance abuse services: State of the art and early results. *Milbank Quarterly, 73,* 19–55.

Migchelbrink, D., Anderson, D., Schultz, P., & St. Charles, C. (1993). Care management model: One hospital's experience. *Nursing Administration Quarterly, 17*(3), 45–53.

Moriarity, J. (1993). The university hospital: Will new strategies keep it in the game? *Minnesota Medicine, 76*(4), 16–23.

Morrow-Howell, N. (1992). Clinical case management: The hallmark of gerontological social work. *Journal of Gerontological Social Work, 18*(3–4), 119–131.

Mumford, E., Schlesinger, H. J., & Glass, G. V. (1982). The effect of psychological intervention on recovery from surgery and heart attacks: An analysis of the literature. *American Journal of Public Health, 72,* 141–151.

National Association of Social Workers. (1992). *NASW standards for social work case management.* Washington, DC: Author.

Oktay, J. S., Steinwachs, D. M., Mamon, J., Bone, J. R., & Fahey, M. (1992). Evaluating social work discharge planning for elderly people: Access, complexity, and outcome. *Health & Social Work, 17,* 290–298.

Parsons, M. L., & Murdaugh, C. (Eds.). (1994). *Patient-centered care: A model for restructuring.* Gaithersburg, MD: Aspen Publishers.

Pawlson, L. G. (1994). Chronic illness: Implications of a new paradigm for health care. *Joint Commission Journal on Quality Improvement, 20*(1), 33–39.

Pear, R. (1993, August 21). Health industry is moving to form service networks. *New York Times,* p. A1.

Rango, R., & Kunes, C. (1995). Outpatient case management: A role for social work. *Social Work Administration, 21,* 3–6.

Robertson, D. (1992). The roles of health care teams in care of the elderly. *Family Medicine, 24,* 136–141.

Robinson, J. C. (1994). The changing boundaries of the American hospital. *Milbank Quarterly, 72,* 259–275.

Rodwin, M. A. (1995). Conflicts in managed care. *New England Journal of Medicine, 32,* 604–607.

Schnall, P. L., Pieper, C., Schwartz, J. E., Karasek, R. A., Schlussel, Y., Devereux, R. B., Ganau, A., Alderman, M., Warren, K., & Pickering, T. G. (1990). The relationship between "job strain," workplace diastolic blood pressure, and left ventricular mass index: Results of a case-control study [published erratum appears in *Journal of the American Medical Association, 267,* 1209]. *Journal of the American Medical Association, 263,* 1929–1935.

Seltzer, M., Litchfield, L., Kapust, L., & Mayer, J. (1992). Professional and family collaboration in case management: A hospital-based replication of a community-based study. *Social Work in Health Care, 17*(1), 1–22.

Shortell, S. M., Gillies, R. R., & Devers, K. J. (1995). Reinventing the American hospital. *Milbank Quarterly, 73,* 131–160.

Sizemore, M. T., Bennett, B. E., & Anderson, R. J. (1989). Public hospital-based geriatric case management. *Journal of Gerontological Social Work, 13*(3–4), 167–179.

Society for Social Work Administrators in Health Care. (1994, July). *A special report of the managed care task force.* Chicago: Author.

Syme, S. L. (1994). The social environment and health. *Health and Wealth, 123*(4), 79–86.

White, M., Simmons, W. J., & Bixby, N. (1993). Managed care and case management: An overview. *Discharge Planning Update, 13*(1), 17–19.

Williams, F. G., Warrick, L. H., Christianson, J. B., & Netting, F. E. (1993). Critical factors for successful hospital-based case management. *Health Care Management Review, 18*(1), 63–70.

Williams, P., & Clare, A. (1979). Social workers in primary health care: The general practitioner's viewpoint. *Journal of the Royal College of General Practitioners, 29,* 554–558.

Williams, R. B. (1990). The role of the brain in physical disease: Folklore, normal science, or paradigm shift? *Journal of the American Medical Association, 263,* 1971–1972.

Wofford, J., Schwartz, E., & Byrum, J. (1993). The role of emergency services in health care for the elderly: A review. *Journal of Emergency Medicine, 11,* 317–326.

Zawadski, R. T., & Eng, C. (1988). Case management in capitated long term care. *Health Care Financing Review* (Annual Suppl.), 75–81.

Zayas, L. H., & Dyche, L. A. (1992). Social workers training primary care physicians: Essential psychosocial principles. *Social Work, 37,* 247–252.

This chapter was originally published in the September 1996 issue of Social Work, *vol. 41, pp. 541–551.*

32

NAFTA, American Health, and Mexican Health: They Tie Together

Dennis L. Poole

At first glance, the North Atlantic Free Trade Agreement (NAFTA) seems to have little to do with health social work in America. The treaty was widely publicized as a pact that opens the economies of industrialized nations (United States and Canada) to a major Third World country (Mexico). It is a type of Marshall Plan in reverse. By liberalizing the movement of goods, services, and capital, NAFTA would help Mexico pay back its debt to these nations.

But closer scrutiny of the treaty unveils another scenario. Two years after the implementation of NAFTA, it is clear that the treaty will have major health and social consequences for people living in this hemisphere. Indeed, history may judge NAFTA as one of the most important social policy decisions of the United States this century.

Although NAFTA brings many risks, the treaty also offers great opportunities for international healing and partnerships. Both are long overdue, especially between citizens of the United States and citizens of Mexico. Many American social workers in health care and other fields have begun the healing process already by forming coalitions and networks with Mexican colleagues and organizations. They know firsthand that American health and Mexican health are inextricably tied. This was evident at the Third International Conference of Social Work, sponsored last summer by the National School of Social Work in Mexico. Appropriately titled "Civil Society: Catharsis or Mobilization?" the conference was strikingly different from most recent social work conferences. The major issues were not managed care, budget cutbacks, and block grants, but democracy, social justice, and civil society.

CIVIL SOCIETY AND HEALTH

Although civil society seldom gets mentioned in American social work literature, the quest for it has much to do with recent changes in health and social services. In the United States, the term "civil society" was established most effectively by Berger and Neuhaus (1977) in the classic *To Empower People*, which entered "mediating structures" into the vernacular of policymakers and professionals. *Mediating structures* are institutions such as families, churches, synagogues, voluntary associations, and neighborhoods that come between individuals and the state. Berger and Neuhaus argued that these structures are essential for a vital democratic society and that public policy should foster and protect these institutions to achieve social goals. A generation of policymakers was later influenced by this view. They believe that mediating structures can, and should, play a pivotal role in social welfare. Hence, decentralization, localism, and non-government interventions rivet their policy-making agendas, which have achieved some success in recent years. Indeed, the movement of many health social workers from institution-based to community-based services stems, in part, from the quest of these policymakers to strengthen civil society in America. They want government to do less and mediating structures to do more in the delivery of services to individuals and families.

But the quest for civil society holds special significance for Mexican health social workers. Because the Mexican constitution explicitly recognizes the civic right to health protection, the national health system is largely governmental. Only 4 percent of the country's population of 90 million people purchase health care through the private sector; everyone else gets care at government hospitals and public clinics (Frenk et al., 1994). As a result, virtually all Mexican health social workers are public employees.

Being employed by the government can put health social workers in a tough position. The Mexican political system cannot be considered democratic. It operates largely as a centralized, one-party state with an extremely powerful presidency and subordinate legislative and judicial branches. The party in power, the Institutional Revolutionary Party (PRI), has run the national government since 1928 and is often charged with vote-rigging and civil rights violations (Heredia, 1994). Hence, political advocacy and social reform efforts carry much risk for health social workers in Mexico who earn their living from the government.

NAFTA has helped to change this situation in ways that were not expected or intended. In the early 1990s, when the Mexican government formed the NAFTA Advisory Council, only PRI-affiliated groups were represented. The Business Organizations for Foreign Trade was assigned public responsibility for coordinating the NAFTA effort. Government officials maintained that NAFTA was an economic issue; the treaty would create jobs and foster economic opportunities in Mexico. Workers, poor people, small farmers, and nongovernmental organizations were generally excluded from the NAFTA agenda-building process because they were not PRI-affiliated or were unlikely to reap benefits from the treaty for a long time (Heredia, 1994). In fact, small farmers and the rural poor population were not expected to fare well under the treaty initially. Early drafts of the trade pact called for a complete overhaul of the land tenure system in Mexico, including cutting agricultural subsidies to traditional farming communities and removing the constitutional guarantee of land grants to indigenous farmers. Revising this system would encourage foreign investors and corporate farmers to purchase land, which provides 70 percent of the nation's rural poor population with sustenance (Cavise, 1994).

The realization that the treaty would have dire consequences for the nation's rural poor population unleashed a supranational, nongovernment movement that has made true democratic reform in Mexico imperative. The movement—which social workers in cross-national coalitions joined—forced changes in the

NAFTA pact to reflect a shared commitment to democratic practices and a respect for civil rights. These changes have put Mexico under greater international scrutiny, and they have increased the influence of nongovernment groups in domestic policy-making.

In this respect, NAFTA provided the political groundwork for the Third International Conference of Social Work, which allowed participants to address substantive issues related to democracy, social justice, and civil society in Mexico. The conference, in turn, directed attention to NAFTA-related challenges and opportunities, including health concerns at the U.S.–Mexico border.

BORDER HEALTH

Indeed, NAFTA has unleashed events that will dramatically affect health in Mexico and the United States, especially in border communities. One event is the sudden rush of U.S. health care companies to Mexico. Over the past two years, medical equipment suppliers, home health care providers, health maintenance organizations, health insurance firms, and American hospital companies have been pouring across the border to get a foothold on Mexico's private insurance market, estimated at about 4.5 million people. Investors are banking that NAFTA will improve the Mexican economy and will fuel the growth of Mexico's middle and upper classes (Mitchell, 1994; Skolnick, 1995).

But there are risks for investors. Mexico recently plunged into a deep economic recession. A free fall in the peso scared off billions of dollars in investments, pushed up inflation and interest rates, and forced people out of work. As a result, many middle-class families have been driven into poverty and forced to receive subsidized care at now overcrowded and underfunded government hospitals and clinics. Inflation and peso devaluation have also eroded the nation's public health budget, reducing government demand for the importation of some health goods (Fineman, 1995).

NAFTA brings other risks for Mexicans as well. In their rush for profits in Mexico, American health care companies could perform unnecessary procedures, discriminate against certain patient groups, or skimp on service quality. Disincentives for them to do otherwise are few. In Mexico, public policy is more lax, and the country lags behind the United States considerably in accreditation of health care facilities and certification of practitioners (Frenk et al., 1994).

In addition, NAFTA will significantly expand the *maquiladora* industry, which consists of "offshore" assembly plants owned mostly by U.S. firms. This industry lures hundreds of thousands of Mexicans from the interior of the country to the border. Although some experts (for example, Guendelman & Silberg, 1993) have reported otherwise, evidence is mounting that work in *maquiladora* industries can be hazardous to one's health. Denman (1990) found that the birthweights of infants of female *maquiladora* workers are significantly below internationally accepted standards. The findings were attributed to harsh working conditions, including exposure to toxins, long working days, and physically demanding work. Kopinak (1995) concluded that foreign capital exploits women at *maquiladora* industries by offering the least desirable jobs to them using the term *personal femenino* ("female personnel") in advertising for unskilled production personnel. Shields (1995) observed that *maquiladoras* avoid payment of health benefits. To avoid providing maternity leave, some companies apparently force pregnant women to quit their jobs by assigning them more difficult tasks to perform. Press and Rose (1995) reported that General Electric and Honeywell recently dismissed 100 workers for trying to establish a labor union at their plants. Thus, complaining about conditions at *maquiladora* plants can jeopardize one's job.

The long-term effects of NAFTA on health in border communities will probably be substantial. In 1990 there were an estimated 7 million people living along the nearly 2,000-mile U.S.–Mexico border. By the year 2000, El Paso, Texas, and its sister city in Mexico, Juárez, will have more than 2.3 million people living in the largest international metropolis in the world (Skolnick, 1995). Many migrants live in *colonias,* or unincorporated settlements on both sides of the border, which usually lack septic tanks, sewers, or running water (Frenk et al., 1994). Other community health problems associated with border life include high fertility rates, disparities in infant mortality, transfer of communicable diseases, pollution, and improper waste management (Shields, 1995; Warner, 1991). Poverty is a severe problem as well. Families often have to "bunch up" in one household to subsist on low-wage jobs in border communities (Kopinak, 1995; Young & Christopherson, 1986).

TIES BETWEEN MEXICAN HEALTH AND AMERICAN HEALTH

NAFTA countries must recognize that investments in economic partnerships will also require substantial investments in health and social services. As one public health official in El Paso observed, citizens on both sides of the border "share the same water, the same air, the same pollution, and the same diseases—none of which have any respect for that line drawn on the map that does little to separate our population" (Skolnick, 1995, p. 1647). The reality is that Mexican health and American health are inextricably and permanently tied together.

One determining factor is economics. U.S.–Mexico trade crossing by land was estimated at $55.4 billion in 1993, and NAFTA partners contributed 50 percent of U.S. export growth in the first quarter and accounted for nearly one-third of U.S. import growth. In the first quarter of 1994, Mexico's imports to the United States expanded by 22 percent, and U.S. exports to Mexico were expected to approach $50 billion by the end of the year, compared with $41.7 billion in 1993. If current trends continue, Mexico will soon surpass Japan as the second largest U.S. foreign market (Bureau of National Affairs, 1994). In addition, the U.S. economy demands Mexican workers. The number of Mexicans who cross the border each day to work is enormous. In New Mexico alone, 60 percent to 70 percent of the state's migrant workers live in Mexico and commute daily to work in New Mexican fields (Skolnick, 1995).

Another determining factor that links Mexican health and American health is immigration. The U.S. Bureau of the Census predicts that the United States will double its number of Hispanic families to almost 46 million in 2015, triple its size to over 68 million by 2035, and expand to almost four times its 1990 size by 2050. Two-thirds of these families will originate in Mexico (Day, 1993). Although it is easy to overestimate the amount of additional immigration that NAFTA will cause, it is clear at this point that the Mexican government has lost control of the single most potent inducement for migration to the United States—inflation (Cornelius & Martin, 1993).

Border states will not be the only states affected by NAFTA and Mexican immigration. Although the additional business brought about by NAFTA will be concentrated in the border states, other states with cities that have a large Mexican American population, like Chicago, will be affected by NAFTA-associated trade, despite the distance to Mexico (Santos, 1994). They, too, will attract emigrants from Mexico to their communities.

CHALLENGES AND OPPORTUNITIES

It is hoped that side agreements during NAFTA's dispute resolution process will allow individuals and nongovernmental organizations to bring health, labor, and quality-of-life issues into the dispute resolution process (Garvey, 1995). Meanwhile, severe challenges are emerging from the growing interaction between Mexico and the United States.

Health social workers can be helpful in at least five ways. First, at the policy level, they can join cross-national coalitions, such as the Tri-National Social Work Task Force and the Coalition for Justice in the Maquiladoras, to monitor the progress of NAFTA and to promote development of service infrastructure to accommodate economic growth. They can also push for changes in the trade pact to protect workers' rights; enforce fair labor standards; and promote environmental, occupational, and personal health. Furthermore, health social workers can support the development of financial mechanisms to pay for health services received on either side of the border as well as the establishment of Mexican medical care facilities for Mexican citizens living in the United States as seasonal workers (Frenk et al., 1994).

Second, health social workers can develop innovative solutions to border health problems. Formal channels of communication, referral, and follow-up between health providers on both sides of the border are urgently needed. El Paso's recent success in increasing its prenatal care and childhood immunization rates by working with leaders on both sides of the border sets a good example (Skolnick, 1995). Working with mediating structures such as families, neighborhood groups, and voluntary associations can be very effective as well. For example, volunteer community health aides can remove barriers to primary and preventive care by developing and implementing culturally appropriate health education and outreach services in border communities (Patton, 1995). The De Madres a Madres Program, started in a Houston inner-city Hispanic community, is a good example. Based on the concept of empowerment, this program uses indigenous volunteer mothers to form coalitions with civic groups and agencies to address health needs of Mexican Americans and other Hispanic immigrants (McFarlane & Fehir, 1994).

Third, NAFTA expands opportunities for international consortia and joint projects in health social work training. Although the treaty provides minimal references to personal health services, Annex 1210 permits "relevant bodies" to negotiate mutually acceptable professional standards and criteria for licensure and certification of professional service providers and to provide recommendations on mutual recognition (Frenk et al., 1994). The Task Force for International Social Work of the Council for Social Work Education has taken the lead in this area by urging faculty exchanges and joint research efforts and by working toward the development of a national accreditation body in Mexico. Several schools of social work have provided leadership as well, including the ones at University of Texas at Pan American, Tulane University, University of Calgary, and University of New Mexico at Las Cruces, to name a few.

Fourth, health social work scholars can help by devoting more research to health and service utilization patterns of Mexican immigrants. Numerous studies (Applewhite, 1995; Chavez, 1986; De la Rosa, 1989; Giachello, 1988; Ginzberg, 1991; Lopez-Aqueres, Kemp, Staples, & Brummel-Smith, 1984; Nichols, Labrec, Homedes, & Geller, 1994; Trevino, Moyer, Valdez, & Stroup-Benham, 1991; Zambrana, Ell, Dorrington, Wachsman, & Hodge, 1994) have reported that families of Mexican origin tend to underuse services in the United States. Most of these studies have been conducted in border cities, where challenges associated with immigration are more obvious and pressing. But little is known about the health and social services utilization patterns of Mexican immigrants in other areas of the country, especially in metropolitan communities of nonborder states. This is unfortunate. The long-term viability of these communities will rest in part on their ability to address the needs of this rapidly expanding population.

Fifth, health social workers can help strengthen interactions between Mexicans and Americans by confronting "moral panic." Hostility surfacing in the form of expressed fears that Mexican immigration will boost welfare rolls, drive up health care costs, or turn the United States into a Third World country must be challenged. Regrettably, much of the debate over NAFTA and immigration has rested on unfounded fears.

In this regard, a few relevant facts can help promote international healing. One is that immigration from Mexico can strengthen American communities. Mexicans traditionally hold family and community values in high regard (Vega, 1990; Vega, Kolody, Valle, & Weir, 1991). Immigration can also improve community health. Mexicans have lower levels of low-birthweight babies, and they are less likely than Anglos to die from many chronic diseases, including cancer, heart disease, and pulmonary diseases (Frenk et al., 1994; Stolberg, 1993). Another relevant fact is that additional patrols at the U.S.–Mexico border cannot stop immigration. Increased apprehension of illegal entrants has never changed the basic pattern of Mexican migration, except perhaps to increase the flow of women and children seeking to be reunited with newly legalized family heads in the United States (Cornelius, 1992; Donato, 1993). Finally, Americans can be gently reminded that Mexican immigrants seek the same thing that attracted their own ancestors to the United States—hope.

REFERENCES

Applewhite, S. L. (1995). *Curanderismo:* Demystifying the health beliefs and practices of elderly Mexican Americans. *Health & Social Work, 20,* 247–253.

Berger, P., & Neuhaus, R. (1977). *To empower people.* Washington, DC: American Enterprise Institute Press.

Bureau of National Affairs. (1994, June 1). NAFTA: U.S., Mexican governors address. *BNA International Environment Daily*.

Cavise, L. (1994). NAFTA rebellion: How the small village of Chiapas is fighting for its life. *Human Rights, 21*, 36–42.

Chavez, L. R. (1986). Mexican immigration and health care: A political economy perspective. *Human Organization, 45*, 344–352.

Cornelius, W. A. (1992). From sojourners to settlers: The changing profile of Mexican migration to the United States. In J. A. Bustamante, C. W. Reynolds, & R. Hinojosa-Ojeda (Eds.), *U.S.– Mexico relations: Labor market interdependence* (pp. 155–195). Stanford, CA: Stanford University Press.

Cornelius, W. A., & Martin, P. L. (1993). The uncertain connection: Free trade and rural Mexican migration to the United States. *International Migration Review, 27*, 484–512.

Day, J. C. (1993). *Population projections of the United States, by age, sex, race, and Hispanic origin: 1993 to 2050*. Suitland, MD: U.S. Bureau of the Census.

De la Rosa, M. (1989). Health care needs of Hispanic Americans and the responsiveness of the health care system. *Health & Social Work, 14*, 104–113.

Denman, C. (1990). La salud de las obreras de la maquila: El caso de Nogales [The health of female assembly plant workers: The case of Nogales]. In G. de la Pena et al. (Eds.), *Crisis, conflicto, y sobrevivencia* [Crisis, conflict, and survival]. Guadalajara, Mexico: Universidad de Guadalajara Press.

Donato, K. M. (1993). Current trends and patterns of female migration: Evidence from Mexico. *International Migration Review, 27*, 748–771.

Fineman, M. (1995, October 1). Economic ills infect Mexicans. *Los Angeles Times*, p. A-1.

Frenk, J., Gomez-Dantes, O., Cruz, C., Chacon, F., Hernandez, P., & Freeman, P. (1994). Consequences of the North Atlantic Free Trade Agreement for health services: A perspective from Mexico. *American Journal of Public Health, 84*, 1591–1597.

Garvey, J. I. (1995). Trade law and quality of life—Dispute resolution under the NAFTA side accords on labor and the environment. *American Journal of International Law, 89*, 439–453.

Giachello, A. L. (1988). Hispanics and health care. In P. S. Cafferty, S. J. Pastora, & W. C. McCready (Eds.), *Hispanics in the United States: A new social agenda* (pp. 159–194). New Brunswick, NJ: Transaction Books.

Ginzberg, E. (1991). Access to health care for Hispanics. *Journal of the American Medical Association, 265*, 238–242.

Guendelman, S., & Silberg, M. J. (1993). The health consequences of maquiladora work: Women on the U.S.–Mexican border. *American Journal of Public Health, 83*, 37–44.

Heredia, C. (1994). NAFTA and democratization in Mexico. *Journal of International Affairs, 48*, 13–38.

Kopinak, K. (1995). Gender as a vehicle for the subordination of women. *Latin American Perspectives, 22*, 30–48.

Lopez-Aqueres, W., Kemp, B., Staples, F., & Brummel-Smith, K. (1984). Use of health care services by older Hispanics. *Journal of the American Geriatric Society, 32*, 435–440.

McFarlane, J., & Fehir, J. (1994). De Madres a Madres: A community partnership for health. *Health Education Quarterly, 21*, 381–394.

Mitchell, L. A. (1994, April 21). Health care revolution in Mexico opens door. *Arizona Business Gazette*, p. 1.

Nichols, A. W., Labrec, P. A., Homedes, N., & Geller, S. E. (1994). The utilization of Arizona medical services by residents of Mexico. *Salud Publica Mex, 36*, 129–139.

Patton, S. (1995). Empowering women: Improving a community's health. *Nursing Management, 26*, 36–41.

Press, E., & Rose, G. (1995). NAFTAmath. *Nation, 260*, 4–5.

Santos, F. (1994). NAFTA in the windy city. *Hispanic Business, 16*, 62–63.

Shields, J. (1995). Border health hazards. *Multinational Monitor, 16*, 22–23.

Skolnick, A. (1995). Crossing the "line on the map" in search of hope. *Journal of the American Medical Association, 273*, 1646–1648.

Stolberg, S. (1993, November 24). Health study ranks Latinos above Anglos. *Los Angeles Times*, p. A-1.

Trevino, F. M., Moyer, M. E., Valdez, R. B., & Stroup-Benham, C. A. (1991). Health insurance coverage and utilization of health services by Mexican, mainland Puerto-Rican and Cuban-Americans. *Journal of the American Medical Association, 265*, 233–237.

Vega, W. (1990). Hispanic families in the 1980's: A decade of research. *Journal of Marriage and the Family, 52*, 1015–1024.

Vega, W., Kolody, B., Valle, R., & Weir, J. (1991). Social support networks, social support and their relationship to depression among immigrant Mexican women. *Human Organization, 50*, 154–162.

Warner, D. (1991). Health issues at the U.S.-Mexican border. *Journal of the American Medical Association, 265*, 242–247.

Young, G., & Christopherson, S. (1986). Household structure and activity in Ciudad Juárez. In G. Young (Ed.), *The social and economic development of Ciudad Juárez* (pp. 229–258). Boulder, CO: Westview Press.

Zambrana, R., Ell, K., Dorrington, C., Wachsman, L., & Hodge, D. (1994). The relationship between psychosocial status of immigrant Latino mothers and use of emergency pediatric services. *Health & Social Work, 19*, 93–102.

This chapter was originally published in the February 1996 issue of Health & Social Work, *vol. 21, pp. 3–7.*

33 Use of Health Insurance in County-Funded Clinics: Issues for Health Care Reform

Cynthia J. Rocha

There is growing concern among U.S. policymakers and the public about how to increase access to affordable health care and still manage rising costs. A number of proposals in Congress have attempted to aid Americans without adequate health care insurance. The Clinton administration's plan called for a comprehensive managed care plan that would provide universal coverage for all Americans (Bureau of National Affairs, 1993). This plan required poor Americans to share the costs but would have subsidized families with incomes up to 150 percent of the federal poverty level (Brown, 1994). Although this plan has been pushed to the back burner in favor of the state-controlled managed care plans in Congress, there is widespread agreement that something must be done to curb both rising costs and an increasing population of uninsured Americans.

Many Americans use public health care facilities to acquire health care services at minimal cost to their family. Generally it is believed that public clinics are used by people without health insurance. It is unknown, however, how many people with health insurance also use public clinics. This article analyzes the characteristics of clients who used four county-funded clinics in the Midwest. Current proposals for policy changes are discussed, and the implications of these changes are assessed.

BACKGROUND

U.S. health care policy traditionally has been viewed as a commodity in a private enterprise system (Estes, 1986). The market model of health care has excluded many Americans who do not have the economic means to participate in the health care market. Medicaid and Medicare attempt to provide care for the most vulnerable members of society (Altman & Beatrice, 1990; Friedman, 1990). The lack of inclusion of all poor Americans in an equitable health care system has derived from effective lobbying efforts against national health insurance by powerful medical and insurance associations (Belcher & Palley, 1991).

As health costs continue to soar and coverage by private insurance companies becomes more difficult to acquire, health care has become unobtainable for many people. Between 1978 and 1986 the number of Americans without health insurance increased by one-third (Children's Defense Fund, 1990). Currently, some 37 million Americans are without any form of health insurance, and millions more are underinsured (Belcher & Palley, 1991; Intriligator, 1994). A major illness can mean catastrophic financial and health problems for uninsured individuals and their families. What these people are unable to pay is passed on to hospitals, the public, and the government.

The Clinton administration's proposal attempted to broaden coverage and control costs federally (Bureau of National Affairs, 1993), whereas Congress continues to examine ways to control Medicaid spending and expand coverage through the state-controlled managed care programs (U.S. General Accounting Office, 1995). Even powerful lobbyists such as the American Medical Association and the Health Insurance Association of America, whose past efforts have kept national insurance from becoming reality, have plans of their own to increase access while keeping health care in the private market (Gorin & Moniz, 1992).

Recent health care proposals can be characterized as single-payer and multiple-payer models (for analyses of the different proposals, see Altman & Beatrice, 1990; Brown, 1994; Gorin & Moniz, 1992). In single-payer models the government is the sole insurer. Private insurers are eliminated, and health care is delivered along federal guidelines. The NASW (1990) health care proposal is an example of this model. In multiple-payer models some form of private insurance coverage remains in place, most often involving subsidizing poor workers and expanding Medicaid. The Clinton plan is an example of this model, also known as "managed competition." Although how to fund a managed competition approach and whether it should be funded at the state or federal level are now being debated in Congress, there is an underlying assumption that by providing some insurance to uninsured people the problem of acquiring the care of private physicians will be resolved.

A number of studies have indicated that health insurance is an important predictor of access to care (Cornelius, Beauregard, & Cohen, 1991; Guendelman, 1991; Hadley, Steinberg, & Feder, 1991; Kirkman-Liff & Kronenfeld, 1992; Solis, Marks, Garcia, & Shelton, 1990; Strogatz, 1990). These and other studies, however, also pointed to income as another important predictor. Some studies have found that income is important to determining access regardless of insurance status (Wood, Hayward, Corey, Freeman, & Shapiro, 1990). Therefore, poor individuals, whether insured privately or publicly, will not fare well in the medical market. If and when the present health care system is overhauled, the question of premiums and copayments will still be an important issue if the working poor population cannot afford the cost-sharing requirements.

LITERATURE REVIEW

Few clinic-based studies have compared insurance status with income characteristics. Studies have been done to determine what type of students use family-planning services in school clinics that provide primary care (Kirby, 1991; Kirby, Waszak, & Ziegler, 1991). Ralph and Edgington (1983) compared low-income areas before and after adolescent care clinics were available to ascertain changes in overall birth rates. Torres and Forrest (1985) analyzed the characteristics of low-income patients at family-planning clinics and found that the number of public assistance recipients declined over time. Radecki and Bernstein (1989) found that the use of family-planning clinics was influenced more by lack of health insurance than by poverty level. Although these studies provide important information on family-planning clinic use, they provide little to inform policy regarding primary care.

To determine what type of patient is expected to use public clinics, population-based studies shed more light. According to Blumenthal and Rizzo (1991), uninsured patients were only 11 percent of the average private physician's caseload in 1986. The likelihood of having a physician's office as a usual source of health care increases with income. Uninsured patients are more than twice as likely as insured or Medicaid patients to use outpatient departments, emergency rooms, or clinics (Cornelius et al., 1991).

Farley (1985) found that people who do not have health insurance through an employer are usually too poor to pay for it individually, although more and more people are denied coverage regardless of their ability to pay (Congressional Budget Office, 1991). Mechanic (1986) found that some uninsured people with the financial means to purchase insurance choose to gamble that they will not incur large medical expenses given their young age and good health status. However, the Health Insurance Association of America (1989) reported that 61 percent of families who are uninsured are classified as poor (below 100 percent of they poverty threshold) or near-poor (below 200 percent).

Whether Medicaid patients use private physicians as their usual source of care has been related to the limitations of each state's reimbursement rates (Blendon, Aiken, Freeman, Kirkman-Liff, & Murphy, 1986). In Missouri, McManus, Flint, and Kelly (1991) found that physician reimbursement was below the national median; Medicaid reimbursed pediatricians at only 57 percent of the market rate for a limited visit and general practitioners at only 65 percent. Also, many doctors prefer not to treat Medicaid patients to avoid the excessive government bureaucracy (Howell & Ellwood, 1991). Although Medicaid recipients have more access to private physician care than poor people without Medicaid, they are still far short of the access "enjoyed by the average American" (Jencks & Benedict, 1990, p. 48).

It is generally believed that Medicare and insured patients are much better off than Medicaid and uninsured patients. Having health insurance is thought to eliminate the price of services as a concern of the patient (Bock, 1988). However, Wood et al. (1990) found that although having health insurance improved access to care, low-income children and children of color continued to have much less access compared with higher income children regardless of insurance status. Furthermore, Medicare beneficiaries face increasing problems of access. Since the 1970s most third-party payers have imposed greater deductibles, higher premiums, or cutbacks in coverage (Rehr & Rosenberg, 1991).

METHOD

Research Questions and Hypothesis

Most efforts to address the nation's growing health care concerns remain focused on the plight of uninsured Americans. However, if insured people are using public clinics for their physician care, then focusing only on uninsured people may mask the problem of high deductibles and copayments that deter low-income people from using private physicians. If efforts simply bring poor uninsured people up to the level of poor insured people, poor people may still use public clinics instead of private physicians. Given these issues, three research questions were asked regarding a sample of clinic patients: (1) What health insurance groups are represented? (2) Is the clinic population homogeneous both demographically and economically regardless of insurance status? and (3) What services are sought most often?

This study compares income, as well as education and occupation, by insurance status; education and occupation are frequently used to determine socioeconomic status (Hansell, 1991; Keil, Sutherland, Knapp, & Tyroler, 1992; Kritz-Silverstein, Wingard, Barrett, & Connor, 1992; Moon & Smolensky, 1977; Susser, 1992). It was hypothesized that if privately insured people used the clinics, they would be as poor as uninsured people.

Sample

The source of data for this study was a database provided by the county health department of an urban midwestern city. The sample included all patients receiving care in four county clinics during December 1991. The sample size of the study was 6,298 patients.

Variables

The variables studied were demographic, socioeconomic, and service utilization characteristics and health insurance status. Demographic variables included family size, marital status, gender, and race. Family size included all members living in the household. Marital status included four categories: single, widowed, separated or divorced, and married.

Socioeconomic variables included education, occupation, and income. Formal education for adults older than 18 included four categories: less than 12 years, high school graduate, one to three years of college, and college graduate. Occupation was determined using the U.S. Bureau of the Census (1980) definitions for white-collar (managerial, professional, sales, clerical, and technical workers), blue-collar (mechanical, machine, construction, and factory workers, laborers, and operators), and service (domestic, protective, food, and personal services workers) occupations. Income was based on U.S. Bureau of the Census (1990) definitions of annual income (the total annual cash receipts before taxes from all sources). Poverty figures were derived using the U.S. Bureau of the Census guidelines for poverty by family size ("Annual Update," 1992).

Service utilization included whether the patient used general medicine, pediatrics, obstetrics/gynecology/family planning, ophthalmology, or immunization services during his or her visit to the clinic. Health insurance status was determined using county payer code lists that included private insurance, Medicaid, Medicare, and no insurance.

Data Analysis

Descriptive statistics were gathered from the clinic population. Chi-square analysis was used to find significant differences among the four health insurance groups and between insured and uninsured groups by demographic and economic characteristics.

RESULTS

Demographic Information

All demographic characteristics significantly differed by overall health insurance status (Table 33-1). Overall, the clinics served more patients of color than white patients and overwhelmingly more African Americans than other patients of color. The proportion of African Americans was slightly higher in the Medicaid group than in other insurance groups.

Uninsured and Medicare patients were much more likely to have only one person in the household than the Medicaid or insured patients [$\chi^2(24, 6,263)$ = 1,047, $p < .0001$]. Interestingly, the insured patients were more likely than all other groups to have four or more people in the household.

Only 6.6 percent of the Medicaid patients were married, compared to 16.1 percent of the uninsured and 24.5 percent of the insured patients [$\chi^2(6, 6,065)$ = 1,016, $p = .0001$]. Consistently more women than men used the clinics in all insurance groups, and the proportion of women in the Medicaid group was slightly higher than in the other groups.

No significant differences were found between uninsured and insured patients by race and gender. Significant differences remained by household size and marital status when tested alone.

Socioeconomic Status

Although there were significant differences between the uninsured and insured patients in annual income [$\chi^2(9, 1,140)$ = 55.5, $p < .001$], overall the sample was very poor (Table 33-1). Of all the patients who reported an annual income, 57.3 percent earned less than $10,000 annually, and 93.7 percent earned less than $20,000. Of the few Medicaid patients who reported an income, 91.3 percent earned less than $20,000; of the uninsured patients 93.6 percent earned less than $20,000. No Medicare patient earned more than $20,000 per year, and 84.1 percent earned less than $10,000. Of the insured patients 74.2 percent earned less than $20,000.

Occupation was significantly different among insurance groups [$\chi^2(14, 1,439)$ = 159.3, $p < .001$]. The uninsured and insured patients were equally as likely to be employed in service occupations. However, the uninsured patients were almost twice as likely to be unemployed, and the insured patients were almost four times more likely to work in blue-collar occupations, which traditionally offer more benefits than service occupations.

There were no significant differences in education between uninsured and insured patients [$\chi^2(4, 528)$ = 2.1, $p = .717$]. However, when Medicaid patients were added for comparison, significant differences emerged [$\chi^2(8, 946)$ = 50.5, $p < .001$). Medicaid patients were more likely to have dropped out of high school and less likely to have a college degree than either the uninsured or insured patients. All three groups had the same likelihood of attending some college.

TABLE 33-1

Demographic, Socioeconomic, and Service Utilization Information of Clinic Patients, by Health Insurance Group

Characteristic	Uninsured	Insured	Medicaid	Medicare
Demographic information (%)				
Race[a]				
White	44.3	36.9	33.5	39.2
African American	53.0	59.6	65.5	60.5
Other	2.7	3.5	1.0	0.3
n	3,436	292	2,143	390
$\chi^2(6, 6,261) = 102.7, p < .001$				
Household size				
1	47.4	20.9	15.9	75.6
2 or 3	29.5	35.9	58.3	22.1
4 or more	23.1	43.2	25.8	2.3
n	3,438	292	2,143	390
$\chi^2(24, 6,263) = 1,047, p < .0001$				
Marital status				
Single	73.5	65.4	86.8	21.6
Divorced, widowed, or separated	10.4	10.1	6.6	56.5
Married	16.1	24.5	6.6	21.9
n	3,300	286	2,095	384
$\chi^2(6, 6,065) = 1,016, p < .0001$				
Gender[a]				
Female	64.7	67.8	71.7	66.7
Male	35.3	32.2	28.3	33.3
n	2,225	198	1,523	260
$\chi^2(3, 4,206) = 124.2, p < .0001$				
Socioeconomic status (%)				
Annual income ($)[b]				
< 10,000	52.8	22.6	56.5	84.1
10,000–20,000	40.8	51.6	34.8	15.9
20,000–30,000	5.6	16.1	8.7	0
> 30,000	0.8	9.7	0	0
n	835	62	23	220
$\chi^2(9, 1,140) = 55.5, p < .001$				
Occupation				
White collar	16.8	26.6	5.9	NA
Service	26.8	25.0	18.9	NA
Blue collar	5.5	23.4	1.1	NA
Student	1.8	0	1.9	NA
Unemployed	49.1	25.0	72.2	NA
n	899	64	476	NA
$\chi^2(14, 1,439) = 159.3, p < .001$				
Education				
Less than 12 years	33.1	23.4	45.2	61.7
High school graduate	42.4	48.9	36.5	26.0
1–3 years of college	18.7	19.2	17.4	9.6
College graduate	5.8	8.5	0.9	2.7
n	481	47	345	73
$\chi^2(8, 946) = 50.5, p < .001$				

(continued)

TABLE 33-1

Continued

Characteristic	Uninsured	Insured	Medicaid	Medicare
Service utilization (%)				
General medicine	30.9	32.9	11.8	85.2
Pediatrics	27.6	45.9	52.6	0
Obstetrics/gynecology/				
family planning	38.4	18.4	33.1	6.1
Ophthalmology	1.9	2.8	1.5	8.7
Immunization	1.2	0	1.0	0
n	3,438	292	2,143	390

NOTE: NA = not applicable.
[a]Insured and uninsured patients not significantly different when tested alone.
[b]Statistical comparisons were run only for insured and uninsured patients because too few Medicaid and Medicare patients had incomes higher than $20,000, making chi-square analysis invalid.

Service Utilization

Uninsured patients were fairly evenly distributed among general medicine (30.9 percent), pediatrics (27.6 percent), and obstetrics/gynecology/family-planning (38.4 percent) services (Table 33-1). The Medicaid patients often used pediatric services (52.6 percent) and obstetrics/gynecology/family-planning services (33.1 percent). General medicine was used by only 11.8 percent of the Medicaid patients.

The Medicare patients most often used general medicine (85.2 percent) and ophthalmology (8.7 percent) services. The insured patients most often used pediatric (45.9 percent) and general medicine (32.9 percent) services.

DISCUSSION

There were several important differences among insurance groups. The insured patients were more likely to be married and to have four or more people in the household, indicating a greater likelihood of having both parents in the home. However, large families may have a harder time using private health insurance if deductibles and copayments are high.

This study supports other research indicating that Medicaid patients use clinics to obtain pediatric and family-planning services. Uninsured patients were more likely to use family-planning and general medicine services, and insured patients were more likely to use pediatric services. Surprisingly few clients used the immunization services at the clinics, perhaps because most children receive their immunizations at the end of the summer before school begins, and the data in this study were collected in December.

The most important results, however, show the similarities among the groups. There were no significant differences between the uninsured and insured patients by race and education. The sample was overwhelmingly poor regardless of insurance status. Only 7 percent of the overall sample earned more than $20,000 annually. Although that percentage was almost entirely made up of the insured patients, almost 75 percent of this group made less than $20,000 annually as well.

IMPLICATIONS FOR SOCIAL WORK

Health care reform efforts must include the integration of Medicaid financing with other employer-based plans, or physicians will continue to have few incentives to treat poor Medicaid recipients. Furthermore, if insured and Medicare patients are using public clinics because of high cost-sharing requirements, these issues need to be taken into account when deciding how best to integrate uninsured patients in reform efforts. If poor Americans who are insured cannot currently meet their deductibles and copayments through private physicians, there is no indication that poor Americans without insurance will have better luck if they are integrated into an existing system through premium subsidies, which still require cost-sharing. The way health care reform is addressed, especially in a managed care environment, will have consequences for social workers trying to locate resources for their clients.

That almost half of the clinic users had some form of insurance yet still used public facilities has important policy implications. If low-income families cannot meet the cost-sharing requirements of the proposed reforms, where will they obtain primary care? Do policymakers want to ensure that people have access to private physician care, or are they willing to create policies that simply increase the use of public facilities? Various public health and social work associations have advocated capping premium payments and eliminating cost-sharing requirements for low-income families (American Public Health Association, 1993).

The secondary data presented in this study cannot completely answer the question of why so many insured people are using public health clinics. More research is needed to further inform social work practitioners in the health care debate. Unless the reasons why insured Americans use public clinics are better understood, any attempt at reform may prove futile and push more and more people into public facilities regardless of insurance status.

REFERENCES

Altman, D., & Beatrice, D. (1990, December). Perspectives on the Medicaid program. *Health Care Financing Review*, pp. 2–5.

American Public Health Association. (1993). *The Clinton Health Care Reform Plan: An APHA perspective on the details* (Report from the 1993 Annual Meeting). Washington, DC: Author.

Annual update of HHS poverty guidelines. (1992). *Federal Register, 57*, 5455–5456.

Belcher, J., & Palley, H. (1991). The prospects for national health insurance reform. *Social Work in Health Care, 15*, 101–119.

Blendon, R., Aiken, L., Freeman, H., Kirkman-Liff, B., & Murphy, J. (1986). Uncompensated care by hospitals or public insurance for the poor? *New England Journal of Medicine, 314*, 1160–1163.

Blumenthal, D., & Rizzo, J. (1991). Who cares for uninsured persons? *Medical Care, 29*, 502–520.

Bock, R. S. (1988). Sounding board: The pressure to keep prices high at a walk-in clinic. *New England Journal of Medicine, 319*, 785–787.

Brown, E. R. (1994). Should single-payer advocates support President Clinton's proposal for health reform? In P. V. Rosenau (Ed.), *Health care reform in the nineties* (pp. 24–34). Thousand Oaks, CA: Sage Publications.

Bureau of National Affairs. (1993, September 10). Clinton health care reform—Administration draft. *Daily Report for Executives*, pp. L-8-L-11.

Children's Defense Fund. (1990). *The health of America's children*. Washington, DC: Author.

Congressional Budget Office. (1991). *Rising health care costs: Causes, implications, and strategies.* Washington, DC: Author.

Cornelius, L., Beauregard, K., & Cohen, J. (1991). *Usual sources of medical care and their characteristics: National Medical Expenditure Survey* (AHCPR Publication No. 91-0042). Rockville, MD: U.S. Public Health Service.

Estes, C. (1986). The aging enterprise: In whose interests? *International Journal of Health Services, 16,* 243–248.

Farley, P. (1985). Who are the underinsured? *Milbank Memorial Fund Quarterly, 63,* 476–503.

Friedman, E. (1990, August 5). Medicare and Medicaid at 25. *Hospitals,* pp. 38–54.

Gorin, S., & Moniz, C. (1992). The national health care crisis: An analysis of proposed solutions. *Health & Social Work, 17,* 37–44.

Guendelman, S. (1991). Health care users residing on the Mexican border: What factors determine choice of the U.S. or Mexican health system? *Medical Care, 29,* 419–429.

Hadley, J., Steinberg, E., & Feder, J. (1991). Comparison of uninsured and privately insured hospital patients. *Journal of the American Medical Association, 265,* 374–379.

Hansell, M. (1991). Sociodemographic factors and the quality of prenatal care. *American Journal of Public Health, 81,* 1023–1028.

Health Insurance Association of America. (1989). *Source book of health insurance data.* Washington, DC: Author, Policy Development and Research Department.

Howell, M., & Ellwood, M. (1991). Medicaid and pregnancy: Issues in expanding eligibility. *Family Planning Perspectives, 23,* 123–128.

Intriligator, M. D. (1994). A way to achieve national health insurance in the United States. In P. V. Rosenau (Ed.), *Health care reform in the nineties* (pp. 53–68). Thousand Oaks, CA: Sage Publications.

Jencks, S., & Benedict, M. (1990, December). Accessibility and effectiveness of care under Medicaid. *Health Care Financing Review,* pp. 47–56.

Keil, J., Sutherland, S., Knapp, R., & Tyroler, H. (1992). Does equal socioeconomic status in black and white men mean equal risk or mortality? *American Journal of Public Health, 82,* 1133–1136.

Kirby, D. (1991). School-based clinics: Research results and their implications for future research methods. *Evaluation and Program Planning, 14,* 35–47.

Kirby, D., Waszak, C., & Ziegler, J. (1991). Six school-based clinics: Their reproductive health services and impact on sexual behavior. *Family Planning Perspectives, 23,* 6–16.

Kirkman-Liff, B., & Kronenfeld, J. (1992). Access to cancer-screening services for women. *American Journal of Public Health, 82,* 733–735.

Kritz-Silverstein, D., Wingard, D., Barrett, C., & Connor, E. (1992). Employment status and heart disease risk factors in middle-aged women: The Rancho Bernardo Study. *American Journal of Public Health, 82,* 215–219.

McManus, M., Flint, S., & Kelly, R. (1991). The adequacy of physician reimbursement for pediatric care under Medicaid. *Pediatrics, 87,* 909–920.

Mechanic, D. (1986). Health care for the poor: Some policy alternatives. *Journal of Family Practice, 22,* 283–289.

Moon, M., & Smolensky, E. (1977). *Improving measures of economic well-being.* New York: Academic Press.

National Association of Social Workers. (1990). *NASW National Health Care Proposal—Executive summary.* Silver Spring, MD: Author.

Radecki, S., & Bernstein, G. (1989). Use of clinic versus private family planning care by low-income women: Access, cost and patient satisfaction. *American Journal of Public Health, 79,* 692–697.

Ralph, N., & Edgington, A. (1983). An evaluation of an adolescent family planning program. *Journal of Adolescent Health Care, 4,* 158–172.

Rehr, H., & Rosenberg, G. (1991). Social-health care: Problems and predictions. *Social Work in Health Care, 15,* 97–121.

Solis, J., Marks, G., Garcia, M., & Shelton, D. (1990). Acculturation, access to care, and use of preventive services by Hispanics: Findings from HHANES 1982-84. *American Journal of Public Health, 80*(Suppl.), 11–19.

Strogatz, D. (1990). Use of medical care for chest pain: Differences between blacks and whites. *American Journal of Public Health, 80,* 290–294.

Susser, M. (1992). Socioeconomic differences in mortality in Britain and the United States. *American Journal of Public Health, 82,* 1079–1081.

Torres, A., & Forrest, J. (1985). Family planning clinic services in the United States, 1983. *Family Planning Perspectives, 17,* 31–35.

U.S. Bureau of the Census. (1980). *Detailed population characteristics: Missouri.* Washington, DC: U.S. Government Printing Office.

U.S. Bureau of the Census. (1990). *Poverty in the United States: 1988 and 1989* (Current Population Reports, Series P-60). Washington, DC: U.S. Government Printing Office.

U.S. General Accounting Office. (1995). *Medicaid: Spending pressures drive states toward program reinvention* (GAO/HEHS-95-122). Washington, DC: U.S. Government Printing Office.

Wood, D., Hayward, R., Corey, C., Freeman, H., & Shapiro, M. (1990). Access to medical care for children and adolescents in the United States. *Pediatrics, 86,* 666–673.

This chapter was originally published in the February 1996 issue of Health & Social Work, *vol. 21, pp. 16–22.*

The Changing Scene of Social Work in Hospitals: A Report of a National Study by the Society for Social Work Administrators in Health Care and NASW

Candyce S. Berger, Jay Cayner, Greg Jensen, Terry Mizrahi, Alice Scesny, and Judith Trachtenberg

The need for radical change in the health care field is gaining support. Hospitals are feeling the pressure of hard economic times as decreasing reimbursements, changing service delivery patterns, and increased competition are forcing them to reduce costs while maintaining quality (Cummings & Abell, 1993; White & Simmons, 1993). As hospitals move to create more cost-effective service delivery, significant changes are occurring in the location, structure, and delivery of services. Such terms as "resizing," "rightsizing," "work redesign," "re-engineering," and "restructuring" are a part of the vocabulary in most hospital settings (Berger, 1993; Hammer & Champy, 1993). These changes offer exciting opportunities in primary care, prevention, health promotion, and delivery system innovations.

Preliminary information suggests that the effects of these changes are being felt by social work departments in hospitals across the country. Anecdotal reports indicate that departments are being eliminated, decentralized, or enlarged to include other departments. Both the Society for Social Work Administrators in Health Care (SSWAHC) and NASW receive numerous requests for information and assistance in responding to these organizational changes. Although these anecdotal reports are important, there is little rigorous research to substantiate what changes are occurring and the effects of those changes on the quality of social work service delivery and professional social work standards.

NASW conducted a preliminary study to explore what was happening to social work departments in hospital settings (Brennan, 1993). The results of this study led to SSWAHC and NASW joining forces to develop a systematic, comprehensive national research project to study the changes occurring in hospitals and the impact of those changes on social work. This article presents preliminary findings from the national study.

METHOD

An exploratory and descriptive survey design was used to study three key research questions: (1) What changes are occurring in hospital environments and, specifically, social work departments? (2) What strategies are being used to achieve these changes? and (3) What effects have these changes had on social work departments? A standardized, self-administered survey instrument was developed for this study. The instrument was composed primarily of fixed-response questions with a few open-ended questions to explore specific issues in depth. To measure change, many questions asked for comparative data from Fiscal Year (FY) 1992 and FY 1994. The instrument underwent multiple revisions using a variety of mechanisms to evaluate its ease of completion and content validity. There was no check on reliability conducted before use of the instrument.

A stratified, random sample of 750 hospitals listing social work as a service provided within their organizations was drawn from the membership list of the American Hospital Association (3,700 hospitals met this criteria). There were two steps to the sampling strategy. First, hospitals were stratified into five study groups (Table 34-1). The first four groups were developed according to the degree of managed care development (group 1 = lowest stage to group 4 = highest stage) within a geographic area to study the effect of managed care on changes within the hospital and social work department. These groupings were created by a national consulting firm. A total of 751 hospitals fell within these four groups, from which half of the sample was pulled. Group 5 consisted of the remaining geographic areas not contained within the four managed care groupings (2,949 hospitals) and provided the second half of the sample. The fifth group was weighted toward small and rural hospitals (50 percent of this group) to compensate for the overrepresentation of urban areas in the first half of the sample. The second step was to stratify the study groups according to number of beds (1 to 300, 301 to 600, and 601 and greater). A proportionate sample was then drawn from each of the five study groups. No distinction was made for specialty hospitals in the sample.

Questionnaires were mailed three times to all social work administrators at the hospitals chosen. The first mailing included a cover letter and a copy of the questionnaire. One week later, a postcard was mailed to encourage participation and to ensure that they had received the original mailing. One week after the second mailing there was a third mailing, which included a cover letter encouraging participation and another copy of the questionnaire. The three mailings yielded a total return rate of 45.3 percent ($N = 340$). As questionnaires were returned, postmarks and descriptive data were used to match respondents with the list of hospitals in the sample, because questionnaires were not coded to identify hospitals before mailing. Accurate identification was not always possible, making evaluation of nonrespondents difficult. Assuming this matching of respondents was correct, there did not appear to be any patterns in response rates that suggested a geographic bias in the sample. Response rates closely approximate the intended sample breakdown, with 57 percent ($n = 193$) of the respondents representing the managed care groups (groups 1 to 4) and 43 percent ($n = 147$) representing the fifth group.

Data from the questionnaires were coded and entered into the computer for data analysis using SPSS as the statistical program (SPSS, 1986). The data were adjusted to remove errors in data entry and incorrect response codes. Confidence intervals were set at $p < .05$ for data analysis.

TABLE 34-1

Geographic Groupings from Which Sample Hospitals Were Drawn

Group 1	Group 2	Group 3	Group 4	Group 5
Omaha, NE	Miami, FL	Orange, CA	Minneapolis/	Nonlisted cities
Nassau County, NY	Louisville, KY	Milwaukee, WI	St. Paul, MN	50% small
Galveston, TX	Fort Worth, TX	San Francisco/	San Diego, CA	or rural
Syracuse, NY	Dallas, TX	Oakland, CA	Los Angeles, CA	
Little Rock, AR	Tampa/St.	Portland, OR	Worcester, MA	
Gainesville, FL	Petersburg, FL	Sacramento, CA		
Chapel Hill (Research	Cincinnati, OH	San Jose, CA		
Triangle), NC	Columbus, OH	Denver, CO		
Birmingham, AL	Atlanta, GA	Detroit, MI		
Harrisburg, PA	Orlando, FL	Middlesex, NY		
Newark, NJ	Jacksonville, FL	Boston, MA		
Columbia, MO	Cleveland, OH	Salt Lake City, UT		
Augusta, GA	St. Louis, MO	Tucson, AZ		
Morgantown, WV	Hartford, CT	Madison, WI		
Charlottesville, VA	New York, NY	Riverside/		
	Kansas	San Bernardino, CA		
	Baltimore, MD	Seattle, WA		
	New Orleans, LA	Phoenix, AZ		
	Indianapolis, IN	Washington, DC		
	San Antonio, TX	Providence, RI		
	Toledo, OH	Houston, TX		
	Richmond, VA	Fort Lauderdale, FL		
	Lexington, KY	Chicago, IL		
	Oklahoma City, OK	Albany, NY		
	Pittsburgh, PA			
	Nashville, TN			
	Philadelphia, PA			

RESULTS

Hospital Demographics

Eighty-eight percent ($n = 299$) of the 340 respondents indicated that they held a social work degree. The affiliations of the other respondents were fairly equally split between nursing (7 percent, $n = 25$) and hospital administration (5 percent, $n = 17$), with 14 percent ($n = 47$) indicating "other" professional affiliations (psychology, business administration, and so forth). Respondents could indicate more than one professional affiliation, so response categories were not mutually exclusive. Of the 299 respondents who held a social work degree, an equal number reported membership in SSWAHC (76 percent, $n = 227$) and NASW (76 percent, $n = 227$), and many respondents were members of both organizations. Responses were received from 45 different states; 58 percent represented urban areas, 19 percent suburban locations, and 23 percent rural areas. All categories of hospital auspices were represented, with private, nonprofit, nonsectarian hospitals representing the largest group (Table 34-2).

A majority of the 340 hospitals reported strong teaching programs, with 59 percent ($n = 200$) indicating that they were university affiliated or offered physician residency programs within their organizations. Respondents offered acute (95 percent, $n = 323$) and ambulatory (89 percent, $n = 302$) services and provided a variety of other programs representing the continuum of care: subacute or extended care (48 percent, $n = 162$), home care (62 percent, $n = 209$), durable medical equipment (36 percent, $n = 123$), home infusion (29 percent, $n = 98$), other nursing facilities (21 percent, $n = 72$), and patient or family housing (14 percent, $n = 48$). Seventeen percent ($n = 58$) of the sample described their facility as a specialty hospital, the largest contingent from pediatric facilities (7 percent, $n = 24$). The hospitals had a mean of 337 licensed beds but staffed only 277 beds for operation.

The average number of hospital admissions per year was 12,273 ($N = 231$), and the median length of stay was 5.9 days ($N = 247$) (the median was used to account for extremes related to specialty hospitals, particularly psychiatric facilities). The average daily census was 68 percent ($N = 240$). Outpatient activity averaged 139,980 visits per year ($N = 186$). The results need to be viewed with

TABLE 34-2

Hospital Auspices

Auspice	n	%
Public, local	39	11.5
Public, state	17	5.0
Public, federal	23	6.8
Private, profit	23	6.8
Private, nonprofit, sectarian	58	17.1
Private, nonprofit, nonsectarian	154	45.3
Public, military	17	5.0
Other	9	2.6
Total	340	100.1

an understanding that there are a large number of missing cases and that responses to these items may not be representative of the sample.

The financial picture was relatively positive. Sixty-three percent ($n = 196$) of the 311 respondents reported a positive financial bottom line, 21 percent ($n = 64$) indicated a break-even situation, and 16 percent ($n = 51$) faced a negative financial status.

An interesting finding was the amount of change reported between FY 1992 and FY 1994 in the ownership status of the hospitals. In FY 1992, 62.5 percent ($n = 205$) of the 328 hospitals that responded indicated that they were free-standing institutions, whereas in FY 1994 only 45.2 percent ($n = 150$) of the 332 that responded were free-standing institutions. This decrease was accompanied by a commensurate increase in multihospital systems, rising from 30.5 percent ($n = 100$) in FY 1992 to 43.4 percent ($n = 144$) in FY 1994.

Activities Related to Changes in the Hospital

A major portion of the questionnaire explored specific changes occurring in the hospital to set the context for the amount of overall change in the institution and to determine if social work was being differentially targeted for changes and reductions. Table 34-3 shows responses to questions about several innovations intended to cut costs highlighted in the literature.

Another set of questions focused on administrative and structural changes within a hospital over the previous year. The greatest change reported was for the chief executive officer, with 51 percent ($n = 171$) of the 338 hospitals indicating that their top administrator had changed. Thirty-eight percent ($n = 127$) of the hospitals indicated that they had used a consulting firm. Only 22 percent ($n = 73$) of the hospitals reported mergers with other hospitals. Hospitals were more likely to have added new product lines (33 percent, $n = 111$) than to have deleted them (10 percent, $n = 32$).

Table 34-4 captures the direction of change in staffing levels and hospital activity. There was a large decrease in the number of personnel, particularly

TABLE 34-3

Hospital Strategies to Reduce Costs

Strategy	n	%	% of Strategies Still Operating in 1995
Care maps	227	66.8	95.4
Decentralization— No departments	74	21.9	88.2
Decentralization—Matrix with departments	74	21.8	95.1
Case management— Benefits	77	22.7	96.6
Case management— Case coordination	156	46.0	98.3

TABLE 34-4
Changes in Hospital Characteristics: FY 1992 to FY 1994

Measure	% Increase	% No Change	% Decrease	N	p
No. of personnel	20.4	17.3	62.3	318	.000
No. of administrative personnel	13.8	36.1	50.2	319	.000
No. of administrative levels	9.5	53.0	37.5	315	.000
No. of staffed acute beds	7.3	45.1	47.6	315	.000
No. of contracted services	47.6	37.0	15.4	246	.000
No. of ambulatory visits	84.0	8.4	7.7	287	.000
Average length of stay	1.9	12.2	85.9	319	.000
Average daily census	16.1	19.3	64.6	311	.000

administrative personnel, although 53.0 percent of the hospitals reported no change in the number of administrative levels. There was little increase in the number of staffed acute beds, with 315 respondents reporting no change (45.1 percent) or decreases (47.6 percent) in number of beds. Dramatic decreases in average length of stay were reported (85.9 percent), with the majority of hospitals also indicating a drop in average daily census (64.6 percent). During this same period, ambulatory visits (84.0 percent) and contracted services (47.6 percent) showed increased activity. Changes in each category were highly statistically significant.

Social Work Characteristics

Respondents were asked to describe the structure of social work services within their hospital. Although this question asked respondents to select the one answer that most closely represented their organizational structure, several respondents indicated more than one response. This occurred only when there was a centralized social work department, although the hospital might also have had unit-based structures as well. If "centralized program" was checked along with any other response, the question was coded as "centralized," although readers should be aware that hybrid structures also existed.

Table 34-5 shows a comparison of departmental structures in FY 1992 and FY 1994. Most of the hospitals continued to have a centralized social work depart-

TABLE 34-5
Changes in the Structure of the Department of Social Work: FY 1992 to FY 1994

Structure	FY 1992 n	FY 1992 %	FY 1994 n	FY 1994 %	p
Centralized	288	84.7	264	77.6	.000
Unit based (centralized)	29	8.5	47	13.8	.000
Unit based (decentralized)	7	2.1	12	3.5	.008
Contract social work service	6	1.8	5	1.5	NS
Other structure	5	1.5	7	2.1	NS
Missing	5	1.5	5	1.5	NS
Total	340	100.1	340	100.0	NS

NOTE: NS = not significant.

ment, but this type of organizational structure had declined by FY 1994. During this same period, the number of unit-based structures affiliated with a central social work department increased dramatically. Total decentralization of social work services showed some increase by FY 1994 but still was reported by a very small percentage of respondents.

A series of questions explored characteristics of the social work director in FY 1992 and FY 1994. Ninety-three percent ($n = 316$) of the 340 respondents reported that there was a social work director or manager who had administrative accountability for the delivery of social work services within their hospitals. The data suggest little change between FY 1992 and FY 1994 in the professional affiliations of directors or managers (Table 34-6). Their span of control increased significantly; by FY 1994 the percentage of social work directors or managers responsible for multiple departments in their hospitals had increased by almost 10 points.

The last question asked respondents to indicate how many administrative levels were above the person responsible for social work services for FY 1992 and FY 1994. The following example was given to explain how to compute the number: "The Social Work Director reports to the Associate Director, who reports to the CEO. This would equal two levels." The data in Table 34-7 suggest a flattening in the administrative structures of the hospitals. The majority of social work directors or managers had two administrative levels above them (that is, the social work department would sit at the third administrative level in the hierarchy). The numbers of responses moving from one to two levels above and from three to two levels above were roughly equal. Very few respondents

TABLE 34-6

Changes in Characteristics of Social Work Directors or Managers: FY 1992 to FY 1994

	FY 1992			FY 1994			
Characteristic	% Yes	% No	N	% Yes	% No	N	p
Graduate social work degree	79.1	20.9	316	77.5	22.5	316	NS
BSW	7.6	92.4	316	8.5	91.5	316	NS
Non–social work degree	13.3	86.7	316	14.9	85.1	316	.026
Responsible for multiple departments	23.4	76.6	316	32.3	67.7	316	.000

NOTE: NS = not significant.

TABLE 34-7

Changes in Administrative Levels above the Social Work Director or Manager: FY 1992 to FY 1994

No. of Levels	FY 1992 (%)[a]	FY 1994 (%)[b]
1	14.5	13.3
2	59.7	63.6
3	21.9	20.3
4	3.9	2.5
5	0.0	0.3

[a]$N = 310$.
[b]$N = 316$.

indicated that there were more than three levels above the social work director or manager. These changes were not found to be statistically significant.

Changes in Social Work Programs

Several questions explored organizational changes in the social work department between FY 1992 and FY 1994 to determine the type and degree of changes affecting social work services. The data revealed important changes. Thirty percent ($n = 99$) of the 333 who responded to these questions reported that the director of social work had changed during this time. Only 6 percent ($n = 19$) reported that the social work department had merged with another social work department, and 21 percent ($n = 71$) indicated that a merger had occurred with a non–social work department. Finally, 31 percent ($n = 103$) of the respondents stated that departmental functions such as productivity and staffing were formally reviewed. These findings were congruent with a second set of questions that examined overall changes in administrative personnel. Table 34-8 shows data related to changes in the number of administrative personnel and the number of administrative levels. In both cases, the majority of respondents reported no change. However, 25.6 percent reported decreases in personnel, and 19.2 percent reported decreases in levels.

A series of questions addressed changes in social work staffing between FY 1992 and FY 1994. A two-part question asked first for the number of full-time equivalents (FTEs) and then for the direction of change in FTE levels within the specified period. Reporting of FTEs was unreliable, so further analysis was conducted only on the second part of the question (Table 34-9). The percentages reflect only those hospitals reporting staffing in the specific category and do not include missing data. The next to last column indicates the number of departments reporting no staffing (this was reported as missing data), providing additional information about staffing mix. MSWs were represented in most of the hospitals, and almost equal percentages of hospitals experienced increases, no change, and decreases in MSW staff. The majority of respondents indicated no change in BSW staff, and equal numbers reported increases and decreases. A small percentage of hospitals reported the use of social workers with a bachelor of arts degree, and their pattern was similar to that of the BSWs.

An interesting finding was related to nursing. Twenty-five percent ($n = 84$) of the 340 hospitals reported nurses as part of their staffing complement in social work services. There was a slight trend toward increased use of nurses in social work departments. Few of the hospitals reported the use of support staff (aides, technicians), and those that did showed a slight overall increase in use.

TABLE 34-8

Changes in Social Work Administrative Personnel and Levels: FY 1992 to FY 1994

Measure	% Increase	% No Change	% Decrease	N	p
Administrative personnel	8.9	65.5	25.6	325	.000
Administrative levels	7.7	73.1	19.2	312	.000

TABLE 34-9

Changes in Social Work Department Personnel: FY 1992 to FY 1994

Measure	% Increase	% No Change	% Decrease	N	No Staff n	No Staff %	p
Personnel							
MSW	32.6	35.9	31.5	270	41	12.1	NS
BSW	22.6	51.2	26.2	168	143	42.1	.000
Bachelor of arts	20.0	56.9	23.1	65	254	74.7	.000
Nurses	33.3	45.2	21.5	84	232	68.2	.028
Support staff (for example, aides)	32.5	53.5	14.0	43	281	82.6	.064
Clerical staff	18.7	60.9	20.4	255	85	25.0	.000
Administrative level							
Senior management	8.3	75.6	16.1	254	31	9.1	.000
Supervisors	16.5	46.8	36.7	139	132	38.8	.000

NOTE: NS = not significant.

Support staff (clerical help) was the only group with a greater decrease than increase in staffing, although this difference was only slight (Table 34-9).

Whereas staffing of most types of personnel was fairly even, staffing at the administrative levels showed a decreasing trend. Three-quarters of the hospitals reported no change in departmental senior management levels. Those reporting changes clearly favored decreases in staffing; the number of hospitals reporting increases in senior management was half the number reporting decreases at this level. Supervisory levels experienced greater change, with only 46.8 percent of the hospitals reporting no change in this area. Again, decreases were reported twice as much as increases (Table 34-9).

Finally, respondents were asked if the changes affecting social work departments were also occurring in other departments and programs. This question addressed the issue of whether social work was being differentially targeted for change. Of the 189 individuals responding to this question, 96 percent indicated that these changes were also happening elsewhere in the hospital.

Impact of Changes on Social Work

The remaining questions examined the perceived effect of departmental changes on various groups (Table 34-10) and activities (Table 34-11). More respondents viewed the effects of changes on patients and families as positive than as neutral or negative. They rated the effects of changes slightly more positive for social work management and more negative for social work clinical staff.

The more negative effect on clinical staff may be related to the increased clinical activity revealed in the data. Fifty-five percent ($n = 168$) of the 308 who responded

TABLE 34-10
Effect of Changes on Various Groups

Group	% Positive	% Neutral	% Negative	N	p
Management staff	37.2	32.5	30.3	274	NS
Clinical staff	33.1	27.1	39.8	269	.04
Patients and families	39.7	36.4	23.9	247	.006

NOTE: NS = not significant.

TABLE 34-11
Effect of Changes on Social Work Activities

Activity	% Positive	% Neutral	% Negative	N	p
Recruitment	19.7	65.6	14.7	244	.000
Staff development	30.1	45.3	24.6	276	.000
Clinical services	34.6	37.2	28.2	266	NS
Student programs	20.0	57.6	22.4	245	.000
Research	11.9	70.4	17.7	135	.000
Quality assurance	32.6	51.7	15.7	267	.000

NOTE: NS = not significant.

reported increased social work clinical activity in the ambulatory area, and 84 percent ($n = 263$) of the 312 who responded reported no change or an increase in activity in the inpatient area. In addition, nearly 72 percent of the respondents felt that the effects of changes on clinical services were either neutral or positive, suggesting that clinicians may be working harder to ensure the same level of quality service (Table 34-11).

Most respondents rated the effects of changes as neutral for all categories of activities (Table 34-11). When comparing positive and negative ratings, the effects of changes on activities were most often rated more positively, except for student programs and research.

There has been much concern that the decreases in administrative positions in social work departments would negatively affect clinical supervision of social work staff. Table 34-12 reveals changes in the supervisory process occurring between FY 1992 and FY 1994. The data show only a slight decrease in supervision by an MSW, which was still the most common approach. Slight increases occurred in peer supervision and supervision by a non-social worker.

Finally, the effects of the changes on the delivery of discharge planning services were evaluated (Table 34-13). Social work responsibility for discharge planning decreased slightly; other structures experienced a commensurate increase. An analysis of the descriptions of these other structures has not yet been completed, but a cursory inspection suggests that they involve social work sharing responsibility with another department, primarily nursing.

TABLE 34-12

Changes in the Supervisory Structure for Social Workers: FY 1992 to FY 1994

	FY 1992			FY 1994			
Structure	% Yes	% No	N	% Yes	% No	N	p
Supervision by social worker with MSW	82.0	18.0	333	80.4	19.6	336	NS
Peer supervision	35.1	64.9	333	39.3	60.7	336	.019
Supervision by non-social worker	12.0	88.0	333	16.1	83.9	335	.001

Note: NS = not significant.

TABLE 34-13

Changes in the Structure of Discharge Planning: FY 1992 to FY 1994

Structure	FY 1992 (%)[a]	FY 1994 (%)[b]	p
Social work is responsible	79.0	71.3	.000
Separate department reporting to social work	2.1	1.8	NS
Separate department independent of social work	8.1	8.6	NS
Other structures	10.8	18.3	.000

Note: NS = not significant.
[a]$N = 333$.
[b]$N = 334$.

DISCUSSION

Before discussing the data, a note of caution is warranted. Some of the data may have been influenced by a sampling bias; differences between respondents and nonrespondents may have influenced particular variables. For example, decentralized social work departments may have been overrepresented in the nonresponding group, perhaps accounting for their nonparticipation in the study. In addition, hospitals were not required to identify themselves. Although it was possible to do some matching from post office codes, this was not an exact process, making it impossible to test for this type of sampling bias. Although the adequate response rate does allow some confidence that the data are representative, some questions may have been susceptible to a sampling bias.

Although social work services have undergone many changes, the data suggest both positive and negative outcomes. It does not appear that social work departments were being singled out as a target of change; respondents reported that changes were also occurring with other departments and programs throughout the hospital.

Changes affecting social work departments must also be viewed within the context of what is happening in the health care industry. Respondents indicated that the number of staffed acute care beds and occupancy levels were dropping. A large majority of the hospitals reported a decrease in average length of stay, with significant drops in average daily census. These decreases suggest that there is less patient activity and that patients are moving through the system at a much faster pace. Hard economic times and greater competition for inpatient care appear to characterize the hospitals participating in this study and corroborate industry reports on these phenomena.

Hospitals are using a variety of strategies to respond to this changing environment, many of them focused on reducing costs while maintaining the quality of clinical services to patients. Care maps and case management approaches, both mechanisms to manage the utilization of resources, appear to be common innovations (Hagland, 1993; Koska, 1990; Shoor, 1993). The literature suggests that utilization management techniques are the most successful to date in managing costs without significantly compromising quality of care (Henderson & Collard, 1992; Tischler, 1990).

Hospitals are also restructuring and resizing. Restructuring involves changing the shape of the organization. Sixty-two percent ($n = 136$) of the 220 hospitals that responded to this question indicated that restructuring was a strategy used in their institution. Decentralization models, one type of restructuring strategy, appeared about equally distributed among the 340 hospitals between total decentralization, which has no departmental structure (19.7 percent, $n = 67$), and decentralization with matrix management, in which the department exists but accountability is shared with the patient care area (22.6 percent, $n = 77$).

Another example of restructuring is horizontal (combining departments) and vertical (eliminating management levels) integration within organizational structures. A decrease in the number of administrative personnel could indicate either horizontal or vertical integration, and a decrease in management levels directly measures vertical integration. The data suggest trends in both of these indexes, although more hospitals had reductions in administrative positions. Such reductions need to be examined more closely over time but do suggest that restructuring strategies are being used to deal with retrenchment in hospitals.

Although some health care programs were experiencing decline, others were growing. About one-third of the hospitals reported new product lines. For example, a strong majority of the respondents indicated that ambulatory activity was increasing in their facilities. This finding correlates with the literature, which emphasizes the move to less costly, community-based models of care (Lumsdom, 1994). Hospitals are also expanding their involvement in other programs along the continuum of care, including subacute and extended care, home care, durable medical care, and home infusion.

The question is, To what extent is social work involved in these community-based programs? Social work clinical activity in the ambulatory area is increasing, according to 55 percent ($n = 168$) of the 308 respondents, but not commensurate with the dramatic increase in ambulatory programs. In addition, although the number of acute care beds in hospitals was decreasing, social work clinical activity on the inpatient units either was increasing (41 percent, $n = 127$ out of 312 respondents) or showed no change (44 percent, $n = 136$ out of 312 respondents). Unless there are social work staffing increases or major work redesign, it is unlikely that hospitals will have sufficient staffing to respond to the increase in ambulatory care programs. Building and maintaining a social work presence in ambulatory and community-based programs may be one of the greatest challenges for social work in the future but is essential to the survival of social work programs in health care settings.

Staffing for social work appears to be stable overall. Equal numbers of departments reported increases, decreases, and no changes in social work staffing. Although one-third (33 percent, $n = 112$) of the 336 hospitals that responded reported decreases in social work staffing, considerably more (62 percent, $n = 198$ out of 318 that responded) reported decreases in overall staffing. This is not to say that decreases did not occur or were not of concern, but the cuts were less dramatic than the anecdotal reports and cries of doom citing the decimation of social work programs in health care.

Two findings may shed some light on this fear and anxiety among social workers in hospitals: About one-third of the departments reported changes in the social work director, and an equal number of respondents indicated that departmental functions had been reviewed. These two factors could combine to create a feeling of departmental instability and vulnerability. Threats to the department may take on greater significance in the absence of stable leadership. Even a small reduction could be interpreted as impending doom if staff do not perceive that their leadership is capable of providing direction and protection during such chaotic times.

An interesting trend is the reported increases in nursing personnel within social work departments. It is not possible to explain these increases until further data analysis is conducted. For example, is this increase a byproduct of horizontal integration (such as departmental mergers), are nurses replacing social workers, or are nurses being added through work redesign efforts? Given the increasing reports that nurses are absorbing social work functions, further study, even beyond that which is possible in the present research, is warranted.

Anecdotal reports indicate a related trend: that discharge planning in many hospitals is being taken over by nursing. Our data do not support this characterization. Social work continued to assume responsibility for this critical function in most of the hospitals participating in this study. During the two-year period, there was only a 0.5 percent increase in the number of respondents reporting that a separate department independent of social work assumed responsibility for discharge planning (Table 34-13). The largest increase occurred in the response category "other structure." Cursory examination suggests that many of these respondents described a shared responsibility between social work and another discipline, such as nursing. Even though the majority of social work departments retained responsibility for discharge planning, the number declined. Further analysis is needed to better understand discharge planning trends and to monitor them over time.

Questions dealing with changes in the social work director or manager position also merit some discussion. It appears that social worker directors or managers were more likely to have expanded their span of control between FY 1992 and FY 1994. There were only slight decreases in the number of directors or managers with MSW degrees, with commensurate increases in those with BSW or non–social work degrees. The affiliations and qualifications of social work heads should be monitored closely. The slight increase in non–social work degrees may have resulted from consolidation of multiple departments, including social work, with a non–social work manager assuming the leadership of the newly constructed group.

Although there have been many anecdotal reports of decentralization of social work departments, the data do not suggest that this is a major force in changing social work services. Over three-quarters (78 percent, $n = 264$) of the 340 respondents indicated that they continued to operate with a centralized structure. Only a very small percentage of social work departments had been a part of decentralization processes (4 percent [$n = 12$] of the departments experienced total decentralization, and 14 percent [$n = 47$] reported decentralization with matrix management). The data suggest that the trend toward decentralization was greater in hospitals than in social work departments within these facilities.

Restructuring also appears to be affecting social work departments. About one-fourth of the respondents reported decreases in the number of social work administrative personnel, and about one-fifth indicated that administrative levels also declined. These decreases were more likely to occur at supervisory levels, although senior management within the departments also declined. Even though decreases were being reported, they were consistently less than decreases in the hospital environment in general (50.2 percent reported decreases in administrative personnel and 37.5 percent in administrative levels). This trend may reflect the already lean administrative structures within social work departments.

What is the impact of these dramatic changes in hospitals on various constituencies and social work activities and programs? Respondents were less likely to rate the effects of changes on patients and families as negatively as they rated the effects on social work management and clinical staff. Clinical staff were most likely to have been rated as negatively affected by the changes, perhaps because social work staff are indeed doing "more with less," contributing to a sense of being overwhelmed. They may be working harder to ensure that patients and families are not affected. This hypothesis cannot be tested adequately in the present study but would be an interesting area for further research.

The effects of hospital changes on social work activities were most often rated as neutral. The highest negative ratings were given to student programs and research. This finding may be of concern to schools of social work, particularly because of its implications for student practica. Schools of social work may need to become more involved in the changes affecting social work in health care settings if they plan to ensure quality field placements for future students.

Finally, there are claims that reductions in social work administrative personnel negatively affect the supervision of social work staff. Further analysis is needed, but preliminary data analysis does not support this contention. Over four-fifths of hospitals reported that staff continued to be supervised by social work personnel, although there was a slight decrease between FY 1992 and FY 1994. The use of non–social work supervisors increased, but this study is not able to discern the character of this supervision. A similar increase appeared in the use of peer supervision. An area for further analysis would be to examine if increases in peer supervision are related to increases in non–social work department heads. Peer supervision allows social work staff whose supervisors are not social workers to continue receiving social work supervision.

CONCLUSION

There is still much more to be done with the data from this study. Further analysis is needed to determine what factors are related to the changes hospitals are experiencing. For example, how do the stages of managed care development influence restructuring and resizing activities, social work leadership, and perceived effect of the changes? How do changes in social work leadership influence supervisory patterns and span of control? Also, it would be important to replicate this study for FY 1996 to see if present trends continue or if new patterns emerge.

Changes in hospital settings are affecting social work departments, but not to the same degree experienced by hospitals as a whole or suggested through anecdotal reports. We do not intend to minimize the significance of these changes, only to create a balanced view within the context of overall change in the health care industry. It does not appear that social work is being singled out or subjected to greater demands for change. Social work needs to maintain this balanced view to prevent practitioners and managers from assuming a stance of victimization. Victimization implies powerlessness and will lead to behaviors that will only exacerbate problems for social work. For example, a stance of victimization can lead to increased concern over turf and efforts to prevent change. This is not a time to put energies into stopping change in hospitals and social work services, but rather a time to mobilize change efforts and participate in the change process.

It is critical that social workers continue to monitor changes and trends in health care. The future is likely to hold even more change as health care moves quickly toward managed care and capitation. Only through knowledge and understanding of what is occurring can individuals increase their ability to predict future directions. Social workers must become architects of this process, shaping the profession's role and position in rapidly changing environments.

REFERENCES

Berger, C. (1993). *Restructuring and resizing: Strategies for social work and other human services administrators in health care.* Chicago: American Hospital Association.

Brennan, J. (1993, October). *NASW Hospital Social Work Reorganization Survey* (Report to the Board). Washington, DC: NASW Press.

Cummings, K. C., & Abell, R. M. (1993). Losing sight of the shore: How a future integrated American health care organization might look. *Health Care Management Review, 18*(2), 39–50.

Hagland, M. (1993). Mapping care. *Hospital and Health Networks, 67*(20), 34–40.

Hammer, M., & Champy, J. (1993). *Reengineering the corporation.* New York: HarperCollins.

Henderson, M. G., & Collard, A. (1992). Measuring quality in medical case management. In S. Rose (Ed.), *Case management and social work* (pp. 170–183). New York: Longman.

Koska, M. T. (1990). Case management: Doing the right thing for the wrong reasons. *Hospitals, 64*(10), 28–30.

Lumsdom, K. (1994). Beyond four walls. *Hospital and Health Networks, 68*(5), 44–45.

Shoor, R. (1993). Looking to manage care more closely. *Business and Health, 11,* 46–48, 50, 52–53.

SPSS, Inc. (1986). *SPSS user's guide.* New York: McGraw-Hill.

Tischler, G. L. (1990). Utilization management of mental health services by private third parties. *American Journal of Psychiatry, 147,* 967–973.

White, M., & Simmons, W. J. (1993). Managed care and case management: An overview. *Discharge Planning Update, 13*(1), 18–19.

This chapter was originally published in the August 1996 issue of Health & Social Work, *vol. 21, pp. 167–177*

35 Medicaid Managed Care and Urban Poor People: Implications for Social Work

Janet D. Perloff

Managed care is rapidly becoming the predominant method of financing and delivering health care to Medicaid recipients. The shift from Medicaid fee-for-service arrangements to managed care has important implications for the health care available to low-income and uninsured people living in U.S. cities. It also presents significant new challenges to the financial viability of urban "safety-net" providers—that is, the public hospitals, academic medical centers, community health centers, local health department clinics, school-based clinics, and other community-based health care providers that traditionally serve residents of low-income urban communities.

Social workers in direct practice and management positions in urban hospitals, clinics, and managed care plans, as well as in policy development and advocacy positions, have many opportunities to influence the transition to Medicaid managed care in cities. This article aims to help equip social workers for broad-scale implementation of Medicaid managed care by describing its theoretical basis and development; presenting reasons for its apparent popularity; and analyzing its likely effects on access to care, the long-term viability of urban safety-net providers, and social workers with Medicaid clients. Steps are identified by which social workers can support clients in the transition to Medicaid managed care and work for the preservation of access to care for disadvantaged urban populations.

MEDICAID MANAGED CARE

Theoretical Basis

Enrollment of Medicaid recipients in managed care reflects the widely held belief that managed care can improve health care access while also promoting cost containment and federal and state budget control (Edinburg & Cottler, 1995; Keigher, 1995). Medicaid managed care seeks to bring increasing numbers of recipients into health care delivery systems that are subject to "the new economics of managed care" (Shortell, Gillies, & Anderson, 1994, p. 48), which is based on the fact that care is provided to a defined number of enrollees at a fixed rate per member per month. Under capitation-based health care, all revenues are earned "up front" when contracts are negotiated. All system components—including hospitals, clinics, imaging centers, and primary care physicians'

418

offices—are transformed from revenue centers to cost centers; these cost centers need to be managed within the capitation-based budget. In theory, these arrangements create incentives for keeping people well and, when they become sick, for treating them at the most cost-effective location on the continuum of care and in the most cost-effective manner. These arrangements also create incentives to underserve patients.

Types

Medicaid managed care plans vary in the strength of their incentives for cost containment. Three major types of Medicaid managed care plans are (1) fee-for-service case management, under which the state pays a health care provider a monthly case management fee to perform gatekeeping and service coordination for each person enrolled; (2) fully capitated systems, under which the state pays a managed care plan, usually some form of health maintenance organization (HMO), a preset, or capitated, rate for each person enrolled, and the plan is then at risk for paying the costs of providing a comprehensive package of services to its enrollees, usually including inpatient, specialty, and primary care; and (3) partially capitated systems, under which the state pays a managed care plan a capitated rate for each person enrolled, but the plan assumes risk for the costs of providing a more limited package of services, usually excluding some specialty and inpatient care but including at least primary care services (Perkins & Rivera, 1995). Fully capitated systems contain the strongest incentives for cost containment; therefore, states are placing the greatest emphasis on developing and enrolling Medicaid recipients in fully capitated plans. As a result, fully capitated systems are the fastest growing type of Medicaid managed care, covering an estimated 63 percent of all Medicaid managed care enrollees in June 1994 (Lewin-VHI, 1995).

Growth

Recent increases in the number of Medicaid recipients enrolled in managed care have been dramatic. In 1983, 750,000 Medicaid recipients—3 percent of the Medicaid population—were enrolled in managed care. In 1994, about 7.8 million recipients—23 percent of all Medicaid recipients—were enrolled in managed care. Between 1993 and 1994 Medicaid managed care enrollment grew 63 percent, from 4.8 million to 7.8 million recipients (Kaiser Commission on the Future of Medicaid, 1995).

Currently, the populations being enrolled in Medicaid managed care are primarily children and adults receiving Aid to Families with Dependent Children and other low-income pregnant women and children. Historically, elderly and disabled Medicaid recipients have been excluded from Medicaid managed care because of their complex service needs, technical challenges in setting appropriate capitation payments, and difficulties finding plans willing to serve these populations. However, the high cost of the care of these Medicaid recipients has increased state interest in serving elderly and disabled people through managed care arrangements (Lewin-VHI, 1995). Some states have also begun to enroll special subpopulations of Medicaid patients in managed care, including patients with AIDS, substance abuse problems, and serious and persistent mental illness (Kaiser Commission on the Future of Medicaid, 1995; State of New York, 1995).

The pervasiveness of Medicaid managed care is indicated by the fact that as of June 1994, all states except Alaska, Connecticut, Maine, Nebraska, Oklahoma, Vermont, and Wyoming had some form of Medicaid managed care program (Kaiser Commission on the Future of Medicaid, 1995). In many states, Medicaid recipients voluntarily enroll in a managed care plan. However, mandatory Medicaid managed care programs are more attractive because they are more likely to yield cost savings (U.S. General Accounting Office [GAO], 1993). Many states are presently requesting and receiving federal approval to implement mandatory Medicaid managed care plans, and indications are that mandatory enrollment of Medicaid recipients in managed care plans will grow exponentially over the next several years (Holahan, Coughlin, Ku, Lipson, & Rajan, 1995; Kaiser Commission on the Future of Medicaid, 1995; Lewin-VHI, 1995).

EMPIRICAL EVIDENCE AND IMPLEMENTATION ISSUES

States are enthusiastic about the promise of Medicaid managed care for improving access, costs, quality, and health outcomes. However, the empirical evidence about Medicaid managed care is equivocal. Several recent reviews of empirical studies concluded that some versions of Medicaid managed care bring improvements in utilization, costs, and access over traditional fee-for-service arrangements (Fox & McManus, 1992; Hurley, Freund, & Paul, 1993; Lewin-VHI, 1995), but others concluded that the available evidence does not support many of the claims about cost savings, improved access, or improved quality (Freund & Lewit, 1993; Rowland, Rosenbaum, Simon, & Chait, 1995).

In the absence of definitive empirical evidence about its impact, Medicaid managed care is perhaps best viewed with a mixture of optimism and caution. Four questions are central to whether state Medicaid managed care initiatives can achieve their full potential: (1) Are managed care plans adequately prepared to meet the unique, pressing, and often complex health care needs of urban poor people? (2) Is the supply and distribution of primary care in cities adequate to ensure that Medicaid recipients enrolled in managed care will be able to find care? (3) What is the future of the health care providers who have traditionally served low-income urban residents? and (4) Will Medicaid recipients be adequately prepared to choose among managed care plans and to protect themselves against managed care's potential for aggressive enrollment and underservice?

Health Care Needs of Urban Poor People

Cities have high incidence rates for health problems such as low-birthweight babies and infant deaths, measles, tuberculosis, AIDS, and sexually transmitted diseases. Many of these problems, particularly those affecting low-income women and children, are concentrated in the most socioeconomically disadvantaged urban communities (Fossett & Perloff, 1995). These urban residents live in states that are the most eager to enroll in Medicaid managed care plans.

Little empirical evidence exists about the impact of Medicaid managed care on service utilization and health outcomes of high-risk populations. Research is needed to fully assess the effects of managed care on urban Medicaid recipients and to develop systems of care that produce the best health and mental health outcomes for these clients. However, the available empirical literature provides reasons to be cautious about the likely impact of Medicaid managed care on service utilization patterns and health outcomes for high-risk, multiproblem, chronically ill, and more expensive patients (Fossett & Perloff, 1995). Most managed care organizations are accustomed to serving employed, low-risk populations and have little experience with providing support services such as outreach, case management, transportation, and other psychosocial services that are beneficial to high-risk populations. In addition, because managed care organizations, especially those participating in full capitation programs, face strong financial incentives to limit utilization, patients enrolled in these plans may encounter difficulties obtaining the full range of health and related social services. As a result, patients needing these services have frequently not fared well in managed care arrangements (Schlesinger, 1986, 1989).

Urban Primary Care Supply and Distribution

There are reasons to be cautious about whether the supply and distribution of primary care in low-income urban neighborhoods will be adequate to meet the needs of Medicaid recipients (Rosenthal, 1993). Most of the nation's metropolitan areas are richly supplied with doctors and hospitals, but embedded in them are areas that lack health care resources adequate to serve the needs of their residents (Fossett & Perloff, 1995; Ginzburg, Berliner, & Ostow, 1993). This maldistribution originates, in part, because private physicians and other health care providers tend to select locations that enable them to attract a large and profitable clientele. As a result of the limited profit-making potential of poor neighborhoods, these areas have historically had very few private health care providers such as office-based physicians or private community hospitals.

The shortage of physicians is aggravated by the fact that many physicians in metropolitan areas do not accept Medicaid patients or limit the number of Medicaid patients they treat (Perloff, Kletke, & Fossett, 1995; Perloff, Kletke, Fossett, & Banks, 1995). The lack of private providers is made worse by some providers' personal inclinations to avoid crime, AIDS, and racial and ethnic diversity, as well as to avoid the challenges posed by patients beset with complex and often unyielding social problems (Physician Payment Review Commission, 1993).

Because many low-income urban neighborhoods already lack an adequate supply of health care providers, there is ample reason to be pessimistic that Medicaid managed care will improve the quantity and quality of health care available in these neighborhoods (Fossett & Perloff, 1995). In theory, Medicaid managed care tries to use the payment system to improve access to care in underserved communities. States set capitation rates at a level that will improve the attractiveness of the Medicaid population to managed care entities and then use mandatory enrollment to ensure HMOs a large and lucrative Medicaid market. It has been argued that the resulting competition among managed care organizations for contracts to serve Medicaid patients will improve the range of available health care alternatives.

However, managed care plans will face equally strong financial incentives to avoid making large investments in developing the health care provider supply. States may set capitation rates at levels that make it attractive for managed care plans to enroll Medicaid recipients, but the supply of care providers in many low-income urban neighborhoods will be inadequate to support mass mandatory enrollment. Without sufficiently generous capitation payments or other financial incentives, managed care plans will unlikely foster significant improvements in the underlying supply of care providers.

Urban Safety-Net Providers

With little access to private physicians and other health care providers, residents of low-income urban communities have come to depend on urban safety-net providers (Fossett & Perloff, 1995). The safety net includes public hospitals and clinics run by cities or counties and also academic medical centers that have historically tended to be in or near urban communities so that physicians, nurses, social workers, and other professionals in training could serve the needs of disadvantaged patients in exchange for rich learning opportunities. The clinics run by county and city health departments, the community health centers funded by federal grants, and the variety of family-planning and other community-based agencies that are supported by a mix of private and public resources have also become important elements in the urban health care safety net.

Safety-net providers offer many features that are valuable to urban poor and uninsured people (Fossett & Perloff, 1995). Providers are often close by, enhancing the probability of their use, and many offer a wider array of enabling services (including outreach, case management, and follow-up) and support services (including transportation, translation, and child care), which are important complements to medical services.

However, managed care organizations will be selective in forming networks, including only those providers who can be successful in keeping down the costs of care. Such network selectivity is likely to result in excluding or drastically reducing the role of the urban safety-net providers in the care of Medicaid patients. Some characteristics typical of safety-net providers may make them less than attractive as network providers for managed care organizations (Fossett & Perloff, 1995). Safety-net providers are often in poor financial condition, undercapitalized, outdated and in disrepair, inefficiently run, lacking in adequate information and management systems, and incompatible with both the mission and the management style of fully capitated health plans. Given the potentially high costs of working with these providers, managed care organizations may not be eager to include them in their managed care network.

Some safety-net providers have benefited from far-sighted and effective leadership and are prepared to be successful in a managed care environment by creating their own managed care plans or securing contracts as providers within the networks of private managed care plans. More typically, however, safety-net providers have had very little experience with managed care. These providers are accustomed to fee-for-service revenues and, in some instances, contributions to their budget from state or local appropriations. For safety-net hospitals, Medicaid's disproportionate share payments, which are made to hospitals that serve more than their share of poor and uninsured people, provide a vital subsidy. Accustomed to the world of fee-for-service with a subsidy, these providers lack experience in competing for patients; their inexperience places them at a competitive disadvantage.

Recent evidence suggests that Medicaid managed care is shifting patients away from urban safety-net providers, although the consequences of this redistribution of patients are not fully understood (Henneberger, 1994; Peck & Hubbert, 1994; Sack, 1995; Winslow, 1995). However, there is ample reason for concern. Exclusion of safety-net providers from managed care networks has the potential to disrupt existing arrangements that residents of underserved neighborhoods have made to obtain care and to shift these patients into the care of providers less responsive to their unique and often complex needs. In addition, the loss of Medicaid patients to managed care plans represents a significant loss of revenues for safety-net providers. Medicaid revenues are used by these agencies and institutions to subsidize the care they provide to the uninsured population. The loss of these revenues will limit the ability of these agencies to care for uninsured people in the future.

Recipient Preparedness

Medicaid managed care is a significant departure from the way recipients have received care in the past and will require a reorientation to the health care system (Perloff, 1993). For the first time, Medicaid recipients will be asked to select a health plan and a primary care provider, limit their use to certain providers, and obtain authorization and referrals before using certain services such as emergency rooms or specialists. Medicaid recipients will need a lot of information if they are to make informed choices about both plan and provider and to be fully prepared to use the health care system in new ways.

In addition, state agencies will need to ensure that Medicaid recipients are protected from overly aggressive marketing by managed care plans (Perloff, 1987). Medicaid managed care plans face strong incentives to earn the up-front revenue from recipient enrollment. Very rapid build-up in Medicaid managed care enrollment and practices that may even be fraudulent can therefore be expected as plans maneuver to lock in enrollees (Gottlieb, 1995; Pear, 1995). In addition, without adequate monitoring by state Medicaid agencies, enrollment can rapidly outstrip the capacity of managed care organizations to provide needed services (Fisher, 1995). Finally, state agencies will need to ensure that both quality assurance mechanisms and legal protection are in place to protect Medicaid recipients from managed care's inherent incentives to underserve (Perloff, 1987).

ROLES FOR SOCIAL WORK

Developments associated with Medicaid managed care will have a significant impact on low-income and uninsured people living in cities and will also pose challenges for institutions traditionally serving this population. Social workers have many opportunities to shape the Medicaid managed care debate and to influence the outcome of these developments.

Direct Practice and Management

Social workers in direct practice can play an important role in helping clients develop the skills needed to obtain health care in the managed care environment. Social workers in settings in which the Medicaid eligibility of clients is being established will have the important task of informing and educating clients about various choices related to their coverage. This role will be particularly important in states implementing mandatory Medicaid managed care plans because, in most instances, clients failing to choose will automatically be assigned to a health plan and a primary care provider. Although the results of automatic assignment may be acceptable to clients, better choices would seem likely to result with client input.

Given that managed care plans have strong incentives to enroll patients and therefore may market themselves aggressively, social workers should place a high priority on helping clients fully evaluate managed care plans and choose the plan through which they will be best served. Clients may face choices between managed care and fee-for-service plans and from among an array of health plans and providers. Carefully assessing a client's situation and helping him or her fully understand and consider the options will improve the probability that good choices are made. For example, noting the existence of transportation barriers or an excellent relationship with a particular primary care provider will improve the likelihood that these situational factors will influence choice.

Social workers will need to be familiar with the rules of Medicaid managed care in their state to help educate clients about new care-seeking requirements and to ensure that these requirements do not become barriers to appropriate care seeking. Changes in care-seeking rules include the requirement to contact one's selected primary care provider before visiting specialists or emergency rooms and, in some states, the possibility that health care previously obtained from public health clinics or community-based agencies (such as immunizations or family-planning services) must now be obtained from one's managed care plan. Clients may also need support to ensure that they are not being underserved by a plan. Social workers can identify instances of potential underservice, compile data documenting such problems, and intervene with managed care plans and state and local Medicaid agencies on behalf of clients whose rights may have been violated.

The informing, educating, and advocating that may be required of social workers in a managed care environment will sometimes put health care social workers at odds with the goals and values of their employers (Cornelius, 1994; Ross, 1993). Social workers will find themselves advocating additional services for a client in an environment that places a premium on cost minimization. Social workers in supervisory positions in hospitals, clinics, and managed care organizations will need to be prepared to help staff social workers satisfactorily resolve such dilemmas arising from the new economics of managed care. To some extent, such dilemmas are inherent in Medicaid managed care. For this reason, social workers outside of Medicaid managed care will have a particularly important role to play in ensuring optimal health outcomes for clients. Because of their independence from the health care system, social workers in other settings—child welfare agencies, community-based social services agencies, mental health agencies, and schools—may be in the best position to help clients judge whether their health care needs are being met, to recognize aspects of Medicaid managed care that are working, and to identify and work toward remedies for aspects that need improvement.

Policy Development and Advocacy

As was the case during the recent federal health reform debate, social workers should be actively trying to influence Medicaid managed care policy development. State Medicaid managed care initiatives entail a planning process, submission of applications for waivers to the federal government, and in many cases passage of state legislation. These and subsequent stages in the policy development process present numerous opportunities for public comment, testimony, and advocacy. Social workers and organizations representing the profession can also take part in emerging coalitions of providers, consumers, and other health and welfare advocates who are committed to sound planning and implementation of state Medicaid managed care initiatives, ongoing monitoring of the impact of managed care, and change.

In the attempt to influence the shape of Medicaid managed care, social work should make efforts to ensure that vulnerable populations will have access to health care. Social workers should be strong advocates for the development of state-level information systems that will monitor the ability of managed care plans to meet recipients' needs and that can produce timely indicators of access problems. Social workers should also advocate for policy proposals that will give managed care plans strong incentives to develop new capacity in underserved areas, including advocacy for payment of higher capitation levels to plans that propose to increase capacity in specific ways. In addition, ensuring access will require strong and continuing advocacy for federal and state policies aimed at developing the supply of primary care providers in underserved communities. Existing federal programs such as the Migrant and Community Health Centers Program and the National Health Service Corps should be preserved; creative new state and local capacity development initiatives should be developed and supported.

High priority should also be given to supporting policy proposals that strike a reasonable balance between protecting the financial viability of urban safety-net providers and fostering cost containment through competition in local health care markets. For example, California's proposed mandatory Medicaid managed care initiative, which is being implemented in 1996, recognizes that safety-net providers have little experience with and lack adequate preparation for managed care, that they are extremely vulnerable to the loss of Medicaid and disproportionate share revenue that may result from increased competition, and that they will need insulation and time to adapt if they are to survive and continue to meet the needs of Medicaid recipients and the growing uninsured population (GAO, 1995). Features that would mitigate some of the harsher effects of managed care on safety-net providers (some of which are included in California's and other state Medicaid managed care plans) include requiring or creating strong incentives for the inclusion of providers in managed care networks; providing technical assistance to providers in key areas such as risk-based financing, negotiating contracts, and developing effective information systems; and ensuring that there is an ongoing subsidy for the services these settings provide to the uninsured population. In the absence of such features, Medicaid managed care will pose a serious threat to the future of urban safety-net providers, to social workers practicing in these settings, and to the people they serve.

REFERENCES

Cornelius, D. (1994). Managed care and social work: Constructing a context and a response. *Social Work in Health Care, 20*, 47–63.

Edinburg, G. M., & Cottler, J. M. (1995). Managed care. In R. L. Edwards (Ed.-in-Chief), *Encyclopedia of social work* (19th ed., Vol. 2, pp. 1635–1642). Washington, DC: NASW Press.

Fisher, I. (1995, August 28). Forced marriage of Medicaid and managed care hits snags. *New York Times*, pp. B1, B5.

Fossett, J., & Perloff, J. (1995). *The "new" health reform and access to care: The problem of the inner city* (Background paper). Washington, DC: Kaiser Commission on the Future of Medicaid.

Fox, H., & McManus, M. (1992). *Medicaid managed care arrangements and their impact on children and adolescents: A briefing report*. Washington, DC: Child and Adolescent Health Policy Center.

Freund, D., & Lewit, E. (1993). Managed care for children and pregnant women: Promises and pitfalls. *Future of Children, 3*, 92–122.

Ginzburg, E., Berliner, H. S., & Ostow, M. (1993). *Changing U.S. health care*. Boulder, CO: Westview Press.

Gottlieb, M. (1995, October 2). A free-for-all in swapping Medicaid for managed care. *New York Times*, p. A1.

Henneberger, M. (1994, June 30). New York hospitals fight to retain Medicaid patients. *New York Times*, p. A1.

Holahan, J., Coughlin, T., Ku, L., Lipson, D. J., & Rajan, S. (1995, Spring). Insuring the poor through Section 1115 Medicaid waivers. *Health Affairs*, pp. 199–216.

Hurley, R., Freund, D., & Paul, J. (1993). *Managed care in Medicaid: Lessons for policy and program design*. Ann Arbor, MI: Health Administration Press.

Kaiser Commission on the Future of Medicaid. (1995, April). *Medicaid and managed care: Policy brief*. Washington, DC: Author.

Keigher, S. (1995). Managed care's silent seduction of America and the new politics of choice [National Health Line]. *Health & Social Work, 20*, 146–151.

Lewin-VHI. (1995, February). *States as payers: Managed care for Medicaid populations*. Washington, DC: National Institute for Health Care Management.

Pear, R. (1995, April 24). Florida struggles to lift Medicaid burden. *New York Times*, p. A2.

Peck, M., & Hubbert, E. D. (1994, July). *Changing the rules: Medicaid managed care and MCH in U.S. cities*. Omaha, NE: CityMatch.

Perkins, J., & Rivera, L. A. (1995, March). EPSDT and managed care: Do plans know what they are getting into? *Clearinghouse Review*, pp. 1248–1260.

Perloff, J. (1987). Safeguards are needed for Medicaid HMOs [Editorial]. *Chicago Sun-Times*, p. 38.

Perloff, J. (1993, April). *Medicaid managed care for women and children: What have we learned?* Paper presented at the National Conference on Managed Care Systems for Mothers and Young Children, Baltimore.

Perloff, J., Kletke, P., & Fossett, J. (1995). Which physicians limit their Medicaid participation and why. *Health Services Research, 30,* 9–26.

Perloff, J., Kletke, P., Fossett, P., & Banks, S. (1995, June). *Medicaid participation among urban primary care physicians.* Paper presented at a meeting of the Association for Health Services Research, Chicago.

Physician Payment Review Commission. (1993). *Annual report to Congress.* Washington, DC: Author.

Rosenthal, E. (1993, October 17). Shortage of doctors in poor areas is seen as barrier to health plans. *New York Times,* p. A1.

Ross, J. (1993). Redefining hospital social work: An embattled professional domain [Editorial]. *Health & Social Work, 18,* 243–247.

Rowland, D., Rosenbaum, S., Simon, L., & Chait, E. (1995, March). *Medicaid and managed care: Lessons from the literature.* Washington, DC: Kaiser Commission on the Future of Medicaid.

Sack, K. (1995, August 20). Public hospitals around the country cut basic service. *New York Times,* pp. 1, 24.

Schlesinger, M. (1986). On the limits of expanding health care reform: Chronic care in prepaid settings. *Milbank Quarterly, 62,* 189–216.

Schlesinger, M. (1989). Striking a balance: Capitation, the mentally ill, and public policy. In D. Mechanic & L. Aiken (Eds.), *Paying for services: Promises and pitfalls of capitation* (pp. 186–214). New York: Jossey-Bass.

Shortell, S. M., Gillies, R. R., & Anderson, D. A. (1994, Winter). The new world of managed care: Creating organized delivery systems. *Health Affairs,* pp. 46–64.

State of New York. (1995, March). *The partnership plan: A public-private initiative ensuring healthcare for needy New Yorkers* [Section 1115 waiver application]. Albany: Author.

U.S. General Accounting Office. (1993). *Medicaid: States turn to managed care to improve access and control costs* (Report No. GAO-HRD-93-86). Washington, DC: Author.

U.S. General Accounting Office. (1995). *Expansion of California's Medicaid managed care program* (Report No. GAO-HEHS-95-87). Washington, DC: Author.

Winslow, R. (1995, April 12). Welfare recipients a hot commodity in managed care now. *Wall Street Journal,* p. A1.

This chapter was originally published in the August 1996 issue of Health & Social Work, *vol. 21, pp. 196–201.*

36 Confidentiality and Managed Care: Ethical and Legal Concerns

Jeanette R. Davidson and Tim Davidson

Before managed care, social work services in the field of mental health tended to be needs driven. Increasingly, these services are resource driven, and there is a profit motive for the managers whether the resource is the public or the private dollar. As managed care companies take over the allocation of funds, the monitoring of treatment, and the measurement of outcomes, social workers encounter an ethical and legal dilemma with the demise of confidentiality in the professional–client relationship. The dilemma appears to be rooted first in the essential difference in primary purpose between social workers and managed care companies and second in the heavy reliance of managed care companies on burgeoning information systems.

Specifically, many social workers providing services within managed care systems are concerned about the quantity of information sought about the client; the sensitive nature of that information (which if exposed leaves the client entirely vulnerable); the way in which the client is, for all intents and purposes, forced to permit the disclosure of the information to ensure third-party payments (unless able to pay directly for services); the potential use of the information to deny rather than provide needed services to the client; and the all-too-often suspect security of the information systems involved. Social workers are also uncomfortable when they consider the potential negative effect that the loss of confidentiality may have on the client–worker relationship as well as the possible liability issues that may ensue.

Given that the profession has long heralded the protection of client confidentiality, it is timely that social workers re-examine traditional guidelines within this new context of managed care. If safeguarding confidences is still valued, then social workers, individually and in consortium, need to negotiate with managed care policymakers and government regulators to develop new mechanisms to protect client information.

CLASH OF ESSENTIAL PURPOSES

Difference in Mission

Social workers need to be aware of the fundamental differences in mission between managed care personnel and themselves as providers and the effect of those differences on the treatment of client data. Because managed care companies primarily serve the funding bodies, they have an essential disparity of purpose from social workers. They are concerned with capitated risk for groups of people, and therefore any individual's particular need is evaluated in the context of all the other covered lives. Thus, managed care companies have gatekeepers in place who examine intimate details about a person from a distance and who may use that information to deny rather than provide needed services. In contrast, social workers' general aim is to work with all who request and need services. With managed care, then, the mission is restrictive and generalized, whereas with social workers service delivery is inclusive and individualized.

Difference in Reasons for Documentation

When care is managed, client data become determinative. Recordings undertaken for managed care companies are first and foremost meant to establish the saving of health care dollars for employers and insurance companies. A document containing highly confidential material, in the hands of a managed care administrator, will be used whatever way is most profitable from a business perspective. This contrasts with the traditional use of social work records, which has been to chronicle, in the context of trust, individuals' treatment and progress for the purpose of assisting recovery.

Difference in Use of Outcome Measures

An impetus for adopting a managed care format in behavioral health care is to promote the measurement of treatment outcomes. This purpose, seemingly laudable at first, belies another agenda. Marketers of managed care companies stress that health professionals will be better prepared to deliver the optimum treatment for each disorder once reams of outcome data are analyzed. Although managed care research is often flawed because of inappropriate questions (Shapiro, 1995), simplistic and reductionistically defined variables, and economic controls over the process, it may in fact produce some interesting and helpful conclusions.

In practice, however, outcome measures for managed care have ultimately been used to determine which populations are healthy and which populations predictably could drain the profits of the managed care company. Chronic, heavy users of health care services are not usually recruited by managed care unless there is a guaranteed safety net provided by state or local governments. The legitimate clinical principle of "least-restrictive alternatives" has been transliterated by managed care to mean "severely restricted alternatives." "Stop-loss" and "hold harmless" are fundamental operating procedures written into managed care contracts. Stop-loss clauses require the government to step in when providing care for those who are needy proves too costly, and hold harmless clauses require providers to shoulder the burden of further treatment and liability when managed care companies discontinue payments because it does not appear that a positive treatment outcome is cheap and imminent.

Social workers have traditionally advocated for people who need services, and so it seems perverse to contribute client data to a system that takes that information and uses it to figure out who should not receive treatment. For clients who have been approved for some managed care payments, the social worker's report of positive treatment outcomes frequently inclines the case reviewer to stop payment for further services because the clients' needs are then determined to be not great enough. Outcome measures are used, then, both to disenfranchise those most in need and to limit funding for others. Social workers support efficacy studies, but not at clients' expense.

PROBLEMS WITH MANAGED CARE'S RELIANCE ON INFORMATION SYSTEMS

Irrespective of the form of managed care, whether a health maintenance organization, an employee assistance program, a preferred provider network with horizontal or vertical layers, or a management service designed to manage these and other kinds of managed care, client information is now shared in a much less discriminate manner than traditionally occurred in fee-for-service delivery systems. Before managed care, even in agencies with several layers of bureaucracy, strict guidelines governed the release of information to the various levels of administration and accounting.

With the use of managed care information systems that include telephone reviews, voice mail, faxes, cellular telephones, and highly unregulated computerized databases, there are few guarantees, if any, that sensitive information is stored securely. Rather, it appears that information, once passed from the social worker to a managed care service and logged into the medical database of a third-party insurance payer, may be as accessible as credit card information or mortgage payment records to people who know how to proceed with the electronic inquiry. As noted by the Legal Action Center (LAC) (1995), "The potential for wrongful disclosure of confidential information has expanded right along with the expansion of the capability of computers to move information from location to location" (p. 104).

Unprotected Databases

Press reports from a number of sources delineate various problems within the managed care industry with respect to information systems. In an article in the *New York Times,* concerns about unprotected databases were cited and clearly indicated a clinical predicament involving trust for both clinicians and clients (Henneberger, 1994). A scathing article in the *Wall Street Journal* noted how "open" all medical information is as "it lies unprotected in a patchwork of databases where it is so easy to see" and how people who file for managed care visits to psychotherapists "build up especially detailed records" (Schultz, 1994, p. A5) that are easy to access. One defense lawyer, representing insurance companies and employers on work-related cases, blatantly admitted that he examined confidential therapy notes within managed care files to see if he could get clients to "look like Charlie Manson" (Schultz, 1994, p. A5). Not surprisingly, the public's generally held belief that sensitive records are protected by doctor–patient confidentiality is considered by lawyers to be more myth than reality. Medical benefits experts report that once therapy files are in the possession of employers and insurance companies, "so are the temptations to tap it, for a variety of reasons that have nothing to do with keeping employees healthy" (Schultz, 1994, p. A1).

Violation of Federal Law

Federal law is in place to protect certain client rights, but managed care companies often do not adhere either to disclosure or to redisclosure regulations. Even in the area of alcohol and drug abuse treatment, for which by law confidentiality requirements are very strict (Confidentiality Law, 1992), private insurance carriers and managed care entities "routinely share information through vast computerized networks" (LAC, 1995, p. 19). For example, one insurer "placed information about claims for reimbursement for drug abuse treatment on recorded telephone messages easily retrievable by anyone who has access to the patient's social security number" (LAC, 1995, p. 19). Such a cavalier approach to sensitive information is reflected again by managed care personnel who "frequently redisclose to third parties (e.g., insurance companies, other health care providers, or governmental agencies) information that identifies the client as having received alcohol or drug services" (LAC, 1995, p. 86), even though such a practice is prohibited by statute and tradition.

Violation of Research Protocol

It is important to recognize that research conducted within managed care systems, based on client information submitted by providers, ostensibly may be very helpful with regard to "practice guidelines" and "efficacious, effective and efficient" treatments (Landers, 1994, p. 3). However, reflecting managed care companies' general tendency to conduct business in an unregulated fashion, the collection of such data may well be out of compliance with accepted guidelines for scholarship and research as outlined in the *NASW Code of Ethics* (NASW, 1994) and federal guidelines about alcohol and drug abuse client records (*Regulations for Confidentiality of Alcohol and Drug Abuse Patient Records*, 1987). In drug and alcohol treatment, for example, when programs permit access to patient-identifying information without the client's specific consent for purposes of research, there must be compliance with a protocol that is independently reviewed and approved by a group of three or more individuals; with regulations about securing data, including electronically stored data; with procedures for locking and blocking protected information; and with rules about access to the data only by authorized and qualified researchers (*Regulations for Confidentiality of Alcohol and Drug Abuse Patient Records*, 1987, § 2.52). In the evolving managed care industry, it is evident that such protection of research data is frequently breached.

Absence of Known Boundaries for Information Transfer

Before managed care and the widespread use of information systems, social workers could more reasonably assume that those who were privy to client information were identifiable, occupied a role specific to the provision of client care, were relatively motivated by the best interests of the client, and were able to safeguard the information disclosed by the client. Similarly, the location of hard copies of client records, which were gathered and stored by the clinician or agency, was "more knowable and securable" (LAC, 1995, p. 103) than is presently the case with managed care systems. Now, with a revolving system of unidentified case reviewers, social workers may not know who knows what or who will have access in the future to client disclosures they divulge for the purposes of being included in a managed care network.

Pressures on Social Workers and Clients to Comply

Clients in managed care environments find themselves compelled to sign consent forms to release information from the social worker to the gatekeeper of managed care services in the hope that doing so will ensure that third-party payments are paid to the provider. Social workers find themselves prevailing on clients to sign these release forms, which in effect relinquish the client's right to privacy, for management purposes, without there being a valid clinical reason to do so.

CONFIDENTIALITY AS A CORE VALUE AND ETHICAL STANDARD

Confidentiality has traditionally been regarded as a core value of the social work profession (Lindenthal, Jordan, Lentz, & Thomas, 1988; Loewenberg & Dolgoff, 1992; McGowan, 1995). The importance of confidentiality has been emphasized by its inclusion as an ethical standard in the *NASW Code of Ethics*, adopted in 1979 and revised in 1990 and 1994, to "serve as a guide to the everyday conduct of members of the social work profession" (NASW, 1994, p. v).

The *NASW Code of Ethics* (NASW, 1994) exhorts practitioners to "respect the privacy of clients and hold in confidence all information obtained in the course of professional service" (p. 6) and guides social workers to "share with others confidences revealed by clients, without their consent, only for compelling professional reasons" (p. 6). Furthermore, social workers are directed to "inform clients fully about the limits of confidentiality in a given situation, the purposes for which information is obtained, and how it may be used" (p. 6) and "to obtain informed consent of clients before taping, recording, or permitting third-party observation of their activities" (p. 6).

A resource guide on managed care recently published by NASW specifies that "it is imperative that all clinicians continue to protect the confidential nature of the patient–therapist relationship" (Jackson, 1995, p. 8.5). The guide urges managed care managers and agency staff to develop clear protocols for communicating about clinical issues, and it states that these protocols should be comfortable to clinicians and in accord with state laws and statutes.

LEGAL RESPONSIBILITIES TO THE SOCIAL WORK CLIENT

It is clear that the social worker's ethical responsibilities and legal duties converge. McGowan (1995) observed that confidentiality is protected legally by a number of case decisions and by statutes granting licensed or certified social workers privileged information status in many states. Schwarz (1989) stressed the legal rights of clients, pointing out that because the law was created for the protection of the client, technically the privilege belongs to the client, not the professional. He explained, "If a client authorizes the disclosure of a privileged communication for purposes of obtaining insurance, such a client is not deemed to have waived the privilege for other purposes" (p. 224), and "the client has the right to limit to whom and for how long the privileged communication will be disclosed" (p. 224).

Social workers have serious legal obligations to maintain confidentiality. Of the six primary legal duties listed by Cournoyer (1991), two refer directly to the obligation to uphold confidential relationships. Besharov and Besharov (1987), examining categories of lawsuits filed against social workers, found that two of the prominent causes for action included breach of confidentiality and violation of clients' civil rights. Kutchins (1991) emphasized that the social worker has a strict fiduciary responsibility to keep information confidential, to tell the client the truth, and to be loyal to the client. He added that the ethical principles outlined in the *NASW Code of Ethics* "are not just desirable conduct to which social workers aspire" but that "if they ignore these ethical mandates, the law governing fiduciary relationships can make them pay dearly" (p. 107), even if the professional's defense is that he or she acted in accordance with accepted practice. The dilemma facing social workers who practice within a managed care environment is that they have a fiduciary responsibility to clients (which by definition is one that is power laden, protective, based on trust, and without any conflict of allegiance) (Kutchins, 1991) and at the same time are asked to give primary loyalty to the managed care network.

INFORMED CONSENT TO RELEASE INFORMATION

Informed consent is much more than the simple matter of signing a piece of paper (Reamer, 1987; Torczyner, 1991). Torczyner and Reamer highlighted as essential standards for valid consent that the person making the decision be competent; that the decision be voluntary and not a result of coercion or captivity or undue influence; and that the client know all the necessary facts, choices, and risks.

With managed care, the technicalities of consent to release information forms, dutifully signed by the client, have been taken to a new level of complicity. A proper legal format for consent to release information about clients in drug or alcohol treatment as defined by the U.S. Department of Health and Human Services includes among other items the name of the individual or organization that will receive the disclosure, how much and what kind of information is to be disclosed, and a statement that the patient may revoke the consent at any time (*Regulations for Confidentiality of Alcohol and Drug Abuse Patient Records*, 1987, § 2.31). With managed care systems the reality is often that the name of the individual or organization receiving the disclosure may change without notice, the information to be disclosed may consist of a verbatim account of the client's most sensitive information given to persuade a gatekeeper to continue to authorize services, and the statement about the client's being able to revoke consent at any time is an illusory proposition given the virtual irretrievability of electronic transmissions of data that are stored in various locations.

Under the auspices of managed care, both the spirit and the letter of social work guidelines relating to confidentiality and informed consent are broken regularly. What the social worker may want to give the managed care company— a molehill of sufficient detail about the client—too often develops into a mountain of intimate detail on computer files, the access to which is outside of the worker's control. And although some social workers may believe they are protected legally by formal consent agreements, it should be clear that technical permission to disclose information does not solve the ethical problem of clients losing their right to confidentiality, nor does it excuse the social worker from fiduciary responsibilities to the client.

Rather, when social workers prevail on clients to give consent to release information to obtain third-party payments, the ethical problems around the issue of confidentiality are compounded, either by the social workers' active role in soliciting the consent or by their passive role in not advising the client fully of the uncertainty of keeping the information private. Kutchins (1991) put it succinctly: "Informed consent is a time bomb ticking away for social workers and other mental health professionals" (p. 111).

QUESTIONS FOR THE PROFESSION

A number of ethical questions emerge with the demise of confidentiality in the context of managed care. Some of these questions concern ethical decision making by the social worker regarding participation in managed care systems, legal issues, social work purpose, fiscal matters, and professional status.

Deciding to Participate

Social workers may find these questions of importance as they decide whether, or how, to participate with managed care systems:

- With managed care, is more good extended to more people, and is the sacrifice of confidentiality necessary for this to occur?
- Do the ends justify the means (that is, cooperation with managed care)?
- If a utilitarian philosophy rules the day, how might the most vulnerable members of society be protected (see Rawls, 1971)?
- Is confidentiality fundamentally good, and to what degree should it be extended or limited in a health enterprise?
- Does managed care perpetuate a class distinction whereby poor and middle-class clients are expected to give up the right to a confidential relationship with social workers while wealthy people who can pay independently are not required to do so?
- How much should the client bear the responsibility for his or her own decision about trading the right to confidentiality for services, and how much responsibility should the social worker bear?

Legal Issues

Questions social workers may have related to legal issues include the following:

- Is a social worker's cooperation with a managed care company inherently in conflict with his or her fiduciary responsibilities related to confidentiality, truth telling, and loyalty to clients?
- Are social workers colluding with managed care personnel to violate clients' civil rights?
- Because it may not be possible to have a clear understanding or accurate knowledge of the accessibility and distribution potential of information released to a managed care entity, are the customary consent to release information forms valid?

- To what degree is the social worker liable should an unforeseen outcome occur about which the client was given no warning?
- Is it always in clients' best interests for social workers to attempt to explain the limits of confidentiality in a managed care environment (what about the very fragile client?), and if not, how will the social worker justify ignoring the duty to tell clients the truth?

Social Work Purpose

Social workers may need to ponder some of the following questions about professional purpose when working with managed care companies:

- Does the social worker's primary duty shift from the client to the managed care company?
- In a bureaucracy where individual rights have been supplanted by principles of group management, are social workers moving subtly into a role in which they will function as agents of social control?
- Is the relationship with managed care a slippery slope, wherein the social worker initially discloses benign information but may be called on later to reveal information that could be used to discriminate against vulnerable individuals (for instance, to identify clients in gay relationships, who may be considered high risk for insurance purposes)?
- What are the ethical obligations of social workers to clients as a collective group who appear to have little freedom to challenge this loss of rights to confidentiality or otherwise influence their situation as an organized group?
- Does this situation with managed care constitute a social justice struggle (forecast by Reid & Billups, 1986) against disentitlement and the emphasis on "the minimal rights and statuses of individuals" (p. 14)?

Fiscal Matters

A number of questions arise related to social workers' fiscal concerns:

- Because of the need to be paid for services by third-party payers, are social workers and social services agencies forced to sacrifice clients' rights in order to be recompensed?
- How far does the social worker's duty to aid go when there is an "inconvenience" to the self (for example, "punishment" by exclusion from managed care provider lists if designated "uncooperative") (Shapiro, 1995)?

Professional Status

Social workers have been diligent in developing standards of practice and a professional image, both of which are now threatened by dictates of managed care organizations. Practitioners concerned about professional status may ask,

- Does the advent of managed care accelerate declassification (Meyer, 1983) of the profession, with social workers being compelled to adhere to the managed care companies' directives that breach confidentiality?
- Is it right for managed care companies to have external authority over traditional social work standards of ethics, hierarchical ethical guidelines

developed within the profession (Loewenberg & Dolgoff, 1992; Reamer, 1987; Rhodes, 1991), and even the social worker's internal ethical judgments?

■ What are the costs of turning back the clock on social workers' fight for privileged communication with their clients?

■ By agreeing to an administrative plan that undermines confidentiality, have social workers and social services agencies allowed professional honor to give way to expedience?

RECOMMENDATIONS FOR CHANGE

Managed care appears to be here to stay, and soon almost all social work services, whether public or private, will be influenced by managed care systems. It is hoped that because managed care is a new and developing industry, the profession can influence its various forms and levels of administration. Given that managed care originated from cost-containment efforts of insurance companies and employers, there now needs to be a strong countermovement from social workers intent on serving clients fairly and not simply managing organizations efficiently.

To regain some of the ground that has been lost with regard to confidential care, the following changes are proposed:

■ A depersonalized coding system should eventually replace all permanent entries into the computer databases maintained by managed care companies, with the main objective being to camouflage client identifying information. If managed care companies' genuine purpose in monitoring clients' progress is to improve treatment and to track effective interventions, then these depersonalized records can be used to achieve this end.

■ In keeping with NASW guidelines (Jackson, 1995), the computer software used in the transfer of client data should be restricted to certain personnel and should block sensitive information that could lead to patient identification. At the same time, tight confidentiality protocols should be maintained by all employees.

■ All contracts with managed care companies should state explicitly the expectation of confidentiality in writing (Corcoran & Vandiver, 1996).

■ Providers should refuse managed care contracts that include nondisclosure clauses (which restrict clinicians' discussion with clients about limitations imposed by the managed care organization). Social workers and their professional organizations should give unequivocal support to members of the profession taking such a stance.

■ Outpatient case notes or hospital files should not be copied in part or whole into the databases of managed care or insurance companies.

■ Clients should have the opportunity to review records that have been given by the social worker to the managed care company. This review should be made easily and routinely, if desired.

■ Any personal information that is put on the files of managed care companies should be destroyed after service is concluded, and managed care companies should comply with federal regulations requiring the elimination of all patient-identifying information on completion of an audit or evaluation.

- If one managed care company is purchased by another company, clients should be notified of the change and guaranteed access to their records.
- If a government body, agency, or person wishes to gain access to information in the database of a managed care company, clients should be notified before the access is made and given veto power over dissemination of the records. In the event this does not occur, managed care companies should be liable for any personal injury that may ensue, based on violations of disclosure or redisclosure laws.
- Gatekeepers and case reviewers for managed care companies should be identifiable and held to the same standards of keeping information confidential as the professionals providing services.
- Managed care companies should be required to have periodic reviews of their record handling and storage of client data by an independent, external examiner with the authority to establish penalties if confidentiality has not been safeguarded.
- Individual social workers, groups of social workers, and organizations such as NASW must recognize their obligation to refuse to comply with managed care directives that contravene clients' rights and should work collectively in this regard.

Implementation of these recommendations would serve to address some of the ethical and legal questions that have been raised. If these recommendations are put into effect, social workers could better work with managed care systems without abrogating their legal and ethical responsibilities to protect confidentiality.

CONCLUSION

Managed care, with its many facets, has developed with the political, economic, and moral changes in American culture. Health and mental health care costs are high, emphasis is shifting from the care of one to the management of many, and the economic climate is such that managed care personnel are positioned to limit services to clients and to limit the power of social work professionals to provide these services. It would be naive to assume that landmark achievements relating to ethical and legal protection of clients would remain unchallenged when economic determinants are so different.

Within this context, it is important for social workers to resist the temptation to "go along to get along" in an effort to survive alongside an industry that is apparently adjusting to a downsizing economy. Clients' rights and the social work ethical and legal commitment to confidentiality are worth fighting for, particularly given that the managed care approach to confidentiality is determined by business interests in controlling resources, not the scarcity of resources. Huge windfall profits, coupled with the understanding that private client information is essential to the cost-containment efforts of managed care, debunk claims to the contrary.

Like any other industry, however, managed care will seek to protect its consumer base to whatever degree is feasible, including safeguarding confidential information, if doing so retains high currency in the culture of providers and consumers. Social workers can defend the value of confidentiality rationally on the basis of good business practices in a free-enterprise system. Specifically, they can highlight to managers the business merits of pleasing the customer by honoring confidentiality and treating client data with respect and of removing the risks of legal action. Thus, social workers' ethical and altruistic endeavors to salvage confidentiality and protect clients can be framed as compatible with businesses' self-interested motives to avoid punitive damages in court and to keep customers satisfied. Alternatively, social workers can develop and support provider-run networks committed to managing data responsibly, maintaining high professional standards, and using sound management principles.

At the same time, social workers must engage in social action to lobby for changes in managed care organizations' approach to confidentiality and for legislative restrictions on dissemination of private client data. Social work leaders, theorists, and researchers need to publicly address the problems around confidentiality that practitioners face on a daily basis. Sadly, members of the profession have been largely silent about these critical challenges to confidentiality or have tended to gloss over problems with euphemistic language or naive optimism.

Because of technological changes and new management initiatives, clients no longer have the right to confidential relationships with their social workers. Confidentiality used to be set within an environment of restrained disclosure but now is lost in a culture of information processing. Social workers need to be clear that client information passed on to managed care companies is data with a purpose beyond the health care needs of a particular individual. Social workers need to reexamine their ethical and legal responsibilities to clients and to challenge managed care personnel to protect the clients' right to confidentiality.

REFERENCES

Besharov, D. J., & Besharov, S. H. (1987). Teaching about liability. *Social Work, 32,* 517–522.

Confidentiality Law, 42 U.S.C. § 290dd-2 (1992).

Corcoran, K., & Vandiver, V. (1996). *Maneuvering the maze of managed care: Skills for mental health practitioners.* New York: Free Press.

Cournoyer, B. (1991). *The social work skills workbook.* Belmont, CA: Wadsworth.

Henneberger, M. (1994, October 9). Managed care changing practice of psychotherapy. *New York Times,* pp. A1, A50.

Jackson, V. H. (Ed.). (1995). *Managed care resource guide for social workers in agency settings.* Washington, DC: NASW Press.

Kutchins, H. (1991). The fiduciary relationship: The legal basis for social workers' responsibilities to clients. *Social Work, 36,* 106–113.

Landers, S. (1994, September). Managed care's challenge: "Show me!" *NASW News,* p. 3.

Legal Action Center. (1995). *Confidentiality: A guide to the federal law and regulations* (3rd ed.). New York: Author.

Lindenthal, J. J., Jordan, T. J., Lentz, J. D., & Thomas, C. S. (1988). Social workers' management of confidentiality. *Social Work, 33,* 157–158.

Loewenberg, F. M., & Dolgoff, R. (1992). *Ethical decisions for social work practice* (4th ed.). Itasca, IL: F. E. Peacock.

McGowan, B. G. (1995). Values and ethics. In C. H. Meyer & M. A. Mattaini (Eds.), *The foundations of social work practice* (pp. 28–41). Washington, DC: NASW Press.

Meyer, C. H. (1983). Declassification: Assault on social workers and social services [Editorial]. *Social Work, 28,* 419.

National Association of Social Workers. (1994). *NASW code of ethics.* Washington, DC: Author.

Rawls, J. (1971). *A theory of justice.* Cambridge, MA: Harvard University Press.

Reamer, F. (1987). Informed consent in social work. *Social Work, 32,* 425–429.

Regulations for Confidentiality of Alcohol and Drug Abuse Patient Records, 42 C.F.R. Part 2, §§ 2.31, 2.52 (1987).

Reid, P. N., & Billups, J. O. (1986). Distributional ethics and social work education. *Journal of Social Work Education, 22*(1), 6–17.

Rhodes, M. L. (1991). *Ethical dilemmas in social work practice.* Milwaukee, WI: Family Service America.

Schultz, E. E. (1994, May 18). Open secrets: Medical data gathered by firms can prove less than confidential. *Wall Street Journal,* pp. A1, A5.

Schwarz, G. (1989). Confidentiality revisited. *Social Work, 34,* 223–226.

Shapiro, J. S. (1995). The downside of managed mental health care. *Clinical Social Work Journal, 23,* 441–451.

Torczyner, J. (1991). Discretion, judgment, and informed consent: Ethical and practice issues in social action. *Social Work, 36,* 122–128.

This chapter was originally published in the August 1996 issue of Health & Social Work, *vol. 21, pp. 208–215.*

37

Social Work and Health Care Practice and Policy: A Psychosocial Research Agenda

Kathleen Ell

I t has been almost 15 years since social work researcher Rosalie Kane (1982) accurately predicted many of the changes occurring in health care today. Observing that social work had no monopoly on concern for the whole person and for the psychosocial well-being and quality of life of the individual, Kane also predicted that psychosocial research would influence health care decision making, that researchers from other professions and disciplines would conduct basic and applied psychosocial research, and that social workers would have to live with the results. Cautioning that research by others might fail to address problems and services of particular concern to social workers, Kane called on social work to empirically examine its practice by specifying the interventions and outcomes of social work services.

In recent years, research on social and psychological factors and health has matured into a broad and increasingly respected science. Striking advances have been made in methodologies, and hybrid disciplines (for example, psychoneuroimmunology) have emerged that reflect critical linkages among biological, social, and psychological factors. Barriers to conducting large-scale controlled studies of psychosocial interventions are being surmounted. For example, the National Heart, Lung, and Blood Institute is currently conducting a four-year, multisite clinical trial of a psychosocial intervention among 3,000 post–heart attack patients. At the same time, policymakers' concerns about the cost, quality, and outcomes of health care have spawned the area of health services research, including effectiveness research and the RAND Medical Outcomes Study (Roper, Winkenwerder, Hackbarth, & Krakauer, 1988; Stewart et al., 1989; Wells, Burnam, & Camp, 1995). As a result, increasingly sophisticated services research methodologies and outcome measurement (Ware & Sherbourne, 1992) are being developed that can be applied to studies of the delivery of psychosocial services in real-world health care systems (Narrow, Regier, Rae, Manderscheid, & Locke, 1993; Regier et al., 1993; Sharfstein, Stoline, & Goldman, 1993; Taube, Mechanic, & Hohmann, 1989).

Since Kane's (1982) call for increased social work research, social work contributions to the growing body of health-related psychosocial and services research have increased significantly. Indeed, social work researchers have produced two of the leading studies in mental health research (Hogarty et al., 1986; Test & Stein, 1980). Social workers are also increasing research on behavioral and supportive group interventions for patients with life-threatening physical illness (Evans & Connis, 1995; Subramanian, 1990; Toseland, Blanchard, & McCallion, 1995). However, the majority of studies have been conducted by researchers from other professions and disciplines.

This article addresses the question, What are the implications of extant psychosocial health-related research for a future social work research agenda? In focusing on next steps for social work research, emphasis is given to gaps in the existing research on basic psychosocial research, psychosocial treatment and intervention research, and health services research (including managed care, outcome and quality of care, and intervention effectiveness research). The examples cited have been brought to the attention of the Institute for the Advancement of Social Work Research (IASWR) and are among the current priorities of national research funding organizations. The article concludes with recommended actions to increase social work's use of and contributions to the development of empirically based knowledge for health care practice and policy.

BASIC PSYCHOSOCIAL RESEARCH

An extensive body of research documents the profound effects of behavioral and social factors on the etiology, course, and management of illness (Anderson & Armstead, 1995; Berkman, 1995; Kaplan, 1995; Kiecolt-Glaser & Glaser, 1995; Manuck, Marsland, Kaplan, & Williams, 1995; Scheier & Bridges, 1995). Indeed, such factors contribute to at least 50 percent of all annual deaths in the United States (Anderson, 1995). Moreover, significant advances have been made in understanding the etiology, detection, diagnosis, and epidemiology of mental disorders (National Advisory Mental Health Council, 1993). Many types of research logically fall under what might be termed basic psychosocial research; particularly important are epidemiological studies to identify behavioral and social risk factors for illness, disease, and health outcomes and studies of interactions and mechanisms linking psychosocial factors and biological factors (Anderson, 1995).

Identifying human problems that are most frequently encountered by social workers in health care is one way of prioritizing areas for future research. For example, social workers in the general health care sector frequently provide services for people who are not easily classified, including people with general functional limitations and degrees of disability and people with comorbid physical illnesses, mental disorders, and substance abuse problems. Many of these individuals require integrated services and combined interventions such as cognitive behavioral treatment plus case management services. Similarly, research on subthreshold and stress-related clinical syndromes that are commonly seen in primary care and that precede or accompany life-threatening physical illness is needed. Studies of social and psychological factors associated with adherence to life-saving medical regimens, of family support giving (Ell, 1996), and of patient and family decision making (Coulton, 1990) are also needed.

Etiologic studies are needed on developmental, cognitive, peer pressure, family, media, psychological, pharmacological, behavioral, attitudinal, and expectancy factors related to substance use and abuse among children and adolescents.

Little is known about risk and protective factors associated with drug abuse among women and people of color and within families. Other studies might examine drug use and abuse among individuals with serious physical illnesses and disabilities and among elderly people. Indeed, the need for future research on the relationship between poverty and health (Anderson & Armstead, 1995) might preoccupy social work researchers for many years.

PSYCHOSOCIAL TREATMENT AND INTERVENTION RESEARCH

Consistent with the mounting evidence on the relationships between psychosocial factors and illness and disease is a small but growing body of psychosocial intervention research that documents the efficacy of health-related psychosocial interventions that are community based and focused on groups, families, and individuals (Altman, 1995; Fawzy, Fawzy, Arndt, & Pasnau, 1995; Hill, Kelleher, & Shumaker, 1992; Lipsey & Wilson, 1993; Padgett, Mumford, Hynes, & Carter, 1988; Sobel, 1995). Controlled clinical treatment trials have led to dramatic improvements in the pharmacological and psychosocial (often in combination) treatment of severe mental disorders (Ballenger, 1993; Frank, Karp, & Rush, 1993; Gelenberg & Hopkins, 1993; Jenike, 1993; Klein & Slomkowski, 1993; Schneider, 1993; Schooler & Keith, 1993; Wallace, 1993).

Faculty of schools of social work and social work researchers and practitioners in other academic, research, and health care organizations have made important contributions to this growing area of research. Social workers are developing methods to specify interventions, including multidimensional interventions such as case management, that target both personal and environmental elements of the problem and family-focused interventions (for example, Hogarty et al., 1986; Hughes, 1992; McFarlane et al., 1995; Toseland et al., 1995). Interventions that have been studied with controlled clinical trial designs and that have demonstrated efficacy are among those most widely accepted in health care. For example, the Assertive Community Treatment model is the most widely used community-based intervention for people with psychiatric disabilities (Burns & Santos, 1995; Stein & Test, 1980; Test & Stein, 1980). Social workers have made significant contributions to research on substance abuse (Schinke, Botvin, & Orlandi, 1991; Siegal et al., 1995), Interpersonal Psychotherapy (Weissman & Markowitz, 1994), and behavioral and supportive group therapies (Evans & Connis, 1995; Subramanian, 1990; Subramanian & Rose, 1988; Toseland et al., 1995).

Types of Psychosocial Intervention Research

Psychosocial intervention studies aim to develop and test strategies that are potentially effective, interpretable, and replicable. Each stage of intervention research requires attention to specification of the psychosocial interventions, selection of the appropriate population for the intervention, explication of the conceptual and theoretical framework that acts as a rationale for expecting the intervention to achieve its desired outcomes (that is, the relationship among factors that is being addressed by the intervention), application of methods to ensure intervention fidelity (to ensure that the actual intervention provided matches that which was originally proposed), and use of outcome measures appropriate to the intervention.

In the stage 1 studies, new approaches are specified based on theories derived from existing social and behavioral research. For example, prevention intervention studies delineate how mechanisms of risk or protection are affected by the intervention and how this process is linked to expected outcomes. Small-scale studies and then pilot studies are conducted with targeted populations. The elements of the intervention are specified in a detailed services protocol or treatment manual. Provider training activities and intervention monitoring techniques are used to ensure that the designated intervention is actually carried out. On the basis of results from the small-scale and pilot studies, the intervention is further refined.

The efficacy of the intervention is assessed through stage 2 studies. Stage 2 studies include large-scale experimental or quasi-experimental studies and multisite clinical trials conducted and replicated on different populations, frequently resulting in further refinements of the intervention. Finally, to determine the effectiveness of the interventions in health care delivery systems, stage 3 studies are conducted in which interventions are tested in real-life settings. Effectiveness studies, including natural experiments, program evaluation, and outcome studies, are discussed in greater detail in the section on Health Services Research.

Increasing Social Work Intervention Research

Given that social work is a practice-based profession, it is both surprising and cause for concern that there have been few controlled studies of social work interventions. Recent experience by the author in working with national policymakers underscored Kane's (1982) observation that unproved assertions about the value of psychosocial interventions and social work services will continue to fall on skeptical or even deaf ears, whereas rigorous efforts to evaluate interventions will more often be supported. There is a need for intervention studies on a broad range of social work interventions. In fact, NASW's government relations staff developed a lengthy list of substantive areas in which research is needed on the efficacy and effectiveness of social work interventions to support the profession's public policy advocacy efforts (personal communication with Sandra Harding, government relations associate, and Madeleine Golde, government relations staff associate, NASW, December 1994).

Irrespective of whether social work conducts psychosocial intervention research, others will. Indeed, one argument frequently proposed by national policymakers suggests that social workers are skilled service providers and that research is better conducted by professions with a scientific tradition and culture. However, failure to dramatically increase empirical research on interventions developed by social workers presents numerous risks for patients and the profession. These risks include relinquishing to those outside of social work "the tasks of defining the important practice questions, selecting the appropriate research methodologies, interpreting the data, and developing the implications for practice" (Kirk, 1991, p. 4); failing to rigorously test services and interventions that are designed based on social work practice experience; failing to provide the most effective services for those with the greatest need (Toseland et al., 1995) or in some circumstances doing harm (Kane, 1982); and increasing the likelihood that social workers will be called on to provide services that have been designed and tested by others, even when the designated service fails to address elements of the problems that social workers know are critical in affecting health outcomes.

The latter circumstance is already occurring. For example, primary care patients should not be denied alternatives to pharmacological treatments for depression because social workers failed to rigorously examine cost-effective and organizationally feasible interventions for patients who prefer interpersonal over drug therapy or who need environmental assistance (Munoz, Hollon, McGrath, Rehm, & VandenBos, 1994). And people of color and socioeconomically disadvantaged consumers should not be effectively denied potentially beneficial treatments for depression because intervention research among these groups has been sparse. At issue is no longer whether controlled psychosocial intervention studies will be conducted, nor whether the results of that research will be used to influence health care policies and practices. The question is, Will social work significantly increase its contributions to this area of research?

HEALTH SERVICES RESEARCH

Health services research is a new field of study that calls for interdisciplinary research on financing, organization, access, utilization, effectiveness, and outcomes of services. Included are studies of health care delivery systems and of health care provided within other human services systems such as mental health services for children and families provided by the child welfare system and health and mental health services provided in schools or senior centers. Services research aims to answer questions about the effectiveness of treatments, interventions, and service delivery mechanisms in actual health care settings and about the impact of organizational and financing mechanisms on the cost, quality, and outcome of health care services.

Recent changes in health care have been propelled by concerns about the rising cost of health care precipitated by changing national demographics and dramatic advances in medical technology. Preoccupation with cost, coupled with failure to marshall the necessary public will to provide health care as a public good, has spurred the current industrialization of health care. As a result, managed care is today's dominant economic and organizational force in health care delivery. Indeed, the managed care movement in this country might be characterized as a giant unplanned natural experiment aimed at reducing health care costs. Results are yet unclear, and little is known about its effects on access to and quality of health care.

Numerous policy questions raised by the rapid growth of managed care fall within a services research agenda. Does managed care reduce health care costs (versus which other systems of care)? If so, which costs does it reduce? And whose costs? Is it possible to reduce the cost of health care and at the same time maintain quality of care (including quality psychosocial care) and obtain positive consumer outcomes? What outcomes will be assessed? Will adequate, accessible, and quality psychosocial services be provided within the general medical and public health care sectors? Will mental health care and substance abuse services be designated (and adequately financed) as essential general health care benefits and services?

To aid them in addressing these primary issues, policymakers, health care administrators, payers, consumers, and the public at large are increasingly demanding research-based evidence of cost-effective services for individual and communitywide health problems. Health services research is likely to be further developed and to be an important element in health policy analysis. Methods for this type of research are advancing, and the complexity of issues calls for interdisciplinary research teams. Therefore, social workers will have new opportunities to help set research agendas and to contribute directly to future health services research on managed care, quality of health care (particularly psychosocial care), health care outcomes, and intervention effectiveness.

Availability, Access, and Utilization of Health Care Services

Questions about availability, access, and utilization of services for vulnerable populations are likely to rank high on a list of needed research as defined by social workers. Currently, managed care is the dominant system for the provision of privately insured mental health and drug and alcohol abuse services (Mechanic, 1994; Mechanic, Schlesinger, & McAlpine, 1995). At the same time, managed care is rapidly growing in the publicly funded health sector (Freud & Hurley, 1995). To begin to address important questions, social work researchers might collaborate with state agencies to monitor and critically analyze utilization data and to develop data-gathering mechanisms and measurement tools for multidimensional outcome assessment. Social workers will want empirical evidence on potential underutilization of services by highly vulnerable groups and on discrimination or preferential selection in managed care enrollment practices or in full access to services.

The types of services and the organizational mechanisms through which services are provided raise further questions of concern to social workers. For example, what services are provided by managed care programs as they assume responsibility for the care of high-risk patients from the public care sector? How is the role of gatekeeper carried out by social workers and other health care providers, and what knowledge base is used to make decisions about access to services? How will public health and preventive, communitywide health services be provided when health care dollars are lodged within managed care industries?

In another recent trend under managed care, mental health and drug and alcohol treatment services are combined into the broader area of managed behavioral health care; frequently these services are provided through the development of "carve-out" plans, in which one vendor manages the utilization of all the behavioral health care benefits (Garnick, Hendricks, Dulski, Thorpe, & Horgan, 1994). Questions include, When mental health services are provided in carve-out managed care programs, is stigmatization of the consumer increased?

Is this negative outcome offset by the greater likelihood that the consumer with special needs will get specialized care from mental health professionals? In what ways is mental health and other psychosocial care provided in the general medical care system (including in primary care) differentially affected by integrated versus carve-out managed care programs?

The development of screening and detection tools is another critical area for research. The recent development of a screening tool for diagnosing mental disorders in primary care is an excellent example of this type of research (Spitzer et al., 1995; Williams et al., 1995).

Effectiveness, Outcome, and Quality of Care Research

Studies are needed on the effectiveness of psychosocial interventions, including interventions previously tested under ideal controlled circumstances, in real-world health care systems. This growing area of research affords social work opportunities to conduct research on actual programs and services (for example, Proctor, Morrow-Howell, Albaz, & Weir, 1992). Research is urgently needed to identify specific features of psychosocial interventions and processes in managed care programs that control costs and maintain quality of care and achieve the intended outcomes (Peak, Toseland, & Banks, 1995). The growing use of brief treatments and of episodic treatment requires further study, particularly as it is used with severely and persistently mentally ill people and with children.

To ensure that effective services are widely accepted, there will be a greater need to conduct effectiveness studies across multiple caregiving sites, as in the multisite studies of Assertive Community Treatment (McGrew, Bond, Dietzen, McKasson, & Miller, 1995). When examining program outcomes or the effectiveness of specific interventions, it will be particularly important to document the fidelity of the intervention. Fidelity monitoring includes checks on whether the treatment, intervention, or service model being studied was actually provided; what elements varied between the services or intervention actually provided and the original specification of the intervention; and potential differences in outcomes obtained in day-to-day practice versus outcomes expected on the basis of laboratorylike circumstances (Essock & Kontos, 1995; Teague, Drake, & Ackerson, 1995).

Again, as Kane (1982) accurately predicted, "Accountability—the catchword of the 1970s—was largely geared toward a productive and appropriate use of time and resources. In the future, accountability will focus more on achieved results. Such analyses will require baseline measurements before intervention and follow-up measurements afterward" (p. 319). Today, outcome-driven psychosocial practice in health care must consider both economic and functional outcomes; the critical question is what outcomes will be measured. Therefore, social workers must develop measurement tools to assess the outcomes sought by social workers, as demonstrated by a recent study by Segal, Silverman, and Temkin (1995) that included the development of a measure of empowerment among people with persistent and severe mental illness. Outcome measurement is particularly salient in light of current efforts to develop quality assurance databases that will increasingly influence evaluation of health and mental health care delivery systems and providers.

To date, studies of managed care have focused foremost on its influence on utilization and cost, whereas studies of quality have been more sparse. How should quality of social work psychosocial care be measured? In another recent study, Segal, Egley, Watson, and Goldfinger (1995) found that although the technical quality of psychiatric emergency services was unrelated in the short term to improved functioning, an interpersonally sensitive approach to the patient was associated with both improved functioning and release from acute care. Similar studies of the nature and effects of the therapeutic alliance in case management services are also needed to determine the effects of social workers' use of clinical guidelines, treatment protocols, and standardized decision rules when evaluating quality of care in relation to outcomes of care.

IMPLICATIONS FOR SOCIAL WORK

What are the implications of the current state of psychosocial research for social work in health care? Undoubtedly, social work has a major stake in the extent to which psychosocial health care services will be available, accessible, and utilized (particularly for the most vulnerable members of society). Given the scientific progress discussed in this article as well as gaps in knowledge, what actions might social workers take? The data suggest that social workers should be encouraged to use available research in advocating their positions, apply well-founded research-based knowledge in their clinical and administrative practice, and increasingly produce research to address identified gaps in the current psychosocial knowledge base (particularly those items that are most likely to be overlooked by other professions and disciplines).

Research and Advocacy

Research findings can be used to advocate for the provision of psychosocial services in the general health care sector, commensurate coverage of mental health and substance abuse services under general health care benefits, and community and organizationally based preventive services. Having empirically grounded evidence on specific elements of social work practice and of its positive effects on health outcomes will add an important element to advance health care practices and policies preferred by social workers. And because social workers often decry the lack of funding for research of interest to social work, it is imperative to increase the profession's advocacy for funding for social work research priorities.

By highlighting research to inform health care practice and policy, I do not intend to prescribe research as a panacea for making life, health, or health care delivery better. Certainly, the seismic change that has characterized health care and health care delivery in recent years would look much the same irrespective of whether social work had committed more resources to conducting research on its practice. Values, value conflicts, and long-held beliefs will often override wise application of knowledge gained from sound research (Rogers, 1986): Witness the current difficulty in convincing policymakers and a general public, blinded by old attitudes, that drug abuse prevention and treatment can be effective.

However, it is also a fact that the lack of convincing empirical data on cost-factored solutions to health problems makes it easier for policymakers to cloud an issue with ideological rhetoric, thereby weakening social workers' ability to maximize their advocacy. Moreover, when credible data exist on the benefits and costs of specific interventions, value-driven choices (and political ideology) are brought into clearer focus, providing social workers with the opportunity to strategically target the more visible underlying value issues. Fortunately, the recently formed Action Network for Social Work Education and Research (ANSWER), a coalition of social work organizations, is strategically organized to begin to exert social work influence in these areas (Hooyman, 1996).

Social Work Intervention and Services Research

Intervention research is costly and time-consuming. Social work is also disadvantaged in that it has yet to fully develop natural practice–research partnerships between researchers and service providers. Helpful lessons can be learned from the experience of other professions that have identified an area of needed research and then acted through a special and targeted initiative to jump-start the necessary infrastructure and commitment within their ranks. For example, in 1984, the nursing profession embarked on a mission to advance science to strengthen nursing practice and health care that promotes health, prevents disease, and ameliorates the effects of illness and disability. This professionwide endeavor culminated in the creation of the 17th institute within the National Institutes of Health (NIH): the National Institute of Nursing Research. The psychology profession developed the Human Capital Initiative, which identifies substantive gaps in existing knowledge on major social problems and mobilizes external funding and intra-professional research resources to address the related issues.

Several efforts are currently under way within social work to advance intervention research on social work practice. For example, the IASWR is exploring ways to support a catalytic initiative to further the development of health-related psychosocial intervention research and is cosponsoring with the Office of Behavioral and Social Science Research of NIH a meeting that will be held during 1996 to showcase psychosocial treatment and intervention research to staff from several institutes within NIH. However, the collective commitment of the profession is needed to successfully address the current gaps in research on social work interventions.

CONCLUSION

The overall state of psychosocial research for health care practice is more convincing than ever before. Social work should take heart in the scientific evidence that supports many of the profession's long-held beliefs about the importance of social and psychological factors. The current state of the science, including technological advances in methods, provides opportunities to advance knowledge even faster as we enter the 21st century. Empirical data will be a formidable tool in social work's efforts to influence the shape of health care delivery in ways that are consistent with its most basic values and goals. There is every indication that history will record this time as one during which social work accepted the challenge to increase its application of and contribution to its scientific knowledge base to improve the health and quality of life of the nation, including its most vulnerable people.

REFERENCES

Altman, D. G. (1995). Strategies for community health intervention: Paradoxes, pitfalls. *Psychosomatic Medicine, 57,* 226–233.

Anderson, N. B. (1995). Integrating behavioral and social sciences research at NIH. *Academic Medicine, 70,* 1106–1107.

Anderson, N. B., & Armstead, C. A. (1995). Toward understanding the association of socioeconomic status and health: A new challenge for the biopsychosocial approach. *Psychosomatic Medicine, 57,* 312–325.

Ballenger, J. C. (1993). Panic disorder: Efficacy of current treatment. *Psychopharmacology Bulletin, 29,* 477–486.

Berkman, L. F. (1995). The role of social relations in health promotion. *Psychosomatic Medicine, 57,* 245–254.

Burns, B. J., & Santos, A. B. (1995). Assertive community treatment: An update of randomized trials. *Psychiatric Services, 46,* 669–678.

Coulton, C. J. (1990). Research in patient and family decision making regarding life-sustaining and long-term care. *Social Work in Health Care, 15,* 63–77.

Ell, K. (1996). Social networks, social support and coping with serious illness: The family connection. *Social Science & Medicine, 42,* 173–183.

Essock, S. M., & Kontos, N. K. (1995). Implementing assertive community treatment teams. *Psychiatric Services, 46,* 679–688.

Evans, R. L., & Connis, R. T. (1995). Comparison of brief group therapies for depressed cancer patients receiving radiation treatment. *Public Health Reports, 110,* 306–311.

Fawzy, F. I., Fawzy, N. W., Arndt, L. A., & Pasnau, R. O. (1995). Critical review of psychosocial interventions in cancer care. *Archives of General Psychiatry, 52,* 234–244.

Frank, E., Karp, J. F., & Rush, A. J. (1993). Efficacy of treatments for major depression. *Psychopharmacology Bulletin, 29,* 457–476.

Freud, D. A., & Hurley, R. E. (1995). Medicaid managed care: Contribution to issues of health reform. *Annual Review of Public Health, 16,* 473–495.

Garnick, D. W., Hendricks, A. M., Dulski, J. D., Thorpe, E. E., & Horgan, C. M. (1994). Characteristics of private-sector managed care for mental health and substance abuse treatment. *Journal of Hospital and Community Psychiatry, 45,* 1201–1205.

Gelenberg, A. J., & Hopkins, H. S. (1993). Report on efficacy of treatments for bipolar disorder. *Psychopharmacology Bulletin, 29,* 457–466.

Hill, D. R., Kelleher, K., & Shumaker, S. A. (1992). Psychosocial interventions in adult patients with coronary heart disease and cancer. *General Hospital Psychiatry, 14,* 285–425.

Hogarty, G. E., Anderson, C. M., Reiss, D. J., Kornblith, S. J., Greenwald, D. P., Javna, C. D., & Madonia, M. J. (1986). Family psychoeducation, social skills training and maintenance chemotherapy in the aftercare treatment of schizophrenia. *Archives of General Psychiatry, 43,* 633–642.

Hooyman, N. R. (1996). A day on the hill. *Journal of Social Work Education, 32,* 2–3.

Hughes, S. (1992). A randomized trial of the cost of VA hospital-based home care for the terminally ill. *Health Services Research, 14,* 13–21.

Jenike, M. A. (1993). Obsessive-compulsive disorder: Efficacy of specific treatments as assessed by controlled trials. *Psychopharmacology Bulletin, 29,* 487–500.

Kane, R. A. (1982). Lessons for social work from the medical model: A viewpoint for practice. *Social Work, 27,* 315–321.

Kaplan, G. A. (1995). Where do shared pathways lead? Some reflections on a research agenda. *Psychosomatic Medicine, 57,* 208–212.

Kiecolt-Glaser, J. K., & Glaser, R. (1995). Psychoneuroimmunology and health consequences: Data and shared mechanisms. *Psychosomatic Medicine, 57,* 269–274.

Kirk, S. (1991). Scholarship and the professional school [Editorial]. *Social Work Research & Abstracts, 27*(1), 3–5.

Klein, R. G., & Slomkowski, C. (1993). Treatment of psychiatric disorders in children and adolescents. *Psychopharmacology Bulletin, 29,* 525–536.

Lipsey, M. W., & Wilson, D. B. (1993). The efficacy of psychological, educational, and behavioral treatment. *American Psychologist, 12,* 1181–1209.

Manuck, S. B., Marsland, A. L., Kaplan, J. R., & Williams, J. K. (1995). The pathogenicity of behavior and its neuroendocrine mediation: An example from coronary artery disease. *Psychosomatic Medicine, 57,* 275–283.

McFarlane, W. R., Lukens, E., Link, B., Dushay, R., Deakins, S. A., Newmark, M., Dunne, E. J., Horen, B., & Toran, J. (1995). Multiple-family groups and psychoeducation in the treatment of schizophrenia. *Archives of General Psychiatry, 52,* 679–687.

McGrew, J. H., Bond, G. R., Dietzen, L., McKasson, M., & Miller, L. D. (1995). A multisite study of client outcomes in assertive community treatment. *Psychiatric Services, 46,* 696–701.

Mechanic, D. (1994). Integrating mental health into a general health care system. (Special Section: Health reform and mental health care). *Hospital and Community Psychiatry, 45,* 893–897.

Mechanic, D., Schlesinger, M., & McAlpine, D. D. (1995). Management of mental health and substance abuse services: State-of-the-art and early results. *Milbank Quarterly, 73,* 19–55.

Munoz, R. F., Hollon, S. D., McGrath, E., Rehm, L. P., & VandenBos, G. R. (1994). On the AHCPR depression in primary care guidelines: Further considerations for practitioners. *American Psychologist, 49,* 42–61.

Narrow, W. E., Regier, D. A., Rae, D. S., Manderscheid, R. W., & Locke, B. Z. (1993). Use of services by persons with mental and addictive disorders. *Archives of General Psychiatry, 50,* 95–107.

National Advisory Mental Health Council. (1993). Health care reform for Americans with severe mental illnesses. *American Journal of Psychiatry, 150,* 1447–1465.

Padgett, D., Mumford, E., Hynes, M., & Carter, R. (1988). Meta-analysis of the effects of educational and psychosocial interventions on management of diabetes mellitus. *Journal of Clinical Epidemiology, 41,* 1007–1030.

Peak, T., Toseland, R. W., & Banks, S. M. (1995). The impact of a spouse-caregiver support group on care recipient health care costs. *Journal of Aging and Health, 7,* 427–449.

Proctor, E., Morrow-Howell, N., Albaz, R., & Weir, C. (1992). Patient and family satisfaction with discharge plans. *Medical Care, 30,* 262–275.

Regier, D. A., Narrow, W. E., Rae, D. S., Manderscheid, R. W., Locke, B. Z., & Goodwin, F. K. (1993). The de facto U.S. mental and addictive disorders service system: Epidemiologic catchment area prospective 1-year prevalence rates of disorders and services. *Archives of General Psychiatry, 50,* 85–94.

Rogers, J. M. (1986). Income maintenance experimentation and welfare policy: The role of value conflict in research utilization. *Knowledge, 8,* 323–348.

Roper, W. L., Winkenwerder, W., Hackbarth, G. M., & Krakauer, H. (1988). Effectiveness in health care: An initiative to evaluate and improve medical practice. *New England Journal of Medicine, 319,* 1197–1202.

Scheier, M. F., & Bridges, M. W. (1995). Person variables and health: Personality predispositions and acute psychological states as shared determinants for disease. *Psychosomatic Medicine, 57,* 255–268.

Schinke, S. P., Botvin, G. J., & Orlandi, G. J. (1991). *Substance abuse in children and adolescents: Evaluation and intervention.* Newbury Park, CA: Sage Publications.

Schneider, L. S. (1993). Efficacy of treatment for geropsychiatric patients with severe mental illness. *Psychopharmacology Bulletin, 29,* 501–524.

Schooler, N. R., & Keith, S. J. (1993). The clinical research base for the treatment of schizophrenia. *Psychopharmacology Bulletin, 29,* 431–446.

Segal, S. P., Egley, L., Watson, M. A., & Goldfinger, S. M. (1995). The quality of psychiatric emergency evaluations and patient outcomes in county hospitals. *American Journal of Public Health, 85,* 1429–1431.

Segal, S. P., Silverman, C., & Temkin, T. (1995). Measuring empowerment in client-run self-help agencies. *Community Mental Health Journal, 31,* 215–227.

Sharfstein, S., Stoline, A., & Goldman, H. (1993). Psychiatric care and health insurance reform. *American Journal of Psychiatry, 150,* 7–18.

Siegal, H. A., Rapp, R. C., Kelliher, C. W., Fisher, J. H., Wagner, J. H., & Cole, P. A. (1995). The strengths perspective of case management: A promising inpatient substance abuse treatment enhancement. *Journal of Psychoactive Drugs, 27,* 67–72.

Sobel, D. S. (1995). Rethinking medicine: Improving health outcomes with cost-effective psychosocial interventions. *Psychosomatic Medicine, 57,* 234–244.

Spitzer, R. L, Williams, J. B., Kroenke, K., Linzer, M., deGruy, F. V., Hahn, S. R., Broody, D., & Johnson, J. G. (1995). Utility of a new procedure for diagnosing mental disorders in primary care: The PRIME-MD 1,000 Study. *Journal of the American Medical Association, 272,* 1749–1756.

Stein, L. I., & Test, M. A. (1980). Alternative to mental hospital treatment: I. Conceptual model, treatment program, and clinical evaluation. *Archives of General Psychiatry, 37,* 392–397.

Stewart, A. L., Greenfield, S., Hays, R. D., Wells, K., Rogers, W. H., Berry, M. A., McGlynn, E. A., & Ware, J. E. (1989). Functional status and well-being of patients with chronic conditions: Results from the Medical Outcomes Study. *Journal of the American Medical Association, 262,* 907–913.

Subramanian, K. (1990). Structured groupwork for the management of chronic pain: An experimental investigation. *Research on Social Work Practice, 1,* 32–45.

Subramanian, K., & Rose, S. (1988). Social work and the treatment of chronic pain. *Health & Social Work, 13,* 49–60.

Taube, C. A., Mechanic, D., & Hohmann, A. A. (1989). *The future of mental health services research.* Rockville, MD: National Institute of Mental Health.

Teague, G. B., Drake, R. E., & Ackerson, T. H. (1995). Evaluating use of continuous treatment teams for persons with mental illness and substance abuse. *Psychiatric Services, 47,* 689–695.

Test, M. A., & Stein, L. I. (1980). Alternative to mental hospital treatment: II. Social cost. *Archives of General Psychiatry, 37,* 409–412.

Toseland, R. W., Blanchard, C. G., & McCallion, P. (1995). A problem-solving intervention for caregivers of cancer patients. *Social Science Medicine, 40,* 517–528.

Wallace, C. J. (1993). Psychiatric rehabilitation. *Psychopharmacology Bulletin, 29,* 537–548.

Ware, J. E., & Sherbourne, C. D. (1992). The MOS 36-Item Short-Form Health Survey (SF-36). *Medical Care, 30,* 473–483.

Weissman, M. M., & Markowitz, J. C. (1994). Interpersonal psychotherapy: Current status. *Archives of General Psychiatry, 51,* 599–606.

Wells, K. B., Burnam, M. A., & Camp, P. (1995). Severity of depression in prepaid and fee-for-service general medical and mental health specialty practices. *Medical Care, 33,* 350–364.

Williams, J.B.W., Spitzer, R. L., Linzer, M., Kroenke, K., Hahn, S. R., deGruy, F. V., & Lazev, A. (1995). Gender differences in depression in primary care. *American Journal of Obstetrics and Gynecology, 173,* 654–659.

This chapter was originally published in the November 1996 issue of Social Work, *vol. 41, pp. 583–592.*

38 Shaping the Policy Practice Agenda of Social Work in the Field of Aging

Roberta R. Greene and Ruth I. Knee

The social work profession has long struggled with how to realize its dual mission: to enhance people's well-being by improving individual functioning and to promote societal reform. But a clear integration of this dual mission has often eluded the profession. Although social workers have consistently engaged in individual and collective action to change societal conditions, they also have often adopted practice theories that do not support changes in the environment or secure social resources (Greene, 1994). Many social workers believe they should take a neutral stance in practice rather than interject political philosophy into a clinical encounter.

Social workers, however, are increasingly recognizing that social work practice is not neutral, value free, or divorced from major social, political, and cultural concerns (Greene, 1994). A growing number of practitioners are engaged in traditional advocacy strategies such as write-in campaigns and are placing more emphasis on the societal inequities related to age, gender, and socioeconomic status that may be mirrored in treatment (Doherty & Boss, 1992; McNamee & Gergen, 1992). However, many social workers have yet to realize their potential to engage in social reform at the local level and to perceive the person as political.

Now is the time for the profession to more fully address the artificial schism between personal and environmental change. The dramatic events during the 1994-95 and 1995-96 congressional sessions have made it even more imperative that the social work profession examine, respond to, and set new agendas for the changing policy practice context of social services delivery. The need to strengthen and redefine social work practice proactively is inherent in the very nature of social work's dual mission. The urgency of this need is fueled also by the massive changes proposed by the Congress and by the increasing need for agencies to develop innovative programming, evaluate practice effectiveness, and compete for funding. Social work practitioners in all roles will be challenged to refine or redefine their goals while remaining true to social work values and ethics. Contemporary social work practice will, of necessity, involve a politically active stance.

Within the framework of this issue of *Social Work* on social work in an era of diminishing federal responsibility, this article explores past societal contexts at the local and national levels affecting policy and practice with older adults. Using insights from an interview conducted February 15, 1996, with Ruth I. Knee, a long-term care mental health counselor in Fairfax, Virginia, this article discusses and illustrates relatively successful traditional advocacy strategies used to develop policy in the field of aging. Ideas are offered for proactive steps to shape services for elderly people and their families.

CONCEPT OF POLICY PRACTICE

Policy practice is a growing area within the profession; it has been viewed as both a problem-solving process of intervention and a field of practice (Iatridis, 1995; Wenecor & Reisch, 1989). Policy practice may be viewed as a "historically situated construct" to connote the interaction among sociopolitical and economic factors, policy initiatives, and clinical social work practice (Goldstein, 1993). This perspective acknowledges that social work practice, which is affected by demographic and socioeconomic trends and the prevailing cultural and political contexts, can contribute to the shift in direct service practice paradigms.

Increasingly, social workers are recognizing that revolutions in epistemologies affecting the arts, humanities, and social sciences must also influence social work (Laird, 1993). A refashioning of curricula and teaching is under way as part of the historical effects of larger social change on the reformulation of research, theory, and practice in the profession: "At the center of this construction is a new relationship among theory, values, and practice" (Weick, 1993, p. 11).

It is difficult to delineate the policy practice context of the field of aging. Understanding policy necessitates awareness of everything that government does, including engaging in debate, making choices, making value preferences, and taking action to solve a problem (Dear, 1995). It is easier to understand the context of social welfare policy if the genesis of social welfare is viewed as a moral and human obligation expressed at any time in response to recognized social problems. As an integral societal obligation, social welfare can be understood as the ethos of the time as well as the worldview of the right order.

Perceptions of what constitutes the ideal society, what makes for a "suitable" way of life, and how society believes valued resources should be distributed are the multiple issues that are at the heart of social welfare policy development. For example, every society has an age-based definition of social roles and ascribes certain qualities to its elderly members (Greene, 1994). In the youth-oriented society of the United States, the older person is frequently portrayed as unproductive. This view is so pervasive that the term "ageism" was coined to describe prejudices and stereotypes applied to older people solely on the basis of their age (Butler, 1969).

Social workers in the field of aging have long combated myths about and stereotypes of their clients, including the view that most older adults are garrulous and "senile"; alienated from their families; incapable of learning new roles, skills, and competencies; and unsuitable candidates for insight-based therapies (Greene, 1986). Older adults may internalize such views. The general acceptance of negative views may limit opportunities for older adults. Furthermore, myths and stereotypes may affect policymakers' thoughts about older service recipients: As Knee put it, "The 10-year campaign of portraying the elderly as 'greedy geezers' has finally taken hold in the 1995 Congress."

To add to the complexity, the development of social policy and the enactment of social and distributive justice are increasingly understood to involve actions at the direct local level as well as in the macro-level ideological, political, and economic realms (Goldstein, 1993). This understanding relates to the idea that power resides not only at the legislative levels, but also at the group, dyadic, and individual levels (Wilson, 1973).

HISTORICAL PERSPECTIVES ON SERVICES IN THE FIELD OF AGING

During the past century, social work practice has evolved into a professional discipline, focusing the bulk of its efforts on assisting people and, to a lesser extent, on effecting social and environmental reforms (Brieland, 1995). It is critical that practitioners continue their interest in both social change and social services—or cause and function—which have so long characterized social work as a profession. Several major themes that illustrate the dual mission of social work have been evident in practice with elderly people and their families at both the local and macro levels.

Services to the aged population have been a logical development of "old age assistance" at the state level. Given the stark effects of the Great Depression, even the most skeptical people recognized that families were ill equipped to give their relatives financial help and that public assistance to older adults was a survival mechanism. Knee observed, "While wealthy people were expected to take care of their own, local-level politicians often bragged that 'no one is turned down for old age assistance.' The acceptance of need at the local level during the Depression appeared to reduce the stigma of financial assistance once associated with the county poorhouse."

Most benefits and services for older adults and their families, however, originated at the federal level, with the federal government outlining eligibility requirements, administrative support structures, and funding levels. The major legislation that determined the basic levels of health, income, and social services reveals a pattern of public responsibility. Other themes also become clear, such as the dovetailing of formal or public services with family caregiving. Much of the collaboration with the family in caregiving or effective aftercare can be traced to the efforts of social workers at both the local and national levels. The early role of social work in promoting family involvement set the stage for later intergenerational approaches to programming and advocacy through groups such as Generations United that have emphasized the need to rationalize the budget in ways that provide security for all. In addition to promoting intergenerational family involvement, social workers were active, if not leaders, in the movement to use federal funding for institutional and community-based care. Knee reflected, "These social work advocates knew that they could build their case through collecting data, directing surveys, conducting field studies, serving as consultants, and speaking to administrative and political officers. It was an interactive process at all levels—a hunt for every last solution."

The enactment of the Social Security Act (1935), the Older Americans Act (OAA) of 1965 (P.L. 89-73), and the Health Insurance for the Aged Act (Medicare Act) (P.L. 89-97) and the creation of Medicaid established more securely the government's responsibility for addressing citizens' social needs (Dickinson, 1995; Torres-Gil & Puccinelli, 1995). From 1935 until the late 1960s, the federal government expanded its role to provide a series of entitlements to selected groups of citizens, forming a safety net of income supports and social services to meet basic human needs (Byers, 1995).

The OAA of 1965, which was founded on a wellness or prevention philosophy, created a national network of Area Agencies on Aging to sponsor training and nutritional and homebound services (Dickinson, 1995). According to Knee, the act "intended that older adults perceive senior centers as a nonstigmatizing, supportive environment in which the older adults could interact with peers. These concepts of prevention and supportive services, often brought forth by social workers, were the foundation of community development efforts."

Title III of the OAA provided funding for older adults to receive chore services, transportation, and home-delivered meals and to engage in congregate meals. Title III also created the nursing home ombudsman advocacy program that safeguards the rights of older adults living in nursing homes (Garner, 1995), which Knee observed was "a key victory because before the passage of this title, the prevailing attitude was that people on public money had no constitutional rights." Through 670 local agencies, the OAA provided for age-based, non–means-tested, universal, accessible, and visible coverage. The Administration on Aging of the U.S. Department of Health and Human Services, which oversees OAA services, also provided a focal point for aging policy within the federal government (Torres-Gil & Puccinelli, 1995).

Medicare, the single largest medical program for older U.S. citizens, largely grew out of the advocacy efforts of the 1961 White House Conference on Aging (NASW, National Committee on Aging, 1980), which emphasized the burden of health care costs for older citizens. The prevailing mood of the country at the time was one of readiness for the Great Society programs; this belief system gave impetus to the passage of the Medicare Act. Through a combination of payroll taxes, premiums, and government revenues, Medicare and Medicaid established the federal government's role in ensuring medical services for older adults and low-income people (Dickinson, 1995). These well-recognized programs, which constitute the largest proportion of the federal budget, provide a health safety net for older adults and a "basis for the social contract—an implicit understanding that if a person has made contributions, he or she will receive social security benefits and the government will not significantly alter the benefits or manner of funding" (Torres-Gil & Puccinelli, 1995, p. 160).

Mental health services also were given public support through the enactment of the National Mental Health Act (1946) and the Community Mental Health Centers Act of 1963 (P.L. 88-164). An important milestone in publicly financed care for elderly mentally ill people was the inclusion of psychiatric benefits in the Social Security Amendments of 1965 (P.L. 89-97). In 1967 the U.S. Senate Finance Committee held hearings to determine the effectiveness or limitations of mental health care financing under Medicare and Medicaid provisions. An ad hoc task force consisting of staff members from the Social Security Administration, Social Rehabilitation Service, and Health Services and Mental Health Administration conducted a comprehensive study of the use of psychiatric benefits. The task force reported that Medicare and Medicaid benefits significantly improved the care of elderly psychiatric patients; they emphasized utilization review of services as essential to understanding how benefits were used (Rice, Knee, & Conwell, 1970).

Long-term benefits, which include services ranging from nursing home care to community-based care, have gradually come under public funding, often through the advocacy of social workers working in coalition groups. These services were designed to promote an optimal level of functioning through health care, personal care, and social services delivery including transportation, homemaker and chore services, and telephone reassurance (Kropf, 1992). According to Knee, "The role of the federal government in improving quality of care was established through grants to establish model programs, sponsorship of conferences, and the publishing of manuals on best practices."

Through coalition groups, social workers also have effected change in nursing home practice. The 1986 Institute of Medicine report *Improving the Quality of Care in Nursing Homes,* which documented abuses and established criteria for quality of care in nursing homes, provided the impetus for federal reform legislation. In 1989 Congress enacted nursing home reforms as part of the Omnibus Budget Reconciliation Act (P.L. 101-239), legislation that reflected the best in research-supported coalition building. This knowledge base set the stage for the National Citizens' Coalition of Nursing Home Reform to advocate for best practices in the nation's nursing home industry. Nursing home social workers presented and heard testimony that illustrated the effective use of social work services in nursing homes. Clinical social workers suggested that clients might want to "march on Washington" (Greene, 1986). In addition, Knee remembered, "the use of research to support program development, including that conducted at the National Institute of Mental Health, was an important feature among such advocacy groups."

However, the federal government has been gradually transferring social services responsibilities to state and local communities. From the 1960s until 1980, established federal programs had expanded in scope and cost as more citizens met eligibility criteria. During the 1980s, the Reagan administration's agenda was to dismantle the federal role in the provision of social services and income supports to everybody except people who received social security. Conservatives emphasized the use of private and volunteer efforts to meet locally defined needs. The momentum for such devolution and privatization processes has continued, culminating in the present debate about the public and private sectors' roles in the provision of human services (Byers, 1995; Humphreys, 1995).

ACTIONS IN RESPONSE TO ATTACKS ON SERVICES FOR OLDER ADULTS

Because the range of services to elderly people and their families is broad, encompassing multipurpose centers, mental health clinics, hospitals, area offices on aging, adult protective services, and nursing homes, core policy change might transform the service industry. Reforms in the size and shape of Medicare and Medicaid, for example, could most seriously affect older adults and their families. During the 1995 congressional budget battle, Republicans planned to eliminate $270 billion from Medicare spending. A number of organizations representing older adults have been deeply engaged in the debate over federal spending cuts. According to American Association of Retired Persons (AARP) legislative director John Rother, if cuts of the magnitude proposed are realized, "payments to hospitals and doctors could be greatly squeezed" (quoted in Hey & Carlson, 1995, p. 1).

Social work professional associations also have been involved in activities to influence policy making (NASW, 1995b, 1995c). These efforts have been intensified through the coalition known as ANSWER (Action Network for Social Work Education and Research), comprising the Council on Social Work Education, Baccalaureate Program Directors, Group for the Advancement of Doctoral Education, Institute for the Advancement of Social Work Research, National Association of Deans and Directors, and NASW. Coalition members have been making their positions known to members of Congress and to the Clinton administration. Topics have included protecting the needs of low-income families and children, balancing the budget through specific nonsocial program cuts, and preserving welfare entitlement (Newsome & Beless, 1996). Social workers' involvement in lobbying was evident at the February 1996 CSWE meeting on public policy challenges for social work education, during which faculty and students were urged to lobby their representatives and senators (Newsome & Beless, 1996). Moreover, NASW, through several key government relations publications, alerted social workers to spending cuts and regulations aimed at gutting Medicare, Medicaid, and federal nursing home standards. For example, a 1995 Government Relations Alert (NASW, 1995a) urged members to voice to their elected officials their opposition to Medicaid and Medicare cuts and to entreat the White House to veto any legislation that would create block grants for Medicaid or impose severe program cuts.

Other print media have addressed the budget struggle. In the *AARP Bulletin*, Lewis (1995) suggested that the sheer numbers of baby boomers (the 76 million people born between 1946 and 1964, the first of whom reached age 50 on January 1, 1996), sometimes called the "Me Generation," will redefine what it means to grow old in America. In the *New York Times* section "Week

in Review," Toner (1995) discussed long-predicted generational tensions between young and old:

> It is a chilling vision of a not-so-distant future, as the first boomers, born in
> 1946, begin to turn 50 tomorrow: The elderly and the soon-to-be elderly
> angrily protecting their benefit programs; the young increasingly resentful
> as programs for increasing numbers of elderly take a greater share of fed-
> eral resources; the whole system growing more precarious as the popula-
> tion gets older, putting more and more of a burden on people still in the
> workforce. (p. 1)

However, Toner (1995) also reported that some pollsters believe that this
prediction, as advanced by some policy analysts, is largely a myth. Both Republican and Democratic pollsters found little evidence of generational conflict in 1995; most younger people were as interested as their parents in protecting Medicare and social security. These programs are likely to continue
to be supported, because as many as 85 percent of elderly people who need
care receive care from family members and, furthermore, because a "sand-
wich generation," those people caught between parents and children who
need help, will need outside assistance (Toner, 1995).

PRACTICE TRENDS WITHIN THE SOCIAL WORK PROFESSION

Clearly, a review of the ways in which social workers and others have effected change through traditional advocacy roles points to many successes.
Yet current political changes seem to have propelled the social work profession into a period of self-doubt. Why do many social workers feel powerless? What more can be done to ensure that basic social work services reflect
current needs? What trends in practice have changed and will continue to
change the design, delivery, and financing of human services?

Because social work is intimately tied to societal institutions, it is naturally affected by social and demographic changes such as increased immigration, modifications in family structure, and an aging population. Since
the 1980s, accelerated social change has had a concomitant effect on the profession. As social work is redefined at the local level, opportunities abound
for practitioners to participate in the new shape of human services. The
reconfiguration of social work practice, including the provision of aging programs, may require that social workers

- operate with blurring of professional boundaries and participate in collaboration and training across disciplines
- provide community-based and family-centered care
- differentiate practice to work effectively with diverse groups
- act as interchangeable members of health and mental health teams
- work in a managed care environment
- enact performance-based outcome measures and evaluate practice
  effectiveness
- seek new revenue streams
- aim for cost-effectiveness and cost-containment

- increase the use of technology
- collapse the boundaries between education and practice
- forge new community partnerships
- increase the use of case management
- use wellness models
- involve families further as partners in care.

These practice trends challenge each practitioner to work at the local level to define social work in the 21st century. They offer social workers positive and daily opportunities to shape the definition of social work services while keeping that effort within the purview of the profession. Social workers in the field of aging have often acted as catalysts for the creation of ethics committees and family councils in nursing homes and hospitals; in the same vein, they can respond to new practice needs. For example, as social workers increasingly work on multidisciplinary teams, often in the absence of a social services department, it is critical that they "elect" leadership and collect, analyze, and act on data related to practice effectiveness. Practitioners can lead the way in suggesting cost-effective measures that reflect client perspectives. They can devise peer supervision strategies that enhance managed care treatment.

Given the growing numbers of older adults, the need for professionally trained social workers in the field of aging to triage, to use wellness and prevention models, and to further involve families in treatment strategies has never been so great. According to Knee, for successful adaptation to the shifting environment,

> Each of us would be careful about data collection about the nature of our practice, knowledgeable about best practice strategies, and conscious of cost containment. . . . Social workers would continue to involve the family and to promote a client's maximum functioning through prevention and wellness models. We would understand that social work's role in the 21st century will be to provide excellent minimal service and get people on the way.

CONCLUSION

More than 15 years ago, social workers were feeling somewhat successful in promoting aging services. Social policies for older adults had already moved "toward selective societal responsibility, and away from reliance on exclusive kin or filial responsibility, toward acceptance of rightful entitlement benefits" (Lowy, 1980, p. 7). Social workers continue to work to improve social conditions and gain resources for social services clients and others through active involvement in political activities. Their participation in election campaigns, as well as their efforts to inform officials of alternative policy actions and build coalitions on behalf of social causes, is on the upswing (Weismiller & Rome, 1995). Practitioners apparently have become more aware that the skills they use to provide services can be instrumental in formulating and executing policies (Dolgoff, 1981). Social workers are increasingly engaging in *policy analysis*—a systematic, evaluative process of using social sciences methods to describe and prescribe the nature of policy and to choose among policy alternatives (Einbinder, 1995).

However, the progress of the past several decades is threatened. Both traditional and new initiatives are needed. The profession must emphasize localized experiences and the political nature of daily interaction. By learning from past examples, every social worker has the potential to take a political role and effect change. The notion that communal belief systems were and are shaped through daily human interaction adds a powerful dimension to the dynamics of social exchange. Building coalitions, evaluating practice, and providing therapeutic and other intervention strategies, then, are political acts (Allen, 1993). This notion also assumes that concerted local experiences, that is, one-to-one daily activities, are a part of the political equation (Blundo, Greene, & Gallant, 1994).

The policy practice approach to social work is based on the idea that the social work profession is a social invention. Social workers have often referenced the need to see beyond the client to others in the same situation—"case-to-cause." Practitioners also have argued that the target of change is whatever community structure is impeding or oppressing the client. If positive structures do not exist, it is "good" social work practice to "invent one" (Middleman & Wood, 1993, p. 135). Although, in general, social workers have seen themselves as advocates ready to lobby and influence public policy, in reality "we treat it [meaning] as though it is constructed by powers outside ourselves . . . while the power to revise flows from the assumption that what has been constructed can be reconstructed" (Weick, 1993, p. 12).

The nature of social work as a profession, then, is an evolutionary process, one that ensures its authority as a profession over time (Goldstein, 1993). If the social work profession is seen as a "cultural artifact" as Goldstein (1993, p. 166) suggested or as "a societally prescribed system" carried out by "authorized personnel" as purported by Siporin (1975, p. 9), then the extension of this view is to see social service designs as social artifacts with historical origins that members of the profession can construct.

This potentially powerful policy practice perspective views social workers as "meaning makers" (Weick, 1993). This perspective also may take social workers beyond policy analysis or problem-solving interventions to a more active construction of social work services in the 21st century. This policy practice approach calls on the profession to proactively shape and evaluate new service paradigms in the field of aging and to advocate for the adoption of new forms that represent the profession's ethos and values. The profession is in danger of losing not only funding for particular programs, but also the philosophy on which the programs are based.

REFERENCES

Allen, J. A. (1993). The constructivist paradigm: Values and ethics. In J. Laird (Ed.), *Revisioning social work education: A social constructionist approach* (pp. 31–54). New York: Haworth Press.

Blundo, R., Greene, R. R., & Gallant, P. (1994). A constructionist approach with diverse populations. In R. R. Greene (Ed.), *Human behavior: A diversity framework* (pp. 115–132). New York: Aldine de Gruyter.

Brieland, D. (1995). Social work practice: History and evolution. In R. L. Edwards (Ed.-in-Chief), *Encyclopedia of social work* (19th ed., Vol. 3, pp. 2247–2257). Washington, DC: NASW Press.

Butler, R. N. (1969). Directions in psychiatric treatment of the elderly: Role of perspectives of the life-cycle. *Gerontologist, 2,* 134–138.

Byers, K. (1995, October). *Introduction: The great debate.* Paper presented at the annual meeting of the National Association of Social Workers, Philadelphia.

Community Mental Health Centers Act of 1963, P.L. 88-164, 42 U.S.C.A. §§ 2681-2687.

Dear, R. B. (1995). Social welfare policy. In R. L. Edwards (Ed.-in-Chief), *Encyclopedia of social work* (19th ed., Vol. 3, pp. 2226–2237). Washington, DC: NASW Press.

Dickinson, N. S. (1995). Federal social legislation from 1961 to 1994. In R. L. Edwards (Ed.-in-Chief), *Encyclopedia of social work* (19th ed., Vol. 2, pp. 1005–1013). Washington, DC: NASW Press.

Doherty, W. J., & Boss, P. G. (1992). Values and ethics in family therapy. In A. D. Gurman & D. P. Kniskern (Eds.), *Handbook of family therapy* (pp. 606–637). New York: Brunner/Mazel.

Dolgoff, R. L. (1981). Clinicians as social policy makers. *Social Casework, 62,* 284–292.

Einbinder, S. D. (1995). Policy analysis. In R. L. Edwards (Ed.-in-Chief), *Encyclopedia of social work* (19th ed., Vol. 3, pp. 1849–1855). Washington, DC: NASW Press.

Garner, J. D. (1995). Long-term care. In R. L. Edwards (Ed.-in-Chief), *Encyclopedia of social work* (19th ed., Vol. 2, pp. 1625–1633). Washington, DC: NASW Press.

Goldstein, H. (1993). Field education for reflective practice: A re-constructive proposal. In J. Laird (Ed.), *Revisioning social work education: A social constructionist approach* (pp. 165–182). New York: Haworth Press.

Greene, R. R. (1986). *Social work with the aged and their families.* New York: Aldine de Gruyter.

Greene, R. R. (1994). *Human behavior theory: A diversity framework.* New York: Aldine de Gruyter.

Health Insurance for the Aged Act (Medicare Act), P.L. 89-97, 79 Stat. 290 (1965).

Hey, R. P., & Carlson, E. (1995). Budget struggle simmers: Medicare, Medicaid cuts still at stake in talks. *AARP Bulletin, 36*(11), 1, 6.

Humphreys, N. (1995, October). *A defense of federal and public responsibility: The great debate.* Paper presented at the annual meeting of the National Association of Social Workers, Philadelphia.

Iatridis, D. S. (1995). Policy practice. In R. L. Edwards (Ed.-in-Chief), *Encyclopedia of social work* (19th ed., Vol. 3, pp. 1855–1866). Washington, DC: NASW Press.

Institute of Medicine. (1986). *Improving the quality of care in nursing homes.* Washington, DC: National Academy Press.

Kropf, N. P. (1992). Home health and community services. In R. L. Schneider & N. P. Kropf (Eds.), *Gerontological social work knowledge, service settings, and special populations* (pp. 173–201). Chicago: Nelson Hall.

Laird, J. (1993). Introduction. In J. Laird (Ed.), *Revisioning social work education: A social constructionist approach* (pp. 1–10). New York: Haworth Press.

Lewis, R. (1995). The "youth generation" nears major milestone as the country watches. *AARP Bulletin, 36*(11), 1, 10.

Lowy, L. (1980). *Social work with the aging.* New York: Harper & Row.

McNamee, S., & Gergen, K. J. (1992). *Therapy as social construction.* Newbury Park, CA: Sage Publications.

Middleman, R., & Wood, G. G. (1993). So much for the Bell Curve: Constructionism, power, conflict, and the structural approach to direct practice in social work. In J. Laird (Ed.), *Revisioning social work education: A social constructionist approach* (pp. 129–146). New York: Haworth Press.

National Association of Social Workers. (1995a, July 20). *Action needed to confront severe funding cuts in the Medicaid and Medicare programs* [Government Relations Alert]. Washington, DC: Author.

National Association of Social Workers. (1995b, December 6). *Federal nursing home standards gutted in reconciliation conference* [Press release]. Washington, DC: Author.

National Association of Social Workers (1995c, November 14). *Social workers urged to take action to save Medicaid and Medicare* [Government Relations Alert]. Washington, DC: Author.

National Association of Social Workers, National Committee on Aging. (1980). *A social work agenda for the '80s.* Washington, DC: Author.

National Mental Health Act, ch. 538, 60 Stat. 421 (1946).

Newsome, M., & Beless, D. (1996, February). *President's and executive director's message.* Program message at the Annual Program Meeting of the Council on Social Work Education, Washington, DC.

Older Americans Act of 1965, P.L. 89-73, 79 Stat. 218.

Omnibus Budget Reconciliation Act of 1989, P.L. 101-239, 103 Stat. 2106.

Rice, D. P., Knee, R. I., & Conwell, M. (1970). Financing the care of the mentally ill under Medicare and Medicaid. *American Journal of Public Health, 60,* 2235–2250.

Siporin, M. (1975). *Introduction to social work practice.* New York: Macmillan.

Social Security Act, ch. 531, 49 Stat. 620 (1935).

Social Security Amendments of 1965, P.L. 89-97, 79 Stat. 286.

Toner, R. (1995, December 31). No free rides: Generational push has not come to shove. *New York Times* [Week in Review], pp. 1, 4.

Torres-Gil, F. M., & Puccinelli, M. A. (1995). Aging: Public policy issues and trends. In R. L. Edwards (Ed.-in Chief), *Encyclopedia of social work* (19th ed., Vol. 1, pp. 159–173). Washington, DC: NASW Press.

Weick, A. (1993). Reconstructing social work education. In J. Laird (Ed.), *Revisioning social work education: A social constructionist approach* (pp. 11–30). New York: Haworth Press.

Weismiller, T., & Rome, H. S. (1995). Social workers in politics. In R. L. Edwards (Ed.-in-Chief), *Encyclopedia of social work* (19th ed., Vol. 3, pp. 2305–2313). Washington, DC: NASW Press.

Wenecor, S., & Reisch, M. (1989). *From charity to enterprise: The development of American social work in a market economy.* Chicago: University of Illinois Press.

Wilson, W. J. (1973). *Power, race, and privilege.* New York: Free Press.

This chapter was originally published in the September 1996 issue of Social Work, *vol. 41, pp. 553–560.*

Part V

MENTAL HEALTH

39 Managing Mental Health: Whose Responsibility?

Susan J. Rose and Sharon M. Keigher

A famous landmark and social center near the University of Wisconsin–Milwaukee campus, the Oriental Drugstore, recently shut its doors. Having served a cross section of Milwaukeeans since 1926, its lunch counter was a place where a frail old cloudy-eyed black man mumbling to himself, a purple-haired chain-smoking young woman with a twitch in her cheek and a tremulous hand on her coffee cup, and a gaunt young man with AIDS all could chat comfortably with other customers as they waited for their prescriptions in the familiar sociable surroundings. The waitresses and the pharmacists knew their customers' names; the food was plain and affordable. Immortalized on the neighboring movie marquee as "a place where people really cared," this public space represented what Putnam (1995) called "institutions of civic engagement"; the social exchanges that occurred there spilled over, generating community "social capital."

The Oriental Drugstore sold out to a national discount drugstore chain. The pressure to sell came from competition and from the preference of local managed care companies for contracting with large chain drugstores offering administrative convenience and discount pricing. The big shiny new drug emporium a half mile away has no food service, no place to linger with other people. Large corporations are too big to deal with independent pharmacies or small private independent vendors catering to poor clients. The loss of the neighborhood drugstore portends an erosion of social care for poor and mentally ill residents.

The enormous growth in managed care, recently documented in this column (Keigher, 1995), has staggering implications for people with mental illnesses in the United States and for social workers employed in the mental health care field who recognize the value of familiarity, affordability, and personal compassion. Managed care, working its way into physical health care for the past 20 years, has emerged as a vendor of mental health care in the form of "behavioral health care plans" in the past 15 years. Managed behavioral health care organizations' interest in patients with severe and persistent mental illnesses has been sparked largely by recent government efforts to reduce their costs of caring for chronically mentally ill people, spurring the Medicaid "experiments" now developing in many states (Essock & Goldman, 1995).

Social workers in mental health care settings are reacting dramatically to the cost-containment changes being imposed on them. In 1992 NASW found that 37 percent of its surveyed membership had already changed their treatment approach because of managed care. A recent survey of 173 mental health practitioners in San Francisco found that 44 percent were considering leaving the field of mental health treatment because of managed care (Hymowitz & Pollock, 1995).

Although social work practice with all populations stands to be fundamentally altered by the incursion of managed care's cost containment strategies into previously foreign territory, practice with seriously and persistently mentally ill clients is especially vulnerable. The large numbers of social workers in mental health transform the issue into one of imminent concern to the profession. Mental health is the leading field of social work practice; the National Institute of Mental Health reported that 47 percent of the patient care staff in outpatient psychiatric clinics are social workers (Hopps & Pinderhughes, 1987).

Although the cost of health care has grown to 12 percent of the gross national product (Dorwart, 1990), only 12 percent to 14 percent of total health care dollars are for mental health services. The total estimated spending on mental health services, both public and private, was approximately $42.5 billion in 1990 (*Medicaid and Mental Health*, 1995). The pattern of use by mental health care consumers is not unlike that of users of physical health care—about 10 percent of mental health care users account for about 50 percent of all outpatient expenditures (Durenberger, 1989), and another 10 percent account for 60 percent of the inpatient days (Scharfstein & Beigel, 1985). In private health insurance plans, mental health care represents no more than 25 percent of total health care costs (Levin, 1992).

MANAGED BEHAVIORAL HEALTH CARE

An oligopoly has emerged among the key corporate players in the managed behavioral health care agenda in the past five years. The vendors with the largest total enrollment at the beginning of 1995 were Human Affairs International, Medco Behavioral Health Care, Value Behavioral Health, and Green Spring Health Services. These four managed care organizations are responsible for directing the care of over 51 million "covered lives" (individuals who are eligible for care under specific care plans financed either by employers or by some type of public funding)—47 percent of the market. With a total enrollment of 111 million people, 40 of the largest managed behavioral health program vendors reported total annual revenues of approximately $2.1 billion (Oss, Winters, Stair, & Mackie, 1995).

Assumptions of Managed Behavioral Health Care

Managed behavioral health care is driven primarily by two assumptions about the bases of costs. The first assumption is that unnecessary care is being provided, so that tight controls should be directed at reducing the frequency of care. The second is that inappropriate types of care for patients' conditions (inpatient, partial hospitalization, intensive outpatient care) are being provided, so close case review can be used to reduce the intensity of care.

Techniques for Controlling Costs

Techniques to control the frequency of mental health care use include cost shifting (copayment), which lowers the probability of use by increasing the patient's share of costs (Keeler, Manning, & Wells, 1988). Increasing the patient's cost of care has always been the fear of providers who care for poor sick people. Containing the intensity of care per user is accomplished through the use of health maintenance organizations (HMOs), precertification, and concurrent approval for care by managed care organization reviewers (Wells, Manning, & Benjamin, 1986).

Credentialing is the process of "certifying" practitioners for inclusion in a given managed care network and thereby making them eligible to receive referrals. This controls both frequency and intensity by routing more enrollees to providers with preferred cost-effective practices.

The reductions in frequency and intensity of use initially accomplished by insurance companies were quickly followed by public jurisdictions that adopted creative reimbursement strategies such as capitation. In a capitation scheme, a provider is paid a flat fee per year for each covered life and then bears the cost for additional services provided above a break-even amount; for example, in 1994 Tennessee providers were paid $1,200 per year for each Medicaid-eligible patient, regardless of the actual cost of the services provided ("Switch to Managed Care," 1995). Capitation serves as a strong disincentive for service provision as it transfers the financial risk to the provider. It reduces costs to the insurer, quickly constraining access for the high-use client. Although 40 percent of preferred provider organizations nationally used this method in 1986, only 25 percent were using it by 1990 (Hoy, Curtis, & Rice, 1991). The financial risks for patients with chronic conditions were too great.

Reducing use through prospective review (precertification) and retrospective review (utilization review) has been less effective for managed behavioral health care organizations. As vendors have moved away from these methods, concurrent review has become the cornerstone of cost containment in managed behavioral health care today; it exerts tight control by reviewing frequency and use at specified intervals so that use (and thus costs) stay within the bounds prescribed by the "protocols."

Requiring all patients to have a DSM-IV (American Psychiatric Association, 1994) diagnosis has become the major method of retrospective review. Sixty percent of behavioral health care insurers use the DSM-IV diagnosis plus a minimum dollar threshold of claims to determine review, and 30 percent use the diagnosis only (Hoy et al., 1991).

MENTAL HEALTH AS A LONG–TERM CARE ISSUE

There is an emerging national uneasiness about the lack of fit between chronic mental illness and the acute care treatment model practiced in managed behavioral health care, because the care of severely mentally ill patients has been built on a different set of assumptions. The major mental health disorders—schizophrenia, major depression, bipolar disorder—are assumed to be incurable (Torrey, 1988); management of symptoms is the primary intervention strategy (Dawson, Blum, & Bartolucci, 1983). Keeping the person in regular continuing contact with a provider over time is recognized as a necessary and cost-effective method of managing the disturbing symptoms of chronic mental illness (Hudson & DeVito, 1994). Psychoeducational approaches assume that people with mental illnesses can and should be taught to manage their own symptoms (Anderson, Reiss, & Hogarty, 1986), and periodic hospitalization is considered a predictable part of the disorder (Anthony, 1993).

Care of people with severe and persistent mental illnesses is guided by two primary assumptions. First, people with a chronic mental illness, who often have spotty employment records because of their disability, must have access to care despite their inability to pay (Dorwart & Hoover, 1994). Second, there must be continuity of care across all levels of intensity of care (Foley & Sharfstein, 1983). These principles, which may well contradict an acute care model that attempts to control frequency and intensity of care, have been integral parts of state and community care delivery systems.

Data on managed care treatment for people with severe and disabling mental illnesses are disturbingly sparse. The assumptions underlying managed behavioral care for acute mental illness, as opposed to care of chronic and disabling mental illness, may not be compatible, but little empirical data exist to evaluate this.

STATE EXPERIMENTS IN MANAGING MENTAL HEALTH CARE

Despite the dearth of research and substantial questioning of the "goodness of fit" of managed care with chronically mentally ill people, states are busily forging ahead, crafting new initiatives to treat this population. To experiment with managed care for mental health services under Medicaid, states must apply for and receive a waiver under Section 1115 of Title XIX of the Social Security Act. These waivers require that research and demonstration be a part of the project but allow states to waive eligibility and HMO requirements and to have some noncovered services. As of July 1995, 11 states had waivers approved, nine states had applications pending, and eight were preparing waiver requests. States with approved waivers include Arizona, Florida, Hawaii, Kentucky, Massachusetts, Minnesota, Ohio, Oregon, Rhode Island, South Carolina, and Tennessee. These state demonstration projects differ in their eligibility requirements, benefits provided, managed care design, financing arrangements, and structure. Although these projects have generated only beginning empirical data for comparison, they illustrate national trends in state efforts to privatize mental health services.

In Arizona all mental health and substance abuse services for seriously mentally ill adults are provided on a capitated basis through the Arizona Department of Health Services (ADHS). Federal funds are passed through the ADHS, which then contracts with Regional Behavioral Health Authorities on a capitated basis. Arizona currently offers no Title XIX mental health or substance abuse services to adults with mental illnesses not deemed serious (American Managed Behavioral Healthcare Association [AMBHA] & National Association of State Mental Health Program Directors [NASMHPD], 1995).

In Oregon mental health and substance abuse services are currently provided through the counties. Physician care organizations will soon assume responsibility for screening, assessment, and treatment of substance abuse patients. Mental health services will be developed through a statewide system beginning in 1996 (AMBHA & NASMHPD, 1995).

Massachusetts, the first state to introduce a statewide specialty mental health managed care plan into the Medicaid plan (Callahan, Shepard, Beinecke, Larson, & Cavanaugh, 1995), was approved for a second demonstration project in April 1995. The newer Section 1115 waiver relies on both primary care case management (PCCM) and HMOs; HMOs will provide mental health services on an integrated, capitated basis, and the PCCM will contract out for mental health services on an individual risk basis (Elias & Navon, 1995).

In Hawaii and Rhode Island, health care plans deliver a basic package of mental health services to Title XIX-eligible people, but there is a "carve out" with expanded benefits for seriously mentally ill adults. (Carve outs reserve specific programs or populations for continued public support, thereby removing them from a managed care system.) People with serious mental illnesses receive services from a contractor on a capitated basis, but use of services is controlled through narrow definitions of "serious mental illness" (AMBHA & NASMHPD, 1995).

It seems likely that most states will propose some type of capitation reimbursement with a carve out for specific populations. Using a carve out is one way of reserving some programs for continued public support (perhaps as an entitlement) so they are not included in a managed care system. Capitation is the preferred method for state contracts because once the number of eligible recipients has been established, the costs of care are fixed and known. Costs might be controlled by limiting those eligible for enrollment (for example, by narrowing definitions as Hawaii and Rhode Island have done). Limits appeal to legislators who see entitlements as having ever-growing costs. Costs for mental health care under Medicaid are expected to be more stable or at least more predictable.

However, the risks are not eliminated. The accuracy of cost estimates for both use and capitation are critical. If the costs of care for those with disabling mental illnesses are underestimated, managed behavioral health care programs will be reluctant to continue nonprofitable business ventures, and states will be back where they started but with a weakened administrative structure less capable of delivering services. If the costs of care are overestimated, managed care organizations stand to make substantial profits, and the states stand to waste significant amounts of money.

The key to this equation seems to be the carve outs. Populations that are too risky in terms of the states' ability to predict their use of care might be carved out and their care contracted out. States have suggested a variety of populations for these carve outs, including children with serious emotional disorders, dually diagnosed adults, people with serious mental illnesses, or elderly people with disabling mental illnesses.

CONCLUSION

The implications of this shift from public responsibility to publicly funded private responsibility for the care of people with mental illnesses are enormous. The shock waves will be felt by the people needing the care, by social workers in community mental health centers, and by state-level administrators of services.

For people in need of the care being "sold," mental health treatment becomes inevitably medicalized. Using DSM-IV or any other medically based taxonomy to determine the course of treatment and the likelihood of reimbursement runs the risk of pathologizing all human behavior and conditions. Is the profession's level of confidence in these categorization schema so great that it would subjugate ideas about appropriate treatment to them? Where will the role of social conditions and environmental factors fit into the development and treatment of mental illness? Will they continue to be relegated to the nonreimbursable, "tacked on" Axis IV (psychosocial and environmental problems) and Axis V (global assessment of functioning) of DSM-IV's diagnostic system?

The implications for social workers in mental health practice are serious, more so for those practicing in local community mental health agencies than for those concerned with the narrower interests of private practice. Traditional tasks of social work agencies serving mentally ill clients have encompassed prevention, education, advocacy, and other activities that are clearly not reimbursable under managed care. How important are these activities in the treatment of mentally ill people? How long will agencies continue to perform these tasks if no one is paying for them?

The continuous buying, selling, and merging of large national corporations in the managed behavioral health care business have consequences for the states' administration of mental health programs. Larger corporations may have little connection to the local community, yet smaller corporations may not have the expertise to manage the complex care of chronically disabled people. Will states turn to the few managed care corporations that attempt to work through local provider systems, even if they are costlier? How will quality be assessed?

Social work continues to value familiarity, affordability, and personal compassion. Services provided in a local context are more attuned to the individual needs of a population and have greater potential to be creative, innovative, and in the end less costly. Social work has a commitment to vulnerable populations and a responsibility not to subject them to greater vulnerability in the name of efficiency, cost-cutting, and professionalism.

REFERENCES

American Managed Behavioral Healthcare Association & National Association of State Mental Health Program Directors. (1995, July). *Public mental health systems, Medicaid re-structuring and managed behavioral healthcare* (White paper in progress). Washington, DC: American Managed Behavioral Healthcare Association.

American Psychiatric Association. (1994). *Diagnostic and statistical manual of mental disorders* (4th ed.). Washington, DC: Author.

Anderson, C., Reiss, D., & Hogarty, G. (1986). *Schizophrenia and the family.* New York: Guilford Press.

Anthony, W. A. (1993). Recovery from mental illness: The guiding vision of the mental health service system in the 1990s. *Psychosocial Rehabilitation Journal, 14*(4), 11–24.

Callahan, J., Shepard, D., Beinecke, R., Larson, M., & Cavanaugh, D. (1995). Mental health/substance abuse treatment in managed care: The Massachusetts Medicaid experiment. *Health Affairs, 14,* 173–184.

Dawson, D., Blum, H., & Bartolucci, G. (1983). *Schizophrenia in focus.* New York: Human Sciences Press.

Dorwart, R. A. (1990). Managed mental health care: Myths and realities in the 1990s. *Hospital and Community Psychiatry, 41,* 1087–1091.

Dorwart, R. A., & Hoover, C. (1994). A national study of transitional hospital services in mental health. *American Journal of Public Health, 84,* 1229–1234.

Durenberger, D. (1989). Providing mental health care services to Americans. *American Psychologist, 44,* 1293–1297.

Elias, E., & Navon, M. (1995). The Massachusetts experience with managed mental health care and Medicaid. *Health Affairs, 14*(3), 46–49.

Essock, S., & Goldman, H. (1995). States embrace of managed mental health care. *Health Affairs, 14*(3), 34–44.

Foley, H. A., & Sharfstein, S. S. (1983). *Madness and government.* Washington, DC: American Psychiatric Press.

Hopps, J. G., & Pinderhughes, E. B. (1987). Profession of social work: Contemporary characteristics. In A. Minahan (Ed.-in-Chief), *Encyclopedia of social work* (18th ed., Vol. 2, pp. 351–366). Silver Spring, MD: National Association of Social Workers.

Hoy, E. W., Curtis, R. E., & Rice, T. (1991). Change and growth in managed care. *Health Affairs, 10,* 18–35.

Hudson, C. G., & DeVito, J. A. (1994). Mental health under national health care reform: The empirical foundations. *Health & Social Work, 19,* 279–287.

Hymowitz, C., & Pollock, E. (1995, July 13). Psychobattle: Cost-cutting firms monitor couch time as therapists fret. *Wall Street Journal,* pp. A1, A4.

Keeler, E. B., Manning, W. G., & Wells, K. B. (1988). The demand for episodes of mental health services. *Journal of Health Economics, 7,* 369–392.

Keigher, S. M. (1995). Managed care's silent seduction of America and the new politics of choice [National Health Line]. *Health & Social Work, 20,* 146–151.

Levin, B. L. (1992). Managed mental health care: A national perspective. In R. W. Mandersheid & M. A. Sonnenschein (Eds.), *Mental health: United States, 1992* (DHHS Publication No. SMA92-1942, pp. 208–218). Washington, DC: U.S. Government Printing Office.

Medicaid and Mental Health: Hearings on Perspectives on Transformation of the Medicaid Program. Hearings Before the Subcommittee on Health and Environment, Committee on Commerce, U.S. House of Representatives, 104th Cong., 2d Sess. (1995, August 1) (testimony of C. Koyanagi).

National Association of Social Workers. (1992). *Managed care update: A report of the National Managed Health Care Congress.* Washington, DC: Author.

Oss, M. Winters, C., Stair, T., & Mackie, J. (1995). *Managed behavioral health market share in the United States, 1995/1996.* Gettysburg, PA: Open Minds Publications.

Putnam, R. D. (1995, January). Bowling alone: America's declining social capital. *Journal of Democracy, 6*(1), 65–78.

Scharfstein, S., & Beigel, A. (1985). *The new economics and psychiatric care.* Washington, DC: American Psychiatric Press.

Social Security Act, Title XIX § 1115, P.L. 89-97, 79 Stat. 286 (1965).

Switch to managed care tricky. (1995, July 13). *Chicago Tribune,* p. 10.

Torrey, E. F. (1988). *Nowhere to go.* New York: Harper & Row.

Wells, K. B., Manning, W. G., & Benjamin, B. (1986). Use of outpatient mental health services in HMO and fee-for-service plans: Results from a randomized controlled trial. *Health Services Research, 21,* 453–474.

This chapter was originally published in the February 1996 issue of Health & Social Work, *vol. 21, pp. 76–80.*

40

Are Mental Illnesses Biological Diseases? Some Public Policy Implications

Philip D. Arben

In the recently published *Diagnostic and Statistical Manual of Mental Disorders-Fourth Edition* (DSM-IV) (American Psychiatric Association [APA], 1994), APA departed from its historically dichotomized classification of mental illnesses as being of either "organic" or "functional" etiology. In all previous diagnostic manuals, beginning with the DSM-I in 1952, APA had categorized a mental disorder as organic if it was associated with an observable or patently inferable brain tissue impairment or lesion, such as vascular dementia or Alzheimer's disease, and as functional if no such association could be established. The primary causes of functional mental disorders were assumed to be psychological factors, social factors, or both. In one simple and breathtaking sentence contained in DSM-IV, the reader is informed that "The term 'organic disorder' is no longer used in DSM-IV because it incorrectly implies that the other mental disorders in the manual do not have a biological basis" (APA, 1994, p. 10). When one examines the range of human behaviors designated as mental disorders in DSM-IV (some 300 entities, compared to about 100 in DSM-I), it is obvious that there is a wide spectrum in terms of presumed severity—for example, "paranoid type schizophrenia" at one end to "caffeine-induced sleep disorder" at the other.

PARTIES TO THE DEBATE

Today a major contentious issue among mental health professionals and others is whether the severe mental illnesses that were formerly regarded as functional in origin are in fact caused by biological or physical abnormalities—that is, whether they are organic diseases. Attention in this debate has tended to focus mostly on schizophrenia, manic depression (now known as bipolar disorder), and severe depression (now referred to as major depressive disorder). In addition to these profound clinical entities, the debate has often spread to other, and in a sense less dramatic, psychiatric classifications such as panic attacks, substance dependence, bulimia, obsessive–compulsive disorder, and attention deficit disorder.

The chief proponents of a biological–physical etiology for the major mental illnesses tend to be found among biopsychiatrists and behavioral geneticists, advocacy groups whose membership consists for the most part of mothers and fathers of mentally ill people, and pharmaceutical companies that have high-volume sales of psychoactive drugs. The dissenters and the agnostics are a more diffuse group who are less proactive and visible. They include mental health professionals from all disciplines (psychiatry, psychology, and social work) and social scientists whose clinical experiences or research attest to the view that environmental, psychological, and social factors can be significant causative agents of serious mental illnesses. The dissenters also include a number of loosely organized former mental patient groups whose members had often been involuntarily committed and who had been forced to submit to somatic therapies, including drugs and electroconvulsive therapy. The agnostics include a large segment of the medical and scientific communities who adhere to the fundamental precept that there is a distinction among a hypothesis, a theory, and a fact.

THE DEBATE

To understand the intellectual underpinnings of the debate, it is useful to dispose of a number of semantic and logical confusions or contortions. First, because all human thought and behaviors associated with those thoughts are associated with human brain activity, it should be obvious that any thought–behavior activity, whether normal or disordered, is happening through some biological process.

Second, although studies show that close relatives of individuals with schizophrenia or bipolar disorder are more susceptible to these disorders than the average person, studies also show that the close relatives of individuals manifesting almost any of the lesser mental disorders are also more susceptible to these disorders than the average person. In fact, any specific normal behavioral trait or personality characteristic tends to be more common among close relatives than in the average population.

Third, the fact that many people feel less depressed while on fluoxetine (Prozac), which apparently increases the quantity of the neurotransmitter serotonin in the brain, does not demonstrate that depression is the result of an inadequate level of serotonin any more than drinking an alcoholic beverage to reduce tension indicates that that tension is caused by an insufficiency of alcohol in the brain.

Fourth, a study in which the results indicate that some individuals with schizophrenia manifest certain brain irregularities does not speak to the issue of whether these brain irregularities caused the schizophrenic symptoms (an organic etiology) or whether environmental or psychological stressors produced these brain irregularities (a functional etiology).

Bearing in mind that the core element in this debate is the matter of causation or etiology—biological versus environmental, organic versus functional, or nature versus nurture—where do we seem to be? In terms of public perceptions it would appear that the biological exponents are well ahead. Driven by a variety of motivations, the biopsychiatrists and behavioral geneticists, some parents' advocacy groups, and the manufacturers of psychoactive drugs, with huge assistance from a generally accommodating media, seem to have engendered a public consciousness that perceives most serious mental illnesses as medical diseases with biological causations. Alcoholism was probably the first disorder to achieve that status; it was soon followed by others. This occurred despite the fact that the field is strewn with headlined "discoveries" of genes for alcoholism, manic depression, schizophrenia, and depression that were either subsequently retracted or that no other investigator has been able to replicate and also despite the fact that even the most favored of the physiological or biochemical causation explanations are usually designated as simply hypotheses. For example, the favored physiological causation explanation for schizophrenia is known by its proponents as the "dopamine hypothesis," which means that schizophrenia is caused by an excess of dopamine activity in the brain.

The phrase "a chemical imbalance" has become part of the popular lexicon when people speak about mental illness these days. It may be that because the ingestion of certain drugs ameliorates the symptoms of certain mental disorders, then it must follow that the drug is correcting "a chemical imbalance," or so runs the logic of this popular discourse. In fact, the drug may be producing any number of physiological or biochemical effects, none of which need have anything to do with correcting a chemical imbalance.

Certainly the popular press has played a major role in propounding the biological thesis by reporting, often on the front page, highly tentative findings of small single studies as proven scientific fact and then failing to report or barely reporting that the study's results have been retracted by its authors or that subsequent studies have failed to confirm the original findings.

As for the dissenters to the biological point of view—and I speak now of the mental health professionals—their views are heard much less often for at least three discernible reasons. First, what they have to offer is not "news"; there are few breakthroughs to report. Second, one can perceive an unwillingness on their part to appear antiscientific, particularly about scientific fields in which their training has been minimal or nonexistent. Third, and paradoxically, to the extent that their work is viewed as "medical," they often stand to gain in both status and insurance reimbursements. As for the ex-mental patient groups, their organizational existence tends to be transitory, they usually are made up of individuals who have a whole lot of other things to contend with, their financial resources are usually quite limited, they have few if any forums in which to express their views, and even when they do manage to gain an audience their views are usually patronizingly heard and then rather quickly dismissed.

The agnostics, who probably constitute the largest segment of the general scientific community, await verifiable evidence. It should be noted, although it seldom is, that despite all the self-interested and media hoopla, the present scientific fact is that there is not any biological marker or biological test of any kind that can be used to establish a diagnosis of any of the previously designated functional mental disorders, particularly schizophrenia, manic depression, and depression. There are, perhaps surprisingly to many, no blood, urine, biochemical, genetic, or brain-imaging examinations or tests that can establish such a diagnosis. A diagnosis of schizophrenia, manic depression, or clinical depression is made today—as it always has been—by the subjective judgment of an examiner based on an individual's reported history and observed appearance and behavior and the examiner's personal interpretation of the individual's expressed speech, emotions, perceptions, and thoughts.

PRESENT STATUS OF THE DEBATE

How then could one summarize the status of the present debate?

1. Most of psychiatry (particularly the younger psychiatrists), with the aid of neuroscientists and other interested groups, is pushing to define mental illness as a biological, medical, brain disease.
2. Although enormous sums of money have been spent on research to establish such an etiology, the results to date can best be described as consisting only of a number of hypotheses and theories.
3. Despite the inability of psychiatry to scientifically demonstrate a biological causation for any of the functional disorders, the general public, influenced by a somewhat breathless mass media, seems to have accepted the general view that at least most mental illnesses in some undefined way are biological disorders.

PUBLIC POLICY ISSUES

How does this muddied state of affairs affect public policy issues that deal with mental illness? There are several issues on the public agenda for which the perception of whether a mental illness is organic or functional can influence how it might be dealt with, including the following:

1. Should health insurance coverage for mental illness be as extensive as coverage for physical illness?
2. Should mental illness be treated in the same manner as physical illness for purposes of the Social Security Disability program, the Supplemental Security Income (SSI) program, and the Americans with Disabilities Act? (Not well known is the fact that as of 1994, 57 percent of adults receiving SSI disability payments did so based on a diagnosis of a mental disorder and that federal spending on SSI exceeded federal spending on Aid to Families with Dependent Children by some $7 billion [Weaver, 1995].)
3. How should public research funds be allocated between biologically oriented mental illness research and psychosocially oriented research?
4. Is violence among youths a biological or a psychological–social problem?
5. If mental illness is a biological brain disease, should civil commitment standards be relaxed and should forced medications, forced electroconvulsive therapy, and even forced brain surgery become more acceptable? (A perspective to keep in mind relative to this question is that if a mental illness is perceived as being the result of a biologically diseased brain, then should someone with that mental illness be permitted to make treatment choices? For a presentation by two authors who think not, see Isaac & Armat, 1990.)
6. Should the traditional rules of confidentiality and privilege between doctor and patient (therapist and client) apply if the mental illness is biological in nature?

7. If someone is found not guilty of committing a crime by reason of insanity, should some biological proof be required?

Obviously, with DSM-IV listing over 300 different types of mental disorders, dealing with these questions can become remarkably complex. And now the authors of DSM-IV state that it is "incorrect" or at least inappropriate to distinguish among mental illnesses with a known organic etiology, mental illnesses with a hypothesized or theorized organic etiology, and mental illnesses that in the future may or may not be hypothesized or proved to have an organic etiology, so the complexity of dealing with these public issues becomes even more confounding. The one undeniable fact about mental illness, however, remains fixed: Dealing with it is never easy.

REFERENCES

American Psychiatric Association. (1952). *Diagnostic and statistical manual of mental disorders.* Washington, DC: Author.

American Psychiatric Association. (1994). *Diagnostic and statistical manual of mental disorders* (4th ed.). Washington, DC: Author.

Isaac, R., & Armat, V. (1990). *Madness in the streets.* New York: Free Press.

Weaver, C. (1995, January-February). Welfare payments to the disabled. *American Enterprise,* pp. 61–64.

This chapter was originally published in the February 1996 issue of Health & Social Work, *vol. 21, pp. 66–69.*

Primary Health Care and Severe Mental Illness: The Need for National and State Policy

King E. Davis

Widespread insecurity about health care coverage in the U.S. population was the major impetus for recent attempts to craft a national health care system reform policy (Bureau of National Affairs, 1993). The Clinton administration and Congress have conceptualized the U.S. health security problem in two related dimensions: limited coverage and rising costs. Part of the policy solution proposed by Congress and the president is managed health care.

Data that support the need for reform forecast that by 1998, 63 million Americans will be unable to maintain their existing health care coverage (Bureau of National Affairs, 1993). Up to 37 million Americans reportedly lacked insurance coverage in 1993, and nearly 22 million Americans had coverage considered insufficient to meet their needs in an emergency (Bureau of National Affairs, 1993). Almost 15 percent of gross domestic product (GDP) is now being spent on health care. Unless strict policy measures are enacted to contain costs, approximately 22 percent of GDP will be spent on health care by the year 2010 (Bureau of National Affairs, 1993).

In a cash-based economy, health care has become just another commodity, subject to the same market forces as other products and services. Individuals who lack sufficient insurance, income, status, or transfer payments cannot obtain health care services at a level they need to sustain their health or the health of their family members. In this fiscally driven environment, individuals or groups who lack access to quality medical care are more likely to have undiagnosed illnesses, untreated diseases, and higher rates of mortality at younger ages.

In the ongoing debate over the direction of national health care policy and how to pay for it, politicians and policymakers should note that one of the most medically insecure populations is people with severe mental illnesses. This population often lacks basic health insurance coverage. People with severe mental illness have limited employment opportunities and thus lack the insurance protection that insulates them from having to personally bear escalating medical costs.

Although the need for psychiatric care generally has been part of the national debate over health care reform, the extensive health care needs of people with severe mental illness raise a number of very complicated legal, ethical, organization, fiscal, medical, and regulatory issues that have been minimally addressed at the national, state, or local levels. Given the multiple health and mental health problems of this population and the national efforts to reduce health care costs, the future health status of this population seems at great risk.

STUDIES ON MENTAL HEALTH AND PHYSICAL ILLNESS

Since the 1930s there has been an increased interest in understanding the relationship between physical disease and mental illness. This interest has taken two directions: Some research has sought to identify the extent to which a relationship exists between mental illness and excessive mortality rates (Allebeck & Wistedt, 1986; Eastwood, Stiasny, & Meier, 1982; Kendler, 1986; Malzberg, 1934), and other research has taken a similar approach to the presumed relationship between mental illness and excessive rates of disease (Herridge, 1960; Koranyi, 1979; Maguire & Granville-Grossman, 1968; Marshall, 1949).

At least 13 studies completed during the past 60 years have confirmed that individuals with various forms of mental illness have rates of physical illness far in excess of the expected frequency of such illnesses in the general population (for example, Davies, 1965; Koran, 1989; McCarrick & Manderscheid, 1986). In 1936, Comroe conducted one of the earliest studies and noted that in a sample of 100 individuals diagnosed with neurosis, 24 percent developed a significant physical illness over the eight months of the study.

Koranyi's (1979) work was among the first to use large samples of patients. In a study of over 2,000 psychiatric patients, he found that 43 percent had at least one medical illness. Nearly 46 percent of these illnesses had previously gone unrecognized by the physicians who made the referral for psychiatric examination and treatment. Koranyi also noted that in 20 percent of the patients, the physical illness was the only identifiable cause of the psychiatric symptoms that formed the basis of the initial referral. He observed that the failure to recognize illness was highest (84 percent) when the patient was self-referred, second highest (83 percent) when the patient was referred by a social services agency, and third highest (48 percent) when the patient was referred by a psychiatrist. The lowest rate (32 percent) of failure to recognize existing illness was by primary care physicians and medical-surgical clinics. Koranyi concluded that in 69 percent of the patients seen, the medical condition contributed significantly to the psychiatric illness. He also concluded that overall rates of physical disease in psychiatric patients far exceeded the rates found in the general population.

When rates of physical illness were examined in low-income individuals with severe mental illness, 80 percent had serious untreated medical problems (Hall, 1978). In addition, Hall proposed that nearly 46 percent of the psychiatric symptoms appeared to have been caused by unrecognized and untreated physical illness. Hoffman and Koran (1984) reviewed several studies that showed that the rate of unrecognized physical illness was higher in patients who were hospitalized than in patients in community outpatient programs. Almost 50 percent of medical problems in psychiatric inpatients had not been identified previously. These researchers noted that the illnesses ranged from endocrine disorders to adverse drug reactions.

In a more recent study, Farmer (1987) focused on "chronic" patients in a community support program and found that 53 percent had undiagnosed medical problems. Of note in this study, 88 percent of the patients with severe mental illness did not have a physician in the community with whom they maintained an ongoing relationship. Over 60 percent of these consumers also reported that their only primary medical examinations occurred when they received psychiatric hospitalization. Because inpatient psychiatric hospitals apparently identify physical illnesses correctly in half or fewer of the cases where they exist, a sizable number of individuals who rely on psychiatric hospitalization for medical care are likely to have untreated illness before, during, and after such hospitalization.

The studies cited, and others conducted over a 60-year span, support the conclusions that individuals with severe mental illness have a higher than expected frequency of coexisting physical illness and that the rates of physical disease increase with severity of the psychiatric illness and lower socioeconomic status. Of import, too, is the finding that the chances that physical illness, when it co-occurs with mental illness, will go unrecognized ranged from 30 percent to 87 percent (Comroe, 1936; Eastwood et al., 1982; Knutsen & DuRand, 1991; Koran, 1989; Maguire & Granville-Grossman, 1968). Also, when individuals with severe mental illness are in community living situations, they are infrequently connected with a primary health care provider or system that would offer routine or preventive health care. These findings may help explain what Kendler (1986) termed excessive mortality rates of psychiatric patients and may provide support for social policy to ensure access to primary health care for this population.

EXPLORING HYPOTHESES

Several hypotheses have been proposed to explain the disproportionate rate of undiagnosed and untreated physical illness in psychiatric patients with severe mental illness (Farmer, 1987; Knutsen & DuRand, 1991; Koranyi, 1979; Lamb, 1989). These hypotheses include factors such as the training emphasis in medicine, physicians' time constraints, service fragmentation, limited resources at the state level, the difficulty patients have in accurately describing their symptoms, society's willingness to fund services, physician skills and attentiveness, poverty, and the extent to which physical symptoms in psychiatric patients are considered part of the psychiatric sequelae (Farmer, 1987; Knutsen & DuRand, 1991; Koranyi, 1979; Lamb, 1989).

In addition to the etiological factors, the ability of mental health and health care systems to resolve the problem of health care for people with severe mental illness also seems dependent on two additional factors: the level of human resources and state responsibility for primary health care.

Human Resources Management

Quality of health care for people with severe mental illness seems related to the number and distribution of primary care physicians and related medical personnel and their ratio to the number of psychiatric facilities, psychiatric episodes, and patients. It can be assumed generally that one of the most significant factors in determining the general health status of patients in public psychiatric hospitals is the number of appropriate medical personnel available and their deployment. The fewer primary health care staff available and the more inappropriately deployed, the greater the chances that people with severe mental illnesses will not receive adequate primary care while hospitalized. Because of inadequate and declining health care budgets, the ratio of patients to health care personnel in state psychiatric hospitals historically has been extremely high (Manderscheid & Sonnenschein, 1992).

Changes in the number of psychiatric facilities, the locus of episodes, and the overall census of patients become meaningful when they are compared with the human resources available during the same period. Between 1969 and 1990, overall staff in all mental health facilities increased by 155,000, or 41 percent, and the number of facilities increased from 3,000 to 5,000 (Manderscheid & Sonnenschein, 1992). However, not all of this growth occurred in professional staffs or in primary health care services. For example, all mental health facilities reported a total of 3,991 primary care physicians in 1969. By 1978, when the number of psychiatric facilities, episodes, and patients had increased markedly, the number of primary care physicians had declined by 23 percent, or 957 physicians, and by 1988 was still lower than in 1969.

When the number of physicians in psychiatric settings is looked at as a proportion of full-time equivalent staff, the picture worsens. In 1969 only 1 percent of all full-time equivalent staff in psychiatric facilities were primary care physicians. By 1990 only 0.8 percent of the total full-time equivalent staff in these facilities were primary care physicians. Of additional importance, psychiatrists as a proportion of total full-time equivalent staff remained at 3.4 percent between 1969 and 1990, while patient numbers grew 155 percent in psychiatric hospitals and 100 percent in general hospitals with psychiatric units (Manderscheid & Sonnenschein, 1992).

States and People with Severe Mental Illness

Because of their disabilities, people with severe and chronic mental illness historically have come under the protection of state governments for both mental health and health coverage. As state governments shift more of their psychiatric care to Medicaid managed care and as the Republican Congress pushes to shift control of Medicaid to the states, the effects on people with severe mental illness and high levels of health care needs are as yet unknown.

During the four years I served as commissioner of mental health in the Commonwealth of Virginia, the medical problems of psychiatric patients in public hospitals became increasingly clear. Far too many patients were admitted to state hospitals with untreated medical illnesses and diseases. My department estimated that nearly one-third of patients admitted to state hospitals had ailments that exceeded the capacity of the facilities to manage, putting the consumer and the facility at risk (Forbes, 1992). Under commitment laws, however, state hospitals were required to admit such patients with minimal regard to the level and quality of medical care available.

The courts are not required to take a patient's general medical condition into consideration in determining commitment. I would not be surprised to find that judges believe that state psychiatric hospitals are as able to provide primary care as general medical hospitals. However, consumers and family members often charge that the level of primary medical care available in state psychiatric facilities and in community outpatient programs is so inadequate that patients' health and lives are in jeopardy. In many instances, federal investigators have identified and documented the inadequate levels of health care that are present in psychiatric settings in many states (S. Rep. No. 416, 1979).

CALL TO ACTION

The U.S. health care system has failed to find ways to provide adequate primary care to people with severe mental illness and other vulnerable populations who lack financial resources and political power. Not only is the absence of national health policy inhumane, it is also costly. The absence of routine medical care for people with severe mental illness can lead to unnecessary and inappropriate hospitalization and use of emergency services (Koranyi, 1979; McCarrick & Manderscheid, 1986) The failure to provide routine medical care on an outpatient basis leads to unnecessary hospitalizations that may account for over 50 percent of hospital bed use nationwide. The failure to recognize and treat diseases at their earliest stages contributes to the need for more expensive medical care. The failure to accurately diagnose illness can lead to the exacerbation of poor health and the need for longer-term medical services.

This historical problem requires that social workers help gather data and translate this information into national and state health care policies containing guidelines and standards for the delivery of medical care to people with severe mental illness. Social workers must help ensure that these new policies apply in all psychiatric care settings—public, private, inpatient, outpatient, and partial.

Social work professionals must remain involved in the political debate over health care to help ensure that access to medical care for people with severe mental illness is seen clearly as the pronounced need it is. State governments must be urged to recognize that their mental health care consumers are in as much need of primary health care as of psychiatric care, if not more. In this regard, social policy advocates must insist that state governments carry out their statutory responsibilities by improving the overall quality and quantity of medical care resources in their facilities. State governments also have the option of contracting with primary care providers for this care or being held legally accountable for the violation of the constitutional rights of people with mental disabilities in their care (Patrick, 1994).

Community mental health programs must also form or join vertical health care networks to ensure primary care for the population with severe mental illness in their communities. However, the most far-reaching solution must be found in a comprehensive national health care policy. The health plight of people with severe mental illness should not be left to loose networks of managed care in which they are seen as just more covered lives. The interrelated health and mental health problems of this population require that society conceptualize integration of health care systems in different ways. Public health advocacy and policies must be based on the explicit needs, help-seeking patterns, and risks of this special population, already thoroughly identified and discussed in over 60 years of research.

REFERENCES

Allebeck, P., & Wistedt, B. (1986). Mortality in schizophrenia: A ten-year follow-up based on the Stockholm County Inpatient Register. *Archives of General Psychiatry, 43,* 650–653.

Bureau of National Affairs. (1993). *Description of the president's health care reform plan.* Washington, DC: Author.

Comroe, B. (1936). Follow-up study of 100 patients diagnosed with neurosis. *Journal of Nervous and Mental Disease, 83,* 679–684.

Davies, D. W. (1965). Physical illness in psychiatric outpatients. *British Journal of Psychiatry, 3,* 27–33.

Eastwood, M. R., Stiasny, S., & Meier, H. (1982). Mental illness and mortality. *Comprehensive Psychiatry, 23,* 377–385.

Farmer, S. (1987). Medical problems of chronic patients in a community support program. *Hospital and Community Psychiatry, 38,* 745–749.

Forbes, R. (1992). *Deaths in Virginia's state mental hospitals: A report to the commissioner and state board.* Richmond, VA: Department of Mental Health.

Hall, R.C.W. (1978). Physical illness presenting as psychiatric disease. *Archives of General Psychiatry, 35,* 1315–1320.

Herridge, C. F. (1960). Physical disorders in psychiatric illness. *Lancet, 2,* 949–951.

Hoffman, R. S., & Koran, L. M. (1984). Detecting physical illness in patients with mental disorders. *Psychosomatics, 25,* 654–660.

Kendler, K. S. (1986). A twin study of mortality in schizophrenia and neurosis. *Archives of General Psychiatry, 43,* 643–649.

Knutsen, E., & DuRand, C. (1991). Previously unrecognized physical illnesses in psychiatric patients. *Hospital and Community Psychiatry, 42,* 182–186.

Koran, L. M. (1989). Medical evaluation of psychiatric patients. *Archives of General Psychiatry, 46,* 733–740.

Koranyi, E. K. (1979). Morbidity and rate of undiagnosed physical illnesses in a psychiatric clinic population. *Archives of General Psychiatry, 36,* 414–419.

Lamb, H. R. (1989). Improving our public health systems. *Archives of General Psychiatry, 46,* 743–744.

Maguire, G. P., & Granville-Grossman, K. L. (1968). Physical illness in psychiatric patients. *British Medical Journal, 115,* 1365–1369.

Malzberg, B. (1934). *Mortality among patients with mental disease.* Utica: New York State Hospital Press.

Manderscheid, R. W., & Sonnenschein, M. A. (1992). *Mental health, United States, 1992* (SMA Publication No. 92-1942). Washington, DC: U.S. Government Printing Office.

Marshall, H.E.S. (1949). Incidence of physical disorders among psychiatric inpatients. *British Medical Journal, 97,* 468–469.

McCarrick, A. K., & Manderscheid, R. W. (1986). Chronic medical problems in the chronically mentally ill. *Hospital and Community Psychiatry, 37,* 289–291.

Patrick, D. (1994). The Civil Rights of Institutionalized Persons Act. *Newsletter of the Association for Persons with Severe Handicaps, 20,* 13–15.

S. Rep. No. 416, 96th Cong., 1st Sess. (1979).

This chapter was originally published in the May 1996 issue of Health & Social Work, *vol. 21, pp. 83–87.*

Managed Care and People with Severe Mental Illness: Challenges and Opportunities for Social Work

Wes Shera

I n many ways the proposed Health Care Security Act of 1993 (White House Domestic Policy Council, 1993) was a final opportunity to develop a publicly controlled health care system that would provide a reasonable level of care for most Americans, particularly vulnerable citizens such as low-income working people and those with severe mental illness. Major factors contributing to rejection of the president's proposal were its complexity, the perception that consumers would give up choice in health care providers, and sophisticated and expensive lobbying by groups that wished to maintain the status quo. Since the demise of the act, there has been a rapid increase in the creation of for-profit health and mental health care organizations in the United States (Arnould, Rich, White, & Copeland, 1993; Cornelius, 1994). This article discusses the managed care initiatives sweeping the nation and their profound effects on the way social workers deliver services to people with severe mental illness.

EVOLUTION OF MANAGED CARE

Gorski (1995) described the evolution of managed care as comprising five distinct phases: (1) carrying out utilization reviews and restricting access, (2) managing benefit use, (3) managing care with a primary emphasis on cost control, (4) managing outcomes, and (5) integrating managed care systems horizontally and vertically. For social workers the language associated with this paradigm shift has been new and somewhat foreign. "Medical necessity," "differential benefit packages," "penetration rates," "capitation contracts," "cost offsets," "carve outs," "cost bands," and "report cards" are but a few of the terms in the new lexicon.

Although managed care is the current buzzword in the human services, numerous health care organizations, supported by provisions of the Health Maintenance Organization Act of 1973 (P.L. 93-222), have been experimenting with this approach for many years. Managed mental health care is a relatively more recent phenomenon and has unfolded in a variety of forms since the early 1980s (MacLeod, 1993).

States and Managed Care

Many states have not waited for federal reform because cost containment is a pressing necessity for them (Patterson & Sharfstein, 1992). Medicaid now constitutes 20 percent of most states' budgets, a larger proportion than higher education; therefore, states are turning to managed care to control this growing budget component (McGuirk, Keller, & Croze, 1995). At least 35 states already have some form of capitated payment system for Medicaid clients with severe mental illness (McFarland, 1994). The U.S. Health Care Financing Administration has awarded more than 17 Medicaid waivers for states providing mental health and substance abuse services (Manderscheid & Henderson, 1995). These waivers allow states to change the type of services provided, the method of delivery, and the population to be served.

Massachusetts, Washington, Utah, Tennessee, and Oregon have been the major pioneers in managed mental health care in the United States. The Mental Health Program of the Western Interstate Commission for Higher Education (WICHE) has attempted to capture their experiences by developing a set of "blueprints for managed care" (McGuirk et al., 1995). The managed care models used in each of these states were compared by mapping their overall system of care and reviewing each of the following core components: beneficiaries and enrollment process, benefits package, benefits management model, managed care technologies, provider participation, financing plan, contracting arrangements, and accountability requirements.

The pictorial blueprints derived from this exercise are intended to provide guidance in describing and clarifying mental health system status; modeling state or local managed mental health care plans; designing regional, county, or community systems of care; explicating the role of state hospitals; designing information systems; conducting staffing analysis; and developing interactive blueprints (McGuirk et al., 1995). Although these blueprints, as a tool for designing coherent mental health systems, appear to be a step in the right direction, some observers of managed care have suggested that a more chaotic, out-of-control nonsystem of care has emerged (Shera, 1996).

Numerous criticisms against managed mental health care have been voiced. Problems identified include unrealistic limits on the number of units of service, a reversion to a more medically driven model of care, lack of emphasis on community-based outreach and psychosocial rehabilitation, little reference to the efficacy of psychosocial interventions, inadequate evidence of cost-effectiveness, and the danger of lowest-bid providers (Bernstein, 1994; Bickman et al., 1995; Corcoran & Vandiver, 1996; NASW, New York City Chapter, 1994; Stern, 1993; Woolsey, 1993).

Market Forces

Some authors suggest that market mechanisms in health and social care do not function like markets in the business sector (Flynn & Hurley, 1994). Le Grand and Bartlett (1993) described them as "quasi-markets" because they differ significantly from traditional markets in both demand and supply characteristics. Social care has many characteristics that make it incompatible with an unfettered, unregulated market. People with mental illness often experience unpredicted service needs that will not wait for the negotiation or renewal of contracts. Contracts covering groups of individuals often homogenize rather than individualize service users. On the other hand, individualized contracts do not give providers the funding base they need to survive. In rural areas of the country, a person is often fortunate to find one agency willing to provide a needed service.

Although a private sector managed care carve out may be the temporary mechanism of choice in some states, optimum use of available resources for people with severe mental illness can often be best achieved through a public sector managed care approach (Hoge, Davidson, Griffith, Sledge, & Howenstine, 1994; Paulson, 1996). (Carve outs are special financial arrangements whereby specific health care services are provided to a target population separate from general health services.) Undoubtedly, a new generation of studies is needed to inform the profession about the most cost-effective ways of organizing managed care services for the population with severe mental illness.

ROLE OF SOCIAL WORK

Wintersteen (1986) argued that the profession of social work, with its unique history and conceptual framework, is in the most advantageous position to provide leadership in the organization of networks of support and services to facilitate the rehabilitation of people with severe mental illness. He said,

> It is not contended that social work is the only, or most important, profession that deals with the long-term mentally ill: It is only argued that the conceptual framework and nearly a century of experience in helping clients with the complexities of social interaction give social work a track record that places it in an optimal position to provide leadership in this developing field, should its members wish to rise to the challenge. (p. 332)

Gerhart (1985), however, claimed that social work had not fully accepted people with severe mental illness as an area of responsibility. Social workers have expressed little interest in working with this group (Atwood, 1982; Johnson & Rubin, 1983; Werrbach & DePoy, 1993) and prefer to work with more intellectually and emotionally rewarding clients.

In spite of these and other difficulties, many social workers are providing a wide array of services to clients with severe mental illness. These workers too have found themselves swept along by managed care mania and have often been passive rather than active participants in the massive changes taking place. Carve outs in some jurisdictions have resulted in the closing of community mental health centers. And in many cases, private sector managed care companies are hiring the best personnel from these facilities. These private sector companies run the gamut from those that do not meet contract obligations so as to maximize profits ("Massachusetts Accuses," 1995) to those who take a longer-term, more holistic view and invest resources in service system development to generate cost savings over the long haul (Stauffer, 1996). The former use the least expensive workers available, such as bachelor's degree–level workers or licensed practical nurses. The latter typically employ more professional staff, and social workers frequently find themselves doing assessment, service planning, and service development.

More and more social workers find themselves working with a group of providers who contract with managed care companies. In this context, social workers can provide therapy, family intervention, group work, and a variety of other services (NASW, New York State Chapter, 1993).

In public sector managed care organizations, the shift has been to increased emphasis on using resources efficiently, monitoring for quality, and focusing on outcomes (Freeman & Trabin, 1994). In addition, there has been increased competition from other disciplines. Both psychiatry and nursing have embraced the biopsychosocial model, and current training materials emphasize the importance of working with families and communities (Group for the Advancement of Psychiatry, 1993; Silberman, Comer, & Butler, 1995).

MEETING THE CHALLENGE OF MANAGED CARE

If social work is to thrive in an environment of managed mental health care, the profession must act on a number of fronts. Three major areas of action for enhancing social work's role in managed care include (1) understanding current knowledge and practice in managed care, (2) using efficacy information to design systems of care, and (3) supporting consumer involvement in the design and monitoring of managed mental health care.

Understanding Managed Care

It is critical for social workers to stay abreast of developments in the managed mental health care field. Groups such as WICHE and the Center for Mental Health Services and journals such as *Behavioral Health Care Tomorrow* and *Psychiatric Services* provide information on state-of-the-art developments. The Managed-Behavioral-Healthcare Listserv on the Internet is another excellent resource.

Schools of social work must update their curricula and continuing education courses to reflect the realities of the managed care revolution (Mizrahi, 1993; Strom & Gingerich, 1993). Managed care systems require practitioners to conceptualize their practice differently and significantly modify clinical assessments, therapeutic interventions, and practice protocols (Corcoran & Vandiver, 1996; Paulson, 1996). Enhanced knowledge and awareness should also be used to identify and act on policy initiatives and to take legal action essential to furthering the greatest good for clients in these systems (NASW, New York City Chapter, 1994). Areas for advocacy by social workers include insurance reforms, reform of Medicaid and Medicare, essential community providers legislation, and establishment of accreditation procedures for utilization review firms (Manderscheid & Henderson, 1995). Numerous changes and improvements in these and other areas of managed care have already resulted from legal action brought forward by a variety of stakeholders, including social workers (Corcoran & Vandiver, 1996; Durham, 1994).

Using Efficacy Information

In addition to this policy practice role, social workers have an enormous role to play in identifying and implementing interventions that have demonstrated efficacy for people with severe mental illness. Bachrach (1993) identified nine essentials for successful rehabilitation of people with severe mental illness: (1) individualized treatments, (2) environmental adaptation, (3) a focus on client strengths, (4) an emphasis on restoring hope, (5) optimism about the individual's vocational potential, (6) a range of comprehensive services, (7) client–consumer involvement in the treatment process, (8) continuity of care, and (9) a therapeutic relationship between the client–consumer and caregiver. With these nine concepts as a contextualizing set of principles, social workers need to carry out holistic assessments of individuals and target populations and identify the interventions and systems of care that have the best probability of achieving positive outcomes for consumers in a cost-effective manner (Jerrell, Hu, & Ridgely, 1994). Recent studies have suggested that the long-term outcomes for people with severe mental illness are better than previously assumed (Harding & Zahniser, 1994; Harding, Zubin, & Strauss, 1992) and that helpers' positive attitudes toward these clients are critical to developing working relationships in which helpers connect with the person behind the disorder (Shera & Delva-Tauili'ili, 1996; Strauss, 1992).

Social workers can also use the opportunity that managed care provides to design new systems of services for people with severe mental illness (NASW, New York City Chapter, 1994; Simmons, 1994; Vaccaro, Young, & Glynn, 1993). Differential treatment packages should be specifically designed for subgroups of this population. In developing these protocols, social workers must draw on the latest efficacy information on the disorders involved and on appropriate interventions (Jerrell et al., 1994; Vaccaro et al., 1993)—for example, individual and family psychoeducation (Lefley & Wasow, 1994), supportive psychotherapy (Novalis, Rojcewicz, & Peele, 1993), assertive community treatment (Santos, 1996), multiple family support groups (McFarlane, 1994), psychosocial rehabilitation (Bedall, 1994), social network intervention (Biegel, Tracy, & Corvo, 1994), and self-help groups (Segel, Silverman, & Temkin, 1993).

Social workers working with clients with severe mental illness must have the commitment to practice in multidisciplinary settings and the ability to negotiate across systems of care. Social workers can be cost-effective coordinators of care, balancing consumer and organizational needs (NASW, New York City Chapter, 1994).

Supporting Consumers' Involvement

Social work, more than any profession in the field of mental health, can and must support the involvement of consumers in the development, implementation, and monitoring of managed care (Cornelius, 1994). In the transition to managed care in the United States, consumers have generally had little say; whenever consumer involvement has happened, it has been in locations where an infrastructure of consumer involvement already existed. Health care consumers must be included in planning councils (as specified in the Health Maintenance Organization Amendments of 1986, P.L. 99-660), protection and advocacy offices, state and national self-help groups, and a variety of agency-based mechanisms for consumer input. National organizations such as the National Alliance for the Mentally Ill (NAMI) provide a forum for consumers to advocate on their own behalf. There are also consumer-run services such as Mind Empowered in Portland, Oregon (Nikkel, Smith, & Edwards, 1992), and Mindstar in San Diego.

Maximizing consumer involvement in managed mental health care reforms requires action on a number of issues: individualized capitation, flexible funding, consumer-run services, accreditation standards for consumer involvement in managed care, and innovative approaches for services in rural areas. An example of a consumer-driven capitated approach to managed health care is the Village in Long Beach, California (Goodrick, 1995). This innovative program merges capitation financing with state-of-the-art community support system policies and practice. Building on lessons from the Program for Assertive Community Treatment in Madison, Wisconsin, and Rapp's strengths model of case management (Kisthardt, 1992), the Village provides a positive model of a consumer-guided outcome-focused managed care system (Goodrick, 1995). Strategies used in this system of care include assisting members in their homes, neighborhoods, and work settings; placing high priority on prevention of relapse; teaching consumers to advocate for themselves; focusing on work as a normalizing activity; and emphasizing quality in the delivery of services (Goodrick, 1995).

NAMI recently published a managed care primer for families and consumers (Malloy, 1995) that covers basic concepts, alternative models, state experiences, and a checklist of ideal attributes of a system of managed care. Consumers have also organized the Consumer Managed Care Network (CMCN) as a vehicle for information and knowledge exchange on mental health managed care. At present, the National Association of State Mental Health Program Directors hosts the CMCN, which already has memberships in 35 states. Social workers must work in partnership with consumer groups to ensure that consumers' voices are heard and that systems of managed mental health care are as empowering as possible (Fisher, 1994).

CONCLUSION

Managed care is here to stay, and social workers must rise to the challenge or let others take the lead. Managed care has forced the profession to think more critically about how its members provide care and how they can provide the best quality of services to the most people under increasing resource constraints. The practice wisdom gained through years of providing case management services to people with severe mental illness and state-of-the-art efficacy information are critical to the development of responsive, individualized, and cost-effective mental health services. The involvement of consumers as partners in the development of managed mental health care is also critical to its success. Social workers have a unique role and responsibility in ensuring that this vision of consumer involvement is realized.

REFERENCES

Arnould, R. J., Rich, R. F., White, W. D., & Copeland, C. (1993). The role of managed care in competitive policy reforms. In R. J. Arnould, R. F. Rich, W. D. White, & C. Copeland (Eds.), *Competitive approaches to health care reform* (pp. 83–104). Washington, DC: Urban Institute Press.

Atwood, N. (1982). Professional prejudice and the psychotic client. *Social Work, 27*, 172–177.

Bachrach, L. (1993). Continuity of care and approaches to case management for long-term mentally ill patients. *Hospital & Community Psychiatry, 44*, 465–468.

Bedall, J. R. (1994). Social skills training. In J. R. Bedall (Ed.), *Psychological assessment and treatment of persons with severe mental disorders* (pp. 95–119). Washington, DC: Taylor & Francis.

Bernstein, C. (1994). Is managed care good for mental health clients? No. In S. Kirk & S. Einbinder (Eds.), *Controversial issues in mental health* (pp. 247–250). Boston: Allyn & Bacon.

Bickman, L., Guthie, P. R., Foster, E. M., Lambert, E. W., Summerfelt, W. T., Breda, C. S., & Hefinger, C. A. (1995). *Evaluating managed mental health services: The Fort Bragg experiment.* New York: Plenum Press.

Biegel, D., Tracy, E., & Corvo, K. (1994). Strengthening social networks: Intervention strategies for mental health case managers. *Health & Social Work, 19*, 206–216.

Corcoran, K., & Vandiver, V. (1996). *Maneuvering the maze of managed care: Skills for mental health practitioners.* New York: Free Press.

Cornelius, D. S. (1994). Managed care and social work: Constructing a context and a response. *Social Work in Health Care, 20*, 47–63.

Durham, M. L. (1994). Health care's greatest challenge: Providing services for people with severe mental illness in managed care. *Behavioral Sciences and the Law, 12*, 331–349.

Fisher, D. B. (1994). Health care reform based on an empowerment model of recovery by people with psychiatric disabilities. *Hospital and Community Psychiatry, 45*, 913–915.

Flynn, N., & Hurley, D. (1994). *The market for care.* London: London School of Economics and Political Science, Public Sector Management.

Freeman, M. A., & Trabin, T. (1994). *Managed behavioral healthcare: History, models, key issues, and future course* (Report prepared for the Center for Mental Health Services). Washington, DC: U.S. Department of Health and Human Services.

Gerhart, U. C. (1985). Teaching social workers to work with the mentally ill. In J. P. Bowker (Ed.), *Education for practice with the chronically mentally ill: What works?* (pp. 50–67). Washington, DC: Council on Social Work Education.

Goodrick, D. (1995). Integrating values, resources, and strategies to achieve outcomes. *California Alliance for the Mentally Ill, 4*(2), 61–65.

Gorski, T. (1995, Spring). The evolution of managed care practices. *Treatment Today*, pp. 10–12.

Group for the Advancement of Psychiatry. (1993). *Residents' guide to treatment of people with chronic mental illness.* Washington, DC: American Psychiatric Press.

Harding, C. M., & Zahniser, J. H. (1994). Empirical correction of seven myths about schizophrenia with implications for treatment. *Acta Psychiatrica Scandinavica, 90*(Suppl. 384), 140–146.

Harding, C., Zubin, J., & Strauss, J. (1992). Chronicity in schizophrenia: Revisited. *British Journal of Psychiatry, 161*(Suppl. 18), 27–37.

Health Maintenance Organization Act of 1973, P.L. 93-222, 87 Stat. 914.

Health Maintenance Organization Amendments of 1986, P.L. 99-660, 100 Stat. 3799.

Hoge, M. A., Davidson, L., Griffith, E., Sledge, W. H., & Howenstine, R. A. (1994). Defining managed care in public sector psychiatry. *Hospital and Community Psychiatry, 45*, 1085–1089.

Jerrell, J., Hu, T., & Ridgely, M. S. (1994). Cost-effectiveness of substance disorder interventions for people with severe mental illness. *Journal of Mental Health Administration, 21*, 283–297.

Johnson, P. J., & Rubin, A. (1983). Case management in mental health: A social work domain? *Social Work, 28*, 49–55.

Kisthardt, W. (1992). A strengths model of case management: The principles and functions of a helping partnership with persons with persistent mental illness. In D. Saleebey (Ed.), *The strengths perspective in social work practice* (pp. 59–83). New York: Longman.

Lefley, H., & Wasow, M. (1994). *Helping families cope with mental illness.* Langhorne, PA: Harwood Academic Publishers.

Le Grand, J., & Bartlett, W. (1993). *Quasi-markets and social policy.* London: Macmillan.

MacLeod, G. K. (1993). An overview of managed health care. In R. R. Pongstredt (Ed.), *The managed care handbook* (pp. 3–11). Gaithersburg, MD: Aspen.

Malloy, M. (1995). *Mental illness and managed care: A primer for families and consumers*. Arlington, VA: National Alliance for the Mentally Ill. (Available from NAMI, 200 North Glebe Road, Suite 1015, Arlington, VA 22203-3754)

Manderscheid, R. W., & Henderson, M. J. (1995). *Federal and state legislative and program directions for managed care: Implications for case management*. Washington, DC: U.S. Department of Health and Human Services, Center for Mental Health Services.

Massachusetts accuses 12 HMOs of plundering mental health funds. (1995, April 27). *Boston Globe* [Metro edition], p. 1.

McFarland, B. H. (1994). Health maintenance organizations and persons with severe mental illness. *Community Mental Health Journal, 30*, 221–242.

McFarlane, W. R. (1994). Families, patients and clinicians as partners: Clinical strategies and research outcomes in single and multiple-family psychoeducation. In H. Lefley & M. Wasow (Eds.), *Helping families cope with mental illness* (pp. 195–222). Langhorne, PA: Harwood Academic Publishers.

McGuirk, F. D., Keller, A. S., & Croze, C. (1995). *Blueprints for managed care: Mental healthcare concepts and structure*. Boulder, CO: Mental Health Program of the Western Interstate Commission for Higher Education. (Available from WICHE, P.O. Drawer P, Boulder, CO 80301)

Mizrahi, T. (1993). Managed care and managed competition: A primer for social work. *Health & Social Work, 18*, 86–91.

National Association of Social Workers, New York City Chapter. (1994). *An evaluation of Medicaid managed care: Social work issues and recommendations and social work role in managed care*. New York: Author.

National Association of Social Workers, New York State Chapter. (1993). *Managed care in New York State: Implications for social workers and health care consumers*. New York: Author.

Nikkel, R., Smith, G., & Edwards, D. (1992). A consumer-operated case management project. *Hospital and Community Psychiatry, 43*, 577–579.

Novalis, P., Rojcewicz, S., & Peele, R. (1993). *Clinical manual of supportive psychotherapy*. Washington, DC: American Psychiatric Press.

Patterson, D., & Sharfstein, S. (1992). The future of mental health care. In J. L. Feldman & R. J. Fitzpatrick (Eds.), *Managed mental health care: Administration and clinical issues* (pp. 335–343). Washington, DC: American Psychiatric Press.

Paulson, R. (1996). Swimming with the sharks or walking in the Garden of Eden: Two versions of managed care and mental health practice. In P. Raffoul & C. McNeece (Eds.), *Future issues for social work practice* (pp. 85–96). Boston: Allyn & Bacon.

Santos, A. (1996). Assertive community treatment. In S. Soreff (Ed.), *The seriously and persistently mentally ill: The state-of-the-art treatment handbook* (pp. 411–431). Seattle: Hogrefe & Huber.

Segal, S. P., Silverman, C., & Temkin, T. (1993). Empowerment and self-help agency practice for people with mental disabilities. *Social Work, 38*, 707–712.

Shera, W. (1996). Market mechanisms and consumer involvement in the delivery of mental health services: A UK-US comparison. *Journal of Sociology & Social Welfare, 23*(1), 13–22.

Shera, W., & Delva-Tauili'ili, J. (1996). Changing MSW students' attitudes towards the severely mentally ill. *Community Mental Health Journal, 32*, 159–169.

Silberman, D., Comer, R., & Butler, B. (1995). Introducing community-based care of the chronically ill. *Academic Psychiatry, 19*, 132–141.

Simmons, J. (1994). Community based care: The new health social work paradigm. *Social Work in Health Care, 20*, 35–46.

Stauffer, M. (1996). Public-private partnerships: What's in the public interest? *Behavioral Healthcare Tomorrow, 5*(2), 19–20.

Stern, S. (1993). Managed care, brief treatment, and treatment integrity. *Psychotherapy, 30*, 162–175.

Strauss, J. (1992). The person—Key to understanding mental illness: Towards a new dynamic psychiatry. *British Journal of Psychiatry, 161*(Suppl. 18), 19–26.

Strom, K. , & Gingerich, W. J. (1993). Educating students for the new market realities. *Journal of Social Work Education, 29*, 78–87.

Vaccaro, J., Young, A., & Glynn, S. (1993). Community-based care of individuals with schizo-phrenia. *Psychiatric Clinics of North America, 16*, 387–399.

Werrbach, G. B., & DePoy, E. (1993). Social work students' interest in working with persons with serious mental illness. *Journal of Social Work Education, 29*, 200–211.

White House Domestic Policy Council. (1993). *The President's health security plan.* New York: Time Books.

Wintersteen, R. (1986). Rehabilitating the chronically mentally ill: Social work's claim to leadership. *Social Work, 31*, 332–337.

Woolsey, S. L. (1993). Managed care and mental health: The silencing of a profession. *International Journal of Eating Disorders, 14*, 387–401.

This chapter was originally published in the August 1996 issue of Health & Social Work, *vol. 21, pp. 196–201.*

Part VI

EDUCATION AND SCHOOLS

43

President Clinton and the 104th Congress: The Nightmare on Capitol Hill

Edith M. Freeman

The budget standoff between President Clinton and Congress is like a frightening nightmare from which one is afraid to awaken. There is a gnawing fear that as scary as the nightmare may be, the reality, on awakening, could be worse. Speaker of the House Newt Gingrich has predicted a reality that undoubtedly would be worse than the present nightmare: that the standoff could last until the November elections. He says the Republican leadership wants to prove to the American people how strongly it is committed to producing a balanced budget by achieving certain deficit-reduction targets within the next seven years. Media coverage of the standoff has effectively obscured the real issue for families and children in this country: that life is likely to be much harder for them in the future, no matter which side wins.

OPPOSING SIDES

Gingrich and other conservatives are trying to balance the budget by dismantling much-needed medical and social programs that affect poor families, children, and elderly people, including the Aid to Families with Dependent Children program, Medicare, Medicaid, and the Earned Income Tax Credit (NASW, 1996). These budget proposals would also lead to reductions in or elimination of the Emergency Food Assistance Program for soup kitchens and food banks, the Low Income Heating and Energy Assistance Program, the School Breakfast program, and the Community Services and Maternal and Child Health Block Grant Programs (Keigher, 1994, 1995).

The Republican leadership has implied, and in some instances stated directly, that the blame for continuing poverty and escalating national debt in the United States rests with poor people and social programs. Therefore, the strategy has been to cut out or drastically reduce those programs by tying approval of their budget reconciliation bill to appropriations for fiscal year 1996. This strategy has led to a massive disruption in federal services and programs. Proposing these budget cuts on the backs of poor people without changing some of the structural causes of poverty (Freeman, 1996), including the availability of jobs and job training, is indefensible (Poole, 1995). Predictably, the Republicans did not recommend reductions in funding for larger priorities in the national budget, such as defense spending.

Clinton wants to maintain or increase funding for many social programs including the Special Supplemental Food Program for Women, Infants, and

Children (WIC), Head Start, the Child Care Block Grant for low-income families, and family preservation programs, as well as services for childhood immunizations and for homeless people (Keigher, 1994). He has recommended cuts in other programs that he believes have not been effective or have been mismanaged, although his cuts are not as drastic as the Republicans' for entitlement programs such as welfare, Medicaid, and Medicare.

Like Gingrich and company, Clinton acknowledges that alternative approaches are needed to address some of this country's complex social problems; the two sides disagree on the causes of the problems, however, and thus on the means for resolving them. Meanwhile, two supplemental appropriation bills have been passed to maintain some of the government's "essential services" (NASW, 1996). But the standoff and the budget crisis continue. And President Clinton and the 104th Congress continue to disagree on how close they are to reaching a consensus about how to achieve a balanced budget. Clinton says they are only $100 billion apart on cuts in key areas, while the Republicans disagree.

Balancing the budget is extremely important, but some of the recommended cuts from both sides are in effective programs that are essential for the survival of families and children in particular (for example, WIC, school lunches, and immunization programs). This process of deficit reduction requires thoughtful attention, research, and analysis rather than the public posturing that has been featured so prominently in the media. What purpose did the standoff serve except to heighten partisan politics and delay the work of Congress and the executive branch of government? Perhaps the greatest damage that occurred in the process was the emphasis on conflicts and de-emphasis on the areas of agreement between the two sides.

COMMON GOAL

If the purpose of the confrontation was to press for a balanced budget, and both sides agree that this is the priority, then there should be a willingness to negotiate and compromise to reach the common goal. This goal and budget reduction bills of the late 1980s have already begun to pay off. The country is close to having "the smallest deficit as a percentage of gross domestic product since 1979" (Keigher, 1994, p. 143). But to actually reach the ultimate goal, both sides must give up the political agenda of crisis.

Ginsberg (1988) indicated that politicians can "become accustomed to and perhaps habituated to crises" like addicted gamblers for whom "the next best thing to gambling and winning is gambling and losing" (pp. 246–247). If we follow Ginsberg's metaphor, the gamble, or standoff, can be maintained only if key people enable or allow it to continue. The common goal could be lost in a self-destructive gamble that both sides are committed to winning at any cost. Examining the costs and consequences of the standoff clearly indicates the risks this country is taking by failing to stop it soon.

COSTS AND CONSEQUENCES

Federal employees and residents of the Washington, DC, area are undoubtedly among those most immediately affected by the problem. For some federal employees in Washington, DC, and elsewhere, some of these effects have been psychological as well as financial. Employees were either labeled essential but not paid fully or on time or considered nonessential and furloughed without a clear understanding of when and if they would return. Residents of Washington who are not employed by the federal government were probably frustrated and angry about the lack of services, because taxes that pay for those services continued to be deducted from their wages.

Other issues had already created a charged atmosphere in the DC area before the current budget crisis. For example, Congress has been discussing the possibility of replacing home rule with federal rule in the area because of a local budget crisis caused by DC government mismanagement. The federal standoff has simply added to the existing problems in Washington.

The standoff has consequences for people in other parts of the country as well. People are clearly polarized about these issues. Many middle- and upper-income people believe they need and deserve a tax cut, but not all of them agree that massive cuts in all social programs are necessary to achieve that goal. They are looking to Congress and the president for leadership in articulating the issues clearly and accurately; instead, many have become frustrated by an absence of leadership and by the confusing partisan politics. The ideological rhetoric has caused divisiveness and resentment among the people of this country and has stigmatized poor people (Poole, 1995).

Perhaps the greatest consequence of the nightmare will affect the families and children served by school social workers across the country as cuts in education and social programs designed to benefit children and youths directly take effect. Because funding for the Department of Education has been approved by a continuing resolution for a limited period, funding for education programs remains at its fiscal year 1995 level. The continuing resolution was necessary after the House and Senate failed to produce an education bill in a joint appropriations conference or to approve Clinton's funding request for education (NASW, 1996). As a consequence, it is possible that the remaining education funding for 1996 may be appropriated through another continuing resolution. Essential regular and special education services may be denied to many children and youths because of these funding limitations. Important educational gains may not occur for some students, and for others, stresses that contribute to school failure and other social problems could be exacerbated by these disruptions.

A second consequence is equally important for children and youths in shaping their perspectives about the use of power and about their relative value to the country's policymakers. The standoff models an inappropriate use of power to enforce the important principle of achieving a balanced budget. The message to youths is, "Those with the most power should always fight to win, and by any means necessary." Another implied message is even more toxic to young psyches: Education programs, and thus children and youths, are of lesser value and priority than other federal responsibilities. Such a message is disempowering. It undermines special programs and other efforts designed to help youths gain the collective voice that women, people of color, elderly people, disabled citizens, and other devalued groups have worked toward in recent years.

COLLECTIVE ACTION IS NECESSARY

School social workers, as pupil services personnel, are affected by these events as well. Many have expressed concerns about families and children similar to those discussed in this editorial, along with concerns about the impact on themselves. They should voice their views about the budget crisis and standoff as parents, taxpayers, and advocates for the children they serve. NASW has developed a set of strategies to address many of these concerns that can provide guidance and support for the collective action necessary to resolve this crisis and influence long-term national funding policy. Involvement can be accomplished by following those guidelines once they are publicized or by selecting other planned social and political action strategies.

Everyone has a stake in the outcomes and, therefore, an important role to play by getting involved. We cannot wait for President Clinton and Congress to stop gambling with this country's future. Although President Clinton has espoused support for many of the recommendations made by NASW regarding social programs (in contrast to the Republican leadership), at this point neither side is remembering that real people are and will be seriously affected by its actions.

REFERENCES

Freeman, E. M. (1996). Community practice and policy issues revisited [Editorial]. *Social Work in Education, 18,* 3–6.
Ginsberg, L. (1988). Social workers and politics: Lessons from practice. *Social Work, 33,* 245–248.
Keigher, S. M. (1994). The morning after deficit reduction: The poverty of U.S. maternal and child health policy [National Health Line]. *Health & Social Work, 19,* 143–147.
Keigher, S. M. (1995). Naive, not stupid [National Health Line]. *Health & Social Work, 20,* 70–75.
National Association of Social Workers. (1996). *Highlights of legislative and executive branch issues.* Washington, DC: Author, Office of Government Relations.
Poole, D. (1995). Beyond the rhetoric: Shared responsibility versus the Contract with America [Editorial]. *Health & Social Work, 20,* 83–86.

This chapter was originally published in the April 1996 issue of Social Work in Education, *vol. 18, pp. 67–70.*

44 The New Federal Role in Education and Family Services: Goal Setting without Responsibility

Paula Allen-Meares

The school system has been increasingly unable to support the myth of equal opportunity and full personal development.

(Bowles & Gintis, 1976, p. 4)

At a time when public schools are under enormous pres-sure to address a variety of social and educational needs and to achieve substantial re form, implement mandates, and respond to the growing diversity of pupils, the U.S. House of Representatives voted in July 1995 to drastically reduce education funding by over $4 billion in fiscal year 1996. In mid-September, the Senate committee that has jurisdiction over education spending approved a plan to cut education funding by approximately $2.5 billion. At the same time, human services, welfare, and health care were also targeted for reduction.

These actions have both symbolic and real meanings. A consistent theme throughout these political maneuverings is the reduction in the role of the federal government in education, welfare, and health care to ensure greater state flexibility and autonomy. Entitlements are to be replaced with block grants.

There has been no discussion of the importance of state and federal partnerships, of inequities among the states in terms of resources, and of the consequences of eliminating basic entitlements. Presently, there are large differences in education expenditures per student and welfare expenditures per recipient within individual states as well as among the states. It is predicted that these gaps will continue to grow in the proposed environment.

In the past the nation's schools have been given the burden of addressing inequities in society, whether attributed to class or racial characteristics. In some instances the family has been blamed for the high rates of educational failure among youths. But neither the school nor the family should be singled out. Neither institution is in a position to eradicate all social injustices or to create equality of educational opportunity unless other supports and social institutions are part of the solution. Public schools alone cannot remediate the effects of the structural shifts in the U.S. economy or the consequences of escalating poverty rates.

Powerful economic forces and technological advancements are driving the structural shifts in the economy. For about three decades differentials in economic status have widened both between and within demographic groups; the result has been a rising tide of inequality (Danziger, 1995). The difference in earnings between blue-collar and white-collar workers has increased, but earnings have eroded both for people with marginal educational or technical skills and for an increasing number of skilled and highly educated workers.

Who will advocate for the disenfranchised members of this society—for children and their families? Who will hold state and federal governments accountable? This article examines the diminishing and ambivalent role of the federal government in addressing the growing inequalities in a democratic society; it pays particular attention to public education and its effects on and approaches to the family. This article addresses inequalities in economic and educational opportunity, the transformation of the family in the United States, structural inadequacies in the educational system, efforts currently under way to reform schools, and the implications for the social work profession.

During the historical evolution of the profession, social workers were consistent vocal advocates for social justice—whether the concern was for immigrants during the settlement house movement of the 19th century or the rights of racial or ethnic groups in the United States during the 1960s. "Advocacy is the premise on which the social work profession is founded and an ethical obligation for the practitioner. However, this advocacy must be informed advocacy—proceeding from knowledge of the U.S. legal system, laws, etc." (Lynch & Mitchell, 1995, pp. 10–11). The time has come for the profession to reaffirm its commitment to social justice both in principle and in practice.

INEQUALITY OF ECONOMIC OPPORTUNITY

According to Thurow (1995), threats to the social order and some sense of equality of educational opportunity in a democratic society are found within the nation. In the United States inequalities between members of the low- and middle-income populations and members of the upper-income population are growing; the gap in earnings between the top 20 percent of U.S. wage earners and the bottom 20 percent doubled in $2^1/_2$ decades. Knitzer and Aber (1995) found that between 1987 and 1992 the number of children six years old and younger growing up in poverty increased from 5 million to 6 million, the highest rate of poverty in over 25 years. The poverty experienced by these children and their families is deep and severe (National Center for Children in Poverty, 1990). Twelve percent of all U.S. children under age six live in families with incomes that are 50 percent or less of the federally established poverty level. Fifty-seven percent of all poor children under six live in families where one or both parents work full-time. Even with full-time jobs, these parents do not earn enough to move toward economic security (Knitzer & Aber, 1995). Thirty-nine percent of poor children have parents who hold part-time jobs. These parents are being responsible even though there are few incentives. Although the work ethic persists, for many moving out of poverty is more dream than reality.

An additional 4 million children under age six live in near-poverty. It is not known how many of these children move in and out of the poverty and near-poverty categories (Knitzer & Aber, 1995). Studies such as the U.S. Panel Study of Income Dynamics (Gottschalk, McLanahan, & Sandefur, 1994) have confirmed that families move in and out of poverty.

Young children of color are disproportionately poor (33 percent of poor children are black, and 21 percent are nonwhite Hispanic). Poverty is both an urban and a rural phenomenon. Although a disproportionate number of poor children and families are people of color and live in urban ghettos, the majority of those who fall below the poverty threshold in the United States are white (Connell, 1994). These data and trends suggest that the current welfare and workfare policies and the proposed new policies fail to address these stark realities.

Economic conditions strongly influence whether a family can provide adequate health care for its children and affect children's readiness to learn. Children who come from poverty-stricken backgrounds face more challenges in today's educational system. They are not inherently less intelligent than children from middle- or upper-socioeconomic groups, but they may be less prepared because their families can provide fewer resources that prepare them for the cognitive tasks required for academic success; these children also face environmental barriers to adequate schooling. Low-income children are more likely than other children to be poor achievers, repeat one or two grades, find themselves at the bottom of the academic heap, be welfare dependent, and earn less when they are employed (National Center for Children in Poverty, 1990).

In a very thought-provoking article, Thurow (1995) raised the following question:

> How much inequality can a Democracy take? The income gap in America is eroding the social contract. If the promise of a higher standard of living is limited to a few at the top, the rest of the citizenry, as history shows, is likely to grow disaffected, or worse. . . . Democracies have a problem with rising inequality precisely because they believe in political equality—one person, one vote. (p. 11)

Thurow also suggested that this society should learn from the Roman Empire, whose downward spiral began not with external forces but with a period of uncertainty and disorientation. Rome lost its ability to share its wealth, opportunities, and ideals.

Thurow (1995) suggested that individual disaffection, social disorganization, and fading incomes could cause a slow downward spiral in the country as well. He criticized the Republican party's solution to balancing the budget by raising taxes on working Americans while offering tax advantages to wealthy Americans on the assumption that this will create jobs and opportunities. He referred to this strategy as "survival-of-the-fittest capitalism," which assumes that those controlling capital will lead the economic renewal of the nation. He suggested that the federal government should instead be considering how to enhance the human infrastructure of the nation in terms of economic and educational opportunities, health, and human services.

Oversimplification and reliance on myths about poor people and welfare recipients do not yield a useful analysis for building solutions. Many politicians and citizens want simple, single-focus, quick fixes to very complicated and interrelated phenomena. How can one speak of the issues confronting public education and equality of opportunity without attention to poverty, the transformation of the U.S. family, and the fact that the current operationalization of capitalism needs to be balanced with compassion and social justice?

The replacement of entitlements with block grants is surely not the answer. Under entitlements, the amount of money each state receives from the federal government rises or falls in response to changing needs. If and when there is a recession or the number of needy children increases, the entitlement automatically increases (Children's Defense Fund, 1995). In contrast, a block grant provides a state with a fixed amount of dollars, and when this amount is exhausted or the need increases there are no automatic adjustments. The states then face the predicament of either adding their own resources, if they are available, or developing ways to serve only the most urgent cases. Thus, social equity and economic justice become a function of the prosperity of the state. A case in point is that 20 states have been sued for severe shortcomings in their efforts to help abused and neglected children (Children's Defense Fund, 1995). These states need federal assistance to carry out this important responsibility. Block grants will not remedy this situation; in fact, they could intensify it.

INEQUALITY OF EDUCATIONAL OPPORTUNITY

Murnane (1994) maintained that there are growing inequalities in educational and job productivity attainment for certain groups of youths. Children who grow up in poverty, many of them children of color, need extra educational intervention if they are to achieve economic independence and self-sufficiency as adults. Although Presidents Bush and Clinton both consistently articulated national educational goals (see Table 44-1) as a part of their respective agendas to reform U.S. education and to bring about improved performance outcomes for all children, neither proposed large-scale interventions. The educational goals listed in Table 1 are laudable but unrealistic given the daily struggle of some children and families to secure adequate food, health care, shelter, and feelings of security in their homes and communities.

Although the United States over several decades pursued a series of federal mandates that moved the country in the direction of equal opportunity for various ethnic groups, women, poor people, and people with disabilities, the goal of achieving equality of educational opportunity for these groups has not been achieved. For example, the Emergency School Aid Act (P.L. 89-10, 1978) sought to accelerate school integration, the Education for All Handicapped Children Act of 1975 (P.L. 94-142) mandated equal treatment in schools for children with disabilities, and the Education Amendments of 1972 (P.L. 92-318) sought to prohibit sexual discrimination in educational practices and to enhance the performance of large numbers of underachieving students by improving teachers' bilingual skills.

According to Wells (1990), five major categories of barriers lead to dropout and enrollment failure in the nation's schools:

1. family related—low socioeconomic status, low educational and occupational attainment levels of parents, larger family size, weak family cohesiveness, single-parent households, stressful home environment, poor communication between home and school, racial and ethnic group membership, and few learning materials in the home

TABLE 44-1

Education Reform Goals

America 2000 (President Bush's education reform proposal, 1988)

Promote accountability of schools through creation of world-class standards and voluntary national exams to help parents assess school performance

Empower parents through real choice (vouchers) when deciding which schools are best for their children

Empower educators and administrators with choice by providing reform-minded teachers, principals, and school districts new freedom from bureaucratic controls

Redesign U.S. schools for excellence by creating "New American Schools"; expand use of information technology and new teaching methods to help children better learn basic and advanced subjects

Expand Head Start; promote instruction in math and science; support adult literacy, job training and youth apprenticeships, lifelong learning, the Merit Schools Program, and presidential awards for excellence in education that reward good schools and recognize outstanding teachers

Proposal of six national education goals (see below)

Goals 2000: Educate America Act (P.L. 103-227) (President Clinton's education reform proposal, 1994)

National Education Goals, including the six proposed by President Bush and two proposed by President Clinton:

- All children will arrive at school ready to learn.
- The high school graduation rate will be at least 90 percent.
- Students in grades 4, 8, and 12 will demonstrate competency in subject matter.
- U.S. students will be first in the world in math and science achievement.
- Adults will be literate and able to compete in a global economy.
- Learning environments will be safe, disciplined, and drug free.
- Parental participation will be increased.
- Professional development for educators will be promoted.

Additional goals:

- National performance standards will be developed and adopted.
- Teacher training, instructional materials, technology, and school services will be improved.
- A National Skills Standards Board will be established to promote development of occupational skill standards to define what American workers need to know to create a world-class workforce.
- Administrative and financial flexibility will be increased to allow schools to pursue local reforms.

Other proposed reforms:

Reauthorization of the Elementary and Secondary Education Act ties Chapter 1 monies to school adoption of the national standards.

Legislation is offered to help students who are not bound for college move right from high school into skilled jobs.

Overhaul of the federal student loan program is being explored.

NOTE: From material on federal education reform prepared by Margaret Wheland, University of Michigan, School of Social Work, August 1994. Adapted with permission from Allen-Meares, P., Washington, R., & Welsh, B. (1996). *Social work services in schools* (p. 6). Boston: Allyn & Bacon. ©Allyn & Bacon 1996.

2. school related—poor interpersonal relations, poor academic achievement, feelings of alienation, inflexibility of the structure, and inadequate teaching staff and materials
3. student related—lower self-concept and self-esteem, immature behavior, family problems, lack of social motivation, short attention span, and desire to leave school to help support family
4. community related—too few social services, mental health services, family interventions, preventive services, and transportation services
5. demographic—racial and ethnic group membership.

An analysis of Wells's list makes very clear that poverty affects the capability of the family, school, student, and community to perform their respective and integrative functions in support of the educational process. The lack of financial resources in families, schools, and communities can lead to a deprivation of learning materials and experiences required for academic success. Furthermore, poor prenatal care and the lack of health care for mother and child can lead to a host of developmental delays that compromise a student's educational performance.

TRANSFORMATION OF THE FAMILY

In many areas the United States leads, but in others it fails. For example, national politics has shifted the focus on children and families from how to provide services to help them achieve economic security to whom to blame—institutions or families—for what is perceived as a national moral breakdown. A cross-national comparative analysis found that many countries have established services to children and families as a national priority (Kagan, 1994). The United States has had limited commitment, and the consequences of this stance are inefficiency, inconsistency, and fragmentation as well as enormous inequities in who receives services.

The family as we know it is undergoing a major transformation—it is more heterogeneous and more easily shaken by external forces than in previous decades. For example, the rate of single-parent families has tripled since 1960, from 9.1 percent to 28.6 percent. This drastic increase is largely attributable to increases in the divorce rate, which has doubled since 1960, and out-of-wedlock births (Benson, 1995).

In addition, increases in two-parent working families and single-parent families have moved mothers into the world of work. In 1988, 70 percent of children between ages six and 13 had mothers working outside the home. More and more grandparents who are economically struggling are also raising children.

STRUCTURAL INADEQUACIES IN THE EDUCATIONAL SYSTEM

The educational system does not exist in a vacuum (Allen-Meares, Washington, & Welsh, 1996). It is linked to several contextual structures and systems (for example, community, state, and regional administration and welfare and health care systems) and is acted on by both internal and external forces. Some of these links are weak, and the structures and systems are not as adaptive or even dysfunctional, according to Pallas, Natriello, and McDill (1987):

> We view schools and schooling as part of a configuration of education that locates a set of educating institutions in relation to one another. Whereas families and communities were once strong educating forces, both of these institutions have weakened considerably in post-World War II America. In many cases, schools have been called upon to fill the void left by the breakdown of family and of the community, especially in central cities. (p. 33)

Yet the current educational system is not structured to respond to the complex needs of children in poverty, in inner cities, from single-parent homes, and with psychosocial disabilities. Instead, it perpetuates the status quo:

> Education in the United States plays a dual role in the social process whereby surplus value, i.e., profit, is created and expropriated. On the one hand, by imparting technical and social skills and appropriate motivations, education increases the productive capacity of workers. On the other hand, education helps defuse and depoliticize the potentially explosive class relations of the production process, and thus serves to perpetuate the social, political, and economic conditions through which a portion of the product of labor is expropriated in the form of profits. . . . Schools foster legitimate inequality through the ostensibly meritocratic manner by which they reward and promote students. They create and reinforce patterns of social class, racial and sexual identification. (Bowles & Gintis, 1976, p. 11)

The capacity of our collective human capital depends on equal access to educational resources. Educational reform in the United States must involve a state and federal partnership and must include restructuring of the welfare and health care systems. No longer can we afford to allow educational institutions and dysfunctional social services systems to perpetuate the growing disparities among socioeconomic and ethnic groups in the United States (Connell, 1994; Kagan, 1994). Bowles and Gintis (1976) said two decades ago,

> The halting contribution of U.S. education to equality and full human development appears intimately related to the nature of [the] economic structure into which the schools must integrate each new generation of youth. We have seen both liberal educational reform and the social theories in which reform is based flounder on an incomplete understanding of the economic system. (p. 53)

In the past, state and local governments would target the education, health, or human services systems without regard to their interdependence in responding to the needs of children and their families and in developing the human capital of the nation. The categorical, single-service approach has resulted in fragmentation, professional turfism, and scapegoating; it has undermined a coordinated approach to equal educational opportunity and the development of our human capital. The need to reform the links between systems is urgent.

SCHOOL REFORM EFFORTS

Integrated Services

The integration of education, health, and human services (referred to as "school-linked" or "integrated" services) is a requirement for achieving equal educational opportunity. With school-linked or integrated services, community-based health and human services collaborate with the school system to provide a variety of programs to children and their families. Either these services are located near the school site, or branch offices are located in the school building (Hare, 1995). School-linked services are one example of a new paradigm—the integration of services and public–private partnerships. Some say that this new paradigm was stimulated by the growing concern for the rising rates of poverty among children and families and a host of social problems (for example, homelessness or family problems) (Kirst, 1994). The consistent cry among human services providers for more integration and coordination among the different systems of support for children and families has provided additional impetus.

National Education Goals

National reports calling for the reform of education directed attention to social and economic factors that were impeding school systems from achieving their objectives (National Commission on Excellence in Education, 1983). Advocates believe that collaboration between school and community is necessary to achieve the National Educational Goals established by two presidents (Table 44-1). The advancement of a well-educated workforce for the United States to maintain and surpass other nations is at the core of these goals.

At the time this article was written, there was no definitive way to finance this new service structure. So far, federal grants have funded integrated service demonstration projects, and foundations have also seeded such efforts. A conference held at the Hubert H. Humphrey Center at the University of Minnesota in 1995 indicated that state government and local pooling of funds appeared to be the most frequently used method of funding school-linked or integrated services (Allen-Meares, 1995). However, proposed reductions at the federal level in education and human services will impede this effort.

Educational Paradigms

The conceptual stimulus or intellectual backdrop (Crowson & Boyd, 1993) driving the shift in the educational paradigm is the new ecology of schooling—a new appreciation of the ecological relationship among schools, families, and neighborhoods. Another is the investment perspective—the view that schooling is an invaluable shield against the uncertainty of the future. Society, in principle, believes that investing in education now will reduce and prevent welfare dependency in the future. However, investing in education without investing in housing, health care, and other human services will not accomplish the objective.

In addition, the goals of the school are advanced if the school itself works to create a sense of community and develop productive linkages with family and social supports. Last, there is Comer's (1988) argument that the school should be a caring institution for children and that there are critical developmental pathways in their lives rooted in home and family that, when merged effectively with support from the school, facilitate school achievement.

IMPLICATIONS FOR SOCIAL WORK

Before advocating for service integration across the education, health, and human services systems, the social work profession needs to engage in thorough analysis of these systems. Problematic assumptions and myths about these systems have influenced their evolution over the decades. The profession must first examine, correct, and refuel these faulty systems before they are fit for integration. Research agendas must include attention to these systems of services.

Old and new social work roles and strategies will be required. The advocacy role must intensify in this time of diminishing federal support for promoting equality of educational opportunity. NASW, the National Association of Deans and Directors of Schools of Social Work, the Council on Social Work Education, the Association of Undergraduate Social Work Directors, and the Group for the Advancement of Doctoral Education must come together around this common agenda. Social workers must become social activists and spokespersons for those with weak voices. The need for knowing and using institutional change strategies will become even more important. Interdisciplinary collaboration and new partnerships across a variety of agencies and levels of government will challenge the profession to think differently about how to engage and manage relationships to maximize mutual objectives.

Social work curricula should emphasize social justice and political advocacy as its foundation and should teach political theory, analysis, and strategies for institutional change. Reform of institutions and systems must be the objective if we are to reverse the growing disorientation and inequalities that are strangling the productivity of future generations. Schools are a critical and important institution in the lives of pupils: Why does society hesitate to invest in them and other systems? Unfortunately, poor undereducated children and their families appear to serve a sociopolitical purpose.

Given the current political regression, the interests of social work must be social action in pursuit of social justice and reform and social research to inform policy and practice. Remember the remarkable group of advocates that assembled at Hull House about a century ago: They met the formidable challenges of their time not with passivity, but with strong conviction, vision, and commitment to the advancement of the next generation. Today's social workers must emulate those great role models.

REFERENCES

Allen-Meares, P. (1995, September). *New opportunities for school social work—School-linked/ integrated service programs: Old wine in a new bottle.* Paper presented at the Hubert H. Humphrey Center, University of Minnesota, Minneapolis.

Allen-Meares, P., Washington, R., & Welsh, B. (1996). *Social work services in schools.* Boston: Allyn & Bacon.

Benson, P. (1995). Family patterns today. *Education Digest, 60,* 47–49.

Bowles, S., & Gintis, H. (1976). *Schooling in capitalist America: Educational reform and the contradictions of economic life.* New York: Basic Books.

Children's Defense Fund. (1995). *The child nutrition block grants in the house welfare bill: How would low-income children be affected?* Washington, DC: Author.

Comer, J. (1988). Educating poor minority children. *Scientific American, 259,* 42–48.

Connell, R. W. (1994). Poverty and education. *Harvard Educational Review, 64,* 125–149.

Crowson, R., & Boyd, W. (1993). Coordinated services for children: Designing arks for storms and seas unknown. *American Journal of Education, 101,* 140–179.

Danziger, S. (1995, December). *Rising inequality and the relationship between economic conditions and stress*. Paper presented at the Workshop on Social Conditions, Stress, Resources, and Health, sponsored by the National Institute of Mental Health, Bethesda, MD.

Education Amendments of 1972, P.L. 92-318, 86 Stat. 235.

Education for All Handicapped Children Act of 1975, P.L. 94-142, 89 Stat. 773.

Emergency School Aid Act, P.L. 89-10, 92 Stat. 2252 (1978).

Goals 2000: Educate America Act, P.L. 103-227, 108 Stat. 125 (1994).

Gottschalk, J., McLanahan, S., & Sandefur, G. D. (1994). The dynamics and intergenerational transmission of poverty and welfare participation. In S. Danziger, G. D. Sandefur, & D. H. Weinberg (Eds.), *Confronting poverty: Prescriptions for change* (pp. 85–108). New York: Russell Sage Foundation.

Hare, I. (1995). School-linked services. In R. L. Edwards (Ed.-in-Chief), *Encyclopedia of social work* (19th ed., Vol. 3, pp. 2100–2108). Washington, DC: NASW Press.

Kagan, S. (1994). Families and children: Who is responsible? *Childhood Education, 71*, 4–8.

Kirst, M. (1994, Fall). School-linked services: Pitfalls and potentials. *Spectrum*, pp. 15–24.

Knitzer, J., & Aber, L. (1995). Young children in poverty: Facing the facts. *Opinion, 65*, 174–176.

Lynch, R., & Mitchell, J. (1995). Justice system advocacy: A must for NASW and the social work community. *Social Work, 40*, 9–12.

Murnane, R. (1994). Education and the well-being of the next generation. In S. Danziger, G. D. Sandefur, & D. H. Weinberg (Eds.), *Confronting poverty: Prescriptions for change* (pp. 289–309). New York: Russell Sage Foundation.

National Center for Children in Poverty. (1990). *Five million children: A statistical profile of our poorest young citizens*. New York: Columbia University School of Public Health, Author.

National Commission on Excellence in Education. (1983). *A nation at risk: The imperative of educational reform*. Washington, DC: U.S. Department of Education.

Pallas, A., Natriello, G., & McDill, E. (1987). Changing students/changing needs. In J. I. Goodlad (Ed.), *The ecology of school renewal: Eighty-six yearbook of the National Society for the Study of Education* (Part 1, pp. 30–56). Chicago: University of Chicago Press.

Thurow, L. (1995, November 6). Why their world might crumble. *New York Times Magazine*, p. 11.

Wells, S. (1990). *At-risk youth: Identification, programs and recommendations*. Englewood: Colorado Libraries Unlimited.

This chapter was originally published in the September 1996 issue of Social Work, *vol. 41, pp. 533–540.*

45 Appropriate versus Least Restrictive: Educational Policies and Students with Disabilities

James C. Raines

Equality and freedom are deeply held values in the United States, but there are circumstances under which they can-not be pursued as a single goal. One of these circumstances has occurred in the field of educational policy. Providing students with disabilities equal access to education has often meant segregating them in special programs specifically designed to meet their needs. In short, society has improved their access to equal education by decreasing their freedom to associate with their peers without disabilities. This unfortunate state of affairs has forced a re-examination of the balance between an "appropriate education" and an education administered in the "least-restrictive environment."

This article evaluates three very different paradigms for achieving the integration of students with and without disabilities. To put these in perspective, it examines three epochs in the education of students with disabilities. It identifies three current approaches to balancing the two primary mandates of providing an appropriate education in the least-restrictive environment. Finally, this article studies the class action and civil suits brought by parents and interpretations of relevant constitutional amendments by federal courts and the U.S. Supreme Court. The results are important for students with disabilities because they provide guidelines for people with disabilities in U.S. society. They have implications for the inclusion of all excluded or segregated groups in the educational system.

HISTORY: EXCLUDED AND UNEQUAL

Four early influences led to the practice of categorizing students during the late 19th and early 20th centuries. The first was a large influx of immigrant children from non-English-speaking countries. Although bilingual education had existed extensively during colonial times (Pennsylvania, Maryland, Virginia, and the Carolinas offered education in German), Theodore Roosevelt was committed to the idea of a single-language nation. He suggested that "We should provide for every immigrant by day schools for the young and by night schools for the adults, the chance to learn English; and if after say five years, he has not learned English, he should be sent back to the land from whence he came" (1917, quoted in Allen-Meares, Washington, & Welsh, 1986, p. 181). Thus, when schools were unprepared to teach immigrant students in their own language, special "opportunity" schools were created until they were ready for entry into the regular public schools (Allen-Meares et al., 1986).

The second factor was the industrialization of U.S. society, which provided the vision of a population differentiated by skills (into management and labor). This idea affected both teachers and their students: Teachers were categorized by the subjects they taught, and students were classified by their ability to learn. Pupils who were deemed unlikely to become management material were considered unfit for the investment of educational currency (Allen-Meares et al., 1986).

The third influence was the development of standardized intelligence tests. The Binet-Simon test was developed in France in 1905 expressly to predict school performance. It was translated into English in 1908 by Henry Goddard and was quickly endorsed by the National Education Association as useful for mentally retarded children. It was then revised by Lewis Terman of Stanford University and published as the Stanford-Binet Intelligence Test in 1916. Since then, intelligence tests have been used widely in the United States to track students into ability groupings (Hardman, Drew, Egan, & Wolf, 1990; Reynolds & Birch, 1988).

Finally, in 1922 a group of teachers and other human services professionals established the Council for Exceptional Children. These advocates for children with disabilities found it pragmatic to separate from general education, because it made their students more visible, encouraged philanthropic support, and avoided confrontation with administrators in regular education who wanted to rid themselves of problem students (Reynolds & Birch, 1988).

TRANSITIONS: SEPARATE BUT EQUAL

Constitutional Law

Brown v. Board of Education (1954) was the turning point in educational policy and law. *Brown* is a landmark case for many reasons. It demonstrated through constitutional litigation that educational issues are social and political issues. It showed that very difficult educational issues can be contested in a civil rights arena. It also illustrated how litigation can provide the bedrock for legislation on both the state and federal level.

Brown marked the entry of the federal government into educational policy, an area that had previously been the sole province of state and local governments. In addition, it proved that although the U.S. Constitution did not guarantee public education, its principles of equal protection and due process applied. It typified the kind of case (that is, civil action) used to address inequities in educational law. And by repudiating the "separate but equal" doctrine it had ratified in *Plessy v. Ferguson* (1896), it provided a "right to equal education" for a class of people. If one substituted the word "disabled" for "Negro" and the word "abled" for "white" in *Brown*, then it becomes clear how the Fourteenth Amendment became the constitutional basis for the rights of children with disabilities to be educated (Turnbull, 1993).

Federal Legislation

Another development in the 1950s was the advances of Samuel Kirk, who started the first teacher preparation and research programs in special education (Allen-

Meares et al., 1986). In 1958 Congress passed P.L. 85-926, which authorized $1 million for universities to train professional educators for mentally retarded students (Reynolds & Birch, 1988). This led a few states (New York, New Jersey, and Massachusetts) to enact mandatory special education legislation. Most states, however, passed legislation that allowed, but did not require, school districts to provide special education services (Hardman et al., 1990).

The federal government finally got directly involved when it passed the Elementary and Secondary Education Amendments of 1966 (P.L. 89-750); these amendments created Title VI, which founded the Bureau of Education for the Handicapped. The bureau established a grants program for innovative educational programs for children with disabilities.

In 1970 Congress replaced Title VI by passing the Education for the Handicapped Act (P.L. 91-230). Part B of the act provided for a grants program with guidelines for states to develop resources and train personnel for special education.

By 1974, however, Congress was becoming impatient with the lack of progress made by the states. Senator H. A. Williams (D-NJ) reported that "the most recent statistics provided by the Bureau of Education for the Handicapped estimate that . . . 1.75 million handicapped children do not receive any educational services, and 2.5 million handicapped children are not receiving an appropriate education" (121 Cong. Rec. 19,486, 1975). With this in mind, Congress passed an interim measure, the Education of the Handicapped Act Amendments of 1974 (P.L. 93-380), which increased funding and required states to adopt the goal of providing full educational opportunities to all children with disabilities. The next year, Congress would pass the most comprehensive legislation for the education of handicapped children.

Litigation

In 1967 the first school classification case, *Hobson v. Hansen*, was heard. It concerned the misuse of intelligence tests to place predominantly poor black children into the lower tracks of Washington, DC's, educational program. The court ruled that this violated the due process clause of the Fifth Amendment, thus reaffirming *Brown's* contention that a class of people cannot be denied educational rights.

During the 1970s, two landmark cases redefined the public schools' obligation to educate children with disabilities. The first was *Pennsylvania Association for Retarded Citizens (PARC) v. Commonwealth of Pennsylvania* (1971). *PARC*, part of a parent movement to advocate for the rights of children with disabilities, relied on four arguments:

1. Expert testimony indicated that all mentally retarded individuals were capable of benefiting from an educational program.
2. The state of Pennsylvania undertook to provide a free public education to all of its children regardless of ability.
3. Therefore, Pennsylvania must provide any mentally retarded child with a free educational program.
4. Further, the state was obligated to place children according to their ability with a preference for placement in a regular public school class rather

than placement in a special public school class or in a nonpublic school program.

The second case was *Mills v. Board of Education of the District of Columbia* (1972), a class-action suit filed on behalf of children who had been suspended or expelled from the schools because of behavior related to their mental retardation, hyperactivity, emotional disturbances, or behavior disorders.

The court required the District to provide a free and appropriate publicly supported education regardless of the degree of disability or the cost involved (even if this meant private tuition). Finally, the school board was forbidden to make disciplinary suspensions for longer than two days unless there was a due process hearing before the suspension and the child's education was continued during the suspension. Thus, the *Mills* case expanded the *PARC* decision by including a broad range of children frequently excluded from the public schools.

REFORM: INCLUDED AND EQUAL

The Education for All Handicapped Children Act of 1975 (P.L. 94-142) was a watershed for many reasons. It established a "zero reject" principle, which said that the states could not refuse an education to any child within their jurisdiction and must locate previously unserved children. It required nondiscriminatory evaluations by a multidisciplinary team and a battery of nonbiased tests administered in the child's native language or normal mode of communication. The act instituted an appropriate education standard that was to be documented in writing (the individualized education plan [IEP]) and that included the child's present level of functioning, annual goals, specific services to be provided, the extent to which the child would participate in regular education, projected date of initiation, anticipated duration of services, and criteria for determining the achievement of objectives.

P.L. 94-142 also required the maximal use of the least-restrictive environment to reduce the segregation of special education children from their nondisabled peers. It demanded fairness in the form of procedural due process whereby parents must be notified and give their informed consent before any evaluation. It also established a principle of shared decision making whereby parents and professionals communicated and collaborated in the best interests of the child. Finally, it clarified which students were to be regarded as disabled and thus eligible for funds through the federal grant program (for example, learning disabled, yes; culturally disadvantaged, no; severely emotionally disturbed, yes; socially maladjusted, no).

Despite this landmark legislation, several problems remained to be resolved. The two most important were, What does "appropriate" education mean? and What does "least restrictive" mean? The answers were not forthcoming from Congress, so the judicial system decided.

Appropriate Education

The Supreme Court defined appropriate education in *Board of Education v. Rowley* (1982), the first special education case to reach the high court. The case involved a deaf student with minimal residual hearing but excellent lip-reading skills. She was placed in a regular kindergarten class and provided with an FM hearing aid. During her first-grade year, her IEP recommended that she be educated in a regular classroom and receive instruction from a tutor for the deaf for one hour each day and three hours of speech therapy each week. Her parents insisted on a sign-language interpreter for all of her academic classes, and the school board balked.

The court declared that the legislative intent was only to provide disabled children the same basic educational opportunities as their nondisabled peers, not maximal development of their potential. Thus, the key to determining appropriateness is "educational benefit." If the student was making progress (not necessarily optimal progress), then the educational program met the standard. The court set forth a process definition that an appropriate education was one that followed the protocol of identification, nondiscriminatory evaluation, and an IEP. If the school district failed to follow these procedures, the education could not be appropriate, but a small mistake would not invalidate the process. Nonadherence to procedures must result in actual or potential harm (Saltzman & Proch, 1990; Turnbull, 1993).

Least-Restrictive Environment

The principle of least-restrictive environment came from many quarters, including corrections and mental health policies (Turnbull, 1993). It was a reaction against special education's practice of segregating students in separate and unequal education. Children in special education classes were often taught by less-capable teachers in worse facilities with fewer resources and for an indeterminate period of time. Thus, least-restrictive environment became a broad approach designed to correct several inadequacies. It remains ill defined, however, because the law has always allowed for segregation through a broad continuum of placements from inpatient hospital care to the regular classroom. There are three very different interpretations of this principle: mainstreaming, regular education initiative, and full inclusion.

Mainstreaming. Neither P.L. 94-142 or its 1990 amendments, the Individuals with Disabilities Education Act (IDEA) (P.L. 101-476), chose to narrow the continuum of services that has made more restrictive programs permissible. Deno's (1973) "cascade model" is a good example of how the most-restrictive placements should serve the fewest number of students and how the continuum should broaden so that the least-restrictive placements serve the greatest number of students. Advocates of this system contend that some students' disabilities are so severe that an appropriate education cannot be achieved in an integrated setting and that the student is more likely to maximize his or her development in a segregated setting, that the inclusion of students with disabilities in the regular classroom deprives nondisabled peers of their right to an appropriate education, that the economic costs of adapting the regular classroom depletes the financial resources available to other students, and that teachers may never be prepared to teach such a diverse group of learners (Kauffman, 1989).

Thus, mainstreaming advocates continued to place children in segregated classes for most of their academic classes but integrated students with disabilities during nonacademic times (lunch, recess, gym, music, and art) and occasionally for an academic class at which the student with a disability excelled. This type of mainstreaming might best be called "physical mainstreaming," because although it brought students together in the same physical space, it did not necessarily lead to social interaction or integrated instruction (Reynolds & Birch, 1988). Under physical mainstreaming, special education teachers were to teach self-contained academic classes while allowing students more freedom of association during nonacademic periods.

Regular Education Initiative. Early case law (for example, see *PARC*) indicated a clear preference for educating children with disabilities in regular classrooms in public schools. Indeed, the "separate but equal" concept was repudiated by *Brown* in 1954. Advocates for integration have noted that left to its own devices, special education has become a "second system" for educating children (Wang, Reynolds, & Walberg, 1988). Both P.L. 94-142 and IDEA emphasized the need for special efforts to integrate children with disabilities and their peers without disabilities.

The prescription for what ailed the educational system had three parts: (1) integration, not only of students but also of systems (that is, special education and general education); (2) large-scale mainstreaming into regular education classrooms; and (3) improvement of achievement levels of children with "high-incidence" disabilities such as mild mental retardation, learning disabilities, and behavioral disorders (Fuchs & Fuchs, 1994).

Integration would require special educators and general educators to work together in the best interests of all children, with special educators serving as consultants to regular teachers on a wide variety of students, not just those labeled as disabled. Teachers would have to become skilled at working with a wide variety of students, thereby improving their ability to teach all learners, not just "normal" ones.

Two highly individualized forms of mainstreaming other than physical were envisioned: social interaction mainstreaming and instructional mainstreaming. Some children by the nature of their disability (for example, hearing impairments) have very little social interaction mainstreaming even though they may be able to participate intellectually in the regular educational program. Other children by the nature of their mental disability (for example, learning disorders or mild mental retardation) can participate socially but have difficulty keeping up with the instructional level of the regular class.

To improve achievement levels, several strategies were suggested: continuous assessment of student achievement, use of alternative methods of instruction, availability of a variety of teaching materials, explicit IEPs, student self-management for parts of the school day, peer assistance among students, team teaching by teachers and other support staff, and use of consulting teachers (that is, special educators) (Wang, Anderson, & Bram, 1985).

An important caveat, however, is that the advocates of the regular education initiative have allowed some room for exceptional children to be educated outside of the mainstream. Reynolds and Birch (1988) identified four types of children who should not be mainstreamed: (1) children who are dangerous to themselves or others, (2) children with severe and profound multiple disabilities, (3) children with traumatic injuries that require extensive rehabilitation, and (4) children who require maintenance environments such as mechanical respirators or dust-free living spaces.

Full Inclusion. As early as 1968 Dunn had come to the conclusion that

> our past and present practices are morally and educationally wrong. We have been living at the mercy of general educators who have referred their problem children to us. And we have been generally ill-prepared and ineffective in educating these children. Let us stop being pressured into continuing and expanding a special education program that we know now to be undesirable for many of the children we are dedicated to serve. (p. 5)

The IDEA amendments reinforced the concept of full inclusion by placing special emphasis on the integration of students with severe disabilities (Section 1426(a)(3) and (4), cited in Turnbull, 1993). The full-inclusion movement sees only "two roads: the road of inclusion and the road of exclusion. We choose the other road—inclusion. The simple starting point for this road is to include everyone. Educate all children in *regular* classrooms and communities" (Stainback & Stainback, 1992, p. xv).

Advocates of full inclusion accept no compromise because the issue is seen as a moral one, not an educational one. Stainback and Stainback (1992) rejected the term "integration" because it implied previous exclusion, and they rejected the term "mainstreaming" because it inferred a need to fit students into an existing program. They argued that responsibility should be "placed on school personnel to arrange a mainstream that accommodates the needs of all students" (Stainback, Stainback, & Jackson, 1992, p. 4). Whereas the proponents of the regular education initiative aim primarily to include children with high-incidence handicaps, the proponents of full inclusion aim to include children with low-incidence handicaps as well. To achieve this goal, they have taken a radical stance to some revered concepts. First, they take a "social constructivist" approach to curriculum:

> Socialization and friendships are among the major educational goals to enable students to become active members of the community. When adults focus on and foster buddy systems, circles of friends, and other friendship facilitation activities, children start to gain what will be most important to them in their lives—a range of people who genuinely care about them as individuals. Thus, if a child never learns any math, history, or other subject, it is critical that he or she be included. (Stainback, Stainback, & Moravec, 1992, pp. 66–67)

The "standardized" curriculum is rejected for several reasons:
- In a changing society, there is no static body of knowledge that will produce success.
- The standardized curriculum does not accommodate the diversity of learning styles and interests.
- It focuses educators on the content rather than the child.
- It is uninteresting and irrelevant for many students.
- It disempowers teachers who want to use their own approaches.

Full-inclusion advocates want to dismantle the entire special education system. They reason that because all students are in the mainstream full-time, all personnel and resources can be in the mainstream full-time. In addition, valuable resources and time would not be spent classifying, labeling, and making placement decisions: "'General' educators and 'special' educators are able to focus on providing every student challenging and appropriate educational programs geared to his or her unique needs and capabilities" (Stainback, Stainback, & Jackson, 1992, p. 7).

The full-inclusion movement would also like to demythologize the professional disciplines for three reasons: (1) expertise is not a prerequisite for providing educational support, (2) strictly defined boundaries between professions are illusory, and (3) just because two individuals have the same educational degree does not mean that they have the same competencies (York, Giangreco, Vandercook, & Macdonald, 1992). In addition to a de-emphasis on professionalization, there is a focus on peer-assisted learning through cooperative group learning systems, where students are responsible not only for their own learning but also for the learning of every pupil within a heterogeneous group (Villa & Thousand, 1992).

Most important, the full-inclusion movement makes no room for exceptions, even for the physically dangerous child. Educators are encouraged to recognize "disruptive, even dangerous, acts as communication" (Hitzing, 1992). Once the "sign language" is understood, the student should then be taught how to "communicate in ways that are equally effective and adaptive, but are not disruptive or dangerous" (p. 147).

CLARIFICATION AND CONTROVERSY

The battle among the approaches to creating a least-restrictive environment is clearly related to how one views the right of every student to an appropriate education. Because Congress and the state education agencies have been unable to devise a solution, the judicial system has been forced to develop some guidelines.

Provision of Nontraditional Services

The Supreme Court has made it very clear that schools must provide heretofore nontraditional related services. In *Irving Independent School District v. Tatro* (1984), a girl with spina bifida suffered from a neurogenic bladder, which prevented her from emptying her bladder voluntarily. She needed clean intermittent catheterization (CIC) every three to four hours to prevent damage to her kidneys. The child's IEP provided early child development classes and physical and occupational therapy but made no provision for CIC. The state argued that CIC fell outside the definition of a related service as defined by Congress, which included only diagnostic and evaluative medical services.

The Court held that CIC was a necessary supportive service for the child to remain in school. Because CIC could be administered by a layperson, the Court did not view it as a "medical service," which required a licensed physician, but a "school health service" that could be performed by a school nurse or other qualified person. Finally, it defined related services as those performed by a qualified person, not a requirement for supplying equipment (Lantzy, 1992).

Cost–Benefit Analysis

The Supreme Court has made it clear that the costs to others can be taken into account when determining least-restrictive environment. In *Roncker v. Walters* (1983), the Sixth Circuit Court of Appeals decided in favor of mainstreaming a student diagnosed as trainable mentally retarded even if the segregated facility was academically superior. The opinion rendered, however, specifically allowed that "cost is a proper factor to consider since excessive spending on one handicapped child deprives other handicapped children" (cited in Turnbull, 1993, p. 186). The court then specified three possible exceptions to the integration requirement: (1) if the handicapped child would receive no benefit from mainstreaming, (2) if it is not feasible for the regular education facility to be modified adequately, or (3) if the handicapped child is too disruptive a force in the integrated setting.

In sum, the court adopted a "competing equities" approach to the issue of least-restrictive environment. This cost–benefit reasoning has several sources. The courts are reluctant to rule on school financing issues. The courts have acknowledged that congressional intent was to leave financing decisions in the hands of the states, not the federal government. The courts also have been reluctant to overstep the natural law that parents have a right to educate their children as they see fit without undue influence by the government (Turnbull, 1993).

Emphasis on Social Goals

There is growing evidence that courts are placing a greater emphasis on the social goals of the least-restrictive environment provision than the need for educational progress. In *Daniel R. R. v. State Board of Education* (1989), the Fifth Circuit Court of Appeals ruled that a boy with Down syndrome could be removed from a general education classroom for four periods a day because he was not participating or making progress in his regular class. The court then created a two-pronged test to determine if the least-restrictive environment mandate had been met: (1) whether education in the regular classroom, with supplementary aids and services, could be achieved satisfactorily and (2) if the school district intended to remove the student to a self-contained classroom, whether the school had mainstreamed the student to the maximum extent feasible.

Further Refinements

In *Greer v. Rome City School District* (1990), the federal court for the Northern District of Georgia cited *Daniel R. R.* in its ruling that a nine-year-old student with Down syndrome could be mainstreamed in a general education kindergarten class for three years because she was making some progress and was not disruptive to other students. The court then created three more standards to determine what cases met the appropriate and least-restrictive environment demands (Osborne & DiMattia, 1994). First, a school district may compare the benefits received from placement in a regular classroom with the benefits received from placement in a self-contained classroom.

Second, the school board could consider what effect the presence of the disabled child would have on the education of other children in the regular classroom. Last, the school district could consider the cost of the supplemental aids and services necessary for the disabled child in a general education classroom to achieve progress. The school district must balance the needs of each disabled child against the needs of other children in the district (Turnbull, 1993).

DISCUSSION

It is clear that the move toward integration will continue to move forward. The United States has moved beyond the old medical, economic, and functional definitions of disability to a psychosocial model in which people with disabilities are regarded as a disadvantaged group whose problems in the social environment are not based solely on personal inadequacy but on the discriminatory practices of society (Karger & Stoesz, 1994). Although social workers must support antidiscrimination practices and policies for disabled people, does it logically follow that they must accept full inclusion as an educational mandate? I think not.

The New Federalism

We should remember where the call for inclusion originated. In 1985 Reagan appointee Madeline Will, the assistant secretary for the U.S. Department of Education, addressed the Wingspread Conference. After affirming Reagan's commitment to excellence in education, she decried the proliferation of federally funded special education programs. Will (1986) reported that over 4.3 million children were eligible for these federally funded programs and asserted the "need to *more efficiently use resources* to accommodate the burgeoning number of students who are failing to learn" [italics added] (p. 413). To meet this need, she recommended that special education form a partnership with regular education to assess and intervene with all children with special learning needs.

There are several reasons to suspect that the rhetoric of academic excellence was actually a guise for the new federalism of disengagement and decreasing financial support. Verstegen and Clark (1988) reported that from 1981 to 1988, federal funding for elementary and secondary education dropped by 28 percent, with the biggest decrease (76 percent) in special education. Albert Shanker, president of the American Federation of Teachers, remarked with skepticism in 1994,

> given the financial situation of our states and school districts, and given the fact that the federal government has never met its commitment to fund its share of education for the disabled, does anybody really believe that the large amount of money that's necessary to provide these services in individual classrooms is going to be made available? (p. 316)

In 1984 the U.S. Department of Education, where Will was the director of the Office of Special Education, recommended to Congress that lawmakers not change the term "emotionally disturbed" to "behavior disorders" because adopting a less-stigmatizing label would increase the number of students eligible for service (Turnbull, 1993). Clearly one of the major reasons behind the Reagan–Bush educational agenda was solely financial and certainly not in the best interests of children with disabilities. This is especially relevant in large, poorly funded cities (Jackson, 1993).

Naive Liberalism

A second reason to remain cautious about full inclusion has to do with the naive liberal idea that underneath, all people are the same. Stainback and Stainback (1984) argued that there are not two kinds of children—with and without disabilities—but that children are more alike than different. The fallacy of this approach is clear from the racial analogy on which the civil rights of disabled people are based. Multicultural education gave up the "melting pot" idea long ago in recognizing that differences are not just skin deep. Taking such a "color blind" approach to children with disabilities will inevitably lead to failing to provide for their differences (Kauffman, 1989). Although many would agree with the idea that true education involves learning how to learn more than it does learning to recite facts, the fundamental purpose of the education system is to foster learning, not socialization. Socialization must be a shared goal of cultural institutions such as families, religious groups, and communities. It is not the sole province of the school system, and separated from these institutions, it would be doomed to failure.

Self-Determination

The profession would do well to listen to the people most affected by these educational policies—the families of children with disabilities. Before 1975 parent advocacy groups frequently sued school boards to include their children in regular education classrooms. Presently, parents are as likely to sue to maintain their children in special education classes as otherwise. Clearly, special education is doing something right. A study of five large school districts by Singer and Butler (cited in Kauffman, 1989) reaffirmed this; the study found that parents of special education students were generally very satisfied: "They were satisfied with their children's overall educational program and related services, with their social interaction with other students, with the administration and teaching in the special education program, and with the facilities" (Kauffman, 1989, p. 269). Most parents do not want their children with disabilities mainstreamed because of an abstract agenda, but only after a careful biopsychosocial assessment of their individual child (American Council of the Blind, 1993; Children and Adults with Attention Deficit Disorders, 1993; Consumer Action Network of, by, and for Deaf and Hard of Hearing Americans, 1993; Learning Disabilities Association of America, 1993).

Although many would agree that a student's destructive acts are communicative, they may also interpret them as an indirect request for a more restrictive placement where both the emotionally disturbed student and his or her peers are safe. Few would relish the thought of explaining to the parents of a student who was violently victimized why the school system did not ensure the safety of all the students in the class and school.

Room for Research

It seems reasonable to study what approaches are most effective for children with various disabilities of various severities. During the 1990–91 school year, the U. S. Department of Education (1993) counted over 4.7 million children with disabilities; of these, 45 percent were diagnosed with specific learning disabilities, 21 percent with speech or language impairments, 11 percent with mental retardation, 8 percent with serious emotional disturbances, and 9 percent preschool children with noncategorical disabilities. Clearly, there are enough children to participate in large-scale studies. In the evaluation research on inclusion so far, the results have been mixed at best (Hepler, 1994; McIntosh, Vaughn, Schumm, Haager, & Lee, 1994; McKinney & Hocutt, 1988).

CONCLUSION

The success of special education is still in doubt. Of the 248,590 students with disabilities who left the educational system during the 1988–89 school year, only 53 percent graduated from school, whereas at least 27 percent dropped out compared with an average of 11 percent in the general school population (Chronicle of Higher Education, 1994, p. 6). In addition, of the special education students who had been out of high school for more than one year, only 29 percent found full-time employment, and only 17 percent earned part-time wages. Fully 69 percent were still living with their parents, and only 17 percent were living independently, whether alone, in military housing, or in a college dormitory (U.S. Department of Education, 1993).

These percentages provide a strong reason to implement the 1990 IDEA amendments calling for increased transition services as part of an appropriate education. This coordinated set of services is designed to promote a variety of outcomes after graduation, including postsecondary education, vocational training, employment, and independent living. These should be the ultimate "benefits" of an education, and equity should be decided on "the quality of instruction, not the place of instruction" (Kauffman, 1989, p. 258).

These services would also be more in keeping with the spirit of the Goals 2000: Educate America Act of 1994 (P.L. 103-227), which seeks to improve the quality of education for all students, both with and without disabilities, by putting an emphasis on results in eight areas: school readiness; school completion; student achievement and citizenship; teacher education and professional development; mathematics and science; adult literacy and life-long learning; safe, disciplined, and alcohol- and drug-free schools; and parent participation. These are goals social workers can affirm for all students with and without disabilities. Thus, the profession should embrace the regular education initiative in principle and apply it with careful deliberation in practice.

The NASW Standards for School Social Work Services (1992) suggest several ways that school social workers should be involved with this issue. School social workers have a responsibility to be ethical professionals. They should stay current on educational policy, including knowing and complying with federal and state legislation, state board of education regulations, and local administrative rules.

Social workers must also be educators to their colleagues. They can provide or arrange in-service training to teachers and other personnel on this issue. School social workers should be systems coordinators by providing creative educational plans that meet the goals of education and socialization through the involvement and collaboration of other community agencies and groups (for example, park districts, libraries, and church programs).

Social workers can act as change agents within various levels of the educational system: the local school, the school district, and state or national organizations. They should regularly communicate problems to the principal, local administrators, or other professionals and work together toward solutions. In addition, social workers can act as mediators between families and the local education agency, helping both avoid expensive and adversarial due process procedures. Conflict resolution strategies can go a long way toward building cooperation. Finally, the profession must advocate for students whose rights have been ignored by the educational system; they must empower families to have a voice in their child's education as well as be a consultant to school personnel about policy issues.

Freeman (1995) noted that "the traditional role of education has changed; its mission cannot be carried out in isolation from the social and economic changes that are occurring in the larger environment" (p. 2097). As a result, there have been changes for school social workers, too. Everything they do within the local school is affected by social and economic policies at state and national levels.

REFERENCES

Allen-Meares, P., Washington, R. O., & Welsh, B. (1986). *Social work services in schools*. Englewood Cliffs, NJ: Prentice Hall.

American Council of the Blind. (1993). Full inclusion of students that are blind and visually impaired: A position statement. *Braille Forum, 32*(1), 44–47.

Board of Education v. Rowley, 458 U.S. 176, 102 S. Ct. 3034, 73 L. E.2d 690 (1982).

Brown v. Board of Education, 347 U.S. 483 (1954).

Children and Adults with Attention Deficit Disorders. (1993). CHADD position on inclusion. In J. H. Kaufman & D. P. Hallahan (Eds.), *The illusion of full inclusion: A comprehensive critique of the current special education bandwagon* (pp. 319–321). Austin, TX: Pro-Ed.

Chronicle of Higher Education. (1994). *Chronicle of Higher Education almanac*. Washington, DC: Author.

Consumer Action Network of, by, and for Deaf and Hard of Hearing Americans. (1993). Position statement on full inclusion. In J. H. Kaufman & D. P. Hallahan (Eds.), *The illusion of full inclusion: A comprehensive critique of a current special education bandwagon* (pp. 322–328). Austin, TX: Pro-Ed.

Daniel R. R. v. State Board of Education, 874 F.2d 1036 (5th Cir. 1989).

Deno, E. (Ed.). (1973). *Instructional alternatives for exceptional children*. Reston, VA: Council for Exceptional Children.

Dunn, L. M. (1968). Special education for the mildly mentally retarded—Is much of it justified? *Exceptional Child, 35*, 5–22.

Education for All Handicapped Children Act of 1975, P.L. 94-142, 89 Stat. 773.

Education of the Handicapped Act, P.L. 91-230, 84 Stat. 175 (1970).

Education of the Handicapped Act Amendments of 1974, P.L. 93-380, 88 Stat. 579.

Elementary and Secondary Education Amendments of 1966, P.L. 89-750, 80 Stat. 1191.

Freeman, E. M. (1995). School social work overview. In R. L. Edwards (Ed.-in-Chief), *Encyclopedia of social work* (19th ed., Vol. 3, pp. 2087–2099). Washington, DC: NASW Press.

Fuchs, D., & Fuchs, L. S. (1994). Inclusive schools movement and the radicalization of special education reform. *Exceptional Children, 60*, 294–309.

Goals 2000: Educate America Act of 1994, P.L. 103-227, 108 Stat. 125.

Greer v. Rome City School District, 762 F. Supp. 936 (N.D. Ga. 1990).

Hardman, M. L., Drew, C. J., Egan, M. W., & Wolf, B. (1990). *Human exceptionality: Society, school, and family* (3rd ed.). Boston: Allyn & Bacon.

Hepler, J. B. (1994). Mainstreaming children with learning disabilities: Have we improved their social environment? *Social Work in Education, 16*, 143–154.

Hitzing, W. (1992). Support and positive teaching strategies. In S. Stainback & W. Stainback (Eds.), *Curriculum considerations in inclusive classrooms: Facilitating learning for all students* (pp. 143–158). Baltimore: Paul H. Brookes.

Hobson v. Hansen, 269 F. Supp. 401, 514 (D.D.C., 1967).

Individuals with Disabilities Education Act, P.L. 101-476, 104 Stat. 1142 (1990).

Irving Independent School District v. Tatro, 468 U.S. 883, 104 S. Ct. 3371, 82 L. Ed. 2d 664 (1984).

Jackson, D. (1993, April 1). Failure track: Mainstreaming can put kids in over their heads. *Chicago Tribune*, Sec. 1, pp. 1, 18–19.

Karger, H. J., & Stoesz, D. (1994). *American social welfare policy: A pluralist perspective* (2nd ed.). New York: Longman.

Kauffman, J. M. (1989). The regular-education initiative as Reagan-Bush education policy: A trickle-down theory of education of the hard-to-teach. *Journal of Special Education, 2*, 256–278.

Lantzy, M. L. (1992). *Individuals with Disabilities Education Act: An annotated guide to its literature and resources, 1980–1991*. Littleton, CO: Fred B. Rothman.

Learning Disabilities Association of America. (1993). Position paper on full inclusion of all students with learning disabilities in the regular education classroom. In J. H. Kaufman & D. P. Hallahan (Eds.), *The illusion of full inclusion: A comprehensive critique of the current special education bandwagon* (pp. 340–341). Austin, TX: Pro-Ed.

McIntosh, R., Vaughn, S., Schumm, J. S., Haager, D., & Lee, O. (1994). Observations of students with learning disabilities in general education classrooms. *Exceptional Children, 61*, 249–261.

McKinney, J., & Hocutt, A. (1988). The need for policy analysis in evaluating the regular education initiative. *Journal of Learning Disabilities, 21*(1), 12–18.

Mills v. Board of Education of the District of Columbia, 348 F. Supp. 866 (D.D.C. 1972).

National Association of Social Workers. (1992). *NASW standards for school social work services*. Washington, DC: Author.

121 *Congressional Record* 19,486. (1975). (statement of Sen. H. A. Williams of New Jersey, June 18, 1975)

Osborne, A. G., & DiMattia, P. (1994). The IDEA's least restrictive environment mandate: Legal implications. *Exceptional Children, 61*, 6–14.

Pennsylvania Association for Retarded Children v. Commonwealth of Pennsylvania, 334 F. Supp. 1257, 343 F. Supp. 279 (E.D. Pa. 1971, 1972).

Plessy v. Ferguson, 163 U.S. 537 (1896).

Reynolds, M. C., & Birch, J. W. (1988). *Adaptive mainstreaming: A primer for teachers and principals* (3rd ed.). New York: Longman.

Roncker v. Walters, 700 F.2d 1058 (6th Cir. 1983), *cert. den.* 464 U.S. 864, 104 S. Ct. 196, 78 L. Ed.2d 171 (1983).

Roosevelt, T. (1917). *The foes of our household*. New York: George Doran.

Saltzman, A., & Proch, K. (1990). *Law in social work practice*. Chicago: Nelson-Hall.

Shanker, A. (1994). Where we stand on the rush to inclusion. *Vital Speeches of the Day, 60*, 314–317.

Stainback, S., & Stainback, W. (Eds.). (1992). *Curriculum considerations in inclusive classrooms: Facilitating learning for all students*. Baltimore: Paul H. Brookes.

Stainback, S., Stainback, W., & Jackson, H. J. (1992). Toward inclusive classrooms. In S. Stainback & W. Stainback (Eds.), *Curriculum considerations in inclusive classrooms: Facilitating learning for all students* (pp. 3–18). Baltimore: Paul H. Brookes.

Stainback, W., & Stainback, S. (1984). A rationale for the merger of special and regular education. *Exceptional Children, 51*, 102–111.

Stainback, W., Stainback, S., & Moravec, J. (1992). Using curriculum to build inclusive classrooms. In S. Stainback & W. Stainback (Eds.), *Curriculum considerations in inclusive classrooms: Facilitating learning for all students* (pp. 65–84). Baltimore: Paul H. Brookes.

Turnbull, H. R. (1993). *Free appropriate public education: The law and children with disabilites* (4th ed.). Denver: Love.

U.S. Department of Education. (1993). *Digest of educational statistics, 1993*. Washington, DC: U.S. Government Printing Office.

Verstegen, D. A., & Clark, D. L. (1988). The diminution in federal expenditures for education during the Reagan administration. *Phi Delta Kappan, 70,* 134–138.

Villa, R. A., & Thousand, J. S. (1992). Student collaboration: An essential for curriculum in the 21st century. In S. Stainback & W. Stainback (Eds.), *Curriculum considerations in inclusive classrooms: Facilitating learning for all students* (pp. 117–142). Baltimore: Paul H. Brookes.

Wang, M. C., Anderson, K. A., & Bram, P. J. (1985). *Toward an empirical data base on mainstreaming: A research synthesis of program implementation and its effects.* Pittsburgh: University of Pittsburgh.

Wang, M. C., Reynolds, M. C, & Walberg, H. J. (1988). Integrating the children of the second system. *Phi Delta Kappan, 70,* 248–251.

Will, M. C. (1986). Educating children with learning problems: A shared responsibility. *Exceptional Children, 52,* 411–415.

York, J., Giangreco, M. F., Vandercook, T., & Macdonald, C. (1992). Integrating support personnel in the inclusive classroom. In S. Stainback & W. Stainback (Eds.), *Curriculum considerations in inclusive classrooms: Facilitating learning for all students* (pp. 101–116). Baltimore: Paul H. Brookes.

This chapter was originally published in the April 1996 issue of Social Work in Education, *vol. 18, pp. 113–127.*

46 School Social Worker Certification in a Climate of Educational Reform

Gary L. Shaffer

Since the mid-1980s, professional education associations, government and private commissions, schools of education, and the general public have engaged in ongoing efforts to redesign and reform education. These efforts have received such great attention that deregulation, school-based management, improved student performance, public-private partnerships, and higher teacher standards have become part of common parlance.

Whatever their ultimate shape or form, the accomplishment of these reforms will require a foundation of successful teaching, teacher preparation, licensing, and professional development. (For the purpose of this editorial, "licensure" will be used to refer to legislation that establishes minimal requirements for general practice in education or social work. "Certification" will refer to those statutes that specifically regulate school social work practitioners. A variety of terms are used in specific professional regulation statutes.) In recognition of this fact, high-profile initiatives to radically alter teacher status, education, and effectiveness have been set into action during the past 10 years. Witness the creation of the National Board for Professional Teaching Standards as recommended by the Carnegie Forum on Education and the Economy (1986); the evolution of community-based professional development schools for teaching, training, and research (Holmes Group, 1990); state adoption of model licensing standards proposed by the Interstate New Teacher Assessment and Support Consortium (INTASC) (1992); and standard revisions by the National Council for Accreditation of Teacher Education (Darling-Hammond & Berry, 1995).

IMPACT ON SCHOOL SOCIAL WORK REGULATION

The education reform movement's impact on school social work education and certification, although not always as explicit as the initiatives outlined above, has influenced and will continue to influence school-based and school-linked practice and practitioners. Educational reform and concomitant changes in teacher preparation and licensure statutes will no doubt cause us to re-examine the regulation of school social work practitioners. Although there is no known effort in place to decertify school social work personnel, several trends exist that may have a similar impact and that will need to be addressed in the near future.

CERTIFICATION IN REVIEW

Almost 40 states are considering the adoption of the INTASC model licensing standards, a program sponsored by the Council of Chief State School Officers. Implementation of the INTASC standards may require some modification of all school personnel licensing and certification requirements, and social work licensing and certification regulations will not escape this scrutiny. Our bargaining position may be strengthened by recent changes in our own professional regulatory climate. It is important to note that in the past 12 years over 25 states have passed social work licensing legislation. Today, social work licensure in some form exists in every state, the District of Columbia, Puerto Rico, and the U.S. Virgin Islands (American Association of State Social Work Boards [AASSWB], 1996). All states except Michigan require licensing examinations prepared by the AASSWB; practice protection is provided in 40 jurisdictions; licensure is limited to BSW, MSW, and DSW professionals with supervised experience; and privileged communication provisions are found in all but four licensing statutes.

Unfortunately, the movement to certify school social work practitioners does not reflect a similar growth in number or quality. If legal regulation exists to protect the public, ensure practitioner competency, and provide professional incentives, then serious questions should be raised about the effectiveness of school social work certification. Since the late 1970s, the number of jurisdictions certifying school social work practice has remained at about 30 (Hawkins, 1980; Torres, 1996). Although certification in some jurisdictions is sound and rigorous, considerable variance exists among the certifying jurisdictions' entry-level, credentials, experience, and examination requirements (NASW, 1996). Preprofessional training varies widely, differential levels of practice are not articulated, and personnel lack privileged communication protection in many areas. Fully a third of the jurisdictions require no supervised school practica for initial certification, and states with large student populations such as Michigan, Pennsylvania, and Texas have no school social worker regulations. Much work remains to be done in this area.

The licensure of social work has had both positive and negative implications for school personnel. Currently, several jurisdictions, notably those in Kansas and Minnesota, are questioning whether certification of school social workers should be eliminated and replaced by their existing general social work licensing statutes. Those in favor of eliminating certification hold that the licensing statute provides adequate protection to the public and that "dual licensure" is unnecessary. Those opposed argue that school social workers hold a specialty status within the social work profession similar to that held by school psychologists, school counselors, and school nurses and that dual licensing and certification provide better protection for clients and encourage the employment of the best-qualified personnel. Marshaled by groups like the Kansas Association of School Social Workers (KASSW), certification supporters assert that much more is involved than statute redundancy and that differential regulation is necessary. Respondents to a recent survey administered to members of the KASSW (personal communication with N. Hermreck, president, KASSW, and S. Terrill, chairperson, Regulations Committee, Kansas State

Board of Education, May 1996) indicated that they believe the loss of certification might lead to

> (1) reduced representation by their union bargaining agents (NEA/AFT), (2) loss of certified status as an employee, (3) erosion of the high practice standards now enforced by certification, (4) fewer uniform quality control standards for clients/consumers within the educational setting, with less specialized practitioners being hired, (5) possible changes in Special Education reimbursement patterns, and (6) less effective teaming, in that one or two essential points of view (those of the school social worker or school nurse) may be inadequately presented or may not be present at all.

Neither state has resolved this issue to date. Dual licensure may remain, certification may be eliminated, or other creative options may be articulated that will serve to protect the public and support professional development and practice.

INCREASED USE OF UNCERTIFIED SCHOOL–BASED PERSONNEL

A greater challenge to school social work certification will come from the employment practices adopted by the many school-based and school-linked programs now emerging in schools across the country. The success of programs such as school-based health clinics and youth and family resource centers often depends on year-round accessibility, collaborative efforts by multiple agency personnel, and mixed funding streams. School-linked and integrated practice models require staffing, service, and program structures far different from those traditionally offered in the public schools (Hooper-Briar & Lawson, 1994).

As these programs expand, so will the use of uncertified student support staff. There are not enough available educational and student support personnel, and school budgets are too small to provide the quality and variety of programs that can be offered through innovative school–community partnerships. The introduction of a large number of uncertified personnel has met with resistance from unionized and nonunionized student support personnel concerned about job security issues as well as from state professional associations concerned about the use of personnel who lack the skills, knowledge, and values required of school-based practice.

Should these staff be required to meet school personnel licensing and certification standards? If not, should their services and interventions be supervised and coordinated by regulated personnel? What other alternatives need to be examined? The full impact of these programs on certification remains to be seen, but it is clear that currently advanced educational reforms will require a nurturing and flexible school climate and depend on a broad spectrum of educational and social services, school- and community-based collaboration, transdisciplinary teamwork, and educational and student support personnel able to cross bureaucratic boundaries and redefine their roles. Traditional staffing patterns are in flux, and current certification standards do not adequately address the staffing needs of these alternative programs.

NEED TO DEMONSTRATE SERVICE EFFECTIVENESS

Whether we are concerned about the impact of the multitude of school reforms, reviews of and challenges to school social worker regulation, or the influx of uncertified personnel, steps must be taken to better identify and articulate our practice effectiveness and to encourage collaboration and communication among educators and social workers at the local, regional, and national levels. The efforts of the National Center for Social Work and Education Collaboration are an example of such activity at the regional and national levels. Perhaps the expansion of professional development schools will foster the growth of similar efforts at the local level among school districts, schools of education and social work, and cooperating agencies. The upcoming practice effectiveness series to be edited and distributed by the American Association of School Social Workers should also help to identify best-practice exemplars and areas in need of further evaluation and research. Ultimately, a collective database must be established that will demonstrate school social work effectiveness and help promote, define, and defend our contribution to America's schools and the children and families we serve.

REFERENCES

American Association of State Social Work Boards. (1996). *Social work laws and board regulations: A state comparison study.* Culpeper, VA: Author.

Carnegie Forum on Education and the Economy. (1986). *A nation prepared: Teachers for the 21st century.* New York: Carnegie Corporation.

Darling-Hammond, L., & Berry, B. (1995). Teacher professionalism and the commission reports: The prospects for creating a learner-centered profession of teaching. In R. Ginsberg & D. Plank (Eds.), *Commissions, reports, reforms, and educational policy* (pp. 151–169). Westport, CT: Praeger.

Hawkins, M. (1980). Survey of state certification standards for social work practice in schools. In *Papers from the National Invitational Workshop on School Social Work and the Law* (pp. 83–95). Washington, DC: National Association of Social Workers.

Holmes Group. (1990). *Tomorrow's schools: Principles for the design of professional development schools.* East Lansing, MI: Author.

Hooper-Briar, K., & Lawson, H. A. (1994). *Serving children, youth and families through interprofessional collaboration and service integration: A framework for action.* Oxford, OH: Danforth Foundation and Institute for Educational Renewal at Miami University.

Interstate New Teacher Assessment and Support Consortium. (1992). *Model standards for licensing teachers: A resource for state dialogue.* Washington, DC: Council for Chief State School Officers.

National Association of Social Workers, Office of Quality Assurance. (1996). *School social work certification requirements from state departments of education: What you need to know to apply for a school social work position.* Washington, DC: Author.

Torres, S., Jr. (1996). The status of school social workers in America. *Social Work in Education, 18,* 8–18.

This chapter was originally published in the October 1996 issue of Social Work in Education, *vol. 18, 195–198.*

47 Regulating School Social Work Practice into the 21st Century

Isadora Hare

Gazing into a crystal ball is a precarious occupation at best. In attempting to predict the future of social work licensing, school social work certification, and NASW's school social work credential, prognosticators risk failure as circumstances and trends change and new factors enter the situation. Nevertheless, reviewing the legal and professional regulation of school social work practice against the backdrop of health care reform, the expansion of managed health care services, and education reform can be instructive.

Clearly, the environment within which social work services will be delivered in schools is changing quickly and dramatically. Managed care will increasingly be a factor to be reckoned with, whether through Medicaid-funded services, school-based health centers, or child welfare agencies involved in school-linked services. Managed care companies, in their efforts to demonstrate a concern for quality as well as cost containment, place major emphasis on the credentialing and recredentialing of their service providers. The National Committee for Quality Assurance (NCQA, 1996) in its *Standards for the Accreditation of Managed Care Organizations* defined *credentialing* as "the process by which the managed care organization authorizes, contracts with, or employs clinicians who are licensed to practice independently, to provide services to its members. Eligibility is determined by the extent to which applicants meet defined requirements for education, licensure, professional standing, service availability and accessibility" (p. 64). New companies are springing up to undertake credentialing services on behalf of managed care organizations (MCOs). One of these has contracted with NASW for its data on NASW credential holders, including those who have the School Social Work Specialist (SSWS) credential. The American Behavioral Health Care Association will also establish a centralized credentialing service for its member organizations in late 1996. Because of these developments, school social workers will have to pay greater attention in the future to licenses, certifications, and credentials that will be necessary or desirable for social work practice in schools.

The author acknowledges with appreciation the contribution of Marianne Josem, MSW, ACSW, senior staff associate, Quality Assurance, NASW, and Janis Burke, student intern, Radford University School of Social Work, Radford, Virginia, to this article. The views expressed are the author's alone.

CREDENTIALING IN AN ERA OF EDUCATION AND HEALTH CARE REFORM

Education Reform

It has been 13 years since the publication of *A Nation at Risk: The Imperative for Educational Reform* (National Commission on Excellence in Education, 1983) propelled the United States into an era of education reform. Although the momentum of reform has slowed somewhat, the national education goals formulated in 1989 remain intact (Hare, 1991). Underlying them is the theme of raising performance standards for teachers and other school staff. One of two goals added to the original six by the Goals 2000: Educate America Act (P.L. 103-227, 1994) was Goal 4: Teacher Education and Professional Development, which states, "By the year 2000, the nation's teaching force will have access to programs for the continued improvement of their professional skills and the opportunity to acquire the knowledge and skills needed to instruct and prepare all American students for the next century" (National Education Goals Panel, 1995, p. 2).

If we extrapolate this goal to school personnel in a wider sense, it clearly points to the advantage of school social workers achieving and maintaining a national credential that goes beyond entry-level certification. Teachers have developed a private-sector credentialing program that indicates excellence of performance well beyond the entry-level proficiency signified by certification (Carnegie Corporation of New York, 1989). Based in Detroit, the National Board for Professional Teaching Standards (NBPTS) was created in 1987 as an independent, nonprofit, and nongovernment organization "to develop and operate a national voluntary system to assess and certify teachers who meet . . . high and vigorous standards for what accomplished teachers should know and be able to do" (NBPTS, 1996, p. 1). Although NBPTS certification for teachers has thus far received more support from state government than school social work credentialing, it does set an example that school social workers could emulate if they so chose.

Health Care Reform

The effect of health care reform on schools is another cogent reason for school social workers to consider the advantages of professional social work credentialing. Although President Clinton's health care reform proposals were defeated, the health care delivery system is undergoing major changes nevertheless. These changes are affecting the schools and the context in which school social work is practiced.

Managed Care. The past decade has seen the emergence and rapid growth of managed health care in the United States. Contributing to these changes is the fact that health care costs in the United States escalated rapidly during the 1980s. Yet advances in information technology revealed that in spite of its advanced medical technology and huge expenditures, the United States was less successful in improving the health of its citizens than many other industrialized nations (Rice, 1995). *Managed health care* has been defined as "a generic term used to describe a variety of methods of financing and delivering health care services delivery while maintaining a defined quality of care" (Jackson, 1995, p. 1.1). The development of managed care has generated much controversy, partly because for-profit companies dominate the delivery of services, and reports appear periodically alleging that needed services are denied purely for financial reasons.

Yet managed care is an established fact in the United States, and the number of people covered by MCOs for medical and behavioral health services (including mental health and substance abuse services) is growing rapidly. From 1993 to 1995 alone, the number of U.S. citizens in specialized managed behavioral health programs grew from 86 million to 107 million (Oss, 1995). Furthermore, managed care principles are being used in general assistance as well as child and family welfare programs. The Child Welfare League of America (1995) has established a Managed Care Institute "to advance best practice in children's services in a managed care environment and to ensure that all children and families in need have access to high quality, appropriate, affordable, and effective health care, behavioral health care, and child welfare services" (p. 2).

Medicaid. Medicaid programs are also moving rapidly toward managed care. Added to the Social Security Act in 1965 as Title XIX, Medicaid is a joint state-federal program to help finance health services for people in poverty. From 1985 to 1995, the costs of Medicaid more than tripled, and increasingly state Medicaid programs have received waivers from the federal Medicaid rules to enable state governments to mandate that Medicaid recipients enroll in MCOs. In 1991 only 6 percent of Medicaid recipients were in managed care plans. By 1994, it was 23 percent. By 1995, 43 states were using managed care companies to deliver Medicaid-funded services to over 8 million beneficiaries (Vandivort-Warren, 1995).

School-Linked Health-Related Services

The trend in Medicaid-funded health care will increasingly affect schools that have been billing Medicaid for health-related services since the late 1980s. Some states began using Medicaid funding after 1972, when Congress expanded Medicaid to include the Early Periodic Screening Diagnosis and Treatment (EPSDT) Program (NASW, 1995). For example, federal monies were used to provide medical, vision, and hearing screening by school nurses in Louisiana. Later Congress enacted the Medicare Catastrophic Coverage Act of 1988 (P.L. 100-360), which authorized Medicaid funds for education-related health services provided to children with special needs in special education programs.

The Omnibus Budget Reconciliation Act of 1989 (P.L. 101-239) went further and mandated EPSDT health services in all states if they were "medically necessary" to treat a condition found in an EPSDT screening of children eligible for Part H or Part B services to children with disabilities (Danilson, n.d.). Medicaid funding could therefore be used for case management and other social work services authorized by statute. A survey in 1993 revealed that 41 states were using Medicaid as a source of revenue for special education (Malone & Yeater, 1993).

As school-linked services and school-based health centers proliferate, more and more Medicaid dollars are being claimed by school systems and other organizations offering health and social services in school buildings (Advocates for

Youth, 1995; Farrow & Joe, 1992; Hare, 1995b). Of the 607 school-based health centers in 41 states and the District of Columbia existing in November 1994, nearly half received Medicaid support, and 28 percent of students using the centers had Medicaid coverage (Advocates for Youth, 1995). However, as more states have initiated Medicaid managed care programs, the process of securing payments for services to Medicaid beneficiaries has become more complicated (Schlitt & Lear, 1995).

As MCOs emphasize the credentialing of their service providers, they are focusing more on provider profiling as a means of ensuring the best quality, cost-effective services to clients (Wadell, 1996). This is an outcomes-oriented approach in which credentialing is but the first step. It goes much further to consider utilization and cost patterns, clinical outcomes, case manager evaluations, incident reports, and patient satisfaction both with the therapist and with the environment in which services are delivered. The goal is to achieve the best match possible between client need and provider skill.

Acquiring and documenting specialized qualifications will therefore become increasingly significant for practitioners. At the same time, it is possible that in the future licensure laws will be amended in the direction of more generalized licensing of mental health professionals. The Pew Health Professions Commission Taskforce on Healthcare Workforce Regulation has issued a set of recommendations to make such regulation more appropriate to the changing environment of health care in the United States (Finocchio, Dower, McMahon, Gragnola, & Taskforce on Healthcare Workforce Regulation, 1995).

REGULATING SCHOOL SOCIAL WORK PRACTICE

Undoubtedly, the increase in managed care will lead to expanded therapeutic services in schools. Social workers will need to document their special qualifications to provide psychosocial services in this environment. School social workers must understand the many levels of regulation that are used to maintain standards of performance and specialization.

The regulatory system is complex, and this complexity is compounded by the fact that there is no clear nomenclature. The same terms are used interchangeably to refer to different forms of regulation. It is therefore important to gain conceptual clarity, irrespective of the particular titles used. In general, regulation takes two forms: legal and professional.

Legal Regulation

Legal regulation is undertaken by public bodies at the state level, such as state legislatures, state boards of education, or state departments of education. As Biggerstaff (1995) stated, "Licensing and other forms of legal regulation are an exercise of the state's police power to protect consumers. Legal regulation, a form of public policy that allows government to intervene in the private sector, is protective regulatory legislation implemented through state agencies" (p. 1617). Legal regulation can be divided into two types: (1) regulation of social work practice in general and (2) field-specific regulation of school social work practice.

Regulation of Social Work Practice in General. There are three types of legal regulation of social workers: licensing, statutory certification, and registration. Licensing laws establish the minimum standards that practitioners must meet to enter the profession. The primary purpose of licensing is consumer protection, and licensure requirements therefore prohibit unqualified persons from providing the services offered by the profession. Although social work licensing laws can regulate up to four levels of practice, ranging from the baccalaureate level to clinical or advanced levels (which require two to three years of experience), the intent of the law is to establish entry-level standards for each type of licensed practice (American Association of State Social Work Boards [AASSWB], 1995).

Statutory certification and registration laws, unlike licensing laws, are "voluntary statutes applying only to social workers who wish to use a particular title" (Biggerstaff, 1995, p. 1617). According to the AASSWB (1996), a national membership organization of state regulatory boards established in 1979, by 1993 all states had some form of legal regulation. By 1996, 40 states had acts licensing social work practice, and 13 had title protection statutes (the total of 53 includes the District of Columbia, Puerto Rico, and the Virgin Islands). Social work regulatory boards are housed in a variety of state departments such as departments of health or departments of regulation and licensing. In seven states, including Georgia, New Jersey, and Ohio, school social workers are exempted from the requirement of state licensing as social workers per se (AASSWB, 1995, 1996).

Field-Specific Regulation of School Social Work Practice. Most school social workers are employed in public school systems, which constitute a major social and governmental institution in every state. Many states have therefore developed governance systems for regulating education professionals who work in the schools (Clark, 1994; Hawkins, 1982). This type of regulation is generally called "certification" (although in some states it is referred to as "licensing" or "credentialing"). An NASW survey conducted for the 1995–96 period revealed that 31 states and the District of Columbia require certification of school social workers, and one additional state, Alaska, has voluntary certification. Twelve states (Delaware, Idaho, Indiana, Iowa, Louisiana, Minnesota, Nevada, New Hampshire, New Mexico, New York, Rhode Island, and Utah) and the District of Columbia require dual licensure; that is, they require practitioners to hold their state license as social workers in addition to their certification as school social workers in public school systems (NASW, 1996b).

Professional Regulation

Professional regulation comes from the private sector, usually from national professional associations, or boards constituted by members of a particular profession or subspecialty. To differentiate this type of national, voluntary, private-sector regulation from state-sponsored, statutory licensing and certification, this article uses the term "credentialing," although some authorities recommend the use of the term "certification" in this context (Finocchio et al., 1995). Various organizations issue credentials that are relevant to social work practice (for example the Board Certified Diplomate [BCD] from the American Board of Examiners in Clinical Social Work) and credentials for substance abuse counselors and case managers.

NASW, established in 1955, mandates a credentialing program in its bylaws (NASW, 1993) and reaffirmed the importance of credentialing in its Strategic Plan adopted in 1991. NASW now issues four credentials:

1. The Academy of Certified Social Workers (ACSW) was adopted in 1960 as "the benchmark of practice for practitioners with a master of social work (MSW) degree" (Biggerstaff, 1995, p. 1619). This credential has general applicability and is available to social workers in all fields and methods who have had two years of approved, supervised post-MSW practice and are members of NASW.
2. The Qualified Clinical Social Worker (QCSW) and
3. The Diplomate in Clinical Social Work are clinical credentials for MSW graduates with two and five years of approved practice experience, respectively. Social workers holding these credentials can be listed in NASW's *Register of Clinical Social Workers*, published biennially since 1976 (Hare, 1995a).
4. The SSWS credential is available to MSW graduates with two years of approved, supervised practice in public schools and other educational settings. (One of these years can be a field placement in the second year of the MSW program.)

SCOPE AND PURPOSE OF THE SSWS CREDENTIAL

The SSWS credential is a national, voluntary qualification. Initially offered in 1992, it was NASW's first field-specific professional credential, and it requires the necessary supervised practice stated earlier, professional references from a supervisor and a colleague, and adherence to the *NASW Code of Ethics* (NASW, 1996a) and *NASW Standards for School Social Work Services* (NASW, 1992a). Membership in NASW is not required. In addition to these requirements, candidates must achieve a passing score on the National Teachers Examination (NTE) School Social Worker Specialty Area Test.

Why were the specialty test and credential for school social workers created? At the time they were developed, NASW was receiving complaints from school social workers, primarily in the northeast, that to achieve the state certification they needed for their jobs, they were being required to take the NTE core battery, which included a test of professional practice for teachers. Although the full battery of NTE tests contained a variety of specialized tests for pupil services providers, such as school psychologists and speech and language pathologists, there was no test for school social workers.

In collaboration with the Educational Testing Service (ETS), NASW developed the School Social Worker Specialty Area Test, which became a part of the NTE battery of tests; this test is based on the results of a national survey of school social work practice conducted for the 1989-90 period. This survey was the third in a series begun in 1968 by Lela Costin (1969) and continued by Paula Allen-Meares (1977). It used Allen-Meares's 1974 inventory as adapted by a 19-member committee of school social work experts appointed by NASW, with Allen-Meares's advice and consultation. This panel of experts was selected because they had extensive first-hand experience with school social work or had an academic background in teaching courses in school social work. They also represented the gender, ethnic, and geographic diversity of the United States.

On the basis of a return of 862 questionnaires (49.5 percent of the original sample), the survey results provided a rich source of demographic data and data on the tasks performed by school social workers and the knowledge, skills, and abilities required to perform the tasks effectively at the entry level (Allen-Meares, 1994; Nelson, 1990). Such data are essential to ensure the validity and legal defensibility of a test-based credentialing process.

The NTE-SSWS test examines knowledge of social work ethics; social work modalities and procedures; theories of human behavior and development; models of school social work practice; research; multidisciplinary activities; program development and managerial skills; characteristics of pupil populations; public education legislation, case law and due process; and financing. With the exception of a test developed in Illinois, the NTE test developed by NASW in collaboration with ETS remains the only test specifically for school social workers constructed by their professional peers in accordance with standards set by them.

Norms for the test were developed in 1992, when 2,272 candidates took the test and were grandparented into the program if they met all the other criteria for the credential. Presently there are 2,025 active and 823 inactive credential holders.

State departments of education are beginning to adopt the test as a means of certifying school social workers (for example, Colorado, Florida, Louisiana, Missouri, West Virginia, Tennessee, and Washington). Other states such as North Carolina and Oklahoma have expressed interest in the test.

However, the chief purpose of the credential program was to set a national standard of excellence for school social workers over and above the requirements of state certification. It was designed to promote the use of *NASW Standards for School Social Work Services* (NASW, 1992a), to enhance recognition of school social workers' contributions, and to encourage continuing professional development for school social workers. Additional goals included to promote uniform credentialing standards across states, agencies, and training institutions; to ensure a consistent level of training and experience in service providers who earn the credential; and to provide a model for states who are considering the introduction of certification for school social workers (NASW, 1992b). In short, the overarching goal is to promote the professional identity of school social workers as specialists in solving psychosocial problems in schools and their own sense of professional pride. It is interesting to note that these goals are remarkably similar to those enunciated by the National Association of School Psychologists (NASP) for their Nationally Certified School Psychologist program (NASP, n. d.).

CONCLUSION

Managed care principles are rapidly entering the public child welfare system and are being implemented in the delivery of therapeutic services in schools. Within this environment, professional credentials and high standards for practice are of paramount importance. School social workers would be well advised to look beyond entry-level certification by state departments of education to social work licensing and to professional credentialing that documents their specialized qualifications to provide educationally necessary psychosocial services in the school environment.

REFERENCES

Advocates for Youth. (1995). *School-based and school-linked health centers: The facts.* Washington, DC: Author.

Allen-Meares, P. A. (1977). Analysis of tasks in school social work. *Social Work, 22,* 196–201.

Allen-Meares, P. (1994). Analysis of tasks in school social work. *Social Work, 39,* 560–565.

American Association of State Social Work Boards. (1995). *Social work laws and board regulations: A state comparison study.* Culpeper, VA: Author.

American Association of State Social Work Boards. (1996). *Social work laws and board regulations: A state comparison study.* Culpeper, VA: Author.

Biggerstaff, M. A. (1995). Licensing, regulation, and certification. In R. L. Edwards (Ed.-in-Chief), *Encyclopedia of social work* (19th ed., Vol. 2, pp. 1617–1624). Washington, DC: NASW Press.

Carnegie Corporation of New York. (1989). Certifying and rewarding teaching excellence: The National Board for Professional Teaching Standards. *Carnegie Quarterly, 34*(2), 1.

Child Welfare League of America. (1995). *Ensuring quality in the managed care environment* [Brochure]. Washington, DC: Author.

Clark, J. P. (1994). Unraveling the licensing, credentialing, and certification maze: A guide for school social workers. *Iowa Journal of School Social Work, 7*(1), 6–15.

Costin, L. B. (1969). An analysis of the tasks in school social work. *Social Service Review, 43,* 274–285.

Danilson, S. (n.d.). *Medicaid and the schools: The Louisiana experience.* Unpublished paper distributed at the Annual Conference on Medicaid, sponsored by the Department of Health and Hospitals and Medicaid of Louisiana, Baton Rouge, 1992.

Farrow, F., & Joe, T. (1992). Financing school-linked, integrated services. *Future of Children, 2*(1), 56–67.

Finocchio, L. J., Dower, C. M., McMahon, T., Gragnola, C., & Taskforce on Healthcare Workforce Regulation. (1995). *Reforming healthcare workforce regulation: Policy considerations for the 21st century.* San Francisco: Pew Health Professions Commission.

Goals 2000: Educate America Act, P.L. 103-227, 108 Stat. 125 (1994).

Hare, I. (1991). School social work and its social environment. In R. Constable, J. P. Flynn, & S. McDonald (Eds.), *School social work: Practice and research perspectives* (2nd ed., pp. 71–86). Chicago: Lyceum.

Hare, I. (1995a). *Analysis of NASW's credentialing program.* Unpublished manuscript, National Association of Social Workers, Office of Quality Assurance, Washington, DC.

Hare, I. (1995b). School-linked services. In R. L. Edwards (Ed.-in-Chief), *Encyclopedia of social work* (19th ed., Vol. 3, pp. 2100–2109). Washington, DC: NASW Press.

Hawkins, M. T. (1982). State certification standards for school social work practice. *Social Work in Education, 4,* 41–52.

Jackson, V. H. (Ed.). (1995). *Managed care resource guide for social workers in agency settings.* Washington, DC: NASW Press.

Malone, L. D., & Yeater, J. (1993). *States summary: Medicaid billing survey.* Indianapolis: Indiana Department of Education, Division of Special Education.

Medicare Catastrophic Coverage Act of 1988, P.L. 100-360, 102 Stat. 683.

National Association of School Psychologists. (n. d.). *Nationally certified school psychologist: Application and information.* Bethesda, MD: Author.

National Association of Social Workers. (1992a). *NASW standards for school social work services.* Washington, DC: Author.

National Association of Social Workers. (1992b). *School social work specialist (SSWS) credential: Information bulletin.* Washington, DC: Author.

National Association of Social Workers. (1993). *Bylaws of the National Association of Social Workers.* Washington, DC: Author.

National Association of Social Workers. (1995). *Third-party reimbursement for clinical social work services.* Washington, DC: Author.

National Association of Social Workers. (1996a). *NASW Code of ethics.* Washington, DC: Author.

National Association of Social Workers. (1996b). *School social work certification requirements from state departments of education.* Washington, DC: Author.

National Board for Professional Teaching Standards. (1996). *Backgrounder.* Detroit: Author.

National Commission on Excellence in Education. (1983). *A nation at risk: The imperative for educational reform.* Washington, DC: U.S. Department of Education.

National Committee for Quality Assurance. (1996). *Standards for the accreditation of managed care organizations* (1996 ed.). Washington, DC: Author.

National Education Goals Panel. (1995). *The national education goals report executive summary: Improving education through family–school–community partnerships.* Washington, DC: Author.

Nelson, C. (1990). *A job analysis of school social workers.* Princeton, NJ: Educational Testing Service.

Omnibus Budget Reconciliation Act of 1989, P.L. 101-239, 103 Stat. 2106.

Oss, M. (1995, April). *Trends in behavioral health financing.* Paper presented at the National Managed Health Care Congress, Behavioral Health Care Track, Washington, DC.

Rice, D. P. (1995). Health care: Financing. In R. L. Edwards (Ed.-in-Chief), *Encyclopedia of social work* (19th ed., Vol. 2, pp. 1168–1175). Washington, DC: NASW Press.

Schlitt, J., & Lear, J. G. (Eds.). (1995). *Medicaid, managed care, and school-based health centers: Proceedings of a meeting with policy makers and providers on state and local partnerships to establish school-based health centers.* Washington, DC: George Washington University, Making the Grade: State and Local Partnerships to Establish School-Based Health Centers.

Vandivort-Warren, R. (1995). *Merging managed care and Medicaid: Private regulation of public health care.* Unpublished manuscript, National Association of Social Workers, Office of Policy and Planning, Washington, DC.

Wadell, D. (1996, February). *Provider profiling: A look at today's state-of-the-art approaches.* Paper presented at a Conference on Behavioral Healthcare Provider Profiling, sponsored by Global Business Research, Ltd. (New York), New Orleans.

This chapter was originally published in the October 1996 issue of Social Work in Education, *vol. 18, pp. 250–258.*

Index

The Editors

Patricia L. Ewalt, PhD, *is dean and professor, School of Social Work, University of Hawaii, Honolulu. She has a master's degree in social work from Simmons College School of Social Work and a PhD in health care policy, research, and administration from the Florence Heller School for Advanced Studies in Social Welfare, Brandeis University, Waltham, Massachusetts. She is the editor of* Social Work.

Edith M. Freeman, PhD, ACSW, *is professor, University of Kansas School of Social Welfare, Lawrence. She has an MSW from the University of Kansas School of Social Welfare and a PhD from the Departments of Psychology and Human Development and Family Life. She is the editor of* Social Work in Education.

Stuart A. Kirk, DSW, *is Marjorie Crump Professor of Social Welfare, School of Public Policy and Social Research, University of California, Los Angeles. He has an MSW from the University of Illinois at Urbana and a DSW from the University of California, Berkeley. He was the editor of* Social Work Research *from 1992 to 1996.*

Dennis L. Poole, PhD, *is professor of social work and public administration in the School of Social Work, College of Health and Public Affairs, University of Central Florida. He has an MSW with a specialization in community development from West Virginia University and a PhD in social policy, planning, and research from the Florence Heller Graduate School for Advanced Studies in Social Welfare, Brandeis University, Waltham, Massachusetts. He is the editor of* Health & Social Work.

The Contributors

Paula Allen-Meares, PhD, *is dean and professor, School of Social Work, University of Michigan, Ann Arbor.*

Catherine F. Alter, PhD, *is dean and professor, Graduate School of Social Work, University of Denver, Colorado.*

Ann Rosegrant Alvarez, PhD, *is assistant professor, Wayne State University, Detroit.*

Philip D. Arben, DBA, MPH, *is professor, Department of Management and Law, Central Michigan University, Mt. Pleasant.*

Darlyne Bailey, PhD, *is dean and associate professor, Mandel School of Applied Social Sciences, Case Western Reserve University, Cleveland.*

Candyce S. Berger, PhD, *is director of social work and director of patient care services for admitting and maternal and infant support services, University of Michigan Health System, and associate professor and assistant dean, Graduate School of Social Work, University of Michigan, Ann Arbor.*

Barbara Berkman, DSW, *is assistant hospital director and director, Social Work Research, Department of Social Services, Massachusetts General Hospital, Boston.*

Catherine E. Born, PhD, *is research associate professor, School of Social Work, University of Maryland at Baltimore.*

Jay Cayner, MSSW, *is assistant hospital director and director, Social, Patient, and Family Services, University of Iowa Hospitals and Clinics, Iowa City.*

Philip W. Cooke, DSW, *is professor and chair of the management concentration, School of Social Work, University of North Carolina at Chapel Hill.*

Claudia J. Coulton, PhD, *is professor and codirector, Center on Urban Poverty and Social Change, Mandel School of Applied Social Sciences, Case Western Reserve University, Cleveland.*

Sandra K. Danziger, PhD, *is associate professor of social work, School of Social Work, University of Michigan, Ann Arbor.*

Jeanette R. Davidson, PhD, ACSW, *is associate professor, School of Social Work, Columbia University, New York.*

Tim Davidson, PhD, *is director, Putnam County Mental Health Services, Carmel, New York.*

King E. Davis, PhD, *is professor, School of Social Work, Virginia Commonwealth University, Richmond.*

Liane V. Davis, PhD, *was associate dean and professor, School of Social Welfare, University of Kansas, Lawrence. She died October 18, 1995.*

Richard L. Edwards, PhD, ACSW, *is dean and professor, School of Social Work, University of North Carolina at Chapel Hill.*

Kathleen Ell, DSW, *is professor, School of Social Work, University of Southern California, Los Angeles.*

Irwin Garfinkel, PhD, *is Mitchell I. Ginsberg Professor of Contemporary Urban Problems, School of Social Work, Columbia University, New York.*

Roberta R. Greene, PhD, *is dean, School of Social Work, Indiana University, Indianapolis.*

Lorraine Gutierrez, PhD, *is associate professor, School of Social Work, University of Michigan, Ann Arbor.*

Jan L. Hagen, PhD, ACSW, *is professor of social work, State University of New York at Albany.*

Anthony P. Halter, DSW, *is associate professor, School of Social Work, University of Illinois, Urbana.*

Isadora Hare, MSW, ACSW, SSWS, *was most recently director, Quality Assurance, National Association of Social Workers, Washington, DC.*

Julia R. Henly, PhD, *is assistant professor of social welfare, School of Public Policy and Social Research, University of California, Los Angeles.*

Susan Hoechstetter, ACSW, *was most recently government relations director, National Association of Social Workers, Washington, DC.*

Bruce S. Jansson, PhD, *is professor, School of Social Work, University of Southern California, Los Angeles.*

Greg Jensen, ACSW, LISW, *is director, Department of Social Service, University of Iowa Hospitals and Clinics, Iowa City.*

Sheila B. Kamerman, DSW, ACSW, *is Compton Foundation Centennial Professor for the Prevention of Children and Youth Problems, School of Social Work, Columbia University, New York.*

Sharon M. Keigher, *is editor of the* National Health Line *in* Health & Social Work, *and professor, School of Social Welfare, University of Wisconsin–Milwaukee.*

Rebecca Y. Kim, PhD, is assistant professor, College of Social Work, Ohio State University, Columbus.

Ruth I. Knee, MSSA, ACSW, is consultant, mental health/long-term care, Fairfax, Virginia.

Kelly McNally Koney, MSSA, is research assistant, Mandel School of Applied Social Sciences, Case Western Reserve University, Cleveland.

James P. Kunz, MSW, is doctoral candidate and research fellow, Program on Poverty and Social Welfare Policy, School of Social Work, University of Michigan, Ann Arbor.

Edith A. Lewis, PhD, is associate professor, School of Social Work, University of Michigan, Ann Arbor.

Yat-sang Lum, MSW, is a doctoral student, George Warren Brown School of Social Work, Washington University, St. Louis.

Daniel R. Meyer, PhD, is associate professor, Institute for Research on Poverty, School of Social Work, University of Wisconsin–Madison.

Frederick B. Mills, PhD, is assistant professor, Department of History and Government, Bowie State University, Bowie, Maryland.

Linda Mills, JD, PhD, LCSW, is assistant professor, Department of Social Welfare, School of Public Policy and Research, University of California, Los Angeles.

Terry Mizrahi, PhD, is professor, School of Social Work, Hunter College, New York.

Elizabeth A. Mulroy, MSW, PhD, is associate professor, School of Social Work, University of Hawaii, Honolulu.

Peter A. Neenan, PhD, is senior research associate, Jordan Institute for Families, School of Social Work, University of North Carolina at Chapel Hill.

Howard Nemon, BA, is student, School of Social Work, University of Michigan, Ann Arbor.

Paul M. Ong, PhD, is professor and chair, Department of Urban Planning, School of Public Policy and Social Research, University of California, Los Angeles.

Dennis K. Orthner, PhD, is professor and associate director, Jordan Institute for Families, School of Social Work, University of North Carolina at Chapel Hill.

Martha N. Ozawa, PhD, is Bettie Bofinger Brown Professor of Social Policy, George Warren Brown School of Social Work, Washington University, St. Louis.

Janet D. Perloff, PhD, *is associate professor, School of Social Welfare and School of Public Health, State University of New York at Albany.*

James C. Raines, MSSW, ACSW, *is school social worker, Wilmette Public Schools, Wilmette, Illinois, and doctoral candidate, School of Social Work, Loyola University, Chicago.*

P. Nelson Reid, PhD, *is professor and chair, Department of Social Work, North Carolina State University, Raleigh.*

Cynthia J. Rocha, PhD, *is assistant professor, College of Social Work, University of Tennessee, Knoxville.*

Susan J. Rose, PhD, *is assistant professor, School of Social Welfare, University of Wisconsin–Milwaukee.*

Alice Scesny, MSW, *is director, Social Work Department/Child Life Program, Cleveland Clinic Foundation, Cleveland.*

Gary L. Shaffer, PhD, *is associate professor, School of Social Work, University of North Carolina at Chapel Hill.*

Wes Shera, PhD, *is dean and professor, Faculty of Social Work, University of Toronto, Ontario.*

Michael Sherraden, PhD, *is Benjamin E. Youngdahl Professor of Social Development, George Warren Brown School of Social Work, Washington University, St. Louis.*

Susan Smith, PhD, *is assistant professor, School of Social Work, University of Southern California, Los Angeles.*

Judith Trachtenberg, MSW, *is chief learning officer, Office of Organizational Learning, New York Hospital, New York.*

Lynn Videka-Sherman, PhD, *is dean and professor, School of Social Work, University at Albany, State University of New York.*

Pamela Viggiani, PhD, *is lecturer, School of Social Work, University at Albany, State University of New York.*

Marie O. Weil, PhD, *is professor and director of the Community Social Work Program, School of Social Work, University of North Carolina at Chapel Hill.*

Gautam N. Yadama, PhD, *is associate professor, George Warren Brown School of Social Work, Washington University, St. Louis.*

Cover Design by Gehle Design

Interior Design by Bill Cathey

Typeset in Lucinda Sans and Palatino by Patricia D. Wolf, Wolf Publications, Inc.

Printed by Boyd Printing Company on 60# Windsor

ORDER THESE COMPREHENSIVE RESOURCES ON SOCIAL POLICY AND ETHICS FROM NASW PRESS

Social Policy: *Reform, Research and Practice*, *Patricia L. Ewalt, Edith M. Freeman, Stuart A. Kirk, and Dennis L. Poole, Editors.* The editors developed this important text to help social workers understand and cope with the current maelstrom of change in social policy. Includes analyses of current economic, political, and social contexts.

ISBN: 0-87101-279-0. Item #2790. Price $38.95

Ethical Standards in Social Work: *A Critical Review of the* NASW Code of Ethics, *by Frederic G. Reamer.* Here is the first comprehensive, in-depth examination of the code of ethics of the social work profession. With this practical guide, which includes many case examples, you'll have a firm foundation for making ethical decisions and minimizing malpractice and liability risk.

ISBN: 0-87101-293-6. Item #2936. $24.95

Prudent Practice: *A Guide for Managing Malpractice Risk, by Mary Kay Houston-Vega and Elane M. Nuehring with Elisabeth R. Daguio.* Social workers and other human services professionals face a heightened risk of malpractice suits in today's litigious society. NASW Press offers practitioners a complete practice guide to increasing competence and managing the risk of malpractice. Included in the book and on disk are 25 sample forms and 5 sample fact sheets to distribute to clients.

ISBN: 0-87101-267-7. Item #2677, Word for Windows disk. Item #2677A, Macintosh disk. $42.95

Social Work Speaks: *NASW Policy Statements, 4th Edition.* Contains the latest unabridged collection of policy statements adopted by NASW's key policy-making body, the Delegate Assembly. This new edition has been updated and thoroughly revised, now packed with 82 statements on social policy and social policy issues.

ISBN: 0-87101-273-1. Item #2731. $36.95

The Legal Environment of Social Work, *by Leila Obier Schroeder.* This book focuses on the legal system as it influences the social work profession and highlights the laws that affect the delivery of social work services. Covers the criminal justice system, juvenile courts, marriage and filiation and adoption concerns, and legislation such as the Americans with Disabilities Act.

ISBN: 0-87101-235-9. Item #2359. $34.95

(Order form on reverse side)

ORDER FORM

Title	Item #	Price	Total
___ Social Policy	2790	$38.95	_____
___ Ethical Standards in Social Work	2936	$24.95	_____
___ Prudent Practice (Word for Windows disk)	2677	$42.95	_____
___ Prudent Practice (Macintosh disk)	2677A	$42.95	_____
___ Social Work Speaks	2731	$36.95	_____
___ The Legal Environment of Social Work	2359	$34.95	_____
		Subtotal	_____
	+ 10% postage and handling		_____
		Total	_____

❏ I've enclosed my check or money order for $ _____.

❏ Please charge my ❏ NASW Visa* ❏ Other Visa ❏ MasterCard

_____   _____

Credit Card Number   Expiration Date

Signature _____

Use of this card generates funds in support of the social work profession.

Name_____

Address _____

City _____ State/Province _____

Country _____ Zip _____

Phone _____ E-mail _____

NASW Member # (if applicable) _____

(Please make checks payable to NASW Press. Prices are subject to change.)

NASW PRESS

P. O. Box 431
Annapolis JCT, MD 20701
USA

Credit card orders call
1-800-227-3590
(In the Metro Wash., DC, area, call 301-317-8688)
Or fax your order to 301-206-7989
Or order online at http://www.naswpress.org

Visit our Web site at http://www.naswpress.org.   SPBI98